THE MEANINGS OF DRESS

P9-AGK-038

THE MEANINGS OF DRESS

SECOND EDITION

Mary Lynn Damhorst Iowa State University

Kimberly A. Miller-Spillman University of Kentucky

Susan O. Michelman University of Kentucky

Fairchild Publications, Inc.
New York

Executive Editor: Olga T. Kontzias
Acquisitions Editor: Joseph Miranda
Assistant Acquisitions Editor: Jason Moring
Art Director: Adam B. Bohannon
Director of Production: Priscilla Taguer
Associate Production Editor: Beth Applebome
Assistant Editor: Suzette Lam
Publishing Assistant: Jaclyn Bergeron
Copy Editor: Monotype Composition Co.

Interior Design: Jeanne Calabrese
Cover Design: Adam B. Bohannon

Second printing, 2006
Second Edition, Copyright © 2005
Fairchild Publications, Inc.

First Edition, Copyright © 1999
Fairchild Publications, Inc.

Library of Congress Catalog Card Number: 2004108967

ISBN: 1-56367-366-5

GST R 133004424

Printed in the United States of America

CONTENTS

CHAPTER 5   **Appearance for Gender and Sexuality**   153

Susan O. Michelman

CHAPTER 6   **Modesty and Immodesty**   193

Susan O. Michelman

PREFACE

Much has happened since the summer of 1999 when the first edition of *The Meanings of Dress* hit the shelves. A new century and millennium dawned, making it awkward to refer to turn-of-century dress. September 11th shocked the world. The meanings of Islamic dress became an acute concern in the United States as we confronted life under terrorism. Unfortunately, Muslims became the target of profiling based on appearance.

We had never had our shoes so carefully examined by strangers and for the good of the nation before, nor did we used to worry about whether we'd forgotten and left those fingernail scissors in our carry-on luggage. "Hanging chads" became a commonly used phrase, and political conservatism took over in Washington again . . . just while young women were showing cleavage, midriffs, and bra straps on campus and fashions got tinier and skinnier. The phrase "wardrobe malfunction" has now officially entered the lexicon. Internet shopping really did take off, despite the doubts of some merchandising professors we know. And all three editors went through major life realignments, causing interruptions in getting out this second edition but giving us new perspectives on our identities.

Our delay had a silver lining: The number of useful articles about the body and dress seemed to explode during the last three years. Perhaps we are just more attuned to finding them, or maybe writers are getting more into the surface level and deciding that appearance is interesting. We have a hunch that it is slowly becoming more acceptable to consider the body as important to society and worthy of scholarly analysis.

Some things haven't changed. On the whole, our classes still cater to an increasingly diverse body of students—diverse in age, gender, ethnicity, and country of origin. Many of us teach classes fulfilling diversity requirements, a curriculum addition that became common throughout U.S. colleges and universities in the late 1990s. And we still face the same quandary: How can we engage students in our subject matter and in the wide array of resources that facilitate learning?

This book does not answer all teaching needs for introductory classes on the social, psychological, and cultural aspects of dress. But we've updated a resource that we think is a valuable supplement to existing and future textbooks. *The Meanings of Dress* provides readings that are compelling and that expand our notions of what dress does for the individual and society. It introduces basic concepts likely to be covered in classes related to dress and psychology, sociology, cultural studies, and consumer behavior.

This book is about dress, that is, all the things human beings do to the surfaces and appearance of their bodies. Dress is an essential part of human experience. Perhaps because of its closeness to the body, dress has a richness of meanings that express the individual, as well as groups, organizations, and the larger society in which that person lives. Understanding its function helps us relate to other cultures, facilitates our interactions with others, and moves us to reflect upon and understand ourselves. We can also gain insight into how and why consumers buy clothing and other products related to dress.

Emphasis on Diversity

Diversity is an important fulcrum for the book. We have tried to incorporate perspectives offered by a variety of disciplines, cultures, and issues. We look to voices of multiple authors to help us understand dress.

These authors vary in gender, ethnicity, cultural backgrounds, age, and work roles. We hear from academics, journalists, business professionals, novelists, and students. They demonstrate how dress is a central factor in most areas of everyday life, such as work, school, sports, rituals and celebrations, intimate relationships, fantasy and play, and aging and development throughout a person's lifespan. The authors talk about dress and the body as a means of communication, but one that also contributes to problems of stereotyping, discrimination, and exclusion from power in society. They describe the richness of meanings of the body and dress that vary as a result of age, gender, sexual orientation, ethnicity, culture, immigration, position in society, and era. Dress is also examined as a reflection of larger social processes such as fashion systems, political conflict, hegemony, technological changes, organizational evolutions, and generational experiences, as well as cultural change in general.

The Meanings of Dress takes an interdisciplinary approach. Articles relate to psychology, sociology, anthropology, material culture, history, communications, semiotics, aesthetics, consumer behavior, marketing, business management, consumer economics, popular culture, gender studies, feminist scholarship, minority studies, and more. Dress is a multifaceted phenomenon. One viewpoint is just not enough.

Plan of the Book

Writings and visuals from popular magazines, newspapers, scholarly journals, books, advertisements, and cartoons contribute the illustrative material of the book. Some of the articles are carefully selected reprints, while others are new and written specifically for this book. Our aim was to build a collection of thought-provoking and easy-to-read works. Chapters 4, 6, and 13 are new. A surprising number of articles related to interpersonal relationships and dress, modesty, and the technology of appearance came to our attention, so we devoted chapters to each of those topics. The collection of readings throughout the book also makes each chapter very new. We have carried over 19 of the first-edition articles and added 67 new articles.

Chapter 1 introduces the essential concepts used throughout the book, including those of culture, hegemony, self, identity, social role, meaning, stereotyping, conformity, individuality, and fashion. Chapter 1 establishes the centrality of diversity, pluralism, relativism, and holism to understanding dress.

Chapters 2 through 13 introduce a variety of concepts and issues and include pedagogy and readings. Key terms and concepts are emphasized in bold in the chapter introductions. Each article is highlighted in its chapter introduction to explain the relevance of the article to chapter issues and themes. Suggested readings at the end of each introduction encourage the reader to explore topics further. The learning activity, also at the end of each introduction, helps students experience the ideas and concepts in the chapter. Discussion questions following each reading encourage critical thinking about the articles. In general, chapters are arranged in a micro to macro organization, starting with discussion of some basic components of human life in relation to dress and moving to larger societal systems. Throughout all chapters, however, we consider the perspectives of individual, group, and larger society and culture.

The integral relationship of the body to dress, self, and society is introduced in Chapter 2. Chapter 3 unpacks the process of communication and the creation of meanings of dress through human interaction.

Chapters 4 through 10 focus on various social roles and how dress helps us express, perform, and experience those roles. Chapter 4 examines how relationships are reflected in and influence dress through symbolic interaction. Family relationships and group relationships, particularly subcultural groups, are included. Gender and sexual identity are examined in relation to the self within various cultural contexts in Chapter 5. Chapter 6 looks at modesty—not a social role per se, but a meaning that is tied to definitions of gender and religion. Chapter 7 focuses on the function of dress in the work environment. Chapters 8 and 9 chart dress as a reflection of age roles throughout the lifespan, from infancy to elder years. The roles of race and ethnicity are examined in Chapter 10. The chapter addresses the importance of body and dress to issues of minority status, hegemonic power, and exclusion and inclusion from power bases.

Moving to still larger systems in society, Chapter 11 examines the fashion process as part of the dynamics of cultural change. Religion is the focus of Chapter 12. Religious ideology is a major influence on larger cultural organizations and values, and dress is a reflection of religion. Finally, Chapter 13 ties image-driven technology to techniques that keep the body looking young, taller, and electronically wired. Ethical issues of new technology are considered.

The Meanings of Dress ends with Chapter 14, a look at major societal trends in the near future that may affect dress. Future shifts of age and ethnic representation, technology as it affects modes of access to procuring apparel, and genetic engineering are examined for impact on dress and how we think and feel about the body. The book closes with a learning activity in which students are asked to write their own scenario of the future.

Five years from now, if we compile a third edition, it will be interesting to see the topic shifts that unfold. As mentioned, we found more articles on family and dress, modesty, and the technology of appearance for this edition. Will these topics be "hot" five years from now? We greatly cut the number of articles on the casual work dress trend. It's still around but seems less crucial. Five years from now will there be more coverage of extreme body modifications? Will these have any impact on fashion? And will this book be accessed by students through the Internet?

ACKNOWLEDGMENTS

This second edition of readings and activities is the result of the collective efforts of many individuals. We thank all our helpers for their generous time, effort, and support.

We thank the writers who willingly let us include their work. They have told engrossing and valuable stories. We especially thank the contributors of original manuscripts for their enthusiasm for the book and their willingness to entertain our editorial requirements.

Our editor, Beth Applebome, deserves high praise for her patience and kindness in dealing with our endless spurts and stops of activity. She is a great cheerleader, and she and Jaclyn Bergeron took on the enormous task of tracking permissions for articles and art. Beth and Olga Kontzias, our first edition editor and guiding light, have sent many an interesting article our way. We thank them for their tremendous interest in and support of this book.

Mary Lynn Damhorst would like to thank her colleagues Jane Farrell-Beck, Jennifer Ogle, Nancy Miller, Geitel Winakor, Harriet McLeod, Ann Marie Fiore, and Lisa Heidger for funneling interesting books, articles, Web sites, and cartoons her way. They are all talented scouts, and I am indebted to them for their interest in this ongoing project. I am especially grateful to my department chair Mary Gregoire for giving me encouragement to continue on with a book, a work focus not always praised by upper administrators at a Research 1 university. I thank my coeditors for their continuing and astute contributions to the book. Without them, such a diverse and rich array of materials could not be assembled. I thank the students in my Appearance in Society class for getting interested in the course, finding new materials for me, and serving as guinea pigs for learning activities. Their comments on the WebCT discussion board were crucial in making decisions about readings for the book. I thank Iowa State University for investing in electronic teaching resources and library indexes. The indexes have opened up easy access to an amazing array of articles. And finally, I thank my parents, Florence and the late Clarence Damhorst, for their interest in the book. Mom has clipped enough cartoons and articles to fill a bushel basket.

Kimberly Miller-Spillman would like to acknowledge and thank her coeditors. The experience of creating this text and revising it for the second edition was an extremely invigorating and positive one. Second, I would like to thank my family for love and support during this process. My husband, Charles L. Spillman, and my children, Charles Lee and Audrey, provided a supportive environment that made working on the book possible. Third, I would like to thank all of the students I have worked with over the past 16 years, who continue to challenge me to grow.

Susan Michelman acknowledges the many students who have shared their interest and enthusiasm for this topic with me and helped motivate me to provide them with a text that would draw them into critically thinking about the diversity of appearance. Thanks to my great coeditors as well as my husband John, who has not only listened but provided great suggestions—both personal and professional. My son Adam and daughter Adria always keep me current on the topic of contemporary culture.

2004

Mary Lynn Damhorst
Kimberly A. Miller-Spillman
Susan O. Michelman

CHAPTER 1
Introduction

Mary Lynn Damhorst

AFTER YOU HAVE READ THIS CHAPTER, YOU WILL COMPREHEND:

- How dress is a multifaceted behavior.

- How dress is a part of culture and society, reflecting how people think and organize themselves.

- That fashion is social and collective behavior.

- How meanings of dress are relative to cultural, historical, social, and individual contexts.

- The relationship between dress and the self.

- The value of diversity in dress across cultures and within U.S. society.

This book is a compilation of readings about **appearance,** including all aspects of the human body that have the potential to be observed by other human beings. We focus particularly on **dress,** which we define as any intentional modification of appearance (see Kaiser, 1997; Roach-Higgins & Eicher, 1992). Dress is what people do to their bodies to maintain, manage, and alter appearance; therefore, dress is behavior.

Dress includes more than clothing—those three-dimensional objects that enclose and envelop the body in some way (Roach-Higgins & Eicher, 1992). Dress includes a wide array of other supplements and attachments to the body, such as makeup, nose rings, masks, shoes, headdresses, wigs, and hair plugs. Dressing may include application of chemicals, heat, and light to change color, texture, and odor, as people do with perfumes, deodorants, tanning, facial peels, hair straightening or curling, tattoos, scarification, and branding. Removing noticeable portions of the body can also be an act of dress, such as cutting hair, shaving a beard, removing a facial mole, removing fat through liposuction, or getting a nose job. Extreme body modification of cutting off a body part for non-medical reasons is practiced by some groups—such as the Dani women in Irian Jaya who amputate to the joint of a finger to honor ancestors when a relative dies (Sims, 2001)—or by some individuals who feel that removing a body part is an important expression of identity or psychological release (Favazza, 1996). Dieting and exercise are also, in part, a type of dress—if those activities are undertaken to change weight, muscle definition, or body shape in any way. Extremes of purging or self-starvation can also be dressing activities when they are adopted as strategies for losing weight. The dressed (or even undressed) body is very much a project under continual construction (Brumberg, 1997).

Roach-Higgins and Eicher (1992) contend that dress is intentional, but in accidental circumstances, this requirement of intention becomes complex. For example, getting splashed and covered with mud by a passing truck is not an act of dress, but how one deals with mud all over one's clothing is an act of dress, even though there might not be complete freedom of choice in how the mud problem is solved.

Dress and appearance are worthy of study because they are laden with meanings. Appearance and dress often provide the most immediate and apparent visual cues about age, gender, ethnicity, social status, and social roles. The shape of the body, as we shall examine in Chapter 2, has significant meanings. In addition, dress protects the body from the physical, psychological, and social environments. It expresses relationships (Chapter 4), steers individuals toward or away from others, shapes actions toward others, reflects how people feel about themselves, and expresses personal values and values of the society in which an individual lives. Dress is more than the mere objects and materials people put on their bodies. Dress can be a sign or symbol that refers to and stands for **meanings** not inherent in the material or object.[1] In sum, the physical body when dressed reflects the "social body" or surrounding societal system (Turner, 1991).

Dress is a chronicle of a historical era. As fashions or norms of dressing change over time, trends in technology, the economy, religion, the arts, notions of morality, social organization, and patterns of everyday living are reflected in dress. Chapter 13 looks at technological changes reflected in dress. We can learn much about people in any society through the way they dress and the meanings assigned to their dress. For example, Ellen Melinkoff in *What We Wore* (1984) compared the late 1960s and early 1970s to the previous ten years:

> The hippie look was many things: sloppy, creative, unstudied, studied, uniform, eccentric, and most of all, casual. That casualness is its legacy. Of course, true hippie garb went to the extreme of casualness, unkempt. But it drew our attention to just how uptight, plastic, cookie-cutter-correct we had been in our dress.
>
> Whether in Jackie Kennedy A-line outfits or Mary Quant minis, we dressed in packs. The only avenue open to us to impress other people was through correctness. The hippies spit on that idea. They felt clothes should be a form of expression and people should be comfortable as well. (p. 170)

PREVAILING CONCEPTS

Several themes and concepts are introduced in this first chapter so that we can draw on them in the following chapters and readings. The concepts include culture and society, fashion, relativism, self, individuality vs. conformity, diversity, and pluralism.

A Cultural Perspective

Culture is an elusive and complex concept. Throughout a person's lifetime, culture surrounds and shapes the individual in ways that he or she can barely recognize.

Linton (1936) pointed out that culture is a complex whole that includes any capabilities and habits held by members of a society. Culture is a system that is learned and reflected in behavioral patterns characteristic of the members of a society (Hoebel, 1958). Spradley (1972) neatly summarized culture as "what people know, feel, think, make, and do" (p. 6). The behavior patterns under focus in this book are the many forms of dress. As we attempt to understand dress from a cultural perspective, a **holistic** approach must be adopted in which all aspects of a culture are considered as potentially shaping the meanings of dress and the choices people make when choosing forms of dress.

WHAT PEOPLE THINK.   What people know and think are the **mentifacts** of a culture, which include ideas, ideals, values, knowledge, and ways of knowing (Spradley, 1972). Knowing how to dress is a part of any cultural knowledge base. How, indeed, do so many people know they should wear jeans on their legs and not on their heads? This seemingly obvious rule is very much a part of many cultures today, as jeans are a garment worn by people all around the globe. We will examine the complexity of unwritten rules for dress in Chapter 3.

In any one appearance, a person may express personal and cultural values simultaneously. For example, a culture that creates changing fashions may be expressing a general belief that change and newness are positive (Sproles & Burns, 1994). In contrast, a culture that values tradition and doing things the old way will likely produce clothing that changes very little over time, as among the Old Order Amish in the United States, who wear clothing similar in style to what Amish wore in the 1800s (Schweider & Schweider, 1975).

People also learn meanings of different styles or types of dressing; meanings are another component of cultural knowledge. Dress may elicit a **stereotype,** or a network of meanings assigned on the basis of appearance. Appearance stereotypes are mentifacts shared by members of a cultural group. Stereotypes are based on limited information, such as appearance, and result in a network of inferences about characteristics of the person. Even though the stereotype rarely fits any individual completely, believers of the stereotype generalize its characteristics to all members of the group. The stereotyper tends to be blinded to other characteristics that make the individual unique. Some individuals hold to a negative stereotype so rigidly that they become **prejudiced** against a group and discriminate against the group regardless of information that the stereotype is unfair or untrue (Aronson, 1999). When a stereotype is widely held in a culture, prejudicial treatment of the group on a broad scale is likely to occur in that society.

What makes stereotyping particularly dangerous is that many people are unaware that they apply a stereotype consistently to a group. Human beings have a natural tendency to attempt to classify others into familiar types to simplify the task of making sense of the surrounding social world. Only by recognizing that we all, at some time, use stereotypes can we become more diligent at avoiding erroneous stereotyping and labeling.

WHAT PEOPLE DO. What people do are the sociofacts of a culture (Spradley, 1972). Sociofacts are social behaviors or how people organize themselves in relation to one another. In fact, the term society is often used to refer to a group of people living and working together in a systematic way. George Herbert Mead (1934) contended that society requires coordinated interaction of individuals. Dress can help in coordinating interaction. For example, uniforms can help people know whom to ask for help if an auto accident has occurred and whom to ask for water in a restaurant. Dress gives clues to the age of individuals, their gender, and their attractiveness, which are all helpful in deciding, for example, whom to ask to dance at a campus bar (even though dress cues can be deceiving). In some cultures dress helps identify who should be accorded special respect and courtesies and who should be ignored or barred from entry to "polite" public areas.

Societies often have a group that dominates and leads minorities and less powerful groups in society. This situation of dominance is referred to as **hegemony**. The powerful group tends to set standards for behavior and ways of thinking (Gramsci, 1971). We will examine how hegemony in the United States has an influence on standards of attractiveness (Chapter 2), business appearance norms (Chapter 7), gender dress (Chapter 5), and social status of ethnic groups (Chapter 10).

Characteristic of hegemonic societies is underrepresentation of less powerful groups in leadership roles and leading institutions. Groups not seen as mainstream, desirable, or attractive are often made "invisible" through consistent omission from media and positions of prestige in society. We will see in Chapters 2, 5, 9, 10, and 11 that persons of larger body size, female sex (in certain jobs and social roles), alternative sexuality, middle and older age, and minority ethnicity have been almost absent from or grossly

underrepresented in U.S. media and are often ignored or underserved by the apparel industry. When the underrepresented are portrayed in mainstream media, it is often as insultingly clichéd or negatively stereotyped figures. Purposely or unconsciously omitting groups of people from media and valued societal roles helps to maintain power and the status quo for the most powerful group.

Shows such as *Will & Grace* are evidence of the modest progress made in featuring men of alternative sexuality on network TV as positive characters. The mail-order Dooney & Bourke catalog featured the woman in Figure 1.1 in 2003, consistent with 1990s trends of featuring a few more women of color in fashion advertising. That her hairstyle is an updated revival of 1970s Afros, never a mainstream white look, is another small example of inclusion of minority appearances in the media. But more progress is needed. For instance, job discrimination for people of size is still practiced and, to some extent, legal in the United States.

Social organization is reflected in and facilitated by dress in many facets of society. In

FIGURE 1.1 *The model with her updated Afro hairdo— not a style characteristic of mainstream whites—is a sign of progress in depicting ethnic diversity in fashion promotions. (From the summer 2003 Dooney & Bourke catalog.)*

fact, fashions cannot exist without coordinated interaction of individuals acting as a collective in wearing similar looks, lengths, and silhouettes. **Fashion** is a way of behaving that is temporarily adopted by a discernible portion of members of a social group as socially appropriate for the time and situation (Sproles & Burns, 1994). Without some similarity and coordination in behavior among individuals, a society would have only unique, idiosyncratic expressions rather than fashion. In Chapter 11 we look at the individual and group behaviors that shape fashion systems.

WHAT PEOPLE MAKE.   The things that people make are sometimes called the artifacts of culture. Dress includes manufactured and handmade objects and materials. These objects also are products of the processes and technologies a culture develops to make things. Both sociofacts and mentifacts become encoded in artifacts, such as dress, made by people in a culture. Chapter 12 looks at how the sociofacts and mentifacts of religion are reflected in dress. Chapter 6 examines how dress incorporates societal notions of modesty.

The Relativity of Meanings

Throughout the readings in this book, the authors do not merely describe dress and physical features of individuals or cultural groups, but continually strive to understand the meanings dress and the body have for those individuals and societies. Dress and the body have meanings that are relative to culture and historical times. For example, Mamie Van Doren (see Figure 1.2a) was a popular pinup girl in the United States during the 1940s. Her thighs, ample according to present U.S. standards, might preclude someone like Mamie from attaining national popularity as a sex symbol today. Yet, she was considered quite shapely and attractive 60 years ago. Compare Mamie with the model in the 2003 Louis Vuitton ad (Figure 1.2b). Similarly, a woman in Jamaica is more apt to be considered attractive if she is pleasingly "plump," a larger and rounder body ideal than is currently fashionable in mainstream American culture (Sobo, 1994).

Meanings are not usually handed down by some inhuman force of cultural or political correctness, however. Meanings are created by individuals living day by day within cultures and interacting daily with the objects and materials of dress. As Herbert Blumer (1969) proposed, the meanings of things (e.g., objects, ideas, behaviors) are directly attributable to the social interaction one has with others. Meanings emerge as people hear others talk about the way people look, see each other dressed in certain ways, and react to people on the basis of appearance. Meanings of dress and appearance are created, maintained, and modified as individuals collectively deal with dress and the people wearing each style of dress.

It is people, then, who assign meanings to dress and who develop shared consensus about what dress means. To create shared meanings about any type of dress in most cultures in the world today requires a convoluted process of meaning transfer and transformation. Various media, such as fashion magazines, films, and television shows, contribute greatly to the transfer and transformation of meanings of dress around the world. Meanings may constantly change as people of diverse ages, shapes, roles, and backgrounds decide to wear the same style. The occasions and activities for which they wear a particular style influence meanings assigned to the style.

Time and number of adopters are important factors in the development of dress meanings. For example, Lind and Roach-Higgins (1985) found that dress worn to express radical and liberal political ideas on U.S. college campuses in the 1970s became

FIGURE 1.2 *(a) Mamie Van Doren was a popular pinup girl and actress during the 1940s, admired most for her "vital statistics." (b) This 2003 Louis Vuitton ad is reminiscent of the 1940s, but note the slender thighs and overall thin body of the model, which are not reminiscent of that era.*

less clear in meaning as more and more students adopted the styles originally worn by and associated only with radical students. The meanings changed from "radical" and "political liberal" to general campus fashion. The same type of dissolution of meanings has occurred more recently during the 1990s with the adoption of black rap styles throughout suburbs and small towns in the United States. A look that was on the cutting edge and a statement of difference from white society was adopted by white male adolescents (Spiegler, 1996).

Change in fashion over time adds to the relativity of meanings of dress as fashion ideas **diffuse** or spread throughout a society (Sproles & Burns, 1994). New ideas for fashion may first be introduced by designers or innovative individuals. Fashion magazines, advertising, retail displays, and celebrities may promote a style as fashionable, the latest thing, and attractive. If a significant number of consumers decide to adopt the style, it actually becomes a fashion, though only certain segments of consumers may wear the style. The style may take on added meaning of representing the lifestyles of people who adopt the new look. For instance, a style might be associated with women business executives. Then several years later, when the style is no longer featured as new and fewer people wear it, its meaning may change to "passé," "boring," "dowdy," or "out of it" (for example, see Figure 1.3). Every chapter in this book deals with change of meanings of dress over time.

The Individual Self

> . . . appearance is a primary mark of identification, a signal of what they consider themselves to be. (Banner, 1983, p. 3)

When do individuals get to be themselves in the midst of all this collective action and shared meanings? Symbolic interactionist Mead (1934) proposed that the **self** is defined through interaction with other people. Dress is part of our interactions with others who react to us, in part, on the basis of the meanings of our dress. Dress is part of defining self-identity to others (Chapter 4): we choose items that reflect our interests, personality, roles, membership in groups, age, gender, socioeconomic status, and more. Of course, some situations or roles limit the amount of choice in self-expression; an extreme example of conformity is found in the dress of prison inmates, who wear uniforms that mask personal identity and emphasize only the prisoner role (Goffman, 1961).

FIGURE 1.3 *Personnel interviewers rated this suit as attractive and highly appropriate for business interviews in 1985. Twenty years later the outfit looks a bit frumpy and out of date.*

Learning about the self is a lifelong process (examined in Chapters 8 and 9). Cooley (1902) suggested that we use other people as mirrors to tell us who we are in a "looking glass self" process. Continuous presentation of **programs** of dress (programs could include other types of behavior, of course) and reflection upon others' **reviews** or reactions to dress allow an individual to gain a sense of how others see and assign meaning to him or her (Stone, 1962). We use others in this process of **self-indication** to learn who we are (Blumer, 1969). Meanings of dress are part of what is learned through the self-indication process.

An integral part of the self is the roles we take on. **Roles** are positions that people occupy in a group or society (Biddle & Thomas, 1966). These positions are defined by social relationships; people take on roles in relation to other persons. Performance of a role is guided by social expectations for the role-player's behavior (including dress), knowledge, and attitudes.

Adult individuals tend to have multiple roles that define parts of the self. At any one time, a man may be 42 years old (age role), male (gender role), Puerto Rican (ethnic role), a chef and a boss to junior chefs (employment roles), a father, a husband, a brother, a son (family roles), a best friend of another man (social role), and a coach for a girls' soccer team (community leadership role). He may express some of these roles through dress, but not all of these roles in any one appearance. These roles are parts of the puzzle that make up the man's **identity.** Other aspects of identity include unique personal traits and interests that are not necessarily role related. The Puerto Rican man might run five miles alone every morning and think of himself as defined in part by running. He, in a sense, has many identities that make up his total self. We would need to examine his total wardrobe to begin to grasp the multiple identities of this man, but some of his identity might never be expressed through dress.

Individuality vs. Conformity

Can anyone truly be an individual if we rely on others to tell us who we are and how to behave in roles? To be a human being, interaction with other human beings is essential. It is the complex combination of unique experiences and reviews from a wide array of others that makes every individual a unique self. Given some amount of personal freedom, we have the human capacity to choose from reviews we receive to define the self. We can decide whose compliments or insults about our hair to consider valid when getting a haircut. Or we may choose to get the regulation haircut for army recruits because we want to become part of that occupational group. To some extent, however, cultures limit the choices we have. Some haircuts might never be considered or known as a possibility in some cultures.

FIGURE 1.4 *The man and his children depicted in front of their modest home in Tanzania are wearing world dress—contemporary styles that are similar to garments worn throughout most of the world. The mother wears traditional dress; women often maintain dress traditions more than do men in economically developing countries.*

Conformity to role dress and cultural norms is a common theme throughout this book. **Conformity** is actually change in behavior to achieve consistency with real or imagined expectations and behaviors of groups or other individuals (Kiesler & Kiesler, 1970). The opposite desire to express the self as a unique individual and set oneself apart is also a common theme in dress (Horn, 1965). A tension between dressing to fit in and dressing to be unique is an essential component of fashion change (Sproles & Burns, 1994). Fashion innovators tend to have a greater need for individuality in dress. In contrast, fashion opinion leaders enjoy **individuality** but also see a need for some conformity (Davis & Lennon, 1985). To inspire others to adopt new fashion ideas, opinion leaders must be somewhat like their followers (Leavitt & Kaigler-Evans, 1975).

In the United States, conformity has gotten a bad rap. We greatly value the concept of individuality but do not always notice the degree of conformity that shapes our everyday lives. Uniforms and looking too much like others often are seen as undesirable ways of dress. In more **collectivistic** cultures, individuals tend not be so negative about conforming to traditions and group norms of behavior (Triandis, 1995). Dressing similarly to others is seen as appropriate and functional in some contexts. In many Asian cultures, for example, conformity to norms of showing respect and modesty is considered essential for the good of society and family. Chapter 12 examines how some religious groups value conformity in dress to state adherence to and belief in religious doctrine.

A World of Diversity

Although people in cultures throughout the world are diverse in the way they dress and the meanings they assign to dress, a network of connections—business, political, media, electronic, migratory, family, and friendships—has emerged among nations to make the present-day world a shrinking "global village" (McLuhan & Powers, 1989) (see Figure 1.4). Many of us no longer live in isolation from other cultures outside our borders. In addition, within any society multiple cultures may be living together or in close proximity. The United States is a prime example of a society that incorporates people from many cultures within its boundaries—a multicultural society.

Appreciating cultural difference in dress is a complex process, especially when confronted with an appearance that is culturally quite different from one's own. The attachments to the face of the Yanomano woman in Figure 1.5 might be difficult for you to understand if you are not used to this type of body modification. But in her own community in the Amazon Basin, she is probably considered attractive and appropriate.

Keep in mind, however, that dress in the United States may look ugly or ridiculous to people in other cultures. High heels, lipstick, cosmetic surgery, and tanning practices seem strange or even dangerous from other cultural viewpoints. Dress that is commonly accepted in one's own country may be considered inappropriate or immodest in another culture. For example, exposure of women's bare upper arms is seen as immodest in many Moslem cultures, even during hot weather. To prevent insults when traveling in those cultures, women from Europe and the United States may cover up more than they would at home during hot weather.

We have attempted to include articles in most chapters that give viewpoints from cultures outside the United States or from minority groups within the United States. One reason for including diverse perspectives is to encourage a move away from **ethnocentrism**—the judging of people from other cultures and backgrounds by one's own cultural standards and beliefs. To function adequately in the global and multicultural workplace and neighborhoods of today requires the development of the ability to accept and respect differences and to strive for relativity in understanding. The perspective of **pluralism**—the acceptance of differences in others while not necessarily wanting to adopt those differences for the self—is increasing in the United States (Light, 1988). It is a perspective that will be increasingly expected on the part of mature individuals in the United States and will be a requirement for getting and keeping many jobs now that a great variety of business and government organizations have become global in their customer/client base and span of operations.

FIGURE 1.5 *Multiple face ornaments are commonly worn among the Yanomano people, native to the South American Amazon River Basin.*

The added benefit of pluralism is the depth of understanding of the self that comes from developing skill in analyzing one's own personal reactions to diversity. In addition, moving away from a smaller, ethnocentric way of thinking to seeing and appreciating a wide array of possibilities for dress adds richness to life. It is fun and rewarding to expand our ideas about what is attractive, aesthetically pleasing, and interesting. Awareness of variety in the world facilitates creativity in dressing and expression of the self.

Summary

In this chapter we have considered how dress is meaningful human behavior that includes a wide array of modifications to the body. Dress may reflect many aspects of cultures, including the ways in which people think, organize themselves, behave toward others, and make things. Individual choice in dress is strongly shaped by culture, fashion (if present in the culture), and the social roles the individual performs. However, a unique self may be expressed through dress because of the complex mix of role identities and individual preferences held by any individual. In the shrinking global society of today, acceptance of diversity of appearances due to individual and cultural differences is becoming a highly important social skill.

Note

1. We do not delve into the technical difference between "sign" and "symbol" in this text and use the terms interchangeably. Various scholars use the two terms differently, and there is wide disagreement over how the terms apply to dress. See Lyons (1977) for a discussion of varying definitions in the field of semiotics.

References

Aronson, E. (1999). *The Social Animal* (8th ed.). New York: Worth Publishers.

Banner, L. W. (1983). *American Beauty*. New York: Alfred A. Knopf.

Biddle, B. J., & Thomas, E. J. (1966). *Role Theory: Concepts and Research*. New York: Wiley.

Blumer, H. (1969). *Symbolic Interactionism: Perspective and Method*. Englewood Cliffs, NJ: Prentice Hall.

Brumberg, J. J. (1997). *The Body Project*. New York: Random House.

Cooley, C. H. (1902). *Human Nature and the Social Order*. New York: Charles Scribner's Sons.

Davis, L. L., & Lennon, S. J. (1985). Self-monitoring, fashion opinion leadership, and attitudes toward clothing. In M. R. Solomon (Ed.), *The Psychology of Fashion*, pp. 177–182. Lexington, MA: Lexington Books.

Eicher, J. (1995). Dress, identity, culture, and choice: The complex act of dress. In C. M. Ladisch (Ed.), *ITAA Proceedings*, pp. 8–11. Monument, CO: International Textile and Apparel Association.

Favazza, A. R. (1996). *Bodies under Siege: Self-Mutilation and Body Modification in Culture and Psychiatry*. Baltimore: Johns Hopkins University Press.

Goffman, E. (1961). *Asylums: Essays on the Social Situation of Mental Patients and Other Inmates.* Garden City, NY: Doubleday.

Gramsci, A. (1971). *Selections from the Prison Notebooks of Antonio Gramsci* (Q. Hoare and G. N. Smith, trans.). London: Lawrence and Wishart.

Hoebel, E. A. (1958). *Man in the Primitive World: An Introduction to Anthropology* (2nd ed.). New York: McGraw-Hill.

Horn, M. (1965). *The Second Skin.* Boston: Houghton-Mifflin.

Kaiser, S. B. (1997). *The Social Psychology of Clothing: Symbolic Appearances in Context* (2nd ed. rev.). New York: Fairchild.

Kiesler, C. A., & Kiesler, S. B. (1970). *Conformity.* Reading, PA: Addison-Wesley.

Leavitt, C., & Kaigler-Evans, K. (1975). Mere similarity versus information processing: An exploration of source and message interaction. *Communication Research,* 2: 300–306.

Light, P. C. (1988). *Baby Boomers.* New York: Norton.

Lind, C., & Roach-Higgins, M. E. (1985). Fashion, collective adoption, and the social-political symbolism of dress. In M. R. Solomon (Ed.), *The Psychology of Fashion,* pp. 183–192. Lexington: Heath/Lexington Books.

Linton, R. (1936). *The Study of Man: An Introduction.* New York: D. Appleton-Century.

Lyons, J. (1977). *Semantics,* Vol. 1. Cambridge: Cambridge University Press.

McLuhan, M., & Powers, B. R. (1989). *The Global Village: Transformations in World Life and Media in the 21st Century.* New York: Oxford University Press.

Mead, G. H. (1934). *Mind, Self, and Society* (Charles W. Morris, Ed.). Chicago: University of Chicago Press.

Melinkoff, E. (1984). *What We Wore: An Offbeat Social History of Women's Clothing, 1950 to 1980.* New York: Quill.

Roach-Higgins, M. E., & Eicher, J. B. (1992). Dress and identity. *Clothing and Textiles Research Journal,* 10(4):1–8.

Schwieder, E., & Schwieder, D. (1975). *A Peculiar People: Iowa's Old Order Amish.* Ames: Iowa State University Press.

Sims, C. (2001, March 11). Stone age ways surviving, barely. *New York Times International,* 8.

Sobo, E. J. (1994). The sweetness of fat: Health, procreation, and sociability in rural Jamaica. In N. Sault (Ed.), *Many Mirrors: Body Image and Social Relations.* Piscataway, NJ: Rutgers University Press.

Spiegler, M. (1996, November). Marketing street culture: Bringing hip-hop style to the mainstream. *American Demographics,* 18(11):29–34.

Spradley, J. P. (1972). *Culture and Cognition: Rules, Maps, and Plans.* San Francisco: Chandler Publishing.

Sproles, G. B., & Burns, L. D. (1994). *Changing Appearances.* New York: Fairchild.

Stone, G. P. (1962). Appearance and the self. In A. M. Rose (Ed.), *Human Behavior and Social Processes: An Interactionist Approach,* pp. 86–118. New York: Houghton-Mifflin.

Triandis, H. C. (1995). *Individualism and Collectivism.* Boulder, CO: Westview.

Turner, B. S. (1991). Recent developments in the theory of the body. In M. Featherstone, M. Hepworth, & B. S. Turner (Eds.), *The Body: Social Process and Cultural Theory,* pp. 1–35. London: Sage Publications.

CHAPTER 2

The Body in Cultural Context

Kimberly A. Miller-Spillman

AFTER YOU HAVE READ THIS CHAPTER, YOU WILL COMPREHEND:

- Frameworks for viewing the body and dress.

- The history of Euro-American body ideals.

- How to critically analyze media images of the body.

- Cultural stereotypes of the body and their potentially negative consequences.

- Cross-cultural alternatives to the U.S. ideal of thinness.

The purpose of this chapter is to engage the reader in a critical thinking process about the body. The body has many possibilities for adornment; it can be considered a canvas for self-expression. Body piercing and tattooing are two types of body adornment that have become increasingly popular in recent years, especially among young people. Body piercing includes those piercings that are visible in public settings (e.g., lip, nose, and eyebrow rings) and those that are not typically visible in public settings (e.g., genital, nipple, and navel rings). Similarly, tattooing can be publicly viewed or hidden (Luzier, 1998; Sanders, 1989). Other forms of body adornment include measures taken to conceal hair loss for men and women. These measures may include the use of wigs or toupees, hair dyes that give the illusion of more hair, or hair transplants. Cosmetic procedures alter bodies of both men and women. Botox injections, facial peels, liposuction, and face-lifts are a few examples. Regular visits to the dermatologist can alter the body through the removal of skin tags, moles, and warts in an effort to achieve a smooth and even skin tone. Most hair salons will remove facial hair by waxing lips, chins, and eyebrows.

Clearly, there are numerous ways to adorn the body. This chapter will draw on the reader's sensitivity to explore the many ways that we dress our bodies. Most of the readings in this chapter focus on body weight, which reflects a Euro-American—and increasingly global—obsession. But other body issues are also present, such as self-acceptance of one's body, challenging the thinness ideal, cultural definitions of beauty, and gym attendance as religion.

FRAMEWORKS FOR VIEWING THE BODY

Because the body is so rarely seen without clothing, dress and the body are closely connected—hence the need to address the body in a discussion about dress. To illustrate this close relationship between dress and the body, disposal of a deceased family member's clothing can be a difficult and emotional task. Handling clothing frequently worn by a loved one, now gone, is often as difficult (if not more difficult) as viewing the body at a funeral. Because clothing is so personal and so intimately associated with the body, clothing elicits strong emotions.

Several scholars have devised ways to view the clothed body, and their work provides a basis not only for viewing the body but also for performing research studies on dress. Eicher and Roach-Higgins (1992) created a classification system for types and properties of dress. Body modifications and supplements can be classified according to their respective properties. For example, skin can be transformed by tattooing (modification), which alters its color (property) and surface design (property). Body piercing not only modifies the body's skin, but allows for a ring to be attached to the body (supplement).

Susan Kaiser (1997) proposed a contextual perspective when viewing the body and dress. Awareness of the social, cultural, and historical influences at any given time is essential to understanding dress and its meaning, according to Kaiser. The contextual perspective draws from the fields of sociology, psychology, and anthropology, allowing researchers to understand meanings below the surface. Mary Lynn Damhorst created a model that considers the context of a person's dress and appearance (see model in Chapter 3). Underlying the contextual model are two premises: (1) in real life, we seldom see clothes divorced from social context, and (2) it has been demonstrated that interpretations of clothing vary along contextual lines (Damhorst, 1985).

Still other scholars view and study dress with an emphasis on visual perception. Marilyn DeLong (1998) presents a method for analyzing appearance that includes a sensitivity to visual aesthetic dimensions of perception. Robert Hillestad (1980) uses a structural approach to explore interactions between the body and clothing. Whether we approach the study of the body from a social, psychological, cultural, historical, or aesthetic perspective (or a combination of perspectives), one overarching concept remains clear: The body and all its attachments communicate volumes of information about an individual, a society, a culture, and a time in history.

CRITICAL THINKING ABOUT THE BODY

To begin the process of critically thinking about the body, it is instructive to examine one's own cultural ideals. A **cultural ideal** is the type of person a culture identifies as highly desirable or attractive. Jennifer Aniston and Brad Pitt are two examples of ideals in U.S. culture in 2004; you can probably think of many others. When we examine a cultural ideal, we begin by asking questions:

- Where did these ideals come from? (Informs us of our ethnic heritage.)

- When did these ideals develop? (Provides a historical context.)

- Who do these ideals benefit? (Gives us an idea of the cultural rewards for ascribing to an ideal.)

- Who do they hurt? (Tells us the negative consequences for not ascribing to an ideal.)

After the reader has examined his or her cultural ideals, it is especially informative to compare ideals from several cultures. This chapter is intended to generate critical questions about cultural body ideals.

The readings in this chapter will certainly stimulate your thinking about the body. You may agree with some of the ideas presented in the readings and disagree with others. That's fine; there are no absolute right or wrong answers. Rather than deciding what is right or wrong, there is value in examining these issues so you can determine your own personal philosophy.

ANALYZING U.S. IDEALS

Before embarking on an examination of dress and appearance from many cultures, it is helpful to create a list of culturally ideal characteristics for U.S. women and men. Each semester I enlist the help of students in my courses at the University of Kentucky to create this list. What are the ideal characteristics for women? What are the ideal characteristics for men? The "thin-but-toned" ideal is often a topic of discussion as students point out that just being thin is not enough. Ideals such as "tall, dark, and handsome," "no pain, no gain," and "one can never be too rich or too thin" are often mentioned as the list develops.

This exercise is often fun and invigorating, and most students are eager to chime in; momentum builds. Other students sit quietly and watch with skepticism as the list of characteristics fills the chalkboard. Not surprisingly, the same list occurs semester after semester, indicating the enduring nature of cultural ideals in the United States. After the list is complete, we step back and take a hard look. How many people can actually attain these ideals? Ten percent of the U.S. population? Five percent? Less than five percent? How realistic are these ideals to the average man and woman in the United States? What are the payoffs for approximating the ideal? What are the risks for not being anywhere near the ideal or intentionally challenging the ideal? The readings in this chapter should help you arrive at some answers to these questions.

Ideals and Power

The "root of power" for women and men is also part of our class discussion. Typically, women are viewed as powerful if they are attractive and fit the cultural ideal. Men are deemed powerful if they have high earning ability or potential. Clearly, one is based more on the physical body and the other is based on skills/abilities. And since we know that physical bodies are likely to decline with age, and skills and earning power are likely to increase with age, we begin to notice some interesting gender differences. Susan Kaiser (1997) regards these gender differences as an artificial dichotomy between agonic and hedonic power, or "doing versus being."

Agonic power refers to power that is active and direct (in other words, "doing"), and **hedonic power** is indirect and passive and relates to "being." The cultural ideal for men is more toward the agonic end of the continuum, while the ideal for women is more toward the hedonic end. Women achieve their power in society through "being" attractive and spending time, money, and energy on their appearance. Men achieve their power in society through "doing" and spending time and energy achieving skills. Kaiser refers to this dichotomy as artificial because we all know women who are highly skilled and men who are preoccupied with their appearance (see "The New Puritans").

Ideals and Gender

Given the previous information about cultural ideals and social power, it seems logical that men and women would pursue activities that are rewarding. But when did these expectations of men and women begin? Gendered dress expectations for the twentieth and twenty-first centuries were possibly affected most by late-nineteenth century ways of thinking. Because of the Industrial Revolution and growing capitalism in the United States, men's dress and demeanor in the late nineteenth century took on a somber appearance. The three-piece business suit came into use at this time and set the stage for men's business wear for years to follow. Fred Davis (1988) compares men's restricted dress code to their strong desire for economic success.

During the nineteenth century, women's dress continued to follow the same elaborate dress code it had followed for centuries. In large part, this happened because men and women were assigned different daily tasks. Because men would be interacting with others in the business world (i.e., the public sphere), men had to take their dress seriously. Because women would be at home raising children and managing households (i.e., the private sphere), their dress could follow the whims of fashion. How has today's dress changed for men and women compared with the late nineteenth century?

There are minimum dress expectations for both men and women. For example, women are not supposed to have facial hair and men are not supposed to have large breasts. But there is a big difference between minimum expectations and ideal expectations. **Stigma** is assigned to those who do not (or cannot) meet minimum dress expectations. Physical disabilities, obesity, hair loss, and postmastectomy are all conditions that can cause a person to be socially stigmatized. Most people are judged physically attractive if they *exceed* minimum expectations and demonstrate some effort toward approximation of the cultural ideal. Since no one is perfect and certain ideal characteristics are simply not genetically transmitted to all (see suggested reading "The Perfect Body"), generally society is accepting of the ordinary person.

Is it easier for men to achieve the ideal than it is for women? Certainly men and women are socialized differently about topics of dress and appearance. This socialization leads to less tolerance in society for men who adopt traditional feminine dress (i.e., skirts) as compared with women who adopt traditional masculine dress (i.e., trousers). Men, however, are not exempt from the pressure of living up to an ideal. Two readings in particular are informative about male body ideals. "The New Puritans" and "No Days

Off Are Allowed, Experts on Weight Argue" both speak to men's obsession with body weight and, in particular, working out. "The New Puritans" addresses similarities between gym attendance and religion. For example, going to the gym offers structure and a familiar (although boring) routine. Working out also allows one to atone for sins of the flesh and relieve feelings of guilt. In a similar article, "No Days Off Are Allowed, Experts on Weight Argue," we are told that those annoying calorie counters among us might be right! Keeping a daily record of calories consumed and calories burned may be the only way to maintain a healthy weight. One man cited in the article has stayed at the same Paris hotel while traveling for the past 15 years because it is the only hotel in Paris with a StairMaster.

Critical Analysis of Media Images

How much impact does a cultural ideal have on an individual? Ideals are pervasive throughout the media. Airbrushed photographs of fashion models and the use of body doubles in popular movies are two ways that unrealistic ideals are perpetuated. All humans are adversely affected by these fake images (see Bordo, 2004), and young girls are especially vulnerable (see "Web of Deceit" and Box 1, "Media's Effect on Girls"). One Web site offers teenage girls an alternative to thin and unrealistic body images (see "An Alternative Voice amid Teen 'Zines" in suggested readings). Two readings in this chapter, "Young and Chubby" and "Proud to Be Big," also provide evidence that some women actively oppose the thin ideal.

One study of Americans found that 15 percent of women and 11 percent of men surveyed would trade more than five years of their lives to be at their ideal body weight (Garner, 1997). This finding is a strong indication that media ideals do affect us on an individual level. Another result of the same study found that men and women find the stomach to be the most problematic area of the body. Is the desire for a slim waistline a twentieth century phenomenon carried into the twenty-first century? Just when did this fixation with the stomach begin? There is archaeological evidence that today's desire for a slim waistline began with the ancient Greeks. Minoan (ancient Greek) artifacts, dating from 2900–1150 BC illustrate both men and women with extremely tiny waists (Tortora & Eubank, 1998, p. 48). Whether these artifacts reflect actual practices of young children wearing tight belts to shape the waist, or the artist's convention, one thing is clear: the desire for a small waist was valued by both men and women. Another historic example of obsession with the body can be found in Box 2, "Concerning the Ear." *Harper's Bazaar* published this helpful note in 1896 for women wishing for a beautiful ear.

Researchers and health professionals typically blame media images of thinness for incidents of anorexia and bulimia among adolescents. To measure exactly how women have been portrayed in magazines, Paff and Lakner (1997) conducted a study of advertisements in *Vogue* and *Good Housekeeping* from 1950 to 1994. The researchers found that the way women were portrayed (dress and body position) in 1994 did not differ much from the way women were portrayed in 1950. An indication that even though women's roles changed considerably between 1950 and 1994, the way women were portrayed in popular magazines did not. Additional research has been conducted to extend Paff and Lakner's analysis to 2002 (Sprigler & Miller-Spillman, 2004). Preliminary indications are that women's portrayals in *Vogue* and *Good Housekeeping* advertisements between 1994 and 2002 are creeping, slowly, toward a less stereotypical feminine presentation. Although these researchers did not set out to make a direct link between media

BOX 1
Media's Effect on Girls: Body Image and Gender Identity

Did You Know?

Gender identity begins in toddlerhood (identifying self as a girl or boy) with gender roles being assigned to tasks early in the preschool years (Durkin, 1998).

A child's body image develops as the result of many influences:

• A newborn begins immediately to explore what her body feels like and can do. This process continues her whole life.

• A child's body image is influenced by how people around her react to her body and how she looks.

• A pre-adolescent becomes increasingly aware of what society's standards are for the "ideal body."

Media's Effect on Body Image

The popular media (television, movies, magazines, etc.) have, since World War II, increasingly held up a thinner and thinner body (and now ever more physically fit) image as the ideal for women. The ideal man is also presented as trim, but muscular.

• In a survey of girls 9 and 10 years old, 40% have tried to lose weight, according to an ongoing study funded by the National Heart, Lung and Blood Institute (USA Today, 1996).

• A 1996 study found that the amount of time an adolescent watches soaps, movies and music videos is associated with their degree of body dissatisfaction and desire to be thin (Tiggemann & Pickering, 1996).

• One author reports that at age thirteen, 53% of American girls are "unhappy with their bodies." This grows to 78% by the time girls reach seventeen (Brumberg, 1997).

• In a study among undergraduates media consumption was positively associated with a strive for thinness among men and body dissatisfaction among women (Harrison & Cantor, 1997).

• Teen-age girls who viewed commercials depicting women who modeled the unrealistically thin-ideal type of beauty caused adolescent girls to feel less confident, more angry and more dissatisfied with their weight and appearance (Hargreaves, 2002).

• In a study on fifth graders, 10 year old girls and boys told researchers they were dissatisfied with their own bodies after watching a music video by Britney Spears or a clip from the TV show "Friends" (Mundell, 2002).

• In another recent study on media's impact on adolescent body dissatisfaction, two researchers found that:

1. Teens who watched soaps and TV shows that emphasized the ideal body type reported higher sense of body dissatisfaction. This was also true for girls who watched music videos.

2. Reading magazines for teen girls or women also correlated with body dissatisfaction for girls.

3. Identification with television stars (for girls and boys), and models (girls) or athletes (boys), positively correlated with body dissatisfaction (Hofschire & Greenberg, 2002).

Media's Effect on Gender Identity

Many children watch between two and four hours of television per day. The presence or absence of role models, how women and men, girls and boys are presented, and what activities they participate in on the screen powerfully affect how girls and boys view their role in the world. Studies looking at cartoons, regular television, and commercials show that although many changes have occurred and girls, in particular have a wider range of role models, for girls "how they look" is more important than "what they do."

Reprinted by permission of National Institute on Media and the Family. www.mediafamily.org

- In a 1997 study designed to study how children described the roles of cartoon characters, children (ages four to nine) "perceived most cartoon characters in stereotypical ways: boys were violent and active and girls were domestic, interested in boys, and concerned with appearances" (Thompson, 1997).

- In another study, three weeks of Saturday morning toy commercials were analyzed. Results found that:
  1. 50% of the commercials aimed at girls spoke about physical attractiveness, while none of the commercials aimed at boys referenced appearance.
  2. Boys acted aggressively in 50% of the commercials aimed at them, while none of the girls behaved aggressively.
  3. With regard to work roles, no boys had unpaid labor roles, and girls were mainly shown in traditional female jobs or roles of unpaid labor (Sobieraj, 1996).

- Dr. Nancy Signorielli, Professor of Communications at the University of Delaware examined the types of media most often viewed by adolescent girls: television, commercials, films, music videos, magazines and advertisements. While the study did find positive role models of women and girls using their intelligence and acting independently, the media also presented an overwhelming message that girls and women were more concerned with romance and dating (and it follows how they look), while men focus on their occupations (Signorielli, 1997).

Sources

Brumberg, J. J. (1997). *The Body Project: An Intimate History of American Girls*. New York: Random House.

Durkin, K., & Nugent, B. (1998, March). Kindergarten children's gender-role expectations for television actors. *Sex Roles: A Journal of Research,* 38:387–403.

Hargreaves, D. (2002). Idealized women in TV ads make girls feel bad. *Journal of Social and Clinical Psychology,* 21:287–308.

Harrison, K., & Cantor, J. (1997). The relationship between media consumption and eating disorders. *Journal of Communication,* 47:40–67.

Hofschire, L. J., & Greenberg, B. S. (2002). Media's impact on adolescents' body dissatisfaction. In J. D. Brown, J. R. Steele, & K. Walsh-Childers (Eds.), *Sexual Teens, Sexual Media*. Mahwah, NJ: Lawrence Erlbaum Associates, Inc.

Mundell, E. J. (2002, August 26). Sitcoms, videos make even fifth-graders feel fat. Reuters Health. Accessed September 16, 2002, at story.news.yahoo.com/news?tmpl=story2&cid=594&ncid=594&e=2&u=/nm/20020826/hl_nm/obesity_television_dc_1.

Signorielli, N. (1997, April). Reflections of girls in the media: A two-part study on gender and media. Kaiser Family Foundation and Children NOW. Accessed September 6, 2002, at www.childrennow.org/media/mc97/ReflectSummary.html#top.

Sobieraj, S. (1996). Beauty and the beast: Toy commercials and the social construction of gender. American Sociological Association, *Sociological Abstracts,* 044.

Thompson, T., & Zerbinos, E. (1997). Television cartoons: Do children notice it's a boy's world? *Sex Roles: A Journal of Research,* 37:415–433.

Tiggemann, M., & Pickering, A. S. (1996). Role of television in adolescent women's body dissatisfaction and drive for thinness. *International Journal of Eating Disorders,* 20:199–203.

USA Today. (1996, August 12). p. 01D.

BOX 2

Beauty and Hygiene, XV. — Concerning the Ear.

A beautiful ear may be best defined by negatives. It must be neither too large nor too small, too fleshy nor too thin, too broad nor too narrow, too red nor too pale; it must be set neither too high nor too low on the head, and must neither stand out unduly from it nor lie too close against it. Where these defects exist, however, they may be remedied in some degree, if not altogether corrected.

For the lobe which is too large there is but one remedy, excision of the superfluous part by the surgeon's scissors, an operation which, although it is said to be almost painless and to be attended by no bad results, one would hesitate a little about submitting to. But a lobe which is too thin or too short may be easily stimulated to growth in the desired direction by pinching and pulling it persistently, using at the same time the aromatic tincture for promoting the growth of the muscular tissues, for which a receipt has been given in a previous paper. In the same way the vessels of nutrition may be stimulated to increased action in any other part of the ear which has not developed in harmony with the line of beauty.

When the ear is set too close against the head a wedge-shaped fold of linen worn for a time at night between the ear and the head will generally suffice to separate them somewhat. When the fashion of wearing the hair will admit of it, this result may be hastened by letting a lock of hair take the place of the wedge of linen during the daytime.

Where the opposite defect exists, that is to say, where the ear stands out too far from the head, an opposite course of treatment is to be pursued. The ear is to be bound to the head at night and, as far as may be possible, during the daytime, by a band of linen, or a ribbon, or by the hair. Only time and perseverance are needed to correct both of these defects.

Where the ear is deformed beyond all hope of remedy, a judicious arrangement of the hair will do much to disguise the deformity, the present fashion of drawing the hair down over the ears is advantageous in such cases.

Beauty and Hygiene, XV. — Concerning the Ear. (1896, August 29). *Harper's Bazaar*, 29(35):724.

images and eating disorders, stereotypical images of women in magazine advertisements is one of the many ways that the thin ideal is promoted in the Western world (Bordo, 2004).

One way to combat pervasive idealized images is to become a critical viewer of media. Rather than zoning out in front of the TV and passively ingesting idealized images, begin by actively critiquing what you see. Is it healthy (or even attractive for that matter) for collarbones and ribs to protrude from the body? This became commonplace on sitcoms such as *Friends* and *Ally McBeal*. Can feet and lower backs survive a constant regimen of 4-inch stilettos, as routinely seen on *Sex in the City*? There is evidence that being a critical viewer of media images can help you resist unrealistic images and the effect they have on you. Research indicates that African American adolescent females are less likely to be affected by media images than white adolescent females (Parker et al., 1995). Remember, being thin is not idealized everywhere. In the reading "The Weight of the World," Peck notes that in Africa thinness is stigmatized. Those afraid of contracting the AIDS virus avoid thin individuals. Among the Kalabari, also in Africa, fatness for women indicates a woman's fertility and therefore her value (see "Is Thin In?" in this chapter). In Jamaica, a thin person is viewed as someone who has low status and is not loved or cared for by others (Sobo, 1994). In Africa, a beauty pageant is held to celebrate a woman's plumpness (Knickmeyer, 2001). The suggested reading by Knickmeyer (2001) includes the interesting cross-cultural observation that Americans focus on the size of a woman's bustline (as illustrated by Barbie, originally a German invention), while Africans focus on the size of a woman's derrière. An examination of many cultures and their approaches to dress and body size can be enlightening (Eicher, 1995).

Many of the Euro-American ideals for women are directly related to a patriarchical society, that is, a society that traces descendants through the father and makes men the center of hegemonic power. In patriarchical societies, females are supposed to be less powerful than, and even subordinate to, males. This passive ideal is expressed through a thin, childlike body and a high-pitched voice — in other words, a dependent who needs a strong man to care for her. However, the growing Hispanic and African American segments of the American population are challenging this hegemonic power (see "Young and Chubby"). In addition, female bodybuilders (Schulze, 1990) and homosexuals further challenge traditional patriarchy by daring to thrive without dependence on heterosexual males for money, power, or sexual pleasure.

All of the readings in this chapter address a person's body image in some way. **Body image** is the mental picture one has of her or his body at any given time (Fisher, 1968). You may know someone who has a terrific body. Then, after you get to know her or him, you discover that the individual is very critical of his or her own body. This is an indication that a perfect body does not guarantee a positive body image. "To Apu, with Love" is a first-hand account of a young girl's struggle for self-acceptance. Arriving in the United States from India at the age of four, this young girl developed a longing for blonde hair and white skin. Her journey ends with acceptance of her body after graduation from college.

Several researchers have looked for a connection between body perception and self-esteem. **Self-esteem** involves individual feelings of self-worth (Rosenberg, 1985). Not surprisingly, when we feel better about our bodies, we feel better about ourselves. "Young and Chubby" reports that young women are learning to love their bodies even though they do not fit the thin ideal. Some insightful retailers have recognized that young women want body-conscious styles regardless of their body weight. As Jennifer Lopez and Serena and Venus Williams challenge body ideals, young girls are hearing more messages to take pride in normal bodies. The promise from this reading is increased self-esteem for young girls. The danger in this reading is apathy about health, leading to obesity and type 2 diabetes. Concern about the increase in obesity is the subject of "The Weight of the World." Peck notes that the world's population is suffering from what he calls the diseases of affluence, that is, heart disease and diabetes.

"Proud to Be Big" also describes a journey to self-acceptance. Fat women are less likely to marry and more likely to be poor than their thin counterparts because of negative stereotypes toward fat people in North America. And Hollywood is the last place you would expect to find a fat woman being rewarded. Camryn Manheim, while accepting an Emmy award in 1998, held her gold statuette above her head and stated: "This is for all the fat girls!" This statement was a culmination point for Manheim, but it was the beginning point of self-acceptance for many of her fans.

Body cathexis is the degree of satisfaction with the body (Secord & Jourard, 1953). Body dissatisfaction is incredibly high among the U.S. population and can lead to excessive exercise and dieting, self-induced vomiting, and plastic surgery. The extent of self-hatred is alarming, especially when it is estimated that 50 percent of all nine-year-old girls have dieted. Certainly all this obsessiveness surrounding the body begs the question: Why don't we like what we have?

Critical analysis of U.S. cultural ideals for men and women is a process of examining our present-day society. Who benefits from all this hype surrounding body perfection? Who loses? Where will all this focus on the body lead us as a nation? Will it enhance our position as a global player on economic and social issues? These are critical questions that do not have easy or immediate answers.

CULTURAL STEREOTYPES

A person's body carries with it a set of characteristics that are categorized by others. When meeting someone for the first time and prior to that person's speaking, we assess their age, sex, body weight/size, ethnic background, level of attractiveness, and how much effort they put into their appearance. First impressions are often lasting ones; even though a first impression may be inaccurate, we are often reluctant to let go of our initial assessments. Because humans do not have the time to mentally process each individual they encounter daily, we develop shortcuts to manage this visual information overload. Unfortunately, these shortcuts can lead to stereotypes that can result in discrimination. To **stigmatize** a group is to brand them as unworthy of respect. Take, for example, the statement: All overweight people are lazy and have no self-control. This stigmatization often leads to prejudiced behavior in which all large-size persons we encounter are treated the same despite their individual uniqueness. For example, Barbara Wickens in "Proud to Be Big" tells us that prejudice against obese individuals in North America is the last socially accepted form of discrimination.

Many of the readings in this chapter posit the argument that obesity is caused (at least partially) by environmental factors (see suggested reading "Fixing a Fat Nation"). With fast food restaurants on every street corner offering huge portions of fat-laden foods, the question we should be asking is: Why isn't every single American obese? Often criticized are those who keep a close watch on their calories. We label them as vain and self-absorbed. Gina Kolata, in "No Days Off Are Allowed, Experts on Weight Argue," presents the view that those who appear to be obsessed with food are individuals who are doing what they must to maintain a healthy weight. In "The New Puritans," gym attendance is compared to religion. We apparently love to devote time and energy to our bodies and criticize those who are at a healthy weight as obsessive calorie counters and those who are overweight as lacking self-control. Does that mean perfection is the goal?

When we consider the global marketplace, cultural stereotyping can be especially fatal to business success. Many businesses today serve customers from a wide array of cultural, ethnic, and racial backgrounds, resulting in a wide variation of physical characteristics. The fast pace of business presents additional challenges to resist stereotyping as a means of saving time. One must carefully balance the need to get things done efficiently with the understanding that an individual's background cannot be assumed or stereotyped.

CULTURAL STANDARDS OF BEAUTY

One way to protect oneself from unrealistic ideals and gain some perspective is to look at several other cultures' definitions of beauty. One connecting factor among all cultures is that we are all human beings, and we simply are not satisfied with what nature has given us. It seems to be human nature to want to "improve" upon the characteristics with which we were born. Because all cultures define ideals for their members, most individuals will spend time and energy trying to attain that ideal. As social beings, we also want acceptance from others. One way to demonstrate that need for acceptance is the effort put into some approximation of one's cultural ideal.

One of the purposes for identifying U.S. ideals through the class exercise described earlier is to acknowledge cultural biases before viewing other cultures and their practices. **Ethnocentrism** is the belief that one's own culture has the "right" way to do things. But when we make comparisons cross-culturally, can one honestly say that there is a difference between wearing high-heeled shoes and the bound lily foot? Is scarification different from having a face-lift or a nose job? Euro-American ideals often seem harsh when compared with other cultures.

"Is Thin In? Kalabari Culture and the Meaning of Fatness" offers the reader a cross-cultural comparison of female body ideals. The Kalabari body weight ideal for women has traditionally been much heavier than the American ideal. The Kalabari ideal, however, is currently affected by a global ideal heavily influenced by Western culture. The globalization of female beauty is creating ambivalence among young Kalabarian women regarding their traditional definition of female beauty. (See "The Miss Heilala Beauty Pageant" for a Polynesian approach to female beauty.)

Another direct comparison between cultural standards of beauty can be found in the reading "To Apu, with Love." As an Indian girl growing up in the United States, the author questions her own beauty and eventually learns to value it. Newman, in "The Enigma of Beauty," points out just how elusive a definition of beauty can be. How do you describe beauty? How do you know it when you see it? Is beauty found only in physical characteristics? Or does "personality" factor into the equation? See suggested readings by Teilhet-Fisk (1995) for a Polynesian definition of beauty—that includes personality—and Knickmeyer (2001) for beauty pageants that celebrate a woman's (large) size. One way scientists have tried to quantify beauty is through symmetrical facial features (see Figure 2.1). Newman's article includes an array of cultural and historical examples of beauty. One unfortunate consequence of the globalization

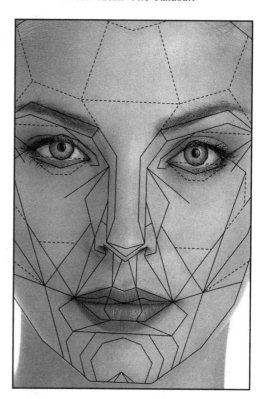

FIGURE 2.1 *Stephen Marquardt's beauty mask.*

of beauty is that one day (if not already) all humans may look alike and the diversity of the past will be lost forever.

Summary

In this chapter, we hope to make the process of "reading the body" a more conscious one. Rather than disregarding the categories in your head and the ten-second (or less) process of putting a person in one category or another, we hope that you will become more aware of how much information you may currently take for granted. This information is important because you may be acting on it in ways you are unaware of. If you ignore or disregard people because of their appearance, this behavior may not be serving you well. The consciousness of reading the body becomes especially important in a global economy as students graduate from college and begin careers with individuals from various ethnic backgrounds. One can no longer assume that they will spend their career working with people who look "just like me."

Suggested Readings

Barnette, M. (1995). The perfect body. In M. E. Roach-Higgins, J. B. Eicher, & K. K. P. Johnson (Eds.), *Dress and Identity*, pp. 51–55. New York: Fairchild.

Etcoff, N. (1999). *Survival of the Prettiest*. Doubleday: New York.

Farley, T., & Cohen, D. (2001, December). Fixing a fat nation. *The Washington Monthly*, 33(12):23–29.

Gardyn, R. (2003, July/August). The shape of things to come. *American Demographics*, 25–30.

Goodman, E. (2001, June 20). Better dead than fat? Women are targets for foolish choices. *The Des Moines Register*, 13A.

Knickmeyer, E. (2001, August 7). African beauty pageant a celebration of size. *The Toronto Star*. Accessed February 19, 2004, at seattlepi.nwsource.com/national/34191_pageant07.shtml.

Ogle, J. P., & Thornburg, E. (2003). An alternate voice amid teen 'zines: An analysis of body-related content in *Girl Zone*. *Journal of Family and Consumer Sciences*, 95(1):47–56.

Rafferty, T. (2001, May). Kate Winslet, please save us. *GQ*, 107–108, 110.

Teilhet-Fisk, J. (1995). The Miss Heilala beauty pageant: Where beauty is more than skin deep. In C. Cohen, R. Wilk, & B. Stoeltje (Eds.), *Beauty Queens on the Global Stage*. New York: Routledge.

Wolf, N. (1991). *The Beauty Myth: How Images of Beauty Are Used against Women*. New York: Doubleday.

Selected Images of Pregnancy through Time

Objective: To examine cultural standards of pregnancy over time.

Pregnancy is an interesting stage of a woman's body that is associated with cultural expectations. For example, in the Arnolfini Wedding Portrait from 1434 (see Figure 2.2), the bride appears to be pregnant when in reality she is not. Her appearance is fulfilling a social expectation. In Europe at that time, great emphasis was placed on replenishing society because of losses from wars and plagues.

Most Americans reacted similarly after World War II by replenishing society, resulting in the Baby Boom generation. Postwar fashions for women are often noted for emphasizing a woman's reproductive capacities (Storm, 1987). A common example of this is Dior's New Look in 1947.

Moving ahead to the early 1970s, we see women exposing their pregnant bellies unapologetically (see Figure 2.3). One might assume that these women are hippies or women who adopted the philosophy of "let it all hang out" quite literally. No bashful pretenses here!

In the 1980s, Princess Diana (see Figure 2.4) took a very conservative approach to her dress for impending motherhood. Note the details of Princess Diana's dress: ruffles around the neck and wrists, white hose, and black patent leather shoes with bows. It appears as if Princess Diana is dressed as the child she is about to have! Certainly, cultural expectations of Diana would have greatly affected her choice of dress while pregnant with the future king of England. This is quite a shift from the previous 1970s illustration.

Also during the 1980s, there was a need for more professional dress than what Princess Diana was wearing (Miller, 1985). Many women in the 1980s were working to establish a career before having a family. You can imagine how difficult it might be for a lawyer or medical doctor to instill confidence in her abilities while wearing ruffles and bows to the office (see Belleau, Miller, & Church, 1988). Several companies during the 1980s developed a line of maternity clothing especially for professional women (see Figure 2.5).

Now let's turn our attention to the 1990s. Demi Moore was pictured on the cover of *Vanity Fair*, pregnant and nude, in 1992 (see Figure 2.6)—quite a bold step for Demi and *Vanity Fair* that resulted in an interesting reaction to this issue. Some cities in the United States required that the magazine be wrapped in brown paper (much like pornographic magazines), while other

FIGURE 2.2 *In Jan van Eyck's Arnolfini Wedding Portrait (1434), the bride is conforming to the fifteenth-century body ideal for European women.*

FIGURE 2.3 *Exposing their abdomens, these women from the early 1970s are visually challenging cultural expectations of pregnant women.*

FIGURE 2.4 *Princess Diana conservatively dressed in maternity attire.*

cities banned the sale of the magazine issue completely. These reactions raise some interesting questions. Why was the cover of *Vanity Fair* so disturbing that it had to be covered or banned? Why are Americans so uncomfortable with the sight of a pregnant woman (a natural state of the body)?

It would appear as though Demi Moore was making a brave and somewhat risky career move by posing nude for the magazine cover. It would also seem likely that she was interested in challenging cultural norms on the expectations of pregnant women. During the Victorian era in America, women were expected to stay at home and out of view when they were "in the family way." Demi very visibly challenged that old notion. How would you describe Demi Moore's body? Do you consider her body beautiful or repulsive? If you were the parent of small children, would you have left this issue of *Vanity Fair* on the coffee table in the living room for your children to see? Why or why not?

Writing Activity

Write a paragraph or two about your thoughts on why the Demi Moore photograph was covered in brown paper or banned. Also include any ideas that came to mind while you looked at the images of pregnant women (real or imagined). How have ideas about preg-

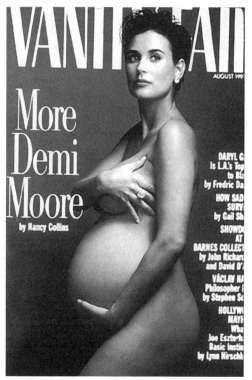

FIGURE 2.5 *Career maternity apparel worn by professional women in the 1980s.*

FIGURE 2.6 *Demi Moore challenges American sensitivities by appearing pregnant and nude on the cover of* Vanity Fair *in 1992.*

nancy changed over time? How have those changes been reflected in dress? In the 1990s, concern for body weight affected women's decisions regarding childbirth. More women were deciding not to have children because of the potential weight gain and difficulty in losing pregnancy weight (Garner, 1997). What implications does the decision not to have children have for American society? Also, consider the social class and status of the women illustrated. How might Princess Diana's status affect her dress as compared with the women from the early 1970s?

Group Activity

After writing down your thoughts, divide into small groups and share your ideas with your fellow classmates.

References

Belleau, B. D., Miller, K. A., & Church, G. E. (1988). Maternity career apparel and perceived job effectiveness. *Clothing and Textiles Research Journal,* 6(2):30–36.

Bordo, S. (2004). *Unbearable Weight: Feminism, Western Culture, and the Body.* Berkeley: University of California Press.

Damhorst, M. L. (1985). Meanings of clothing cues in social context. *Clothing and Textiles Research Journal,* 3:39–48.

Davis, F. (1988). Clothing, fashion and the dialectic of identity. In D. R. Maines & C. J. Couch (Eds.), *Communication and Social Structure*. Springfield, IL: Charles C Thomas.

DeLong, M. R. (1998). *The Way We Look: Dress and Aesthetics* (2nd ed.). New York: Fairchild.

Eicher, J. B. (1995). *Dress and Ethnicity*. Oxford: Berg Press.

Eicher, J. B., & Roach-Higgins, M. E. (1992). Definition and classification of dress. In R. Barnes & J. B. Eicher (Eds.), *Dress and Gender: Making and Meaning*, pp. 8–28. Oxford: Berg Press.

Fisher, S. (1968). Body image. In D. Sills (Ed.), *International Encyclopedia of the Social Sciences*, Vol. 2. New York: Macmillan.

Garner, D. M. (1997, January/February). The 1997 Body Image Survey results. *Psychology Today*, 30(1):30–44, 75–76, 78, 80, 84.

Hillestad, R. (1980). The underlying structure of appearance. *Dress*, 5:117–125.

Kaiser, S. B. (1997). *The Social Psychology of Clothing* (2nd ed. rev.). New York: Fairchild.

Knickmeyer, E. (2001, August 7). African beauty pageant a celebration of size. *The Toronto Star*. Accessed February 19, 2004, at seattlepi.nwsource.com/national/34191_pageant07.shtml.

Luzier, L. A. (1998). Tattooing as a vehicle for expressing aspects of the self. Unpublished master's thesis, University of Kentucky.

Miller, K. A. (1985). Clothing preferences for maternity career apparel and its relationship to perceived job effectiveness. Unpublished master's thesis, Louisiana State University, Baton Rouge.

Ogle, J. P., & Thornburg, E. (2003). An alternate voice amid teen 'zines: An analysis of body-related content in *Girl Zone*. *Journal of Family and Consumer Sciences*, 95(1):47–56.

Paff, J. L., & Lakner, H. B. (1997). Dress and the female gender role in magazine advertisements of 1950–1994: A content analysis. *Family and Consumer Sciences Research Journal*, 26:29–58.

Parker, S., Nichter, M., Nichter, M., Vuckovic, N., Sims, C., & Ritenbaugh, C. (1995). Body image and weight concerns among African American and white adolescent females: Differences that make a difference. *Human Organization*, 54(2):103–114.

Rosenberg, M. (1985). Self-concept and psychological well-being. In R. L. Leahy (Ed.), *The Development of the Self*. Orlando, FL: Academic Press.

Sanders, C. R. (1989). *Customizing the Body: The Art and Culture of Tattooing*. Philadelphia: Temple University Press.

Schulze, L. (1990). On the muscle. In J. Gaines & C. Herzog (Eds.), *Fabrications, Costume and the Female Body*, pp. 59–65 (excerpt). New York: Routledge.

Secord, P. F., & Jourard, S. M. (1953). The appraisal of body cathexis: Body-cathexis and the self. *Journal of Consulting Psychology*, 17:343–347.

Sobo, E. J. (1994). The sweetness of fat: Health, procreation, and sociability in rural Jamaica. In N. Sault (Ed.), *Many Mirrors: Body Image and Social Relations*. New Brunswick, NJ: Rutgers University Press.

Sprigler, M. J., & Miller-Spillman, K. A. (2004). *A Postmodern Portrayal of Women: A Content Analysis of* Vogue *and* Good Housekeeping, *1994–2002*. Manuscript in preparation, University of Kentucky.

Storm, P. (1987). *Functions of Dress*. Englewood Cliffs, NJ: Prentice Hall.

Teilhet-Fisk, J. (1995). The Miss Heilala beauty pageant: Where beauty is more than skin deep. In C. Cohen, R. Wilk, & B. Stoeltje (Eds.), *Beauty Queens on the Global Stage*. New York: Routledge.

Tortora, P., & Eubank, K. (1998). *Survey of Historic Costume* (3rd ed.). New York: Fairchild.

1   The New Puritans

WORKING OUT IS PAINFUL AND BORING. SO WHY BOTHER?

At an hour when he would usually prefer to be asleep, your correspondent drags himself into an LA Fitness gym in north London. In the changing room, he finds a reassuringly fat man forlornly weighing himself; but the other early birds wrestling with the weights machines look dauntingly fit and expert. Nursing a mild hangover and grave doubts about his vocation, he prepares to meet his nemesis.

His nemesis is an affable personal trainer, who is initiating him into the cult of the gym. Questioned about his exercise regime, your correspondent mumbles something about playing soccer from time to time. The instructor is not impressed, and introduces him to a series of contraptions that look like instruments of torture. The new boy and the step-trainer do not see eye to eye. After much sweating and huffing, the instructor estimates that it will take six months for the novice to get into shape, if he eats healthily and sticks to mineral water. The pupil makes his excuses and leaves just before the "fat burner" class begins; the trainer amicably promises to take the relieved smile off his face if he shows it in the gym again.

This humiliating ordeal is of course familiar to millions. It will soon be familiar to many more: the busiest time for gym recruitment is just after Christmas, when seasonal gluttony and optimistic new-year resolutions impel the slothful to take drastic action. The other bumper recruitment times tend to be just before the summer holidays (for which people want to look nice) and just after them (when they realise that, alas, they didn't).

THE FIT AND THE SAVED

The modern gym craze grew out of the aerobics fad of the 1970s and 1980s. In Britain, the industry really took off in the 1990s, when private companies entered a market that had previously been dominated by local councils. Membership of private British gyms, and their revenues, more than doubled between 1996 and 2001, according to the International Health, Racquet & Sportsclub Association (IHRSA). The leading gym franchises have rapidly become fixtures in high streets and shopping arcades. The LA Fitness chain, for instance, one of the country's most successful, was founded in 1996 and will, according to Fred Turok, its chief executive, have 73 outlets by July 2003; the (relatively modest) average monthly fees are currently £38 ($58). Likewise, gym revenue in Germany has almost quadrupled in a decade.

But the beefiest market by far is in America. There are three times as many health clubs in America as there were 20 years ago; around 13% of Americans were members at the last count, and many more attend casually. Companies hoping that the odd work-out will improve their employees' productivity and perhaps contain their health-insurance bills, along with growing numbers of older recruits, have helped to sustain the boom. All this represents quite a big change in how people in rich countries—particularly the young and affluent—spend their time and money.

To anthropologists of the future, however, the gym boom may look as much like a sinister cult as a commercial triumph. Gym-going, after all, has all the basic lineaments of a religion. Its adherents are motivated by feelings of guilt, and the urge to atone for fleshly sins. Many visit their places of worship with a fanatical regularity: a third of LA Fitness members, for instance, go virtually every day. Once there, believers are led by sacerdotal instructors, who either goad them into mass ecstasy during aerobics classes, or preside over the confessional tête-à-tête of personal training. Each devotee has his own rituals, though most rely on the principles of self-mortification and delayed gratification. The extremist cult of body-building, whose Mecca is Gold's Gym in Venice, California, has become a mass movement.

After escaping from a brush with the horizontal leg press, the question that troubles this slobbish journalist is: why? What inspires the armies of devout body-worshippers? What is the point?

Today's young professionals are not the first people in history to devote so much time and cash to the cultivation of their bodies. The word "gymnasium" comes from the Greek word *gumnos*, meaning "naked", which is how many ancient Greeks practised wrestling, boxing and running in their gymnasia (or *palestra*). Gymnasia were part of Plato's ideal city; the Romans inherited this corporeal preoccupation from the Greeks. Ancient gyms shared some features with their modern equivalents: for instance, well-heeled exercisers could engage the services of the classical version of personal trainers. There was a fair bit of ogling. But one essential difference was that one of the purposes of gym-attendance was to prepare young men for war; it was essential for the warrior classes in martial societies such as ancient Sparta.

Conventional religiosity motivated a 19th-century form of body-worship. Christianity had traditionally regarded the body as something of an embarrassment; but with the Victorian rise of "muscular Christianity", looking after the body became a way of worshipping the creator. Christian gentlemen were obliged to attend to their muscles as well as to their minds. Exercise was also embraced to quell the unruliness of poor, urban youths, who were shepherded into boxing clubs. And it answered worries about the sturdiness of the national gene pool, which was required to generate enough able-bodied young men to govern an empire. So the cult of the body spilled out of public schools and into the slums (and across the Atlantic to America).

Unfortunately, these precedents offer little insight into the motives of today's mostly civilian, often godless gym-goers. But there is one concomitant phenomenon that might supply an obvious explanation for the rise of the fitness religion: fat. The exercise boom has coincided with an epidemic bulge in waistlines in many rich countries: an astonishing number of Europeans and Americans are either overweight or obese. So perhaps gym-attendance can be explained as a logical consequence of gluttony—a prophylactic or remedy for fatness in particular, and a sensible way to stay healthy in general?

One problem with this neat explanation, as a visit to almost any gym will reveal, is that most gym-goers are already depressingly svelte. According to Mintel International, a British market-research firm, more people visit gyms to tone up than to lose weight. As one personal trainer confides, fat people are generally too self-conscious to subject themselves to comparison with the flabless forms of most gym users (though some clubs are attempting to entice the shy with euphemistically named "beginners' sessions"). Society, it seems, is becoming polarised between the fat and the fit.

Moreover, if better health is what the running-machine acolytes are looking for, the gym is not always the place to find it. Cardio-vascular exercise has undeniable benefits. (The calculation made by one waggish sceptic—that the amount of time exercise adds to a life is approximately equal to the amount of time spent exercising, yielding a net gain of zero—is no doubt unreliable.) Working out can, says Jeremy Shearman, a specialist in exercise psychology at Britain's University of Essex, have wider benefits, including increased productivity. However, gyms are quite often bad for their devotees' health. That is partly because, as in any gold rush, some unscrupulous entrepreneurs have cut corners on staffing, and regulations have evolved belatedly. So, in Britain, there is no industry-standard qualification for fitness instructors, who often boast only one of many more or less bogus diplomas, or none at all. Some inflict cruel and unusual punishments on their flocks. Even adherents of sedate sub-cults such as yoga are liable to have their limbs damagingly contorted by maverick instructors.

Jonathan Betser, an osteopath in Harley Street, London, says he spends much of his time treating back problems and neck strains incurred by gym-users who have been badly advised or are over-ambitious—compensating for their sedentary jobs with lunatic and damaging work-outs. Others concentrate too much on improving one particularly beloved muscle and end up with dangerously imbalanced bodies. The peak time for such self-inflicted injuries, Mr Betser says, is (be warned) during the penitential January rush.

THE SWEAT AND THE STUPOR

Whatever they do to the body, gyms are certainly numbingly bad for your mind. This is not simply the partisan judgment of a self-vindicating slob. The biggest problem the fitness industry faces is retaining club members, who, when their original zeal wears off, get bored with all the lonely and repetitious rituals. To combat the threat of boredom, gyms have installed distracting televisions and (in the posher ones) Internet connections to entertain the Sisyphean toilers on bikes and rowing machines. Most chains have devised zany-sounding exercise classes to bedazzle flagging members. LA Fitness, like most others, offers a range of unpronounceable varieties of yoga: *Astanga, Iyenga, Sivananda,* and so on.

At the plusher end of the market, the techniques deployed against boredom are much more elaborate. After a generous recovery time—and a more substantial lunch than was technically advisable—this correspondent subjects himself to one such elaboration at the Third Space, a swanky gym in Soho. With membership costing around £1,000 a year, the Third Space is not quite London's priciest outfit, but is probably its most chic. He heads for the club's full-sized boxing ring for an hour's instruction with Martin, a charismatic and patient professional light welterweight. Martin assures him that learning to box is a good way to get fit (the possibility of concussion notwithstanding), and one which is surprisingly popular with women. Martin doesn't seem to mind—or perhaps he doesn't notice—when his pupil breaks a promise to go easy on him, accidentally biffing him on the chin. Martin graciously allows that your correspondent could indeed be a contender, though suggests he comes down a few weight divisions before turning professional.

The boxing ring, which hosts regular "fight-club" nights for emasculated city and media types, is—says Ollie Vigors, a co-founder of the Third Space—one of the ways in which the gym tries to differentiate itself, and keep its visitors entertained. Mr Vigors includes bowling alleys and bars, as well as other gyms, among his competitors. Other features designed to give the Third Space the edge include an altitude-controlled running chamber; a reduced-chlorine swimming pool in which members can learn to scuba dive; a climbing wall; and the opportunity to be serenaded by DJs or (on Sunday mornings) a gospel choir while you work out. There is also on-site alternative therapy, including "neuro-linguistic programming" and other offerings from the outer reaches of medicine and the English language.

Many American gyms, especially those in New York, have devised even more unlikely and exotic novelties to dispel the danger of somnolence. In New York's gyms, experimental exercisers can work-out by pretending to be fire fighters; participate in a "striptease aerobics" class (not an activity likely to appeal to beginners); or engage in the oxymoronic "bootcamp yoga". Rick Caro, who founded the IHRSA and now runs Management Vision Inc, a specialist American consultancy, says that as the fitness business becomes more competitive—and with mini-gyms opening in, among other places, airports and shopping malls—more and more facilities are carving out specialist niches for themselves. Mr Caro believes that group work-outs are one of the best ways to counteract boredom (partly because wavering participants can see that some other people are in a worse shape than they are).

So what, this sweating scribbler continues to ask himself, are the compensations of a pastime whose physical benefits are variable, and which is so dull that all manner of improbable hybrids and gimmicks have to be invented to keep people at it? Why do hordes of already-fit people devote so much of their time to such a boring and self-punitive pursuit? Most other forms of entertainment that have evolved with mass affluence—

such as, say, the rise of foreign holidays—are more obviously enjoyable. Indeed, one standard critique of Anglo-American capitalism argues that, at a certain point, the puritanism that originally sustained it evaporated, to be replaced by a callow and self-indulgent hedonism; whereupon pleasure replaced graft as capitalism's ultimate good. What explains this masochistic anomaly?

HELP THOU MY UNBELIEF

Perhaps the answer lies in the access gyms offer to gaggles of lithe and scantily clad (if not entirely *gumnos*) strangers. Many gyms are indeed designed with plenty of glass and mirrors to facilitate mutual admiration. As Tris Reid-Smith—editor of the *Pink Paper*, a gay British weekly—says, there are some gyms that attract large numbers of "muscle Marys" or "gym bunnies", as stereotypically muscle-bound gay men are known among their peers.

In some of these, gratification is not always exactly delayed. But the etiquette in most gyms, and the strict concentration on personal salvation that prevails, precludes much in the way of flirtation. Most of the admiration is of the narcissistic variety (it is the men, fitness instructors report, who are especially besotted by the mirrors).

Changes in the structure of relationships outside the gym may be part of the explanation: the increased likelihood of divorce and separation may have persuaded attached people, unconsciously or otherwise, that they ought to stay in shape, just in case. Along with the growing demand for male-grooming products, gym attendance among men may also reflect the growing power of women in the singles market: more and more men are now afflicted by the same sort of bodily anxieties that women have endured for decades. (A contrary explanation is that the emasculation wrought by women's gains at work and home has driven some men to fall back on muscular notions of masculinity.) Perhaps, for both sexes, muscles have come to signify prosperity, just as a suntan used to be the mark of an agricultural labourer but now denotes wealth.

Explanations based on the potential rewards of swelling biceps and flat tummies assume that, at some level, gym-going is motivated by the rational pursuit of happiness. According to a more pessimistic view, going to the gym is not pleasurable (however indirectly) but pathological. Oliver James, a clinical psychologist, thinks that the fitness cult is part of a wider pattern of self-flagellation, induced by the drawing of comparisons with inappropriate role models. More and more people feel inadequate, he believes, because the standards by which they judge themselves are the visions of perfection purveyed by seemingly benign television programmes such as "Friends". Meanwhile, too many people fail to derive any solace from comparisons that are flattering to themselves, such as with the fat man in the changing room.

The result is an "horrendous perfectionism" which, Mr James believes, prevents people from enjoying the fruits of their affluence. Few will take this "horrendous perfectionism" to the same extreme as did Yukio Mishima, a celebrated Japanese novelist who, after building a splendidly buff torso from years of pumping iron, committed *hara-kiri* rather than grow old and ugly. But still, Mr James speculates that for every person who goes to the gym for a legitimate health reason, many more are engaging in low-grade attacks on their bodies, which, in most cases, are already absolutely fine. An extreme form of this can be found among bodybuilders, some of whom suffer from a pathological belief that they are puny. According to researchers in Melbourne, "muscle dysmorphia" (or "bigorexia"), as the delusion is known, often leads sufferers to exercise obsessively and gobble steroids.

There is some evidence to support the view that working out, and other forms of body-anxiety, may be sicknesses of affluence—driven by unreasonable and unachievable expectations about where the rowing machine can take you. One personal trainer confides that, whenever a client successfully hardens or tightens one targeted part of the body, he or she invariably moves on to the improvement of another part. Research suggests that twenty-somethings are more dissatisfied with their bodies than anybody else, when, in fact, they tend to be in the best condition. Anxieties about body-shape, epidemiologists in Canada have found, are most prevalent in affluent areas. On this analysis, going to the gym will only make things worse, condemning users to an endless and destructive cycle of perfectionism.

A slightly less depressing possibility is that the appeal of the gym cult lies in the structure of religion itself. Perhaps hedonism is losing its lustre, and rich westerners once again crave the shape and strictures, however masochistic, that orthodox religion once supplied. Like Christian salvation, the holy grails of gym-goers may be distant and unattainable, and the paths towards them painful,

but the rules and routines that their pursuit involves seem to provide comfort to a new and growing breed of secular puritans.

In the end, gym-attendance, like most popular religions, probably has something to do with fear of death and the quest for immortality—as if a well-toned body could somehow stave off the day of judgment. Which, unfortunately, is just another way in which it is liable to lead to disappointment. Gyms may not actually be bad for most people who go to them; but, as a wise man once inquired about hard work, why take the risk?

DISCUSSION QUESTIONS
The New Puritans

1. How often do you "work out"? The author makes some interesting points in comparing gym attendance to religion, such as ritual, repetition, boredom, pain, self-punishment, etc. Do you see similarities between your workout routine and religion?

2. Do you think that American society is "becoming polarized between the fit and the fat"? Why do only fit people go to the gym? Why should fat people feel self-conscious while exercising in a gym?

3. Why do you think so many people who are already in shape continue to go to gyms? Is

it to ogle strangers' bodies? Is it the increased rate of divorce and the fear of what may happen if they don't stay in shape? As women's power in the singles market grows, do men feel anxious about their bodies? Is it the search for perfectionism? The need for self-flagellation? A method of counteracting low body esteem? How do you feel about these arguments? Are they plausible explanations or silly theories about gym attendance?

4. Why has the author chosen this title for the article? Explain the title of this article.

2 No Days Off Are Allowed, Experts on Weight Argue

Gina Kolata

No one looking at her would ever guess that Eileen Barton has a food obsession. She seems so utterly normal: a part-time administrative assistant at her church, Crosspointe Church at Cary, N.C., part-time freelance writer and a conservatively dressed mother of a 12-year-old boy. She is a woman whose calm demeanor indicates a life that is balanced and in control.

At a recent dinner at an Italian restaurant in Raleigh, N.C., Ms. Barton spent no time thinking out loud about what to eat. With little ado, she had a tossed salad, a glass of wine, monkfish, one slice of bread and, after her plate was cleared, one cup of decaffeinated coffee. It was almost unconscious for her to refrain from the appetizers, to abstain from the dessert, to keep her hands out of the bread basket.

But eating, for Ms. Barton, is anything but impulsive. She is acutely aware of what she is eating, privately contemplating eating, privately contemplating what to eat, how much to eat, and whether she has had too much to eat. She weighs herself to make sure that her weight never exceeds 145 pounds on her 5 foot 7 frame, she exercises every day, and she dreams of losing those 5 to 10 pounds that she believes would make such a difference in her appearance.

Ms. Barton is the chronic dieter. Food, her weight, her exercise program, she says, are "always on my mind."

A recent national survey of 107,804 adults by the Centers for Disease Control and Prevention found that more than two-thirds of Americans, 64 percent of men and 78 percent of women, are either dieting to lose weight or watching what they eat to prevent themselves from gaining weight.

Not all are as skillful as Ms. Barton. Dr. Mary K. Serdula, who led the survey, said many tried to control their weight by controlling their fat intake, a strategy that Dr. Serdula and other experts said was ineffective. Or they fail to exercise. But Dr. Serdula said she was not at all surprised that so many Americans were trying so hard to keep their weight under control.

"Weight is a big concern in America," she said.

Until recently, obesity experts would have wrung their hands in dismay over such statistics. Chronic dieters, they would have said, either have eating disorders or are on their way to developing them.

Now, however, increasing numbers of experts say that view is woefully wrong. In today's society, where ever greater varieties of food, in larger and larger portions, always beckon, these experts have concluded that the only way for most people to control their weight is to be like Ms. Barton, exquisitely aware of food, planning their eating and planning exercise to burn off calories and never letting a day go by when what to eat and how much to eat and how much to exercise is not on their minds.

"How many people eat because they're hungry?" asks Dr. James Hill, an obesity researcher at the University of Colorado Health Science Center in Denver. "We eat because it's 12 o'clock."

While there are what Dr. Hill calls "the genetic superstars" who are naturally thin and who naturally stop eating when their body tells them they have had enough, "the data suggests that they are in the minority," he said.

"The only way to keep from gaining weight is to make gaining weight a conscious activity rather than an unconscious activity," Dr. Hill said. "If you leave it to your physiology, you're going to gain weight. You have to plan."

Dr. Madelyn H. Fernstrom, director of the weight management center at the University of

Pittsburgh Medical Center Health System, put it bluntly: "The term 'chronic dieter' is not a negative one."

And, Dr. Hill added, it is the responsibility of obesity researchers to tell the public that they really do have to think about food and exercise all the time.

EVER VIGILANT ON REGIMENS

For years, the great hope and promise of diet programs had been to get people's weight down and then allow them to, in essence, forget about food, living the rest of their lives like someone who was naturally thin.

"That was the meta-message. You go on a diet for short period of time and then the diet's over," said Dr. Gary D. Foster, who is the clinical director of the Weight and Eating Disorders Program at the University of Pennsylvania School of Medicine.

If only it were so simple, chronic dieters say.

Mary Litman began dieting years ago, when she was 20. She remembers the moment she resolved to lose weight, at the end of a date with a good-looking young man.

He walked her to her door, she recalled, and said, "It's a good thing you have a pretty face because you're really fat."

Ms. Litman was 5 foot 2 and weighed 125 pounds. Her date was right, she decided. All that oblivious eating of cakes and pies that her mother, a farmer's wife, had made for the family had taken their toll.

"I was farm-girl fat—pretty, but chubby," Ms. Litman said.

She began a life of dieting, first losing about 10 pounds, then learning to maintain it. She walks at least four miles a day, makes deliberate food choices and bargains with herself in a constant internal conversation.

The other day, for example, one of the women in her office at the University of Pittsburgh Health System, where she is an administrative coordinator, brought in homemade cannoli.

"I said to myself, 'I'm going to eat it,' " Ms. Litman declared. But then, she told herself, "If you do, you have to walk home from work and eat a salad for dinner." Which is exactly what she did.

She plans ways to keep her portions small. "If I buy a pound of grapes and leave them in a big package, I'll eat every one of them," she said. "If I put them in baggies, I'll eat what's in a baggie." When she wants mint candy, she buys Junior Mints rather than a large mint patty and eats a few at a time. "If you buy a mint patty, it's gone," Ms. Litman said.

OTHERS HAVE MORE EXTREME REGIMENS

"I've been in pretty good shape now for decades," said Dr. Richard Wurtman, who directs the clinical research center at the Massachusetts Institute of Technology. "But it's only because of being concerned every day with what I eat and what I burn up."

Dr. Wurtman, who describes himself as a fat person in a thin person's body, says he is so concerned about getting his aerobic exercise every day that he calls hotels before he visits them when he travels to make sure they have stair-stepping machines.

"There's one hotel in Paris that I've gone to for 15 years because they had the only StairMaster in town," he said.

He also keeps a mental tally of the calories he consumes each day, aiming for a total of about 2,000. Breakfast is always grapefruit juice, black coffee and a bran muffin made by his wife, Dr. Judith Wurtman, who directs Triad, a commercial weight-loss center in Belmont, Mass. No bakery muffins for the Wurtmans. They can have 600 calories, Dr. Wurtman said.

Lunch for Dr. Wurtman is either a cup of soup or nothing at all, unless he has a visitor and goes out to eat. "Then I compensate later," he said, eating less for the rest of the day. After work, Dr. Wurtman has "a dab of cottage cheese—we buy the fat-free kind—and I pour some soy sauce on it to make it taste good." Then he goes to the gym. After working out, he and his wife have dinner. "It's very spartan—fish and lots of vegetables and good bread." For dessert, he gets a treat—some frozen yogurt.

"I don't want to be fat," Dr. Wurtman said. "I don't want my clothes to be tight on me. I like the sense of looking in a mirror and not being displeased."

CONTROL, A RELATIVE TERM

In a sense, Ms. Barton, Ms. Litman and Dr. Wurtman are lucky. With chronic dieting, they have learned to stay thin. Not everyone is able to do so, obesity researchers say. Some are simply misinformed about how to do it. Others are biologically unable to become thin—the most they can realistically hope for is to be less fat.

In recent years, an ever-accumulating body of evidence has led most obesity researchers to a troubling conclusion: except within certain narrow limits, people may not be able to control their weight completely. Each individual, they say, inherits genes that predetermine a range of body weights—varying about 10 percent from a midpoint, that they can maintain. The chronic dieters, through their constant vigilance, are keeping their weights as low as their genes will allow. The notion of natural weight ranges can be hard for many people to accept, obesity experts say. The idea that anyone who wants to could be thin, is "the biggest misunderstanding in medicine," said Dr. Jules Hirsch, an obesity researcher at Rockefeller University.

Dr. Hirsch and others point out that years of research consistently show that if someone's weight gets out of her genetically determined range—either because she has managed to eat so much that she becomes fatter or because she diets so much that she becomes thinner—her body is driven to lose or gain weight to force her weight back in line. Those who are above their range lose their appetites and lose interest in food. At the same time, their body's metabolism actually speeds up to push their weight back down. Those who are below their range become obsessed with food and unable to control their urges to eat. In that situation, the body's metabolism slows down to make the pounds creep back on, researchers find.

That, of course, does not mean that environment plays no role in making people grow fat. After all, researchers add, genes cannot change overnight, but environments can. And something must be making people gain weight. Many experts say that more and more Americans are responding to a society that insidiously encourages them to be as fat as their genes will allow them to be. Instead of being at the bottom of their weight range, like the chronic dieters, many people are at the top.

But what is it that tempts people to eat so much? Hypotheses abound.

"Portion sizes are enormous," said Dr. F. Xavier Pi-Sunyer, a professor of medicine at St. Luke's-Roosevelt Hospital. "People are walking around with liter cups of milkshakes. And people nibble all the time. They're eating on the street, they're eating all night while they watch television."

Americans are eating more and more meals away from home, too. Fast foods are notoriously fattening. But expensive restaurants, too, have been known to ladle on the fat, knowing it makes their food taste good.

Mashed potatoes at luxury restaurants may contain one part butter to two parts potatoes and even vegetables often get a tablespoon of butter per serving added on their way out of the kitchen. At Union Pacific, a Manhattan restaurant, the menu correctly said that its halibut was poached, but it did not say in what. The answer, said the proprietor and chef, Rocco DiSpirito, was goose fat.

"Fat is an important element of flavor," Mr. DiSpirito explained.

Dr. Jeffrey M. Friedman, an obesity researcher at Rockefeller University, likes to explain weight ranges by analogy with height. With height, he said, people—and animals—are pretty much at the mercy of their inheritance, but the environment can—and does—make a big difference. After all, he said, the average height of soldiers during the Civil War was 5 foot 4. But while diet can make people grow taller, the upper and lower limits of an individual's height is set by genes. The same may be true with weight, Dr. Friedman said.

"There's an illusion that you can control weight," he said, "but the facts don't support that."

EXPECTATIONS VS. REALITY

Researchers who have seen what they describe as overwhelming evidence of biologically determined weight ranges say they are becoming weary of hearing promoters of weight-loss programs insist that people could be really thin if they truly wanted to.

"They insist that if you would just eat less," Dr. Hirsch said. "How many calories would it take? Come on, a mouthful less a day. Can't you do that," he said, adding, "Everyone wants to focus on the behavior side, as though people are perversely eating one bite more."

But behavior has failed to explain why people stay fat, Dr. Hirsch and others say. Studies searching for behavioral characteristics, like binge eating, eating too quickly or skipping meals that typified obesity failed to find consistent patterns. Every behavior by fat people was found just as often in thin people.

It is a lesson that has been met with denial or disbelief, even by some who run research programs on obesity. These experts say that until recently they would point to height-weight charts and tell fat people that their goal should be to get to what the chart said was an optimal weight for their height. Only a few got their weights down that low and even fewer could maintain them. Now, these researchers say, they are citing what is a more realistic weight goal—a loss of about 10 percent of body weight, which often is enough to make people healthier, lowering their blood sugar and blood pressure.

But such modest goals are not always easy for fat people to accept, Dr. Foster said. Achieving them requires great effort—and constant vigilance for life—but it also means coming to terms with the fact that, for many, being slender will always be a fantasy.

In a recent study, Dr. Foster and his colleagues asked 60 obese women to reveal what they hoped for, and what they dreamed of, when they began a diet and exercise program. The women, whose average weight was 218 pounds, said their goal was to lose, on average, about a third of their body weight, or 71 pounds for a new weight of 146 pounds. They said that their dream would be to get down to 135 pounds.

But after 48 weeks of diet and exercise, their average weight loss was just 37 pounds, a loss that they had described before the study as "disappointing and could not be viewed as successful in any way." And that was before they tried to maintain what they had lost.

Obesity experts say that many fat people will have to lower their expectations and realize that they can look and feel better even though they will not be thin.

"Most of us have a little bit of an unrealistic idea of what we should look like," said Cathy Monas, the director of the weight management and nutrition center at St. Luke's-Roosevelt Hospital in New York.

Ms. Monas reminds patients of how much better their lives are with even a small but sustainable weight loss. "We say, 'Look, you're maintaining your weight. Your blood pressure has gone down, your cholesterol has gone down, you're playing tennis again. This is terrific.' "

That, of course, is not the message that many fat people want to hear.

Dr. Foster says he tries to explain to patients that they must be realistic. But, he said, "when you tell a woman who weighs 220 pounds that she has to lose 22 pounds, she looks at you like you've got three heads."

PLANNING DIET AND EXERCISE

Dr. Fernstrom says she is still dumbfounded when she sees what many do to try to lose weight. Over and over again, she says, her patients will tell her they drank fruit juice with abandon or ate bags of fat-free pretzels, reasoning that because these foods had no fat, they are not fattening.

"Sometimes I call it the great hope of American eating, that nonfat means non caloric," Dr. Fernstrom said. "This has been a sabotage."

Dr. Serdula of the Centers for Disease Control and Prevention found the same thing in the national survey she directed. About 35 percent of the men and 40 percent of the women who were trying to lose weight said they were controlling their food intake by eating less fat. That simply does not work, Dr. Serdula said. "Calories do count," she said.

While high-fat foods typically have many calories, so do many low-fat foods, including ones like nonfat cookies or muffins that dieters buy in place of the real thing, obesity experts point out.

Because the total number of calories, a measure of the energy value of food, is what determines whether a person loses weight, stays the same, or gains weight, people ignore calories at their peril, obesity experts say.

It is one thing for someone to want to be at the bottom of their weight range, obesity experts said. It may be quite another for them to know how to do it.

"The people who watch and know the calorie content of foods are labeled as overzealous and obsessed with foods," Dr. Fernstrom said. But, she said: "You do need to learn the calories that are in certain portions of food. You do have to have some control over the types and amounts of foods that are going into your mouth."

It is all too easy for people to eat more than they realize, obesity experts said. In a recent study, Dr. George Bray, an obesity expert at the Pennington Biomedical Research Center at Louisiana State University, asked dietitians to estimate the number of calories they were consuming, thinking that if anyone should get it right, it was these professionals.

"They underreported by 10 percent," Dr. Bray said.

Many Americans also delude themselves about how much benefit they are getting from exercise, researchers say. In Dr. Serdula's national survey, about two-thirds of the people who were trying to lose weight said they were increasing their physical activity. But only 21 percent reported exercising at least 150 minutes a week, which is the minimum recommended for weight loss.

The goal now, Dr. Hill said, should be to teach people what is really required to control their weights. It means showing people what the participants in his registry of successful dieters do.

"These people have figured out that they can't just leave it to chance," Dr. Hill said. "They have to plan their diet and they have to plan their exercise."

A CHOICE FOR A LIFETIME

Growing up, Eileen Barton had seemed like one of those girls who would never have to worry about her weight. She gave no conscious thought to what she was eating yet remained slender and healthy. In fact, she says, the first time she even thought about her weight seems silly in retrospect.

She was a junior in high school, 5 foot 6 and weighing 115 pounds. Anyone would say she was thin, but she decided she had a weight problem because she thought her hips bulged too much when she wore a bikini. "I thought I had this disgusting problem," she said. The next year, however, she weighed even more—120 pounds. "I remember thinking, 'This is all wrong. I was supposed to go down. I wasn't supposed to go up,'" Ms. Barton said. "I was flipping out."

Then came college, and the beginning of a real weight problem. At Wheaton College, an all-woman institution in Massachusetts, the students would joke about "the freshman 20," the 20 pounds that freshmen often gained. Ms. Barton far exceeded it. In her first two years, she gained 60 pounds, topping the scales at 180. Her weight gain was no mystery. "I was bingeing," she said. Miserable about the way she looked, she tried desperately to lose weight.

"I remember the feelings and the thoughts were, 'How did I ever allow it to get out of my control? This wasn't supposed to happen to me,'" Ms. Barton said. She tried fad diets, like a high-protein diet and the Scarsdale diet. Once she fasted for two weeks. But the pounds she lost came right back.

Alarmed, her mother took her to a doctor because she was convinced that Ms. Barton must have a thyroid problem. She turned out to be perfectly healthy. Just fat.

After college, Ms. Barton moved to Denver. There, over two years, she assiduously dieted and exercised and the weight slowly came off. With her weight down to 135 pounds, a perfect size 8, Ms. Barton decided that that awful period of her life as a fat woman was behind her. Now that she was thin she would never have to think about dieting again.

It was not to be. The only way to maintain her weight, Ms. Barton learned, was to watch what she ate and to exercise regularly, walking or riding her bike for an hour to an hour and a half each day. Even so, staying at 135 pounds was be-

yond her. At that weight, she found herself obsessed with food and unable to control her eating. She let her weight creep up to 140 to 145, and now carefully keeps track of it so it goes no higher. She also gave away her size 8 clothes.

"I'm at the point where I say, 'O.K. I've got more on my hips than probably exceeds my best desire, but I feel great,' " Ms. Barton said.

When she gets depressed about her weight, she goes to a Web site that gives body mass indices, a measurement of obesity, and verifies that she is not even close to being too fat.

But still, Ms. Barton said, she often wishes she could just forget, for once, about what she is eating.

"I'd like to just live my life and not think about it," she said.

DISCUSSION QUESTIONS

No Days Off Are Allowed, Experts on Weight Argue

1. Where is the balance between the extremes of obesity and thinness? It appears from the articles in this chapter that Americans are either obsessed with becoming overweight from overeating and lack of exercise, or they are obsessed with dieting, by constantly counting calories and exercising. With so many mixed messages, how do you find a balance?

2. What do you think America needs to do to remain healthy eaters and exercisers? List your ideas, regardless of how outlandish

they may sound, and discuss them with a small group of your classmates.

3. The author states: "the perception that chronic dieters are individuals who are on their way to eating disorders is the wrong view." Since Americans no longer have to physically work to earn a living and support a family (in contrast to much of the U.S. population around the 1900s), how do we replace that physical activity in a healthy way?

3 A Web of Deceit: Internet Sites Encouraging Anorexia Draw Alarm from the Medical Community

Dawn Sagario

Trudy Randall starved herself for almost 25 years. Randall, 35, is recovering from a disorder that has plagued her since she was 11, growing up in Algona, Ia. During the bleakest days of her fight against anorexia she remembers her weight dipping to 80 pounds.

She was 19.

Recovery is still new to her. Every day, she deals with the disease that consumed her for nearly three-quarters of her life. Sometimes, she can still recall the delirious high of denying herself food.

Her recovery has been slow and painful, but ultimately successful. At 5-foot-1, she now weighs 140 pounds.

Then something scared her on the Internet.

She discovered a Web site that actually encourages pro-anorexic behavior.

"It was too psycho," Randall said.

For women like her, the site could reverse all the hard-earned efforts to return to a normal life.

In scores of chat rooms and message boards, those suffering from anorexia share dieting tips and "thinspiration"—words of encouragement to keep starving themselves. Their lifestyle is to be celebrated, they say, rather than dismissed as a disease that needs to be treated.

In a disorder where competition can become the motivation to lose weight, sites like "Pro-Anorexia!" "Stick Figures" and "Anorexic Nation" are drawing more players into a contest to be the thinnest.

The growth of this network of support groups is attracting attention from doctors and therapists, who have every right to worry about the trend. Anorexia has the highest mortality rate of any psychiatric disorder, claiming more lives than schizophrenia and depression.

Comments left on these sites are ones of adoration, relief and gratitude. They shed light on the tortured thinking that drives women who have the disorder.

A posting on "Pro Anorexia's Dreambook" from Danielle is an example: "I love your site. Thank you so much. I just started a 100-hour fast 12 hours ago, and your site has given me the inspiration I need to get through it!!"

Pictures of women with jutting shoulder bones, prominent ribcages and concave stomachs are posted, all intended to help fellow anorexics abstain from eating.

Log on to the "Stick Figures" Web page to find an emaciated Angelina Jolie with a gray pallor and sunken cheekbones. A red "X" stitches her mouth shut.

The site's message is spelled out clearly: "Stick Figures is a club for people with eating disorders who are not ready to recover yet and will do anything they have to, to meet their weight-loss goals."

"Anorexia is a lifestyle, not a disease" appears in bold letters.

"Let the bones define the beauty of your body," is one of at least a dozen sayings that accompany images of super-thin models on the site.

"Food is a hindrance to your progress. Nothing tastes as good as being thin feels."

Stick Figures' ticker shows more than 61,000 hits since January.

Web master "dietpepsi_uhhuh" delivers her own "Thin Commandments":

"If you aren't thin you aren't attractive.

"Being thin is more important than being healthy.

"You must buy clothes, cut your hair, take laxatives, starve yourself, do anything to make yourself look thinner. Thou shall not eat without feeling guilty.

"Being thin and not eating are signs of true willpower and success."

The reaction to these pro-anorexia sites has been swift, and to some extent, worthwhile. Groups have rallied for their removal, with one association claiming a victory earlier this month.

Yahoo! began deleting the pro-anorexic sites from its servers at the beginning of August, responding within days of requests made by the National Eating Disorders Association, said Holly Hoff, director of programs for the Seattle-based group.

Hoff reports that at least 100 sites have been erased so far.

Initial attempts to dissuade the founders of the pro-anorexia forums went unheeded, said Hoff, whose organization first heard of the online eating disorder support system in May.

The Web masters are "physically starving," she said, "so they're not able to comprehend the damage they're doing, or they aren't able to be enough concerned about it."

Swapping tips among anorexics online is dangerous, helping to maintain unhealthy behavior, said Dr. Wayne Bowers, an associate professor of psychiatry at the University of Iowa College of Medicine.

"It's taking a serious illness and saying it's a lifestyle," said Bowers, who for two decades has counseled patients recovering from the disease. "It's part of the huge denial factor of anorexia that says, 'This is all right.' That's what's most disconcerting."

Those toying with the thought of anorexia could be swayed by the pro-anorexia sites and are highly vulnerable, he said.

Anorexia is still misunderstood, he said, and more education at the junior high level is needed. He also cited lack of support for effective treatment, with many insurance companies refusing to fully cover what could be years of recovery.

Officials at Yahoo! wouldn't comment on the pro-anorexia sites but said the company prohibits "harmful, threatening, and abusive" content.

Yahoo! spokeswoman Mary Osako did say complaints about Web page content are handled within 24 hours. "We will evaluate it, and in extreme cases, remove it," she said.

Patients at the Eating Disorder Treatment Center at Iowa Lutheran Hospital heard about the online groups last month, said Carrie Peitzmeier, a dietitian and mental health specialist.

"My first reaction was, 'I can't believe it,'" Peitzmeier said. "They're already trying to fight those eating disorder messages, then you've got someone who's pushing them harder."

The center, an intensive outpatient program, has seen enrollment surpass totals from last year, said Sharon Check, a registered nurse and counselor. Those with less severe conditions are referred to weekly outpatient programs.

For many suffering from anorexia, restricting food intake is a way to deal with their problems and achieve a form of control, Peitzmeier said.

"These Web sites are teaching them to get that control in an unhealthy way."

Randall said her anorexia began when she was sexually abused at the age of 11. It would be another 10 years of water, fruit and diet soda before she would receive formal treatment at 21.

"When I look at my life and everything that's happened in it, my eating disorder has totally been a means of control for me," said Randall, whose weight would fluctuate between 70 and 90 pounds during high school. "When something would happen, the eating disorder would come out."

Randall said access to the pro-anorexia sites might have killed her.

"If I had that extra help, I wouldn't be here."

After going through treatment at eating disorders clinics in Minnesota and Des Moines,

Randall found a counselor she trusts in Omaha and schedules visits every other week.

Wanting health and happiness won out over her disease, Randall said. Those with eating disorders need to learn how to cope with their troubles and move on.

"You can't shift the blame," she said. "We all make choices. It's all about choices with eating disorders."

A Web of Deceit

1. Have you ever seen a Web site that promotes anorexia? If fat people have an organization that promotes their "lifestyle," why shouldn't people with eating disorders have Web sites that promote their "lifestyle"? If being fat should be regarded as "just another characteristic of a person" (see "Proud to Be Big"), why shouldn't anorexia be viewed in the same way? If search engines are blocking Web sites that promote anorexia, why shouldn't search engines also block Web sites that promote being fat?

2. Consider this: Anorexia kills more than schizophrenia and depression, but does it kill more than diabetes and heart disease (the results of being overweight)?

3. Do you think that search engines such as Yahoo! are limiting free expression by deleting anorexia promotion Web sites?

4. Make a list of all the ways you can think of to combat images of thinness. These could be individual ways (i.e., self-esteem and self confidence, "I feel good about myself no matter what my weight or size") or they could be on a societal level (i.e., include information about dangers of dieting in health education classes for elementary kids).

4   The Weight of the World

Don Peck

Obesity may soon surpass both hunger and infectious disease as the world's most pressing public-health problem.

In 2000, for the first time in history, the number of overweight people in the world—more than a billion of them, 300 million of whom were obese—matched the number of underweight people. (Obesity is defined as a specific ratio of weight to height: someone standing five foot five, for instance, would be considered obese at 180 pounds or more, whereas someone six feet two would be considered obese at 233 pounds or more.)

The United States contains more fat people—by a large margin—than any other nation. Sixty-four percent of American adults are overweight, versus 47 percent in 1980. Some nine million Americans are now "morbidly obese," meaning roughly a hundred pounds or more overweight, and weight-related conditions

This article originally appeared in the June 2003 issue of *The Atlantic Monthly*. Reprinted with the permission of Don Peck.

cause about 300,000 premature deaths a year in this country—more than anything else except smoking.

Yet, surprisingly, health problems associated with obesity may be more severe in poor countries than in the United States, according to a recent World Health Organization report, in part because such countries lack the resources to treat diabetes, heart disease, and other frequently fatal illnesses linked to excess weight. Another WHO study notes that although both hunger and infectious disease remain major problems, particularly in some regions, obesity will soon surpass them as the most severe public-health problem facing the world as a whole.

The extent of global obesity is striking. For instance, 71 percent of women in Egypt are overweight or obese. Even in countries that are still struggling to feed many of their people, unhealthy weight gain is increasing; 15 percent of Kenyan women and 26 percent of Zimbabwean women are overweight. (Corresponding figures for men are typically higher.) Childhood obesity rates in many developing countries are rapidly converging with those seen in this country. In China, for example, childhood obesity—a phenomenon unknown in previous generations—has risen as high as 13 percent in urban areas. Twenty-nine percent of urban Chinese children are overweight.

What accounts for such rapid gains in weight worldwide? Declining physical activity has undoubtedly played a role, but greater food availability and changing eating habits have probably played larger ones. In the United States families now eat fewer home-cooked meals, which tend to have about half as many calories as restaurant or takeout meals. This shift has driven perhaps two thirds of the country's weight gain since 1980. And in developing countries increased dietary fat—largely attributable to the spread of cheap, high-quality cooking oil—has helped to raise daily caloric intake by an average of 400 calories per capita since 1980. People in the vast majority of countries now have access to an average of more than 2,500 calories a day.

Until recently frequent food shortages may have masked a genetic vulnerability to obesity that is carried by a significant share of the world's people—perhaps billions of them. The evidence is most striking in Pacific Islanders, Central Asians, and other populations that have seen food availability rise to near-Western levels in recent years and are now experiencing rates of obesity as high as 80 percent. And in any population, whatever its genetic predisposition, malnutrition during gestation heightens the risk of obesity, diabetes, and heart disease during adulthood; it may be that when fetuses are undernourished, they are "programmed" to overeat during times of abundance, storing fat for presumed lean times ahead. Many of the world's people were conceived and brought to term in a very lean era yet now face a wealth of affordable, high-fat food—meaning that untold children may avoid starvation and diseases related to poverty only to die early from diabetes, heart disease, or other "diseases of affluence."

Obesity is often discussed as an American cultural phenomenon, closely intertwined with a taste for fast food, soft drinks, television, and video games. But it is more accurately seen as a broader economic phenomenon, its growth driven by such changes as cheaper food, urbanization (less walking and agricultural work), the increasing prevalence of desk jobs, and the delegation of food preparation to professionals who—whether gourmet chefs or fast-food executives—are skilled at making food taste good, and making us want more of it. None of these trends has run its course (in fact, the biggest cause of increased obesity in the United States recently—the decline of home cooking—has yet to become a major factor in most of the world). Overall, obesity looks like an epidemic still in its infancy. Its worst consequences are yet to come.

DISCUSSION QUESTIONS

1. Without stating it directly, Peck appears to blame America for exporting the "diseases of affluence" to other countries. How do you feel about this issue? Do you believe that America is responsible for the increase of diabetes and heart disease worldwide?

2. How could American culture change to make gaining weight more difficult? Limit the number of fast food restaurants per mile? Increase walking paths and bike routes? What types of environmental changes would reverse the trend toward increased obesity in American culture?

3. Peck states that the worst is yet to come since the obesity epidemic is still in its infancy. What do you predict will happen over the next 100 years? Will Americans slow down and begin to cook more meals at home in the future to preserve their longevity?

5 Is Thin In? Kalabari Culture and the Meaning of Fatness

Susan O. Michelman
University of Kentucky

It will be of no surprise to those reading this article that most women in America today aspire to an aesthetic of thinness and are constantly seduced into thinking that "you can neither be too rich nor too thin." Although this is historically quoted from the Duchess of Windsor, the statement bears contemporary truth because many women equate thinness with happiness and financial success (Bordo, 1993).

How dominant an ideal is this aesthetic of thinness? Every culture ascribes to a body ideal for both men and women. A body ideal is a size, age, and a combination of physical attributes that society deems to be the most desirable for each gender. For example, the current popular ideal for American women emphasizes a youthful, slim, athletic, and well-toned physique. Although most apparel designers both promote and design for this image, in reality, only a small percentage of the population fit these stringent criteria. Recent studies have found that the average American woman is 5 feet 4 inches tall, weighs 142 pounds, and wears a size 14.

Not every culture on the globe ascribes to an ideal of slimness. As the apparel industry is both motivated by and addresses an increasingly diverse multicultural market, both designers and merchandisers will need to be sensitive to cultural body ideals. Asia's rapidly expanding market of fashion consumers is an example of this trend. Currently, some Indonesian designers are attaining success by designing for Asian women's tastes and body size, frequently smaller in proportion to an American or European woman's body frame.

In each historic era, the American women's body ideal has changed based upon society's motivations and resulting characteristic forms of dress. At the turn of the 20th century, women's corsets enhanced an S-shaped ideal with an ample bustline, tiny waist, rounded hips, and long hair. Couturier designers, such as Charles

---

Original for this text.

Worth, extolled these ideals in lavish, hand-constructed designs for wealthy women. Only 20 years later, along with the advent of mass production of apparel and social changes such as women attaining the vote, the "flapper era" extolled a youthful, slim, almost boyish physique for women, with short, bobbed hair. This ideal for women was literally the antithesis of designs at the turn of the century.

My objective in writing this article is to demonstrate that there is no one universal body ideal for women. I will discuss the tradition of *iria* among the Kalabari people of Nigeria. In 1990, I did fieldwork and research among the Kalabari (Michelman, 1992). In contrast to American culture, I discovered that fatness or plumpness is considered a sign of beauty for Kalabari women. Understanding the body ideals of another culture, the Kalabari, will help you gain a greater understanding of the diversity and cultural meaning of body ideals, particularly for women (Michelman & Eicher, 1995; Michelman, 1995).

THE KALABARI AND THE TRADITION OF *IRIA*

The Kalabari are an ethnic group who reside in the Niger River delta of southern Nigeria in West Africa (Figure 2.7). The Kalabari form a distinct cultural and linguistic subgroup that is a comparatively small population of approximately one million within the total Nigerian population of 120 million. The eastern Niger River delta, where the Kalabari live, is a saltwater swamp. Exploitable resources from this environment are limited, and people have relied primarily on occupations of fishing, salt-making, and trading, along with exchanging produce from inland areas. Although most Kalabari are Christians, precolonial beliefs and practices still pervade their daily and ritual life.

Kalabari dress has been examined by several authors from different points of view. Erekosima and Eicher have discussed the concept of cultural authentication expressed through Kalabari dress (Erekosima, 1979; Erekosima & Eicher, 1981). Through trade, foreign goods and European cloth

were introduced into the Niger River delta area as early as the sixteenth century (Alagoa, 1972, p. 291). The Kalabari incorporated these western items into their indigenous system of dress and aesthetics, modifying them to make them part of their own ethnic identity.

The Kalabari celebrate the female appearance known as *iria*, a cultural celebration of womanhood characterized by dress and body modifications. *Iria* marks the period of transition in the female life cycle from late childhood through childbirth. According to Akobo's (1985) accounts of the oral tradition of *iria*, in early puberty young women underwent the ceremony of *ikuta de* (i.e., decoration with beads), which was a cultural acknowledgement of their femininity. As adolescents, these young women performed the *pakiri iwain* ceremony where they became "social debutantes." With subsequent ceremonies and physical maturity, they revealed less of their bodies to the public. *Konju fina* was

Celebration of female maturity & development

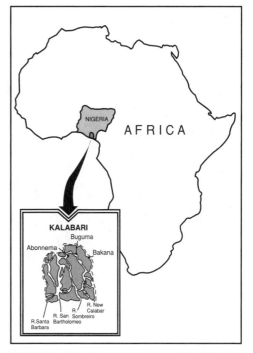

FIGURE 2.7 *The Kalabari reside in the Niger River delta of southern Nigeria in West Africa.*

the ceremony that indicated their readiness for marriage. *Bite sara* was peformed when they became betrothed, with the final stage *iriabo* indicating their childbearing status (see Figure 2.8).

After the adolescent "coming out," Kalabari men were historically able to openly admire the young woman's appearance and approach the parents concerning marriage. As the female body matured and rounded out, clothing became less important as it obstructed the visibility of the body's development. Well-developed breasts and, more important, protruding buttocks indicated the ability to wear wrappers properly. Wrappers are large, rectangular pieces of cloth that are literally wrapped around the body at the waist and

FIGURE 2.8 *Examples of how two Kalabari women incorporated Western items into their indigenous system of dress and aesthetics, modifying them to make them part of their own ethnic identity.*

extend to the ankles. Wrappers are worn by both men and women.

Historically, after the birth of their first child, a woman stayed in a fattening room for about two months, necessitating a substantial financial commitment from the woman's and husband's family (Daly, 1984). While in the fattening room, the woman was attended by other female family members, who nurtured the *iriabo*'s child while the woman was instructed in dance. Dancing was performed publicly at the end of the confinement.

Today, because of contemporary demands of education and employment, women are less willing to devote time to complete the full process of becoming an *iriabo*. *Iria* is now performed by women at cultural events and particularly at family funerals.

Nonetheless, cultural ideals of female beauty are still associated with public acknowledgement and approval of female fecundity. The ideal adult Kalabari female figure is "substantial and thick or plumpy" (Daly, 1984). The expression "to be up to a woman" is to be rounded, particularly in the breasts and buttocks. The practice of seclusion or fattening after pregnancy further enhances the image of the plump Kalabari woman. Historical photographs reveal women in the desirable state of roundness (see Figure 2.9).

The midsection of the female Kalabari body is emphasized by clothing more than any other area. This body aesthetic, admired by both Kalabari men and women, indicates an intense interest in recognizing and revering the reproductive capacity of the female. There is no apparent comparable interest in a plump body for Kalabari males.

BODY IDEALS IN CROSS-CULTURAL CONTEXT

Even among the Kalabari of Nigeria who have an essential cultural belief in the beauty of a plump female body, contemporary influences

FIGURE 2.9 *A historic portrait reveals the desirable state of roundness in Kalabari women.*

ologies of a culture are inscribed. Mary Douglas (1982) suggested that the human physical body in any culture symbolically represents important aspects of the social "body." How the physical body serves as a medium of expression varies with ethnicity and religious and political beliefs. This could include ideals related to modesty, size, and importance of various body parts—some that are covered and some not. Body ideal varies from culture to culture and can change over time.

References

Akobo, D. I. (1985). *Oral Traditions of Buguma: Iria Ceremony a Case Study.* Ibadan, Nigeria: Ibadan University Press.

Alagoa, E. J. (1972). *A History of the Niger Delta.* Ibadan, Nigeria: Ibadan University Press.

Bordo, S. (1993). *Unbearable Weight: Feminism, Western Culture, and the Body.* Berkeley: University of California Press.

Daly, M. C. (1984). Kalabari female appearance and the tradition of iria. Unpublished doctoral dissertation, University of Minnesota, St. Paul.

Douglas, M. (1982). *Natural Symbols.* New York: Pantheon Books.

Erekosima, T. V. (1979). The tartans of Buguma women: Cultural authentication. Paper presented at African Studies Association, Los Angeles.

Erekosima, T. V., & Eicher, J. B. (1981). Kalabari cut-thread and pulled-thread cloth. *African Arts,* 14(2):48–51, 87.

Michelman, S. (1992). Dress in Kalabari women's societies. Unpublished doctoral dissertation, University of Minnesota, St. Paul.

Michelman, S. O. (1995). Social change and the symbolism of dress in Kalabari women's societies. *Family and Consumer Science Research Journal,* 23(4):368–392.

Michelman, S. O., & Eicher, J. B. (1995). Dress and gender in Kalabari women's societies. *Clothing and Textiles Research Journal,* 13(2):121–129.

conveyed through international media are having their effect by creating ambivalence about plumpness, particularly among younger women. The globalization of body ideals is a contemporary issue and makes it impossible for them to exist in cultural isolation.

The Kalabari women and their desired body aesthetic are a striking contrast to the images of thin women prevalent in American media. By understanding that there are cultural alternatives to this ultra-thin image, readers may begin to think more critically about alternative ideals of beauty. Dress, in all cultures, has a unique and critical role because of its proximal relationship to the body. The body and how we dress are a medium of culture, a powerful symbolic form, a surface on which the rules, hierarchies, and ide-

Is Thin In?

1. Can you identify any ethnic influences on your current body weight/size? If so, what are they? If you cannot identify any ethnic influences on your current body weight, why not?

2. Why do you think the midsection of the plump traditional female Kalabarian figure (emphasized by clothing) is the body part many American women try to de-emphasize? Reflect on the different ideologies that would lead to such opposite approaches to viewing the body.

3. Speculate as to why Kalabari men do not also have a plump body ideal.

4. Would you characterize the following statements as ethnocentric? Why or why not? "What they do in Africa has nothing to do with me. I don't care what people think about me being too skinny. They are not me."

6   To Apu, with Love
Bhargavi C. Mandava

Shortly after arriving in New York in 1971 from Hyderabad, India, I remember skipping ecstatically behind my father as he carried a naked, used, black-and-white Zenith television through the streets of Astoria, Queens. Since he hadn't learned to drive yet, there was no candy-apple-red Impala to transport the beast. And we couldn't afford to take a taxi—a rickshaw, certainly, but not a taxi. So my father crouched into an Atlaslike stance, and up went the TV onto his shoulders.

"Can you see?" my mother asked him nervously. "Careful, it's wet over there. Are you breathing?"

Her voice faded as I became lost in the appliance teetering above me. Soon, this innocuous gray box would become my savior in a new country where I had no grandfather to tell me stories, no rickshaw drivers to take me for rides, no evening walks with my mother and sister to pluck jasmine blossoms for our hair.

It didn't matter that the channel featuring *The Wonderful World of Disney* was a mess of lines and squiggles. At four years of age, I sat with my ear to the speaker, using the TV like a giant radio and listening raptly to the magic dust spilling from Tinkerbell's wand. When I think about it now, I know it was a blessing in disguise that I had to fashion my own images of Snow White and Sleeping Beauty.

One day, after a healthy dose of that wascally wabbit, I discovered that NBC was coming in loud and *clear*. Finally, I could put pictures to words! Little did I know that fairy skin was a smooth and hairless alabaster—or that fairy hair was blond and flowing.

And so marked the start of my re-education.

During the year's wait to enroll in nursery school, I sat glued to the TV set, a bowl of Spaghetti-Os in hand, and absorbed the world inside the tube. By day, I was bombarded with pitches for Barbies in evening gowns and townhouses and for giant doll heads on which I could smear Avon pinks and blues. By night, my one-eyed doll Judy and I slept in between my parents, my head reeling with wishes that my sister and brother would soon come live with us and that I could play on *Romper Room*.

Well, one of those wishes came true when my siblings joined us in New York a couple years later. I welcomed their companionship, which I had sorely missed. My sister and brother, who are seven and six years my elder, respectively, were flung into the turbulence of an alien culture rather suddenly, since they had to start school as soon as they arrived.

While whisking them off to the local Salvation Army for school clothes, my mother and I bestowed bits of American culture. We taught them English (according to Bugs Bunny) and how to ride the subway (never get on the train going into Manhattan) and which foods were "safe" to eat (pizza and peanut butter and jelly sandwiches). What we couldn't quite impart to them was the scoop on American style. My mother, who had always been a step ahead of the Hyderabad fashion world, was still contemplating whether the ruffles on a pair of American-made panties went in the front or the back. In India, we all had our clothes custom-tailored to suit my mother's tastes. In Astoria, thrift stores became our fabric shops and my mother, the family tailor.

Silently, we were all going through some kind of transformation, which we faced with a mixture of resistance and naive enthusiasm. While my parents struggled to support us, my sister and brother were trying to fit in at Junior High School 141 and I was wending my way through Public School 122. At first, there were the usual complaints of not having many friends or not receiving any Valentine's Day cards. But

FIGURE 2.10 *An Indian girl.*

by kindergarten's end, I started to feel a visible separation between myself (see Figure 2.10) and the rest of the children. Through the third grade, I complained that I never looked like the other kids, that my mother didn't know how to dress me, that my hair was ugly. My mother never denied her cluelessness about kindergarten couture. However, what she absolutely couldn't understand was my fervent hatred for what she saw as a thick head of beautiful, satiny black hair.

In India, she had massaged oil into my scalp and plaited my hair into two ribboned loops. That practice continued even though we were on another continent.

"But no one in school puts oil in their hair," I would argue.

"That's because they don't have such thick black hair like yours," she would reply. "Don't you want it to grow longer and more beautiful?"

Longer? It was quickly approaching my ass; pretty soon, I'd be able to sit on it. Although there was a healthy mix of ethnicities at P.S. 122, I was the only Indian kid going there at the time. No one else's mother wore a *sari* to pick them up from school.

Wasn't she listening to me? I wanted hair with springy waves. I wanted Dippity-Do curls and bangs, and that cropped, tousled look. Anything but straight, black, boring hair.

My mother finally succumbed to my miserable whining and cut my hair into a shoulder-length *That Girl* flip. Unfortunately, this only fueled my pining to meet Hollywood's narrow definition of beauty. The truth was, there was no going back until the demon seed planted by the Breck Girl had played itself out in my beating heart.

As I stood poised with a hammer and chisel, ready to crack the dark brown stone and unearth the more beautiful American me sculpted in glowing white marble, my mother stood vehemently in the way. I couldn't fully comprehend why her ideals of beauty didn't match up with society's. At the time, I felt her insistence that I keep my hair long and avoid the sun was ridiculous—more absurd than my fantasies of waking up white and blonde.

Still, somewhere beyond our many battles over hair, a new seed was planted. I was able to grasp that by eschewing my heritage, I would not be losing something precious, but giving it away. And what was that something—that *it*? That was the question.

So, I started growing my hair again.

The fourth grade was one of my most pleasant school years, mostly because of my teacher Mrs. Rodvien. She was a wonderfully alert and caring woman who nurtured her students' strengths. She picked up on my writing interest and enticed me to include a poem with each of my reports. No one else had to write a poem about Spain or the Middle Ages, but I did so anyway. I was rewarded with a glimpse beyond the physical into the intriguing beauty that lay within me.

Perhaps that precious experience gave me strength to face the times ahead—the changes that menstruation would bring by the fifth grade. Along with this rite of passage arrived hormonal imbalances and a disinterest that shifted my priorities from playing basketball with the boys to gawking at them from the sidelines. I stepped back and looked into the mirror, wondering what the hell was going on with my body.

Actually, I was excited about getting my period and growing breasts, because it proved that there was nothing wrong with me—that everything was going according to plan. Or so I thought. But then my true hair problems began. No, not with the hair on my head, though my mother still insisted on parting it down the middle and tightly plaiting it into two braids. The problem was the hair growing—with more ferocity every day—all over my fifth-grade body. It wasn't so much the sprouting of pubic and underarm hair that concerned me. It was all the *other* hairs rearing their ugly heads—between my eyebrows, above my upper lip, around my jawline, down my neck, around my new breasts, down my front to my navel, over my arms and knuckles, right down my legs to my toes. I didn't recall ever seeing a woman shaving her face and "taking it all off" on that Noxema commercial. None of the other girls at school appeared to be walking carpets.

It wasn't long before a bully picked up on my insecurities and dubbed me an inhabitant of the Planet of the Apes. When I complained to my mother and my sister, they said not to worry about it and to concentrate on getting good grades.

"Did you know that when you were born, your head was already covered with hair?" my mother said proudly. "It's perfectly natural. Your hair shows up more because it's black, that's all."

"So, what you're telling me is this is some kind of birth defect?" I asked with terror.

"No, Nana, you have good genes," she said with a laugh.

That didn't help. Neither did Marcia bonking her nose with a football or Jan's hatred of her freckles; Tabitha's spells or Jeannie's magic; not even Mr. Softie bomb pops.

So what if my mother, a doctor, was telling me I was healthy? The rest of the world was telling me otherwise. I had to take action.

While doing my homework in front of the Sony Trinitron (my father had traded in the black-and-white Zenith), I took my cue from a Nair commercial. Happily singing, "Who wears short shorts," I slathered the stinky goop on my arms. When my skin started burning, I panicked and quickly washed it clean. After toweling off, I gaped in horror at my arms, which were all patchy. I grabbed a Bic razor and shaved the skin.

My peace, however, was short-lived.

In the lunch line the next day, Susan screamed after brushing past me. "Eww! What happened to your arms—they're prickly!"

Everyone turned and stared. I wanted to crawl under the table. I wanted to grab that blond cheerleader ponytail, wrap it twice around her neck and yank. I wanted to choke the last drop of sky from her heavily-lined eyes. But I didn't say or do anything. For the next few weeks, I just wore a hooded zip-up sweatshirt to school.

Despite my mother's predictions, my arm hair grew in much thinner than before. I was thankful for that, but was still quite disconcerted about my facial hair. I couldn't very well cover it up. Would it ever stop growing? Would it vanish one day as mysteriously as it had appeared?

I became distracted from my hair problems when my parents announced we were moving to Long Island. I left the warmer, melting-pot ambiance of Astoria and was thrust into the cold, suburban homogeneity of green lawns and swimming pools. My parents were on their way to fulfilling the American Dream, and who was I to question it?

So I bucked up. I tried to ignore that people's jaws dropped when I walked into the lunch room, that I was the darkest kid in my junior high school, that they told me I talked funny, that all eyes were on me.

Hanging up my street-smart, blue-and-gold Pumas, I tried to get excited about the latest Sassoon and Jordache jeans. I tried to fit in, but how could I with all that hair? I was wearing it down now, pinned up at the sides with Goody barrettes. The long locks fanning out behind me

served to draw some attention away from my facial hair, but I still wasn't happy.

This time, I turned to my college-bound sister and Jolene Bleach. Naturally, the bleached facial hair provided an interesting contrast against my chestnut skin. My new vanishing act was particularly noticeable when the sun hit my face during a game of field hockey.

"Hey, you got blond hair on your face. It's so weird!"

"Big deal," I responded coolly, stalling for an ample retort. "What would you know about it? I got a cousin with blue eyes."

I guess some of the girls and boys at my junior high honestly believed that Indians had jet-black hair on their heads and golden hair on their faces, and that some of us even had blue eyes. More stupid questions and more stupid answers were to follow.

And so began the re-education of my fellow students.

I should have been happy to get them off my back, but my explanations only sufficed to buy me time. Through high school, I focused most of my energy on SATs rather than dating, but I silently floundered to make sense of those much sought-after adjectives: beautiful, gorgeous, sexy, hot.

New York University and the death of my father dumped me into the abyss of an identity crisis. Soon, I was attempting to eradicate societal norms and expectations by cutting my long tresses into a short buzz and donning asexual clothing. Enraged by all the lies I had been radiated with since I stepped on American soil, I spurned fashion, nutrition, television, medication, transportation and mechanization. I delved into an underground world of the non-glamorous, the non-plastic and that hyper-reality New York City is known for.

As I moved past the anger and on to resolution, I toyed with formulas inspired by college Zen courses: Education + Faith + Truth = Beauty. I committed myself to my writing and it propelled me into a deeper search for the purpose of my existence. I realized that with the wink of an eye, we could render ourselves blind or restore our vision. It was as easy as clicking off the television—not just the ones in our living rooms, but the ones droning in our heads. The '70s had brought us Nair; the '80s, electrolysis; and the '90s the "miracles" of laser technology. The one constant has been that droning from television and print advertising—and eventually our own heads—a droning that makes us feel thirsty, hungry and in dire need of looking like "the Other," whatever or whomever that might be. So we continue to shave, bleach and dye our way toward an ideal.

At a local hangout, a female bartender wears a baseball cap etched in glitter with the words "Sexy M.F." *Why not sexy M.F.A.?* I muse. My chuckle is cut short when I spy the glint of something on her forehead. It's a sparkling *bottu* perched on her Third Eye. The same symbol of Hindu faith that propels bigoted groups like the Dot-Busters to commit hate crimes against Indians? The same little thing that made me cringe whenever people stared and pointed at my mother in a mall? It's hard to believe the sacred *bottu* is flaunted by goddess wannabes these days. Wearing crucifixes was popularized by rock musicians, and now it's Hinduism's turn, I suppose. Sipping a club soda, I consider if it's a positive or negative thing that the *yarmulke* hasn't been honored so.

With 1997 marking India's fiftieth year of independence from Britain, I have to wonder if all the hype further exoticized Indians, or if it pulled us from obscurity and pinned us under a small cultural limelight? After all, it was also the year that Mother Theresa's funeral was televised; the year that Arundhati Roy, the author of the Booker Prize-winning novel *The God of Small Things*, was lionized in the media; the year that Deepa Mehta's film *Fire* put a spin on Indian domesticity; and the year that the ancient art of *mehndi* was translated explosively into temporary tattoos for the fashionably enlightened and the culturally fashioned. Is America caught in the full-blown phase of exoticizing Indian people, or is it in the next phase of re-exoticizing them? And if so, when will the deconstruction of this stupidity begin?

On that same Sony Trinitron from my Astoria days, I watch Apu (the only regular cast member of Indian origin on a prime-time sitcom) have an arranged marriage in Springfield on *The Simpsons*, and *Seinfeld*'s Elaine (wrapped in a *sari* and sporting a pierced nose and jasmine flowers in her hair) attend a love marriage in India. Over the next week, the episodes pop up in conversations with people, and I laugh.

These days, I meet people who tell me how much they love my skin and hair, which, by the way, is once again long. "You have such a nice complexion," they say. "Aren't you glad you don't have to lie out on the beach? You're so lucky. I'm *sooo* jealous."

My partner, like most people I've met in my post-college world, doesn't find the hair covering my body out of the ordinary. I suppose this has every bit to do with the fact that I don't either anymore.

Instead, he compares three white hairs streaking the black around my temples to comets in a night sky.

"Do you see them?" he asks.

"I see constellations on your shoulder," I reply, stroking my index finger across his freckles and moles.

"Oh, I have old Jew skin," he mumbles.

"I love your skin," I say.

"Here they are," he says, as he touches my forehead. "Beautiful."

"Yes," I say as I kiss his shoulder.

To Apu, with Love

1. This article gives a personal and endearing account of self-acceptance. Reflect on your own journey toward self-acceptance of your body. What experiences have marked your journey? Do you constantly compare your body to others? Or have you reached self-acceptance?

2. Imagine yourself being whisked off to another culture when you were a pre-schooler. What challenges come to mind? If you have moved often, perhaps you can relate to the author's story. What are some of the similarities between your moves and the author's story? What are some of the differences?

3. A bully called the author "an inhabitant of the Planet of the Apes" because of her body hair. Do you have a personal example of someone calling you names because of one of your physical characteristics? Write a reflective statement or two about your experience and how it compares to the author's.

4. Can you remember a particular incident when you were obsessed with someone else's appearance? Did you ever want your hair to be curlier, straighter, shorter, longer, or another color? Did you ever want to be taller, shorter, thinner, heavier, more muscled, or less muscled? Write down your most memorable incident and reflect on the impact of the media on your memory

7   Young and Chubby: What's Heavy about That?

Ginia Bellafante

On the corner of Seventh Avenue and Lincoln Place in Park Slope, Brooklyn, Ozzie's, a coffee bar, exists as a refueling point for teenagers attending Berkeley Carroll, the private school down the block, and for grown-ups on their way to Manhattan offices, thus making it an ideal laboratory each weekday morning to observe the signifiers of the modern generation gap.

After near daily visits over the past few years, what this reporter has concluded is that teenage girls do not seem to share the adult woman's fear of starch. Nor, more significantly, do they appear to share her belief that a body betraying a love of such an enemy substance need be veiled like a public monument given over to Christo. Adhering to the dress code mandated by Britney Spears—tight low-riding jeans, tighter truncated tank tops—teenage girls unabashedly show their bellies even when they have actual bellies to show. What this stylistic phenomenon may represent is a significant shift in the way young women think about their bodies—the first stage of a revolt against the assumption that no Pilates class can be missed in the pursuit of a figure resembling the neck of a giraffe.

The evidence that an evolution is taking place in young women's attitudes is preliminary—eating disorders do, after all, remain a serious health hazard—but glimmers of a new mind-set are emerging from teenagers, from professionals who deal closely with them and even from images purveyed by the mass media.

"There is now a greater awareness among teenagers of any race and ethnicity of not falling into the trap of 'I have to be thin,'" said Dr. Andrea Marks, a co-author of the forthcoming book "Healthy Teens, Body and Soul" (Fireside) and a specialist in adolescent medicine who practices on the Upper East Side.

"I don't think that there is a major backlash across the culture against that kind of Twiggyish ideal," Dr. Marks added, "but girls are hearing more messages to take pride in normal body shapes."

Torrid, a national chain of clothing stores that sells size 14 and above, has been built successfully from a realization by its founder, Betsy McLaughlin, that young women, no matter how they are proportioned, maintain an affinity for body-conscious styles.

"The overriding factor is that these girls want to look like their friends," said Ms. McLaughlin, who opened the first Torrid outpost in 2001, expanded by 21 branches last year and plans 25 more stores for 2003. Low-cut jeans, vinyl jeans and glittery lingerie in so-called plus sizes are the specialty. "The paradigm that the larger girl does not want to show skin does not hold," Ms. McLaughlin said.

An Internet company with a similar target market, Alight.com, has had an increase in its sales of 42 percent in two years, Norman Weiss, the company's president, said. "We sell a ton of tank tops, halter tops, camisoles, shorts—these girls are really flaunting it," Mr. Weiss said.

Atoosa Rubenstein, the 30-year-old editor of *Cosmo Girl*, which has used plus-sized models, said her teenage readers are less obsessed with dieting and exercise to reach the traditional model-thin ideal. "These girls no longer see their bodies as tools for wooing men," Ms. Rubenstein said. "My generation was self-hating—we really thought we had to look like Niki Taylor."

The debut issue of *Teen Vogue*, just out, features as one of its cover lines, "Making it big: How curvy girls are changing Hollywood's stick-thin standard." An overstatement, perhaps, but inside, the magazine does offer homage to performers and personalities like Pink, Beyoncé

Knowles, Sara Rue and Kelly Osbourne, all zaftig and none wearing sackcloth.

Dr. Marks said she was surprised and delighted two weeks ago to hear a patient—a college student whom she described as healthfully big—express absolutely no interest in dieting. "She said: 'This is just the way I am. This is who I am. This is my set point,'" Dr. Marks said.

The reasons for the attitude shift among a new generation of girls, experts surmise, include the influence of, notably, Jennifer Lopez, and of muscular athletes like Serena and Venus Williams who are more visible than they would have been before Title IX, the law that bars sex discrimination at institutions receiving federal funds.

"The ideal body is really the athletic one," said Emily Leslie, a junior at Bronxville High School in Bronxville, N.Y. "The emphasis is on being healthy. My friends all do sports, and you can't eat cucumbers for lunch."

Another possible factor is the influence of blacks and Latinos on the broader culture, since some studies show that these minorities favor a more rounded feminine beauty ideal.

"What I've noticed is that kids who are part of multiethnic communities really broaden their idea of the social norms," said Dr. Jon Klein, a specialist in adolescent medicine and an associate professor at the University of Rochester.

But perhaps the most significant factor is the expanding body size of Americans generally, and therein lies the downside of the trend. With 14 percent of American adolescents already overweight—triple the rate two decades ago—the danger in an increased acceptance of bigness is that young people will balloon to perilously greater proportions, threatening their health. Overweight adolescents are at increased risk of heart disease and of a type of diabetes once found only in adults, according to the Surgeon General's office, which said in a 2001 report that "the most immediate consequence" of being overweight was children's poor self-esteem and depression.

That finding challenges the notion of a growing acceptance of a larger physical form. One important measure of girls' unhappiness with their bodies—the prevalence of eating disorders like anorexia and bulimia—has not changed over the past decade, experts say.

There is a distinction between the healthfully round body and the overweight one. According to standards of the Centers for Disease Control and Prevention, a girl of 15 who is 5-foot-1 is overweight at 128 pounds, and one who is 5-foot-7 is overweight at 155 pounds.

On a recent afternoon at the Garden State Plaza in Paramus, N.J., none of the young shoppers interviewed at the Torrid shop sounded tormented by their weight. Diana Trampler, a full-figured six-foot-tall college freshman, was visiting for the second time. Earlier, she had bought a camisole; on this excursion she was trying on a fitted knit top, ruched in the front.

Ms. Trampler said she cared little about what people thought of her proportions. "I always seem to find people who accept me as I am," she said.

Neysha Marek, a robust-looking blonde of 23, was shopping for a sheer black evening blouse. She said that she would like to be a size 12 but that she was not dieting toward that goal. "When I was 17 I dieted down to a size 8," she said. "I looked at a picture of myself, and my collarbone was sticking out. I didn't like it. I'd really rather be my size than a size 2." She is a size 14.

"I think larger women really are more accepted today," Ms. Marek continued. "There are stores like this, and the marketing of plus-sized images." She mentioned Mia Tyler, a half-sister of Liv Tyler who has modeled for Lane Bryant. "Skin and bones just aren't everyone's cup of tea," she said.

This was a view shared by Janell Tatis, a 5-foot-8 high school junior who weighs 170 pounds. "I don't think I'm big," she said. "I'm voluptuous. I just look like I eat."

"My best friend, Charmaine, wears skirts and tank tops, and she's bigger than I am," Ms. Tatis said. "She's 5 feet 5 inches and 200 pounds—like a little circle. She says, 'As long as it fits and everything's not hanging out, I'll wear it.'"

A teenager of Charmaine's size is considered unhealthfully overweight by medical authorities, but the power of her self-confidence speaks to the emerging mood. It suggests both the promise (increased self-esteem) and the danger (complacency about health) of the new attitude.

"I spend a lot of time in focus groups and a lot of time talking to teenagers," Amy Astley, the editor of *Teen Vogue*, said. "They really don't want to be told that they have to change. They don't want to fight their natural body type."

"They refer to certain Hollywood starlets as 'skinny,'" she said, "and they see this as passé."

DISCUSSION QUESTIONS

Young and Chubby

1. Do you see a difference between a healthy round body and an overweight one? If yes, please list the differences. If no, why not?

2. How might this acceptance of a healthy round body play out between adult women and teenage girls? For instance, what might be some of the issues between a mother who believes that a healthy body should be thin and her daughter who believes that a healthy body should be round?

3. Choose one week to be conscious of all the media (television, newspapers, movies, Internet, billboards, etc.) images of women you see and answer the following questions:

- Do you think African American and Latino body types have affected the images you see?

- Estimate the percentage of images that follow the thin ideal. Estimate the percentage of images that follow a round body ideal.

- Do you predict that the thin ideal will change as African Americans and Latino Americans become larger segments of the U.S. population? Why or why not?

- Do you predict that the thin ideal will change as the baby boomers age? Why or why not?

8 Proud to Be Big: The Fat Fight Back against Insults and Discrimination

Barbara Wickens

The message came through loud and clear. In September, when Hollywood's Camryn Manheim won an Emmy for best supporting actress in a television drama series, she held the gold statuette high over her head and boldly declared: "This is for all the fat girls!" The statement helped propel Manheim, who portrays lawyer Ellenor Frutt on ABC and Global's The Practice, onto People magazine's bellwether year-end list, "The 25 most intriguing people of the year." Broadway Books will publish her autobiography, Wake Up, I'm Fat, based on her 1995 one-woman play of the same name, in May. And countless people have written to the 37-year-old actress or stopped her on the street to thank her for her gesture. Thrilled as she is by the reaction, however, that is not why she did what she did. "I was doing it for myself," Manheim told Maclean's. "Winning an Emmy was the culmination of a long struggle."

Like many large people, Manheim says she fought for years to get her weight under control, damaging both her body—she was addicted to amphetamines at one point—and her psyche. Many casting directors, looking through the loopy lens of thin-obsessed Hollywood, magnified her problems, telling her she would never find work. "I felt that I had three choices," she says. "I could either destroy my spirit, I could change myself so I could learn to love myself, or I could love myself just the way I was. Well, I tried to destroy my spirit with drugs, and I tried to lose weight and I almost killed myself. So I was left with what I think was the most difficult choice, loving myself just the way I am. That's my goal and I'm close enough to enjoy my life and laugh everyday." Encouraged by the Sacramento, Calif.-based National Association to Advance Fat Acceptance, Manheim used the word "fat" at the Emmys deliberately. "If we are going to say that being fat is not bad and it is simply a characteristic of somebody," she says, "then we have to say it loudly and we have to say it with pride."

As the self-declared "poster girl for fat acceptance," Manheim is at the forefront of a movement gaining momentum throughout North America. Groups like NAAFA have lobbied for years to lighten the crushing load of prejudice society piles on the obese. Other organizations have followed suit, including the Toronto-based Canadian Association for Size Acceptance (CASA), founded just over a year ago by NAAFA's Canadian representative, Helena Spring, a large-sized nurse. The groups' message: although most modern societies have legislation prohibiting racism, sexism, religious intolerance and discrimination against the disabled, the obese are still fair game. "It's the last socially sanctioned form of discrimination," says Toronto writer Kerry Daniels, founder of Heavy Girl Press, a quarterly magazine that promotes fat acceptance.

The notions that fat people are lazy, have no self-control, are by definition unhealthy or could lose the weight if they really wanted to are just myths, say those who advocate acceptance. The public, in general, may take a lot of convincing. One 1993 Harvard School of Public Health study found that, compared with thinner women, obese females were 20 per cent less likely to marry and 10 per cent more likely to be living in poverty. That was regardless of how and where they grew up or of how they had scored on achievement tests as teens.

Still the lobbyists have one plus on their side: demographics. With increasing numbers of baby boomers hitting their 50s, many are putting on the pounds known as middle-aged spread. It is the marketplace—not social conscience— that will likely nudge attitudes along. And there

This article originally appeared in the January 11, 1999, issue of Maclean's Magazine. Reprinted with the permission of Maclean's Magazine.

are signs that it is already happening. Newsstands are offering fashion magazines, such as *Mode*, aimed at the 30 per cent of North American women who wear size 14 or larger. And more so-called plus sizes are available in department stores and specialty shops.

In some cities, dating services have sprung up to cater to large people. *More to Love*, a Canadian feature film to be released next summer, tells the story of a heavy woman who finds self-acceptance and then true love with a handsome—and average weight—man she meets at a social club. For director Paul Lynch, who wanted to show that large women have lives that are as rich and varied as their slender sisters', it was important that the actress who played the lead role of Maryanne be attractive. "This is not in any way a freak show," says Lynch. "This is a romance." After trying unsuccessfully to find a Hollywood actress to fit the bill, he heard from Louise Werner, a five-foot, 9-inch, 229-lb. former model who lived in Santa Monica, Calif. The Swedish beauty, who studied with the late famed acting coach Lee Strasberg, had been unable to find work when she could not lose the 110 lb. she had put on in two pregnancies.

Still, getting the film made took four years, says Lynch, who explains the entertainment industry's fat phobia made it difficult for him to find a backer. Toronto's Crystal Films Inc., which was interested in producing a low-budget art film, finally took on the project. Of course, it's not just in Hollywood where fat is reviled. In Canada, the satirical biweekly *Frank* routinely refers to Mike Duffy, the Ottawa-based host of CTV's *Sunday Edition* newsmagazine, as "The Puffster." Because of a pending lawsuit, he declines comment on *Frank*. Duffy says, however, that while "it is clear to anybody who has their eyes open" society is biased, being heavy has not been an issue in his TV career. "I've been lucky because I've had bosses who were prepared to ignore that and allow me to be a journalist." Perhaps no one has been as cruelly savaged as singer Rita MacNeil. In her new autobiography, *On a Personal Note*, the Nova Scotia entertainer writes that despite all her achievements she could never escape the issue of her size. "My appearance was usually an issue, no matter if I was interviewed for television, radio or print. I was a 'heavyweight challenger for the title of pop queen,' an 'unlikely star.'"

Celebrities are humiliated publicly—but they also receive support from their fans. Ordinary heavy folk are more likely to suffer the reproaches and insults in silence. But it is time to draw the line, says CASA's Spring. "If I hear someone muttering behind me about how fat I am," she says, "I turn around and politely say, 'You said it to my back, now say it to my face.' They usually back down."

Meanwhile, there is a bit of a backlash developing towards the emaciated image promoted by the wraithlike Kate Moss and her ilk. In recent months, many fashion publications have declared "the supermodel is dead." A similar uproar occurred after Calista Flockhart, the slim star of FOX TV's hit comedy *Ally McBeal*, looked especially gaunt at the same Emmy Awards where Manheim took home her statuette. Reacting to reports that she was anorexic, Flockhart's publicist denied the actress was ill and declared she would go home and eat "a bucket of chicken." But the rebuttal did little to calm the controversy that raged in the entertainment media for weeks afterward. A sign, perhaps, that thin is not quite so in any more.

Proud to Be Big

1. In direct contrast to "The Weight of the World" article, Wickens' article celebrates an appreciation of fat people or, at least, the fight to end discrimination against fat people. Where is the balance on the issue of body weight?

2. Once a group is stigmatized, it is economically disadvantaged and must exist on the periphery of society. With a system in the United States that systematically discriminates against groups outside the norm, obese women are 20% less likely to marry than thinner women and 10% more likely to live in poverty. There are no laws that prevent discrimination against the obese. Do you think there should be? How do you feel about this issue?

3. Are you surprised to find out that a movie about a heavy woman who finds true love with an average size man was difficult to fund? Why or why not?

9   The Enigma of Beauty

Cathy Newman

Sheli Jeffry is searching for beauty. As a scout for Ford, one of the world's top model agencies, Jeffry scans up to 200 young women every Thursday afternoon. Inside agency headquarters in New York, exquisite faces stare down from the covers of *Vogue*, *Glamour*, and *Harper's Bazaar*. Outside, young hopefuls wait for their big chance.

Jeffry is looking for height: at least five feet nine. She's looking for youth: 13 to 19 years old. She's looking for the right body type.

What is the right body type?

"Thin," she says. "You know, the skinny girls in school who ate all the cheeseburgers and milkshakes they wanted and didn't gain an ounce. Basically, they're hangers for clothes."

In a year, Jeffry will evaluate several thousand faces. Of those, five or six will be tested. Beauty pays well. A beginning model makes $1,500 a day; those in the top tier, $25,000; stratospheric supermodels, such as Naomi Campbell, four times that.

Jeffry invites the first candidate in.

"Do you like the camera?" she asks Jessica from New Jersey.

"I love it. I've always wanted to be a model," Jessica says, beaming like a klieg light.

Others seem less certain. Marsha from California wants to check out the East Coast vibes, while Andrea from Manhattan works on Wall Street and wants to know if she has what it takes to be a runway star. (Don't give up a sure thing like a well-paying Wall Street job for this roll of the dice, Jeffry advises.)

The line diminishes. Faces fall and tears well as the refrain "You're not what we're looking for right now" extinguishes the conversation—and hope.

You're not what we're looking for. . . .

Confronted with this, Rebecca from Providence tosses her dark hair and asks: "What are you looking for? Can you tell me exactly?"

Jeffry meets the edgy, almost belligerent, tone with a composed murmur. "It's hard to say. I know it when I see it."

Reprinted by permission of The National Geographic Society.

What is beauty? We grope around the edges of the question as if trying to get a toehold on a cloud.

"I'm doing a story on beauty," I tell a prospective interview. "By whose definition?" he snaps.

Define beauty? One may as well dissect a soap bubble. We know it when we see it—or so we think. Philosophers frame it as a moral equation. What is beautiful is good, said Plato. Poets reach for the lofty. "Beauty is truth, truth beauty," wrote John Keats, although Anatole France thought beauty "more profound than truth itself."

Others are more concrete. "People come to me and say: 'Doctor, make me beautiful,'" a plastic surgeon reveals. "What they are asking for is high cheekbones and a stronger jaw."

Science examines beauty and pronounces it a strategy. "Beauty is health," a psychologist tells me. "It's a billboard saying 'I'm healthy and fertile. I can pass on your genes.'"

At its best, beauty celebrates. From the Txikão warrior in Brazil painted in jaguar-like spots to Madonna in her metal bra, humanity revels in the chance to shed its everyday skin and masquerade as a more powerful, romantic, or sexy being.

At its worst, beauty discriminates. Studies suggest attractive people make more money, get called on more often in class, receive lighter court sentences, and are perceived as friendlier. We do judge a book by its cover.

We soothe ourselves with clichés. It's only skin-deep, we cluck. It's only in the eye of the beholder. Pretty is as pretty does.

In an era of feminist and politically correct values, not to mention the closely held belief that all men and women are created equal, the fact that all men and women are not—and that some are more beautiful than others—disturbs, confuses, even angers.

For better or worse, beauty matters. How much it matters can test our values. With luck, the more we live and embrace the wide sweep of the world, the more generous our definition becomes.

Henry James met the English novelist George Eliot when she was 49 years old. *Silas Marner, Adam Bede,* and *The Mill on the Floss* were behind her. *Middlemarch* was yet to come.

"She is magnificently ugly," he wrote his father. "She has a low forehead, a dull grey eye, a vast pendulous nose, a huge mouth, full of uneven teeth. . . . Now in this vast ugliness resides a most powerful beauty which, in a very few minutes, steals forth and charms the mind, so that you end as I ended, in falling in love with her."

In fairy tales, only the pure of heart could discern the handsome prince in the ugly frog. Perhaps we are truly human when we come to believe that beauty is not so much in the eye, as in the heart, of the beholder.

The search for beauty spans centuries and continents. A relief in the tomb of the Egyptian nobleman Ptahhotep, who lived around 2400 B.C., shows him getting a pedicure. Cleopatra wore kohl, an eyeliner made from ground-up minerals.

Love of appearance was preeminent among the aristocracy of the 18th century. Montesquieu, the French essayist, wrote: "There is nothing more serious than the goings-on in the morning when Madam is about her toilet." But monsieur, in his wig of cascading curls, scented gloves, and rouge, was equally narcissistic. "They have their color, toilet, powder puffs, pomades, perfumes," noted one lady socialite, "and it occupies them just as much as or even more than us."

The search for beauty could be macabre. To emphasize their noble blood, women of the court of Louis XVI drew blue veins on their necks and shoulders.

The search for beauty could be deadly. Vermilion rouge used in the 18th century was made of a sulfur and mercury compound. Men and women used it at the peril of lost teeth and inflamed gums. They sickened, sometimes died, from lead in the white powder they dusted on their faces. In the 19th century women wore whalebone and steel corsets that made it difficult to breathe, a precursor of the stomach-smooshing Playtex Living Girdle.

The search for beauty is costly. In the United States last year people spent six billion dollars on fragrance and another six billion on makeup. Hair- and skin-care products drew eight billion dollars each, while fingernail items alone accounted for a billion. In the mania to lose weight 20 billion was spent on diet products and services—in addition to the billions that were

FIGURE 2.11 *Chinese lily foot.*

What's an attractive face? It's a symmetrical face [see Figure 2.1]. Most important, it's an averaged face, says Langlois. Averaged, that is, in terms of position and size of all the facial features. As the slides flash in front of the baby, I see what she means. Some faces are more pleasing to look at than others. It's a question of harmony and the placement of features. The picture of the young girl with wide-set eyes and a small nose is easier on the eye than the one of the young girl with close-set eyes and a broad nose. Extremes are off-putting and generally not attractive, Langlois says.

The idea that even babies can judge appearance makes perfect sense to Don Symons, an anthropologist at the University of California at Santa Barbara.

"Beauty is not whimsical. Beauty has meaning. Beauty is functional," he says. Beauty, his argument goes, is not so much in the eye as in the brain circuitry of the beholder.

In studies by psychologists such as Victor Johnston at New Mexico State University and David Perrett at St. Andrews University in Scotland, men consistently showed a preference for women with larger eyes, fuller lips, and a smaller nose and chin. Studies by psychologist Devendra Singh at the University of Texas show a preference for the classic hourglass-shaped body with a waist-hip ratio of seven to ten.

"That men prefer women with smooth skin, big eyes, curvaceous bodies, and full lips is anything but random," Symons insists. All these traits are reliable cues to youth, good health, and fertility. Take lips, which, plumped up by estrogen, reach their fullness at 14 to 16 when women enter the fertile stage of their life. With menopause and the loss of fertility, lips lose their fullness. Likewise lesions or sores on the skin signal the presence of infectious disease or parasites. Clear, smooth skin speaks of youth and good health.

In the scenario envisioned by Symons and other evolutionary scientists, the mind unconsciously tells men that full lips and clear skin equal health, fertility, and genetic soundness. It's an instinct honed over a hundred thousand years of selection, Symons believes. Because we are

paid out for health club memberships and cosmetic surgery.

Despite the costs, the quest for beauty prevails, an obsession once exemplified by the taste of Copper Eskimo women for a style of boot that let in snow but was attractive to men because of the waddle it inflicted on the wearer—a fashion statement not unlike the ancient Chinese custom of foot binding [see Figure 2.11] or the 20th-century high heel shoe.

I am standing behind a one-way mirror watching a six-month-old baby make a choice. The baby is shown a series of photographs of faces that have been rated for attractiveness by a panel of college students. A slide is flashed; a clock ticks as the baby stares at the picture. The baby looks away; the clock stops. Then it's on to the next slide.

After more than a decade of studies like these, Judith Langlois, professor of psychology at the University of Texas in Austin, is convinced that this baby, like others she has tested, will spend more time looking at the attractive faces than the unattractive ones.

mortgaged to our evolutionary history, the instinct persists.

Not everyone agrees. "Our hardwiredness can be altered by all sorts of expectations—predominantly cultural," says C. Loring Brace, an anthropologist at the University of Michigan. "The idea that there is a standard desirable female type tells you more about the libidinous fantasies of aging male anthropologists than anything else."

Douglas Yu, a biologist from Great Britain, and Glenn Shepard, an anthropologist at the University of California at Berkeley, found that indigenous peoples in southeast Peru preferred shapes regarded as overweight in Western cultures: "A fuller evolutionary theory of human beauty must embrace variation," Yu says.

To think you've found a cultural universal is thrilling, says Elaine Hatfield, professor of psychology at the University of Hawaii, "but you don't want to deceive yourself into thinking that biology accounts for everything. The sociobiologists say we're trapped in our Pleistocene brains. The idea can be slightly bullying, as well as chauvinistic."

What about those who are not so symmetrical or well formed? Is anyone immune to feelings of inadequacy? Eleanor Roosevelt was once asked if she had any regrets. Only one, she said. She wished she had been prettier.

I knew I was an ugly baby when my parents gave me an electric toaster as a bathtub toy. . . . The joke is told by Joan Rivers, so I call her up—she lives in New York these days—to ask if the humor isn't just a little too dark.

"I always wonder what my life would have been if I had had that wonderful ingredient called beauty," the unmistakable raspy voice responds.

"Marilyn Monroe said to a friend of mine, 'I knew I had power when I was eight. I climbed a tree and four boys helped me down.'

"On the other hand, not being pretty gave me my life. You find other ways. It made me funny. It made me smarter. I wasn't going to get into college as Miss Cheerleader."

There's a hint of wistful in the voice. "Beauty is based on youth and on a certain look. When you're old, you're invisible. No matter how they lie to us and tell us Barbra Streisand is beautiful, if you woke up without her enormous talent would you rather look like her or Michelle Pfeiffer?"

In the world of beauty there are many variations on a theme, but one thing seems clear. Every culture has its bad hair day. In central Australia balding Aranda Aborigines once wore wigs made of emu feathers. Likewise, the Azande in Sudan wore wigs made of sponge. To grow long hair among the Ashanti in Nigeria made one suspect of contemplating murder, while in Brazil the Bororo cut hair as a sign of mourning.

Hair has other shades of meaning. Although the archetypal male hero in Western civilization is tall, dark, and handsome like Cary Grant, blond women have sometimes been imagined as having more fun.

Blond is the color of fairy-tale princesses like Cinderella and Rapunzel, not to mention the siren in *Farewell, My Lovely*, of whom Raymond Chandler wrote: "It was a blonde. A blonde to make a bishop kick a hole in a stained glass window."

Jean Harlow was a blonde. So were Carole Lombard and Marilyn Monroe (only their hairdressers knew for sure), who said she liked to "feel blond all over." A dark-haired colleague admits to "blonde anxiety," adding her observation that in California blondes have blonde insecurity. "They don't feel they're blond enough."

Hair-care product companies estimate that in the U.S. 40 percent of women who color their hair choose blond, a choice women also made in ancient Greece. From a biological perspective some researchers say blondness suggests a childlike appearance. Many newborns are blond and darken with time.

What other signals does hair send? In most societies, short hair means restraint and discipline: Think West Point, Buddhist monks, and prison. Long hair means freedom and unconventional behavior: Think Lady Godiva and Abbie Hoffman. Hair says I'm grown-up, and let's get that first haircut. It's the stages of life, from pigtails to ponytail to gray hair.

"This is what I looked like at age five," Noliwe Rooks, a visiting assistant professor of history and African-American studies at Princeton, tells me.

We're at her dining table drinking tea and talking about hair—specifically African-American hair—and how it defines culture, politics, and the tension between generations. The photograph she shows me is of a little girl with a big puff ball of an Afro staring up at the camera.

"My mother was a political activist, and so I wore my hair like this until I was 13," Rooks says, smiling.

"My grandmother had this huge issue with it. I was her only grandchild, and she couldn't stand it. It wasn't cute. It wasn't feminine. You couldn't put little bows in it. Every summer my mother would take me down to Florida to stay with her. As soon as my mother left, my grandmother would take me to Miss Ruby's beauty parlor and straighten my hair. Issues between my mother, my grandmother, and me got worked out around my hair."

While in college Rooks decided to let her hair "lock," or grow into a mass of pencil-thin dreadlocks.

"Before I was able to tell my grandmother, she had a stroke. I found myself on a plane flying to her bedside, rehearsing how I was going to explain the locks. The doctors didn't know the extent of the damage. She hadn't spoken. All she could make were garbled sounds. I couldn't wear a hat to hide my hair. It was Florida. It was 80 degrees. I walked into her hospital room, expecting the worst, when all of a sudden she opened her eyes and looked at me.

"'What did you do to your hair?' she said, suddenly regaining the power of speech."

After her grandmother died, Rooks found herself in front of the mirror cutting her hair in a gesture of mourning.

"When my grandmother was in the hospital, I'd brushed her hair. I pulled the gray hairs out of the brush, put them in a plastic bag, and put it in front of her picture. That was hair for me. There was so much about it that defined our relationship. It meant closeness, and then, finally, acceptance."

Gravity takes its toll on us all. That, along with time, genetics, and environment, is what beauty's archenemy, aging, is about. "The bones stay upright until you go permanently horizontal," says Dr. Linton Whitaker, chief of plastic surgery at the University of Pennsylvania Medical Center. "As the soft tissue begins to sag off the bones, the rosy cheeks of childhood become the sallow jowls of the elderly. What was once jawline becomes a wattle."

Blame the vulnerability of flesh on collagen and elastin—materials found in the second layer of our skin that give it elasticity.

"Collagen under a microscope is like a knit sweater," Whitaker explains. "After the 10,000th wearing and stretching, it becomes baggy, and the same with skin. When the knit of collagen and elastin begins to fragment, skin loses its elasticity." Then gravity steps in.

"If aging is a natural process, isn't there something unnatural about all this surgical snipping and stitching to delay the inevitable?" I ask.

"I guess it's not natural, but what is?" Whitaker sighs. "It's the world we live in. Right or wrong, it's a judgment. But it's doable and makes people happy."

It makes many people happy. According to the American Society for Aesthetic Plastic Surgery, almost three million cosmetic procedures were performed in the United States in 1998. Baby boomers (35 to 50) accounted for 42 percent.

The quest for the perfect look is global. In Russia cut-price plastic surgery lures patients from as far away as London and Sydney. In Australia, where a short-lived magazine called *Gloss* trumpeted the glories of cosmetic surgery, penile enlargements are among the six cosmetic procedures most popular with males, along with nose jobs, eyelid lifts, liposuction, face-lifts, and ear corrections.

In China plastic-surgery hospitals are sprouting up faster than bamboo shoots in spring. Patients can check into a 12,000-square-foot palace of plastic surgery called the Dreaming Girl's Fantasy on Hainan Island.

In Brazil, says Dr. Ivo Pitanguy, a world-famous plastic surgeon, "women get liposuction at 18 and breast reduction at between 16 and 22. They prefer small breasts and big derrieres, whereas Americans want big chests. In the 1970s only 8 percent of my patients were men. Now it's 25 percent. Today society accepts the idea of improving one's image."

The line between self-improvement and neurosis can blur. I hear about a town in Texas where breast augmentations are given as graduation gifts. And how to make sense of singer Michael Jackson with his reported inventory of four nose jobs, a chin implant, eyelid surgery, a face-lift, lip reduction, skin bleaching, and assorted touch-ups?

("Michael designed the way he wants to look," said a source close to the star. "It's no different from choosing your jewelry, your clothing, or your hairstyle.")

"Suppose I'm not so cute when I grow up as I am now?" Shirley Temple is said to have asked with some prescience when she was eight. Fret not. What goes down, comes up. For falling hair, Rogaine. For the drooping face, Retin-A. Prozac for the sagging soul and Viagra for the sagging penis.

"Old age is not for sissies," I say to a friend, quoting one of Bette Davis's favorite lines.

"No, no," she corrects. "Old age is not for narcissists. If you are wrapped up in yourself, you have nothing but the potential for loss."

Even non-sissies have trouble with aging. Martha Graham, a powerful woman and possibly the most influential force in modern dance, grew bitter as she grew old. She would call Bertram Ross, one of her dancers, in the middle of the night. "Die while you're young and still beautiful," she would hiss into the phone, then hang up.

At 48, gravity has taken its toll on me. I look at the mirror and note the delta of wrinkles starting to branch from the corners of my eyes. My chin has begun to blur into my neck. There is a suggestion of jowliness.

Of course I could consult a plastic surgeon like Dr. Sherwood Baxt. On the day I visit his office in Paramus, New Jersey, Baxt, a tall man with a sweep of graying hair, is dressed in a well-cut charcoal double-breasted suit with a pinstripe shirt, yellow silk tie affixed by a gold safety pin, and a pair of black tasseled calf loafers.

You might say that Baxt, who has not one but three different lasers for sculpting, peeling, and taming the bumps and wrinkles of imperfect flesh, offers one-stop shopping for cosmetic surgery. The centerpiece of his office complex is an operating suite that would be the envy of a small community hospital.

"Plastic surgery is exciting," Baxt tells me in calm, reassuring tones. "We're lifting, tightening, firming. We change people's lives."

"How and why?" I want to know.

"Most of my patients work," he says. "I see a lot of high-power women who can't fit into a suit anymore because of hormonal changes and pregnancies. They're in a competitive world. Liposuction is the most common procedure. The face is the next order of business—the eyes, double chins. All of that says to the workforce, 'You look a bit tired. You're a bit over the hill. You're having trouble keeping up.'"

Wondering how I'd fare with nip and tuck of my own, I've asked for a consultation. Thanks to computer imaging, I can get a preview. An assistant takes front and side views of my face with a Polaroid camera and scans them into a computer. As I watch, my face pops up on the screen and then morphs as Baxt manipulates the image. The softness under my chin retracts into firmness; the circles under my eyes disappear; wrinkles smooth out. I'm looking younger—not the hard, stiff, pulled-tight mask-look that screams "face-lift! face-lift!"—but more subtly younger.

"First I did your upper eyelids," Baxt explains, pointing at the screen. "I removed a bit of fatty tissue. I also took off some of the fat pockets over the lower lid, then lasered the skin smooth and tight. Next I did some liposuction on the wad of fat under the chin and brought the chin forward with an implant. You've got two things going for you: good skin and a full face. You age better if you have a full face. You don't need to be lifted and pulled at this point. Maybe in ten years."

The tab? About nine or ten thousand dollars. Of course my insurance would never pay this bill. It's strictly out-of-pocket. No problem. Baxt offers an installment plan.

Back home, I stare at myself in the mirror. I've always scoffed at plastic surgery. Then 50 loomed into view. Now I'm more tolerant. We are living longer. We are healthier. Today the average life expectancy is 76 years. Fifty years ago it was 68. One hundred years ago it was 48. The face in the mirror doesn't always reflect how old or young we feel.

The sad, sometimes ugly, side of beauty: In a 1997 magazine survey, 15 percent of women and 11 percent of men sampled said they'd sacrifice more than five years of their life to be at their ideal weight. Others were prepared to make other sacrifices. One 25-year-old Maryland woman said: "I love children and would love to have one more—but only if I didn't have to gain the weight."

Is life not worth living unless you're thin?

"Girls are literally weighing their self-esteem," says Catherine Steiner Adair, a psychologist at the Harvard Eating Disorders Center in Boston. "We live in a culture that is completely bonkers. We're obsessed with sylphlike slimness, yet heading toward obesity. According to one study, 80 percent of women are dissatisfied with their bodies. Just think about how we talk about food: 'Let's be really bad today and have dessert.' Or: 'I was good. I didn't eat lunch.' "

In one of its worst manifestations, discontent with one's body can wind up as an eating disorder, such as anorexia, a self-starvation syndrome, or bulimia, a binge-and-purge cycle in which people gorge and then vomit or use laxatives. Both can be fatal.

Today eating disorders, once mostly limited to wealthy Western cultures, occur around the world. "I was in Fiji the year television was introduced," says Dr. Anne Becker, director of research at the Harvard center. "Eating disorders were virtually unknown in Fiji at that time." When she returned three years later, 15 percent of the girls she was studying had tried vomiting to lose weight.

In Japan anorexia was first documented in the 1960s. It now affects an estimated one in one hundred Japanese women and has spread to other parts of Asia, including Korea, Singapore, and Hong Kong. In the U.S., according to the Menninger Clinic in Topeka, Kansas, the proportion of females affected by eating disorders is around 5 to 10 percent.

To say that all women with eating disorders want to look like runway models is to gloss over a complex picture that weaves biology and family dynamics in with cultural influences. One thing can be said: Eating disorders are primarily a disease of women.

"It's easy to be oversimplistic in defining causes," says Emily Kravinsky, medical director at the Renfrew Center in Philadelphia, a treatment center for women with eating disorders. "Some of these women don't know how to cope or soothe themselves. They have low self-esteem. Also, there's increasing evidence that biology and genetics play a role. Finally, the distance between the cultural ideal of what we would like to look like and the reality of what we actually look like is becoming wider. If Marilyn Monroe walked into Weight Watchers today, no one would bat an eye. They'd sign her up."

Late one winter afternoon at Renfrew I sat in what once was the drawing room of an elegant mansion—it is now a space used for group therapy—and had a conversation with two young women who are patients. The subject was beauty and self-image and how that sometimes goes uncontrollably awry. The two sat next to each other on a sofa, occasionally turning to tease or reassure the other, in the easy, bantering way that friends do. One, a former gymnast, was short and compact and very overweight. The other, a former dancer, was tall, and very, very thin.

"My family moved here so I could attend the gymnastics academy," said the former gymnast we'll call Sarah. "I was three years old. Every week they would put us on the scale and call out our weight so everyone could hear. By 13, I was anorexic. And then I started eating and couldn't stop. I became bulimic."

"For me it was the mirrors and being in leotards and tights," said the former dancer we'll call Leah. "It was seeing the parts go to the prettier girls. I thought: 'If only I were thinner.' "

It has been a long struggle and will continue to be so, both said. There are no shortcuts in the search for equilibrium of the soul.

"I want a relationship," Leah said wistfully. "I say to myself: You don't have to be thin. Then I open a magazine and see these gorgeously thin women, and they all have a handsome guy next to them. I tell myself, oh, so you do have to be thin."

And yet, despite setbacks and constant self-vigilance, both could finally begin to see the glimmer of another possibility. There are other ideas of beauty, the two agreed.

"Beauty is all the wonderful creative things that a person is, how they handle themselves and treat other people," Sarah said. "My brother has Down's syndrome, and I judge people by how they treat him. It doesn't matter if you weigh 600 pounds. If you treat him well, you are beautiful."

There is a pause, then a quiet moment of insight offered in a very small voice: "Of course it's a lot easier for me to see beauty in others than in myself." She takes a breath and goes on. "Still, I know more than ever before that there are things about me other than my body. Things that—I can almost say—are beautiful."

The preoccupation with beauty can be a neurosis, and yet there is something therapeutic about paying attention to how we look and feel.

One day in early spring, I went to Bliss, a spa in New York. It had been a difficult winter, and I needed a bit of buoyancy. At Bliss I could sink back in a sand-colored upholstered chair, gaze at the mural of the seashore on the walls, and laugh as I eased my feet into a basin of warm milk. I could luxuriate in the post-milk rubdown with sea salts and almond oil. Beauty can be sheer self-indulgent pleasure as well as downright fun, and it's best not to forget it.

"People are so quick to say beauty is shallow," says Ann Marie Gardner, beauty director of W magazine. "They're fearful. They say: 'It doesn't have substance.' What many don't realize is that it's fun to reinvent yourself, as long as you don't take it too seriously. Think of the tribesmen in New Guinea in paint and feathers [see Figure 2.12]. It's mystical. It's a transformation. That's what we're doing when we go to a salon. We are transforming ourselves."

Until she was a hundred years old, my grandmother Mollie Spier lived in a condominium in Hallandale, Florida, and had a "standing," a regular appointment, at the beauty salon down the street. Every Friday she would drive, then later be driven, for a shampoo, set, and manicure.

This past year, too frail to live on her own, she moved to a nursing home and away from her Friday appointment.

A month before she died, I went to visit her. Before I did, I called to ask if she wanted me to make an appointment for her at the salon.

"I could drive you, Grandma. We could take your nurse and wheelchair. Do you think you could handle it?"

"Of course," she replied, as if I'd asked the silliest question in the world. "What's the big deal? All I have to do is sit there and let them take care of me."

FIGURE 2.12 *Young Asaro mudman from Papua New Guinea.*

On a Friday afternoon I picked my grandmother up at the nursing home and drove her to the salon she hadn't visited in more than a year. I wheeled her in and watched as she was greeted and fussed over by Luis, who washed and combed her fine pewter gray hair into swirls, then settled a fog of hair spray over her head.

When he was finished, Yolanda, the manicurist, appeared. "Mollie, what color would you like your nails?"

"What's new this year? I want something no one else has," she shot back, as if in impossibly fast company at the Miami Jewish Home for the Aged.

Afterward I drove my grandmother back to the nursing home. She admired her fire engine red nails every quarter mile. Glancing in the car mirror, she patted her cloud of curls and radiated happiness.

"Mollie," said the nurse behind the desk when I brought her back. "You look absolutely beautiful."

DISCUSSION QUESTIONS

The Enigma of Beauty

1. Write down your definition of beauty. Be specific in your definition as to what beauty includes and what it excludes. Swap definitions with someone else in your class. How are your definitions similar? How are your definitions different?

2. List current "beauty" practices that can be fatal, dangerous, or unhealthy. Which ones have you engaged in? Which ones have you avoided? Why?

3. What do you think the consequences would be of everyone looking alike? Would this be a positive outcome? Why? Would this be a negative outcome? Why?

4. Pick out all of the cultural and historic examples of beauty given in the article. Do you know the reasons behind these beauty practices? How/Where could you learn more about these practices?

CHAPTER 3

Dress as Nonverbal Communication

Mary Lynn Damhorst

AFTER YOU HAVE READ THIS CHAPTER, YOU WILL COMPREHEND:

- The substantial complexity underlying communication through dress.

- The basic components of the structure of dress communication systems.

- How people put together appearance according to "rules" or guidelines for dress shaped by cultural, historical, and group factors as well as personal tastes and preferences.

- The characteristics of the present era in time that influence the way consumers "produce" appearances.

We express much through dress, including our personal identities, our relationships with others, and the types of situations in which we are involved. A phenomenal amount of information is transmitted in one's appearance, and human beings have an amazing capacity to make sense of a substantial amount of detail in a very short time. In this chapter we will consider both the complexity of communicating through appearance and factors that influence messages sent through dress. We will look closely at the process of creating meanings about the self and society through dress.

WHAT IS NONVERBAL COMMUNICATION?

Dress is one of several modes of nonverbal communication that does not necessarily involve verbal expression through speaking or writing.[1] Other types of nonverbal communication include facial expressions, physical movement and actions (kinetics), the physical distances people maintain from one another (proxemics), touch (haptics), the sound of the voice while delivering verbal communications (paralinguistics), and hand gestures. All of these types of nonverbal communication involve behaviors that are informative and meaningful to people.

Dress serves as a backdrop while other forms of communication—verbal and nonverbal—occur. Unlike many other modes of communication, dress often tends to be stable or unchanging for many hours of the day. Dress, then, is usually **nondiscursive** behavior rather than behavior that dynamically changes or unfolds moment by moment as do words in a conversation or movements in a dance (McCracken, 1988).

Two different definitions of communication are useful in understanding dress. One definition, mapped out by Burgoon and Ruffner (1974), contains a number of premises about sending and receiving messages:

FIGURE 3.1 *Jennifer Lopez at the 2004 Golden Globes ceremony.*

1. *Communication is an interactive process between two or more people.* Millions of people can be involved when television and other media send messages to a vast audience. The performer may never interact directly with most viewers, but an interaction nonetheless occurs. For example, when Jennifer Lopez appeared on the Golden Globes awards show on January 25, 2004, her gown, jewelry, and hairstyle were perused by the vast TV audience. (See Figure 3.1.) Many fans were checking out how she looked in the aftermath of her breakup with actor Ben Affleck just days earlier. Commentary on morning shows the next day indicated that people had been watching.

2. *Communication involves the sending of messages to at least one receiver who, for a complete act of communication, sends a feedback message to the original sender.* Feedback messages sent about dress are not always obvious and overt. Occasionally, one may receive a direct compliment or insult about dress. Or a long stare or whistle may be the feedback. In many instances, lack of comments serves as feedback that nothing was terribly wrong with one's appearance. Getting a job or a date may indicate that one's dress was appropriate or approved.

3. *Communication is a process that is ongoing and dynamic. Meanings are negotiated and created to reach common understanding.* According to the three-part definition of communication, sender and receiver must come to a minimal level of agreement about the meanings of dress for a complete communication interaction to occur. This may happen to some extent in purposeful efforts at impression management, such as a suit worn to a job interview, a wedding dress, or a uniform for a job role. But for most dress, wearer and observer never converse specifically about dress and often do not completely agree on what each other's dress means (Tseëlon, 1992). Dress is so **polysemic** (i.e., sends a great amount of messages all at one time) that it is difficult to find agreement on all the meanings packed into one appearance.

A second, broader definition of communication emphasizes that dress is "the production and exchange of meanings" (Fiske, 1990, p. 2). A wearer puts clothing, hairdo, accessories, and grooming together to produce an appearance and may assign meanings to that assembled appearance. Each observer of that appearance may agree on some meanings but may also have a unique interpretation of the appearance. According to the second definition, disagreement does not mean that communication stops or fails. It is the sum of how wearer and observers interact (or do not interact) on the basis of appearance that produces meanings for the wearer and the observers.

FIGURE 3.2 *During the traditional portion of a Korean wedding, the groom wears* sadae kwon mo *and the bride wears* hwal-ot *while the couple is presented to his parents. Koreans assign deep meanings to the garment forms and embroidery designs of traditional wedding dress.*

Throughout much of the world during the early twenty-first century, dress meanings tend to be vague and hard to verbalize. A picture, such as an appearance, tells a thousand words, but those thousand words are difficult to pin down precisely. In addition, changing fashion trends continually modify meanings of dress, adding further to lack of clarity of meanings. Umberto Eco (1976) refers to this vagueness of meanings as undercoding. Meanings of dress in U.S. society today are coded only generally and imprecisely, leaving much to the imagination of the perceiver.

In contrast to "modern" attire worn throughout the world today, dress in traditional cultures tends to change slowly over time and may incorporate long-used symbols that are steeped with meanings. The dress worn by a bride and groom at a Korean wedding in Seoul (see Figure 3.2) reflects hundreds of years of tradition. The colors, patterns, and shapes of garments are highly meaningful to Koreans. Similarly, some uniforms in mainstream U.S. society, such as police and military uniforms, rely on long familiar symbolic components to express the role of the uniform wearer.

FIGURE 3.3 *Adolescent boy experiences the communication channel of taste in dress.*

The Structure of Dress Communication Systems

CHANNELS OF TRANSMISSION. Dress as a communication system is extremely complex. In any one appearance, messages may be sent simultaneously through a variety of channels. Berlo (1960) defined **channels** of communication as the five physiological senses. We often study how dress is used to communicate via the visual channel. However, we might also send messages via the hearing channel (e.g., the clanging of bangle bracelets, the clickety-clack of high heels coming down an uncarpeted hallway, the rustle of taffeta) or via the sense of smell (e.g., perfumes, deodorants to mask body odor, new leather). The sense of touch is inherent in perceiving clothing, as textiles have a tactile component. We can often look at a fabric and guess that it is soft (e.g., corduroy, velvet) or slick (e.g., vinyl). These sensory transmissions may have meanings for observers. For example, many business dress advisors suggest that clanging jewelry and obvious perfumes convey an image that is less than professional in the office environment (Fashion Workshop, 1989; Fiore & Kimle, 1997; Roscho, 1988).

Notice that we have not discussed the sense of taste. Perhaps because of the low level of development of that sense in humans, it is not commonly used as a message channel in dress. Other than flavored lipsticks (such as the lip gloss experienced by Jeremy in Figure 3.3), only a few amusing and/or erotic novelty dress products are flavored. We won't describe those here.

GRAMMAR. An array of things may be compiled on the body to complete a dressed appearance. When hairdo, facial grooming or makeup, clothing, scents, jewelry, shoes, and accessories are all combined, a tremendous amount of organization has taken place. The rules we use to put all of these components together on the body are loosely held guidelines for what is appropriate, fashionable, and attractive. The rules are a sort of grammar of dress. We learn the grammar of dress through the media and through groups and families to which we belong.

Any dress grammar rules can be broken; however, some rules are held seriously in some societies. For instance, in most communities in the United States today, it is against the law for women to go topless and for men to display genitals in public. These laws stem from moral taboos related to a sense of modesty and sexual behaviors. In France recently, a presidential commission proposed a law that would prohibit students from wearing veils or head scarves to school for religious reasons (Ganley, 2003). Banning of other forms of religious dress in schools was under consideration. Government authorities contended that religious expression through dress might be undermining the constitutional guarantee of secular control. Some government officials feared that communities with high levels of immigration of fundamentalist Muslims could be threatening preservation of France's secular identity.

Banning students from wearing certain forms of dress is not always an easy means of controlling student behaviors in the United States. The "Symbols in School" article outlines cases in which the right to freedom of expression in student dress has become highly problematic. In separate incidents in high schools in a number of states, students were suspended for wearing T-shirts printed with images of the Confederate flag and other racially divisive messages. The courts have supported the rights of students to wear the flag symbols in some cases, leaving schools with no other options than mandatory school uniform policies.

For most of what we wear, however, rules are not seriously enforced but are shaped by personal tastes, fashion trends, and group habits and conventions. For example, many people in the United States tend not to wear red and pink garments together in one ensemble. However, a print or multicolored garment may combine those two colors in ways that appear attractive. Some organizations may have rules for dress of members when they attend meetings or represent the group. In "It's All Greek to Me," Miller and Hunt report data from a study of sorority women attending the University of Kentucky. In contrast to common stereotypes about conformity within college sororities, the members of Greek organizations did not feel that their houses required strict adherence to particular ideals of appearance. They felt that rules for dress were very tolerant and general; they needed to attend to basic elements of hygiene and cleanliness, but had no particular style requirements.

Youth gangs in urban areas in the United States often adopt dress symbols such as colors, tattoos, or headwear that indicate gang membership. Brian Palmer reports in "True Colors" that to thwart bans by school officials and detection by police, some gangs change their group symbols from week to week or abandon sartorial signs altogether in favor of current fashion trends. The grammar of gang dress changes continually and sometimes covertly.

ELEMENTS OF DRESS SIGNS.   Elementary components of clothing that may convey messages are listed in Figure 3.4 within the inner oval of the diagram. These are "perceptual elements" that are the integral units of fabric and apparel that can be perceived by human beings. Many of these elements are the basic elements of design (Davis, 1980; Fiore & Kimle, 1997). Some of the elements have multiple subcomponents that influence meaning; for example, color has hue (the color family), value (lightness versus darkness), and intensity (brightness versus dullness). Fiber names can be meaningful (i.e., silk is a luxury fiber) as are fabrics such as denim (Berger, 1984). These elementary units are relevant for clothing, but other aspects of dress such as hair, tattoos, and shoes have different sets of elementary perceptual units.

During the twentieth century in North America, rounded design lines and flowing and delicate, translucent fabrics (such as voile) could be worn by women but were not traditionally seen in men's dress. Men tended to wear angular lines and sturdy, smooth, "hard" woven fabrics (McCracken, 1985). These differences in lines and fabrics reflected differences in traditional concepts of what is male (e.g., active, sturdy, strong) and female (e.g., soft, fragile). Today, women borrow masculine fabrics and design lines freely, as they take on roles and behaviors traditionally reserved for men. The increasing

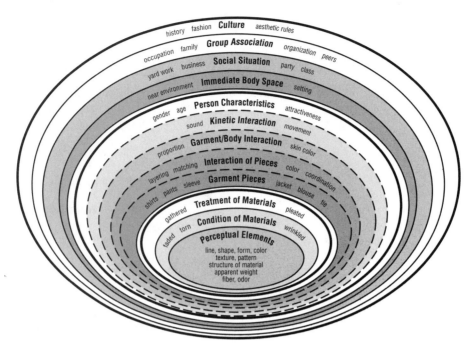

FIGURE 3.4 *Model of clothing in context.*

incorporation of menswear symbols into womenswear is helping (along with other societal changes) to obscure the traditional gender meanings of design lines and fabrics.

CONTEXT OF USE.   In any appearance, a great number of perceptual elements are combined according to or in violation of some rules of grammar. How elements are combined and placed on the body, who wears them, and in what situation they are worn shapes meanings of perceptual elements. Combinations of elements and surrounding situations make up **context** (cf. Bateson, 1979). Figure 3.4 maps components of context that may shape meanings of clothing.

The inner ovals of Figure 3.4 that surround the core perceptual elements pertain to clothing materials and how they influence meanings. Condition of fabrics, such as stains or tears, could degrade the impression given by a job applicant. The meaning of fading and tears can vary with the whims of fashion, however. Distressed and stonewashed jeans have been popular for casual clothing. Treatments of materials such as gathers may add fullness and softness to clothing, whereas pressed pleats may appear precise and sharp.

The next several layers of the clothing context model relate clothing to the body of the wearer. Garment pieces become familiar objects in a culture and are usually associated with coverage of one area of the body. Certain arrangements of elements (i.e., lines, shapes, fabrics, patterns) within a garment piece may then add meanings. For instance, denim jeans are a highly familiar garment symbol worldwide.

Garment pieces are combined in an ensemble with accessories and worn on the body. In some cultures, infinite arrangements and meanings are possible. Susan Kaiser discusses in "Identity, Postmodernity, and the Global Apparel Marketplace" how choice is a characteristic of dress during the current era in time. Consumers collect an array of garment pieces and accessories that can be used to produce a different look or unique expression of identity.

The wearer's shape fills out a garment, and skin and hair coloring interact with garment elements. Body size also influences meanings of clothing. Clayton, Lennon, and Larkin (1987) found that garments worn by larger-size female models tended to be evaluated as less fashionable. This could pose a problem in marketing to larger-size women via catalogs and magazine ads. Do larger-size women themselves see plus-size models as less fashionable than slim models? Certainly, more research is warranted. To approach the size issue cautiously, many mail-order firms feature plus-size models who are actually only a size 12 or 14, larger than average fashion models (size 0 to 4) but not in the size ranges offered in women's larger sizes (16W and up). (See "Plus-Size Modeling" in Chapter 11.)

Body movement may add meanings to clothing. In "Kimono Schools" Liza Dalby explains how movement and posture are essential for achieving a graceful presentation of kimono. Displaying the same movements while wearing modern dress makes an individual look pigeon-toed and awkward.

Numerous characteristics of the wearer can influence interpretation of clothing meanings. For example, an ice-cream stain on the shirt of a toddler may be perceived as cute or amusing, but might not be so cute on a 42-year-old. Some individuals adopt dress that becomes their signature style. Johnny Cash (Figure 3.5), famous singer and songwriter who died in 2003, expressed his unconventional performance persona through clothing. Long before the 1990s when black became a conforming fashion color, Cash symbolized his uniqueness from mainstream country and western performers through his characteristic color choice. He was known as "The Man in Black."

The outer layers of the model in Figure 3.4 relate to the situation surrounding the wearer. Let's leap to the outer rim and examine the all-encompassing context of culture (Firth, 1957). Elements and grammar of clothing take on meaning in cultural context. Consider the color red, for example. Red is an appropriate color for traditional Chinese bridal dresses, but what would the meaning of red convey in an American bride's dress? Similarly, bright red is the traditional color for funerals in Ghana, Africa, but is not usually an appropriate color to wear to funerals in the United States. In "India Examines Color of Beauty," Tim Sullivan reports that lighter skin color in India is considered beautiful and a sign of higher social caste.

FIGURE 3.5 *Johnny Cash was known as "The Man in Black."*

In Chapter 10 we examine whether lighter skin color indicates higher social status and attractiveness in the United States. For ethnic minority groups lighter color is often considered more attractive (see "Complex Issues of Complexion Still Haunt Blacks" in Chapter 10), but among whites, a tanned skin is more attractive.

Moving to the "group association" level of the clothing in context model, groups and organizations vary with each culture and over time, and role dress varies across groups. In North America, the medical doctor's white coat is associated with laboratory science, cleanliness, purity, godlike control over life, and impartial treatment of all— concepts relevant to modern medicine (Blumhagen, 1979). But by the end of the twentieth century, as doctors took on a more egalitarian role with patients and emphasized preventive medicine, many doctors abandoned the white coat for street wear more similar to patients' attire. Similarity and casualness were expected to reduce barriers to effective communication, essential to fully assessing the patient's health status. However, some patients still feel more comforted by the white coat, a familiar symbol of medical authority and expertise.

Dress helps us define social situations. Some social critics fear that the invasion of casual dress into business organizations will degrade the seriousness and professionalism of business interactions, while many workers enjoy the relaxed tone set on "casual days." Similarly, a party to which everyone wears tuxedos and formal gowns might have a different atmosphere or definition than a party to which everyone wears T-shirts and jeans.

Immediate surroundings of space and people can influence interpretations of dress. Damhorst (1984–1985) asked employees of private business firms in Texas to describe what they thought was happening in different pictures of men and women interacting in various office settings (Figure 3.6). Dress of the pictured people clearly shaped stories told about the pictures and influenced meanings of adjacent persons' dress.

a   b

FIGURE 3.6 *The two stimulus pictures (Damhorst, 1984–1985), with formality of clothing worn by the man and woman reversed, elicited different stories. The respondents in the study described the informally dressed woman in (a) as causing problems for the man who was "obviously" high in status and competence. In contrast, the woman in (b) was seen as managerial and having to reprimand or fire the incompetent worker who was crouching behind his desk.*

To sum up the model of clothing in context, it is not individual colors or garment pieces that dominate an appearance to create meanings. How all elements are combined on the body within cultural context is crucial for meanings. As Roach-Higgins and Eicher (1992) emphasized, dress is an assemblage. How the wearer uses clothing and other components of dress in context makes dress meaningful.

Meanings of Dress Messages

Recall from Chapter 1 that meanings of symbols such as clothing are something other than the clothing object itself. Dress refers to or indicates qualities or meanings more abstract than the actual physical objects of dress. For example, dress makes visual proclamations such as "this person is male," "the wearer is competent at her job," "this person is fashionable," "this person is Nigerian," "I'm attending a black-tie affair," "I completed the 2002 10 K Fox Valley Run," or "I wanna be like Britney Spears." Many dress messages are such that we might feel a bit silly having to verbally pronounce them upon first meetings with others.

McCracken (1988) contended that, because dress remains fixed or unchanged during most interactions, it tends to communicate stable characteristics of the wearer. Keep in mind, however, that many of us change our clothing and sometimes other aspects of grooming every day or several times a day. The "stable" characteristics we communicate may be stable only for a few hours. On one day, a student might throw on a sloppy sweat suit to go to class because he's having a bad day and doesn't want to pay much attention to dress. Usually, however, that same student rarely wears sweats to class, preferring jeans and sweaters. Another student might dress in sweats every day; his attire might indicate personal attitudes about school, self, and dress. The meanings of his dress may be far more complex than not caring about his appearance, however. In the student's mind, and to the group he hangs out with, sloppy may be "cool." Surface-level interpretations do not always accurately tap the meanings of dress.

THE PRESENT-DAY CULTURAL "MOMENT"

The present situation in U.S. culture very much shapes how consumers assemble appearances and send messages through dress. The characteristics of U.S. culture, as well as many cultures around the world, at the end of the twentieth century and the beginning of the twenty-first century were sometimes referred to as "**postmodern**" (Gitlin, 1989). We will not try to pinpoint when postmodernism started, to assume that now is totally different in every way from prior eras, or to trace the philosophical or political bases of postmodern theory; the term is useful in summarizing some present-day trends in consumer life. Morgado (1996) thoroughly analyzes postmodern influences on dress. We will focus our look at four characteristics of consumer culture—eclecticism, nostalgia, questioning of rules, and simulation—that are reflected in how we purchase and present our appearances today.

Postmodern appearances are **eclectic** in that consumers often mix-and-match a diverse array of styles and influences in any one appearance or throughout a wardrobe. For example, African-inspired fabrics (e.g., kente cloth) are sewn into American styles; a Peruvian-knitted alpaca sweater may be worn with jeans. Consumers and designers borrow fabrics, hairstyles, jewelry, and diverse symbols across cultures, making the market for clothing very globally inspired (even though many consumers do not know the origin and

FIGURE 3.7 *The ensembles worn by these models include combinations of patterns not usually seen together, a mix of more formal and casual pieces, and an unconventional play on proportion and length. Is this postmodern chic, or does it work only because it appears in a Prada ad?*

meaning of their borrowings). Postmodern consumers are prone to mix diverse brands and designers in one appearance and buy parts and pieces of an ensemble at an array of price levels. Mixing Target and Gucci can be cool (Agins, 1999). Buying separates and mixing them with diverse accessories is quite common. Consumers mix-and-match not just to save money, but also to have more freedom in putting unique looks together. Susan Kaiser in "Identity, Postmodernity, and the Global Apparel Marketplace" describes how consumers actively put looks together to "produce identity."

Perhaps because the postmodern era continues on while we move into a new millennium, people might become **nostalgic** for times past as we know we are leaving them behind. Fashion trends tend to highlight a past decade every few years. Currently, flared pant legs are inspired by 1960s and 1970s bell-bottoms. Tie-dyeing, popular in the 1960s, reemerged in the late 1980s and early 1990s.

Questioning of traditions and rules seems to be a given during the current times (Featherstone, 1991). We see fashionable combinations of masculine and feminine symbols, casual combined with formal, and interesting mixes of fabrics that challenge old rules about not mixing patterns in one look (see Figure 3.7). During a time when many traditional aspects of culture, such as gender roles, sexuality, bases of economic power distribution, and ethnic hegemony, are questioned, it is no wonder that questioning of traditional rules for dress should occur. By the early 1990s, black rap groups (certainly not mainstream power leaders) became a major source of fashion inspiration for young men in the

United States (Spiegler, 1996). And tattoos and piercings became both fashionable and a statement of defiance against mainstream norms of body modification (Peace, in press).

The ethics of global apparel production systems and consumers in economically advantaged countries have also been questioned. Controversy abounds about the hiring of poor people of the world to sew garments for incredibly low pay so that North American and European consumers can purchase an endless array of fashions for relatively low prices. Our freedom of choice has consequences, such as slave wages for many workers, some of whom are children.

Finally, Baudrillard (1983) suggested that during the postmodern era, **simulations** are becoming as valuable as what is real and rare. Since the late 1980s, animal prints and fake furs have been featured even in top designer lines, perhaps to save endangered species while affording enjoyment of natural forms, even if they look fake. We also live in an era when cosmetic surgery is on the rise. It seems to be increasingly acceptable to modify the natural body and acquire a "simulated" perfect figure or face. Simulations in general probably are increasing because of technological innovations that allow us to simulate materials (and bodies) effectively.

Kaiser, in "Identity, Postmodernity, and the Global Apparel Marketplace," discusses the overall trends in postmodern consumer culture—choice, creativity, and resulting complexity and confusion. With so many consumers mixing and matching, breaking old rules in novel ways, and borrowing across cultures and times, it becomes increasingly difficult to read appearances clearly (and it may take greater time to make decisions while getting dressed in the morning). Communicating through dress is increasingly complex.

Summary

The vast complexity of communicating through dress has become heightened during the postmodern era. Old rules of dress are questioned, symbols are borrowed and used out of historical and cultural context, and what is real can be simulated and faked. Communicating through dress may less often involve clearly shared meanings. The perceiver may have to work hard at making sense of an appearance produced during postmodern times. Nevertheless, dress is still significant human behavior that takes on a rich array of meanings within the surrounding context of individual wearer, social interactions, family, organizations, and culture.

Note

1. Verbal communications may be transmitted via dress, as when a brand logo (e.g., Calvin Klein Jeans, Wrangler) is emblazoned on a garment or a saying is printed on a message T-shirt.

Suggested Readings

Barnard, M. (1996). *Fashion as Communication*. London: Routledge.

Gitlin, T. (1989, July/August). Postmodernism defined, at last! *Utne Reader*, 52–61.

McCracken, G. (1988). *Culture and Consumption*. Bloomington: Indiana University Press.

Morgado, M. A. (1996). Coming to terms with postmodern: Theories and concepts of contemporary culture and their implications for apparel scholars. *Clothing and Textiles Research Journal*, 14(1):41–53.

LEARNING ACTIVITY

Dressing out of Context

Objective: The experience of how others respond when your dress does not match with the social context in which you appear will demonstrate how context affects meanings of dress. Using systematic observation techniques, record other people's reactions to your dress and your own reactions to their feedback.

Procedure

Select one of the levels of context from the model in Figure 3.4. Plan to wear dress that is incongruent with that component of context during one day of the week when you will interact with other people during several hours of the day. For example:

Level of Context	Incongruent Dress Possibility
Culture	Wear dress that is normative to a culture other than the one in which you live or are from. (Wear a sari or a Scottish kilt to classes in the United States.)
Social Situation	Wear a formal gown or a tuxedo to classes.
Person Characteristics	Wear an outfit that is appropriate for a much younger or much older person than yourself.
Garment/Body Interaction	Wear an outfit that is too small for you or extremely large.
Interaction of Pieces	Wear unmatched plaids and prints together in one ensemble.
Garment Pieces	Wear a pair of jeans on your head all day.
Condition of Materials	Wear a garment that is notably stained or ripped to classes.

Wear your out-of-context dress for at least six hours in one day. Try to wear it on a day when you will be seen by and interact with a variety of people you know, as well as people you know very little or not at all.

Pretend that you think nothing is odd about your appearance. Let others react to you before explaining to them that what you are doing is an experiment.

Recording Your Experience

Carry a notebook to record your reactions and the reactions of others as the experiment progresses. Record information on the following:

- Positive and negative responses.
- Responses from males and females.
- Verbal and nonverbal responses.
- Responses from acquaintances, friends, and strangers.
- Your feelings and thoughts about yourself before you venture out wearing the costume and as the experiment progresses.
- Comparisons of yourself with others' appearances.

Also, describe the places you went, situations you were involved in, types of people with whom you interacted, types of people you were seen by but with whom you did not specifically interact, date and times of day for each entry in your recordings, and weather conditions you may have experienced.

Questions to Ponder

1. Did you learn anything about how people respond to others on the basis of appearance? What types of meanings did various others seem to assign to your dress?

2. Was there more than one aspect of context affecting how your dress was interpreted?

3. What factors may have affected your accuracy in interpreting responses from others?

4. Will you ever dress this way again?

References

Agins, T. (1999, June 11). Fashion: Cheapskate chic. *Wall Street Journal*, W1.

Barnard, M. (1996). *Fashion as Communication*. London: Routledge.

Bateson, G. (1979). *Mind and Nature*. New York: E. P. Dutton.

Baudrillard, J. (1983). *Simulations* (P. Foss, P. Patton, & P. Beitchman, trans.). New York: Semiotext(e), Inc.

Berger, A. A. (1984). *Signs in Contemporary Culture*. New York: Longman.

Berlo, D. K. (1960). *The Process of Communication*. New York: Holt, Rinehart and Winston.

Blumhagen, D. W. (1979). The doctor's white coat: The image of the physician in modern America. *Annals of Internal Medicine*, 91:111–116.

Burgoon, M., & Ruffner, M. (1974). *Human Communication*. New York: Holt, Rinehart and Winston.

Clayton, R., Lennon, S. J., & Larkin, J. (1987). Perceived fashionability of a garment as inferred from the age and body type of the wearer. *Home Economics Research Journal*, 15:237–246.

Damhorst, M. L. (1984–1985). Meanings of clothing cues in social context. *Clothing and Textiles Research Journal*, 3(2):39–48.

Davis, M. L. (1980). *Visual Design in Dress*. Englewood Cliffs, NJ: Prentice Hall.

Eco, U. (1976). A *Theory of Semiotics*. Bloomington: Indiana University Press.

Fashion workshop: Real life cues to clothes for your job. (1989, October). *Glamour*, 203–206.

Featherstone, M. (1991). *Consumer Culture and Postmodernism*. London: Sage.

Fiore, A. M., & Kim, S. (1997). Olfactory cues of appearance affecting professional image of women. *Journal of Career Development*, 4:247–264.

Fiore, A. M., & Kimle, P. A. (1997). *Understanding Aesthetics: For Merchandising and Design Professionals*. New York: Fairchild.

Firth, J. R. (1957). *Papers in Linguistics, 1934–1951*. London: Oxford University Press.

Fiske, J. (1990). *Introduction to Communication Studies.* London: Routledge.

Ganley, E. (2003, December 12). French group backs ban on head scarves. *The Des Moines Register,* 3A.

Gitlin, T. (1989, July/August). Postmodernism defined, at last! *Utne Reader,* 52–61.

McCracken, G. (1985). The trickle-down theory rehabilitated. In M. R. Solomon (Ed.), *The Psychology of Fashion,* pp. 39–54. Lexington, MA: Lexington Books.

McCracken, G. (1988). *Culture and Consumption.* Bloomington: Indiana University Press.

Morgado, M. A. (1996). Coming to terms with postmodern: Theories and concepts of contemporary culture and their implications for apparel scholars. *Clothing and Textiles Research Journal,* 14(1):41–53.

Peace, W. J. (in press). The artful stigma. *Disability Studies Quarterly.* Journal available at www.afb.org/dsq/.

Roach-Higgins, M. E., & Eicher, J. B. (1992). Dress and identity. *Clothing and Textiles Research Journal,* 10(4):1–8.

Roscho, L. (1988, October). The professional image report. *Working Woman,* 109–113, 148.

Spiegler, M. (1996, November). Marketing street culture: Bringing hip-hop style to the mainstream. *American Demographics,* 18(11):29–34.

Tseèlon, E. (1992). Self presentation through appearance: A manipulative vs. a dramaturgical approach. *Symbolic Interaction,* 15(4):501–513.

10   Symbols in School

The Southern Legal Resource Center (SLRC) claims that *Castorina v. Madison County School Board*, 246 F.3d 536 (6th Cir. 2001), is "first and foremost the ONLY pro-Confederate student free speech case in any of the United States Circuit Courts of appeals." But given the SLRC's penchant for exaggeration, it should surprise no one that *Castorina* not only is not "the ONLY pro-Confederate" appellate decision, it is not even the most significant one. That distinction belongs to *Sypniewski v. Warren Hills Regional Board of Education*, 307 F.3d 243 (3rd Cir. 2002), a case that originated north of the Mason-Dixon Line and has the potential to give school administrators fits.

More than three decades ago, the Supreme Court ruled that students do not shed "their constitutional rights to freedom of speech or expression at the schoolhouse door." *Tinker v. Des Moines Independent Community School District*, 393 U.S. 503 (1969). To prohibit student expression—be it speech, the wearing of black armbands as a sign of protest, or the wearing of Confederate flag emblems as a sign of regional or ethnic pride—school officials must point to more than an "undifferentiated fear or apprehension of disturbance." Instead, they must point to evidence that they have reason to anticipate that the expression will "substantially interfere with the work of the school or impinge upon the rights of other students."

The *Castorina* decision is simply an application of these same principles. The case was filed after two Kentucky students were suspended from school for insisting on wearing T-shirts emblazoned with the Confederate flag and the slogan "Southern Thunder." Because it was not clear that the school had experienced any racial unrest from past displays of Confederate symbols and because the suspended students claimed that the school had let black students wear clothing with racially divisive messages, the appellate court

ruled that the lower court had erred in ruling for the school district without a trial.

The school in the *Sypniewski* case, in contrast, had experienced significant racial turmoil. A group of white students known as "the Hicks" had marked what they called "White Power Wednesdays" each week by sporting Confederate flag clothing. After racial tensions escalated into threats and fights, the school board enacted a policy that prohibited students from wearing "racially divisive" clothing. The policy was even-handed—it referred to both white supremacist and black power fare.

Thomas Sypniewski was one of the students who wore a Confederate flag shirt during the period of racial unrest. His shirt carried the slogan "Not only am I perfect, I'm a Redneck too!" The Confederate battle flag could be seen through the letters in the word "redneck." Less than ten days after the school board enacted its new policy prohibiting "racially divisive" clothing, Thomas showed up at school wearing a T-shirt that listed the "Top 10 reasons you might be a Redneck Sports Fan" inspired by comedian Jeff Foxworthy. "The thought crossed my mind," Thomas was quoted in his local newspaper as saying, that the shirt was "going to piss people off." (Thomas later denied making the remark.) When Thomas refused to remove the shirt, he was suspended. With the backing of the Center for Individual Rights, a conservative law firm best known for bringing challenges to university affirmative action policies, Thomas and his brothers filed suit.

In a split decision, the court of appeals ruled that school officials had probably violated Thomas' First Amendment rights when they

This article originally appeared in the Southern Poverty Law Center's *Intelligence Report* (Spring 2003) Issue 109, pages 70, 72. Reprinted by permission.

suspended him. In an opinion more notable for its verbal gymnastics than for its realism, the court ruled that the term "redneck" was not sufficiently similar to the expressions and symbols that had caused racial problems at the school despite the fact that Thomas had worn a shirt with the word "redneck" and a Confederate flag on it during the period of racial unrest, despite the racial connotations of the term "redneck," and despite the in-your-face timing of the incident.

The *Sypniewski* decision has the potential to cause tremendous headaches for school officials. Even if they are justified in prohibiting racially divisive clothing because of a history of racial turmoil at their schools, they will likely face challenges from belligerent, but clever students wearing clothing sufficiently similar to the banned fare to threaten problems, but sufficiently different to make the issue a debatable one. Faced with the prospect of federal judges second-guessing their decisions, prudent school officials will be tempted to adopt broad, but easy-to-administer policies requiring student uniforms rather than narrow, but difficult-to-enforce policies banning only the kind of clothing that has caused problems. Student self-expression will be sacrificed in the process, but school administrators will avoid lawsuits. *Sypniewski* may be a First Amendment victory for Thomas and his brothers, but it may lead school administrators to stifle the rights of future students.

Perhaps the most ironic thing about the *Sypniewski* case is that it arose in a northern state like New Jersey. The champions of the word "redneck" were not Southerners, but proud Polish-American brothers living less than 100 miles from New York City. They claim that there was nothing racial in their actions. But to us, the case looks like a reflection of the ethnic nationalism that is growing throughout the country.

DISCUSSION QUESTIONS

Symbols in School

1. Do you think that schools should have the right to ban forms of dress such as message T-shirts? If so, who should decide what is offensive—the principal, faculty, parents, students? How should the process to consider bans be conducted?

2. What if students were allowed to wear T-shirts with images of the Confederate flag? What might be the consequences of allowing that to happen at school?

11   It's All Greek to Me: Sorority Members and Identity Talk

Kimberly A. Miller and Scott A. Hunt
University of Kentucky

This article examines how identities are developed and maintained through talk about dress and appearance. In 1965, the sociologist Gregory Stone indicated that dress was equally as important as speech to the task of establishing and maintaining one's identity. More recently, Boynton-Arthur (1992) and Holloman (1990) have studied the use of dress in Greek (i.e., fraternities and sororities) organizations.

We approached our task by analyzing the identity talk of sorority women from a single university in the southeastern United States.[1] In 1993, 16 campus sorority presidents were contacted about the study. When sorority presidents agreed to announce the study at their next chapter meeting, some members volunteered to participate because of interest, while others participated in order to meet a community service requirement.

The information in this article is based on eight in-depth interviews with 18 sorority members. All interviews were held in sorority houses in semiprivate meeting rooms. The interviews were open-ended, question-and-response sessions that lasted 45 to 75 minutes each. An analysis of the interviews revealed that many of our questions asked respondents to "evaluate" their appearances as well as the appearances of others. The responses indicate that evaluating appearances is a complex task with many possibilities. Therefore, the interview data reflected respondents' efforts to explain the rules of appearance evaluation to naive outsiders.

THE INTERVIEWS

An important theme that occurred again and again in the interviews with sorority members was that of respect for individual identity. Suggestions of an "ideal" appearance were rejected by respondents, and factors such as personality, culture, and circumstances were emphasized. To illustrate, when asked about paying attention to appearances, one respondent stated:

> I guess if you look presentable—but who's to say what's presentable, you know? One person might pay attention a lot to their appearance and think that they look really good, and someone else might [not].

The sorority members we interviewed often questioned the "legitimacy" of an ideal that would govern dress and appearance—for example, "who's to say what's presentable?"

Responses from sorority members indicated a high tolerance of different "personalities" or "cultures." This tolerance was revealed in an interview with four sorority members who were asked about their views on the existence of an "ideal" appearance:

> First Respondent: I think there is a difference between a person who likes to dress preppy and a person who likes to dress all in black....I think it depends on your personality.
>
> Second Respondent: I think it depends on your organization or what group you want to surround yourself with....They have different ideas of what is beautiful or what is in style for your group.
>
> Third Respondent: Your culture too. I have a friend in Europe now and she dresses sexy now. So I think it depends on where you grow up.
>
> Second Respondent: I don't think there is really an ideal way to look....I don't think there is an ideal. I think it varies from person to person.

Original for this text.

Fourth Respondent: I don't think there is an ideal person. I think it's whether they are happy with the way they want to look. [If they are], then that's all that really matters. You can't say they are wrong because they are not wearing the same things you are.

In another interview, a different sorority member made similar comments:

I think a lot of it [dress and appearance expectations] is regional. I went home last year and I wore bows, but nobody had bows [there]. I think that's [wearing bows] more [common in local college town]. People will say why do these people [sorority members] have ribbons around their waist and bows in their hair. I have never seen it [bow wearing] but here in [local college town]. Last year I went to Alabama for a talent contest with sorority women from the Southeast. It's so funny when people say that [bow wearing] is the sorority look. When you see some girls from sororities you are totally shocked. It went from extremes. Girls wore boots and high heels and all done up from head to toe. All the way down to girls who looked like they just rolled out of bed, hair was a mess, and no makeup.

Another respondent made a similar point:

…if you had big hair and a lot of makeup and slutty-looking clothes, to us that are in the middle class, then you were lower income [sic]. A lot of stuff I wear you wouldn't dream of wearing, because you would think it was the slutty-looking female. Where I'm from, it's perfectly acceptable.

According to the above statements, a person's dress and appearance were viewed as a reflection of an individual's "personality" or "culture." In addition, the respondents generally agreed that it would be "inappropriate" to assume certain kinds of personalities or cultures were superior to others.

Another aspect of tolerance was respect and understanding of the situation and surrounding circumstances. One respondent commented on this view by comparing summer camp to every-day life on a college campus:

At summer camp nobody cared [about appearances] because we were out in the middle of the woods, but here we have our shirts tucked, belts with the little thing over here on the side.

Another respondent indicated that situations were heavily influenced by the individuals within a given situation and that dress and appearance were affected by these interactions with others:

Every day you go to high school. I cared more there than I do now, because on campus you don't [sic] hardly see anybody you know. If you go back to high school, you're still going to look good because you don't want them to think you gained a few pounds and they don't think you look as good.…When you go out to the bars you want to look attractive because there are guys there. You want to look attractive when you come to meetings because you want to keep up a nice image.…I don't try to impress my parents or my family. That [appearance] doesn't matter. They are family.

In addition to personality, cultural, and situational circumstances, the respondents suggested that set expectations were not possible because images given are not always identical to images given off (Goffman, 1959). One respondent gave this example:

If you should wear, like, those warm-up suits, like, you know, jogging suits or something you wear after you play tennis, exercise, people might think, "Oh, they're into sports and fitness," but really it's kind of more of a fashion statement.

Later in the same interview, this respondent also said:

Like with the example of the exercise suit, I mean I think the way dress…definitely can be a big reflection of your personality, but in a situation like that it can definitely not be.…if you're just looking at a person and all you have to go by is what they have on, then you can judge them by that, but so often it ends up that the way they dress is not [a reflection of their real personality].

To summarize, the sorority members we interviewed communicated a commitment to respect for individual identity. Their interpretations of individuals' dress and appearance depended on understanding a variety of factors (i.e., personality, culture, and situation).

While there was general disagreement regarding an ideal appearance, sorority members did agree that "minimal" standards were expected. These expectations revolved around "minimal" hygiene and grooming. For example, in one interview, two respondents articulated minimal expectations:

> First Respondent: Keeping up with general maintenance of personal appearance [means] keeping up with a haircut, clean fingernails. Just keeping up with your appearance on a general basis. Have your shirttail tucked in and things of that sort.
>
> Second Respondent: Have your hair cut regularly and things like that.
>
> Interviewer: How can you tell if someone is not paying attention to their appearance?
>
> Second Respondent: Just the opposite. Sloppy hair, dirty face, shoes untied, nails are not filed, neck can be dirty.

In a different interview, another sorority member said that those with "offensive" body odor were violating a fundamental, universal standard. She said:

> Body odor. I know people will say that other people from foreign countries smell bad, but this is just part of our culture. More than 95% of the people are opposed to body odor and that has become a symbol of uncleanliness. That's something I find to be very uncomfortable and difficult to work next to someone. You can't concentrate.

Almost all of the respondents suggested that "appropriate" appearance included bathing on a regular basis, washing and combing one's hair, brushing one's teeth, and practicing "basic" hygiene. One sorority member said, "People tend to not socialize with people that are obviously offensively dirty." Several respondents admitted being annoyed when people appeared to have "just rolled out of bed" without making any effort at minimal hygiene. However, as we shall see below, the sorority members also suggested that there are "exceptions" for occasions when minimal hygiene is not met. Sorority members indicated that there were times when the lack of minimal hygiene was necessary, but it really did not cause "any great harm." For example, one respondent denied that her lack of attention to her appearance caused her personal identity any harm:

> Today I was late for my eight o'clock class. I put on a pair of sweats and a T-shirt. I really didn't care because I really don't know anybody in class.

This quote suggests that because the respondent did not "really know" anyone in her class, her appearance did not cause any permanent damage to her personal identity. Along similar lines, another respondent offered this statement:

> My friends I have in class that I feel close to, I don't think they are going to dislike me if I walk into class one day looking bad or not having paid much attention to try to look nice.

Again it was denied that a single bad day would cause significant harm to personal identity. Several individuals also denied that their "deviant" appearances injured their sororities' collective identities, because they would not wear their sororities' letters on such occasions.

Condemnation of the condemners (Sykes & Matza, 1957) allows the "offender" to shift "…the focus of attention from [his/her] own deviant acts to the motives and behavior of those who disapprove of his violations." One sorority member spoke for herself and her friend on this matter:

> If people aren't going to, you know, like you because you don't look nice, then neither one of us want to hang out with people like that.

Most often, respondents referred to physical comfort to neutralize a "dressed down" look. For instance, one sorority member claimed that "…there are times when I just want to be comfortable and just wear some T-shirts or something." Physical comfort, as the following quote implies, goes beyond comfortable clothes:

> When people just go on what I look like, I have been termed granola [i.e., natural look]. People say, "There goes that granola girl over there." I'll tend to look at girls who always have the bow in their hair, makeup on, always fixed up, and I can't understand why somebody would get up at seven in the morning every day to make themselves look like that. I guess that is more of a lifestyle choice. I enjoy sleeping.

This respondent believed that comfort (i.e., sleep) has a higher priority and therefore justified her "granola" look.

Psychological comfort, in addition to physical comfort, was mentioned by several sorority members. One respondent explained her typical dress and appearance this way:

> I guess some women feel they need makeup and a nice outfit. It is part of their self-confidence, and if they don't have that then they don't feel like a whole person. You can feel comfortable with yourself and have to put on makeup and wear fancy outfits. I guess I'm comfortable with myself the way I look so I don't feel I have to go through this big ritual to be ready to face the world.

However, explanations that emphasized psychological comfort tended to justify why individuals "dressed up." For example, one sorority woman explained the rings that she usually wore:

> If I leave and forget to put on my rings, no one else will notice. But I feel I notice if it is not there....There is some degree of personal comfort there. If I feel comfortable then I feel that I am acting comfortable and other people are going to get along with me more.

Making a similar claim, another sorority member reported:

> I feel, in classes, the nicer I look, the better I feel. That goes for every day, not just when I go to class. The better I look, I feel better about myself. Especially in class, I pay more attention. Things go smoother if I look nicer.

> You carry yourself better around campus maybe when you look better and hold your head up high and just carry yourself better than you would if you didn't have time to do all you wanted to do in the morning because you wanted to sleep that extra 15 minutes.

However, another sorority member gave an opposite opinion, citing school obligations (i.e., a test) as more important than appearance. She said:

> Sometimes if I have a big test, and I have been up late, or I get up early to study, and the shower comes later and stuff like that.

In summary, sorority members used comfort (i.e., personal, physical, and psychological) to rationalize a variety of looks, from "natural" to "dressed up."

Conclusion

Our findings suggest a belief held by sorority members that one should respect individual identities and tolerate differences in personalities. Perhaps this belief is a practical one because those who live in sorority houses live in close proximity to one another, and tolerance enables the house to function smoothly. To support this claim, sorority women interviewed repeatedly mentioned that gossiping about another member was a bad trait for a sorority sister to have. This respect for others, however, seemed to extend only as far as one's own sorority, as it was mentioned in every interview that "our sorority has all kinds [of people]" but respondents were quick to stereotype other campus sororities. These stereotypes invariably included comments about what the typical dress of another sorority member might be.

Note

1. This study is part of a larger project that includes surveys of: (1) sorority rush participants, and (2) non-Greek male and female students at the same southeastern university. The survey data are not analyzed here. An expanded version of this article was published in *Symbolic Interaction*, Vol. 20, in 1997.

References

Boynton-Arthur, L. (1992). Idealized images: Appearance and the construction of femininities in two exclusive organizations. Unpublished doctoral dissertation, University of California, Davis.

Goffman, E. (1959). *The Presentation of Self in Everyday Life.* Garden City, NY: Doubleday.

Holloman, L. O. (1990). Clothing symbolism in African American Greek letter organizations.

In B. Starke & L. Holloman (Eds.), *African American Dress and Adornment.* Dubuque, IA: Kendall/Hunt.

Stone, G. P. (1965). Appearance and the self. In M. E. Roach & J. B. Eicher (Eds.), *Dress, Adornment and the Social Order,* pp. 216–245. New York: John Wiley & Sons.

Sykes, G., & Matza, D. (1957). Techniques of neutralization: A theory of delinquency. *American Sociological Review,* 22:664–670.

DISCUSSION QUESTIONS

It's All Greek to Me

1. Give several examples of situations in which dress may affect the self-perception of sorority members.

2. Why do you think the sorority members interviewed rejected suggestions of an "ideal" appearance? Is that a typical response of other college students as well?

3. Individual identity was stressed by sorority members who were interviewed. Why do you think stereotypes of sorority members as women who "all look alike" continue?

12   True Colors

Brian Palmer

When Vice President Gore added a ban on "gang-related clothing" to his platform, he gave a boost to a growing national movement. Especially popular with school officials and police officers, the drive to prevent gang activity by outlawing gang symbols is so well established that, though some debate its constitutionality, few public figures question its effectiveness.

But gangs are often two or three plays ahead of the law-enforcement officials who try to block them—and miles ahead of the impressionable kids who try to imitate them. These days, the styles are highly localized and fragmented, just like the gangs themselves. And to avoid detection by police, many true gang members have given up the obvious symbols in favor of an extremely subtle visual vocabulary that shifts week to week and is visible only to its intended audience. Others have given up on such symbols altogether, and now dress in the same expensive sportswear that businessmen or college students might buy.

Says DeWayne Holmes, a former gang member who now works for the California State Senator Tom Hayden, "Individuals today are concentrating on blending in as opposed to standing out."

UNIFORM OF THE DAY

Bloods and Crips are widely associated with red and blue, but to avoid the police, both groups now play down their colors (except at ceremonial events like funerals) and opt instead for Tommy Hilfiger and Fubu. Latin Kings in the East used to wear beads in the gang's color scheme; lately, they've started hiding them in a pocket. For obvious reasons, though, tattoos—like three dots, which symbolize la vida loca—never completely go out of style. Some smaller gangs still wear the old styles, though, for one simple reason: "That's all they can afford," says Detective V. R. Bond of the Harris County, Tex., Sheriff's Department. "If the gang has some form of finances, the identifiers are going to be a little more sophisticated." In search of the old L.A. cholo style—khakis, white undershirt, Pendelton shirt—some even turn to the Salvation Army.

UNDER THE RADAR

The sartorial symbols that currently have the most power are the most inconspicuous. In Chicago, gang members may leave the laces on the left or right sneaker untied, or roll up their left cuff. And in districts with school-uniform policies, gang-affiliated students and their admirers are finding subtle ways to subvert the rules: slitting the bottom of their pant legs, parting their hair a special way, leaving a pocket inside out or one side of a shirt untucked. The codes change so fast that administrators can't keep up with them. But sometimes the ins and outs have nothing to do with gangs: "A lot of these kids have a tendency to be sloppy," says Paul Vallas, C.E.O. of the Chicago Public School System.

HANGIN' IN THE HOMEROOM

Nevertheless, clothing that's described—rightly or wrongly—as gang-identified has an ever-growing market in civilian teen-agers attracted to an outlaw image. "We've got kids here in Bismarck, real North Dakota kids, taking on inner-city gang identities," says Detective Lloyd Halvorson of the Bismarck Police Department. "It's kind of weird. You've got kids calling themselves Black Gangster Disciples—and these are white kids." Not only do these kids deliberately wear far more of a gang's colors than most members comfortably would, they also sometimes get tattoos for which they aren't eligible—like one that indicates a member has officially been "jumped in" to a gang. "The younger kids, half of them don't even know what this stuff means," says Donna DeCesare, a photographer who has documented two Los Angeles gangs. "It becomes real when they find themselves in jail." There, when someone is spotted with a tattoo that he hasn't earned the right to wear, prison gangs often give him a choice: cut it off, burn it off or let us get rid of it.

True Colors DISCUSSION QUESTIONS

1. Were there gangs in the area in which you grew up? If so, did any of the gangs have special clothing codes to identify gang members?

2. What type of system would gang members need to secretly change their dress code every few weeks? How could frequent changes be a problem for the gang at times?

13 Identity, Postmodernity, and the Global Apparel Marketplace

Susan B. Kaiser
University of California, Davis

Today, a visit to another country—or even to another city or state in our own country—often yields surprises when observing what is available for purchase, what people are actually wearing, and—in some cases, most significantly—how people are wearing what they are wearing. For example, one might see the same basic products everywhere, but worn in a variety of ways. Jeans, baseball caps, T-shirts, or other fairly basic items may be worn in many different ways: tight or baggy; shaped in a variety of ways; tucked or loose; and the like. So, it is not only what we buy, but also how we wear what we buy that expresses our identities: that is, who we are and how we see ourselves at any point in time. We can shape these ideas in relation to ourselves as individuals, as well as the groups and communities to which we belong, and even the nations or societies in which we live.

The idea that appearance styles, or "looks," are negotiated as people influence each other on what to wear and how to wear it is fundamental in understanding social processes of fashion (Kaiser, Nagasawa, & Hutton, 1991; Kaiser, 1997). Places and communities have identities, too. The latter, in fact, is no longer restricted to geographic location. Global technologies, the worldwide production and distribution of apparel, and the circulation of images of style across national and cultural boundaries all contribute to what might be characterized as a larger, complicated negotiation of global style, or international dress (Eicher, 1992). It is possible to be influenced not only by immediate, local culture(s), but also by globally circulating images and commodities. Constructing and reconstructing appearance and, in part, identity, becomes a process of figuring out how we "fit" in and "depart" from a vast array of possible looks. The contemporary social and economic conditions that shape the global apparel marketplace and our multiple possibilities for shaping identity within it are often referred to as "post-

modernity" (Lyon, 1994). The commodities and images that were once only available through travel or other cross-cultural contact are now globally and quickly produced, distributed, and consumed. In the process, more and more global locations are touched by "global style" in some way, as apparel manufacturers search around the world for (1) new sources of labor that are less expensive, more timely in response, and higher in quality, and (2) new consuming markets. A nation's level of economic development influences whether it will be regarded as a source of labor or a consuming market, or both. Yet the picture is even more complicated than that: Pockets of poverty exist within relatively wealthy nations, and pockets of wealth exist within relatively impoverished nations. The issue of who can afford to buy which goods in the global marketplace becomes one that is ethical, as well as economic.

What is for sale in the postmodern, global marketplace? Objects, images, and the marketers' constructions of reality. On a daily basis, consumers around the world are bombarded with new ideas and possibilities, whether they can afford to buy them or not. If one can afford to participate, it is possible to be part of larger (even global) communities ranging from the business world to leisure interest groups (e.g., rap or reggae or country western music; skateboarding or biking or golfing) and more fundamental identity-based communities (e.g., gay and lesbian; African diasporas; youth) to the more local hometown community where someone lives. Magazines, catalogs, and television and Internet shopping help to bring a world of possibilities for consuming and shaping identity to the fingertips of global consumers.

How do we make sense of who we are and who we are not in the context of postmodernity: a

Original for this text.

time characterized by media and commodity saturation, in a marketplace that may seem more global than personal? And how does fashion influence individual and collective searches for identity? The term *fashion* implies change; it also implies processes of imitation and differentiation. To some extent, we want to express our inclination and ability to belong to certain groups and communities. Yet somehow we balance this desire with assertions of individual uniqueness. A hundred years ago, sociologist Georg Simmel, who has been described by some as one of the earliest postmodern thinkers, noticed this interplay between imitation and differentiation in fashion change (Simmel, 1904). Even more generally, he indicated that in times of intense societal change or transition, we (collectively) become more concerned about representing who we are by how we consume: by what we buy and how we use and display it in our expressions of identity to others (Lyon, 1994).

Identity politics are involved in processes of imitation and differentiation. The word *fashion* is related to the Latin word *factio*, which implies faction or political distinctions (Barnard, 1996). Issues of gender, race and ethnicity, sexuality, nationality, social class, age, and leisure-time preferences all enter into the creation of the groups in which we see and do not see ourselves. These issues have always been factors in how we consume fashion. Since the late 1960s and early 1970s, however, we have become more aware of these issues due to social movements and related academic areas of study (i.e., feminist, ethnic, and cultural studies). The media have also played a huge role in shaping a larger cultural awareness of identity politics. In 1997, when Ellen "came out" as a lesbian on her television situation comedy, a whole media discourse (on talk shows, in magazines, and on the Internet) emerged to learn more and express views about diverse sexualities.

In addition to promoting awareness of differences through a complex expression and discovery of identity politics, postmodern culture seems to thrive on the juxtaposition of component parts from different social, cultural, and historical contexts. Traditional categories and boundaries collapse, or at least budge, as they are stretched by a bending, blending, and blurring of ideas and images (e.g., gender blending, retro looks, subcultural fusions). It is not so much that this idea of mixing and blending is completely new. The history of clothing and appearance styles has probably always relied on blending to some extent. But now there are technological and economic conditions that bring all of these possibilities into our televisions and computers. And there is a lot of profit to be made. Consider the following:

- Gender and sexual blending is evident in media that highlights drag or cross-dressing. A "lesbian chic" look (short hair, black pantsuits, masculine black shoes) becomes widely popularized in films, television, and in the workplace.

- The growth of casual businesswear creates a need to mix and match separates, potentially blurring a number of boundaries: formality, status, gender, age, and the like.

- Junior high girls wear dresses to dances and parties that would once be reserved for women who are adults: very long dresses (with slits) or very short, sexy black evening dresses worn with high-heeled, strappy black sandals.

Appearance styles ("looks") tend to be eclectic, visually stimulating, and confusing when consciously contemplated. How can we explain this complexity of style in the contemporary marketplace, and what is the impact on our perceptions of identity? On a cultural level, through talk shows or other interactions with media, as well as through "global style" per se, we seem to be collectively working through ideas or conducting "cultural conversations" about what appearances say about individual, community, national, and global identities. We are also interested in how and why we rely on style to work through ideas. These self-examining tendencies are often characterized as indicating a kind of *postmodern reflexivity*. This reflexivity refers, for example, to the media analysis of media coverage (e.g., "Are we paying too much attention to political scandals, showing the same images over and over until they become imprinted in viewers' minds?"), to the self-conscious and critical examination of fashion and beauty issues by fashion and beauty magazines whose pages depict thin models, at least some of whom have undergone breast augmentation surgery (e.g., "Is plastic surgery really necessary?"), and to public discussions of dress codes in the context of concerns regarding gang symbolism (e.g., "Will school uniforms really eliminate violence?").

Are we losing ourselves in a sea of surface-level judgments? In some ways, images are almost amazingly important for politicians and celebrities, as well as for the public in general. Consider the number of times and the variety of ways in which Madonna has "remade" herself. A whole page on the World Wide Web—"Hillary's Hair"—is devoted to Hillary Clinton's changing hairstyles. And, consider the popularity of "makeovers" on daily talk shows. Witness the increase in elective cosmetic surgery, the explosion of the fitness market, incidences of eating disorders, and the importance of designer or status labels in more and more contexts (including the football field).

Or, are we reaching new heights of understanding about ourselves and developing new, integrated ways of relating to one another? In a recent (1998) visit of the Pope to Cuba, communist leader Fidel Castro greeted him in a business suit: a symbol of Western, masculine capitalism. The international media reported on the political significance of this stylistic choice and its global, economic consequences. Did this signal the fall or decline of communism in Cuba? Or is it possible that new models of government could emerge, combining some of the most humane, equitable, and freedom-inspired qualities of communism and democracy with capitalism? Although the media did not comment on it, Castro's trademark beard remained intact. Consistent with his speeches, he seemed to be conveying the idea that his country was moving in new directions and creating new syntheses or collages of political ideas, rather than portraying a mere capitulation to Western, capitalist democracy.

In the everyday context, style affords an outlet for experimenting with a whole host of changing boundaries and collages of ideas and identities. Most likely, those who experiment the most with style have the most to gain from new aesthetic and status boundaries—namely, women, ethnic minorities, and working-class youth. Those whose physical appearances coincide with tradi-tional notions of power (i.e., northern European white male heritage) seem to have the most to lose from changing aesthetic and status boundaries (for example, any move away from the century-old, and remarkably stable, male business suit).[1] Yet there are signs that these boundaries are indeed changing, as evident in the "casualization" of businesswear (that is, the move away from suits toward a mixing and matching of separates, for at least some days of the week). And those who seemingly have the most to lose are participating in the shift to "casual Fridays" or even "casual weeks." Women and ethnic minorities have probably had some visual influence on this trend, because their relative tendency to be "more into style" has added variety and complexity into the visual culture of the workplace. On the other hand, some women and ethnic minorities in mid-management positions worry that the casual businesswear trend may serve to "keep them in their places," with the glass ceiling intact (Janus, 1998).

So style, in many ways, seems to be a "mixed bag." Signs of progressive change, whether anticipated or reflected through style, coincide with the suggestion—so embedded in modern, Western thought—that playing with appearances is shallow or superficial. About 100 years ago, Oscar Wilde (gay author and leader in the "aesthetics movement" who espoused "art for art's sake") said, "It is only shallow people who do not judge by appearances." In other words, the true mystery of our realities may reside in the visible, tangible, and taken-for-granted realm of appearances. We may be able to express something about ourselves and our cultures through the medium of personal appearance that we are unable to get across through other means.

In the postmodern cultural context, it seems as though a lot of the pieces of the puzzle that compose our realities are "up for grabs" or dislodged from their usual locations and juxtaposed with one another in a way that does not seem to fit. Shared yearnings lead us to search for new ways of understanding our identities and communities (hooks, 1990). Simultaneously, advanced-stage or global capitalism compels us to want and "need" more than ever. The promise of improving ourselves (for a price) is alluring and intoxicating, as evident in slogans such as "Shop 'til you drop," "When the going gets tough, the tough go shopping," and "Truth, knowledge, new clothes." Are we in the process of shaping new realities or merely serving as pawns in the marketplace? Let's consider this question by exploring three topics close to the heart of postmodernity: choice, confusion, and creativity.

CHOICE

> Eclecticism is the degree zero of contemporary general culture: one listens to reggae, watches a western, eats McDonald's food for lunch and local cuisine for dinner, wears Paris perfume in Tokyo and "retro" clothes in Hong Kong. (Lyotard, 1988)

Choice is often regarded as the mainstay of freedom. In the global context, the desire for and availability of consumer goods is equated with progress. To a great extent, freedom and democracy are associated with an unlimited range of options in the consumer marketplace. And in the capitalist apparel marketplace, the range of choice is tremendous because goods are produced and distributed worldwide. (Often, textiles and apparel are the first items produced in nations taking the first steps toward becoming more industrialized.) The assortment of styles, colors, and textures is enormous, if not overwhelming. In the apparel marketplace, at least in the industrialized nations, the world is at our fingertips. Yet another trend seems to contradict this idea of increased variety in the marketplace.

In some ways, there is a globalization of style, with some looks (often those associated with Western capitalism, modernity, and democracy) having the most global potency. At the same time, the choice within a given store or community seems to have increased, drawing from (and often appropriating) all kinds of cultural and subcultural traditions and innovations.[2] This tendency toward both increased variety within geographic locations and a homogenizing effect across locations represents a global paradox. Still, catalogs stuffing the mailboxes of middle-class consumers defy any problems with geographic access. The concept of choice itself becomes more complicated and harder to interpret.

Perhaps it is easiest to comprehend choice by examining its limits. The limits to choice are primarily economic. Not everyone can afford the latest, most popular brand of shorts for their children. Not everyone can afford to travel and be inspired by diverse cultural expressions of style. Not everyone can afford to diversify his or her wardrobe to engage in a daily, pleasurable, and postmodern play with style. And often those who actually make our clothes (i.e., apparel workers around the world, including those who live in immigrant communities in postmodern cities such as Los Angeles) are least likely to be able to afford to purchase the clothes for which their labor is responsible.

Yet in many modernized societies, even within very basic categories of commodities, including those at lower price points (e.g., disposable diapers, coffee, pantyhose), there can be a confusing array of choices. Buying even seemingly generic or standard items (e.g., Nike shoes, Levi jeans) requires complicated thought processes as one contemplates the range of features from which to select, the statement he or she will be making, and the contexts in which the item is likely to be worn:

- A woman in her thirties goes to a discount outlet shopping mall to buy a pair of athletic shoes and is confronted with a large store filled with thousands of boxes. What she thought would be a generic item actually presents a vast array of options. She must make numerous choices. Which brand should she choose? Should she go with high tops or the standard models? What color does she want? Will she be using the shoes for aerobics, step class, walking, running, playing tennis or basketball, or some combination thereof? Does she really need the $200 shoes with the air pumps? Can she wear the shoes for multiple functions even though they are intended for specific functions? Should she select leather, vinyl, or canvas? How do the shoes compare in terms of how they fit and feel? And what can she wear with them?

- The same woman stops at a convenience store on her way home to buy pantyhose for the next day. She wants a quick and easy decision, after the multiple choices she has confronted in her purchase of athletic shoes. She walks over to a display of pantyhose in egg-shaped containers. What size is she: A, B, or Queen? She briefly checks the height and weight table to confirm her size and then begins to address the other choices she must make: color, sheer versus reinforced toe, control top versus sheer-to-the-waist versus regular top, and so forth. As she makes her choice, she must: (1) consider what garments she will wear with the pantyhose, (2) analyze her figure and examine how she feels about it, and (3) debate whether the sheer styles will be less durable.

- A 9-year-old boy goes to the department store with his father to buy some jeans for school. The two of them are confronted with rows and rows of jeans, folded neatly in shelves built into the wall. Once they find what they think is his size, they unfold the jeans to examine the stylistic variations. Does he want basic indigo blue or some fashionable color? Faded (and if so, how faded)? Preshrunk or shrink-to-fit? Zipper or button fly? Standard five-pocket or extra pockets on the legs, and if so, how low can they be without suggesting gang membership? Flared, straight leg, or "pipe" style? Then, when beginning to try on some of the options to arrive at the best "fit," questions surface regarding how long, how baggy, and how low the jeans should be worn. And what are the current features and ways of wearing jeans that are associated with gang involvement? Does the school have a dress code — implicit or explicit?

Thus, even in the realm of standard or basic items, the range of choice is evident in today's marketplace. Choice can also be subtle but still require a great deal of thought and attention. In some ways, choices that are not obvious or readily visible when entering a store may be even more complicated. On the surface, one is making a "basic" purchase. So why does so much thought need to go into the decision making? Why are there so many issues to be weighed?

Perhaps we need new ways of thinking about choice in a global economy. For example, how do we perceive choice, and how do these perceptions compare with what apparel producers and marketers are trying to achieve? Whose cultural traditions and innovations become a part of the package of choice, and who receives credit for these traditions and innovations? Who profits? What are the effects of the complexities of choice? One possibility is that too much choice may create a feeling of overload that contributes to a preference for simplicity. Hence, the now "classic" popularity of black and (more recently) dark brown or gray, after every conceivable color combination has been seen on the body and head; the return of basic jeans after the heyday of designer jeans in the 1970s; the return to unisex disposable diapers by one manufacturer, after a decade of gender-coded diapers (for example, blue or male-patterned and "functionally altered" diapers for males). Yet even these "simpler" styles reflect a diversity of choices; the choices are merely more subtle.

Hence, choice can lead to confusion, ambiguity, and a desire for relief. At the same time, diversity in the marketplace can contribute to a celebration of style. The postmodern marketplace allows for a creative search for and expression of identity. In some ways, it is easier to figure out who we are not than it is to affirm a positive identity. In the retail setting, one can survey the options visually, scanning and eliminating the more obvious expressions of "not me," or identity *not* (Freitas et al., 1997). Then comes the even more complex process of gauging, mixing and matching, and the fine-tuning of possible, positive identity expressions ("me" or, more accurately, multiple "me's"). Even if one is not inclined to revel in the play of appearances, a certain amount of energy, in addition to money, is required to put together an appearance. Hence, choice contributes to confusion on the one hand and creativity on the other.

CONFUSION

Culture is in a process of recycling: everything is juxtaposable to everything else because nothing matters. (Gitlin, 1989)

Schizophrenic…an experience of isolated, disconnected, discontinuous material signifiers which fail to link up into a coherent sequence. (Jameson, 1983)

Postmodern eclecticism can foster ambiguity. U.S. culture, for example, is not sending straightforward messages about what is fashionable. We are bombarded with a diverse array of everyday looks of the people around us (intensified in an urban context), commodities in stores, images advertised and promoted in fashion magazines, appearance styles we see in films and television sitcoms, mail catalogs, and music videos.

There is likely to be a confusion about issues of time (e.g., are we looking forward or backward?), place (e.g., is there a local look anymore?), and existence (e.g., why are we so caught up in image?). Image and style seem to be in a constant state of flux:

- Apparel manufacturers traditionally produced only a few lines of garments per year, and retailers could reorder successful styles. Today, some produce as many as 12 lines per year and do not accept reorders.

- One can observe a vast range of styles in media such as music videos. Moreover, characters in the videos frequently change their looks numerous times in the space of a few minutes, suggesting that identity is changeable in the flick of a second. A somewhat similar pattern is found in Hindi films produced in Bombay, India.

- Youth subcultures seem to multiply overnight, and they stylistically blend into one another. The visual images that identify them precede verbal labels (e.g., punk or postpunk, new age, gothic, motorhead, boardhead, skater, or surfer).

Part of our confusion about culture and fashion probably stems from ambivalence, which has always been with us but is probably intensified in the postmodern context. In fact, we seem to be ambivalent about capitalism itself: We both love and hate what capitalism represents and promotes (Wilson, 1985). We also seem to be ambivalent about our identities, and fashion can give aesthetic form to unconscious tensions linked to gen-

der, age, and status (Davis, 1992). And we are probably ambivalent about our own absorption in issues of style, appearance, and image; they seem both trivial and practical, superficial and complex, personal and global. At any rate, the stage is set for experimentation. Fashion seems to provide a way of articulating individual and cultural ambivalences that are not easily expressed otherwise (Kaiser, Nagasawa, & Hutton, 1991; Kaiser, Nagasawa, & Hutton, 1995). In any case, ambivalence and confusion provide creative fuel for aesthetic exploration.

CREATIVITY

According to the French sociologist Jean Baudrillard (1975), it is not so much a matter of being the self as it is producing the self. To consume is to produce again. Part of what we produce as consumers are our appearance styles. In addition to its relation to the word *factio*, the term *fashion* also derives from the Latin *facere*, which means "to make or to do." Using *fashion* as a verb or a process in this way, we can consider how fashioning appearance style is one way—a visual and creative way—of producing identity. In African American culture, the term "style" is often used similarly as a verb or process, in a way that implies that styling is a way of producing not only identity, but also a sense of community with others (Hall, 1993). That is, it becomes a process of creating a cultural bond with others.

We could argue about whether or not we are more likely to experiment with our appearance styles, and hence, our identities, in the postmodern context. Is our current level of "producing identity" at a record high, historically speaking? Clothing historian Rachel Pannabecker (1997) suggests that although there do seem to be some unique aspects of contemporary appearance styles, they need to be examined in the context of larger, historical trends.

What we do know is that today, more than one look can simultaneously be regarded as fashionable. As clothing scholar Jean Hamilton (1990) comments, it becomes an issue of looks for spring, rather than a single look for spring. So there are many ways that we can create our appearance styles and still be considered fashionable. This seems to represent a shift toward a greater plurality of popular styles, perhaps to parallel an increasing awareness of what it means to live in a multicultural society. Yet we also live in a global society, as noted earlier, and our clothes are being produced in a larger array of places around the world, as apparel and retail companies search for or "source" new locations with lower labor costs for sewing clothes. And, perhaps in part as a result, there is a stronger emphasis on mixing and matching separates, because the pieces that are produced and worn together are produced, and often purchased, in different locations. These pieces come together, somehow, in our wardrobes and our appearances.

So, on a daily basis, we engage in the process of managing our appearances, almost unconsciously using our creative abilities. I recently asked a close friend, Carol, and my son, Nathan, to describe where and when they obtained the different pieces comprising their ensembles. Carol, who is 30 years old and from Louisiana, is now living in California and is dressed for a Sunday afternoon play we are attending together. Nathan, who is 20 years old and a student, has come home for Sunday dinner. Both are dressed casually and comfortably, and the total looks they have created are understated and well coordinated. Yet a discussion about each article comprising the look reveals a more complex state of affairs:

- Carol, who is 30 years old, is wearing black straight jeans (relaxed fit) pants bought at Gap and made in the United States. She has on a black leather belt (made in Italy) with antiqued brush silver (scroll design) hardware; her sister bought it for her as a birthday gift while they were shopping together at The Limited a few years ago. Her long-sleeved brown knit top buttons up the front and has a V-neck. It was made in Taiwan, but she bought it at Lerner New York in Baton Rouge, Louisiana. She is wearing a black "pleather" vest over it, made of 100% polyurethane. It was made in China, and she bought it for seven dollars at a discount store in Baton Rouge (where all separates are seven dollars) a few years ago, when she was on a tighter budget. She has only worn it once before, but really likes the way it fits. And this is

the first time she feels as though she has really worn it. She is wearing dark brown boots with heels; she bought them at Mervyn's in Woodland, California, and they were made in China. She's also wearing knee-high black socks purchased at Sears in Sacramento, California; she actually had meant to buy trouser socks. She is also wearing a scarf of 100% polyester that was made in Italy. It is square, with a black border and different shades of beige in an abstract design. She "borrowed" it from her sister. She's also wearing a silver ring with a swirl design; she bought it in San Francisco from an Asian street vendor for five dollars. She is also wearing a sterling silver ring with a V-shaped design; she got it at Rich's department store in Atlanta, in one of her favorite neighborhoods (and stores). She is also wearing silver antiqued drop earrings from The Limited; they were a Christmas gift from her sister. There is another, identical pair that is currently circulating between her and her sisters. Her watch, which she wears every day, is a silver chained style; it was made in Japan, and she bought it at a time that she was consciously moving toward wearing silver. She bought the watch in Marietta, north of Atlanta, at Sears in the Galleria shopping center. She is also carrying a black leather Etienne Aigner purse; it has a drawstring style with gold hardware and a detachable shoulder strap with a fixed shorter strap that can be worn over the wrist, "lady style." It has a matching wallet. She bought it at an outlet mall in Gonzales, Louisiana. She is also wearing a new fragrance (Clinique Wrappings), made in the United States. Overall, she realizes that her outfit is the result of six years of acquisition of goods, although she has never worn all of these pieces together before. She put the overall look together (especially her boots) to go with her recent, short-cropped haircut. She calls the whole outfit a typical "sister style" outfit. The term has a double meaning. She associates the look and some of the component parts with her sisters; they would all "fit" together with a look like this. In a larger sense, the outfit also represents "sistuh style"; it is a "constructed" and "achieved" look that she associated with the process and outcome of African American female styling.

- Nathan, who is 20 years old, begins by describing his gray and black baseball cap with "Oakley" embroidered into it. The cap was made in Bangladesh. He purchased the cap for five dollars from a street vendor in Mexico during spring break about a year ago. After purchasing the cap, he began to compare it with other caps with the same brand name, and he's noticed that the "a" on his cap is shaped differently. He is wearing a T-shirt that says "Glacier Point: Coolest Apartments in Davis." The T-shirt was given to him by his apartment complex about six months ago to celebrate its grand opening. The T-shirt was made in Jamaica. Over the T-shirt, he's wearing a gray, long-sleeved pullover top with a collar and cuffs and a small white stripe as a trim. He bought it at Gap in Sacramento, California, a few months ago, but it was made in the northern Mariana Islands. He's also wearing Gap jeans, worn loose but not too baggy, and just long enough to "scrunch" over his shoes. The jeans were made in the United States. He's also wearing black Nike high tops, with a "swoosh" trademark symbol. He bought them in Texas on a family trip to visit relatives almost a year ago. They were made in Indonesia. He doesn't remember where he got his white socks; he pulls them straight up, but not quite all the way. His Guess watch was a Christmas present from his parents. He realizes that he has only worn this complete outfit a couple of times, but it is a fairly typical "student" outfit for him.

Whether or not we are conscious of it, a lot of effort and eclecticism goes into our created selves. On a routine basis, we assemble elements from different times and places in our lives. The objects themselves are produced in an even wider range of locations throughout the world. The net result of our coordinating efforts may be subtle, or it may reveal a mood celebrating the possibilities of color, texture, and form. In any case, we are participating in a process of producing identity when we construct our looks. Perusing the labels indicating the country of origin also reminds us of the labor "behind the scenes," although this labor, in many ways, remains invisible in a global economy.

Some appearances may seem more postmodern than others, but the point is not one of classifying appearances or styles as traditional, modern, or postmodern. Instead, what seems to capture the idea of postmodern best lies in minding, managing, and perceiving appearance styles and component parts from a perspective that is perhaps more tolerant of diversity and ambiguity, more exploratory, and more "constructed" of elements from various places around the world. We are fashion consumers in a larger, global marketplace that is profit-motivated, often exploitative of developing societies, and endangering to a sense of place. The upshot of the contradictions that seem to be part and parcel of postmodernity is as follows: There is a promise of a new way of seeing the world as at once pluralistic and democratic, expressive and creative. But there are also cultural and personal costs associated with this new insight—namely, the possible threat of further exploitation on a global scale, a blurring of cultural traditions into a vast uniform global context, and a confusion between who we are and how we look. These may be the ultimate choices to which fashion in the postmodern context refers.

Perhaps we will be able to arrive at some form of synthesis through new imagery, new social arrangements, and new ways of viewing ourselves. Hopefully, such a solution will be kinder and gentler to women, ethnic minorities, and people of developing nations. We are at a critical juncture in our global society, and fashion plays a part in shaping and defining this juncture. Consciously or unconsciously, we are both commodity consumers and identity producers as we manage our appearances and continue to create ourselves and our communities. With increased awareness of identity politics, global inequities, and industry and media influences, perhaps we can create new, more complex understandings as well.

Notes

1. The "sack suit" emerged from a longer process of a masculine move away from anything feminine, frivolous, or fussy (see Paoletti, 1985).

2. There is an ongoing debate in the textiles and apparel field on whether the range of choice increases or decreases in the context of global capitalism (see Kaiser, Nagasawa, & Hutton, 1995; Kean, 1997; Kaiser, Nagasawa, & Hutton, 1997; Kaiser, 1997).

References

Barnard, M. (1996). *Fashion as Communication.* New York: Routledge.

Baudrillard, J. (1975). *The Mirror of Production* (M. Poster, trans.). St. Louis, MO: Telos Press.

Davis, F. (1992). *Fashion, Culture, and Identity.* Chicago: University of Chicago Press.

Eicher, J. B. (1995). Cosmopolitan and international dress. In M. E. Roach-Higgins, J. B. Eicher, & K. K. P. Johnson (Eds.), *Dress and Identity.* New York: Fairchild.

Freitas, A. J., Kaiser, S. B., Chandler, J., Hall, C., Kim, J-W., & Hammidi, T. (1997). Appearance management as border construction: Least favorite clothing, group distancing, and identity . . . not! *Sociological Inquiry,* 67(3):323–335.

Gitlin, T. (1989, July/August). Postmodernism defined, at last! *Utne Reader,* 52–61.

Hall, C. (1993). Toward a gender-relational understanding of appearance style in African-American culture. Master's thesis, University of California, Davis.

Hamilton, J. (1990). "The silkworms of the East must be pillaged": The cultural foundations of mass fashion. *Clothing and Textiles Research Journal,* 8(4):40–48.

hooks, b. (1990). *Yearning: Race, Gender, and Cultural Politics.* Boston: South End Press.

Jameson, F. (1983). Postmodernism and consumer society. In H. Foster (Ed.), *The Anti-Aesthetic: Essays on Postmodern Culture,* pp. 111–125. Port Townsend, WA: Bay Press.

Janus, T. (1998). Negotiations @ work: Analysis of the casual businesswear trend. Master's thesis, University of California, Davis.

Kaiser, S. B. (1997). *The Social Psychology of Clothing: Symbolic Appearances in Context* (2nd ed. rev.). New York: Fairchild.

Kaiser, S. B., Nagasawa, R. H., & Hutton, S. S. (1991). Fashion, postmodernity and personal appearance: A symbolic interactionist formulation. *Symbolic Interaction,* 14(2):165–185.

Kaiser, S. B., Nagasawa, R. H., & Hutton, S. S. (1995). Construction of an SI theory of fashion: Part 1. Ambivalence and change. *Clothing and Textiles Research Journal,* 13(3):172–183.

Kaiser, S. B., Nagasawa, R. H., & Hutton, S. S. (1997). Truth, knowledge, new clothes: Responses to Hamilton, Kean, and Pannabecker. *Clothing and Textiles Research Journal,* 15(3):184–191.

Kean, R. (1997). The role of the fashion system in fashion change: A response to the Kaiser, Nagasawa and Hutton model. *Clothing and Textiles Research Journal,* 15(3):172–177.

Lyon, D. (1994). *Postmodernity.* Minneapolis: University of Minnesota Press.

Lyotard, J. F. (1988). *The Postmodern Condition: A Report on Knowledge* (G. Bennington & B. Messumi, trans.). Minneapolis: University of Minnesota Press.

Pannabecker, R. (1997). Fashioning theory: A critical discussion of the symbolic interactionist theory of fashion. *Clothing and Textiles Research Journal,* 15(3):178–183.

Paoletti, J. B. (1985). Ridicule and role models as factors in American men's fashion change, 1880–1910. *Costume,* 19:121–134.

Simmel, G. (1904). Fashion. *International Quarterly.* Reprinted in *American Journal of Sociology,* 62(1957, May):541–558.

Wilson, E. (1985). *Adorned in Dreams: Fashion and Modernity.* London: Virago Press.

Identity, Postmodernity, and the Global Appparel Marketplace

1. How is fashion currently a part of identity politics?

2. How is fashion in the United States global?

3. How does postmodern emphasis on choice and creativity cause confusion? Is confusion an essential part of postmodern dress? What does it accomplish?

14   Kimono Schools
Liza Dalby

Geisha may be the only definable group of women in Japan today who, as a matter of course, wear kimono every day. New members of the profession obtain help in getting dressed from their ex-geisha mothers and their colleague sisters. They soon learn the proper way to move by example and practice. A middle-class woman who takes up kimono as a hobby does not have this surrounding environment to learn from, so instead she may actually take lessons from one of the recently established kimono schools. These institutions capitalize on the fact that many women with the means and desire to cultivate a kimono image do not quite have the required knowledge or confidence. They give classes that range from basic kimono wearing to advanced techniques of tying the *obi* in facsimiles of daffodils or folded cranes.

The kimono schools try to convince the public that they alone hold the secret to kimono success, by having appropriated one particular mode of wearing the garment and elevating it to an ideal. The text of one school calls for an elderly lady to wear her kimono "with dignity"; a middle aged woman, or "missus," to wear it "composedly"; and a young girl to wear hers "neatly and sprucely." All this originates from bourgeois notions of how the upper crust once dressed—and, in particular, from the somewhat stiff samurai class tradition, where propriety was the sole aim of women's dress and demeanor. That the kimono has been and can be very sexy and alluring seems to be systematically ignored by the schools.

A certain amount of judicious padding will help most women achieve a better kimono line, to be sure, but the numerous figure-fillers advocated by the kimono schools mold a woman's figure into an absolute cylinder. A towel around the waist, a V-shaped bust pad that adds substance to the upper chest, a bust suppressor to flatten the breasts, and a back pad to fill in the curve of the lower spine are items recommended as kimono foundation garments. Various sorts of clips and elastic velcro bands are sold to keep the collars in place and the front overlap neat. Such gadgetry is a substitute for the ease that comes with familiarity in wearing kimono. Geisha somehow manage to stay put together without all these aids.

When I first began to wear kimono, I used towels and handkerchiefs here and there as padding devices, as well as alligator clips to keep my underkimono in place. As I became more accustomed to wearing kimono every day, and as my entire way of moving became more attuned to its constraints, I found I could do without all the clips and padding and still maintain a neat appearance. A novice kimono wearer will usually tie the obi too tight, cutting off breath and appetite, yet will still somehow come apart after several hours. A geisha, or other experienced woman, can tie the obi so that it is well secured but not constricting. One of my plump geisha friends, for instance, said she always wore kimono when she was invited out to dinner so she could eat more.

LEARNING A FOREIGN CLOTHING

We are revealed by clothes more than we are clothed by them. Only a sincere attempt to wear foreign dress makes us realize the extent to which we are not just naked without familiar clothing: we are stripped of part of ourselves. A garment as demanding as the kimono, for example, requires a whole new personality, and, like learning a foreign language, it takes a while before we are no longer self-conscious.

"You look like a rabbit, hopping along like that," the sarcastic auntie at the Mitsuba would jibe during my early days of attending parties as one of the geisha. I would then forget the errand I had been sent on while I concentrated on my manner of walking. Eventually the proper movements became natural, but in absorbing them I discovered that I had developed another self in kimono. By no accident are the relatively small gestures of Japanese body language gauged to the kimono, but I was surprised to find that after a while, I actually felt awkward speaking English when dressed as a geisha. American English body language simply does not feel right in kimono.

Much presence of mind is required to switch back and forth easily between Western and Japanese dress. Few geisha can do it. On the whole, they tend to look awkward in dresses and skirts. The stunning and sophisticated older geisha I met at a banquet one evening seemed dowdy on the street the next day in her two-piece navy blue knit. When they wear Western clothes, geisha scrape their feet along as they are used to doing in their zōri. Their manner of walking with turned-in feet, which makes a kimono rustle delicately, looks simply pigeon-toed in shoes and a dress. They seem to be wearing invisible kimono, gesturing as if long sleeves were quietly constraining their arms.

Almost every geisha I know has a weakness for kimono and a passion for collecting them.

FIGURE 3.8 *Contrast in eras: Geisha in traditional kimono passes pedestrian wearing modern dress on the street.*

This is above and beyond the necessity of acquiring the basic number for each season that is considered a geisha's working wardrobe. Kimono are the single greatest expense in a geisha's budget. When a young woman begins her geisha career she will have had to purchase at least ten of them, along with obi, to see her through the changes of season in proper attire. About ten thousand dollars is needed to purchase a minimum wardrobe. A young geisha is thus likely to start her career in debt for the loan to buy kimono.

An old proverb says that Osaka people are *kuidōraku*—prodigal in their expenditures on the delights of eating—whereas Kyoto people would eat plain rice in order to lavish their money on clothes (*kidōraku*). The Kyoto geisha exemplify their city's stereotype perfectly. I know from my own experience, too, that it is difficult to be satisfied with a bare minimum number of kimono. Once wearing kimono becomes a habit, the desire to have a chestful of kimono and obi becomes an addiction. In Kyoto, where the affectionate local dialect term for kimono is *obebe*, women talk about the enviable state of being *obebe mochi*, having lots of kimono. Every geisha wants to be obebe mochi, and she will spend thousands of dollars a year to add to her kimono collection.

Geisha will appear before guests only in silk kimono and, further, only in certain kinds of silk kimono. Although kimono today can be thought of first of all as native dress, as counterposed to Western dress, within the realm of Japanese clothing a number of important distinctions define which kimono can be worn on what sort of occasion.

DISCUSSION QUESTIONS

Kimono Schools

1. How is movement a part of the grammar of wearing kimono and modern street attire?

2. What parts of the clothing in context model (Figure 3.4) are referred to in factors affecting kimono meanings?

15 India Examines Color of Beauty

Tim Sullivan

The pharmacy clerk pulls a box of skin-lightening cream from a glass cabinet, places it on the counter and says it's obvious why he sells so much of it.

Women want to be beautiful, says Vishnu Kayat, and the key to that is inside the box, which has a series of drawings showing a woman growing pale to the point of near invisibility.

"When a woman is more fair, she is more beautiful," Kayat says.

Seemingly, much of India agrees.

In this country of 1.02 billion people, images of fair-skinned women are everywhere. Light-skinned women dominate billboards, magazine ads and fashion-show runways.

Marriage ads, which consume a large part of many Sunday newspapers, are filled with requests for fair-skinned brides. Or, for the particularly choosy: "Very Fair."

Sales of skin lighteners bring in more than $100 million a year.

Not all Indians are comfortable with this celebration of fair skin, however, and the debate over the social divisions of skin tone—divisions that have long been decried by feminist groups and intellectuals—has spilled into newspaper editorials, advertising and politics.

In a nation often tangled in its own cultural contradictions, where ancient traditions jostle against MTV videos and Madison Avenue ad campaigns, it's an often schizophrenic debate, tied to questions of caste, colonialism and the global media invasion.

The result? The past few years have seen both an increase in the use of white women as advertising models—and an increase in acceptance of dark skin as a sign of beauty.

Often, it seems no one is quite sure what they think.

"A face cream that promotes fair complexion among women undoubtedly reduces their worth to the colour of their skin," the Times of India said in a recent editorial. "Yet, is this not a reflection of the premium society places on fair-skinned women?"

Skin tone is an issue across much of the world, and skin lighteners can be purchased from Tokyo to small towns in central Africa. But in India it is an obsession.

"Some people with dark complexions can also be attractive, but when a person is fair she looks very good," said Sunetra Surve, a 52-year-old Bombay housekeeper who uses skin lighteners. "And if a dark person were a little fairer she would look better."

It's an idea that increasingly grates on many in India's elite.

Liberalizing views on race and caste and increasing disquiet over women's often subservient roles have made skin lighteners an embarrassment to many in India's educated classes—even if they remain secretly stocked in the medicine cabinets of many of its women. In April, government broadcasting officials ordered an advertisement for Fair & Lovely, the country's best-known skin lightener, pulled from television. The ad, which showed a father wishing he had a son instead of a dark-skinned daughter, was decried by politicians who felt it disparaged dark-skinned people as well as women.

Prasad Pradhan, a spokesman for Hindustan Lever Ltd., which manufactures Fair & Lovely, said in an e-mailed response that it had "taken note of these objections and will address them."

"People across Asia—from Japan to India—historically have demonstrated a marked preference for skin-lightening and glow," Pradhan added. "It is as much a consumer-desired attribute among people in this region as anti-aging or tanned skin are consumer-desired attributes in the West."

Most of the lightening creams "contain bleaching agents or hydroquinone, which causes lightening of skin over a period of time," said Dr. Pooja Kaushik, a New Delhi dermatologist.

The reality in India is that light skin is often a significant advantage. And it has been for millenniums.

Skin color is not just a mark of beauty here, but an indication of caste, the ancient system of social division that remains an integral part of Indian culture.

The equation is straightforward: Light skin often comes with a high caste, since India's higher-caste people trace their ancestry, in part, to lighter-skinned Central Asian tribes that arrived in India thousands of years ago. Ancient texts, which traditionally were read only by high-caste Hindus, described various treatments to improve the color and quality of skin.

While the rigidity of caste rules has weakened in recent years, members of higher castes still tend to be better educated, wealthier and more politically powerful.

They also make up the largest part of India's ever-expanding army of Western-style consumers. Much of Indian advertising is aimed at them, or at the masses who aspire to be like them.

The result is that it's often light-skinned models appearing in ads, selling everything from DVD players to detergent.

"It starts with the clients, who are reluctant to use anybody who would be dark-skinned," said Farokh Chothia, a fashion photographer in the country. But, he conceded: "They are businessmen responding to sales."

India Examines Color of Beauty

1. Why would lighter skin be considered more beautiful in India, where darker skin has always been common and a part of ethnic heritage? Do you know of any historical situations that may have helped to instill a sense that lighter skin is more beautiful?

2. Why is skin color a symbol of social caste or class in India?

Dress and Relationships

4

Mary Lynn Damhorst

AFTER YOU HAVE READ THIS CHAPTER, YOU WILL COMPREHEND:

- How the self is defined through interactions with others.
- That relationships and interactions with others influence how people dress and how they feel about their appearance.
- That appearance helps to shape interactions.
- How meanings of dress are socially constructed and are a product of relationships.

I have always considered it surprising that I don't wear the color blue much except for some dark denim and don't have much that is blue in my home. I like a wide variety of colors, but for some unconscious reason I limit my personal involvement with blue more than almost any other color. I attribute my blue aversion to my mother. She frequently stated during my childhood that she did not like blue. We did not have blue things around the house much at all. Why I picked this up from my mother and my sister did not (she decorates extensively with blue) is one of those mysteries of family relations.

Our families and our friends have substantial impact upon how we dress and how we feel about our appearance. Often we are unaware of how we are influenced by significant persons in our lives. In other instances, we recognize clearly the opinions of others and purposely try to dress as others wish, carefully copy the dress of others, or deliberately dress the opposite of what is expected. Dress is part of almost any role we take on, and because roles are relationships, we may dress according to expectations of others when we try to carry off a role. We will specifically see in Chapter 5 that gender roles are expressed through dress and in Chapter 7 that work roles often include dress as part of job performance. Age roles (see Chapters 8 and 9) are also indicated in dress. Dress reflects our membership in a culture and the many groups we belong and relate to within a culture.

A variety of scientific theories help us understand interpersonal relationships. One theory that is particularly useful is **symbolic interaction theory.** The theory contains a broad set of premises about how an individual self is defined through interactions and relationships with others. We will focus on only a small portion of the theory. One basic premise of the theory is that the self is defined through interaction with other people (Mead, 1934).

Symbolic interaction theorists contend that to develop a sense of self as a human being, one must interact with other people. Other people respond to an individual (both verbally and nonverbally) about how he or she is doing, what he or she is supposed to be doing, what the value or worth of that individual is, and how the individual is identified (Stone, 1962).

Because dress is a part of our interactions with others, we learn some things about ourselves through the responses others give to our appearance. This is the process of **discourse** involving the presentation of appearance programs and receiving reviews introduced in Chapter 1. In addition, we interact with others on the basis of what their appearances mean to us (Shilling, 1993; Stone, 1962).

Cooley (1902) long ago compared the process of development of self to looking in a mirror. He outlined the general process as:

1. Individuals attempt to perceive themselves by imagining how others perceive them or by reflecting on reviews by others.

2. We may reject or accept other people's reflections of the self, but these reflections nevertheless have an impact.

This process of using other people as mirrors to tell us who we are is the "**looking glass self**" process. So, who we are depends very much on the people with whom we interact, their reactions to us and evaluations of us, and our reflections on these reactions as guides to future behavior, including how to dress. We continually try out new presentations of self through dress or stick to old ways of dressing that we feel are successful or safe. We learn the self, or who we are, through continued reflection and action. This constant experimentation and exploration is, in a sense, a **self-indication process** (Blumer, 1969). Our reflections on others' responses or how we interpret what other people mean is as crucial to self as is our own behavior and the responses of others. Our interpretations may not always be accurate; we develop skills throughout life at placing the self in another person's position in order to understand the other or to understand the self from the other's point of view (Mead, 1934). Taking other people's perspectives to understand their responses is called **taking on the role of the other.** Seeing the self and the world from another person's perspective is crucial to the looking glass self.

SIGNIFICANT OTHERS

Parents and Children

As a child develops, he or she collects increasing numbers of **referents** or people and groups from whom meanings of the self are learned (Charon, 1985). These may include **significant others,** such as parents and family members, who have crucial relationships with the individual and important impact on development of the self. The Osbourne family, whose daily lives are broadcast via the MTV show *The Osbournes,* are truly a unique example of a family (see Figure 4.1). It is clear that the children are not given negative feedback from their parents about their sometimes creative appearances. Several of our readings focus on more ordinary family relationships and dress.

FIGURE 4.1 *Stars of MTV's* The Osbournes—*not your typical family in appearance or behavior, but a real and functioning one nonetheless.*

"Learning the Language of My Daughter's Hair" is a touching story of father–daughter bonding through the ritual of hair braiding. Peter Harris describes how his 7-year-old daughter arrived one summer for their first go at an extended visit. Since his divorce years earlier, he had been unable to spend time with her due to child custody deliberations. He needed to develop a parental relationship with his young daughter and learn to care for her. After many tears and lessons learned, he became adept at braiding her hair. Their hair braiding sessions became a ritual that brought the two close together and helped them to learn about each other. The significance of their relationship increased because of the time they spent on grooming together.

The mother–daughter relationship often has enduring consequences for identity of the daughter. Michelle Stacey, in "Your Mother, Your Body," reviews how mothers can have a strong impact on their daughters' feelings about their bodies and actions toward their bodies. Mothers can influence eating and dieting behaviors of daughters as well as eating disorders. Mothers' influence on their daughters is discussed further in Chapter 8.

Marriage

The marital relationship is a family role that has substantial impact on how one feels about the self and appearance. One study found that, among older married couples, each spouse had a strong impact on how the other felt about his or her own attractiveness. Oh (1999) studied 94 married couples aged 60 and older who lived in Florida. A good predictor of a man's or woman's body satisfaction was what he or she thought his or her spouse thought about his or her attractiveness. But the *best predictor* of the older men's and women's body satisfaction was what the spouse *actually* thought. In a close relationship such as a long-term marriage, spouses serve as mirrors for each other to define, to some extent, the self. But even when a person is not totally aware of what the other thinks, the way in which one spouse acts nonverbally and verbally toward the other spouse over time has a profound influence on feelings of attractiveness and body satisfaction. (See Figure 4.2.)

FIGURE 4.2 *Couples can have substantial influence on each other's feelings about the self. In this case, the wife may have different criteria for assessing attractiveness of her husband than people outside the relationship would use.*

Not all spouses have positive influence on their partners' body satisfaction. A small sample of married women in their 60s and 70s reported that they ignored or rebelled against their husbands' negative comments about their aging bodies (Tunaley et al., 1999). In a huge national sample, Garner (1997) found that women, more than men, listed or checked that comments from a spouse were a common source of negative feelings about the body. Men and women indicated that their marital spouse had both positive and negative impacts on their body satisfaction.

Kyle Munson reports on couples getting romantic tattoos for Valentine's Day in "Erasing Love Never Easy with Tattoos." Sharing the tattoo experience and having their lover's name permanently attached to their bodies is a symbolic relationship-building experience for some couples today. However, when the relationship goes bad, tattoo removal is more painful than the original tattooing and perhaps an addition to the pain of dissolution of the relationship.

Our socialization to marriage begins early in childhood. We learn societal notions of what is expected of husbands and wives. The wedding day is a ritual celebration that symbolically marks passage from singlehood to the relationship of marriage. The marriage ceremony and its costumes for bride, groom, and attendants require extensive planning and preparation before the formal ceremony. In "Princess for a Day" Martha McEnally reports a case study of four women in their late 20s who were planning to get married. Even though they were from different parts of the United States, all of these brides had remarkably similar notions about what they wanted in a wedding dress and the ceremonies they were planning. The traditional wedding dress has common design components that symbolize societal notions of the ideal bride. Members of U.S. culture learn this symbolism and readily incorporate it in their wedding dress choices. Though each wedding dress may be different, a culturally shared rule system guides selection of the dress. Relationships with family and friends helped to narrow the dress choices of the bride-to-be.

REFERENCE GROUPS

Other referents or reference groups with which an individual has relationships may include peers and organizations to which he or she belongs. The individual looks to reference groups for ideas on how to behave and think. Some individuals may not belong to a group (such as cool kids at school, high fashion models), but may learn about the self by observing contrasts and commonalities between self and the reference group.

Dress marks membership in a group and may encode ideals and values of the group (see Figure 4.3). Conformity to group norms is surface indication that the wearer has adopted group ideals and values (Stone, 1962). Group dress marks the individual's relationship to society as well as to group members.

Subcultures

Deviant subcultures are groups that belong to or are a part of a larger culture, but differ in substantial ways from mainstream and hegemonic groups in the culture. The subculture sets itself apart and creates a relationship of contrast to and sometimes rebellion from the mainstream. Polhemus (1994) noted that the deviant subcultural group gives a sense of community and common purpose to its members, who frequently feel that mainstream society lacks values and characteristics that subcultural members desire as a part of their lives.

Members of subcultures may choose to look different from the mainstream majority for a variety of reasons. Groups that express religious identity and difference are discussed in Chapter 12. Some groups express political resistance against the dominant society and gain power through visible resistance (Majors & Billson, 1992). A difference in style can give subcultures an alternative approach to **status attainment** by affording a sort of power through **controlling the gaze** of others (Hebdige, 1997). Those in the mainstream tend to notice those who look different. The deviant appearance also distinguishes the individual as authentic and hip within the subculture (Majors & Billson, 1992). Many subcultures choose the margins of society that they inhabit to be a place of creativity and resistance rather than oppression. Creativity may be expended on appearance style and other forms of expression (hooks, 1990; Majors & Billson, 1992). In sum, appearing different by choice can give a sense of powerful being. The option of expression of deviance through appearance can be a healthy way for society to allow deviance and may help to channel some of the anger of the deviant group away from violent expression.

During the last half of the twentieth century, a subculture that differentiates itself from mainstream society through extreme body modifications emerged in the United States and Europe. Their modifications include multiple piercings, extensive tattooing, branding, scarification, Teflon implants to change the 3-dimensional shape of the body, and sometimes surgical modification of or removal of parts of the body. (See Figure 4.4.) In "A Survey of 'Modern Primitive' Body Modification Rituals," Theresa Winge explains

FIGURE 4.3 *The First Communion ritual is a rite of passage for young children as they become participating members of the Catholic church. Girls wore white dresses and veils in the 1950s (as shown) to symbolize their innocence. Today, white frilly dresses may be worn, but veils are not necessarily worn for the ceremony in the United States.*

FIGURE 4.4 *The body as art: This man may not consider himself part of the Modern Primitives movement. However, his extensive tattoos, reflecting traditional South Pacific Islander styles, and his multiple piercings indicate extreme engrossment in body modification.*

how the experience of pain is central to the meanings of body modifications for this group, meanings that can be spiritual and central to identity. Practitioners often share their experiences and research into body modifications with other members of the subculture and achieve a sense of community and social bonding through their deep interests and involvements. Great creativity is expended in developing the extremely modified body. Gatherings may feature individuals engaged in body modification such as hanging from hooks embedded in the flesh, adding a performance art component to the subculture's ritual events.

In some groups, subcultural dress may be adopted to make deep political or ideological statements. Barbara Brodman describes the rejection of contemporary fashions and wearing of traditional dress on the part of the Maya in Guatemala in the article "Paris or Perish." Mayan native dress became symbolic of the struggle with the government that was systematically trying to destroy native ways of life and superimpose modernization. For many years the government and powerful groups were rounding up and ruthlessly assassinating Native Americans in Guatemala, so the adoption of native dress—a clear symbol of ethnicity—was an act of political courage. In the case of the Mayan Indian subculture, native dress was not originally a deviant subcultural expression but a normal part of daily life. But the wearing of native dress during the times of intensified government pogroms identified the Maya as a deviant and rebellious subculture within Guatemala.

Media and Subcultures

Media are often part of subculture development. Through stereotyping and distortion of subcultural group ideas and behaviors, the media help to get exaggerated views of a subculture into the public mindset. Over time, however, media exposure can help to make some subcultures a familiar and even somewhat acceptable segment of society. Media can help to facilitate **legitimation** of a subculture in the larger society (Hebdige, 1979).

The article "Dress and the Columbine Shootings" provides an example of how media did not legitimize a group but may have influenced development of meanings of dress of a now-famous pair of friends who committed an ultimate act of deviance. Ogle and her coauthors trace media coverage of two students who took their own lives and the lives of 13 other people in the tragic shootings at Columbine High School in Littleton, Colorado, in 1999. The study illustrates how media coverage of the event focused on dress of the students, thereby linking dress and school violence. The press coverage stretched to interpret the boys' motives for dress and may have added to meanings of the long black trench coats worn by the boys to conceal the weapons they brought to school. The study provides an example of how media can shape the meanings we assign to dress.

Summary

Concepts from symbolic interaction theory provide a framework for understanding relationships and dress. The self is defined through interaction with others, and interaction is in part shaped by or focused on appearance. We use other people as mirrors to tell us who we are in the complex process of the looking glass self. Our relationships with significant others such as family members are reflected in dress, and significant others have impact upon our feelings about our appearance and the choices we make for dress. Dress may also reflect the reference groups to which we belong. Dress of subcultures reflects ideals and values of the group and also the relationship of the deviant group to society.

Suggested Readings

Hebdige, D. (1997). Posing . . . threats, striking . . . poses: Youth, surveillance and display. In K. Gelder & S. Thornton (Eds.), *The Subcultures Reader*, pp. 393–405. London: Routledge.

Majors, R., & Billson, J. M. (1992). *Cool Pose: Dilemmas of Black Manhood in America*. New York: Lexington Books.

McVeigh, B. (1997). Wearing ideology: How uniforms discipline minds and bodies in Japan. *Fashion Theory*, 1(2):188–213.

Mechling, J. (1987). Dress right, dress: The Boy Scout uniform as a folk costume. *Semotica*, 64(3/4):319–333.

Polhemus, T. (1994). *Streetstyle: From Sidewalk to Catwalk*. New York: Thames and Hudson.

Szostak-Pierce, S. (1999). Even further: The power of subcultural style in techno culture. In K. K. P. Johnson & S. J. Lennon (Eds.), *Appearance and Power*, pp. 141–151. New York: Berg.

LEARNING ACTIVITY

Unpacking the Meaning of Group Dress

Objective: Examine uniforms and dress of groups to which you have belonged for symbolic expression of group ideals and values.

Procedure

Find pictures of or actual garments that you wore as a part of a group. The group may have been a club, team, or organization to which you belonged. It could have been a work, church, or school group. You might also consider informal friendship groups to which you belonged if there was some similarity in how members of the group dressed. Think of examples from your childhood to the present.

Record characteristics of the dress worn as a part of a group. Did it indicate your particular role in the group?

Then think of what the group believed in and valued. What were ideals of the group? What did the group want to achieve, and why was it a group?

Does the dress you wore as part of the group reflect those ideals and values in any ways? For example, does the group style promote or reflect efficiency, modesty, cleanliness, casualness, formality, or traditional gender norms (see Chapter 5)? Does it reflect team spirit in any way?

How did you feel about dressing as part of the group? Did it give you a sense of belonging? Or did you never like the group symbols? What do your feelings say about your relationship with the group?

References

Blumer, H. (1969). *Symbolic Interactionism: Perspectives and Method.* Englewood Cliffs, NJ: Prentice Hall.

Charon, J. M. (1985). *Symbolic Interactionism* (2nd ed.). Englewood Cliffs, NJ: Prentice Hall.

Cooley, C. H. (1902). *Human Nature and the Social Order.* New York: Charles Scribner's Sons.

Garner, D. M. (1997, January/February). The 1997 body image survey results. *Psychology Today,* 30(1):30–44, 75–76, 78, 80, 84.

Hebdige, D. (1979). *Subculture: The Meaning of Style.* London: Methuen.

Hebdige, D. (1997). Posing . . . threats, striking . . . poses: Youth, surveillance and display. In K. Gelder & S. Thornton (Eds.), *The Subcultures Reader,* pp. 393–405. London: Routledge.

hooks, b. (1990). Choosing the margin as a space of radical openness. *Yearning: Race, Gender, and Cultural Politics,* pp. 145–153. Boston: South End Press.

Majors, R., & Billson, J. M. (1992). *Cool Pose: Dilemmas of Black Manhood in America.* New York: Lexington Books.

Mead, G. H. (1934). *Mind, Self, and Society.* (Charles W. Morris, Ed.). Chicago: University of Chicago Press.

Oh, K. Y. (1999). Body image and appearance management among older married dyads: Factors influencing body image in the aging process. Unpublished doctoral dissertation, Iowa State University, Ames.

Polhemus, T. (1994). *Streetstyle: From Sidewalk to Catwalk.* New York: Thames and Hudson.

Shilling, C. (1993). *The Body and Social Theory.* Newbury Park, CA: Sage.

Stone, G. P. (1962). Appearance and the self. In A. M. Rose (Ed.), *Human Behavior and the Social Processes: An Interactionist Approach*, pp. 86–118. New York: Houghton Mifflin.

Tunaley, J. R., Walsh, S., & Nicholson, P. (1999). "I'm not bad for my age": The meaning of body size and eating in the lives of older women. *Ageing and Society*, 19(6):741–759.

16 Learning the Language of My Daughter's Hair

Peter Harris

In 1987 I learned to love braiding my daughter's hair. That's the year that Adenike, then seven years old, stepped off the plane to begin a summer visit with me in California. She was holding Jessica, the teddy bear she'd brought for protection and comfort, and wearing two neat plaits on either side of her head. Within a week's time, her hair needed washing. The task seemed simple enough. But when I untwined her plaits, my girl looked like Chaka Khan after three encores. Scared me to death.

I had to tame all that? Wash it, dress it, part it, plait it? It was summertime, but the living was not easy. It quickly dawned on me that I had never braided hair in my life. Now, growing up in D.C. I had seen little sisters plaiting each other's hair, or watched as young women in high school sat between each other's legs and spun three strands into gold. A lot of my buddies during the seventies had girlfriends braid their hair before basketball games, or just so they could style. Once I even had my own hair cornrowed before a high school baseball game so my cap could sit firmly on my otherwise flyaway 'fro. And the spring before Ade arrived, I had practiced by weaving, unraveling, and reweaving yarn hanging from a bedpost. But neither memories nor macramé could prepare me for my baby's briar patch. Her mother's words rang in my ears: "She's very very tenderheaded!"

That first session took more than an ouch-filled hour. Throughout the next week, she cried a lot as I tortured her with my dreaded comb and brush. Mornings were especially tense. Tightening up her hair became the A.M. demand that fixing breakfast and lunch could never be. I even stopped playing the radio or listening to Earth, Wind & Fire records, although music had fueled my morning ritual for years.

In the days ahead, as I made the rounds to introduce Ade to friends, at least one of my sister-girls rolled her eyes at my daughter's hair.

"Why don't you bring her on over to my house," she gently suggested.

I told her no out of pride and continued to hack away.

I learned my first lesson about handling hair from my partner's eighteen-year-old daughter during a weekend visit to their home. Before a Saturday outing, she unbraided what I just knew had been a hip ponytail. She combed through kinks in Ade's head that I never knew existed. The reworked do was obviously better than the one I had created. I slumped, but my friend explained without sneering that I hadn't been combing all the way to the roots. She advised me to comb through small sections at a time—starting with the ends—to limit the pressure on the scalp.

Made sense.

I thought I had the hang of it. But later that week, somebody at day camp unhooked Ade's plaits and substituted two smart cornrows.

I got to soul-searching again. Why didn't I let somebody cornrow me out of my constriction and be done with it? I was feeling out my league, locked out of the circle of wisdom where all the grooming secrets are passed on. Deep down, I was also plain embarrassed: There I was, a grown man, and I couldn't even fix my own daughter's hair.

Once I moved past shame, then I arrived at pissed! Here I was braiding Ade's hair, and women were redoing my styles without asking my permission, or even if I wanted their help. Turn the tables. Let me or some other man—day-care director, boyfriend, husband, or candy man on the corner—put his hands on one of their daughters, and be talking about, "Girl, I'm just doing a touch-up"! Sister be cussing him out, dialing 911, and

---

Copyright 2004, Peter J. Harris, excerpted from manuscript, "The Black Man of Happiness: Testimony of a Good Nigger."

feeling around for a knife—all the while holding her daughter close, redoing the hairstyle, and wiping imaginary sleep out the child's eyes!

As mad as this double standard made me, I have to admit, doing hair was proving too tough for the kid. Then I had a breakthrough. It came after an intense conversation with another woman friend, who encouraged me to keep trying. Despite the tears, my friend assured me, Adenike appreciated my hard work and would remember my determination all her life. Then, fingering her own magnificent dreads, she fondly reminisced about the snap, crackle, and pop of *her* mother's hands.

That night I dreamed that I had been going about it all wrong: I saw braiding as a chore, instead of as an opportunity for special intimacy with my daughter. I was too tentative. Every time she whimpered, I eased up and brushed only the surface of her hair.

My dream also offered me some practical advice:

Use more Dax Jack! Don't make her Little Richard or nobody, but spread a little more sheen, boy! Soften the hair so the girl won't need a Mister Ray hair weave after you comb to the roots.

I had a New Attitude at our next session. We had gone swimming, and I got down, if I do say so myself.

After I used shampoo and conditioner, her hair draped damply, defiantly. But this time, with comb in hand, I took a deep breath and easily separated small portions until her scalp peeked out. Section by section, I parted her hair, fingering dressing down each row, until her crown had a fragrant glow to it. Handling Ade's hair gave me chills. Slowly I braided, and to my satisfaction—my sasafaction, to borrow from soul crooner Clarence Carter—deepened twist by tug by criss by cross. I transformed her hair into patterned plaits. Through four well-woven braids, she didn't moan at all. She looked into the mirror, rubbed her hands over the job, and nodded approvingly.

I was fired up. Once again, I felt under control as a father. A part of me—quiet as it's kept—was gleeful that black women aren't born knowing how to braid hair. Mostly, though, I felt good reconfirming that with perseverance, dedication and imagination I could learn to speak a loving,

painless language to my daughter through her thick, healthy hair.

After that, I even got halfway creative. One hairstyle included a braided ponytail and two other braids hanging from the side that had my baby remarking in an airy, awed little voice: "You can't even see the ponytail unless you hold it up."

I could braid hair. Damn! I felt like I had cracked a code or something. In a way I had: the summer of '87 was a turning point for me and Ade. I mean, it was her first visit with me since me and her mother divorced in 1984. I had expected her in the summers of '85 and '86, but custody battles shoved those visits to the back burner. Before Adenike finally came, the only real time I'd had with her was in her first year and a half of life. Even then, I was working out of town, away from our Baltimore home.

By the time Ade visited in '87, she didn't really remember those days. She only knew me through pictures and gifts through the mail, or the occasional long-distance calls in which I talked and she listened, or she spoke with curious detachment in her little-girl voice. Those calls only left me hollow.

I missed her, though, because I remembered what she couldn't. Feeding her. Changing her diaper. Pushing her stroller in the neighborhood around our East Baltimore row house. Letting her fall asleep on my chest. Catnapping myself on our queen-size bed, while she crawled across my face or sat beside me, playing with a toy.

I used to give her baths. Even took baths with her, along with the miniature boat, yellow rubber duck, and plastic soap dish. Man, those baths were peaceful communions. Time slowed to a caring pace. I remember every detail. I'd run the water—warm, but leaning toward cool—until it was high enough only to reach her chest when she sat down.

Once, when she was sixteen months, I remember hollering her nickname down the hall while the water ran: "Ahhhdaaaaayyyy." She waddles out from the bedroom to meet my voice. She sees my toothbrush sticking from my mouth. Her eyes light up, 'cause she's been "brushing" her four front teeth. Pointing toward my mouth, Adenike babbles a request for her brush, which is an orange miniature of my white one. I grab her hand, and we walk to the bathroom. I turn off the water, then hand her the brush full of paste. With her attention diverted, I plop her into the water so she's sitting, even though she always prefers to stand. The toothbrush sticks from her mouth like a toothpick.

Squirming, grabbing the side of the tub, she pulls herself up anyway. With her right hand clutching the rim of the tub, she gathers her balance and stands in triumph. Facing me, she's my grinning Pot Belly Baby. Her pudgy brown left hand holds the brush. Almost falling, her mouth becomes a soft oval of surprise. I can see her gapped top two teeth and her bottom two looking like erect white sentinels. She regains her balance and her black black eyes, with even blacker pupils, dance in some private merry triumph. I crack up at my naked baby clown.

Memories like these fueled me, soothed me, sustained me, when I moved out of our Baltimore house and eventually to California. If Ade remembered anything of baths and naps with Daddy, she didn't show it by the time she visited me in June 1987. Often, "Mommy" slipped out her mouth before she asked me questions. And the first time she fell—while she skipped ahead of me across an empty street—she wailed such a pitiful "Mommy" that I damn near wished her mother would materialize myself and help me check her scraped hands and knees.

Since she was only going to spend two months of that summer with me, I desperately wanted to communicate and commune with her in a special and particular way, so we could lock our thing in the pocket. I wanted to be her daddy, not just her father, complete with our own rituals/language/intimacy, the way I was with her brother, who had been living with me since the divorce.

Looking back on that summer, it's no question that learning the secret language of braiding her hair allowed me and Ade to become daddy and daughter. It was the mutual beginning of our most precious memories. Time began for us after braiding.

Since 1987, we have had miles but no distance between us. We have developed a new confidence, an understanding of how we can, and will, work together to stay close and really get to know each other. We've learned each other's moods and body language. We've developed our own style of discipline and celebration.

During our subsequent visits, I could sense when she really wanted to sleep with me—because missing Mommy, or the group of girlfriends she'd left behind, hung on her too heavy to handle. Or she definitely understood that when I said I hated whining, I hated whining! And that if she really wanted something, she'd best speak up directly and confidently, 'cause if she whined for it I turned deaf, dumb and blind.

She and I learned how to hang. I cooked and cleaned, read to her, took her shopping, to the movies, said yes, said no, laughed at her jokes, told her punch lines of my own, got great big hugs, heard bits of gossip from mom's household, held her hand when we hit the street, bought her En Vogue and Bobby Brown tapes, and played, as I did for all my kids and any youngster within earshot of my turntable, all my classic Temptations records.

In the summer of '90 I took Ade, then ten, and her then-thirteen-year-old brother Ketema to Florida. During our chlorine-and-salt-water-soaked vacation, I braided her hair every day. By then, me and Ade were duet partners. She'd ask for a style, I'd do it. If we were in a hurry to get out the house to go, say, to Disney World, I'd whip her hair into a style that wouldn't come loose with all the running and sweating and waiting in lines. If she'd just washed her hair after we'd all had a dip in the pool in the muggy Florida night, we'd take our time and watch a movie on HBO, the rhythm of combing through hair matching the sundown ease between mellow partners sure of their confidence in each other.

In the summer of '93, Ade turned thirteen. Of course, by then she wanted to style her own hair (even into styles that required hot curlers, which I couldn't get to with my natural- and dreadlock-loving ass). But I couldn't help but dig her independence and creativity. Besides, I was confident (please God!) that all those braiding sessions, the many times I'd taken her to sisters for full-blown cornrows, and the overall, affirmative black vibe of my household would bloom into some consistent natural hairstyle she'd choose for long-term pleasure and reflection.

Meantime, get this, I found myself teasingly spot-checking to make sure she was combing down to the roots. Ain't that a trip! She didn't pay me no mind, either, 'cause she was a big girl. Young woman. Eighth grader. As far from being that caramel toddler in the Baltimore bathtub as I was from being that nervous, second-time father worried that she'd slip out my loving hands and drown in two feet of water.

But I laughed and told her, "You know I can still braid it if I got to," and she cracked up 'cause she knew it was true. She knew her daddy could do her hair. If he wanted to. If she wanted him to!

Looking back, my dreadlocked "counselor" was as right as rain about one thing: braiding Adenike's hair gave me the powerfully intimate way to help my daughter gain confidence in me. These days, I may be out of the hairstyling/hairdressing loop, but in my prime I could ask her to get the comb, brush, and barrettes, and her smile wouldn't hibernate. Sometimes, 'cause turnabout is fair play, and she and I had found what we were looking for, she even sat me down to brush and comb my hair and beard.

At this writing, my daughter, who is now a young woman, wears her hair short. As a member of her college track team (my baby entered the school on a combination academic and athletic scholarship!), she finds it much hipper to sport the wash-and-wear look. Over the years, Adenike has evolved into a powerful, beautiful person, with a sense of humor that delights me. She's also serious and hardworking, and her sensitivity inspires me.

I haven't braided Adenike's hair in years now. Still, I savor the intimacy we created during those times when she squirmed under my hair-hacking, hair-braiding hands. We remain daddy and daddy's baby, you know, having gone beyond just father and daughter, which could have been our fate given the divorce and geographical distance. When we talk by phone or during our visits, we have no taboo subjects. We've grappled with the history of me and her moms, her evolving explorations of sex and relationships, my 40-something life as a single man, her worries, my worries. And of course, we riff on school and sports in that overall silly groove we fall into when we take the time to hang.

DISCUSSION QUESTIONS

Learning the Language of My Daughter's Hair

1. Why do you think that Peter was so resistant to getting help at braiding his daughter's hair at first?

2. How did the braiding sessions shape the father–daughter relationship over time?

3. Do you have any memories of a parent or other relative helping you with clothing or grooming as a child? Are the memories positive or negative? Why?

17 Your Mother, Your Body

Michelle Stacey

Everyone has their own story about mothers and food. The link between the two is, of course, fiercely elemental: Every child's first nourishment flows quite literally from the mother's body (at least it did until the invention of bottles and formula). We feed off our mothers, and when they no longer manufacture our food in the furnace of their bodies they cook it on the stove—oatmeal, macaroni and cheese, hot chocolate.

But in the last generation or so, the story line of mothers and food has changed, at least when it comes to mothers and daughters. It used to go something like this: *Eat your vegetables. Finish your plate. Don't you want to grow big and strong? Why aren't you eating? Are you hungry? Do you want something to eat?*

Now the script is often (though not always) closer to this: *Eat your vegetables* (no escaping that one). *Do you really want to eat that? Too many of those will make you fat. You know, bread has a lot of calories. The women in our family have always been heavy. You'll have to be careful.*

Sometimes the underlying script is revealed less through words than through actions. Here is my friend Elaine's story: Every night at dinner, her (overweight) mother used a smaller plate than the rest of the family in a usually futile attempt to control her own eating. Both Elaine and her younger sister developed borderline anorexic-bulimic behaviors (chronic undereating, occasional purging) that persisted into their adult years. Here is another story, from my childhood friend Anne-Marie: Her mother had struggled against obesity since childhood, and Anne-Marie was always slender. In Anne-Marie's elementary and junior-high-school years her mother bought her chic, body-hugging clothes. I envied her miniskirts and stretchy tops, but Anne-Marie once said to me that she felt her mother dressed her that way because she herself was too fat to wear such things. In high school, Anne-Marie became the first real-life anorexic I ever knew: emaciated, obsessed, and still "too fat."

"HOLD IN YOUR STOMACH"

Mothers have always held powerful sway over their daughters' ideas about food, eating and body shape—feeding their children has been their evolutionary duty for most of human history. The difference, now, is that young adult women currently in their childbearing years are the first generation to grow up with mothers who themselves are firmly ensconced in the modern dieting culture. The 1960s brought us superthin Twiggy-type models, weight-loss centers and *Dr. Atkins' Diet Revolution*, and women's feelings about how to feed themselves have not been the same since.

In fact, according to Debra Waterhouse, M.P.H., R.D., author of *Like Mother, Like Daughter: How Women Are Influenced by Their Mothers' Relationship With Food—and How to Break the Pattern* (Hyperion Press, 1998), we are now embarking on a third dieting generation as baby boomers raise their kids, and a frightening pattern is emerging. Each generation starts dieting at an earlier age. I saw a wrenching example of such multigenerational body anxiety recently when I watched the 10-year-old daughter of a friend prance around the living room showing off her new bikini. Her 62-year-old grandmother, already the veteran of two face-lifts, reflexively said, "Hold in your stomach." I could see those words echoing down the years, until at age 25 she sits in a body-image therapy session recounting how her grandmother said she was fat.

BODY OBSESSION: LIKE MOTHER, LIKE DAUGHTER

"Research has shown that one important way you develop body image is through identification with a same-sex parent," confirms Ann Kearney-Cooke, Ph.D., director of the Cincinnati Psychotherapy Institute, and an expert in body image and eating disorders. Thus, logically, the mother who obsesses about her own thick waist or heavy thighs passes along a view of herself and the world: There's something wrong with you if you're not thin. Embedded in that message is the further idea that being thin will make a crucial difference in your quality of life.

This transmission of values can happen in two different ways, according to Kearney-Cooke. One is the identification process, in which you indirectly absorb your mother's values and worldview even if she never directly comments on it. You watch her trying on 10 outfits, none of which makes her feel attractive; you observe her ordering salads with dressing on the side and chatting with friends about the latest diet. And you understand quite clearly, and at a young age, that women restrict their food, often feel overweight and unattractive, and strive endlessly toward slenderness.

The second way is the internalization process, in which the message is more overt. People make comments to you about your eating and your body, and you take them in and make them part of your psyche—as I imagine my friend's 10-year-old doing. "It's like being branded," Kearney-Cooke says. "Very often the comments come from people who are overly concerned with their own bodies, and they're extending that to their child." The grandmother of the 10-year-old has clearly repeated a litany to herself countless times: "Hold your stomach in."

Kearney-Cooke cites research indicating that when a mother is self-critical of her own body, she is more critical of her daughter's shape, and the daughter in turn tries to control her body in particularly destructive ways: extreme diets, laxative abuse and eating disorders.

A "DIETING" GENE?

An interesting wrinkle has turned up recently in the study of parental effects on eating problems: evidence of a genetic predisposition to eating disorders. Studies of fraternal and identical twins suggest that 30–60 percent of vulnerability to bulimia nervosa is due to genetic factors, and about 58 percent of tendency toward anorexia nervosa may be genetic. Cynthia Bulik, Ph.D., associate professor of psychiatry at Virginia Commonwealth University's Virginia Institute of Psychiatric and Behavioral Genetics, who has conducted some significant twin studies, says further evidence suggests that the deciding factor in who actually develops eating disorders is what she calls "unique environmental events." These unique events could be things like deciding to take gymnastics or dancing (where there is great focus on the body and eating disorders are common), hearing comments about one's weight, or even being exposed to family members who are weight- and dieting-obsessed.

"If eating disorders can be activated in these susceptible individuals by unique events," says Bulik, "perhaps they can also be prevented by protective environments—such as having a mother who has healthy attitudes about eating and weight." Unfortunately, such attitudes seem rarer and rarer in the current thin-focused culture. I have seen young mothers of 3- and 4-year-old girls—girls of an age when baby fat clings and tummies stick out because the abdominal muscles are not yet fully developed—bemoan their daughters' "chunky" physiques.

MOM KNOWS: LIFE REALLY IS HARDER WHEN YOU'RE OVERWEIGHT

Without question, the mother-daughter connection is powerful and convoluted, and, as we all know, often fraught with unstated conflict. A mother may feel jealous of the emerging beauty

How much does your mother influence your attitude toward dieting and body shape?

Researchers have been coming up with some interesting—and sometimes heartbreaking—clues to the mother-daughter relationship:

- **Seventy-six percent of girls** completed the statement "My mother (or stepmother) worries about how her body looks…" with "all the time," "a lot of the time" or "sometimes," according to a survey of more than 200 teen-age girls for the new book *Fat Talk: What Girls and Their Parents Say About Dieting,* by Mimi Nichter (Harvard University Press, 2000). The result was the exact opposite when the girls were asked about their fathers: 69 percent thought their fathers worried about their bodies "hardly ever" or "never."

- **The mothers of adolescent girls** with eating disorders were more likely to have eating disorders themselves, compared with mothers of normal eaters, according to a small Yale University study. These mothers also thought their daughters should lose more weight than mothers of normal eaters, and judged their daughters as less attractive than the girls judged themselves.

- **Eating-disordered mothers** express more concern about their daughters' weight from toddlerhood onward, and make "significantly fewer positive comments about food and eating" during mealtimes, according to two studies, both of which concluded that there is a strong correlation between disordered eating in the mother and higher risk for later eating disorders in the daughter.

of her daughter, or may feel almost too identified with her daughter—that if her daughter is heavy it reflects back on her in some way. A daughter may feel inadequate next to the all-powerful archetypal female exemplified by her mother, as if she will never measure up.

But underlying these tensions is a great love and concern. Many mothers who try to influence their daughters' physical shape have learned firsthand the harsh reality that women are still judged on their appearance, and their weight-loss efforts are aimed at smoothing their daughters' way in the world. It's a fact in our culture today: Your life is harder if you're fat. And, of course, it's also a fact that you can be diet-obsessed while in possession of a perfectly level-headed mother. I am living proof of that. Although she did press a few too many carrots on me, I can't recall my mother talking about dieting or denying herself the good stuff. And, like mothers from time immemorial, she's been known to say, not with approval but with worry, "You're looking a little thin."

DISCUSSION QUESTIONS

Your Mother, Your Body

1. What are possible reasons why the same-sex parent tends to have more influence on how children feel about and act toward their bodies?

2. Do you have any memories of how your mother shaped your attitudes toward eating and satisfaction with your body?

18   Erasing Love Never Easy with Tattoos

Kyle Munson

A rose blooms but once.

Diamonds are forever.

Tattooing your sweetheart's name on your skin falls somewhere in between as a semi-permanent sign of (supposedly) abiding love.

As Valentine's Day approached this week, plenty of Iowa couples were going under the needle to seal their romance with matching tattoos.

Plenty more were ruing the day they got inked in the first place. The tattoo had become a lingering, stinging reminder of an ex-lover who was gone.

That's how Shawna Meyer of Ankeny, 32, found herself face down on a table in a plastic surgeon's office just west of downtown Des Moines Tuesday, her fingers digging into the cushion as she let out low moans and occasionally kicked up her legs.

Susan Schooler, a physician's assistant who has erased tattoos for more than a decade, was using a laser to zap the ink into microscopic particles for Meyer's body to absorb and whisk away through the bloodstream.

Removal is "double the pain of getting the tattoo in the first place," Meyer hissed between clenched teeth.

Six years ago, Meyer and her then-fiancé, Randy, day-tripped to Montezuma, threw back a few drinks and visited the local tattoo parlor to celebrate their impending nuptials. She paid about $80 for the fateful five letters of his name.

"Stupid's the first word I can use," said Meyer, when asked to recall that day. "It was *not* my idea."

When the couple divorced about a year ago, Meyer immediately had a heart-shaped rose-and-vine design tattooed over Randy's name. That wasn't enough closure. Eventually she decided that since she had gotten the guy off her back, his name should follow suit.

"When it's gone, it'll be great," she said. "No memories."

So this week, Meyer endured her third of about a half-dozen monthly, $350 sessions, which last about 15 minutes.

No lie: The Righteous Brothers' "You've Lost That Lovin' Feelin'" was playing on the radio, followed a little later by Paul Simon's "50 Ways to Leave Your Lover."

A day later at Sacred Skin on Southwest Ninth Street, Paula Baker sought out tattoo artist Earl Ramey to cover initials that had been tattooed on her left foot more than 30 years ago when she was a star-crossed 14-year-old marking (gasp!) a three-month anniversary with her boyfriend.

Her husband of 15 years, Edward (not the same guy), came with her to add "Paula" to a mermaid tattoo on his left forearm, dating back to his days in the U.S. Navy.

Ramey, with 17 years in the tattoo business, covers up tear-stained tattoos every week, but he isn't superstitious about it.

Tattoos don't break lovers' hearts, his theory goes. Lovers break lovers' hearts.

"People don't think about what they want for the rest of their life, is what it amounts to," Ramey said. He himself wears a tattoo of his wife's name, Hilary, on his left hand.

Other tattoo artists I spoke to, though, tend to believe romantic tattoos tempt fate.

Chris Murry of Wildside Tattooing in Mount Vernon dissuades his customers from getting them: "Me and my friends always joke, if you're married and you get their name on the tattoo, (the marriage) will last about two more weeks."

"I always call it a curse," said Ryan Anderson, who runs Mojo Tattoo, across the street from the Iowa State Fairgrounds.

"Even your kids can go sour," warned Ike Bills of Ink Addiction in Des Moines.

"I guess I can understand getting someone's name tattooed on you who, say, just died or something like that, some benediction with it," he said. "Really, after they're dead, they can't do anything wrong by you."

Back at the cozy Sacred Skin, Ramey had finished etching a multi-colored butterfly over the initials on Paula Baker's foot for $75.

Ramey pointed to the picture of one of his award-winning tattoos hanging on the wall. A woman from Knoxville had her wedding portrait inked in detail across her back.

"That's the extreme," Ramey said. "That's true love, right there."

As if on cue, Don and Melissa Mesecher waltzed into the shop. Both are police officers in Pleasantville who married about a month ago.

She already had his initials tattooed above her right breast and was looking to add Celtic knotwork.

He would get matching knotwork on his right bicep and maybe her initials as well.

The Mesechers said the tattoos were all about their love for each other, their mutual Irish heritage and family values.

Ramey was all for it. Who was I to throw up a cautionary flag?

With this ring I thee wed, and with this tattoo I thee curse? Could that be true?

Impossible to tell, like everything else about love.

Meanwhile, what are Shawna Meyer's plans this Valentine's Day?

Easy answer. She didn't miss a beat.

"No tattoos."

Erasing Love Never Easy with Tattoos

1. Do you think it is ever a good idea to have someone's name tattooed on your body? Under what circumstances might it be "safe"?

19 Princess for a Day
Martha McEnally

He popped the question and she said, "Yes." Now begins the planning for one of the most elaborate rituals in the U.S.—a wedding. Those who are inexperienced cannot begin to appreciate what is about to happen. From selecting a dress, finding a date when the church or wedding site is available, deciding on receptions, food, music, bridesmaids, endless showers, lunches, to place cards for the guests and the bows on the flower girl's hat, this is a multi-month—frequently a year-long—process. Couples routinely seem to expect six-month engagements, nowadays.

Over 2.4 million couples tied the knot in the year 2000. To do so, they spent over $32 billion dollars with the average wedding costing over $20,000 in the U.S. And the honeymoon will only add to the cost. Who is going to pay for this? The answer to that question fifty years ago or even thirty years ago might have been

McEnally, Martha: *Cases in Consumer Behavior*, Vol. I, 1st Edition, © 2002. Reprinted by permission of Pearson Education, Inc. Upper Saddle River, NJ.

FIGURE 4.5 *The Reem Acra Collection featured this bride dress in 2003.*

might vary, with perhaps the date coming first because of the need to make reservations. Then there may be an interaction between the site and the food (what can be served where). Dates and sites are a matter of what's available around the time that the couple hopes to get married; whereas food is not so much a matter of the actual menu as the type of food—a full meal or just finger foods. Once the date, site and type of food are settled, the bride's attention focuses on selecting the right dress.

To start this process, she has stored memories and dreams from weddings that she has already attended and sessions at sleepovers in which she and her friends giggled, oohed and aahed over bridal magazines when they were growing up. Nowadays, these same brides-in-waiting can buy InStyle Weddings and pore over celebrity weddings. Catherine Zeta Jones and Michael Douglas probably had the most publicized wedding since Princess Di wed Prince Charles (available on videotape). By being willing to sell the rights to photos and "the story of their love and wedding," Catherine and Michael were able to recoup the cost of their more than $1,000,000 wedding.

As if that weren't enough, the young woman and her friends can watch the Wedding Channel—a television show that describes the planning of real weddings. Some young women even admit to watching the show with their boyfriends. (Now, that's throwing the guy a hint.)

But this treasury of stored memories, images and dreams are hard to convert to reality, so brides must turn to "real" information sources. Which ones can or do they use? Recent studies show that 24% of engaged women use the Internet as their *primary* source of information for planning their wedding and a total of 62% do some of their wedding shopping on the Internet. What sorts of web sites do they use? There are two major ones— WeddingChannel.com and TheKnot.com.

When this researcher investigated the WeddingChannel.com, it was obvious that wedding planning and bridal registries were the major items prospective couples were looking for. Under planning, gowns were mentioned first. To get an idea of prices, I asked for gowns of any type by any designer that were over $5,000 and 40 dresses were promptly shown on the

"parents," but today's couple is older and more financially secure. In the last forty years, the average age for men getting married for the first time has risen from 25.2 to 29.5; for women it has increased from 22.5 to 27.4. These older couples are more likely to be college graduates and they have worked for several years. As they take on more of the expenses themselves, they are able to suggest that interfering parents back off. Paying their own way gives them more control over the details of the wedding and the opportunity to do what they *want* rather than what parents think *appropriate*.

Given the elaborate nature of wedding planning, where does the bride-to-be start? It's either the dress, the date and site, or the food for the wedding. The order of these three items screen. In the $2,000 to 5,000 range there were another 200; in the $500 to $2,000 range, there was another 200; in the $200 to $500 range, there were 70 and below $200, there were only two. Thus, 39.1% of the dresses shown were in the $2,000 to $5,000 range and 78.1% of the dresses were in the $500 to $5,000 range. There were considerably more very high end dresses (over $5,000) than there were low-end dresses (under $200). Unwilling to register at another bridal registry (which would mean lying about my identity, age, marital status and being bombarded with hundreds of email wedding ads to go with all the low-rate mortgage and credit offers I already receive via email), I was not able to search TheKnot. However, they claimed to have over 20,000 gowns in their listings in five price ranges (very affordable, affordable, moderately expensive, expensive and very expensive). Expensive seems to account for more of the price ranges and probably more of the dresses.

If you are willing to register at all these sites, the Internet makes comparison shopping easy and provides an incredible variety of dresses, cake styles and flower styles and thousands of wedding tips. This enables the bride to gather a lot of information before she ever sets foot in a bridal salon.

In addition to the Internet, there are magazines that provide information to the bride-to-be. The long-time favorites are *Brides* and *Modern Bride*. Both are fat magazines with what seems like more than 90% advertisements. The average circulation of *Brides* in 2000 was 420,000 and the average page count was 850 pages. For *Modern Bride*, the average circulation was 400,000 and the average page count was 800 pages. Besides those two magazines (weighed in pounds), there's *Bridal Guide* (circulation of about 265,000 and 400 pages) and *Elegant Bride* (circulation of 150,000 and 250 pages). Those four magazines accounted for the vast majority of magazine sales until Martha Stewart entered the market with her publication Martha Stewart *Weddings* which was estimated to have grabbed a circulation of 375,000 with about 400 pages in less than a year.

Traditionally, bridal magazines have featured page after page of wedding dresses, and al-though Martha Stewart's publication is entitled *Weddings*, it's no exception. Although Martha started with a smaller book (as magazines are called), it's getting larger with each addition. All magazines feature planning tips and have articles on cakes, flowers, receptions, bridesmaid gifts and dresses, etc., but Martha Stewart seems to have more ideas for the wedding. Focus group research revealed that nearly all participants (over 50 in total) thought that Martha Stewart would have more ideas. This perception was based on anticipations, not actual experience with the magazine. This means that the image of her magazine is based on other experiences with and knowledge of Martha Stewart. Because she is known for having lots and lots of decorating ideas, readers expect the same to be true of her bridal magazine.

When we think about the positioning of bridal magazines, it becomes clear that publishers have traditionally positioned their magazines to appeal to the first part of the decision process—the dress; whereas Martha Stewart appeared to position her magazine for the wedding planning process rather than selection of the dress. With each successive issue, however, her magazines are getting bigger and they have more dresses in them. Will this change the perception of the magazine?

What other sources of information are available to the bride-to-be? There's word-of-mouth among friends. Discussing weddings is something that many young women want to do. In these sessions, well-thumbed copies of magazines are passed around and evaluations are shared. Weddings of older siblings and then weddings of friends are dissected remorselessly so that young women come to have strongly-held ideas about the wedding that they want before they are even engaged.

While magazines and the Internet can provide a lot of information, no woman is willing to buy a wedding dress without actually feeling the fabric, trying on dresses and closely examining the results. Thus, bridal salons become extremely important. In this cocooned world, the bride-to-be is waited on attentively by sales staff, mothers and friends. The virtues of many dresses may be discussed at length and measurements taken to make the dress fit perfectly. This cosseting experience is the appropriate setting for selecting the wedding dress, which many refer to as *the princess dress*. Selecting the right dress cannot be done without reinforcement from others. The audience has to agree that this is the right princess dress for this bride.

Given high divorce rates, one might think that the importance of weddings would decline, but a look at the generation getting married reveals that that is not so. Most of today's brides are "Generation Xers". They were born between 1965 and 1976. Generation Xers are part of the "I" generation who have been labeled rebels and influencers. They were latchkey children who entertained themselves after school when their parents or more likely (single) parent came home from work. In addition to divorce, this generation witnessed a series of social disappointments such as the Challenger space shuttle explosion in 1986 and the growth and maturity of the AIDS virus. As a consequence, many of these bridal consumers are determined to do better; they are committed to making their marriage a lasting success. They are entrepreneurial, highly educated, very technologically advanced, expect to take charge of their future and are very likely to voice their concerns, and opinions and wedding planning is no exception.

Younger brides (born after 1976) are members of Generation Y which is the "all" generation. They grew up in an age of optimism, recycling, knowing how to live in the present to take care of the future and brand loyalty. They respond to messages that acknowledge their intelligence, share new ideas, are community-oriented and inspire health. They are also very computer literate and process information in a multi-tasking manner.

One might expect very rational decision-making from these groups when they enter the bridal salon, but something else seems to happen. The recognition that this is the bride's day starts to permeate decision-making so that little expense or effort is spared in creating the "perfect" wedding. At this point, what they *want* matters more than what they can *afford* or what makes "sense". Couple that with an ability and willingness to pick up the tab if parents are either unwilling or unable, and one has a recipe for an explosion of wedding spending.

To understand this better, let's listen to four young women (late twenties) describe their attitudes toward wedding dresses.

Alice: "When I was growing up, we lived in northern Jersey and often shopped in New York. Once when I was ten—I think I was ten or about that—we were in Saks and happened to walk past a bridal display. I saw the *most gorgeous* dress and I knew right then that I would buy my dress in Saks. I have always believed that."

Did she? Even though she now lives in the Southeast? Yep, first thing after getting that diamond, she and Mom flew to New York and shopped for nearly a week. Where did they find a dress? Saks of course! It had to be ordered and altered, so she won't even get it for months, but it's the right dress—she knows that in her heart. And she and her friends have discussed it any number of times—they can't wait to see it.

One of Alice's friends who is already married and had had to hold the line on the cost of her dress actually bought hers in a chain of discount bridal salons. According to Vicky:

"I knew I couldn't spend a lot on a dress. After all, my budget was only $15,000. So, I shopped at (name of chain) and out of all the dresses there, I could easily tell which one was right for me. It was satiny and simple with a high waist and was embroidered down the front. It really stood out from the other dresses, because they were all covered in lace. There's lace everywhere—on the bodice and sleeves …and they were all white—really white-white—no cream or ivory."

At this point, Alice chimes in:

"I looked in those places too, not just at Saks. Yeah, the dresses are all lace and have puffy sleeves…and trains. They are too white and so-o-o-o eighties."

Alice and Vicky's two friends, one of whom is engaged, chime in. "It's true. They're all lace and puffy sleeved. They are just too cute—not elegant at all and you want your dress to be elegant."

When asked what constitutes an elegant dress, they look at you as if you are stone stupid not to know…"Why, they're classy, simple, have clean lines and wonderful fabrics. They make you look like what-was-her name? The blonde who married the prince? Oh, yeah, Kelly, Grace Kelly! That's who you want to look like. She would never wear something that was fussy and covered in lace—especially that stiff, cheap lace," says Kelly, Alice's friend.

When asked why they think salons carry dresses like that (lacy and puffy-sleeved), the four women are silent for a few moments and finally, tentatively suggest that well, there are a lot of people who like that kind of thing. And, they point out, that after all, we *are* discussing discount chains.

What is so amazing is the similarity of taste that these four women (all in their late twenties and all doing well in their chosen careers) exhibit. They are all agreed on the appropriate style of dress. They all know about sources of information about dresses—they could name internet sites right away—and can discuss bridal magazines without needing to look at any actual magazines. If Vicky had not had a budget constraint, she would no doubt have flown off to New York as well, but she is not embarrassed about buying her dress at the discount salon.

What magazines do they like? They really prefer *Elegant Bride*. They comment that *Brides* and *Modern Bride* are just page after page of advertisements. When asked if the advertisements are useful in selecting a dress, they ask "Where are you going to buy the dress after you see the ad?" Even Alice (our New York shopper) says, "I looked at those magazines and I couldn't find those dresses in stores!" What do they think of Martha Stewart? They actually seem to wilt over the idea of Martha Stewart and point out that she's good for lots of ideas, but who wants to make their own place cards or tie the bows on the chairs at the reception. As one of them commented, "you might get some ideas there (in Martha's magazine), but you have too many other things to do to actually make all those things for yourself." They all groan just thinking about it.

Those four women are Gen Xers. What would we hear if we listened to a group of Generation Y? A focus group of undergraduate students had very different ideas. They, too, had looked at all the magazines, but because they weren't engaged yet, they really hadn't checked out the Internet. That did not mean that they didn't have strong ideas about dresses. Their preferences were for strapless dresses or dresses with spaghetti straps, form-fitting and low cut—front and back. When discussing dresses, they were all agreeing with this idea of the perfect wedding dress until one of them said "Well, that's what I want, but I probably won't get it." "Why not?" the others asked. "Well," she said, "my grandmother will be there. I couldn't get married without my grandmother, and she would be horrified if I wore a low-cut gown." This caused the others to pause and deliberate for a few moments before agreeing that that would probably be true for them as well until one of them broke in with "Really, I'm a lot less worried about my grandmother than I am my father! He would skin me alive if I walked down the aisle showing too much cleavage!" This produced a lot of laughter and agreement from the others who said things like, "Yeah, my dad would be like that too. He would never let his 'little girl' reveal too much." However, the group seemed reluctant to dismiss the low cut gowns and one girl wistfully said "Well, probably by the time I have a daughter getting married, ideas will change and she can wear my low cut gown—the one I didn't get to wear!" When asked about the lacy dresses, they also look at you like you're stupid—another group that doesn't want that lace.

Their attitudes on magazines diverge from their older sisters, however. They liked *Brides* and *Modern Bride* magazines because these books were so fat that the women assumed that they must have lots of good information. Did the fact that most of the dresses pictured therein were in ads bother them? No. They just wanted to see lots of dresses.

And they had strong ideas about the models on the covers. They preferred models who appeared to be in their mid-twenties and who were relatively serious about this. If the model was standing one-sided, this seemed to connote that she wasn't taking this seriously. Also, she couldn't be laughing—again that wasn't serious. There was a strong relationship between hairstyles and dresses. Long hair should be worn up with regular dresses and down with those strapless dresses. They didn't think brides should wear much jewelry and they didn't like tiaras. They preferred veils. Overall, they seemed to favor models with a somewhat sophisticated, but almost simple appearance—not too much makeup, fussy hair styles (bits of hair dangling everywhere was a no-no) and relatively little jewelry.

When asked about where they would like to have their weddings, there was a sharp division within the women. One group—about 60% of each group—said that they would get married in a church. The primary reason was religion. Several women who were Roman Catholic said that they really didn't have any other option, but most of the protestants agreed that they preferred to be married in a church as that seemed to be more fitting—after all, it is a religious ceremony as well as a civil one they said.

What was of more interest was where the reception would be held. Indeed, the reception seemed to be of more importance to most of them than the wedding. Wedding ceremonies are remarkably similar across churches, but receptions are not. Almost none of the women wanted to have their reception in the church hall—that was very definitely *out*. Instead they wanted to have the reception at more upscale meeting places such as country clubs, local mansions, bed and breakfasts and elegant hotels—even some private dining facilities.

The importance of the reception was apparent in their attitude that one must show guests a good time. The site of the reception, the food and the music set the tone for remembrances of the wedding because the reception actually takes longer. The group of women in the Gen X group remembered Vicky's reception in detail and talked about how great it was. Vicky commented, "I would have been embarrassed if I couldn't have shown the guests a good time. These are my friends from college and childhood. Some of them came all across the United States to the wedding. The family I lived with in Germany (as a high school exchange student)

also came to the wedding. They spent a lot of money. How could I have had a stand-up affair with finger food?"

Her friend Kelly agreed by saying "I'm from Connecticut and Robbie's from Georgia. Where are we getting married? Here (Middle Atlantic), which is sort of halfway for everyone. We aren't inviting them to come all that distance for chicken wings! In Connecticut where I grew up, there was a mansion outside town that would have been perfect for a wedding. It was sort of an Italian villa with large terraces overlooking the ocean. Just think if you had an evening reception with dance music and lights strung around the terrace what a romantic setting..." The other women dreamily agreed.

The younger women had fewer details in mind, but they also expressed an interest in having a big reception and showing guests a good time. They were especially interested in music and hiring the right kind of band (one that could play a wide range of music to suit different guests' tastes) was extremely important. For both groups, dancing seemed to be an expression of enjoyment on the part of the guests. Somewhere in this discussion, one woman said "And let's face it. We have to have a bar. Without alcohol, no one will dance!" No dancing seems to be the seal of doom on a reception. Having guests standing around making chitchat would be most upsetting to these women.

After the wedding and reception, there was actually very little discussion of the honeymoon. It seemed to pale in comparison with the wedding itself.

A few days later, this researcher was having lunch with a friend whose three daughters are between 23 and 30. She has been to a lot of weddings recently—a lot of weddings! When I told her about the research, she said, "That's like my experience. They all want these expensive affairs that go on for hours afterward. The idea of weddings as a celebration has thoroughly permeated this age group. They really want to get all their 'loved ones' together and celebrate the marriage. But you know…there's a sameness about all of these weddings. I can predict what they're going to be like—lots of food, same music/same dancing, expensive dress and while they all have a theme, once you get beneath the theme (outdoors, romantic, Italian, whatever) they're very much the same. Lots of people, sit-down dinners, dancing, smart and witty toasts and fashionable guests. I don't know that they've achieved much individuality beyond the theme." Hm-m-m-m, so much for all this wedding planning.

Some of the most startling statistics about U.S. society concern marriage. Nearly 50% of those $20,000+ weddings ends in divorce. Only 64% of people getting married in the U.S. are getting married for the first time. This means that 36% are getting married for the second, third, fourth, fifth, who knows how many times? Census data from the year 2000 indicate that the percentage of married couple households declined from 55% in 1990 to 52%. The percentage of female-headed households with children in the home increased by 25% in the same period. But that is only part of the picture. The number of unmarried-partner-homes (couples living together) increased from 3 to 5% of the population. These couples cite personal beliefs and the so-called marriage penalty on federal income tax as deterrents to being married. One respondent says "We've talked about it several times and could get hitched in a heartbeat, but we haven't seen a need for it."

Those firms involved in the bridal industry need not cringe, however. The echo boomers (teens and pre-teens) or children of the baby boomers constitute the second biggest population bulge ever in the U.S. They are the mirror for the baby boomers in terms of size and willingness to spend—after all they grew up in homes headed by the boomers who in the eighties were into more, more, more and quality in everything. If bridal trends continue, this could be a very free-spending group.

And if it doesn't work out, does it matter? "No," according to one recent divorcee. "The marriage ended but I still have an investment in the dress. I saved it to keep the happiness of that time alive for my son. It is a piece of my history."

It appears that the wedding ritual has meaning whether the marriage has a storybook ending or not. Could we stretch that to suggest that the ritual is more important than living happily ever after? That it's better to have wed than never to have?

Remember there were four women discussing Vicky and Alice's wedding, but we never heard from the fourth one, Sally, who isn't engaged and has no prospects on the horizon. At one point, she looked thoroughly miserable and almost began crying while staring at the table. "I don't know what I'll do. At the rate I'm going, I may never get married," she whispered. "Don't worry," the others told her. "Your day will come." Unfortunately, she really seems to need that reinforcement.

References

Armas, G. (2001, May 15). Family makeup changed vastly in last decade. *Greensboro News and Record*, A1, A5.

Bridal magazines "gloriously strong." (1988, April 18). *Advertising Age*, 59(17):S22(3).

Bridal magazines open new front in war for ad dollars: "Modern Bride" takes early lead in pages for '97. (1997, June 16). *Advertising Age*, 68(24):3(2).

Bride's. (1996, November 18). *HFN: The Weekly Newspaper for the Home Furnishing Network*, 70(47):34.

Fried, L. (1991, June 1). Battle at the altar. *Folio: The Magazine for Magazine Management*, 20(6):31(4).

Martha Stewart Omnimedia plans internal expansion. (2000, June 26). *Home Textiles Today*, 21(42):29.

McDowell, J. (2000, June). Martha Stewart. *Working Woman*, 25(6):60.

Nelson, L. (1991, June). Dashing down the bridal path. *Business North Carolina*, 11(6):68(6).

Weddings: A $35 billion market. (1998, May). *Target Marketing*, 21(5):66(3).

1. How did the families of the women getting married influence the wedding dress decision process?

2. How did the younger women in the focus group differ from the women getting married in their ideas about wedding dresses? Were any of the differences related to their age, engagement status, or generation?

3. What does the traditional wedding dress symbolize about the bride?

4. Why does the wedding ritual generate such elaborate efforts at consumer behavior?

20 A Survey of "Modern Primitive" Body Modification Rituals: Meanings of Pain

Theresa M. Winge
University of Northern Iowa

"Ritual is performance. Performance is an illusion of an illusion and, as such, might be considered more 'truthful,' more 'real' than ordinary experience"—Richard Schechner, Performance Theory, 1977/1988

The human body can be a vehicle for spiritual, psychological, and physical transformation, primarily through the use of body modifications and associated rituals. Body modifications can be traced back to the earliest human cultures, as evident in the discoveries of the following mummies: the Stone Age hunter, nicknamed Ötzi[1] (Tanaka, 1996); the Siberian Ice Maiden[2] (Campbell, 1994; Polosmak, 1994); and the mummies of Xinjiang, China[3] (Hadingham, 1994). These mummies had numerous tattoos and piercings, which researchers hypothesized were used to represent social status, life-stages, cultural aesthetic ideals, and participation in medicinal and spiritual rituals (Polosmak, 1994; Tanaka, 1996; Siggers & Rowanchilde, 1998).

Body modification has been defined as a general "… term for a variety of techniques aimed at changing one or more parts of the body from the natural state into a consciously designed state" (Camphausen, 1997, p. 110). While some types of body modifications, such as small tattoos and pierced earlobes, are currently accepted and popular in normative or mainstream Western society, body modifications have been embraced by subcultures[4] since World War II (Hebdige, 1979; Polhemus, 1994). As a result, subcultures wishing to differentiate themselves from mainstream society are able to do so with more extreme body modifications than those more widely accepted by the mainstream. Some examples of subcultural body modifications are multiple body piercings, body-sleeve tattoos, brands, cuttings, and three-dimensional Teflon implants. One subculture leading the way with more extreme body

Original for this text.

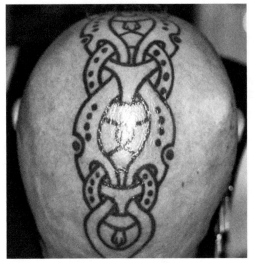

FIGURE 4.6 *Two views of the tattooed head of a man involved in the Modern Primitives movement.*

modifications and related technology is the Modern Primitives (Polhemus, 1994; Mercury, 2000). In this article I examine Modern Primitives and their exploration of experiences of pain and spirituality via body modification rituals.

MODERN PRIMITIVE SUBCULTURE

I first became interested in Modern Primitive subculture in 1995, when I was conducting graduate school research on the adaptive social structures of four subcultures in Minneapolis and St. Paul, Minnesota. During this research, I was introduced to and became fascinated by the Modern Primitives' use of extreme body modifications and associated rituals. Members of the Modern Primitive subculture placed a substantial amount of significance on their body modifications, to such a degree that they conducted extensive research about not only a chosen design but also about the type of technology that would be used to achieve the desired body modification. I later discovered that this group was not just after aesthetic changes, but significant life changes through their chosen body modification rituals.

The Modern Primitive subcultures can be found all across the United States and parts of Europe in heavily populated and industrial urban cities. They can be identified by their use of extreme body modifications, such as multiple piercings, scarification, brands, and/or three-dimensional Teflon implants (Mercury, 2000; Vale & Juno, 1989). Since the late 1960s, in the subculture's early beginnings, Modern Primitives have been wearing body modifications that they refer to as "tribal," "pagan," or "primitive" (Vale & Juno, 1989, p. 7). While the name Modern Primitive appears to be a contradiction of terms, it aptly explains this subculture's ideology. The Modern Primitive subculture was named by a self-proclaimed Modern Primitive and body artist, Fakir Musafar, because the name represents this subculture's connection to the modern, urban world in which they live and to the world of the "primitive" or "other"[5] they tend to idealize and imitate (Camphausen, 1997, p. 114). While the term "primitive" has ethnocentric connotations (often indicating negative bias toward non-Western and "uncivilized" cultures), Musafar selected "primitive" because it also connotes "first" or "primal" and represents the cultures that inspire the

Modern Primitives' body modifications and associated rituals (Musafar, 1996; Vale & Juno, 1989).

According to Musafar, the Modern Primitive is responding to a "primal urge" to modify their bodies and to experience new physical sensations, specifically pain (Favazza, 1987; Vale & Juno, 1989, p. 13). Since the mid-1960s, members of this subculture have been inspired and influenced by photographs and articles in *National Geographic* and *Time Magazine* (Vale & Juno, 1989). Thus, Modern Primitives have been wearing body modifications that are often referred to as "tribal," "pagan," or "primitive" by its members (Vale & Juno, 1989). Modern Primitives derive a great deal of meaning from their body modifications and the experience of pain associated with acquiring them.

To this end, these individuals participate in body modification practices and rituals, utilizing both modern and ancient technology to modify their bodies similar to the idealized cultures (Vale & Juno, 1989). Thus, a member of the Modern Primitive subculture, such as Fakir Musafar, has a distinct appearance; he or she often has numerous piercings, and tattoos, along with more extreme body modifications, such as brands, keloids, and scarifications.

Fakir Musafar

Musafar is an excellent example of a member of the Modern Primitive subculture. He has a distinct appearance with his extreme body modifications, such as numerous surface body piercings and blackwork[6] tattoos (Vale & Juno, 1989; Kleese, 2000). At first glance, Fakir Musafar looks like any other middle-aged male in a business suit, but upon closer examination one might notice his septum or ear piercings or even his blackwork tattoos—visual cues that he is a member of the Modern Primitive subculture. Musafar's real name is not known; he took this name from a *Ripley's Believe It or Not* article. The first Fakir Musafar lived in the nineteenth century and was a Sufi.[7] The original Musafar roamed India and surrounding areas for eighteen years with daggers piercing his skin and heavy metal hanging from his torso (Vale & Juno, 1989, pp. 8–9).

As a Modern Primitive, Musafar derives a great deal of meaning not only from his body modifications, but also from the pain that is a significant part of the ritual experience of acquiring them. Modern Primitives wear their body modifications as badges of enduring and owning that pain, just as (they believe) a member of a "primitive" culture would do during various times of his or her life. Modern Primitives suffer and endure pain so they can achieve the "other," and thereby achieve spiritual transcendence. This is the primary ideology behind the subculture.

Musafar has become well-known in subculture media[8] for his use of extreme body modifications within performative rituals inspired by non-Western cultures. He has participated in numerous body modification rituals inspired by ethnographies about similar rituals of the "other"—that is, "exotic" and non-Western cultures. Moreover, these body modification rituals were and are scripted, with only minor modifications, according to the ethnographic texts that inspired him.

Musafar claims, as do many Modern Primitives, that he has performed these rituals in order to transcend the pain into another realm, to reach spiritual transcendence (Vale & Juno, 1989, p. 13). Modern Primitives believe that spiritual transcendence is attainable by everyone, regardless of ethnicity, religion, social position, and the like, who is willing to endure the necessary pain. In addition, through spiritual experience the individual will be able to connect with cultures of the "other" (Favazza, 1987). Modern Primitives believe this connection is key to finding the real truth in the modern world.

EXAMPLES OF BODY MODIFICATION RITUALS
Ritual Piercing

An example of a Modern Primitive body modification is ritual piercing, which typically yields temporary body modifications. Single-use needles are used to pierce the skin and are placed in a designated arrangement to create a design.

Participants quite often lose consciousness during this process due to the continuous intensity of the pain. A nurse is on hand to revive participants, if necessary, and the ritual continues or ends based on the participant's wishes and/or a determination of health risk.

Once the needles are removed the design remains visible for several days. Usually the piercings heal within a few weeks and there is little trace on the body that the ritual ever occurred. While the pain is a significant part of this body modification practice, the evidence or remaining body modifications—needle marks—fade with time. Therefore, participants often repeat this type of ritual.

Musafar has participated in piercing rituals, such as the Kavandi-bearing ceremony, during which spears of Siva pierced his skin, and the Hindu Ball Dance, during which he wore 48 weighted balls that hung from hooks in his skin (Vale & Juno, 1989). Accounts from participants of piercing rituals indicated they reached an altered state of consciousness and wanted to experience more intense pain in future body modification practices (Vale & Juno, 1989; Winge, 2001). Piercing ritual is often considered a gateway experience with pain that leads Modern Primitives to more intense or extreme rituals.

Ritual Hook Hanging

A growing number of Modern Primitives take ritual piercing to the next level by participating in ritual hook hanging. Similar to ritual piercing, hook hanging ritual begins by piercing the skin; however, this piercing is larger and accomplished with hooks. Since the hooks must support the body, it is necessary to use large hooks and pierce larger areas of skin, such as that on the torso, back, or legs. Modern Primitives often practice ritual hook hanging at parties. Still others participate in cultural hook hangings such as the Sun Dance.

At a hook hanging party, the guest of honor is a modification troop, such as Mind over Flesh, who provide all the needed expertise and equipment for the night's events. Party guests are in-

vited to not only watch, but also participate in hook hanging rituals. A member of the troop begins this body modification ritual by having a professional piercer insert large sterilized hooks into his or her back, usually at the top of the back across the shoulder blades. Then the hooks are attached to a rack, which is raised and suspended above the crowd. The participant swings from the hooks until the pain becomes unbearable and he or she asks to be let down or passes out. Finally, the participant is lowered, and the hooks are removed. If necessary, the participant is revived.

Before the end of the evening there are several other people with fresh body modifications from hook hanging circulating through the crowds of onlookers. These body modifications will not only be displayed at the party, but they will be the center of conversations for months to come. Many participants comment after experiencing ritual hook hanging about a type of transcendence or altered state of consciousness. It is thought that this transcendence is a result of the extreme pain experienced. These same participants have commented on how they wanted to experience that intensity of pain again, perhaps in a more extreme body modification practice.

Sun Dance

Originally, the Sun Dance was an eight-day spiritual ritual practiced by North American Plains Indians. After three days and nights of fasting and dancing, participants would have incisions made in their backs or chests, and pieces of wood connected to leather straps were inserted through the fresh incisions under the chest or back muscles. Then the straps were tied to a sacred pole, located in the center of the ceremonial site, and the participants were hoisted into the air, forcing the dancers to gaze into the sun. This was the pinnacle of the ritual and was called "Gazing-at-the-Sun" (Beck, Francisco, & Walters, 1995). The participants experienced continuous ripping of piercings and endured extreme pain in the remaining days of the ritual in order to achieve spiritual transcendence (Mails, 1972/1995). The participants might hang for days before they were able to rip through the piercings that held them to their bonds. The scars served as reminders of the participation in the Sun Dance and the subsequent spiritual transformation (Beck et al., 1995). This ritual is now illegal, but it is still secretly practiced by some groups of Native American Indians.

One of the first Modern Primitives to participate in the Sun Dance was Musafar, but his Sun Dance was modified from the American Indian versions (Vale & Juno, 1989). He skipped the first part of the ritual and began with the Gazing-at-the-Sun portion. Also, his chest piercings that he hung from were decades old, in that they were healed rather than fresh incisions. Still, Musafar's experience was quite painful, as documented in the *Dances Sacred and Profane* documentary (Jury & Jury, 1985). After nearly 30 minutes, he passed out from the pain. When interviewed after the ritual, he said that he achieved spiritual transcendence via the pain.

Another Modern Primitive who has performed the Sun Dance is Pan Stovall. Stovall's version also skipped the first three days of fasting and dancing and began with the Gazing-at-the-Sun phase. Stovall had fresh incisions made in his chest and was then hung by them. He was able to remain hanging for less than one minute, for two hanging sessions. And Stovall also expressed that he experienced spiritual transcendence during the intense pain associated with the ritual. He also stated that he is quite proud of the remaining body modifications he acquired during the ritual (Eiserer, n.d.)

The two Modern Primitive versions of the Sun Dance emphasize that, while influenced and inspired by what they would call "primitive" cultural practices, Modern Primitives put their own spin on it—a modern and unique spin. The Sun Dance was originally done as a sacrifice ritual for the warriors who had been caught by the enemy; it was a way for those in the physical realm to connect with the spiritual realm to sacrifice for the betterment of the community. For the Modern Primitives, this ritual is about self-sacrifice and self-improvement.

3-D Implants

The most modern technology employed for body modifications was invented by Steve Haworth, a Modern Primitive who creates medical instruments to implant 3-D Teflon and surgical steel shapes (and on rare occasions, coral shapes) both subdermally (i.e., completely under the skin) and transdermally (i.e., through the skin rather than completely under it) for individuals wanting to modify or alter their appearance (Mercury, 2000, p. 65). In 1996, Haworth created a metal Mohawk for Joe Aylward, a thirty-two-year-old man from Arizona. Haworth placed several implants transdermally along the top center of the scalp (Mercury, 2000). The bases of the implants were square in shape with a shallow thread at the center, which held interchangeable metal Mohawk spikes. The skin healed over the base, and all that remained were the spikes that extended along the cranial ridge.

This type of body modification is growing in popularity. Since the mid-1990s, many examples of Haworth's implants have been visible through the skin of members of the Modern Primitives. Circular barbell jewelry has been inserted through small incisions; Teflon shapes have been placed under the skin of the biceps to create new shapes; and threaded bases have been implanted in the center of the chest to hold a variety of jewelry.

PAIN AND SPIRITUAL TRANSCENDENCE

According to many Modern Primitive members, the pain experienced during a piercing, hook hanging, or 3-D implant ritual produces such a unique sensation—a positive pain experience—that each ritual drives him or her to participate in more rituals and acquire more body modifications. They further implied that they are seeking the experience of pain in order to better understand the self and his or her place in the world (Favassa, 1987; Vale & Juno, 1989). Some Modern Primitives even claim that their body modification rituals are a way of seeking spiritual transcendence; through the pain they can cross to another plane of existence—a spiritual plane.

Pain is highly individual and an obvious aspect of nearly any body modification. There is pain involved in the initial procedure, whether a prick of the needle, a slice of the knife, or piercing of a hook, and throughout the healing process as well. However, for Modern Primitives the pain involved in the body modification ritual has additional meaning. For these individuals, pain achieved through a body modification process is seen as a doorway or means to attain wholeness and a spiritual encounter.

What makes Modern Primitives body modification practices so fascinating is not that it is a new idea to use physical pain to re-define one's existence in the world. Pain has been used as a definer in rites of passage for hundreds of years at least. What makes this worthwhile to research is the way the Modern Primitives make these body modification rituals their own and how they use pain to redefine and reinforce their place in a modern world. Defining this pain is not an easy endeavor, primarily because while the construct of pain is universal, it is also extremely subjective for each of us.

The examples demonstrate the importance of physical pain to the Modern Primitives' body modification rituals. The pain reinforces and establishes the certainty of the body's physicality. At the same time Modern Primitives recognize that they are not only of their physical bodies, but also exist in a mental and spiritual realm as well.

Summary

In the late twentieth and early twenty-first century, body modifications such as pierced earlobes and navels and small discreet tattoos became quite popular among many diverse groups in Western cultures. One could conclude that subcultures, such as the Modern Primitives, are pushing the envelope on body modifications to remain outside the norm. While it is true that the Modern Primitive subculture enjoys its fringe existence, I believe it is not the case that their body modifications are extreme only for that reason. Instead, I would argue that they push the envelope on body modifications because they consciously seek pain in their body modification practices, which allows Modern Primitives to have certainty about their physical and spiritual existence in the world. Additionally, members of this subculture gain self-identity and importance by securing a unique place in the world via their appearances and body modification experiences.

As these examples illustrated, Modern Primitive body modifications are representations of the pain experienced during the body modification ritual. These rituals have been inspired by past cultures but have a modern spin. Not only do Modern Primitives utilize modern technology, but many also seek unique experiences with pain and spirituality. It will be interesting to see if this pain seeking for personal meaning becomes more normative. If so, Modern Primitive body modifications may have to become more extreme in the future to accommodate the desire to intensify pain to achieve altered states of consciousness in the hopes of achieving spiritual transcendence.

Notes

1. Ötzi is the Stone Age male mummy that was found in the Ötztal Alps in 1991. The mummy was nicknamed Ötzi because of where he was found. This mummy had numerous tattoos that have been hypothesized to be part of medicinal cures, spiritual ceremonies, and indication of social status (Tanaka, 1996; Siggers & Rowanchilde, 1998).

2. The Siberian Ice Maiden was a well-preserved mummy found on the steppes of eastern Russia in 1993. The mummy is a fifth-century B.C. Ukok priestess. She was about 25 years old and dressed in a fine-woven wool skirt, wild silk blouse, an elaborate headpiece, and jewelry. She had several tattoos and piercings that are believed to have had medicinal, spiritual, or social significance (Polosmak, 1994).

3. The mummies from Xinjiang, China, are about 4,000 years old and in a condition so well preserved that the skin and hair still remain. The mummies varied in age, were both

male and female, and ranged from infants to elderly. Most of the adult mummies had tattoos, which seemed to relate to their gender or social position (Hadingham, 1994).

4. The term "subculture" is often viewed as a value-laden term, due to "sub" indicating less than. I use the term "subculture" because the groups I discuss self-identify themselves as subcultures (Hebdige, 1979). Also, I define a subculture as a group whose numbers are significantly less than the mainstream culture within which they exist and who also share common ideology, activities, geography, etc. with the subcultural group to which they belong (Winge, 2001).

5. Edward Said first used the term "other" when discussing the way in which colonial Europeans studied Asian cultures. The "other" is a cultural generalization about a culture or people based on bias, and often these generalizations do not reflect the actual culture. This term is also often used to refer to those who are subjugated by and who have less power than those in authority (Said, 1978).

6. Blackwork tattoos are created entirely of black ink that is reapplied until the color of the skin is obscured. Blackwork tattoos have been created in many cultures, such as Micronesian and Japanese (Vale & Juno, 1989).

7. Sufism is an Islamic religion that seeks the truth. Sufis are the mystics of Islam and are sometimes known as "whirling dervishes." Dervish is derived from the English translation for Fakir, which means poor in spirit. Whirling literally comes from the twirling style of dancing that some Sufis perform in order to create a trance-like spiritual state (Ling, 1970).

8. Subculture media are magazines, books, and documentaries created outside of popular media, such as *Body Play* and *Bizarre*. Fakir Musafar's Professional Body-Piercing Intensives, an organization that trains piercing professionals, has been in several documentaries, such as the documentary that fo-

cused on the Sun Dance, titled *Dances Sacred and Profane* (Jury & Jury, 1985).

References

Beck, P., Francisco, N., & Walters, A. (Eds.) (1995). *The Sacred: Ways of Knowledge, Sources of Life*. Tsaile, AZ: Navajo Community College Press.

Campbell, M. (1994, June). Ice maiden of the Steppes. *World Press Review*, 41(6):40–41.

Camphausen, R. C. (1997). *Return to the Tribal: A Celebration of Body Adornment*. Rochester, VT: Park Street Press.

Eiserer, T. (n.d.). *The Sundancer*. Accessed February 2001 at www.angelfire.com/me2/gephoto/Unique.html.

Favazza, A. R. (1987). *Bodies under Siege: Self-Mutilation and Body Modification in Culture and Psychiatry*. Baltimore: Johns Hopkins University Press.

Hadingham, E. (1994, April). The mummies of Xinjiang. *Discover*, 15(4):68–77.

Hebdige, D. (1979). *Subculture: The Meaning of Style*. Oxford: Routledge.

Jury, D., & Jury, M. (1985). *Dances Sacred and Profane* [independent documentary film]. United States: Gorgon Video.

Kleese, C. (2000). "Modern primitivism:" Non-mainstream body modification and racialized representation. In M. Featherstone (Ed.), *Body Modification*, pp. 15–38. London: Sage Publications.

Ling, M. (1970). Sufis. In R. Cavendish (Ed.), *Man, Myth, & Magic: An Illustrated Encyclopedia of the Supernatural*, pp. 2713–2716. New York: Marshall Cavendish Corporation.

Mails, T. (1972/1995). *The Mystic Warriors of the Plains Indians*. New York: Marlowe & Company.

Mercury, M. (2000). *Pagan Fleshworks: The Alchemy of Body Modification*. Rochester, VT: Park Street Press.

Musafar, F. (1996). Body play: State of grace of sickness? In A. R. Favazza (Ed.), *Bodies under*

Siege: Self-Mutilation and Body Modification in Culture and Psychiatry, pp. 325–334. Baltimore: Johns Hopkins University Press.

Polhemus, T. (1994). *Streetstyle: From Sidewalk to Catwalk*. London: Thames & Hudson.

Polosmak, N. (1994, October). A mummy unearthed from the pastures of heaven. *National Geographic*, 186(4):80–103.

Said, E. (1978). *Orientalism*. New York: Random House Publishers.

Schechner, R. (1977/1988). *Performance Theory*. New York: Routledge.

Siggers, J., & Rowanchilde, D. (1998). How the iceman was tattooed. In J. Miller (Ed.), *In the Flesh*, pp. 9–11. Hoboken, NJ: Casey Exton.

Tanaka, S. (1996). *Discovering the Iceman: What Was It Like to Find a 5,300-Year-Old Mummy?* Toronto: The Madison Press Limited.

Vale, V., & Juno, A. (1989). *Re/Search: Modern Primitives*. Hong Kong: Re/Search Publishers.

Winge, T. M. (2001). An exploration of the parallels between the Modern Primitive subculture and the framework of complex adaptive systems. Unpublished master's thesis, University of Minnesota, St. Paul.

DISCUSSION QUESTIONS

A Survey of "Modern Primitive" Body Modification Rituals

1. Were you previously aware of the Modern Primitives movement? Have you ever seen anyone with extreme body modifications? If so, what was your reaction to this type of dress?

2. How might belonging to the Modern Primitives subculture affect one's relationships with people outside the subculture?

21   Paris or Perish: The Plight of the Latin American Indian in a Westernized World

Barbara Brodman

I crossed the border carrying dignity…

I carry the huilpil of colors for the fiesta when I return…

I will return tomorrow…

Rigoberta Menchú, *Patria Abnegada*

Like Mother Fashion, Paris delivers her haute couture designs to the world at large. From fashion hub to fashion hub, city to city around the world, disciples of Western fashion bow to their Parisian mecca. Yet, not all have accepted the hegemony of Paris and the West in matters of style and dress. In the Americas, for example, indigenous peoples continue to wear with pride the tribal designs that mark them as Indian. Their dress is an expression of culture as rich in history and symbolism as oral literature or other indigenous art forms. It is part of the glue that holds Indian cultures together and that safeguards them against extinction. Sadly, the price Indians pay for preserving their native fashion is social degradation, persecution, and, often, death. Adoption of Western dress is part of an ongoing process of Western colonialism that began almost five centuries ago, and it may signify the demise of cultures that have existed and thrived for millennia.

In the two areas of the Americas where indigenous populations are most concentrated, the Andean region of South America and Middle America (Mexico and Central America), Indians face economic and legal discrimination, and have even become victims of blatant, sustained genocidal campaigns. Often, the Indians' choice of whether to adopt Western dress or continue to wear native designs determines whether they will live or die. In 1932, for example, after troops of the dictator Maximiliano Hernández Martínez slaughtered 30,000 Indian peasants, indigenous peoples in El Salvador stopped wearing traditional Maya garb, and Indian identity all but disappeared. In Guatemala, however, a particularly brutal conquest led to the creation of a tradition of revolt and the retention of culture. Of today's Guatemalan Indians, some 40 percent speak one of over 120 dialects of 22 Maya languages as their primary tongue and wear with pride one of hundreds of distinct costumes that not only mark them as Indian but also proclaim their village or town of origin.[1]

Considered one of the worst violators of human rights in the Western Hemisphere, Guatemala focuses its pogroms on the elimination of its indigenous people, who are considered naturally susceptible to "communist subversion." With the largest percentage of Indians in Mesoamerica—some 60 percent of the total population—Guatemala provides a fine killing field for death squads and civil patrols for whom the Guatemalan Indian wears his or her native garb like a red flag. It should come as no surprise that Indians make up a large percentage of the estimated 45,000 "disappeared" and 100,000 persons murdered in Guatemala since the mid-1960s.[2]

In Guatemala, as elsewhere in Indo-America, to dress like an Indian is to be an Indian. And to be an Indian is to be socially and economically deprived, at best, and persecuted to death, at worst. Yet, many Guatemalan Indians choose to perish rather than accept the cultural dictates—including fashion—of a world in which indigenous peoples and their cultures have become increasingly expendable.

CULTURAL SIGNIFICANCE OF DRESS

Worldwide, fashion is a clear and definitive expression of the culture from which it derives. Western fashion, for example, reflects

Reprinted by permission of Barbara Brodman.

the dynamism of modern industrial societies characterized by rapid change and innovation, by individualism coupled with an increasingly global perspective, and by a superficiality that, to some, represents a threatening uniformity. Western fashions change with the seasons and at the whim of the fashion industry.[3] By direct contrast, consistency of style and design characterizes native American dress.

Among indigenous Latin American peoples, like the Maya of Guatemala, dress reflects little of the capriciousness and superficiality of Western fashion, because it is linked to cultural survival. It symbolizes a time when ancient American civilizations were among the most advanced in the world, when being Mexican or Maya, Chibcha or Inca, was a source of pride and power, not degradation. In contemporary Middle America, as elsewhere in Indo-America, patterns of native dress reflect not only the rich symbolism that lies at the heart of Indian ritual life, but also the basic institutional framework of the culture. Within this context, native dress helps perpetuate divisions of labor, family systems, and hierarchical orders that have stood the test of millennia and that today are threatened.

Once, the Maya were the greatest cultural force in the Americas. They left copious records of their history, cosmology, and achievements, but most of them were destroyed before or during the Spanish Conquest. Today, the splendor of those times is perpetuated mainly in an oral tradition and in the style and design of traditional Maya clothing. So linked to cultural identity and survival are the sacred symbols and colors that characterize Maya dress and textiles that their mythical origin is recounted in the *Popol Vuh: The Sacred Book of the Ancient Quiché Maya.* It explains that the great god Tohil presented the ancient Maya with the symbols and colors of their being painted on three cloths.[4] Their contemporary descendants use the same designs and colors in memory of that event. They employ the figures of the jaguar, the eagle, wasps, and bees, and the colors of the Maya cosmology: green, the royal color, signifying eternity and fertility; red, the color of the sun and of blood, signifying life; yellow, the color of death and of maize, the staple food of life and the substance of which man was made by the gods; black, the color of obsidian, symbol of war; and blue, the color of sacrifice. All remind the Maya of a time when they communed directly with the gods and produced a high culture unsurpassed in the hemisphere. Indigenous designs thus form a text of Maya origins, religions, and history and, as such, help keep alive a culture that is increasingly threatened. All the colors of the Maya cosmology can typically be seen in contemporary Guatemalan marketplaces, including the flower market in Chichicastenango. The traditionally woven fabrics worn by the flower women are elaborately brocaded and embroidered with designs and colors that reflect both ancient and modern influences. Note, however, that the flower woman's sweater of synthetic fabric, symbol of the encroachment of Western dress into Maya culture, mars the splendor of this display of Maya textile art.

It may be that when the Maya cease to use the ancient symbols on their clothing and textiles, their culture will have died; and they will indeed have been westernized. In the face of genocidal campaigns, planned dislocations, and forced assimilation into a hostile culture and environment, preserving these overt and material vestiges of culture becomes all important. The imposition of Western fashion, within this context, is no less than a subtle form of genocide.

But it is not just the mythical/religious symbolism reflected in Middle American textile and clothing design that renders its preservation essential if Indian cultures are to survive. The "text" of a weaving more often incorporates a broader theme: the worldview and basic institutions founded on that worldview that serves as the framework of Maya culture. Incorporated in native dress is the blueprint of an entire social system: agriculturally based, community oriented, and decidedly non-Western. Within this broader context, dress helps perpetuate divisions of labor that hearken back to earlier periods of cultural development and achievement, when the Indian community offered its members—females included—a level of prosperity, security, and safety that no longer exists, except in the most remote areas.

From ancient times, a woman's life revolved around weaving. The technology and skills used in this all-important female activity were, like the designs and colors they incorporated, gifts of the gods. In ancient codices, Ix Chel, the Mother Goddess, is depicted sitting at her backstrap loom, one end tied to a tree, the other around her waist, her shuttle in hand. According to legend, Ix Chel first attracted the attentions of the sun god by her weaving, and from their union was produced a daughter, Ixchebel Yax, patroness of embroidery. Young Maya girls still pray to Ix Chel, patroness of weaving, for skill with the loom sufficient to attract them good husbands, and some continue to use the bone needle of Ixchebel Yax to create elaborately embroidered huipiles. To the Westerner, this link between industry and myth signifies a level of inefficiency and ignorance that rightfully, in accordance with the Judeo-Christian and capitalist worldview, targets a people for exploitation. To the Maya, however, it represents a continued bond between the people and their tribal gods that is perceived by many as their only hope and protection in an otherwise totally hostile environment. "Children, wherever you may be, do not abandon the crafts taught to you by Ixpiyacoc," the *Popol Vuh* exhorts them, "because they are crafts passed down to you from your forefathers. If you forget them, you will be betraying your lineage."[5] To sever such bonds would not only shatter the cosmic reality of the Maya, but would also upset the very institutions that have helped preserve them as a culture. Although the affluence of others might be enhanced by the destruction of traditional Maya ways, what hope of affluence and harmony remains for the Maya people today and in the future may well rest on their preserving certain divisions of labor and economies upon which their ancient affluent culture rested.

In ancient times, as today, women were responsible for clothing themselves and their families and for producing the exquisitely made textiles that adorned priests and temples. As mothers, they were responsible for passing their skills on to their daughters, whose status in the community rested largely on their skill as weavers. On the basis of their skill, they could, regardless of class, gain prestige and fame. The material from which they wove their cloth and the dye plants they used to color it varied from region to region, but the weaving tools and techniques they used and the style of garments they wore were fairly standardized. Thus, it was the individual skill of the weaver that served to distinguish one garment from another, not innovations in style. Weaving, then, provided not only an essential economic commodity (textiles having been valuable trade items long before the Conquest), but provided as well for a degree of egalitarianism and female mobility that is impressive even by modern standards. In contrast with the extreme "machismo" and socioeconomic disequilibrium that characterize mainstream Latin American culture, such a system seems far less inefficient and born of ignorance.

The construction and tailoring of native garb has always been of the simplest kind, but the textiles of which that garb is made are the product of a complex technology, by which are woven into each piece the threads of a harmonious and affluent village economy. Through weaving and textile design, the ancient American was able to perpetuate symbols and designs that reflected the Indian view of the cosmos and that clearly proclaimed the status and role of the wearer and the weaver. Although Indian dress has changed somewhat over the past half-millennium, it remains an essential expression of cultural continuity.[6]

CONTEMPORARY PATTERNS OF DRESS

Rarely, however, do modern indigenous people completely preserve the ancient style of dress. Even the primitive Lacandon of the Usumacinta River region that separates Mexico and Guatemala have eschewed their traditional bark fiber garments for tunics of cotton—which they wear with high plastic boots for trips to town. When Europeans invaded and conquered the New World, they imposed their manner of dress and customs upon the native peoples of the region. In Mesoamerica, as elsewhere in Spanish America, Spaniards replaced the native elite classes and assumed all power and access to wealth. The Indian assumed the lowest position in society, although always with the option of rising above his humble status merely by assuming the look of the Spaniard. Those who chose to retain their Indian identity paid a heavy price.

Despite this, important vestiges of ancient dress remain, particularly in the Maya heartland. These are most evident in women's dress, which more clearly reflects a pre-Colombian tradition. But they are not lost in the typical male garb. True, in all but the most conservative villages and among older Maya males, the ancient turbanlike head covering (the "tzut") has been replaced by the ubiquitous cowboy hat; and the traditional sandal, often quite elaborate if the wearer were a nobleman, has in most of the region been replaced by shoes and boots of Western design and construction (including, alas, plastic). Nonetheless, in the southern Mexican state of Chiapas, Maya males continue to wear ribbon-strewn straw hats that serve as the post-Colombian equivalent of ancient plumed headdresses, and brightly colored textiles of assorted design continue to distinguish members of one village from another. In Guatemala, it is not unusual to see village men wearing long pants, a Western-inspired garment, made of handwoven Maya fabric and topped with an overpant that resembles the peculiar, short, "eared" trousers of ancient times, the symbols on which identify the male's age group and status in the community.

A visit to any major marketplace in the Guatemalan highlands will reveal the degree to which traditional male garb has been preserved, on the one hand, and has given way to Western influences on the other. In this scene women wear the traditional dress of their village, while the men display a mixture of Western and Maya dress. Their woven short pants and skirt reflect their village and cultural ties, but to this traditional garb they have added Western shirts and the ubiquitous cowboy hat. Some young men have clearly adopted Western dress to the exclusion of any traditional items. For them, as for many, the pressures of modern commercial relations have led to the complete abandonment of traditional dress. For others, the transition has been less complete. Despite some significant additions and modifications, most men preserve key elements of their indigenous heritage through their dress and distinguish themselves from their more Western-influenced compatriots. They are Maya first and Guatemalan second. However, since, traditionally, it has been the indigenous male who has inter-acted most with Spaniards and "Ladinos," often against his will, it is not surprising that male dress should reflect a strong Western influence.[7]

Women's costume has changed little since ancient times. The costume of a conservative Maya woman still consists of a traditional upper garment, the huipil; a wraparound skirt, or "corte"; a woven belt; and a head covering or braid wrap. In the more conservative villages of Mexico and Guatemala, Indian women continue to produce the textiles for these garments on backstrap looms identical to those employed by their earliest ancestors. These looms are light and portable enough to allow a woman to use them when attending to other chores, like tending sheep or caring for home and family. They are also versatile. On a backstrap loom, a woman can produce intricate designs using complicated techniques impossible to replicate on commercial looms. Even a woman of the simplest means can produce a fabric of great intricacy. A textile technique known as brocade allows the Indian woman to weave designs and symbols of ancient origin into the cloth itself. From the textile emerge images of gods and animals who give fertility to the earth, protect the growth of corn, and symbolize the Maya cosmology. Women who devote their lives to brocade and become skillful in the complicated techniques and symbolism it incorporates are venerated. It is through them that ancient myths, symbols, and visions of the cosmos are preserved. To her weaving skills, a woman may also add her skill in embroidery, as she embellishes the seams and borders of her simply constructed garments with traditional designs of great complexity and beauty.[8]

Although dress and class are no longer as indistinguishable as they were in ancient times, traditional village costumes still reflect slight differences in status and wealth. Officeholders generally wear elaborate costumes for ceremonial occasions and often put themselves in debt to do so. In general, though, costume reflects not rank but village affiliation. In less conservative villages and towns, men and women alike have borrowed freely from Western fashion. In addition to garments of Western origin, one sees costumes of machine-made textiles, sometimes machine-embroidered, and incorporating designs of non-indigenous origin. In these places Indian identity is threatened.

In the more traditional villages, this is not the case. Each village has its distinctly colored and patterned costume, in which it takes great pride. Although once a means of distinguishing combatants in war, this custom serves today not only to foster pride and solidarity within villages, but also to promote pride and solidarity among Indian peoples who are fighting for cultural survival. In Guatemala, where almost 300 distinctive village costumes have been identified, Maya Indian culture remains strong even under the impress of Western religion. A woman religious practitioner in native dress may serve as a symbol of religious syncretism in the Maya heartland, where the distinction between Catholicism and indigenous ritual and religion is blurred. Note that in her role of "chuchkajau" (independent native religious practitioner), she displays more of the Indian than Western influence. Her dress is traditional Maya.

But Maya culture is severely threatened. In much of Middle America, the Indian has been forced to assimilate into mixed-blood, Western-based society. Those who have chosen to preserve their ancient customs and way of life have been relegated to the lowest levels of the socio-economic scale. Increasingly, that position alone singles them out for physical destruction.

DRESS AND CULTURAL SURVIVAL

There is no more obvious expression of Indian identity than costume. Perhaps for that reason, so many groups intent on influencing or controlling Indian peoples have attempted to alter their patterns of dress. First the missionary, intent on imposing his religion on the peoples of the New World, forced the Indian to dress like a Christian (who, by some strange coincidence, dressed like a European). Since then, land barons, armies, churches, and guerrilla rebels have attempted to do the same as part of a larger plan to change or adjust the Indians' relationship to their land.

At the heart of genocidal campaigns in Guatemala and elsewhere in this hemisphere is the threat of land reform inspired by the existence of culturally unified peoples who are tied to the land but increasingly landless. In Guatemala, some 80 percent of cultivated land is owned by 2 percent of landowners, who, aided by centuries of institutionalized racism and the ever-increasing rapaciousness of the agro-export sector, continue to rob Indians of land that they need to survive. Agro-exports have made Guatemala one of the strongest economies in Central America. Yet 74 percent of the rural population, most of whom are Maya Indians, live below the level of absolute poverty, while 85 percent of rural households are landless or possess insufficient land to satisfy the basic food needs of their families.[9] Consequently, families routinely watch their children die of malnutrition and find themselves forced to labor on the *fincas* (plantations) of the wealthy Ladinos, separated from their communities and stripped of their dignity as members of a once great and still multitudinous race. On the fincas, Indians endure an appalling deficiency of food and health care, the cruelty of overseers, and backbreaking labor for wages that are criminally inadequate. They often return to communities that are systematically ravaged by the Guatemalan military, whose fear of Maya insurgency, born of deteriorating living standards and an increasingly threatened way of life, inspires them to commit unconscionable acts of brutality. In the last decade alone, the Guatemalan army has razed hundreds of Indian villages, forced tens of thousands of Indians into "model villages" that are little better than concentration camps, and subjected thousands of rural Maya, young and old, male and female, to rape, torture, and murder, often as public spectacle. Nominally, these atrocities are aimed at deterring the growth of "communism"; in reality, they are aimed at discouraging highly justified and growing calls for reform. It is a hope of the privileged class that by "ladinizing" the Indians, they can better control them and assimilate them into systems that favor the interests of the few over the many.

For Ladinos it is enough to glorify ancient Maya culture, as a means of proclaiming ethnic pride and individuality in the face of foreign domination, while denigrating modern indigenous peoples whom they revile and treat as slaves. No better evidence of this Ladino paradox exists than the national Folklore Festival held every August in Cobán. The festival culminates in the selection of an Indian beauty queen. Contestants, selected earlier by the Ladino authorities of towns throughout Guatemala, parade their distinct regional costumes before a largely foreign and non-Indian audience that flocks to Cobán to participate in this widely advertised celebration of national identity. For the contestants themselves, who are required by law to travel from their villages to the festival at their own expense, the spectacle is often a source of humiliation and impoverishment. But for the Ladinos, it is an opportunity to bask in the splendor of Maya textile art—among the best in the world—and a Maya heritage that they rarely associate with modern indigenous peoples about whom they prefer to remain ignorant.

Among those who are regularly drawn to this display of exquisite indigenous fashion are buyers and representatives of designers and clothing manufacturers from around the globe. For them, the festival provides a unique opportunity to view a living catalog of masterfully woven fabrics that can be purchased at astoundingly low prices and fashioned into some of the world's most expensive designer creations. That the weavers and wearers of these incomparable textiles are being exploited, perhaps to the point where their craft will eventually disappear, seems not to occur to these entrepreneurs, for whom the people and culture that produced such beauty are of little interest. Increasingly, Indians realize that as long as they remain unable to communicate with Ladinos in their own language or understand and work within the Ladino system, they will be exploited and robbed of their land, their dignity, and their lives. Although the more conservative Maya still prefer isolation from Ladino society, they cannot escape the degradation of folk festivals in which they are reluctant participants or the brutality of military and civil forces bent on eliminating the call for reformed systems by exterminating the people who would most benefit from reforms.

Growing political activism among the Maya reflects their awareness that to learn about and work within the Ladino system does not require that the Indian *become* a Ladino. Indeed, it may only be through some emergence from cultural isolation and greater dialogue with the outside world that traditional Maya culture can be preserved in the future. It is a lesson of the Conquest that the Indian cannot defeat what he or she does not understand. In the last few years, rural Maya have become active in a burgeoning network of organizations established to deal with issues of labor and land reform, human rights abuses at the hands of the government and military, and the retrieval of bodies of "disappeared" family and community members.

Many of those involved in these organizations have been forced into exile. For them, to leave the communities and land in which their Maya identity is rooted is a personal tragedy. But it has allowed them to bring their struggle to the attention of international organizations without whose support they will probably be unable to counter the genocidal campaigns of the government or accomplish reforms that will improve conditions for the Indian majority. These reluctant refugees proudly continue to wear their native Maya garb in the capitals of Europe and the Americas as proof that political activism need not threaten indigenous culture, but may indeed be a means of preserving it.

There are those who believe that survival of traditional societies in the twenty-first century is impossible. The better-intentioned of these individuals believe that improving the lives of indigenous peoples is more important than preserving their cultures. Others believe that cultural survival is essential at any price. It is often said that the Maya spirit was never conquered, although the Indian was subjugated to Ladino rule. It is this undaunted spirit, kept alive and venerated in oral tradition and dress, that suggests a less radical solution to the problems that confront the Maya today. Survival of Indian culture in Guatemala and elsewhere in Latin America may depend, in the future, upon the ability of indigenous peoples to balance change with tradition. In Guatemala, this balance may be achieved by focusing both on radical, long-term political and social reforms (including land reform) and on increased integration of Indians into the commercial infrastructure of the nation.

Within this context, and assuming an ever-increasing role in the battle for cultural survival through commercial integration, are the Maya women who produce the native garb that helps perpetuate their culture. Perhaps because of the male-centered nature of Spanish society, Maya women have escaped some of the exigencies imposed on Maya males. Being invisible, except when it benefits Ladino culture to put them on display for tourists and entrepreneurs, Maya women have been able to retain their ancient crafts and costumes, even when in fairly regular contact with Westerners. The complex and central role of women in the village life and economy of the Maya has gone largely unnoticed by members of the mainstream culture; and, thus, it is only recently that they have begun to take notice of the growing number of weavers' cooperatives and female-run commercial enterprises through which Maya women may improve their own and their families' standard of living without sacrificing their culture in the process.

Decades of civil war and state-sanctioned genocide have catapulted women into realms of political and economic activism that were formerly closed to them (and largely unnecessary within the traditional balance of power structure of the village). Sheltered (or trapped) under the umbrella of a patriarchal ideology, Maya women have traditionally, and unobtrusively, shouldered a disproportionate burden of labor within the household, serving not only as household managers and agricultural laborers, but as weavers and clothers of their people as well. They are, therefore, well positioned for assuming a dominant role in preserving Maya culture, while at the same time working to achieve greater integration into the national economy, for, next to agriculture, the most important economic activity of the Maya is textile production. The growing demand for Maya textiles, so popular today in the fashion industry, has led to increased use of the foot loom, a method of textile production introduced by the Spanish and, until recently, used only by men. However, the best and most valuable cloth is still that produced (only by women) on the backstrap loom. The work of producing such pieces is slow and painstaking, but thanks to the creation of weaving coopera-

tives, women can, for the first time, receive a fair price for their efforts.

On the other hand, cooperatives are generally viewed as politically subversive. Although eliminating Ladino middlemen is often enough to increase a weaver's earnings several times over, the reaction of those disaffected may be severe. After centuries, conditions established by the Spaniards have not ameliorated. Indians who wish to prosper or, indeed, subsist in the Ladino economy are forced to adapt to the mainstream culture in ways that threaten their indigenous lifestyles, while those who wish to retain key elements of their culture find it increasingly perilous to do so. Today, the Western fashion industry collaborates in a process of oppression and exploitation that goes back centuries. Perhaps it does so unwittingly: first by sanctioning the encroachment of Western dress into non-Western cultures, and next through the co-optation of native textile arts into Western fashion. Co-optation need not signify exploitation, however. If, indeed, imitation is the purest form of compliment, then isn't it also a means of preserving cultures in danger of extinction?[10]

The fashion industry is a powerful special interest. Although it may not recognize itself as actively involved in international affairs, its involvement is considerable. Take the recent case of Liz Claiborne and the "model village" of Acul, in the Guatemalan highlands. In 1983, Acul became Guatemala's first "model village," an army-controlled enclave, inspired by U.S. counterinsurgency in Vietnam, and reviled by Indian and human rights advocates for whom it and others like it are little more than concentration camps. A year ago, Guatemalan officials discovered that the residents of this particular village were skilled at crocheting. They contacted executives of Liz Claiborne in New York, with whom they developed a project that would give the Maya of Acul "a chance at a brighter future."[11] Using seed money from the Guatemalan government, Claiborne and the government-sponsored National Fund for Peace developed a project to teach Acul villagers to redirect their skills toward hand-knitting sweaters for sale in the United States, where they would sell, with Claiborne labels, for up to $200 each. The villagers were to earn up to $40 per sweater, a great deal by regional standards. After two months of knitting, however, villagers were yet to receive any pay for their work, whereas their crocheting had brought them instant earnings. In addition, the sweaters they made, but did not design, did little to perpetuate Maya culture. While Guatemalan officials optimistically billed this project as one that could produce "as many as 20,000 jobs over five years," the people of Acul remained skeptical.[12] All in all, the project promised to do little for the Maya villagers, and Liz Claiborne, however unwittingly, had helped perpetuate the traditionally exploitive relationship between Native Americans and the fashion industry.

Projects like this one can, however, benefit Indians and the fashion industry alike. They can be designed to direct profits to Indians and not to middlemen. And they can be designed to promote the preservation of traditional designs and textile-making skills on which cultural survival in part rests. In the long run, the fashion industry will benefit from preserving important sources of quality textiles and artistic inspiration. To do so, though, will require a greater and more responsible involvement of the industry in the preservation of indigenous cultures. It will, above all, require a commitment on the part of the fashion industry to turn its international lobbying powers in a new direction. First, it must sensitize itself to the practices within the industry that may contribute to the exploitation, oppression, and even extermination of indigenous peoples. It should work hand in hand with organizations already committed to the cause of human rights and cultural survival for indigenous peoples. And, certainly, it should assist directly in the protection and proliferation of weavers' cooperatives, through which women can produce and market their textiles while, at the same time, preserving and perpetuating the ancient designs and techniques that periodically "revitalize" haute couture.

The future of indigenous cultures in the Americas is by no means assured. Already, in many nations of Latin America, Indian identity has disappeared. In other nations of the region, it is severely threatened. The survival of indigenous culture depends, in great part, on the Indians' ability to preserve its essential elements, like dress, while at the same time adapting more and more to the political and economic exigencies of the times. Nothing proclaims the tenacity of Indian cultures more than their refusal to succumb to the hegemony of the West in matters of style and dress. And nowhere is that tenacity more evident than in Guatemala.

In her internationally acclaimed autobiography, Maya political activist Rigoberta Menchú states that "what hurts Indians most is that our costumes are considered beautiful, but it's as if the person wearing it didn't exist."[13] Rigoberta expresses the desire of all Indians in Latin America that they be accorded the respect and opportunity that is their right as human beings and as descendants of once-great civilizations.

After five hundred years, voices like Rigoberta's are being heard. For over a decade, Rigoberta has championed Indian rights from exile. During that time she has continued to wear the traditional dress of her Guatemalan Highlands village. Her style has been a vital part of her message. Rigoberta Menchú's receipt of the 1992 Nobel Peace Prize attests not only to her own tenacity and devotion to culture, but to that of all Native Americans. Tradition tells us that when Indians stop wearing their native garb, they will have lost their culture. Then they will truly not exist. But as long as they preserve the fashions of their ancestors, their culture survives—until better times.

Notes

1. For excellent historical analyses of the role and plight of Indians in Latin America generally and Middle America specifically, see E. Bradford Burns, *Latin America: A Concise Interpretive History*, 5th ed. (Englewood Cliffs, NJ: Prentice Hall, 1990), and Benjamin Keen, *A History of Latin America*, 4th ed. (Boston: Houghton Mifflin, 1992).

2. Recent general data about Guatemala and other Indo-American nations may be obtained through any of the many international human rights organizations dedicated to the protection of indigenous peoples in the Americas and elsewhere. Always reliable sources are Amnesty International and Americas Watch.

3. On the link between Western fashion, modernity, and capitalism, see Elizabeth Wilson, *Adorned in Dreams: Fashion and Modernity* (London: Virago, 1975).

4. *Popol Vuh: The Sacred Book of the Ancient Quiché Maya*, English version by D. Goetz and S. G. Morley, from the translation of A. Recinos (Norman: University of Oklahoma Press, 1983).

5. Quoted in E. Burgos-Debray, Ed., *I... Rigoberta Menchú: An Indian Woman in Guatemala*, trans. A. Wright (New York: Verso, 1984), p. 59.

6. For excellent discussions of the cultural and social significance of Indian dress in Middle America, see D. Cordy and D. Cordy, *Mexican Indian Costumes* (Austin: University of Texas Press, 1978), and S. Annis, *God and Production in a Guatemalan Town* (Austin: University of Texas Press, 1987).

7. In the narrowest sense, "Ladino" refers to persons of mixed race or Indians who speak Spanish as their primary language and wear Western garb. In a broader sense, it refers to anyone who represents a system that oppresses the Indian.

8. For outstanding pictorial analyses of Maya dress, see C. L. Pettersen, *The Maya of Guatemala: Their Life and Dress* (Seattle: University of Washington Press, 1976), and L. Asturias de Barrios, *Comalpa: El Traje y Su Significado* (Guatemala: Ediciones del Museo Ixchel, 1985).

9. These figures come from UNICEF, State of the World's Children, 1989, and the Worldwatch Institute.

10. An interesting case in point is that of artist Frida Kahlo, who wore native Indian garb as a means of discovering her own and the collective Mexican identity.

11. See T. Johnson, "Sweater-Knitting Project Giving Guatemalans Hope for Better Life," *The Miami Herald*, June 29, 1992, 8A.

12. Ibid.

13. Burgos-Debray, Ed., *I...Rigoberta Menchú*, p. 204.

DISCUSSION QUESTIONS

Paris or Perish

1. What political statements do the Maya of Guatemala make when they wear traditional dress and refuse to adopt modern styles?

2. How do the Mayan men and women differ in their adoption of traditional Mayan dress? What does this suggest about their roles?

22 Dress and the Columbine Shootings: Media Interpretations[1]

Jennifer Paff Ogle, Molly J. Eckman,
and Catherine Amoroso Leslie
Colorado State University, Colorado State University,
and Kent State University

On April 20, 1999, at Columbine High School in Littleton, Colorado, Eric Harris and Dylan Klebold took their own lives and those of 12 students and one teacher in the worst school shooting in terms of fatalities on U.S. soil to date. In addition, several other students and staff members were injured from the gunfire or from bombs that Harris and Klebold had planted in the school before the shootings. In the days, weeks, and months that followed the Columbine shootings, the local and national media provided considerable coverage of this act of school violence. By the first anniversary of the shootings, the two major newspapers in the Denver metropolitan area had published over 1,000 articles about it. From the outset, the media made linkages between the Columbine shootings and appearance cues, with numerous references to the appearances of the gunmen and their alleged associates, the appearances of their victims, and the appearances of the many others who were somehow implicated in the incident at Columbine High. Very quickly, appearance had become a factor in the Columbine investigation, or more precisely, a factor in the media's interpretation of the incident, the ensuing investigation, and the public's reaction to the incident and investigation.

It is important to understand the kinds of messages the media send about events such as the Columbine shootings; how the media interpret these events can shape our own thoughts about them (Altheide & Michalowski, 1999; Gerbner et al., 1978). But, media content is not always objective; the messages that we read in newspapers or magazines reflect a certain set of motives and values as well as reporters' personal interpretations. For instance, in describing a crisis situation such as a school shooting, newspaper reporters may be pressured either by the public or by their superiors to present answers or to provide solutions. In turn, this pressure may influence what reporters say in their articles or how they say it (Altheide & Michalowski, 1999).

We were interested in exploring newspaper accounts of the relationship between appearance and the tragedy at Columbine High School. Of particular interest to us was the process by which newspaper coverage transformed the Columbine incident into a social problem linking school violence to appearance. Further, we were interested in examining the role of the popular press in creating meanings about varied appearances that were associated with the shootings.

To examine the media linkage between appearance and the Columbine shootings, we collected and analyzed newspaper articles and editorials addressing the Columbine incident and published in the two major Denver newspapers, *The Denver Post* and *The Rocky Mountain News.* Due to Littleton's proximity to Denver, both of these papers provided ongoing and detailed coverage of the event and subsequent investigation. We identified 1,262 articles and editorials published in these newspapers and related to the Columbine shootings. Of these articles and editorials, 155 (12%) focused upon dress and were selected for examination. The articles and editorials we studied were dated April 20, 1999, through July 1, 1999, when media coverage of the shootings was most active. Articles and editorials also were collected when Columbine-related events, such as the release of *The Columbine Report* and the first anniversary of the shootings, generated additional coverage.

Original for this text.

BRINGING APPEARANCE INTO THE DISCUSSION

Reconstructing the Crime

Within hours of the Columbine shootings, the media's construction of the crime as an appearance-related social problem had begun. By two days after the shootings, *The Denver Post* and *The Rocky Mountain News* had published 31 and 22 references to the appearances of the gunmen and their victims, respectively.

Most initial references to the appearances of the gunmen were made by Columbine students who provided firsthand accounts of the shootings. At the time, little was known about the incident, and the gunmen had yet to be identified. Newspaper reporters used these student accounts to assist in reconstructing for their readers the details of this mysterious and horrific event. For the most part, these earliest accounts were descriptive in nature, including little explanation of the gunmen's dress:

> Sophomore Amanda Stair, 15, was in the library when the shooting started...."We hid under different tables," Stair said. "Two guys in black trench coats walked in. They said 'get up,' or they would shoot us...." (Anton, 1999b, p. 2A)

Numerous witnesses were quoted as saying that the gunmen wore black trench coats. Within days, however, a discrepancy emerged among the witnesses' accounts: some reported seeing a youth wearing a white T-shirt and carrying a gun. This prompted newspaper reporters to suggest that a third gunman may have been involved in the shootings:

> Some students reported seeing two gunmen in black trench coats. Others said one of the teen-agers wore a white tee-shirt—launching speculation that at least one person besides Harris and Klebold was involved. One of the two dead teenagers—it wasn't clear which one—was wearing a white shirt and did not have a trench coat on when officers found his body Tuesday. He may have shed the coat

during the attack.... (Vaughan & Abbott, 1999, p. 23AA)

Once the possibility of a third gunman was made public, news reporters and those whom they quoted pondered who else may have been involved in the crime. These conjectures often were based upon perceived similarities between the appearances of the gunmen and those of additional suspects.

Early news reports also concerned the victims' appearances. Several students were quoted as saying that the gunmen had targeted athletes or "jocks" in their shooting spree and that the gunmen had ascribed "jock status" to students wearing white baseball hats:

> Meanwhile, Brittany Bollerud, 16, hid under a library table and saw only the gunmen's shoes and long trench coats. "They yelled, 'this is revenge,'" she said. They asked people if they were jocks. If they were wearing a sports hat, they would shoot them. (Obmascik, 1999, p. 1A)

In one article, a student was quoted as suggesting that ethnicity also had played a role in the gunmen's selection of victims:

> "They shot a black kid. They called him a nigger. They said they didn't like niggers, so they shot him in the face." (Obmascik, 1999, p. 1A)

Intermingled with the student accounts were the reporters' interpretations. Several reporters reiterated the notion that Harris and Klebold had targeted both athletes and ethnic minorities, despite the fact that only one witness had indicated that ethnicity played such a role:

> The masked shooters first targeted specific victims, especially ethnic minorities and athletes and then randomly sprayed the school hallways about 11:30 a.m. with bullets and shotgun blasts, witnesses said. The bloody rampage spanned four hours. (Obmascik, 1999, p. 1A)

FIGURE 4.7 The Matrix *featured Keanu Reeves as a character who hid machine guns under his long, black trench coat when infiltrating police headquarters. Some suggest this movie inspired the choice of garments worn by the perpetrators of the Columbine shootings.*

Moving Beyond Reconstruction: Building a Foundation for Further Hypotheses

Soon after the media had established what the gunmen had looked like on the day of the shooting, they began to focus more attention upon both the meanings of these appearances as well as the everyday appearances of the two boys. These reports created an image of two young men who routinely adorned themselves in symbols of violence. For instance, reporters estab-

lished the black trench coat as a symbol of violence. In some cases, trench coats were imbued with negative meanings by linking them with the gunmen, characterized by reporters as antisocial and deviant:

> Trouble at Columbine. Gunshots. Suddenly, existence boiled down to what mattered most. And strange kids in trench coats were threatening to yank it away. (Finley & Olinger, 1999, p. 14A)

Reporters also drew upon pre-existing meanings linked to trench coats in other school shootings and the films, *The Basketball Diaries* and *The Matrix* (see Figure 4.7):

> In the enormously popular new movie *Matrix*, Keanu Reeves wears a black duster and battles the forces of evil with two-fisted bursts of gunfire.... The movie already is being mentioned as a possible source of influence on the Trench Coat Mafia, two of whose members entered Columbine High School Tuesday carrying weapons and wearing long black coats. (Denerstein, 1999, p. 17AA)

Some students were quoted as saying that they were frightened of Harris and Klebold, in part because of their dress. Reporters claimed that prior to the shootings, the gunmen had regularly sported trench coats, berets, and T-shirts emblazoned with swastikas and German slogans.

These newspaper reports created an image of two young men who routinely adorned themselves in symbols of violence—both before and during the shootings at Columbine. These reports seemingly established a pattern of potential for violence that led up to the shootings. And, it was this association between the gunmen's dress and violence that provided the platform from which reporters began to speculate about appearance as a possible cause of the shootings.

LOCATING CAUSE: HOW CAN APPEARANCE EXPLAIN WHY THIS HAPPENED?

Within the first week, media attention switched from what the gunmen and their victims were wearing to why they were wearing it and how it may have contributed to violence. In seeking to understand and explain the shootings at Columbine, reporters and the public presented three different claims (i.e., explanations) that were related to dress.

Claim 1: The Subcultural Group Claim

Soon after the shooting, reporters linked the gunmen to various adolescent subcultures whose membership was symbolized in part by appearance. Most often, the gunmen were identified as members of the Trench Coat Mafia—a group of Columbine outcasts who were said to wear black trench coats, embrace violence and hatred, and worship death. Newspaper reporters also drew linkages between the Trench Coat Mafia and other subcultures, primarily the Goths, Marilyn Manson fans, satanic cults, and neo-Nazi groups:

> Masked gunmen Eric Harris, 18, and Dylan Klebold, 17, are said to have hung out with the so-called mafia, a small, self-styled group drawing on the satanic "goth" scene and neo-Nazi paramiltarism. Underlying both those subcultures, experts say, are preoccupation with death, feelings of being misunderstood and isolated, and often unspeakable anger. …Several Columbine students say the group idolized Marilyn Manson, who claims to be a satanic priest. (Greene & Briggs, 1999b, p. 11A)

In drawing linkages between the gunmen and these nonmainstream subcultures, reporters offered one explanation for the shootings. In effect, the association of the gunmen with these groups cast them as deviant. Implicit here was the notion that normal kids could not commit such violent acts. Perhaps, however, kids drawn into the violent underworld of the Trench Coat Mafia or the Goths could:

> Indeed, [Littleton's] corporate office parks, its strip malls, bike trails, and housing tracts contrast with the nefarious, nonconformist image the clique chose. [Littleton], if it were an article of clothing, would be a pastel sundress or Pat Nixon's respectable Republican wool coat compared to the dark trench coats the "mafia" took as its moniker. (Greene & Briggs, 1999b, p. 11A)

The naive theory underlying these interpretations was that appearance can predict tendency for violence. This assumption was underscored by news reports implicating as suspects innocent citizens with appearances similar to those of the gunmen, the Goths, or the Trench Coat Mafia:

> A riveted nation watched Tuesday as heavily armed police descended on three teens dressed in black coats and boots near Columbine High. While two gunmen shot students inside the school, the three teens were handcuffed as suspects. (Hubbard, 1999, p. 16A)

The supposed usefulness of appearance in recognizing potential violence was further highlighted in published checklists about warning signs of violence such as the wearing of trench coats, the adoption of nonmainstream appearances, or general changes in children's appearances:

> Think of this as a new school supply checklist for parents…Forget the notebook, pencil, calculator….Have your children's personalities changed in troubling ways? Have you dismissed these changes—how they look, act, as just normal changes that come with being a child? (Smokes, 1999, p. 9B)

The notion that potentially violent youth could be identified by appearance may have provided some sense of control for a community anxious to understand and remedy a disconcerting situation. However, the use of appearance as a sign of potential violence was not embraced by all, inciting a backlash by subcultural group members and youth whose appearances were outside the norm.

Claim 2: The Social Tensions/Revenge Claim

The idea that the gunmen's involvement in the Trench Coat Mafia contributed to their violence spawned a second, related explanation for the shootings as acts of revenge in response to tensions between the Trench Coat Mafia and the jocks. Students and reporters established that athletes had teased the gunmen and Trench Coat Mafia members, often about appearance:

> "Everywhere they went, they were taunted and teased about how they dress…" says Typher, the girl Harris went out with briefly after his freshman year. ("Harris," 1999, p. 18A)

The revenge hypothesis was further substantiated by claims linking the teasing of the gunmen and their violent acts. The following news report is indicative of this claim:

> But employees and patrons of…Rising Phoenix [a coffee house catering to Goths] also tried to understand how teenage "outcasts" can feel persecuted by a mainstream culture that cannot tolerate their dress, hairstyle, or other statements of individuality. "The kids who did this, something had to push them," [said a disc jockey at the coffee house]. (Leib, 1999, p. 17A)

Claim 3: The Dress as Facilitator Claim

The final media explanation for the role of dress in the shootings concerned the gunmen's use of trench coats to hide guns and bombs and thus, facilitate their crime. These claims were proposed by reporters shortly after the shootings:

> The two came to school Tuesday in fatigues, pipe bombs strapped to their chests and shotguns and high-powered pistols under long black coats. (Anton, 1999a, p. 2A)

Several months later, the release of the Columbine tapes renewed the discussion concerning the use of clothing to hide weapons. According to newspaper reports, the tapes included two separate segments in which Klebold experiments with the use of his trench coat to hide his gun. One of these "experiments," dubbed a "dress rehearsal" by the media, occurred three days prior to the shootings:

> During Klebold's dress rehearsal on April 17…he worries that his gun is making his black trench coat look bulky. (Lowe, 1999, p. 11A)

STAGING A BACKLASH: THE MEDIA AS A FORUM FOR COUNTERCLAIMS

As noted, shortly after the shootings, adolescents whose appearances resembled the gunmen's were suspects in the Columbine investigation. Although each adolescent was eventually cleared of wrongdoing by the police, the media had cast them and others who looked like them or who associated with the same adolescent peer groups as scapegoats for the shootings. In fact, Trench Coat Mafia members and Goths became targets of harassment after the shootings:

> "There are a lot of us [Goths] who are starting to get afraid of the people who think we were part of [the Columbine shootings]," he said. "The jocks and yuppies are constantly driving by, calling us 'faggots' or yelling, 'I'm going to kick your asses.' It's happening a lot more now after Columbine." He said his group is "not about violence or killing." (McPhee, 1999, p. 5A)

Counterclaims challenged accusations of "guilt by association." For instance, subcultural group members tried to distance themselves from Harris and Klebold and the shootings. Members of the Trench Coat Mafia denied that the gunmen were actively involved in their clique:

> The teen said Harris and Klebold were less socially active than other mafia members. From the outside, he said, they must have seemed part of the group because of their black trench coats and their similar Goth style of dress. But, speaking from the inside, he said they really weren't members [of the Trench Coat Mafia]. (Greene, 1999b, p. 15A)

Other citizens disputed allegations that the Trench Coat Mafia and Goths embraced violence:

> "They're [the Goths] not violent. They're not racist. They're not into the whole hate mentality," said Sweet [a researcher who had studied Goth culture]. (Briggs & Greene, 1999, p. 11A)

Counterclaims also challenged the attribution of violence on the basis of appearance:

> "We have three or four kids who wear the long black trench coats, but they are actually great kids. It's a fashion thing"—said Ann Bailey, principal at Jefferson High School in Denver. (Greene & Briggs, 1999a, p. 17A)

Finally, some suggested that the attention paid to appearance represented a misguided investigative effort that should be focused upon factors other than appearance:

> Harris and Klebold didn't try to blow up Columbine…and slaughter its students because they wore black clothes and listened to German music. They did it because…their minds curled in the heat of high school social pressure and because they could get guns and because their parents apparently didn't notice that anything was amiss. To make this an issue of deviant dress is a counterproductive effort on the part of the mainstream. [Comments excerpted from a letter to the editor of *The Denver Post* (Irvine, 1999, p. 7B)]

PROPOSING SOLUTIONS TO THE COLUMBINE PROBLEM

Because the Columbine problem was constructed as appearance-related, proposed remedies also focused upon appearance. Two solutions involved changes in dress.

The Adoption of School Dress Codes or Uniforms

Within just two days of the shootings, news reports addressed the adoption of dress codes or school uniforms as a solution to the Columbine problem.

Proposed dress codes included banning trench coats, baseball caps, and dress, such as leather collars, associated with the Goth movement. In response to these suggestions, news reporters and citizens divided themselves along two lines: those for and those against dress regulation.

Advocates of school dress codes argued that dress can shape the behavior and thoughts of wearers and/or perceivers (see Lennon, Johnson, & Schulz, 1999). Specifically, advocates claimed that the regulation of student appearances had the potential to: (1) decrease gang activity and school violence, (2) increase student achievement, (3) create an environment that facilitates learning, (4) assist in identification of school trespassers, (5) deter students from hiding weapons in their clothing, and (6) deter students from expressing class divisions or hatred against others. Further, school and law enforcement officials suggested that banning trench coats would: (1) protect students who may find trench coats frightening, given the events at Columbine, and (2) safeguard students who may wear such coats from others who may (mis)interpret the garments as indicative of violence:

> "We have excluded the long black coat because it makes it hard for us to guarantee the safety of our students," said Susan Carlson, spokeswoman for the Adams 12 schools. "Wearing such a coat," she said, can also be "alarming enough to others that it disrupts the educational environment." (Brown, 1999, p. 15AA).

> I would also like to suggest we revisit the idea of school uniforms that take away the opportunities to hide weapons and express rage and class divisions within our schools. [Comments excerpted from a letter to the editor of *The Rocky Mountain News* (Nelson, 1999, p. 21AA)]

Those opposing the adoption of school dress codes typically focused upon three issues. First, they argued that regulating dress could represent a form of personal harassment and violate one's freedom of speech and right to self-expression:

> Neil [an Englewood student who was ticketed for the wearing of Gothic-style accessories],

for his part, said, "I should be able to express myself however I want, to wear whatever I want, as long as it's not hurting anybody." (Greene, 1999, p. 5A)

Second, opponents of dress regulation challenged the logic that dress can be an indicator that a wearer may behave in a certain way (e.g., violently) or hold certain attitudes (e.g., hatred toward others). This argument also was used to oppose the claim that individuals with specified appearances were somehow involved in the Columbine shootings:

> One [student] statement read: "I wonder how long it'll be before we're allowed to wear our trench coats anymore. You know those screwed up kids in Colorado were wearing them, so that means I will also kill someone and so will all my friends." ("Complaints Inundate ACLU," 1999, p. 15A)

Finally, those opposing dress codes contended that such a "solution" was a superficial and unrealistic way to address the shootings:

> If Eric Harris and Dylan Klebold had been wearing Denver Broncos jerseys with No. 7 on the back, would school systems be so quick to ban those? This banning of trench coats is a ridiculous response promoted by people who refuse to deal with the real underlying causes of violence. [Comments excerpted from a letter to the editor of *The Denver Post* (Irvine, 1999, p. 7B)]

The Adoption of Columbine RESPECT Patches

A second solution concerned the adoption of RESPECT patches. The patches were created by the Colorado High School Activities Association to be worn by students to reduce social tensions among Columbine's cliques:

> The new patches are meant to spotlight a critical concept that emerged from the Columbine siege and to promote it universally, in a way that speaks to all students and all adults, officials said. (Cornelius, 1999, p. 1A)

CLARIFYING AND REVISITING THE ISSUES: *THE COLUMBINE REPORT*

In May 2000, an official summary of the crime investigation, *The Columbine Report*, was released. Newspaper articles concerning *The Report* clarified and/or revisited prior claims made in the media. For example, despite prior claims by students that they had observed three gunmen—two in trench coats and one in a white T-shirt—newspaper articles about *The Report* cited ballistics evidence to confirm that only two gunmen had been involved. In *The Report*, the confusion concerning the gunmen's dress was attributed to the fact that Harris had shed his coat before entering the school.

Media coverage of *The Report* also suggested that Harris and Klebold did not use appearance as a cue with which to select their victims. It is interesting to note that the reporters labeled the earlier claim that appearance was used to target victims as "MYTH" and the revised claim as "FACT":

> MYTH 6: Harris and Klebold targeted blacks, Christians, and jocks. FACT: No one group or individual was sought out, Battan [a detective with the Sheriff's Office] said. For example, if the two were really looking for jocks, they wouldn't have gone to the library, she said. "This was not about killing jocks or killing black people or killing Christians," Battan said. "It was about killing everybody." Said Kiekbusch [the Sheriff's Division Chief]: "They put themselves above everybody. They hated everybody." ....Nor did Harris and Klebold seek out Isaiah Shoels, the only black student killed, although they did make a racial remark about him, Battan said. (Lowe, 2000, p. 22A)

Finally, media content about *The Report* questioned the gunmen's involvement in the Trench Coat Mafia and the suggestion that the group's members behaved violently or advocated the hatred of others:

MYTH 3: Harris and Klebold were members of the Trench Coat Mafia. FACT: The Trench Coat Mafia was a "tongue-in-cheek kind of thing," Kiebush said, not an organized group or clique. The group was composed of about a dozen students, mostly social outcasts who hung out together. Their picture appeared in the 1998 Columbine yearbook. But Harris and Klebold weren't in the picture and they weren't part of the group....They did wear black, Western-type dusters into the school, but only as a way to hide their weapons. (Lowe, 2000, p. 22A)

According to newspaper articles about the report, the gunmen did not regularly wear symbols of violence or the Goth culture, but rather, "appeared outwardly normal, [sharing] their dark side only with each other" ("The Columbine Report," 2000, p. 1AA). This claim seemingly undermines earlier claims suggesting that an adolescent's appearance is a reliable indication of violent tendencies.

Conclusions

It is important to consider the implications of the media's construction of appearance as part of the Columbine problem. Granted, many of the claims linking appearance to the shootings were eventually revoked. However, these "corrective" claims were published more than a year after the original claims. In the months between, the reality of Columbine as an appearance problem was constructed in the eyes of the public. As a seeming result of this dialogue, innocent individuals perceived themselves as unjustly implicated and were moved to make counterclaims defending their innocence. Further, by constructing Columbine as an appearance-related problem and proposing appearance-based solutions, the media may have shortchanged an opportunity for "real" social change to prevent future school shootings.

Indeed, the growing body of evidence that media reports may impact public policy is a call for continued research related to the media's role in the construction and explanation of issues as

social problems. Further work might focus upon other issues such as the role of appearance in date rape cases or the use of appearance cues to ascertain a criminal suspect's possible guilt or innocence. Finally, more research related to the influence of school uniforms—and more broadly, students' appearances—upon student behavior is needed. Previous work has produced conflicting results regarding the relationship between students' appearances and their behaviors (e.g., academic performance, discipline problems, and student violence). Research examining the reasons for the inconsistencies in prior work would be helpful for school districts considering the implementation of dress code or uniform policies.

Note

1. An expanded version of this article was published in *Sociological Inquiry*: Ogle, J. P., Eckman, M. J., & Leslie, C. A. (2003). Appearance cues and the shootings at Columbine High. *Sociological Inquiry*, 73(1): 1–27.

References

Altheide, D. L., & Michalowski, R. S. (1999). Fear in the news: A discourse in control. *The Sociological Quarterly*, 40:475–503.

Anton, M. (1999a, April 21). Death goes to school with cold, evil laughter. *The Rocky Mountain News*, 2A.

Anton, M. (1999b, April 20). School war zone: Many students wounded in shooting, explosions, fire at Jeffco's Columbine High. *The Rocky Mountain News*, 2A.

Briggs, B., & Greene, S. (1999, April 22). Hate calls, threats target 'goth' youths. *The Denver Post*, 11A.

Brown, S. (1999, April 22). Some districts ban trench coats. *The Rocky Mountain News*, 15AA.

The Columbine Report: Journal entries expose a darker side. (2000, May 16). *The Denver Post*, 1AA.

Complaints inundate ACLU after Colorado school tragedy. (1999, May 10). *The Denver Post*, 15A.

Cornelius, C. (1999, August 4). Students to don 'Respect' badge. *The Denver Post*, 15A.

Denerstein, R. (1999, April 22). Movies echo harsh reality—or do they? *The Rocky Mountain News*, 17AA.

Finley, B., & Olinger, D. (1999, April 21). Panic yields relief for lucky: Parents agonize to find children. *The Denver Post*, 14A.

Gerbner, G., Gross, L., Morgan, M., Signorelli, N., & Jackson-Beeck, M. (1978). Cultural indicators: Violence profile no. 9. *Journal of Communication*, 28:176–207.

Greene, S. (1999a, April 23). Goth-fashion crackdown seen by some as fascism. *The Denver Post*, 5A.

Greene, S. (1999b, April 24). Trench Coat Mafia teen describes school life filled with taunts, abuse. *The Denver Post*, 1A, 15A.

Greene, S., & Briggs, B. (1999a, April 21). Carnage puts spotlight on Trench Coat Mafia. *The Denver Post*, 17A.

Greene, S., & Briggs, B. (1999b, April 22). Comfortable suburbs harbor troubled teens. *The Denver Post*, 11A.

Harris, a consummate actor, hid secret yen for revenge. (1999, May 2). *The Denver Post*, 18A, 23A.

Hubbard, B. (1999, April 26). Three let curiosity get the best of them. *The Rocky Mountain News*, 16A.

Irvine, A. (1999, April 24). Don't ban clothing [Letter to the editor]. *The Denver Post*, 7B.

Leib, J. (1999, April 21). Don't blame 'goth' culture for tragedy, insiders say. *The Denver Post*, 17A.

Lennon, S. J., Johnson, K. K. P., & Schulz, T. L. (1999). Forging linkages between dress and the law in the U.S., part II: Dress codes. *Clothing and Textiles Research Journal*, 17(3):157–167.

Lowe, P. (1999, December 14). Killer's hatred shows in vitriolic 'film festival.' *The Denver Post*, 11A.

Lowe, P. (2000, March 12). Officials separate facts, fiction. *The Denver Post*, 1A, 22A.

McPhee, M. (1999, April 24). Three arrested at rampage say people in black persecuted. *The Denver Post*, 5A.

Nelson, M. (1999, April 22). Tragedy points out great needs in society [Letter to the editor]. *The Rocky Mountain News*, 21AA.

Obmascik, M. (1999, April 21). Columbine bloodbath leaves up to 25 dead. *The Denver Post*, 1A, 5A.

Smokes, S. (1999, April 26). In wake of shooting, a new checklist. *The Denver Post*, 9B.

Vaughn, K., & Abbott, K. (1999, April 25). Journal records details, intent to kill. *The Rocky Mountain News*, 2AA, 23AA.

DISCUSSION QUESTIONS

Dress and the Columbine Shootings

1. The Columbine massacre was a tragic event that haunts the memories of many. Why did the media attempt to analyze and explain meanings of dress worn by the boys on a killing spree?

2. Does attributing the dress of the two boys (erroneously) to a deviant gang help people deal with the tragedy? How so?

3. What consequences has the Columbine event had for school dress around the nation?

4. Has the event changed the meanings of the long black trench coat?

CHAPTER 5

Appearance for Gender and Sexuality

Susan O. Michelman

AFTER YOU HAVE READ THIS CHAPTER, YOU WILL COMPREHEND:

- The comparison of the cultural meaning of being a man or woman, and the link of gender norms to appearance.

- How gender is socially and culturally determined and is a significant component in the study of appearance.

- The diversity of human appearance that may be influenced by sexual orientation.

What do we notice in the first few seconds of encountering someone else? We usually notice skin color, age, body language, appearance (particularly if it is "different" and deviates from the norm), and most critically, a person's sex—at least we think we see whether an individual is male or female. Actually, what we first notice is gender appearance, which we may correctly or incorrectly identify as a sign of their sex. What most people experience on a daily basis is related to fitting into socially accepted gender norms for dress.

FIGURE 5.1 A *Kalabari man from Nigeria, West Africa, in traditional dress, which includes a wrapper, shirt, waist- and head-ties, and beads.*

Clothing does not have inherent meaning: it is culturally defined. Cultural norms and expectations surrounding the meaning of being a man or woman are closely linked to appearance. For example, in many Muslim societies, the practice of women's veiling quickly identifies gender as well as the cultural meaning of being a woman in that society. Women's lifestyles are secluded from the world outside the home, the domain of men. In Indonesia, the *sarong*, a rectangular piece of cloth wrapped and tied around the waist, is worn by both men and women. Similarly, the *wrapper* is worn by both sexes in West Africa (see Figure 5.1). In the culture of North America, the sarong and wrapper, which physically resemble our definition of a skirt, would rarely be seen on men, except perhaps in the theater, on film, or in the context of couture or avant-garde fashion.

What then is meant when we use the terms *gender* and *sex*? Although many people use the terms interchangeably, the two terms do not have the same meaning. **Gender,** determined psychologically, socially, and culturally, refers to "appropriate" behavior and appearance for males and females. Appropriate male and female behavior varies according to time and place. **Sex** refers to the biological aspects of maleness or femaleness. A person's sex is determined on the basis of **primary sex characteristics,** the anatomical traits essential to reproduction. One may assume that determining biological sex is a clear-cut process, but a significant number of babies are born **intersexed.** This is a broad term used by the medical profession to classify people with some mixture of male and female biological characteristics (Newman, 1995). For example, a **true hermaphrodite** is a person who is born with ovaries and testes. Why, then, is there no intersexed category? Parents of such children usually collaborate with a physician to assign their offspring to one of the two recognized sexes.

Secondary sex characteristics distinguish one sex from another. These are physical traits not essential to reproduction (e.g., breast development, quality of voice, distribution of facial and body hair, and skeletal form). Many of the articles in this text are concerned with such aspects of appearance. "Scrawn to Brawn" by Trebay and "Measuring Up" by Dickinson are examinations of how the popular body image for men has changed in the past 30 years and the meaning of such a transition from a "thinner/scrawny/sexy rock-star mode" to a more muscled and buff physique. The author points out that men are now suffering from some of the body ideal maladies that had formerly been reserved for women. Dickinson states in "Measuring Up" that an increasing number of boys suffer from eating disorders. This is due in part to an increased push to obtain the unrealistic goal of a body ideal of the toy icon G.I. Joe.

Gender is a **social construction.** Frequently, differences between males and females are attributed to biology rather than the fact that they may be socially created. For

a   b

FIGURE 5.2 *The dress on the left in (a) follows the S-shaped silhouette that is more typical of the nineteenth century. Gauguin's painting (b) illustrates his observations of Tahitian women.*

example, the French painter Paul Gauguin noted this ambiguity about men and women, which he recorded in a journal that he kept while painting in Tahiti in 1891. His observations were highly influenced by his recollections of the fashion norms of Europe during this period of the late nineteenth century, when women wore tightly laced corsets under their dresses. (See Figure 5.2a and b.)

> Among peoples that go naked, as among animals, the difference between the sexes is less accentuated than in our climates. Thanks to our cinctures and corsets we have succeeded in making an artificial being out of woman . . . . We carefully keep her in a state of nervous weakness and muscular inferiority, and in guarding her from fatigue, we take away from her possibilities of development. Thus modeled on a bizarre ideal of slenderness . . . our women have nothing in common with us [men], and this, perhaps, may not be without grave moral and social disadvantages.
>
> On Tahiti, the breezes from forest and sea strengthen the lungs, they broaden the shoulders and hips. Neither men nor women are sheltered from the rays of the sun nor the pebbles of the sea-shore. Together they engage in the same tasks with the same activity. . . . There is something virile in the women and something feminine in the men. (Gauguin, [1919] 1985, pp. 19–20)

How then are we socialized into an appearance that is either masculine or feminine? This is determined by the culture in which a child is raised. **Socialization** is a learning process that begins immediately after birth and continues throughout life. It is a process that allows individuals to develop their human capacities, acquire a unique personality and identity, and internalize the norms, values, beliefs, and language needed to participate in society (Ferrante, 1995). In the article "In Iran's Hair Salons, the Rebels

Wield Scissors," Sciolino examines the politics of these Muslim women's appearance in light of restrictions on the display of women's hair in public. They can go bareheaded privately in front of a limited group consisting of family and other women, which has created a continuing interest in hair styling at beauty salons.

Socialization involves the cultural context in childhood and adolescence, in which individuals form their concepts of self. For example, when a child is born in any culture, the first question is almost always, "Is it a boy or a girl?" Although the answer to this question is based on a physical examination of genitalia, very quickly in a child's life, gender is established by others observing the way an infant is dressed by the parents. For example, in American hospitals newborn babies are given pink or blue blankets, identification bracelets, or even hair ribbons that give quick visual identification of their gender. Research has shown that children as young as two years of age classify people into gender categories based on their appearance (Weinraub et al., 1984). This is obviously long before they understand the meaning of the biological differences. The article "Day-Care Dress Up Not Amusing to Boy's Dad" points out that young children experiment with gender through dress-up. This normal experimentation by the boy with feminine dress was interpreted by the father as "abnormal." In this chapter, we examine how gender and even sexuality do not exist as a binary opposition of male and female.

Gender socialization regarding appearance is closely linked to learned social roles. Children are highly influenced by gender-specific toys that serve to reinforce social stereotypes regarding femininity and masculinity. Some examples that have come under scrutiny for their influence on the development of children are Barbie for girls and G.I. Joe or Power Rangers for boys. "Life in Plastic" analyzes how Barbie has reflected society as it changes. Currently, the average American girl aged between 3 and 11 owns 10 Barbie dolls, and to date over 1 billion Barbie dolls have been sold. Barbie has been criticized for encouraging an impossible ideal of slimness, as well as beauty and youthfulness, as a prerequisite of feminine success.

Similarly, children's books and media images can reinforce stereotypical gender appearances. *Beauty and the Beast* and *The Little Mermaid* contain classic examples of beautiful young women whose lives are made perfect by a handsome prince. As children grow, they may begin to associate behaviors with gendered dress. The trend for very young children to wear designer clothing may contribute to their overinvolvement, and even preoccupation, with appearance issues while they are very young and vulnerable.

THE SEXUAL IDENTITY KIT

Questions of gender are socially defined, but what about **sexual identity?** Do the anatomical differences in the reproductive systems of men and women provide a foundation for identifying the self as feminine or masculine? Present-day debate on whether sexual identity is biological or constructed (as is gender) has been influenced by social movements dealing with sexual politics (Woodward, 1997). One important example is the feminist movement. In the broadest sense, a feminist is a woman or man who actively opposes gender dogma (i.e., learned patterns of behavior expected of males and females) and believes that self-image, aspirations, and life chances of both women and men should not be constrained by those scripts (Bem, 1993). For some people, the term "feminist" evokes negative images and stereotypes of mannish-looking women who hate men and who find vocations as wife and mother oppressive and unrewarding (Ferrante, 1995).

What do you think of when you hear the word **sexism?** About the male construction worker who whistles and shouts sexual comments at females passing by? About the office worker who makes lewd comments about a co-worker's appearance? Sexism refers to a system of beliefs and behaviors by which a group of people are oppressed, controlled, and exploited because of presumed gender differences (Anderson & Collins, 1992; Rothenberg, 1992). The Civil Rights Act, Title VII, defines sexual harassment as "unwelcomed sexual advances, requests for sexual favors and other verbal or physical conduct of a sexual nature that are connected to decisions about employment or that create an intimidating, hostile, or offensive work environment." Feminist authors have sought to expand the definition of sexual harassment to include any coercive behavior imposed upon members of one gender by those of the other gender, which results in conditions of unequal power and is associated with gender differences (Wise & Stanley, 1987). Gender stereotypes figure strongly in the public's perceptions of both parties in harassment cases. Research consistently finds that the general public assumes that women who wear sexually provocative dress incite, and are in part responsible for, sexual harassment from co-workers (Johnson & Workman, 1992; Workman & Johnson, 1991). However, most evidence indicates that sexual harassment in the workplace is a power issue; an individual in a power position attempts to harass a subordinate regardless of how the individual dresses, because the subordinate is an "easy," powerless target. Dress is an ambiguous form of communication, read incorrectly in many instances, and cannot be considered clear indication of intent of victims to "ask for" sex or sexual attention (Lennon, Lennon, & Johnson, 1993).

Another type of harassment can be related to sexual preference. The article "Northampton Confronts a Crime, Cruelty" reports the violent and tragic consequences of homophobia or fear and harassment of individuals perceived to have a homosexual lifestyle. Homosexuality can be defined as same-sex sexual activity. Although this describes sexual experience, it does not necessarily include a long-term homosexual or gay lifestyle, because many heterosexual individuals have had homosexual experiences. Also, there are some individuals with bisexual desires and activities. A 15-year-old person such as the student described in the *Boston Globe* article may have conflict between sexual desires and activity and may be in a transitional stage of sexual development without coming to a more clearly defined homosexual, bisexual, or heterosexual resolution.

It is hoped that the materials presented in this book, as well as the reader's own thoughtful reflections, will lead to an appreciation of diversity in culture as well as sexual orientation. The double tragedy of homophobic harassment and the victim's violent reaction should be most distressing for students of dress and culture, because the article suggests that the harassment followed an intolerant, and perhaps incorrect, interpretation of dress and appearance.

Cross-Dressing

Popular culture is one venue for us to glimpse "queer practices," which play on masculine/feminine ambiguities, with their deliberate exposure and celebration of the mismatch between gender and sexuality (Woodward, 1997). For example, as discussed in Hegland's article, "Drag Queens, Transvestites, Transexuals," cross-dressers are males who put on feminine dress or females who wear masculine dress for different purposes or effects. Culturally prescribed and proscribed gender norms, manifested by dress and appearance, can be challenged through social interaction. What happens when individuals step across the social boundaries of gender-appropriate dress and appearance by cross-dressing? How does the public respond when confronted with an incongruous or unfamiliar gender appearance? Recent popular movies such as *Tootsie*; *Mrs. Doubtfire*;

Priscilla, Queen of the Desert; and *The Birdcage* have confirmed growing popular interest in gender-bending appearances of men cross-dressing as women. RuPaul, a male-to-female cross-dresser who had his own talk show on television, affects an appearance of a supermodel that is admired by some young women. *Victor/Victoria* was a popular play and movie that considered in a lighthearted way whether or not a woman can successfully "pass" as a man. This, of course, is Hollywood's interpretation of these gender issues. Does it work as well off-screen for those who cross-dress? Hegland's article will give you a more realistic perspective.

Dress and Gender: A Historical Perspective

Examining dress historically gives us perspective on how the relationship between dress and gender has changed. During the twentieth century through the 1950s, men followed a **restricted code** of appearance, limited to angular design lines, neutral and subdued color palettes, bifurcated garments (i.e., pants) for the lower body, natural but not tight silhouettes, sturdy fabrics and shoes, and simple hair and face grooming (McCracken, 1985). This simple, restricted code helped them to focus on work and accomplishments rather than appearance. Their attire (except perhaps for the tie) did not tend to impede physical activity. In sum, men dressed for an agonic role in society.

Women, in contrast, had an **elaborated code** for appearance through the 1950s. They could wear some of what men wore, and a lot more. Their unlimited options for fabrics, colors, design lines, and silhouettes gave them a useful bag of tricks for attending to their hedonic role, emphasizing pursuit of beauty and physical being. Their tight or flowing skirts, high heels, and nylons did not facilitate emphasis on physical activity, however. Women were encouraged to spend a lot of time on clothes, hair, weight control, and makeup to render themselves beautiful for men (who would marry and support women to have children). Women's engrossment in appearance, along with attending to men and children, could easily distract them from pursuing a full-time career.

Since the late 1960s, the pendulum has swung from men and women wearing distinctively different styles to an interest in unisex and androgynous styles. **Androgyny** is defined as a mixing of masculine and feminine qualities in one person's appearance, and **unisex** refers to a style of clothing that could be worn by either men or women. For example, women have adopted some amount of androgyny in business dress. According to McCracken (1985), businesswomen in the United States avidly appropriated the business suit and its corresponding masculine body form in the early 1980s. He believes the motivation was a striving for women to be similar to their male counterparts in business settings, with shoulder pads, conservative fabrics, and a focus on the upper torso and head through contrasting shirt and tie. By the mid-1980s, however, women in business were increasingly moving away from a completely masculine look to a mix of feminine and masculine styling (Ogle & Damhorst, 1999). Along with many business women softening their image, some U.S. men are showing less concern with a traditional masculine physical image, particularly in casual dress. Many men now wear soft pastel colors in shirts, in addition to jewelry, cologne, and skin products that were previously worn exclusively by women.

Goffman (1961) referred to the clothing and other necessary accoutrements of appearance as "identity kits." Today, these "kits" are being rapidly reevaluated according to social perceptions of gender, particularly as traditional social roles for men and women change. Men in the United States are now beginning to experiment with the torments of vanity, the prior domain of women. Men now account for around 25 percent of all cosmetic surgeries. Clearly, men and women are not so different today in their obsession with appearance.

Summary

The articles in this chapter address multiple aspects of our gender appearance. Articles examine how we are socialized into gender, the relationship between sexuality and gender, the politics of appearance, and an examination of a historical practice in Chinese culture that constructed a feminine appearance. The articles allow you to critically reflect on your own thinking and ideas about appearance and its relationship to gender and sexuality.

Suggested Readings

Barnes, R., & Eicher, J. (Eds.) (1992). *Dress and Gender: Making and Meaning.* Oxford: Berg Press.

Bem, S. (1993). *The Lenses of Gender: Transforming the Debate on Gender Inequality.* New Haven, CT: Yale University Press.

Bordo, S. (1993). *Unbearable Weight: Feminism, Western Culture, and the Body.* Berkeley: University of California Press.

Bordo, S. (1999). *The Male Body.* New York: Farrar, Straus and Giroux.

Cahill, S. E. (1987). Directions for an interactionist study of gender development. In M. J. Deegan & M. Hill (Eds.), *Women and Symbolic Interaction.* Boston: Allen and Unwin.

Garber, M. (1992). *Vested Interests: Cross-Dressing and Cultural Anxiety.* New York: Routledge.

Goffman, E. (1976). *Gender Advertisements.* New York: Harper Torchbooks.

Griggs, C. (1998). *S/he: Changing Sex and Changing Clothes.* Oxford: Berg Press.

Kessler, S. J., & McKenna, W. (1978). *Gender: An Ethnomethodological Approach.* Chicago: University of Chicago Press.

Kidwell, C., & Steele, V. (1989). *Men and Women: Dressing the Part.* Washington, DC: Smithsonian Institution Press.

Roach-Higgins, M., & Eicher, J. (1992, Summer). Dress and identity. *Clothing and Textiles Research Journal,* 10(4):1–8.

Woodhouse, A. (1989). Sex, gender, and appearance. In *Fantastic Women: Sex, Gender and Transvestism,* pp. 1–16. New Brunswick, NJ: Rutgers University Press.

Appearance for Gender and Sexuality

Objective: To examine the intimate relationship between what we wear and our perceptions of gender.

This assignment will involve working with a partner to analyze which items of clothing are typically used only by males or females and which forms of dress are worn by both genders.

Procedure

Students should pair up. Ideally, females should pair with a male. This may not always be possible, however. Each student should obtain ten images from magazines, mail-order catalogs, or newspapers that depict items of clothing. To make the images slightly more ambiguous, cut off the head in the image. Try to pick some images that are more androgynous than others. Include some unisex clothing.

Show each image to your partner. Have your partner indicate if the item is typically worn by males or females. If the item is typically used by both males and females, have your partner indicate "both."

Discuss and compare your responses with those of your partner. What are the items of clothing that are worn only by females? What items of clothing are worn only by males? What items are worn by both males and females?

Discussion

As a class, discuss why certain items of clothing are restricted to females. Why are some items worn predominantly by males? Analyze how dress has a role in reinforcing gender stereotypes. How have some of these "rules" of dress and gender changed within the past 10 to 15 years? What social, economic, political, and ideological influences have affected gender and appearance issues? How might different cultures and their dress influence our typically "American" attitudes toward gender and appearance?

References

Anderson, M. L., & Collins, P. H. (1992). *Race, Class, and Gender: An Anthology*. Belmont, CA: Wadsworth.

Bem, S. (1993). *The Lenses of Gender: Transforming the Debate on Sexual Inequality*. New Haven, CT: Yale University Press.

Davis, F. (1992). *Fashion, Culture and Identity*. Chicago: University of Chicago Press.

Ferrante, J. (1995). *Sociology: A Global Perspective*. New York: Wadsworth Publishing.

Gauguin, P. [1919] (1985). *Noa Noa: The Tahitian Journal* (O. F. Theis, trans.). New York: Dover.

Goffman, E. (1961). *Asylums*. Garden City, NY: Doubleday.

Johnson, K. K. P., & Workman, J. (1992). Clothing and attributions concerning sexual harassment. *Home Economics Research Journal*, 21(2):160–172.

Lennon, T., Lennon, S. J., & Johnson, K. K. P. (1993). Is clothing probative of attitude and intent? Implications for rape and sexual harassment cases. *Journal of Law and Inequality*, 11:301–325.

McCracken, G. (1985). The trickle-down theory rehabilitated. In M. R. Solomon (Ed.), *The Psychology of Fashion*, pp. 39–54. Lexington, MA: Lexington Books.

Newman, D. (1995). *Sociology: Exploring the Architecture of Everyday Life.* Thousand Oaks, CA: Pine Forge Press.

Ogle, J. P., & Damhorst, M. L. (1999). Dress for success in the popular press. In K. K. P. Johnson & S. J. Lennon (Eds.), *Power and Appearance*. New York: Berg Press.

Rothenberg, P. S. (1992). *Race, Class, and Gender in the United States*. New York: St. Martin's Press.

Weinraub, M., Clemens, L. P., Sockloff, A., Ethridge, T., Gracely, E., & Myers, B. (1984). The development of sex role stereotypes in the third year: Relationships to gender labeling, gender identity, sex-typed toy preference, and family characteristics. *Child Development*, 55:1493–1503.

Wise, S., & Stanley, L. (1987). *Georgie Porgie: Sexual Harassment in Everyday Life.* London: Pandora.

Woodward, K. (1997). *Identity and Difference*. Thousand Oaks, CA: Sage Publications.

Workman, J., & Johnson, K. K. P. (1991). The role of cosmetics in attributions about sexual harassment. *Sex Roles*, 24(11/12):759–769.

23 Measuring Up
Amy Dickinson

Obesity in young boys is on the rise, and so are eating disorders. Whose fault is that? Try G.I. Joe.

Women my age know whom to blame for our own self-loathing, eating disorders and distorted body image: Barbie. So we're raising our vulnerable, body-conscious girls to beware the perpetually pointy-toed goddess with the impossible body and perfect face. Now it's time to take a good look at our sons and their plastic influences. Studies show that boys increasingly suffer from eating disorders, and if that fact is surprising, the root cause is not—after you take a good look at G.I. Joe.

G.I. Joe, for those of you who haven't raised an eight-year-old boy lately, has evolved from a normally proportioned grunt into a buff, ripped, mega muscular warrior who, if he were a real man, would have 27-inch biceps and other proportions achievable only through years of bench presses, protein diets and the liberal use of steroids.

A recent study shows that 36% of third-grade boys had tried to lose weight. In the past 10 years, more than a million males have been found to have eating disorders. In addition to suffering from anorexia and bulimia at increasing rates, boys are falling victim to a newly named disorder: muscle dysmorphia (also called bigorexia)—the conviction that one is too small. This syndrome is marked by an obsession with the size and shape of your body, constant working out and weight lifting (even if you aren't involved in sports) and the use of supplements to "bulk up." Parents might tell themselves their kids' spending hours in a gym working on "six-pack abs" is better than hanging out on the corner and drinking six-packs, but a true case of bigorexia can be just as ruinous to a boy's health and future.

Dr. Harrison Pope, co-author of *The Adonis Complex*, a helpful book on male body obses-sion, says parents should look at the world through their sons' eyes. "Boys are fed a diet of 'ideal' male bodies, from *Batman* to the stars of the WWF," he says. "So parents need to tell their boys—starting when they are small—that they don't have to look like these characters." Pope, himself an avid weight lifter, says parents should also educate themselves and their sons on the uses and dangers of supplements such as adrenal hormones. "Any kid can go into a store and buy 'andro' [formerly Mark McGwire's bulk-up drug, androstenedione] legally," he says, "but we still don't know what long-term use will do to a boy's health." Pope believes that up to 15% of high school boys use andro, often in dangerous mega-doses. A large percentage will then move on to anabolic steroids.

Boys are hampered by their tendency to stay silent about their anxieties, but parents can help them open up by asking questions rather than making statements. The media are full of unattainable images, so an Abercrombie & Fitch or a Gap ad can spark a discussion about what the proper build for a boy is. Parents of kids involved in such weight-sensitive sports as wrestling should know that crash dieting can trigger health problems and eating disorders. Danger signs include extreme mood changes, compulsive behavior and depression. Parents of very young boys can take a page from the Barbie playbook by asking their sons to compare muscle-bound action figures with real people they know, like Mom and Dad. When we did this in our house, it got a big laugh—maybe too big. But at least it's a start.

Measuring Up

1. What are some ways parents and teachers could use to help boys attain a more positive body image?

2. What aspect of boys' psychology would cause them to be more silent about their body concerns? How could this be addressed?

24   Scrawn to Brawn: Men Get Muscles, or Pray for Them

Guy Trebay

It started with Woodstock—the video, not the event. Although old enough, barely, to have attended the original 1969 festival, I opted to skip the brown acid and spend that fateful weekend working my summer job. I've never regretted particularly that I wasn't on hand at the Yasgur farm for the grooviness, the mud and Jimi Hendrix's wah-wah pedal, although the rampant nudity sounded like fun. I had no idea how much fun until a friend invited me over recently to watch the documentary film on television.

Now, it's a cheap gimmick to quote Oscar Wilde when you've got hold of a tricky thesis, but you'll forgive me, I hope, for invoking him here. "It is only shallow people who do not judge by appearances," Wilde wrote in "The Picture of Dorian Gray." And watching "Woodstock," it was hard to keep from thinking that there was something important to be learned from the way people appeared 30 years back. I don't mean the crocheted ponchos and granny glasses. I mean anatomically.

People were much thinner then, especially guys. They had lean torsos and narrow shoulders and scrawny legs. A lot of them had stoner's swayback, but that's a separate issue. It occurred to me watching "Woodstock" that I'd happened on a piece of evidence documenting a powerful change in the social landscape. You have only to check out MTV's perennially rerun spring break special to see how radical the evolution in men's bodies has been.

The age cohort on spring break is the same as at Woodstock. Any similarity ends with that. Where the average 20-year-old man at Woodstock had a body that looked fine by most objective standards, that same man today would be judged a pathetic dweeb. The women, too, look different, of course, although not as markedly. Even braless hippie chicks knew pretty well what the culture expected of them.

FIGURE 5.3 *Body building and a buff physique have become increasingly important to men.*

But hold a picture of the Woodstock man alongside the MTV guy, and you'll be shocked by the difference. Where one has a perfectly agreeable pectoral arrangement, the other resembles a Playtex model. Where one has a flat stomach, the other possesses an abdominal six-pack with musculature that looks acid-etched.

Woodstock guys were all thin in the fashionably groovy scrawny/sexy/semiwasted rock star mode, while the contemporary guy resembles a plastic action figure. His is the image of a recent New Yorker cartoon in which a woman replies to a hunk's barroom approach by saying, "Sure, we can have dinner," but only if his breasts sign a "noncompete clause."

"Can you imagine today's kids trying to fit into those Woodstock clothes?" asks Lou Schuler, fitness editor for Men's Health, a mass market monthly published by Rodale. Rodale, you may recall, is the Pennsylvania-based press founded on a roster of organic gardening journals. Now, with the phenomenally successful Men's Health and its new teen-age spinoff, MH-18, it has become a publisher of what amounts to eugenics primers—wish books whose surreally godlike cover models provide, as Mr. Schuler says, "the definitive cultural icon of masculinity."

That icon has a thin waist and wide shoulders. He has "muscles that you can see from 50 feet away," Mr. Schuler says. Never mind, he adds, that the actual models chosen for Men's Health covers are members not only of a self-selecting minority but of one that's "super genetically gifted." Few men are physically able to achieve a tiny waist, a washboard stomach and a massive torso, Mr. Schuler concedes, adding: "It's not necessarily an unreachable ideal. But it's an ideal."

The evolution of that ideal is the subject of "The Adonis Complex" (Free Press), a new book that tries to demonstrate how concerns about body image have come to dominate, and tyrannize, many American men.

"There's no question that there's a much greater emphasis on male body image than there was a generation ago," said Dr. Harrison G. Pope Jr., one of the book's three authors and

a professor of psychiatry at Harvard Medical School.

Back in the iconographically innocent era of Woodstock, Dr. Pope said, "men didn't go to the gym five days a week." They didn't employ personal trainers, measure themselves in terms of body fat percentage or spend $2 billion a year on commercial gym memberships, and $2 billion more on home exercise equipment.

They probably read Rolling Stone, too, not muscle magazines. But now even Wenner Media, Rolling Stone's parent company, has gotten into the fitness act, publishing its own regular exhortations, in Men's Journal, on how to achieve six-pack abdominals and a pert behind.

In 1996, "The Adonis Complex" reports, American men underwent 690,361 cosmetic surgical procedures, including 217,083 hair transplant operations and 54,106 liposuction procedures, not to mention surgery to augment their pectoral muscles, their buttocks, their calves and even their penises. A recent survey conducted by Dr. Charles Ysalis, a Pennsylvania State University researcher, also found that—beyond the steroid abuses now considered commonplace among the adult male population—40 percent of American boys 12 and over report that they have experimented with, or plan to use, anabolic steroids to look better naked, as the gym ads say.

Many men, in other words, seem to be suffering a crisis of identity whose remedy is apparently to become cartoons. None of this would particularly shock women, who are accustomed to negotiating a reasonable self-image against body ideals that might include such implausible models as Barbie and Calista Flockhart.

"For men there's something new in all this," said Susan Bordo, a humanities professor at the University of Kentucky and the author of "The Male Body" (Farrar, Straus & Giroux, 2000). On the one hand, Ms. Bordo said, men now "can experience the pleasure of self-display, a pleasure that women have always known, that experience of your body as the erotic center of the world."

But that pleasure is not without cost: many men are now developing women's maladies—a cruel cultural trick if ever there was one. "There's a serious increase of eating disorders among men," Ms. Bordo said, "of steroid abuse, of exercise compulsion."

One result is the beefcake parade you'll see at all the local beaches these last weekends of summer. At Jones Beach recently, there were enough supermanly specimens to give Charles Atlas the willies. Similarly at Fire Island Pines, the beach resembled a "Gladiator" casting call. Even at Robert Moses State Park—never much of a muscle beach—there was so much hypertrophy on display that most guys with ordinary physiques took refuge behind their Igloo coolers.

When Jane Pratt, the editor of Jane, began planning the magazine's August beefcake issue, her intention was parodic. "The idea was to poke fun at Playboy," she said. "We made lists of questions like you'd find in the Playboy centerfold: 'What's your biggest turn-on?' Things like that."

The actors and models approached for the issue were let in on the conceit, and told they would be photographed nearly naked in come-hither poses. "Most of these guys are in good shape to begin with," Ms. Pratt said. "Our idea was to have fun with reverse sexism. But I ended up feeling so bad for these guys, for how distorted their body images were. We've featured women in bathing suits plenty of times, but we've never gotten so many calls from subjects begging us to airbrush their pictures."

Even models with buff bodies were paranoid about love handles. They wanted signed agreements that gave them the right to see how the other men looked.

"When Men's Health started doing covers that said, 'Get abs like this in 10 days!' " Ms. Pratt recalled, "it was a first in terms of putting pressures on men that women's magazines have always promoted. It's been at a ridiculous level for women for so long. I remember when it was just women who were obsessing over every square inch of their bodies. Now, men are going to that place where women always were. It's not that much fun here. I think we should all get out."

DISCUSSION QUESTIONS

Scrawn to Brawn: Men Get Muscles, or Pray for Them

1. This author discusses the difference in men's physiques from the 1960s to the present. What social influences have caused this ideal to change?

2. Why do you think cosmetic surgery is becoming more acceptable and even popular for men?

25   Life in Plastic

Of all the forces against which resistance is futile, Barbie ranks right up near the top. Any poor innocent who assumed that this piece of anatomically challenged plastic, devised in 1959, had been left on the toy shelf beside other relics of the era is evidently not the parent of a pre-school girl. Cult-like, Barbie draws her flock with a heady mix of marketing, magic and the colour pink. "So you think that if you can keep your daughter out of a pink tutu, she'll have more chance of becoming a brain surgeon? Just try it sometime", wailed the novelist Allison Pearson recently of her failed effort to withhold the doll from her daughter. She went on:

> One day, in an attempt to stem the toxic tide, I brought home a Scandinavian doll which looked like a Barbie designed by a feminist committee: a wholesome small-breasted individual wearing khaki, she clearly worked at something useful in developing countries. Alas, this poor social democrat never got to meet the Barbies. "It's a boy!" my daughter yelled in horror, before dropping the liberal compromise in the bucket her baby brother reserved for drowning snails.

Just visit one of the secular temples to Barbie that has opened in recent times. Behind the plate-glass façade of the gleaming Toys "R" Us store in New York's Times Square, which opened last year, some 4,000 square feet are dedicated to the pint-sized princess. This shrine is a riot of regulation (and trademarked) Barbie pink, a peculiarly nauseating hue that lies between a garish fuchsia and a medicinal shade of bubblegum. There, the latest Rapunzel Barbie (plus handsome prince) nestles beside old favourites such as Malibu Barbie, not to mention the Barbie lunch box, jewellery box, cruisin' car, mustang convertible, horse-and-carriage, or "Make-me-pretty talking styling head" play set.

AMERICAN SWEETHEART

To date, over 1 billion Barbie dolls have been sold. The average American girl aged between three and 11 owns a staggering ten Barbie dolls, according to Mattel, the American toy giant that manufactures her. An Italian or British girl owns seven; a French or German girl, five. The Barbie brand is worth some $2 billion—a little ahead of Armani, just behind the *Wall Street Journal*—making it the most valuable toy brand in the world, according to Interbrand, a consultancy. How is it that this impossibly proportioned, charmless toy has endured in an industry notorious for whimsical fad and fickle fashion?

Part of Barbie's appeal is that she has become, according to Christopher Varaste, a historian of Barbie, "the face of the American dream". Barbie is not a mere toy, nor product category: she is an icon. Quite how she became one is hotly debated among the Barbie sorority. Some think she answers an innate girlish desire for fantasy, role-playing and dressing-up. Others that Mattel has simply manipulated girls' aspirations to that end.

Either way, wrapped up in her pouting lips and improbable figure—buxom breasts, wafer-thin waist and permanently arched feet waiting to slip into a pair of high heels—is an apparently enduring statement of aspiration and western aesthetic. She is, according to M.G. Lord, who has written a biography of Barbie, "the most potent icon of American popular culture in the late twentieth century."

Officialdom has recognised Barbie's iconic status. The Americans included a Barbie doll in the 1976 bicentennial time capsule. Earlier this year, the American government buried her in a "women's health" time capsule, alongside a pair

---

of forceps and a girdle. As an emblem of Americana she is subject to pastiche, derision and political statement. Andy Warhol made a portrait of Barbie, the Campbell's soup of toy brands. An exhibition in London earlier this year displayed "Suicide Bomber Barbie" by Simon Tyszko, a British artist. Her hair was blonde, her hair ribbon red, and around her slender waist was wrapped a belt of explosives, attached to a detonator held daintily in her hand.

An industry has even grown up to deconstruct the meaning of this pint-sized piece of pink plastic. Students can enrol on sociology courses in America with such titles as "From Barbie to Superman: images of gender in popular culture". There are shelfloads of books and essays about the toy doll, full of insights such as this:

> Barbie represents the sort of contemporary selfhood some see as embattled and others see as liberated. Hers is a mutable, protean, impression-managing, context-bound self whose demeanour shifts from situation to situation and role to role... Her personality is inchoate, even ethereal; her morals and values are more implicit than expressed or affirmed; her intimate life—her dreams, her passions, her abiding attachments—remains a mystery.

Barbie has not colonised girls' imaginations by accident. Mattel has dedicated itself to promoting Barbie as "a lifestyle, not just a toy". In addition to selling the dolls, Mattel licenses Barbie in 30 different product categories, from furniture to make-up. A girl can sleep in Barbie pyjamas, under a Barbie duvet-cover, her head on a Barbie pillow-case, surrounded by Barbie wall-paper, and on, and on. There are Barbie conventions, fan clubs, web sites, magazines and collectors' events. "She's so much more than a character brand," enthuses a Mattel publicity person, "she's a fashion statement, a way of life."

Most fashion statements made by a 43-year-old woman might be met with scorn. But the secret of Barbie's eternal youth is reinvention. "The brilliance of the brand is that she's a reflection of society as it changes," says Adrienne Fontanella, head of Mattel's girl division. "From a fashion perspective, she's always right there with the latest trend." Every year, Mattel devises about 150 different Barbie dolls, and designs some 120 new outfits. She acquired a mod look in the 1960s, and tie-dyed clothes and a hippie headband in the 1970s. Over the years, she has worn her hair in a ponytail, bubble cut, page boy, swirl and side-part flip. "It is a business-school case study in innovation," says Dan Jansen, at the Boston Consulting Group.

Moreover, Mattel has moved with the times, continually pumping out new messages about women as if to keep its critics at bay. Barbie is no bimbo, it appears. From her early days as a teenage fashion model, Barbie has appeared as an astronaut, surgeon, Olympic athlete, downhill skier, aerobics instructor, TV news reporter, vet, rock star, doctor, army officer, air force pilot, summit diplomat, rap musician, presidential candidate (party undefined), baseball player, scuba diver, lifeguard, fire-fighter, engineer, dentist, and many (many) more. "Barbie as Rapunzel", a computer-animated video, was tipped as one of the top-selling toys this Christmas.

VINYL VAMP

If Barbie appeals because she embodies an American ideal, however, it is the nature of that ideal that so exasperates her critics. They fall crudely into two groups: the "Barbie is the face of wicked American imperialism" camp; and the "Barbie corrupts young girls with shallow messages that promote style over substance" lot.

The first group blames Barbie for promoting rampant consumerism and Americanisation. Naomi Klein, author of "No Logo", lumps Barbie in with MTV, Coca-Cola and Disney as perpetrators-in-chief of American corporate expansionism. Like all toy makers, Mattel has also received its share of complaints about its third-world factories (it has no plants in America). Fair-trade activists have in the past protested about the conditions in such places—and secured improvements to them.

Barbie is charged too with glamorising the white all-American ideal. She may have her African-American, Hispanic and Asian sisters, introduced by Mattel as early as the 1960s, but Barbie's hold on the imagination is as a white, blue-eyed blonde. Indeed, in Iran earlier this year, there was a crackdown on street-sellers trading in this emblem of decadent western culture. Certainly, Mattel's efforts to introduce an international flavour to its dolls border on pastiche. India Barbie, for instance, launched in the 1980s, came in a box stating that most Indians "eat with their fingers, not silverware".

The second lot of critics deplore Barbie for preaching the supremacy of appearance. Girls, they urge, should be out climbing trees and riding bikes, not plaiting Barbie's hair. Mattel thrives on girls' desire for endless new costumes for their dolls. For all the astronaut and army outfits, it is the silky stuff they love. Words like "elegant", "glamorous", "romantic" and "beautiful" pepper Mattel's marketing literature. Dressing and undressing, brushing and grooming, is what Barbie is all about.

More than this, Barbie has joined the gallery of rogues—alongside supermodels, women's magazines and the advertising industry—held responsible for teenagers' weight anxiety, and women's body complexes. The doll, says Mary Rogers, a professor of sociology at the University of West Florida and author of a book on Barbie, "belongs to that chorus of voices extolling not only slimness but also beauty and youthfulness as requisites of feminine success." Naomi Wolf, author of "The Beauty Myth", argues that Barbie shares the blame for the fact that girls are raised with a clear expectation of what a sexually successful woman should look like. The "official breast", Ms Wolf once said, was "Barbie's breast"—and shame on any girl who failed to possess or acquire one.

Indeed, Barbie's preposterous figure would almost cause a grown woman to topple over. Her origins hint at the reason for this. The doll was modelled by Ruth Handler, who founded Mattel along with her husband, Elliot, on a German toy for adult men called Lilli. Mrs Handler discovered this 11½-inch plastic doll while visiting Germany, and named her adapted version after her daughter, Barbara.

Naturally, there are periodic uprisings against Barbie. In the early 1990s, Mattel released a series of talking Barbies, one of which cheeped "Math class is tough". Feminists were irate. A New York group calling itself the Barbie Liberation Organisation swapped the voice boxes inside such dolls with those from GI Joe, a male doll made by Hasbro, a rival toymaker, and slipped them back on the toy-shop shelves. The re-educated Barbies bellowed muscular lines such as "Vengeance is mine!", while the boy dolls chirped "Let's go shopping!"

Other detractors turn to art. There is a whole world of anti-Barbies, devised for reasons of protest and humour. Among the exhibits that have gone on display are Exorcist Barbie, Drag-queen Barbie and Sweatshop Barbie—much to the exasperation of Mattel, which guards its creation's image with ferocity.

When Aqua, a one-time Danish pop group, released a song in 1997 called "Barbie Girl", for example, Mattel promptly took the band to court. Lines included "Life in plastic, it's fantastic" and "I'm a blonde bimbo girl, in a fantasy world." Earlier this year, a judge in San Francisco ruled against Mattel, upholding the group's right to freedom of expression. Nobody, added the judge, would have assumed that Mattel had authorised the lyrics: "Nor, upon hearing Janis Joplin croon 'Oh Lord, won't you buy me a Mercedes-Benz', would we suspect that she and the car maker had entered into a joint venture."

PINT-SIZED, PINK AND PLASTIC

But is Barbie as bad for girls as her critics imply? When Barbie first burst into the toy shops, just as the 1960s were breaking, the doll market consisted mostly of babies, designed for girls to cradle, rock and feed. Such toy babies had swept aside the finely dressed Victorian adult dolls, which were still popular into the early 20th century, and had dominated the doll market since.

Barbie, by contrast, was a go-getting, independent young woman. By creating a doll with adult features, insisted Mrs Handler, Barbie's creator, Mattel enabled girls to become "anything they want". A child of the liberated times, she was an astronaut in 1965, a surgeon by 1973, a presidential candidate in 1992. Barbie, claims Mattel, "has opened new dreams for girls that were not as accessible in the early 1960s." So Barbie empowers girls after all?

The research, such as it is, does not tell whether Barbie fans turn into brain surgeons, but it does seem to reject at least the idea that Barbie squashes the imagination. One study observed that four-year-old girls snatched and bickered more while playing with toy babies than they did with Barbie dolls. Barbie, this study concluded, promoted dramatic play and language development. A separate set of interviews with adults who played with Barbies in childhood concluded that what mattered to them in retrospect was "opportunity" and "human connection", not concern about looks.

Ultimately, it is impossible to prove whether Barbie is a more potent force than any other product of western consumer culture. Indeed, if anything, sociologists have spent more time examining the weird sub-cultures and behaviour that Barbie seems to have provoked than the role she has in gender stereotyping.

One such is the apparent ambiguity of her sexuality. With her skimpy zebra-striped swimsuit, Barbie caused a stir at her launch in the late-1950s. Many condemned the doll as sleazy and provocative. Yet Barbie and her boyfriend Ken, who joined her in 1961, remain curiously sexless. Barbie has no nipples; Ken's anatomy consists of a bump between his legs. There is, asserts the University of West Florida's indefatigable Ms Rogers, "the possibility that Barbie may not be heterosexual. Indeed, she may not even be a woman. Barbie may be a drag queen."

Barbie also seems to have turned into something of a gay icon. Barbie attracts a huge following among adults, for whom collecting is a serious business (a vintage Barbie can fetch nearly $10,000). Steven Dubin, a sociologist, claims that many of these male collectors are gay. He describes their two-step coming out: "First they disclose their sexuality. They later profess their love for Barbie." A study by an American psychiatrist into homosexuality suggested that all the boys he classified as "feminine" played with Barbie, according to their parents; for nearly a fifth of them, she was their favourite toy. Only two-fifths of the "masculine" boys were reported as playing with Barbie even occasionally.

Academics have even tried to theorise about another less-publicised, but apparently widespread, feature of the doll: Barbie mutilation. "Barbie torture", according to one researcher, "commonly involves tearing her head off, ripping her limbs out, and burning her hair off." One male interviewee in a study confessed that "When one day I was mad at my sister, I grabbed her Barbies and burnt all of their hair off and cut their bodies with sharp knives." Another remembered that "I used to have a beheaded Barbie in my fish tank with my dog's toy shark and my goldfish." Some suggest this could represent innate male violence towards women; others that it reflects female resistance to an impossible ideal. Others point out that the plastic dolls are just cheaply made.

FASHION QUEEN

Whatever sociologists say about the diminutive diva, however, Mattel's concerns lie primarily elsewhere. Last year, global sales of Barbie, which supplies nearly a third of Mattel's revenue, fell by 3%, to $1.6 billion, from a peak in 1997 of $1.8 billion. The main trouble is what is known in the industry as "age compression" or "KGOY": kids getting older younger. Girls now grow out of traditional play patterns, such as playing with dolls, earlier than they did in the past.

There was a time when even a 12-year-old might still be playing with Barbie. Today, the prime audience is three to five. Yet, as Rita Clifton, chief executive of Interbrand, puts it: "Barbie has a particular challenge: if she's something your little sister wants, you'll consider her too babyish."

The toy company's answer has been twofold. First, it is introducing more brand extensions—in effect, more Barbie paraphernalia to tempt the tinies. "Barbie in the Nutcracker", for instance, Mattel's first computer-animated video, generated $150m from sales, including associated products. For the second, "Barbie as Rapunzel", Mattel increased from eight to 14 the number of product tie-ins. A third, "Barbie in Swan Lake", is in the works. Mattel's plan, ghastly as it may be for defenceless parents, is to invade every corner of a little girl's life. "I like to think of the brand as the Calvin Klein for girls," says Mattel's Ms Fontanella.

The second strategy is to segment the market. Adapting Barbie for the older, savvier girls, however, is tricky, not least because of competition from cosmetics, music, fashion and—to a lesser extent than for boys—electronic games. Mattel knows full well that it can only stretch so far the Barbie brand beloved of little girls to their older sisters. One variation, launched recently, is "My Scene": this groups three dolls, Barbie being one, but has a hipper look. Mattel expects to develop perfume, cosmetics and music under this brand.

In many ways, it is fitting that Barbie is venturing out to the edgy fringes of the fashion industry. For the entire toy industry is driven by fashion these days. Toys are swept from the shop shelves one year, only to be forgotten by the next, discarded in the recesses of the toy box. Creating children's classics that endure, and turning them into profitable franchises, is the holy grail of the toy business. In that regard, Barbie has few peers. She could topple Spiderman and Action Man with one swing of her dainty handbag. Fashion may undo her rivals. Barbie just remakes fashion.

DISCUSSION QUESTIONS

Life in Plastic

1. The head of Mattel's girl division states "The brilliance of the brand is that she's a reflection of society as it changes." Explain.

2. What are some of the practical ways parents and teachers can help girls attain a more re-alistic and positive body image than through Barbie?

3. Sales of Barbie have been reported to be declining. What social and political factors might cause this to happen?

26 In Iran's Hair Salons, the Rebels Wield Scissors

Elaine Sciolino

Four hundred women from Khuzestan Province gathered in a darkened auditorium here to confront one of the most sensitive issues of the Islamic Republic: hair.

The women, all of them hairdressers, were invited by a hair products manufacturer for a one-day conference in the city's best hotel on how to better cut, bleach, dye, perm and straighten.

Fatimeh Farah, the company's representative, used tables laden with dozens of products and five wigs as visual aids. Her strawberry blond bangs blended nicely with the ivory- and peach-colored scarf on her head.

Ruler in hand, a microphone pinned to her well-cut pantsuit, she took a tough, no-nonsense approach. "So what happens if you want to turn hair blond and it turns green instead?" she asked, answering the question herself. "You have to use purple!"

When one participant suggested that blue would take out the green, Ms. Farah replied: "I want to beat the lady who said you should use blue to take out green. Blue is used only to take out orange!"

The audience applauded.

Ever since Iran's Islamic revolution in 1979, by far the most relentless battle for control of public space has been over the way women look.

The Koran says that "believing women" should "draw their veils over their bosoms and not display their beauty." They can go bareheaded in front of other women, their husbands, fathers, sons, nephews, servants, slaves and small children who "have no sense of the shame of sex."

Still, early in the revolution, women were allowed to go bareheaded. Since the Koranic verse was viewed as subject to interpretation, a law had to be passed requiring women to observe good "hejab" (literally "curtain") by concealing the shape of their bodies and covering their hair.

But that has not stopped women from wanting to look good. Just as hair care is a major industry in Iran, the question of showing or hiding hair is a national obsession. So a guerrilla struggle rages on between women who want to show their hair and conservative elements determined to preserve what they see as Islamic purity.

Hair, in short, has become a measure of resistance to the forced will of the Islamic Republic.

Some women have mastered a gravity-defying trick with bobby pins or clips of showing as much hair as possible without the scarf falling entirely off the head.

Ayatollah Ruhollah Khomeini, the father of Iran's revolution, called beauty salons "dens of corruption" and tried to ban them. He failed. Beauty salons remain safe havens for women, private spaces where men cannot enter. Hair care has become a major industry.

"Having beautiful hair is vital in this country, as vital as electricity or water," said a beautician who has operated a hair salon in Tehran for more than 30 years. "And forcing women to hide it is just part of a bigger power struggle against women. My scissors and combs are my weapons in fighting for the four strands of hair women can show."

There is a sign on the front window of her salon, but the curtains are drawn and the door is locked. Customers have to be buzzed in.

More than the hair on women's heads is at stake. Many Iranian women have facial and body hair, so many salons offer full body depilation and bleaching. One method involves a heavy string slung around the neck of the beautician that removes facial hair from its roots by a painful friction system. Some women wax hair not only from their legs but also from their arms.

Pain is part of the process. "Torture me but make me beautiful," is one saying to describe what women endure in the name of beauty. Another saying to describe the pain of having hair removed from the upper lip goes, "The pain is less than that of your mother-in-law's tongue."

A complicating factor is that in traditional and religious families, all women are forbidden from showing the hair on their heads, while unmarried women are also forbidden from removing facial hair. Preparing a bride for her wedding day can be a lengthy and expensive ritual involving a facial, massage, manicure, pedicure, hair styling as well as plucking and tweezing.

Even men are spending more time and money on their looks. A popular book for barbers displays 51 different combinations of mustaches and beards. More barbers are offering facials and eyebrow shaping along with a haircut.

In a society that encourages men to grow Islamically correct beards but keep their hair short, some men have grown their hair shoulder length or longer. (The Koran does not forbid men from showing their hair.) More men are seen these days wearing telltale bandages of rhinoplasty across their noses, and newspapers advertise hair implant services. In Kurdish areas, some men submit to the painful string technique instead of shaving.

Still, it is in the evolution of women's appearances that change is most evident. Ever since Mohammad Khatami, a midlevel cleric, was first elected president on a platform of reform six years ago, the Islamic Republic has tolerated a relaxation of the hair and dress code.

But the trend is complicated by the fact that enforcement of rules on head covering often involve humiliation more than religion. Both male and female lower-class morals police tend to single out middle-class or foreign women.

The hair issue also remains a political pillar of the Islamic structure. An editorial in the highly conservative daily Kayhan last month criticized the reformist Participation Front Party for "rolling out the red carpet" for a human rights delegation from the European Union. "Now they are saying 30 prisoners must be released," the editorial complained. "And tomorrow they will say we must remove the 'hejab.'"

In Iran's Hair Salons, the Rebels Wield Scissors

1. Hair is discussed as a politically important issue. Why do you think that beauty salons remained popular in Iran despite restrictions on women's public appearance?

2. The article reports that Iranian men are spending more time on their appearance. How do the issues differ for Iranian men and women?

27 Day-Care Dress Up Not Amusing to Boy's Dad

Lisa Respers

When Henry Holmes picked up his 6-year-old son from the day-care center at the Social Security Administration's headquarters last week, he found the boy laughing and playing. And wearing a dress.

Holmes did not think it was funny.

"He was playing in this area they call 'housekeeping,' and he was wearing a shiny, white dress that resembled one a little girl would wear in a wedding," Holmes said.

Now that incident has sparked a dispute over teaching methods at the Social Secur-A-Kiddie Child Care Center's kindergarten program.

An irate Holmes has taken his son, Gerald, out of the program. The center, meanwhile, insists that such dressing up is not unusual or harmful. And the state, asked to investigate, says that dressing up is an appropriate part of a child-care curriculum.

After last week's incident, Holmes, a single parent, complained to officials at the center, which occupies space in the Social Security's Operations Building but is not managed by the agency.

Linda Heisner, executive director of the Child Care Administration, said that "dress up" activities are considered an appropriate part of child-care curriculum.

Lindi Budd, executive director of the day-care center, said the facility provides clothing such as men's shirts and ties, dresses and high heels, and firefighters' and nurses' uniforms for children to use.

Holmes said he discussed the incident with his son and explained that other children might tease him.

To his dismay, he said, the boy responded, "I don't care."

Day-Care Dress Up Not Amusing to Boy's Dad

1. Why was the boy's interest in feminine dress a problem for the father and at the same time age-appropriate for the boy?

2. Give other examples of how young children explore social roles through appearance.

28 Turning Boys into Girls

Michelle Cottle

I love *Men's Health* magazine. There. I'm out of the closet, and I'm not ashamed. Sure, I know what some of you are thinking: What self-respecting '90s woman could embrace a publication that runs such enlightened articles as "Turn Your Good Girl Bad" and "How to Wake Up Next to a One-Night Stand"? Or maybe you'll smile and wink knowingly: What red-blooded hetero chick *wouldn't* love all those glossy photo spreads of buff young beefcake in various states of undress, ripped abs and glutes flexed so tightly you could bounce a check on them? Either way you've got the wrong idea. My affection for *Men's Health* is driven by pure gender politics—by the realization that this magazine, and a handful of others like it, are leveling the playing field in a way that Ms. can only dream of. With page after page of bulging biceps and Gillette jaws, robust hairlines and silken skin, *Men's Health* is peddling a standard of male beauty as unforgiving and unrealistic as the female version sold by those dewy-eyed pre-teen waifs draped across the covers of *Glamour* and *Elle*. And with a variety of helpful features on "Foods That Fight Fat," "Banish Your Potbelly," and "Save Your Hair (Before It's Too Late)," *Men's Health* is well on its way to making the male species as insane, insecure, and irrational about physical appearance as any *Cosmo* girl.

Don't you see, ladies? We've been going about this equality business all wrong. Instead of battling to get society fixated on something besides our breast size, we should have been fighting span-

dex with spandex. Bra burning was a nice gesture, but the greater justice is in convincing our male counterparts that the key to their happiness lies in a pair of made-for-him Super Shaper Briefs with the optional "fly front endowment pad" (as advertised in *Men's Journal*, $29.95 plus shipping and handling). Make the men as neurotic about the circumference of their waists and the whiteness of their smiles as the women, and at least the burden of vanity and self-loathing will be shared by all.

This is precisely what lads' mags like *Men's Health* are accomplishing. The rugged John-Wayne days when men scrubbed their faces with deodorant soap and viewed gray hair and wrinkles as a badge of honor are fading. Last year, international market analyst Euromonitor placed the U. S. men's toiletries market—hair color, skin moisturizer, tooth whiteners, etc.—at $3.5 billion. According to a survey conducted by DYG researchers for *Men's Health* in November 1996, approximately 20 percent of American men get manicures or pedicures, 18 percent use skin treatments such as masks or mud packs, and 10 percent enjoy professional facials. That same month, *Psychology Today* reported that a poll by Roper Starch Worldwide showed that "6 percent of men nationwide actually use such traditionally female products as bronzers and foundation to create the illusion of a youthful appearance."

What men are putting on their bodies, however, is nothing compared to what they're doing *to* their bodies: While in the 1980s only an estimated one in 10 plastic surgery patients were men, as of 1996, that ratio had shrunk to one in five. The American Academy of Cosmetic Surgery estimates that nationwide more than 690,000 men had cosmetic procedures performed in '96, the most recent year for which figures are available. And we're not just talking "hair restoration" here, though such procedures do command the lion's share of the male market. We're also seeing an increasing number of men shelling out mucho dinero for face peels, liposuction, collagen injections, eyelid lifts, chin tucks, and, of course, the real man's answer to breast implants: penile enlargements (now available to increase both length and diameter).

Granted, *Men's Health* and its journalistic cousins (*Men's Journal, Details, GQ*, etc.) cannot take all the credit for this breakthrough in gender parity. The fashion and glamour industries have perfected the art of creating consumer "needs," and with the women's market pretty much saturated, men have become the obvious target for the purveyors of everything from lip balm to lycra. Meanwhile, advances in medical science have made cosmetic surgery a quicker, cleaner option for busy executives (just as the tight fiscal leash of managed care is driving more and more doctors toward this cash-based specialty). Don't have several weeks to recover from a full-blown facelift? No problem. For a few hundred bucks you can get a microdermabrasion face peel on your lunch hour.

Then there are the underlying social factors. With women growing ever more financially independent, aspiring suitors are discovering that they must bring more to the table than a well-endowed wallet if they expect to win (and keep) the fair maiden. Nor should we overlook the increased market power of the gay population—in general a more image-conscious lot than straight guys. But perhaps most significant is the ongoing, ungraceful descent into middle age by legions of narcis-sistic baby boomers. Gone are the days when the elder statesmen of this demographic bulge could see themselves in the relatively youthful faces of those insipid yuppies on "Thirtysomething." Increasingly, boomers are finding they have more in common with the *parents* of today's TV, movie, and sports stars. Everywhere they turn some upstart Gen Xer is flaunting his youthful vitality, threatening boomer dominance on both the social and professional fronts. (Don't think even Hollywood didn't shudder when the Oscar for best original screenplay this year went to a couple of guys barely old enough to shave.) With whippersnappers looking to steal everything from their jobs to their women, post-pubescent men have at long last discovered the terror of losing their springtime radiance.

Whatever combo of factors is feeding the frenzy of male vanity, magazines such as *Men's Health* provide the ideal meeting place for men's insecurities and marketers' greed. Like its more established female counterparts, *Men's Health* is an affordable, efficient delivery vehicle for the message that physical imperfection, age, and an underdeveloped fashion sense are potentially crippling disabilities. And as with women's mags, this cycle of insanity is self-perpetuating: The more men obsess about growing old or unattractive, the more marketers will exploit and expand that fear; the more marketers bombard men with messages about the need to be beautiful, the more they will obsess. Younger and younger men will be sucked into the vortex of self-doubt. Since 1990, *Men's Health* has seen its paid circulation rise from 250,000 to more than 1.5 million; the magazine estimates that half of its 5.3 million readers are under age 35 and 46 percent are married. And while most major magazines have suffered sluggish growth or even a decline in circulation in recent years, during the first half of 1997 *Men's Health* saw its paid circulation increase 14 percent over its '96 figures. (Likewise, its smaller, more outdoorsy relative, Wenner Media's *Men's Journal*, enjoyed an even bigger jump of 26.5 percent.) At this rate, one day soon, that farcical TV commercial featuring men hanging out in bars, whining about having inherited their mothers' thighs will be a reality. Now *that's* progress.

VANITY, THY NAME IS MAN

Everyone wants to be considered attractive and desirable. And most of us are aware that, no matter how guilty and shallow we feel about it, there are certain broad cultural norms that define attractive. Not surprisingly, both men's and women's magazines have argued that, far from playing on human insecurities, they are merely helping readers be all that they can be—a kind of training camp for the image impaired. In recent years, such publications have embraced the tenets of "evolutionary biology," which argue that, no matter how often we're told that beauty is only skin deep, men and women are hardwired to prefer the Jack Kennedys and Sharon Stones to the Rodney Dangerfields and Janet Renos. Continuation of the species demands that specimens with shiny coats, bright eyes, even features, and other visible signs of ruddy good health and fertility automatically kick-start our most basic instinct. Of course, the glamour mags' editors have yet to explain why, in evolutionary terms, we would ever desire adult women to stand 5'10" and weigh 100 pounds. Stories abound of women starving themselves to the point that their bodies shut down and they stop menstruating—hardly conducive to reproduction—yet Kate Moss remains the dish du jour and millions of Moss wannabes still struggle to subsist on a diet of Dexatrim and Perrier.

Similarly, despite its title, *Men's Health* is hawking far more than general fitness or a healthful lifestyle. For every half page of advice on how to cut your stress level, there are a dozen pages on how to build your biceps. For every update on the dangers of cholesterol, there are multiple warnings on the horrors of flabby abs. Now, without question, gorging on Cheetos and Budweiser while your rump takes root on the sofa is no way to treat your body if you plan on living past 50. But chugging protein drinks, agonizing over fat grams, and counting the minutes until your next Stairmaster session is equally unbalanced. The line between taking pride in one's physical appearance and being obsessed by it is a fine one—and one that disappeared for many women long ago.

Now with the lads' mags taking men in that direction as well, in many cases it's almost impossible to tell whether you're reading a copy of *Men's Health* or of *Mademoiselle*: "April 8. To commemorate Buddha's birthday, hit a Japanese restaurant. Stick to low-fat selections. Choose foods described as *yakimono* which means grilled," advised the monthly "to do list" in the April *Men's Health*. (Why readers should go Japanese in honor of the most famous religious leader in *India's* history remains unclear.) The January/February list was equally thought provoking: "January 28. It's Chinese New Year, so make a resolution to custom-order your next takeout. Ask that they substitute wonton soup broth for oil. Try the soba noodles instead of plain noodles. They're richer in nutrients and contain much less fat." The issue also featured a "Total Body Workout Poster" and one of those handy little "substitution" charts (loathed by women everywhere), showing men how to slash their calorie intake by making a few minor dietary substitutions: mustard for mayo, popcorn for peanuts, seltzer water for soda, pretzels for potato chips....

As in women's magazines, fast results with minimum inconvenience is a central theme. Among *Men's Health*'s March highlights were a guide to "Bigger Biceps in 2 Weeks," and "20 Fast Fixes" for a bad diet; April offered "A Better Body in Half the Time," along with a colorful four-page spread on "50 Snacks That Won't Make You Fat." And you can forget carrot sticks—this think-thin eating guide celebrated the wonders of Reduced Fat Cheez-its, Munch 'Ems, Fiddle Faddle, Oreos, Teddy Grahams, Milky Ways, Bugles, Starburst Fruit Twists, and Klondike's Fat Free Big Bear Ice Cream Sandwiches. Better nutrition is not the primary issue. A better butt is. To this end, also found in the pages of *Men's Health* is the occasional, tasteful ad for liposuction—just in case nature doesn't cooperate.

But a blueprint to rock-hard buns is only part of what makes *Men's Health* the preeminent "men's lifestyle" magazine. Nice teeth, nice skin, nice hair, and a red-hot wardrobe are now required to round out the ultimate alpha male package, and *Men's Health* is there to help on all fronts. In recent months it has run articles on how to select, among other items, the perfect necktie and belt, the hippest wallet, the chicest running gear, the best "hair-thickening" shampoo, and the cutest golfing apparel. It has also offered advice on how to retard baldness, how to keep your footwear looking sharp, how to achieve different "looks" with a patterned blazer, even how to keep your lips from chapping at the dentist's office: "[B]efore you start all that 'rinse and spit' business, apply some moisturizer to your face and some lip balm to your lips. Your face and lips won't have that stretched-out dry feeling…Plus, you'll look positively radiant!"

While a desire to look good for their hygienists may be enough to spur some men to heed the magazine's advice (and keep 'em coming back for more), fear and insecurity about the alternatives are generally more effective motivators. For those who don't get with the *Men's Health* program, there must be the threat of ridicule. By far the least subtle example of this is the free subscriptions for "guys who need our help" periodically announced in the front section of the magazine. April's dubious honoree was actor Christopher Walken:

> Chris, we love the way you've perfected that psycho persona. But now you're taking your role in "Things to do in Denver When You're Dead" way too seriously with that ghostly pale face, the "where's the funeral?" black clothes, and a haircut that looks like the work of a hasty undertaker….Dab on a little Murad Murasun Self-Tanner ($21)…For those creases in your face, try Ortho Dermatologicals' Renova, a prescription antiwrinkle cream that contains tretinoin, a form of vitamin A. Then, find a barber.

Or how about the March "winner," basketball coach Bobby Knight: "Bob, your trademark red sweater is just a billboard for your potbelly. A darker solid color would make you look slimmer. Also, see 'The Tale of Two Bellies' in our February 1998 issue, and try to drop a few pounds. Then the next time you throw a sideline tantrum, at least people won't say, 'look at the crazy *fat* man.'"

Just as intense as the obsession with appearance that men's (and women's) magazines breed are the sexual neuroses they feed. And if one of the ostensible goals of women's mags is to help women drive men wild, what is the obvious corollary objective for men's magazines? To get guys laid—well and often. As if men needed any encouragement to fixate on the subject, *Men's Health* is chock full of helpful "how-tos" such as, "Have Great Sex Every Day Until You Die" and "What I Learned From My Sex Coach," as well as more cursory explorations of why men with larger testicles have more sex ("Why Big Boys Don't Cry"), how to maintain orgasm intensity as you age ("Be one of the geysers"), and how to achieve stronger erections by eating certain foods ("Bean counters make better lovers"). And for those having trouble even getting to the starting line, last month's issue offered readers a chance to "Win free love lessons."

THE HIGH PRICE OF PERFECTION

Having elevated men's physical and sexual insecurities to the level of grand paranoia, lads' mags can then get down to what really matters: moving merchandise. On the cover of *Men's Health* each month, in small type just above the magazine's title, appears the phrase "Tons of useful stuff." Thumbing through an issue or two, however, one quickly realizes that a more accurate description would read: "Tons of expensive stuff." They're all there: Ralph Lauren, Tommy Hilfiger, Paul Mitchell, Calvin Klein, Clinique, Armani, Versace, Burberrys, Nautica, Nike, Omega, Rogaine, The Better Sex Video Series….The magazine even has those annoying little perfume strips guaranteed to make your nose run and to alienate everyone within a five-mile radius of you.

Masters of psychology, marketers wheel out their sexiest pitches and hottest male models to tempt/intimidate the readership of *Men's Health*. Not since the last casting call for "Baywatch" has a more impressive display of firm, tanned, young flesh appeared in one spot. And just like in women's magazines, the articles themselves are designed to sell stuff. All those helpful tips on choosing blazers, ties, and belts come complete with info on the who, where, and how much. The strategy is brilliant: Make men understand exactly how far short of the ideal they fall, and they too become vulnerable to the lure of high-priced underwear, cologne, running shoes, workout gear, hair dye, hair strengthener, skin softener, body-fat monitors, suits, boots, energy bars, and sex aids. As Mark Jannot, the grooming and health editor for *Men's Journal,* told "Today" show host Matt Lauer in January, "This is a huge, booming market. I mean, the marketers have found a group of people that are ripe for the picking. Men are finally learning that aging is a disease." Considering how effectively *Men's Health* fosters this belief, it's hardly surprising that the magazine has seen its ad pages grow 510 percent since 1991 and has made it onto *Ad-week*'s 10 Hottest Magazines list three of the last five years.

To make all this "girly" image obsession palatable to their audience, lads' mags employ all their creative energies to transform appearance issues into "a guy thing." *Men's Health* tries to cultivate a joking, macho tone throughout ("Eat Like Brando and Look Like Rambo" or "Is my tally-whacker shrinking?") and tosses in a handful of Y-chromosome teasers such as "How to Stay Out of Jail," "How to Clean Your Whole Apartment in One Hour or Less," and my personal favorite, "Let's Play Squash," an illustrated guide to identifying the bug-splat patterns on your windshield. Instead of a regular advice columnist, which would smack too much of chicks' magazines, *Men's Health* recently introduced "Jimmy the Bartender," a monthly column on "women, sex, and other stuff that screws up men's lives."

It appears that, no matter how much clarifying lotion and hair gel you're trying to sell them, men must never suspect that you think they share women's insecurities. If you want a man to buy wrinkle cream, marketers have learned, you better pitch it as part of a comfortingly macho shaving regimen. Aramis, for example, assures men that its popular Lift Off! Moisture Formula with alpha hydroxy will help cut their shave time by one-third. "The biggest challenge for products started for women is how to transfer them to men," explained George Schaeffer, the president of OPI cosmetics, in the November issue of *Soap-Cosmetics-Chemical Specialties.* Schaeffer's Los Angeles-based company is the maker of Matte Nail Envy,

an unobtrusive nail polish that's proved a hit with men. And for the more adventuresome shopper, last year Hard Candy cosmetics introduced a line of men's nail enamel, called Candy Man, that targets guys with such studly colors as Gigolo (metallic black) and Testosterone (gunmetal silver).

On a larger scale, positioning a makeover or trip to the liposuction clinic as a smart career move seems to help men rationalize their image obsession. "Whatever a man's cosmetic shortcoming, it's apt to be a career liability," noted Alan Farnham in a September 1996 issue of *Fortune.* "The business world is prejudiced against the ugly." Or how about *Forbes'* sad attempt to differentiate between male and female vanity in its Dec. 1 piece on cosmetic surgery: "Plastic surgery is more of a cosmetic thing for women. They have a thing about aging. For men it's an investment that pays a pretty good dividend." Whatever you say, guys.

The irony is rich and bittersweet. Gender equity is at last headed our way—not in the form of women being less obsessed with looking like Calvin Klein models, but of men becoming hysterical over the first signs of crows feet. Gradually, guys are no longer pumping up and primping simply to get babes, but because they feel it's something everyone expects them to do. Women, after all, do not spend $400 on Dolce & Gabbana sandals to impress their boyfriends, most of whom don't know Dolce & Gabbana from Beavis & Butthead (yet). They buy them to impress other women—and because that's what society says they should want to do. Most guys haven't yet achieved this level of insanity, but with grown men catcalling the skin tone and wardrobe of other grown men (Christopher Alien, Bobby Knight) for a readership of still more grown men, can the gender's complete surrender to the vanity industry be far behind?

The ad for *Men's Health's* web site says it all: "Don't click here unless you want to look a decade younger…lose that beer belly…be a better lover…and more! *Men's Health* Online: The Internet Site For Regular Guys." Of course, between the magazine's covers there's not a "regular guy" to be found, save for writers or editors— usually taken from a respectable distance. The moist young bucks in the Gap jeans ads and the electric-eyed Armani models have exactly as much in common with the average American man as Tyra Banks does with the average American woman. Which would be fine, if everyone seemed to understand this distinction. Until they do, however, I guess my consolation will have to be the image of thousands of once-proud men, having long scorned women's insecurities, lining up for their laser peels and trying to squeeze their middle-aged asses into a snug set of Super Shaper Briefs—with the optional fly front endowment pad, naturally.

DISCUSSION QUESTIONS

Turning Boys into Girls

1. As women grow more financially independent, what effect do you feel this has on how men perceive their own appearance?

2. What are some present-day social factors that might make men more insecure about their appearance than in the past?

29 Northampton Confronts a Crime, Cruelty

Jordana Hart

With his earring and black eyeliner, Matthew Santoni was a popular target for boys at Smith Vocational and Agricultural High School.

They would surround him, students recall, and spew "homo," "faggot," and "queer" at him, their words striking with rapier intensity.

Two weeks ago, Santoni, 15, apparently snapped. He allegedly stabbed to death a classmate, Jeffrey LaMothe, 16, amid the trendy boutiques and restaurants of downtown Northampton. LaMothe, according to many, was a ringleader of those who made Santoni's life miserable with their teasing.

While hundreds of teenagers came from schools all over the region to LaMothe's wake and funeral in Easthampton, described as the greatest convergence of young mourners ever at Sacred Heart Church, many other people focused on Santoni: Had teasing been the root of his rage?

LaMothe's murder cut to the core of this counter-culture college town. The affluent center of Massachusetts farm country, Northampton is also know for its open embrace of gay couples, many of whom have moved here from around the country to open businesses and start families.

"We think of Northampton as very progressive, so to hear that this kind of harassment is going on in our school system and that it might have led to such violence is very hard to accept," said Rebecca Lockwood, who runs youth programs, including one for gay and lesbian teens, at the Franklin Community Action Corporation in Greenfield, north of here.

"There is no excuse for that level of violence, no matter how persecuted you feel," Lockwood added. "But I think it gets really intense around sexual orientation, especially for young men. To be perceived as gay contradicts what young men are taught about being masculine."

Santoni never said he was gay, and he apparently was teased simply for his style of dress.

Now, amid increasing reports of school shootings and other acts of violence among young people across the country, specialists are paying more attention to youth culture and how harshly it treats those youngsters who are somehow different. Sexual orientation is but one subject of teasing: Looks, weight, family background, ethnicity, and race all register as fodder for teasers.

"The psychological damage of taunting, name-calling, exclusion, and other ways kids victimize kids is very extensive," said Ervin Taub, a professor of psychology at the University of Massachusetts at Amherst, who studies aggression among teenagers. "It is a significant issue, and one just beginning to be recognized."

Taub warned that parents and teachers must recognize when it is time to step in. "Adult passivity communicates things to kids. Perpetrators tend to interpret this" as tacit approval, he said.

On the sprawling campus of "the Voke," with its squat, red brick buildings set alongside wide-open fields, students said teasing is a familiar part of school life. Santoni, they said, looked like he was gay. And in the corrosive culture of high-school teasing, any distinguishing characteristics are fuel for taunts.

"It's all the time," said junior Becky Ely, 17, surprisingly stoic as she described a year of torment at the vocational school. "The boys call me slut, bitch. They call me a 10-timer, because they say I go with 10 guys at a time. I put up with it because I have no choice. The teachers say it's because the boys think I'm pretty."

Santoni's lawyer, Alan Black, said the boy, from nearby Florence, pleaded not guilty in Northampton District Court May 26 to a charge of murder. He is being held without bail at Plymouth County House of Correction and will be arraigned in Hampshire County Superior Court tomorrow.

Sources said Santoni had complained to administrators about the harassment, and that LaMothe was suspended from school. Ely said she, too, recently complained about the teasing to school officials, who have declined comment on either case.

The jabs at students like Ely and Santoni are hardly unique to this school of 516 students. Taunting and teasing have long been as basic to American high school culture as proms, geeks and jocks, specialists say. Just ask the overweight teenager in thick glasses. Or the girl who everyone says went all the way on a first date. Or the guy with an earring called "homo" or "faggot."

"Teasing happens a lot," said Joseph Laboute, a ninth-grader at Smith Vocational. "If you know them, you know how much they can take. But it is different if it's someone you don't know."

Smith Vocational itself is in a curious situation, existing as it does in what may well be one of the nation's most socially tolerant towns. Principal Veronica Carroll says the school has students who come from 29 towns—ranging from Northampton and Amherst to tiny farm towns like Goshen and Hatfield.

"I think of the school as a safe haven, but it is a lot of work to make it safe," said Carroll, who started teaching there in 1976. "There is less tolerance among kids in general."

Carroll declined to speak about the stabbing and what may have led to it. Since LaMothe's murder, she said, teachers have been meeting with students in small groups to talk about grieving and tolerance. "We have lost two students," she said. "There are rumors about taunting and about what kids were saying."

Carroll also said teachers have suggested starting a Gay/Straight Alliance, similar to those at 140 other Massachusetts high schools.

Lockwood, the youth-center counselor, said gay youngsters at meetings in Greenfield and across the state talk constantly about being harassed, and what it feels like to be ignored, or hear students toss around anti-gay invectives.

"I sat alone in French class because no one would sit next to me," said Emily DeLisle, a 10th-grader at Bromfield High School in Harvard, who came out to her parents and schoolfriends a year ago. "Kids told new students to stay away from me because there were rumors that I was gay. It never bothered me not to fit in with the popular kids, but I want friends and I want people to like me."

Meanwhile, Northampton residents continue to struggle with the realization that their city, known for its acceptance, is not immune to acts of taunting and violence.

Last week, hundreds of people gathered on the steps of Northampton City Hall for a rally against hate crimes, propelled by a May 23 attack by four young men on two others perceived to be a couple. Since that attack, which was reported to police, two others have come to light, said the Rev. Victoria Safford of the Unitarian Society, who has presided over same-sex marriages.

Teaching tolerance "is difficult, painful and dangerous, but it must be done," Safford said. "It is not that we have bad, homophobic children. We have frightened adults who have not done their own homework, and until they are willing to face that, we will continue raising violent, and homophobic children."

DISCUSSION QUESTIONS

Northampton Confronts a Crime, Cruelty

1. Although not specifically stated in the article, what do you think was the nature of the young man's appearance that caused him to be labeled gay? How is this issue related to homophobia?

2. Why is it dangerous to stereotype someone's sexual preference based on their appearance?

30 Drag Queens, Transvestites, Transsexuals: Stepping across the Accepted Boundaries of Gender

Jane E. Hegland
South Dakota State University

A common thread which seems to run through virtually all known societies is that females and males have been visually differentiated by gender-appropriate dress: males in masculine dress and females in feminine dress. The socialization process toward gender-appropriate behavior and appearance begins at birth. Eicher and Roach-Higgins (1992) indicate that at the birth of a child:

...adult caretakers (kin or surrogate kin who come to the aid of the child) act as purveyors of culture by providing gender-symbolic dress that encourages others to attribute masculine or feminine gender and to act on the basis of these attributions when interacting with the child. (p. 17)

Concepts of femininity and masculinity are historically and culturally defined, and are revealed through such observable features as clothing, accessories to the clothing, accessories to the body, hairstyle, facial features, body shape, mannerisms, voice, and gestures.

Rarely do we pause to wonder if an individual is male or female. Rather, perception is immediate and simple because, although we have no direct

---

Original for this text.

knowledge of a person's genital sex, we know what a woman or man is *supposed* to look like. In other words, we do not require locker-room proof as to whether a person is male or female. In short, dress and appearance are key factors in social communication. An initial nonverbal encounter with an individual reveals numerous personality characteristics. Similarly, dress can indicate occupation, religious affiliation, social status, and gender.

This article focuses on what happens when culturally prescribed and proscribed gender norms—manifested by dress and appearance—are challenged through social interaction. What occurs when individuals step across the social boundaries of gender-appropriate dress and appearance by cross-dressing? What if we cannot immediately establish the gender of an individual? What if something doesn't seem quite right? How does the public respond when confronted with an incongruous or unfamiliar image?

For a number of reasons, including the emancipation of women, practicality in the workplace, personal safety, physical comfort, and trends in fashions, women in cosmopolitan[1] societies have adopted and adapted almost every characteristic of "masculine" dress. Because of this, it has often been suggested that there are no female cross-dressers in cosmopolitan societies because women can easily wear "men's" clothing. While this does—at least superficially—seem plausible as an explanation, it is bound by time and place. It is only in the recent past that women have been allowed to don masculine forms of dress. Although there are historical accounts of women who dressed as men, and even convinced others they were men, this was either to facilitate their participation in activities open only to men, such as being a soldier or a sailor; to escape from a situation safely—disguised as a man, they were less apt to be approached or sexually harassed; or to connote sexual orientation, as numbers of homosexual women have traditionally rejected the feminine image and worn masculine dress (Dekker & van de Pol, 1989; Devor, 1989; Maitland, 1986; Wheelwright, 1989).

The adoption and adaptation of men's dress by women is acceptable, so long as women do not attempt to disguise their biological sex.[2] But the reverse has not held true. Men who adopt *any*

feminine forms of dress are viewed—at best—as humorous or peculiar, and—at worst—as an abomination that should be locked up. Generally, males who cross-dress will experience immediate stigmatization if they are exposed, as their discrediting attribute is their incongruous appearance. Evans and Thornton (1989) have attached the concept of stigma to the act of cross-dressing:

> There is less threat in women's cross-dressing; it is a sign of aspiration, moving up the patriarchal hierarchy. The powerful taboo is against male [cross-dressing], partly because of entrenched homophobia, partly because it is a step down the social ladder. (p. 44)

In this article, I examine the visual presentations of males within American and European cultures[3] who don feminine forms of dress. Three types of male-to-female cross-dressers considered are the transsexual, the transvestite, and the drag queen.[4] The act of cross-dressing challenges the accepted boundaries of gender. Existing literature indicates that various types of cross-dressers cross-dress for different reasons (Ackroyd, 1979; Allen, 1989; Benjamin, 1953, 1966; Brierley, 1979; Bullough & Bullough, 1993; Cauldwell, 1956; Dekker & van de Pol, 1989; Docter, 1988; Feinbloom, 1976; Garber, 1992; Gilbert, 1926; Kirk & Heath, 1984; Lynn, n.d.; Newton, 1972; Prince, 1981; Raynor, 1966; Rudd, 1990; Stevens, 1990; Woodhouse, 1989). I have pushed the concept further, and propose that different *reasons* for cross-dressing result in significantly different visual presentations, which ultimately result in varying responses from the cross-dressers' audience.

DEFINING CROSS-DRESSING: DEVELOPING A VISUAL TYPOLOGY

I define *cross-dressing* as those occasions when a male puts on feminine dress or a female adopts masculine dress for whatever purpose or to whatever effect. However, beyond the visual transformation from male to female or female to male through body modifications and body supplements, there is also a change in the individual's

FIGURE 5.4 *A cross-dresser.*

body movements, posture, gestures, facial expressions, eye contact, and often vocal intonation.

Aside from the obvious growth of facial and body hair, there are a number of other visual cues which could expose the biological sex of the most convincing cross-dresser. Foot and hand size tend to be proportionally larger on males than on females. Also, men typically have a stronger, squarer jaw line than women. Makeup can disguise this feature to some extent, but it is difficult to completely hide. The most conspicuous feature cross-dressed males have to contend with is their prominent Adam's apple. If left uncovered, it will certainly reveal their biological sex.[5]

The phenomenon of cross-dressing can be divided into three general categories: the transsexual, the transvestite, and the drag queen (Lynn, n.d.). Within each category, the male cross-dresser modifies and supplements his biological package to create *what* he conceives of as a feminine image. Kirk and Heath (1984) concluded from their pictorial study of men who cross-dress that the dividing lines are often blurred, and that self-definition of *what* one is can change over time. By suggesting that an individual's motivations for cross-dressing can change with time, Kirk and Heath have alluded to a range of reasons for cross-dressing. Although the existing literature has acknowledged the three types of male cross-dressers, the possibility that each type creates a distinct feminine image has not been addressed.

In the next section of this paper, the visual differences between each of the three types of cross-dressers are considered. First, I define the parameters of each type. Second, I include a detailed description of a prototype of the cross-dresser in order to provide a sense of the visual image created by each type. Third, I discuss how the cross-dresser alters his appearance.[6] Finally, I address the possible audience responses to each type's transformed appearance.

The Transsexual

The transsexual has a complete psychological identification with one sex, but the reproductive organs of the other. The male transsexual conceives of himself as both female and feminine. In essence, he feels "trapped" in the wrong body. The adoption of feminine dress seems quite natural for this individual.

There are two general types of transsexuals: preoperative and postoperative. It is within the preoperative stage that I consider the transsexual to be a cross-dresser. If the male transsexual is physically changed into a biological female, *she* dresses in the manner appropriate to her newly acquired sex. Consequently, my definition of a cross-dresser is no longer applicable.

Transsexuals' visual presentations are as varied as the images of biological females. They exist in all shapes and sizes. They can be tall or short, thin or heavy; they have pronounced or nondescript facial features; they wear their hair long or short; they wear masculine or feminine styles of dress.

In the process of becoming female in appearance, the transsexual extensively modifies his body and tends to be meticulous about his transformed appearance, as he is convincing others of his "true" gender identity. All telltale body hair is removed, leaving the hair on his head, which is often grown into a feminine hairstyle.

The transsexual may also choose to modify his appearance through hormone treatments, which tend to stunt the growth of body hair and increase the growth of hair on the head. These treatments also increase breast size and expand hip width, making the transsexual's silhouette even more feminine. If hormone treatments are not taken, the transsexual will likely create the illusion of breasts and hips through padding. Makeup is expertly applied. Fingernails and toenails are apt to be buffed and polished. Ears are often pierced and adorned with earrings, and other jewelry—such as necklaces, bracelets, and finger rings—may decorate the body.

As for supplements to the body, the range of appearances of transsexuals is as great as the range of the appearances of biological females. However, in contrast to the transvestite and the drag queen, the transsexual will often wear trousers and other more casual forms of dress. The transsexual is typically not exhibitionistic in nature, and will tend to wear whatever is considered to be fashionable among women. Great care is taken to create as convincing an image as possible.

If every aspect of the transsexual's dress is carefully attended to, *she* will convince her audience that she is indeed female. Inconcealable characteristics, such as foot size or a prominent Adam's apple, will likely be overlooked. Therefore, the transsexual's presentation will be positively reviewed by her audience. In other words, the public will probably assume the transsexual is a biological female. However, if the transsexual is "read"—or found out—she will endure a stigmatized status because her presentation will have been challenged.

Because the male transsexual believes he is female in every way—except for the annoying fact that he was born with the wrong genitalia—it is essential for him to create an appearance that is unquestionably female. Consequently, in the event that the transsexual's presentation is challenged, the individual will make the appropriate adjustments to be certain it does not happen again.

The Transvestite

The population of transvestites is quite diverse, and therefore not easily categorized. Most male transvestites are heterosexual, married with children, and cross-dressing tends to be linked with sexual activity (Ackroyd, 1979; Allen, 1989; Bullough & Bullough, 1993; Docter, 1988; Prince, 1981; Woodhouse, 1989). However, a transvestite may be homosexual or bisexual, single or divorced, an occasional or frequent cross-dresser, and the activity may not be connected to sexual arousal. Further, a transvestite's cross-dressing activities might remain invisible to the public, and be limited to the wearing of women's undergarments under men's clothing.

As a group, male transvestites differ from male transsexuals in that they are *always* aware of their male identity, and their "maleness" plays a major role in their cross-dressing activities. The male transvestite sees himself as male and masculine when in his gender-appropriate dress, and as very feminine in feminine dress. But he never forgets—and never allows his audience to forget—he is a man in feminine dress, although he does use a feminine name while cross-dressed (Ackroyd, 1979; Baker, 1968; Bullough & Bullough, 1993; Woodhouse, 1989).

Exhibitionism is a crucial factor of transvestism. Baker (1968) reinforces this point with the following statement: "All the transvestites I have spoken to...have, either blatantly or covertly, revealed a strong strain of exhibitionism. In its simplest form it is a need to go out in the street dressed as a woman" (p. 36). Yet, because of possible detrimental repercussions, transvestites generally sequester their cross-dressing activities to a private environment. Some share their activities with their wives, while others keep it to themselves. In her pictorial study of cross-dressers, Allen (1989) includes short biographies of individuals who cross-dress. One interview revealed that a banker from Oklahoma keeps a trailer for his feminine wardrobe. When he feels the urge, he visits this trailer and transforms himself into Samantha, keeping the secret from his wife.

According to Allen (1989), Stevens (1990), and Woodhouse (1989), most transvestites suffer immense anxiety from their condition, which is twofold and cyclical. First, they feel guilty when they cross-dress. Then, they experience uneasiness and depression when they try to suppress their needs or are unable to cross-dress. Many cases can be likened to a binge-and-purge eating disorder, where the transvestite goes through a period of intense cross-dressing, followed by a time period when they feel guilty and quit—often performing a ritualistic destruction of the wardrobe only to return to the shops within a few weeks to begin the cycle again.

Ackroyd (1979) divided transvestism into two broad categories: fetishistic transvestism and feminine passing. Fetishistic transvestites cross-dress in order to experience sexual arousal and generally have no interest in entering the public domain. Rather, their needs are satisfied by cross-dressing in secret, as is the case with those who limit their cross-dressing to the adoption of feminine undergarments. Because of the relative invisibility of this type of cross-dressing practice, it will be excluded from further discussion in this paper.

Transvestites who fall into the category of feminine passing move beyond the private fetishistic stage. They cease to be sexually excited by the act of cross-dressing, but instead cross-dress for exhibitionistic purposes. They dress as women for long periods of time, appear in public as such, and take seriously their aspirations of femininity. They want to prove how beautiful and desirable they can be as a woman, and their primary aim is to deceive other men. Some only want to be recognized as women by women. Others dress in feminine attire, but do not intend to pass as women. They make a genuine attempt to behave as well as dress like women. However, unlike the transsexual, the transvestite's male identity remains firmly intact.

The transvestite tends to create a feminine image that could be characterized as "the woman next door" who is perhaps a bit old-fashioned in her style: a few curls, perhaps a string of pearls, a tweed skirt, sensible shoes, and stockings. He will usually wear conservative styles of women's clothing—concealing body curvatures, or lack thereof. The makeup may not be entirely perfect; the legs, face, and arms not properly shaved; the voice too low; the silhouette may not be convincing; the walk not quite right. Yet, another transvestite may look—in most respects—like a biological female. Although well-disguised, the visual clues to the individual's biological sex are available to the keen viewer. The transvestite will often slip up—accidentally or purposely. Because of their exhibitionistic nature, transvestites tend to enjoy the shock value of their incongruous appearance.

Transvestites will often create a feminine image that is "drab" and "old-fashioned" by contemporary standards (Ackroyd, 1979; Woodhouse, 1989). There are a few possible explanations for this inclination. First, perhaps the transvestite adopts the image of femininity derived from his earliest memories of his mother or another female relative. Or, by avoiding extravagances, the use of nondescript dress may allow the transvestite to pass unnoticed in public. Another possible explanation could be that the dress relates to the age of the transvestite. Younger transvestites may soon be dressing in the manner of contemporary women. Although this is a valid explanation, it seems doubtful, as it is difficult to express femininity and an exhibitionistic nature while in the casual dress of the modern, and often androgynous, woman. Transvestites tend to be attracted to the polarization of masculine and feminine roles *and* appearance characteristics.

All of this highlights the complexities of transvestism, along with the difficulties of visual definition. Yet, some generalizations can be made. Although the transformation of transvestites from male to female may range from extremely convincing to not believable, as a rule, they will adhere to the prevailing gender and social codes. Further, they attempt to create at least the illusion of femininity, whether or not they pass as women in public.

Because there is such a broad range of presentations created by transvestites, there is also an array of perceptions by their audience. While some transvestites will never be "read"—others will endure exposure every time they venture out to public places. Those transvestites who pass as women experience a positive response to their presentation by their audience, while those who are read are challenged and stigmatized. If their goal is to pass, transvestites will strive to create a more believable image. However, for some transvestites, part of the excitement (including risk and danger) of cross-dressing and appearing in public is being found out. They report to enjoy the deviance involved (Ackroyd, 1979; Bullough & Bullough, 1993; Kirk & Heath, 1984). Consequently, it seems that some transvestites *aspire* to a challenge of their presentation.

The Drag Queen

Webster's Dictionary carries this simple definition for drag: slang: woman's dress when worn by a man (Gove, 1993, p. 684). *The American Thesaurus of Slang* states that drag is the female costume of a male homosexual (Berrey & van den Bark, 1953, p. 85). The *Oxford English Dictionary* defines drag as feminine attire worn by a man; also, a party or dance attended by men wearing feminine attire (1989, p. 1010). Partridge (1984), in *The Dictionary of Slang and Unconventional English*, defines drag as the petticoat or skirt used by actors when playing female roles. He suggests that the word derived from "the drag of the dress as distinct from the nondragginess of the trousers" (p. 338). One source proposes that the term drag was coined by Shakespeare as an acronym meaning DRessed As Girls (Lynn, n.d., p. 5).

The ability to *do drag* is concentrated and widespread within the homosexual community. Many social events include or focus on drag—drag balls, drag shows. At these events, cross-dressed males parade in the spirit of satire, imitating female models and celebrities. *Queen* is a descriptive term used within the homosexual community, and is usually reserved for the especially effeminate male. Therefore, a drag queen is often defined as a homosexual male who cross-dresses in the spirit of satire. Although drag queens are almost exclusively homosexual, not all homosexual cross-dressers are drag queens.[7]

Drag queens are generally considered to be a subculture within the homosexual community. While creating a semblance of femininity, the drag queen relies on the fact that his audience is aware of his true sexual identity. In contrast to the transvestite, who usually adheres to the prevailing social and gender codes of behavior while in feminine dress, the drag queen tends to flout and break the rules. Also unlike the transvestite, the drag queen maintains that he does not cross-dress for fetishistic or sexual purposes. Rather, he views dressing in drag as a means of entertainment, and as a mask which allows him an entirely different view of the world.

Drag is a vehicle for satire: it parodies and mocks the ideals of feminine beauty. Ackroyd (1979) suggests that "it is misogynistic both in origin and intent" (p. 14). However, some drag queens who attach themselves to the feminist movement claim to satirize and exaggerate what seems to attract heterosexual men. Others insist their drag routine is a political act of defiance against rigidly stereotyped male and female images and ideals (Kirk & Heath, 1984).

The visual image of the drag queen is quite different from the other categories of cross-dressers, although he will modify and supplement his body in much the same manner as the transsexual and the transvestite. The drag queen creates an appearance that is comparable to that of a showgirl or a prostitute. Men in drag go "way over the top" (Kirk & Heath, 1984, p. 61), with spiked heels, a sequined dress, and a bouffant hairstyle. Body curvatures tend to be well-defined. The hair, makeup, and breasts are exaggerated. The clothing is generally quite slinky and provocative, emphasizing legs, curves, and cleavage. Extreme gestures, carriage, and vocal intonation complete the presentation.

Drag queens' satire on femininity renders an image that typically will not allow them to pass as females (Ackroyd, 1979; Kirk & Heath, 1984; Phillips, Shapiro, & Joseph, 1980; Robinson, 1988; Woodhouse, 1989). Alternative explanations emerged in the following excerpts of interviews from Kirk and Heath's (1984) pictorial survey of males who dress in drag. Reported justifications range from a glorification of the feminine ideal to a rejection of the restrictive masculine role in Western culture:

> Does he ever feel that, in drag, he is satirizing women? "Perhaps that's how women see it, but for me the opposite is true. For me it's a way of glorifying women. I think with drag people get confused sometimes, but it is not my confusion. Drag is a denial of politics. It

takes the reality away, questions the reality of things." (p. 88)

One of the reasons Colin likes to frock up is to go against the whole gay establishment which is so dull..."I like the elegance myself and my image is hopefully the latest over-the-top thing you've seen on the Paris catwalk...That's what it's all about—outrage! Entertainment for everyone." (p. 122)

Whether a queen started wearing drag because he enjoyed doing it or for political reasons—it was usually a combination of the two—it soon became a symbol of separation, a political act of defiance against the stereotyped male image. It was a badge saying you disagreed with "male" values and wanted nothing more to do with them. (p. 100)

Although justifications for dressing in drag seem quite diverse, the images created by all remain relatively constant. During my fieldwork, I observed drag queens—both on and off stage—flouting and breaking prevailing gender and social codes. For example, a performer may appear on stage and work through an extremely delicate routine. In the end, an unexpected crotch gesture will break the spell *she* has cast on her audience. Another common style of performance which emphasizes the incongruence focuses on the interplay between dress and movement. When the spotlight is turned on and a stunning entertainer stands poised at center stage, the irony is soon realized when she begins to move about in a very aggressive—and typically masculine—manner. Both styles of performance are calculated, as the drag queen relies on the fact that the audience is aware that *she* is actually a *he*.

The acceptance or rejection of the female image created by the drag queen is context-bound. Within the walls of gay clubs, men in drag are everywhere, and their presentations are generally appreciated by other customers. However, closing time signifies the ending of the environment that readily accepts cross-dressers. When it came time to go home, there were several occasions when bunches of people were milling around on the sidewalk and street in front of each establishment I visited. At this

time, the cross-dressers endured all sorts of verbal abuse from the "outside world." So, a short time after these individuals received positive responses for their appearance, they experienced verbal and sometimes physical abuse.

There is indication from my fieldwork, as well as the research of others, that those males who dress in drag do so in defiance of established gender and sexual codes. They are fully aware of how their appearance is reviewed by members of the public. However, the stigma attached to cross-dressers by the outside world seems to be offset by the rewards received in an accepting and appreciative environment. Perhaps the presence of difference is desirable for the drag queen. Males who cross-dress in the spirit of entertainment conspicuously defy the deeply ingrained taboo of crossing the lines of rigidly ascribed gender roles. The very act of cross-dressing draws attention to itself and incurs the wrath of a society that has been known to react hysterically to any challenge of nonconformists. By overdoing their appearance, drag queens have opened themselves to the possibility of a negative response from their audience. This makes a certain amount of sense when one realizes they are mocking the prescribed and proscribed boundaries of gender within an essentially heterocentric culture.

UNDERSTANDING CROSS-DRESSING

In developing this visual typology of male-to-female cross-dressers, I have emphasized what visually distinguishes each of the cross-dressing types from the others. In summary, the transsexual becomes female, taking on the acceptable feminine image. The transvestite desires to emulate his conception of femininity, often creating the illusion of the unremarkable woman next door. The drag queen tends to go to the extreme in his transformation, which results in a flamboyant and exotic caricature of the female image.

By placing cross-dressers into these three categories, I have greatly simplified an extremely complex subject. Each of the three types of cross-dressers could have their own continuum, with variances in occurrence and visual success. However, as I indicate in my analysis, the three types create three distinct appearances, which result in three different types of responses through social interaction.

Transsexuals take on a feminine appearance that looks appropriate to the viewer. Femininity is achieved through a modest ensemble of dress, where the body is only subtly defined. Hair is an important framing device. Makeup and jewelry are consistent—but understated—modifications of their appearance. Transvestites tend to look anywhere from incongruous to inappropriate to the viewer. Some will pass as females, while others will not. They generally are conservative in their appearance, wearing clothing styles that may be slightly out-of-date, accented by modest styles of makeup and jewelry. And, in most cases, it is obvious that the transvestites are wearing wigs. Males who dress in drag have been accused of satirizing the female form, resulting in a "bad-girl" look. The makeup is overdone, the jewelry is large and flashy, and hairstyles—which are primarily wigs—are props for the personae created by drag queens. The often exotic and revealing garments define and exaggerate the curves of the body, and tend to emphasize the breasts and legs. The surfaces of the garments are most often reflective, ranging from sequined fabric to lamé to black vinyl.

ACCEPTED BOUNDARIES OF CROSS-DRESSING

Dress is a powerful form of communication. Ideals of femininity and masculinity are deeply entrenched in our culture, and are manifested by how we modify and supplement our bodies. One only needs to look at rest room symbols in most public buildings to realize how concretely defined our images of males and females actually are: bifurcated silhouettes for the men's room and skirted silhouettes for the women's room. It is likely that most of us are not aware of the thoroughness of our gender training until we are confronted by people who cross-dress.

The primary focus of this article has been to consider what happens when culturally prescribed and proscribed gender norms—revealed through dress and appearance—are challenged through social interaction. Equally important and equally compelling are the cultural, social, and personal issues that discourage more people from cross-dressing. For we've all experienced the urge—and the opportunity—to pretend, to play "dress up." In its most innocuous form, the consumer will indulge in some cosmetic extravagance: "It will create a brighter, more beautiful you!" is the basic premise for many advertising campaigns. However, if a person uses dress as a means for disguising his or her biological sex, observers are more apt to consider the cross-dresser as inappropriate.

Although dressing and attempting to pass as the opposite sex is considered by most as inappropriate and unacceptable, as a culture we have been fascinated with the idea and the reality of cross-dressing for as long as it has been documented. Through the ages, we have been titillated, fascinated, annoyed, or frightened by the practice. And yet, cross-dressing marches through generations of people. Recent popular entertainment venues have brought the topic "out of the closet." The music and film industries have done much to publicize and legitimize cross-dressing, gender-bending, gender-blending, and androgyny—at least as entertainment. Prominent musicians such as Laurie Anderson, David Bowie, Alice Cooper, Michael Jackson, Mick Jagger, k. d. lang, Annie Lennox, (The Artist Formerly Known As) Prince, and RuPaul have used dress to challenge the visual constraints of masculinity and femininity. Recent acclaimed films, such as *The Adventures of Priscilla, Queen of the Desert* (1994), *The Birdcage* (1996), *The Crying Game* (1993), and *Paris Is Burning* (1992), have introduced drag to the straight audience (many of whom haven't yet ventured into a place where drag shows are staged).

The male-to-female cross-dressers considered in this paper move through a transformation that may seem to be quite synthetic—bordering on the abnormal, in the sense that male-to-female cross-dressing is not sanctioned as normal behavior in American and European cultures. However, Kuhn (1985) reminds us of the artificial manipulation of appearances by women in the following statement:

A good deal of the groomed beauty of the women in the glamour portraits comes from the fact that they are "made-up," in the immediate sense that cosmetics have been applied to their bodies in order to enhance their existing qualities. But they are also "made-up" in a sense that the images, rather than the women are put together, constructed, even fabricated or falsified in the sense that we might say a story is made up if it is a fiction. (p. 13)

Male-to-female cross-dressing, in light of Kuhn's comment, seems really not that peculiar—except that it is deemed inappropriate human behavior by many in mainstream society.

To make sense of the countless groupings of peoples, objects, and ideals that exist in our world, we create stereotypes or codified categories. These categories are necessary, in that they help us to organize responses to external stimuli. However, codified categories will often encourage the viewer to overlook subtle differences that may be extremely important in understanding and defining a situation. Most people—when they think about male-to-female cross-dressing—tend to clump all males who cross-dress into one category. When this occurs, the differences in appearance are overlooked. In this case, it is the differences that are closely related to the identity of each type of cross-dresser.

A transvestite I met while doing my fieldwork made the following comment that sums up his years of experience as a cross-dresser. In the statement, he also emphasized the meanings people attach to dress and appearance:

People will act and react toward you, and treat you in a certain way—according to your dress and appearance; but when they discover that you are not what they thought you were, the meaning of your appearance changes drastically for them. (Hegland, 1991, p. 183)

Those who cross-dress—whether they fit neatly into the three categories discussed here or fall somewhere in between—force us to face issues that tend to make us feel uncomfortable. The accepted gender boundaries are so intricately woven into daily life, that to encounter one who crosses the line by dressing as the opposite sex often causes many of us to recommit ourselves—with steadfastness and vigor—to the dualities of the prevailing gender ideals, to the pairing of femaleness with femininity and maleness with masculinity, in whatever ways those concepts are defined within the contexts of time and space. For others, the act of cross-dressing is a compelling phenomenon that functions as a catalyst, and forces us to look more critically at culturally constructed gender roles and ideals of appearance.

Notes

1. In 1912, Crawley proposed that *cosmopolitan* be used as an adjective to describe the dress of industrialized (or "Westernized") parts of the world, as *Western* tends to be Eurocentric and pejorative. Baizerman, Eicher, and Cerny (1993) suggest the terms *urban* or *cosmopolitan* instead of *Western* in the search for terms that designate "dress of the other." I agree with these arguments, and use the term *cosmopolitan* in this paper.

2. When females attempt to disguise their biological sex, I consider them to be "cross-dressers" as well. At this point, they are stigmatized in much the same way as male cross-dressers (Devor, 1989; Strega, 1985).

3. This paper focuses on the current phenomenon of male-to-female cross-dressing within American and European cultures. However, the phenomenon is not exclusive to any time or place. Cross-dressing has occurred for as long as humans have been dressing their bodies, or at least to approximately 4000 BC, when the Hebrew prohibition against cross-dressing was alleged to have been written: "Women shall not wear that which pertains to a man, nor shall a man put on a woman's garment, for all that do are an abomination to the Lord God" (The Bible, Deuteronomy 22:5).

Cross-dressing exists in various religious and mythological traditions. A cross-dressed individual has often been considered a sign of an extraordinary destiny. The dualistic symbolism of men who dressed as women were often given divine authority within a community, and were regarded as sorcerers or visionaries. Oddly enough, it is almost exclusively within the religious realm where these men–women, or androgynous figures, have been accepted without reservation. There is an androgynous, or at least bisexual, nature in the deities worshiped in the various creation myths (Ackroyd, 1979; Hauser, 1990; Katz, 1976; Levy, 1971; Wikan, 1977).

Detailed documentation of many tribal traditions describe males who cross-dressed (Ackroyd, 1979; Hauser, 1990; Karlen, 1971; Levy, 1971; Lindholm & Lindholm, 1982; Whitam & Mathy, 1986; Wikan, 1977; Williams, 1986). Native Americans have *berdaches*, who are males who wear women's clothing, engage in culturally defined feminine activities, and are given the status of the third sex. Among the Cocopa Indians, males who displayed feminine characteristics were dressed as women and labeled *e L ha*. In Tahiti, males who cross-dressed were known as *cudinas*, among the California Indians as *i-wa-musp*, among the Aztecs and Incas as *bardages*, and in coastal Oman as *xanith*.

Perhaps the most overt occurrences of cross-dressing can be found through a historical review of the theatre. Female impersonation is one of the oldest thespian traditions, practiced by the Elizabethans, the Chinese, the Japanese, and the ancient Greeks. It seems that whenever and wherever the history of dramaturgy began, it was automatically the man's business to play the female roles (Baker, 1968; Gilbert, 1926).

The act of cross-dressing may be nearly as old as the act of dressing itself. From this, the implication is that—early on—humans developed a strong emotional attachment to the idea that females should appear feminine and males should appear masculine within a specific time and place. As far back as 6000 years, laws were written that admonished cross-dressing; yet, it has been practiced continuously, both covertly and overtly, to the present day.

4. I use these categories with some reservation. We all have been exposed to these labels, but even the most objective among us may experience an unsavory response to the three categories. I do not apologize for that. However, I do encourage the reader to attempt to break away from all the complex preconceptions that surround the issue. Dialogue with numerous faculty, graduate students, and personal acquaintances reinforce and highlight the stigma attached to each of these labels. Further, there seems to be consistent misunderstanding as to how each term is actually defined. I provide a brief definition of each category here, and include a more thorough explanation later in the body of the paper.

The *male transsexual* is a male with the genitalia of one sex and the psychosocial identity of the other. A preoperative male transsexual identifies with femaleness in every way, yet he has male reproductive organs. When he cross-dresses, the male transsexual becomes female.

The *male transvestite* is a male who dresses in feminine attire, ranging from women's underwear worn underneath a business suit to a complete transformation. When cross-dressed, the male transvestite emulates the female form, but never forgets that he is male.

The *drag queen* is a male—often homosexual—who cross-dresses in the spirit of parody and satire.

5. In the film *Victor/Victoria* (1982), Julie Andrews plays a down-and-out singer who becomes a hit musical star by portraying a man who does female impersonations on the stage in the 1930s. While in her role as a man and a female impersonator, she is careful to hide the fact that she does not have a protruding Adam's apple. If discovered, this

would give away her true biological sex. In the same way, males who cross-dress are careful to hide their protruding Adam's apple.

6. While doing my fieldwork, I quickly learned how to address cross-dressed males. The general rule is to simply look at their appearance. Whether they are convincing or not, if you do not want to offend male-to-female cross-dressers, you refer to them with feminine pronouns when they are in feminine dress. In this paper, I use feminine pronouns to reflect the male's change in appearance.

7. Newton (1972) states that "the homosexual term for a transvestite is a drag queen" (p. 3). In my opinion, the issue of male-to-female cross-dressing is significantly more complex than Newton's statement would have us believe. Additional sources such as Ackroyd (1979) and Kirk and Heath (1984) support the notion that drag queens are almost exclusively homosexual males. These sources also imply that all homosexual male cross-dressers are not necessarily drag queens.

Contingent on his intent and visual transformation, the homosexual male cross-dresser could fit into either of the previously delineated categories of transsexualism or transvestism. Similarly, it is possible for a self-defined drag queen to be heterosexual, although I did not come across any in the literature or in my fieldwork. So, the term drag queen is apparently reserved for a homosexual male who cross-dresses in the spirit of satire.

References

Ackroyd, P. (1979). *Dressing Up: Transvestism and Drag, the History of an Obsession*. New York: Simon & Schuster.

The Adventures of Priscilla, Queen of the Desert [Film]. (1994). R. Penfold-Russell (Executive Producer); A. Clark & M. Hamlyn (Producers); S. Elliott (Director & Writer). Australia: Polygram & Latent Image Productions.

Allen, M. P. (1989). *Transformations: Cross-Dressers and Those Who Love Them*. New York: E. P. Dutton.

Baizerman, S., Eicher, J. B., & Cerny, C. (1993). Eurocentrism in the study of ethnic dress. *Dress*, 20:9–32.

Baker, R. (1968). *Drag: A History of Female Impersonators on the Stage*. London: Triton Books.

Benjamin, H. (1953). Transvestism and transsexualism. *International Journal of Sexology*, 7:12–14.

Benjamin, H. (1966). *The Transsexual Phenomenon*. New York: Julian Press.

Berrey, L. V., & van de Bark, M. (1953). *American Thesaurus of Slang: A Complete Reference Book of Colloquial Speech* (2nd ed.). New York: Crowell.

The Bible: Revised Standard Version.

The Birdcage [Film]. (1996). N. Machlis & M. Danon (Executive Producers); M. Nichols (Director & Producer). USA: MGM & United Artists.

Brierley, H. (1979). *Transvestism: A Handbook with Case Studies for Psychologists, Psychiatrists, and Counsellors*. Oxford: Pergamon Press.

Bullough, V. L., & Bullough, B. (1993). *Cross Dressing, Sex, and Gender*. Philadelphia: University of Pennsylvania Press.

Cauldwell, D. O. (1956). *Transvestism: Men in Female Dress*. New York: Sexology Corporation.

Crawley, A. E. (1912). Dress. In J. Hastings (Ed.), *Encyclopedia of Religion and Ethics*, Vol. V, pp. 40–72. New York: Charles Scribner's Sons.

The Crying Game [Film]. (1993). S. Woolley (Producer); N. Jordan (Director & Writer). United Kingdom: Palace Pictures & Miramax.

Dekker, R. M., & van de Pol, L. C. (1989). *The Tradition of Female Transvestism in Early Modern Europe*. New York: St. Martin's Press.

Devor, H. (1989). *Gender Blending: Confronting the Limits of Duality.* Bloomington: Indiana University Press.

Docter, R. F. (1988). *Transvestites and Transsexuals: Toward a Theory of Cross-Gender Behavior.* New York: Plenum Press.

Eicher, J. B., & Roach-Higgins, M. E. (1992). Definition and classification of dress: Implications for analysis of gender roles. In R. Barnes & J. B. Eicher (Eds.), *Dress and Gender: Making and Meaning,* pp. 8–28. Oxford: Berg Press.

Evans, C., & Thornton, M. (1989). *Women and Fashion.* New York: Quartet Books.

Feinbloom, D. F. (1976). *Transvestites and Transsexuals.* New York: Delacorte Press.

Garber, M. (1992). *Vested Interests: Cross-Dressing and Cultural Anxiety.* New York: Routledge.

Gilbert, O. P. (1926). *Men in Women's Guise: Some Historical Instances of Female Impersonation.* New York: Brentano's.

Gove, P. B. (Ed.). (1966). *Webster's Third New International Dictionary of the English Language, Unabridged.* Springfield, MA: G. & C. Merriam.

Hauser, R. E. (1990). The berdache and the Illinois Indian tribe during the last half of the seventeenth century. *Ethnohistory,* 37(1):45–65.

Hegland, J. E. (1991). Drag queens, transvestites, transsexuals: A visual typology and analysis of male-to-female cross-dressing. Unpublished master's thesis, University of Minnesota, St. Paul.

Karlen, A. (1971). *Sexuality and Homosexuality: A New View.* New York: W.W. Norton.

Katz, J. N. (1976). *Gay American History: Lesbians and Gay Men in the USA.* New York: Thomas Y. Crowell.

Kirk, K., & Heath, E. (1984). *Men in Frocks.* London: Gay Men's Press.

Kuhn, A. (1985). *The Power of the Image: Essays in Representation and Sexuality.* London: Routledge & Kegan Paul.

Levy, R. I. (1971). The community function of Tahitian male transvestitism: A hypothesis. *Anthropological Quarterly,* 44(1):12–21.

Lindholm, C., & Lindholm, C. (1982, September). The erotic sorcerers. *Science Digest,* 78–80.

Lynn, M. S. (n.d.). *Definitions of Terms Commonly Used in the Transvestite-Transsexual Community.* Compiled for the International Foundation for Gender Education's Educational Resources Committee, Wayland, MA.

Maitland, S. (1986). *Vesta Tilley.* London: Virago.

Newton, E. (1972). *Mother Camp: Female Impersonators in America.* Englewood Cliffs, NJ: Prentice Hall.

Oxford English Dictionary (2nd ed.). (1989). Oxford: Clarendon Press.

Paris Is Burning [Film: Documentary]. (1992). D. Lacy & N. Finch (Executive Producers); J. Livingston & C. Goodman (Producers); J. Livingston (Director). USA: Offwhite Productions & Prestige Films.

Partridge, E. (1984). *A Dictionary of Slang and Unconventional English: Colloquialisms and Catch-Phrases, Solecisms and Catachreses, Nicknames, and Vulgarisms* (8th ed.). New York: Macmillan.

Phillips, M., Shapiro, B., & Joseph, M. (1980). *Forbidden Fantasies: Men Who Dare to Dress in Drag.* New York: Macmillan.

Prince, V. (1981). *Understanding Cross Dressing.* Tulare, CA: Chevalier.

Raynor, D. G. (1966). *A Year among the Girls.* New York: Lyle Stuart.

Robinson, J. (1988). *Body Packaging: A Guide to Human Sexual Display.* Los Angeles: Elysium Growth Press.

Rudd, P. J. (1990). *Crossdressing with Dignity: The Case for Transcending Gender Lines.* Katy, TX: PM.

Stevens, J. A. (1990). *From Masculine to Feminine and All Points in Between: A Practical Guide for Transvestites, Cross-Dressers, Transgenderists, Transsexuals, and Others Who Choose to Develop a More Feminine*

Image…And for the Curious and Concerned. Cambridge, MA: Different Paths Press.

Strega, L. (1985). The big sell-out: Lesbian femininity. *Lesbian Ethics*, 1(3):73–84.

Victor/Victoria [Film]. (1982). B. Edwards & T. Adams (Producers); B. Edwards (Director & Writer). Great Britain: MGM, Peerford, & Ladbroke Entertainment.

Wheelwright, J. (1989). *Amazons and Military Maids: Women Who Dressed as Men in Pursuit of Life, Liberty, and Happiness.* London: Pandora Press.

Whitam, F. L., & Mathy, R. M. (1986). *Male Homosexuality in Four Societies: Brazil, Guatemala, the Philippines, and the U.S.* New York: Praeger.

Wikan, U. (1977). Man becomes woman: Transsexualism in Oman as a key to gender roles. *Man: The Journal of the Royal Anthropological Institute*, 12(2):304–319.

Williams, W. L. (1986). *The Spirit and the Flesh: Sexual Diversity in American Indian Culture.* Boston: Beacon Press.

Woodhouse, A. (1989). *Fantastic Women: Sex, Gender, and Transvestism.* New Brunswick, NJ: Rutgers University Press.

DISCUSSION QUESTIONS

Drag Queens, Transvestites, Transsexuals

1. In American culture, why do you think the practice of cross-dressing is generally associated more with male-to-female cross-dressing than female-to-male? What are some of the physical cues that could expose even the most convincing cross-dresser?

2. According to the author of this article, why is the term *cross-dressing* not accurate for transsexuals?

3. What is the nature of being a drag queen and why is it hard for him to "pass" as a biological female?

Modesty and Immodesty

CHAPTER 6

Susan O. Michelman

AFTER YOU HAVE READ THIS CHAPTER, YOU WILL COMPREHEND:

- That modesty is socially and culturally constructed and varies historically.

- That fundamental religious values regarding the body frequently influence the proscription of modest dress. This would include some Christian, Jewish, and Muslim beliefs.

- That dress associated with popular culture is frequently immodest. However, a trend toward more modest dress is gaining importance, as demonstrated by an increasing number of publications on the value of modesty.

As you learned in Chapter 5, dress is an important component of conveying gender and sexual identity. This chapter explores some of the complexities associated with gender and sexuality regarding modesty and immodesty of dress. The meaning and interpretation of modesty varies culturally and across historical periods. However, **modesty** is generally understood to be the covering of certain parts of the body that, according to the certain belief systems, have a sexual connotation if exposed in public. Modesty is also frequently related to different religious beliefs and is associated with holiness. For example, many Muslim women cover their heads, necks, arms, legs, and even faces in public because of their belief that it is proper for a woman to show these "sexual" parts of their body only within the confines of their home. Mennonite women (see "Clothing, Control, and Women's Agency" in Chapter 12) have many religious proscriptions about women's dress that relate to their belief that clothing is "a mirror of the soul" reflecting their inner attitudes and values. In contrast, there is much immodesty today in American movies, television, and music. However, you will learn in this chapter that there is an increasing backlash to this current immodesty, particularly among more fundamental religious groups that are having a wider influence on the broader American culture. The following section presents some of the theories for modesty.

THEORIES OF MODESTY

Flugel, in *The Psychology of Clothes* (1930), suggests that dress serves three main purposes—decoration, modesty, and protection. Laver (1969) contends that, until quite recently, it was almost universally agreed that the fundamental reason for wearing clothing was modesty. The Genesis story in the Bible recounts that Adam and Eve, having eaten of the fruit of the Tree of Knowledge, "knew that they were naked" and made themselves "aprons" of fig leaves. In Laver's theory of the **shifting erogenous zone,** he contends that complete nudity is antierotic. Fashion designers continually alter the location of attention on the female body, keeping the continuous cycle of fashion alive through an ever-changing focus of interest. Laver maintained that fashion was essentially a game of hide-and-seek between seduction and "prudery." Although this theory originated many years ago, a current examination of fashions shows that designers and apparel manufacturers frequently raise or lower a hemline, bare a shoulder, or plunge a neckline to create some new interest in their line. In the article "All That's Bare Is Fit to Wear," Bader discusses some of the social complexities associated with showing more skin, ranging from physical discomfort to humiliating inspections of short skirt length in the classroom.

Some people are concerned by the challenge to modesty from exposed skin. Thompson (2000) discovered in a study of 2,000 fashion advertisements published in *Gentlemen's Quarterly* (GQ) and *Vogue* between 1964 and 1994 that there was an increasing amount of skin and/or nudity displayed. This essentially confirms that during this 40-year period less and less modesty in advertising became more and more acceptable. Television, movies, music videos, and, of course, fashion reflect this current trend. Pop icons such as Madonna and, more recently, Britney Spears have gone from relatively modest attire to nudity (see Figure 6.1).

Millions of girls and young women who emulate their success also imitate pop stars' fashion choices. Unfortunately, this means that dress choices that expose a lot of skin are chosen by young women and deplored by parents and teachers. Although this has caused concern with some parents who grew up in a more permissive period regarding dress, the schools say they are protected by court decisions affirming their right to ban clothing that they feel is disruptive in an educational environment. Some parents and educators are concerned that body-exposing clothing is related to a loosening of morals and an increase in sexual behavior in young people.

Goffman (1963), a sociologist, examined the situational context of body exposure. For example, he observed that a certain amount of undress in bathing attire at the beach is tolerated. Undress in the confines of the home may be accepted, but the same clothing in a public setting might be considered totally inappropriate. In the article "Racy School Fashions under Fire" by Kletter and Braunstein, the authors discuss some schools' increasing intolerance with revealing clothing, as well as dress that announces controversial issues related to sexual and religious orientation, and gang- or drug-related imagery. Modesty, therefore, also has its situational relevance, constantly being negotiated in accordance with the mores of the time. An examination of the history of bathing suits from 1900 to the present reveals an ever-increasing tolerance of the display of skin at the beach. In the article "Goodbye Briefs, Hello Jammers," Gray looks at the trend away from men's swim teams wearing skimpy Speedos. Gray indicates that many young men have body image anxiety in such abbreviated attire. Instead, they are choosing a longer suit that covers more of the body and helps obtain faster times in competition. For young women, the prom dress marks a rite of passage out of high school to the larger world. However, in the article "The Pared Down Prom Dress," Merrick points out that dresses have become skimpier and more revealing, causing some to question the appropriateness of this trend. Michelman, in "Reveal or Conceal?," discusses the backlash to this body-baring trend by more religious young women.

Modesty is culturally relative. Research on dress of the Kalabari people of Nigeria in West Africa (see "Is Thin In?" in Chapter 2) shows that dress for women became much more modest after Christian missionaries who came from Europe introduced the concept of sin and shame associated with the nude body. Young girls exposed and drew attention to developing breasts and buttocks as part of the cultural norms of dress. Although now done only for ceremonial reenactment, this was a stage of dress

FIGURE 6.1 *Britney Spears has been criticized for her body-baring fashion choices.*

that exhibited a girl's ability to move to a higher social status through the process of physical maturation and her potential for bearing children. This example demonstrates that, from an anthropological perspective, exposure of body parts is not inherently shameful.

MODESTY AND RELIGION

Modest dress can be frequently associated with fundamental religious beliefs. Generally, the more fundamental the religious belief, the greater degree of modesty is required, particularly for women. Fundamentalism is a conservative religious doctrine that opposes intellectualism and worldly accommodation in favor of restoring traditional, otherworldly religion (Macionis, 1996). Dress is a visible symbol for fundamental beliefs. Religious principles govern all aspects of believers' lives (including dress), and women's roles are more traditional, with individual needs and beliefs relinquished to the greater good of the family and religious group. Some examples of religious groups that mandate modest dress are Muslims, Orthodox Jews, Mormons, and Mennonites.

Recently, political issues in Afghanistan, Iraq, Iran, Egypt, and other Middle Eastern countries have drawn attention to the meanings of the veiling of women. The type of veiling that Muslim women wear and the degree of coverage vary greatly (see Figure 6.2). Some Muslim women dress modestly but do not veil at all. Generally, the more fundamental the religious beliefs, the greater amount of body that is covered. In very extreme cases, literally everything is covered, with a thinner material placed over the mouth and nose. However, in the woman's own residence, a woman does not veil. Veiling is reserved for her public presence only. The article "Men Hear Saudi Women's Unmentionable Details" by Abu-Nasr examines how these veiled women experience the embarrassment of purchasing underwear from all-male vendors. Out of necessity, they must compromise their standards of modesty.

There has been recent worldwide attention regarding the proscribed attire for men and women under the rule of the Taliban in Afghanistan. Since the downfall of the Taliban, these restrictions have lessened. Much of the publicity, particularly regarding Afghani women who were required to wear a complete covering of the body in public, have raised concerns among non-Muslims of oppression of women, particularly as it regards the political control of their bodies. For example, in the article "Hair as a Battlefield for the Soul," Sciolino discusses the forced veiling of Afghani women by the Taliban and the requirement of beards for men. She explains that there is a long history regarding debate over these modesty issues in Islamic culture, which is governed by the interpretation of the Koran, the Muslim holy book.

The issue of veiling for Muslim women is complex, defying the simple interpretation of men's oppression over women. It is critical to place veiling within the context of the belief system, social roles, and issues of personal identity. For example, there is a current movement in Egypt among lower middle-class women to return to veiling practices from secular or Western dress. Many non-Muslims and Westerners view this as a regressive stance in regard to social roles. MacLeod (1991) conveys a complex motivation for this return to veiling, highly rooted in issues of identity and personal beliefs. Rapid social change in Egypt has created cultural discontinuity, causing these largely urban women to "turn back to a more authentic and culturally true way of life, and they perceive the veil as part of this cultural reformation" (MacLeod, 1991, p. 111).

According to the most current conservative viewpoints, it is possible to maintain fundamental religious beliefs, dress modestly, and still be considered quite fashionable. For example, Orthodox Jewish women who observe *Halakha*, Jewish law, frequently wear wigs to cover their hair that, according to the Talmud, exudes sensual energy. However, there is nothing to say that these wigs cannot be stylish. In New York, the most fashionable hairdressers, including Frederic Fekkai, John Barrett, Oribe, John Sahag, and Oscar Blandi, do wigs for Orthodox women. They work to make them modest, not matronly and definitely not "wiggy"—the word Orthodox women use to describe the heavy appearance of wigs (Hayt, 1997). In Hayt's article, "For Stylish Orthodox Women,

FIGURE 6.2 *Muslim schoolgirls in Jakarta, Indonesia, wearing a type of modified veiling.*

Wigs That Aren't Wiggy" (Chapter 12), Rabbi Avi Weiss, of the Hebrew Institute of Riverdale in the Bronx, agreed. "I would distinguish between being stylish and being immodest," he said. "Jewish law is not monolithic, there can be two views, and they can be both opposite and correct."

Within the Roman Catholic Church, nuns and their habits symbolize complete devotion and dedication to their vows as Brides of Christ. Modesty, as it relates to humility, is a central identity of these women, as revealed in the quote from this woman who had worn a habit for many years and recounts the degree to which modesty was a central issue in their everyday lives:

> Oh yes, there used to be an expression "modesty of the eyes." Basically it referred to not being distracted, so you could concentrate on what you were doing. There used to be a monastery right down the hill and they wore a giant heart. When they conversed with one another, they were to address the heart and not look directly at the person. Now picture, they used to do a lot of education with us because they had a seminary and during the time of Vatican II, we took advantage of learning theology. When they addressed us, they would look at our chest.
>
> We had very little privacy. We had a dresser that was about 18" wide. There was a screen curtain and that was the only space you had between you and the person next to you. That was your privacy. You had to dress and undress under your nightgown with your eyes cast down. You wanted the privacy that you were giving everyone else. Because of the lack of privacy, you gave respect to others. (Quote taken from an interview by Michelman with a member of Sisters of Providence, Springfield, Massachusetts, 1995)

Fundamental and evangelical Christians as well as Mormons also promote modest attire. A current Gallup survey discloses that roughly four out of ten Americans identify themselves as evangelical or born-again Christians (Tolson, 2003). Wolfe (2003) argues that religion in the United States is being transformed in radically new directions. Evangelicalism is having an effect on American culture, including promoting more modest fashions for women. Michelman, in the article "Reveal or Conceal?," discusses how, despite highly media-hyped immodest style, an increasing number of modesty-seeking consumers, frequently evangelical or fundamental in their religious beliefs, are having an influence on the production and consumption of fashion. Religious values can lead fashion, as demonstrated in an increasing interest in more modest fashion and the movement against immodesty.

Summary

The articles in this chapter address multiple issues regarding modesty and immodesty. Modesty, which is culturally and historically relative, is related to issues of gender and sexuality and is closely tied to religious views of display of the body. Religions such as Islam, Judaism, and Christianity all have certain proscriptions about display of the body, the degree to which depends on how fundamental the beliefs. Although Western popular culture includes many immodest displays, there is a growing backlash to regain the importance of modest dress.

Suggested Readings

Arthur, L. (1997). Clothing, control, and women's agency: The mitigation of patriarchal power. In M. L. Damhorst, K. Miller, & S. Michelman (Eds.), *The Meanings of Dress*. New York: Fairchild.

Fernea, E. W., & Fernea, R. A. (1995). Symbolizing roles: Behind the veil. In M. E. Roach-Higgins, J. B. Eicher, & K. K. P. Johnson (Eds.), *Dress and Identity*. New York: Fairchild.

Gresh, D. (2002). *Secret Keeper: The Delicate Power of Modesty*. Chicago: Moody Press.

Pollard, D. J. (2001). *Christian Modesty and the Public Undressing of America*. San Antonio, TX: Vision Forum, Inc.

Shalit, W. (1999). *A Return to Modesty*. New York: Free Press.

Storm, P. (1987). *Functions of Dress: Tools of Culture and the Individual*. Englewood Cliffs, NJ: Prentice Hall.

LEARNING ACTIVITY

Modesty and Immodesty

Objective: To understand cultural differences in expression of modesty.

Find a person who is similar in age and gender who comes from a culture different from your own. The objective of this assignment is to compare and contrast cultural definitions of modesty and immodesty. The use of pictures (photographs or images in magazines) is encouraged to illustrate discussed concepts. Each of you should take notes during the discussion, then analyze them at the close of your meeting. Try to draw some conclusions about modesty and immodesty and cultural differences or similarities.

1. Discuss the meaning of modest or immodest dress in each culture.
2. Does this meaning differ for men and women?
3. Does the meaning of modesty or immodesty vary by occasion?
4. Are there generational differences?

References

Flugel, J. C. (1930). *The Psychology of Clothes*. London: Hogarth Press.

Goffman, E. (1963). *Stigma: Notes on the Management of a Spoiled Identity*. Englewood Cliffs, NJ: Prentice Hall.

Hayt, E. (1997, April 27). For stylish orthodox women, wigs that aren't wiggy. *New York Times*, 43, 48.

Laver, J. (1969). *Modesty in Dress: An Inquiry into the Fundamentals of Fashion*. Boston: Houghton Mifflin.

Macionis, J. J. (1996). *Society: The Basics* (3rd ed.). Upper Saddle River, NJ: Prentice Hall.

MacLeod, A. (1991). *Accommodating Protest*. New York: Columbia University Press.

Thompson, M. (2000). Gender in magazine advertising: Skin sells best. *Clothing and Textiles Research Journal*, 18(3):178–181.

Tolson, J. (2003, December 18). The new old-time religion. *U.S. News and World Report*. Accessed February 16, 2004, at www.usnews.com.

Wolfe, A. (2003). *The Transformation of American Religion*. New York: Free Press.

31   Hair as a Battlefield for the Soul

Elaine Sciolino

Celebrating their liberation from Taliban rule in Afghanistan last week, men shaved off their beards, while women unveiled their faces and revealed bits of hair. Suddenly, ordinary people needed to show they had regained control over their looks. But why?

It helps to understand that the Muslim world today is waging two wars on overlapping battlefields: one between traditional interpretations of Islam and modernity, the other between the will of the state and the rights of the individual. Islamic scholars, lawyers and feminists debate laws and traditions governing such obviously-serious issues as freedom of speech, divorce, inheritance, child custody, polygamy, flogging and stoning.

But the most visible manifestation of the Taliban's control over people has been the forced bearding of men and the forced veiling of the bodies and faces of women.

So the subject of hair is anything but trivial.

For women, the rules governing hair-covering stem from a passage from the Koran that states: "Say to the believing women that they should lower their gaze and guard their modesty.... They should draw their veils over their bosoms and not display their ornaments."

"Zinah," the Arabic word for ornament, has come to mean "hair." So, strictly speaking, women can go bareheaded only in front of other women, their husbands, fathers, sons, nephews, servants, slaves and children small enough to "have no sense of the shame of sex."

But the Koranic verse itself is open to interpretation, and the Koran also states in many verses that there is no compulsion in Islam. That has promoted debates about—as well as experimentation with—the extent, color and design of hijab, or Islamic cover.

For men, there is even more confusion because there is no Koranic verse requiring that they grow beards. But the Prophet Muhammad had a beard, as had the prophets of Judaism and Christianity before him. So having a beard can be a visible symbol of being created by God. And many Muslim clerics over the centuries have written opinions strongly recommending beard-growing or even calling it an Islamic duty.

"In the world in which Islam was revealed, men kept their beards whether they were Christian, Jewish or Muslim," said Seyyed Hossein Nasr, professor of Islamic Studies at George Washington University. "There were no beardless prophets. You never had a shaved Moses or Abraham or Jesus." (Even today, he added, practitioners of other religions, like some rigorously Orthodox Jews, place great importance on men retaining facial hair and women not displaying their own hair.)

Over the centuries, the absence of a Koranic dictum on facial hair led to variety. According to some sayings attributed to Muhammad, the mustache should be too short to be placed in the mouth. Some Sufi dervishes responded by growing their mustaches long—to show their independence from the esoteric rules of organized religion. Other clerics claimed that although Muhammad had a good-sized beard, his mustache was thin, which prompted some pious Muslims to clip their mustaches short. Many Muslims who are averse to beards but believe shaving is wrong keep a short growth that they clip every few days. Decades ago, Communists in the Muslim Middle East sported Lenin-like goatees.

Under the Taliban, men were required to grow beards at least four inches long. The order was based on what some Islamic scholars believe is a somewhat spurious Islamic teaching, because traditionally, a man with a long beard meant one of two things: either he was of a venerable age or had great spiritual or intellectual authority. "Even in Egypt today, a long beard on a 22-year-old would be considered a sign of pretension," said Mr. Nasr. "You will not find many ordinary bakers with long beards unless they're 70 years old."

Choice—to veil or not, to shave or not—has been an issue in Islam for more than a century. In 1935, going even further than Turkey's secular modernizers, Reza Shah of Iran decreed that the wearing of traditional dress for both women and men was punishable by a prison term. The army and police roamed through villages to enforce the law, tearing the all-enveloping chador off women and handing out free Western-style suits to men. Reza Shah also forbade men to wear turbans. Mustaches were allowed (the shah wore one) but beards were forbidden, even for clerics, although the ban was only episodically enforced.

To many women, the veil was a source of protection, respect and virtue. In her 1992 memoir, "Daughter of Persia," Sattareh Farman Farmaian, the daughter of an Iranian Qajar prince, recalled her mother's bitter reaction to Reza Shah's edict: "He doesn't fear God, this evil shah—may God curse him for it!" Some women refused to leave home, some because they didn't want to be bareheaded in public, others to protest coercion.

For men of the cloth in Islam, a beard is essential. In the days of the Iranian monarchy, Ayatollah Ali Khamenei, who is now Iran's spiritual leader, was humiliated by having his beard shaved and his turban removed during one period of imprisonment. A former Iranian president, Ali Akbar Hashemi Rafsanjani, a midlevel cleric, is considered most unlucky because he has a few strands of hair on his face.

Perhaps the clearest rules about hair for Muslims govern those making the pilgrimage to Mecca that all Muslims are supposed to do once in their lives. That trip, the hajj, is a ritual of death, purification and renewal, and men are required to remove some of their hair, although they do not have to shave their heads. Men and women clip or shave their underarms and their pubic hair and during the hajj men let their facial hair grow. At the end of the hajj, men must go to barbers to clip or shave their hair.

One of the most confusing moments in the history of hair in the Muslim world in the 20th century came in the late 1960's, when Western hippies trekked through places like Iran and Afghanistan. For the Muslims who lived there, the long hair and beards were confusing. Westerners weren't supposed to look like that.

DISCUSSION QUESTIONS

Hair as a Battlefield for the Soul

1. This article discusses the symbolic importance of hair. What do you feel hair symbolizes? For women? For men?

2. Why were beards for men deemed important under the rule of the Taliban?

32 Men Hear Saudi Women's Unmentionable Details

Donna Abu-Nasr

The Saudi woman, swathed in black with only her eyes showing, held up a lacy orange bra and asked the salesman in a whisper whether he had her size.

"Did you say 36C?" the man replied, loudly enough for other customers to hear. "Are you sure you don't need a bigger size?"

"It was 36C in the past," said the woman.

"Well, the past changes," responded the salesman.

It's not the kind of exchange one might expect in Saudi Arabia, where the sexes are segregated by an unwritten but stringent code. Yet when it comes to lingerie, women often find themselves having to discuss their most intimate details with strange men.

The reason is that in most stores, only men are allowed behind the counter.

The alternative is women-only shopping centers, of which there are few, or department stores, where it's self-service but the selection is narrower.

And once outside the house, women may be seen only as shapeless forms under black cloaks called *abayas*. A visible hand, jeans-clad leg or strand of hair can bring trouble from the *muttawa*, the powerful religious police.

At social functions such as weddings, where the sexes are segregated in different halls, women can wear strapless evening dresses—but they have to arrive covered up and can reveal their gowns only once they are in the women-only hall.

The subject rouses much passion among women.

"Society covers you up, and the salesman strips you down," said Gihan Ramadan, an on-line editor for Arab News daily. "It's outrageous. Nothing could be more humiliating."

Mohammed bin Abdullah al-Hawwas wrote to the newspaper Al Watan recently about accompanying his wife to a store and seeing her "engaged in a very private conversation with a strange man about her body measurements."

"I couldn't take it, and I pulled my wife out," he said.

Jehayeir al-Muassaid, a writer who has tackled this issue in Al Riyad newspaper, was particularly incensed about a two-week book fair that women were allowed to visit on only two half-days, closely watched by muttawa agents.

The reason given was that the vendors were men, said al-Muassaid.

"What makes me livid is that it's OK for a woman to buy underwear from a man who pulls and stretches each piece to show her how it can accommodate a certain body part and then rubs it to show her how she can wash out stains, but it's not OK for her to buy from a man a book that would enrich her as a person," she added. "What kind of logic is that?"

The same logic, apparently, allows lingerie store windows to display full-busted mannequins in skimpy underwear and sheer nightgowns.

Al-Muassaid said one explanation for the contradictions arising from allowing men to sell lingerie while enforcing the rules of the abaya is that "the rush to turn the Saudi society into a consumer society was not matched with a drive to increase social awareness" to the changes.

Reprinted with permission of The Associated Press.

Men Hear Saudi Women's Unmentionable Details

1. What ways have Saudi women found to combat issues of the rule that only men are allowed behind the counter? Are they successful?

2. If the rules regarding Saudi women's public appearance were lifted, what challenges would face them?

33 The Pared-Down Prom Dress

Amy Merrick

In her quest for the perfect prom dress, Rebecca Neal, a high-school senior in Nicholasville, Ky., found frustration rack after rack.

All the dresses left her feeling, well, undressed. Too low-cut in front, and she couldn't bend over. Too low-cut in back—she'd be blushing all night. Too tight, and she couldn't dance.

"I think designers need to actually go to prom and talk to people," says the 17-year-old Ms. Neal, who eventually settled on a classic, burgundy dress with a shimmery black-lace overlay.

With the prom season in full swing, designers are betting more than ever on skimpy, peekaboo offerings. There are the "two-piece gowns," made up of a midriff-baring halter top and skirt. Then there are the thigh-high slits and cleavage-baring numbers.

The dresses have become so daring—so Frederick's of Hollywood—they've begun to stir a backlash. More than a dozen schools nationwide have instituted prom "dress codes," some specifically banning the bare-midriff look. In Arcadia, Fla., DeSoto County High School now insists that some cloth cover the tummy, though "netting or sheer material covering the midriff is acceptable." Dress slit lengths are regulated too; they can't go higher than a girl's fingertips when she hangs her hand by her side. (For boys, sneakers are an infraction.)

Concerned about the growing popularity of skimpy styles in the past few years, DeSoto Principal Steve Cantees rounded up students last fall to flip through magazines and help him write some moderate rules. "When I saw the styles this year, I said, 'Oh my gosh,'" he says.

For high-school boys, meanwhile, the new styles amount to something of a mixed blessing. Faced with a date in a revealing outfit, some are simply flummoxed. With so many strapless or spaghetti-strap dresses, few boys bother to offer up the traditional pin-on corsage. Others aren't sure where to rest their hands while dancing, some girls report. "I think a girl should look more princess-like," says Adam Hansen, an 18-year-old high-school senior from Wood Dale, Ill. "The pictures would look better with a nice full dress."

Designers peg the racy look to pop stars like Britney Spears and Christina Aguilera, both famous for provocative outfits. One two-piece prom dress is even dubbed "Genie in a Bottle," after the pop single that launched Ms. Aguilera's career two years ago.

Prom watchers say girls aspire to a different style than they did in years past. "Instead of looking to be Cinderella, they're looking to their rock-

Wall Street Journal. Eastern Edition (staff produced copy only) by Amy Merrick. Copyright 2001 by Dow Jones and Co. Inc. Reproduced with permission of Dow Jones & Co. Inc. in the format Textbook via Copyright Clearance Center.

star idols, " says Annemarie Iverson, editor-in-chief of teen magazine YM, who says she disapprovingly inserted a line in this year's prom special issue saying "un-dressing like Britney Spears" was "out."

Says the 37-year-old Ms. Iverson: "It sounds old-fashioned, but a sense of appropriateness is really a key lesson for young women."

Clearly, many teens like the minimalist look. Stocking her stores with corset tops and strapless ballgowns, formalwear designer Jessica McClintock says she is having one of her best years in some time. But she also says some customers think the cleavage-baring styles are stepping over the line. "We got an awful lot of letters from parents and kids who said, 'You know, we were just looking for something simpler,'" she says.

Typically known for her more-modest designs and use of chiffon and satin, Ms. McClintock herself admits she has been seeing a lot of "really trashy stuff" in catalogs, especially two-piece styles with bra tops and skirts cut far below the navel.

A group of about 20 high-school girls in Kansas got so fed up with the lack of modest choices that one complained to customer service at a Nordstrom Inc. store in Overland Park. To the group's surprise, Nordstrom executives invited them to explain what styles they would like to see.

For four months, the girls—all members of a Kansas City-area church youth group—combed through magazines and even sketched their own designs. Some asked seamstresses to make the gowns, which included styles in red chiffon, white eyelet and purple satin. Most of the designs were long gowns with covered shoulders, higher necklines and low or no slits.

"I feel more comfortable being a little more covered up," says 16-year-old Annie Kershisnik. "But I don't want to wear a grandma dress."

After their fashion show last month, the Nordstrom executives told the girls over lemonade and cookies that their buyers would look for more demure styles. "I think they had a lot of great ideas," says Lynn Brooks, a regional merchandiser who attended the presentation. "It kind of confirmed what a lot of young girls want out there: trendy, but maybe not so bare and strappy." As word of their presentation spread, the girls say they have received hundreds of letters and e-mails in support.

Some retailers say they are seeing interest in more-glamorous gowns, spurred by actresses like Julia Roberts and Renee Zellweger at this year's Academy Awards. Ms. Roberts's vintage black-and-white Valentino gown was a big hit with teen girls, and designers say they expect a classy look to grow in popularity for next year's prom.

Still, some of the provocative dresses are selling well. The two-piece gown, with its bikini-style top and full skirt, has been something of a hit, retailers report. Vanessa Gouldburn, 17, wore a lavender two-piecer to her senior prom last weekend. "It's not so elegant, and I don't have to be so serious all night," says the Houston teen, who doesn't mind prom dresses being more revealing. "It's cool to get away from the traditional-style prom dresses. A lot of them could be too plain and boring."

The Pared-Down Prom Dress DISCUSSION QUESTIONS

1. If the trend toward more modest prom gowns continues, what effect will this have on designers, manufacturers, and retailers?

2. What is the impetus for more conservative prom dresses? Do you feel it is coming from the fashion world, pop culture, social movements, religion, or politics? Why?

34   Goodbye Briefs, Hello Jammers
Rob Gray

Evolution—in performance swimwear and young men's attitudes—goes beyond a basic theory of survival of the fittest, or the tightest.

The style and science of swimwear is rapidly changing, in Iowa's high school pools and across the country. Suits offering more coverage than the classic skimpy, Speedo-style brief are finding their way onto swimmers' bodies.

Some suits help ease body-image anxiety. Some high-tech suits, such as Speedo's Fastskin, are expensive and worn in hopes of increasing performance.

"One of the things we've discovered about high school boys is they're rather shy," said Mike McWilliams, the Ottumwa boys' coach. "Shyer than I thought they'd be."

Bettendorf coach Mike Ahrens said his team still uses briefs, but estimates up to 50 percent of swimmers in the Mississippi Athletic Conference have changed to more expansive models.

"I've always heard that's one reason boys aren't coming out for swimming," Ahrens said. "They don't want to wear the Speedo."

Des Moines East and Des Moines Lincoln are among the schools that have switched from briefs to suits known as "jammers" that extend to just above the knee.

Both schools adopted the new suits in an effort to halt a decline in participation.

"I've seen a lot of new guys come out," East swimmer Ross Hesseltine said.

Lincoln's Eric Crawford said adjusting to wearing jammers took time.

"At first it's a little tight," Crawford said. "It sort of feels different from Speedos, but after a while it's pretty cool."

East made the change last season. Lincoln is wearing jammers for the first time this season.

"The misconception is they have to wear bikinis, and that's a myth," East boys' coach Susan Monahan-Blair said. "The other is they have to shave their bodies, and that's crazy."

FIGURE 6.3 *Speedo briefs or longer suits are the options for male swimmers.*

Top swimmers have long favored shaving their bodies, or tapering, shortly before important events. The practice makes the body slightly more streamlined, and is believed to help attain faster times.

Whether or not tapering or squeezing into state-of-the-art suits measurably enhances physical performance is a point of contention at all levels of competitive swimming.

But Iowa's top boys' swimmers aren't taking any chances, especially when it comes to districts on Feb. 9 and the state meet on Feb. 15-16 at Iowa City. In addition to tapering, many of the state's best plan to wear or buy a half- or full-length custom suit.

Valley's Michael Burke, who ranks fourth in the state in the 500-yard freestyle, owns a Fastskin jammer for use at major meets, but has trained and swum in briefs for several years.

"If you told me to wear a jammer when I was 10 years old, I probably would have thought you were crazy," Burke said.

Lucas Hale, who swims for Council Bluffs' combined high school team, plans to wear his full-body, sleeveless suit for his second consecutive district meet.

"It kind of makes you feel like you're faster, or it might psyche out the other person," Hale said.

East's Hesseltine is saving money to purchase a custom suit for districts and state. He said the expense of the suits—which cost from about $90 for a leg-length jammer to $350 for a full-body model—limits the local market to those who want to improve their district or state finishes.

"The guys that are close enough, who want that little edge, or the guys who know they are going to be there, they're the ones who might get them," Hesseltine said.

Controlled studies on the effects of full-body or full-leg suits are sparse, but opinions abound.

Dave Johnson, coach of the Canadian men's national swim team, said in a Montreal Gazette article that the line between perception and performance is small.

"You're not going to put this on and become an instant winner," Johnson said.

But Speedo has built an impressive résumé for its frontline suit. According to the company, 27 of 33 Olympic gold medalists in the 2000 Games at Sydney, Australia, wore Fastskins.

West Des Moines Dowling's Josh Otis, the state's second-ranked 100 butterfly swimmer, doesn't want to get ambushed at state if the suit actually does work as touted.

"If it does have an advantage, I don't want to be the only one who isn't getting that advantage," Otis said.

Speedo is banking on—and feeding—the perception that the Fastskin dramatically improves times and has commissioned studies to prove just that. One study found that swimmers wearing Fastskins enjoyed a three percent reduction in drag.

Objective studies are mixed, but Speedo trumpets endorsements from Olympic gold medalists such as Lenny Krayzelburg and Amy Van Dyken.

Swimmers and coaches largely agree it's the work, not the suit, that translates into reduction in times. There's also the question of how high-tech suits—if as effective as advertised—might create a gap between haves and have-nots.

"My belief is the swimmer makes the race," Burke said.

Still, if putting on a pricey or longer suit makes a swimmer feel more comfortable and confident, the investment could be worth it based on perception alone.

"I think if they thought they could wear a loincloth like Tarzan to go faster, they'd go faster," Ottumwa's McWilliams said.

Goodbye Briefs, Hello Jammers

1. Other men's sports have designed their attire to cover more of the body. For what reason(s) was this done, and what were the changes?

2. Because modesty issues have focused more on women, what social concerns prompt male modesty?

35 Racy School Fashions under Fire

Melanie Kletter and Peter Braunstein

When hot pop singer Britney Spears whipped off her clothes to reveal a barely there, flesh-tone halter top and tight pants at the MTV Video Music Awards in early September, many parents were up in arms.

This squeaky-clean teen, who has used her position to extol the virtues of moral living, suddenly became a force with which to be reckoned. In one brief moment, she became a sex symbol more akin to stars such as Madonna and Jennifer Lopez than the youngsters on the "Mickey Mouse Club," where she got her start.

The issue involves more than just another canned "scandalous" teenybopper appearance on MTV. Parents across the country realized immediately that Spears, being both a role model and fashion icon to many teenage—and younger—girls, might inspire her legions of followers to dress in a similarly pseudo-nudist fashion.

As it turns out, too-sexy clothing for teenage girls has become an issue at school and in the wider media—the subject was a recent Time magazine cover feature and the storyline of an episode in last season's HBO series "Sex and the City." The recurring question in all these forums is the same: When it comes to 14-year-old girls, how much is too much or, more appropriately, how little is too little? Should teens and the younger girls who worship them be allowed to wear skimpy clothing a la Christina Aguilera?

Fashions in recent years have gotten tighter and sexier both for teens and women. Recent trends, such as halter and open-back tops, belly-baring shirts and low-cut cleavage tops, are being marketed to teens, pre-teens and girls. So the idea of what is considered "appropriate" has become a contentious topic. Although teens have had a love affair with music and fashion since the days of a crooning Frank Sinatra and a hip-swinging Elvis, today's youngest stars are wearing clothes that rival what's shown in the raciest of men's magazines.

"A lot of it is in the eye of the beholder," said Irma Zandl, president of the New York-based trend and consulting firm The Zandl Group. "The standard of what is considered cute and sexy has been redefined by a new generation. Adults look at it as being sexy, while teens think they are being cute."

Zandl said it has happened before, adding, "What happens is that all of a sudden 90 percent of people start wearing tube tops and at a certain point in time, that becomes OK."

Fashions across the board have gotten racier, and many teens are taking cues from their older siblings and parents, who are heading off to work now in items such as skintight knit sweaters from Wayne Rogers and even snug tank tops from more mainstream stores such as Banana Republic.

Sex isn't the only issue.

Not only have schools around the country banned clothing for being too sexy, but they've also clamped down on apparel deemed gang-related, racist, sexist or even "sociopathic," such as the black outfits worn by the perpetrators of the Columbine High School killings. The list of what has been banned in some schools ranges from understandable to extreme, from two-piece prom dresses and hip-hop gear, to expensive sneakers and skimpy tops and underwear. Many schools have outlawed T-shirts featuring beer and tobacco prints, and what they see as controversial logos, such as "Porn Star."

Among other recent incidents:

Administrators at Sam Barlow High School in Gresham, Okla., banned a 17-year-old gay student from wearing a button that read "Because I'm Gay, That's Why," as well as a T-shirt proclaiming "Sorry Girls, I'm Gay." Angered by what he deemed suppression of free speech, the stu-

Courtesy of Fairchild Publications, Inc.

dent showed up the next day in a black velvet dress, high-heeled pumps and red lipstick.

In an attempt to clamp down on controversial iconography, Lincoln Park High School in Detroit, banned a 17-year-old honor student from wearing a pentacle, or five-pointed star, associated by some with satanism. The school ban also applied to the Muslim crescent and star and Jewish Star of David. The student, a self-described witch and member of the Wicca religion, took her case to the Witches Anti-Discrimination League (WADL) and the American Civil Liberties Union, which filed a lawsuit against the school on her behalf. The school has since changed its policy on this issue.

To combat gang-related violence back in 1996, Calumet High School in Chicago banned black, white and red clothing, including a red and black version of Air Jordans. The colors, incidentally, are the same ones worn by the Chicago Bulls.

The Jordan School Board in Utah instituted a policy banning the word "Vegan" from clothing, and suspended one student who repeatedly defied the prohibition. The school district claimed there was a gang-related faction of potentially violent "straight-edge" vegans who needed to be suppressed. Vegan is a form of dietary regiment that generally excludes dairy and meat products.

Last year, Carver Middle School in Harris County, Ga. suspended several white students for wearing the Confederate flag symbol. In turn, some of the students' parents insisted that black students should not be able to wear the Fubu brand of urban clothing, a brand that has been worn by many high-profile hip-hop stars. While the parents didn't specify why they chose Fubu, they seized on the label, which stands for For Us, By Us.

The Harris County school superintendent responded by temporarily banning both Fubu and the Confederate flag from school premises.

Following the shootings in the spring of 1999 at Columbine High School in Littleton, Colo., some schools began to crack down on what they saw as "subversive" trends. The long trench coats worn by the two Columbine high-school shooters, both of whom were seniors, suddenly became a warning sign of kids who were at risk or potentially dangerous.

Even the Billabong brand—an outdoor label most associated with sports—has been banned because of the name's similarity to the word "bong," a term for a certain marijuana pipe. The principal of Winneconne High School in Winneconne, Wisc. banned clothing with the Billabong name because he felt that the word "bong" should not be advertised in school.

In response to the proliferation of controversial apparel, many schools have instituted dress codes and uniforms. For example, last fall in Kansas City, Kan., the Turner School District instituted for the first time a standardized attire policy for all students, which includes the banning of jeans.

Jim Hass, a spokesman for the district, told local papers that the district thought "there was a lack of distinction between play and outside work and school."

The current spate of banned clothing is reminiscent of the Vietnam War protest days of the late Sixties and early Seventies, where peace signs and radical sayings adorned all sorts of attire and the American flag was sewn into unusual places, leading to suspensions and counter protests and adding to the political rancor of the day.

Of course, today it's also been great publicity for the labels that make the list. Porn Star, a label owned by L&H Apparel in Santa Barbara, Calif., has been at the center of its own controversies since it first opened its doors five years ago, according to Sean Murphy, a founder of the firm.

However, driven by its logo, bawdy slogans and body-conscious silhouettes, the line found a following among flashy customers who wanted to get noticed. Porn Star courts controversy with its racy name, and because it is marketed as a teen brand.

"From the start we have had resistance, but it's been a good way for people to identify us," said Murphy.

As the line became more prominent in the marketplace, several conservative factions, primarily parental groups in the South, refused to let their daughters wear apparel that had the Porn Star logo on it. Many stores, including at least one large specialty chain, Hot Topic, withdrew the line from its shelves.

In 1997, the firm launched a new label called Starlette, which is oriented to younger customers and carries tamer slogans with slightly less attitude, such as "I Rule" and "Talk to the Hand."

Last year, to make up sales from the chains that dropped Porn Star, L&H launched a third label called FOS, or Freedom of Speech. FOS offers many of the same looks as Porn Star, but the shirts do not contain the word "Porn." Among its offerings are shirts with sayings such as "Hucci" and "Drama Queen" and ones with stick figures in sexual acts.

Now the label is sold in fashionable boutiques in the U.S. and in Europe, and has also found a home online. Sales this year are expected to reach about $10 million, according to executives.

"Kids should be able to wear whatever they want," Murphy said. "As long as they are not hurting anyone or doing anything bad."

The firm does have some limits. Murphy, who was featured in a recent episode about risky teen fashion on the "Jenny Jones" show, said he will not put the "f" word on shirts.

"We try not to be too hard core or freaky," he said.

The firm also doesn't do any advertising, but has been recognized by some bands, including Blink 182 and Foo Fighters, who regularly wear Porn Star apparel.

At the same time that schools are cracking down on teen fashions, formerly "subversive" apparel brands are starting to find appeal beyond the underground boutiques found in major cities.

Hot Topic, a fast-growing specialty teen chain, has pushed the limits of mainstream fashion and offers a wide range of labels that were once relegated to streetwear shops. The publicly held, music-oriented chain is located in malls, a typical teen hangout, and it has found wide appeal among young men and women. Its offerings range from gothic to punk, and includes labels such as Lip Service and Serious.

With its chrome fixtures and blaring music, Hot Topic resembles a nightclub more than the traditional teen stores such as Pacific Sunwear of California and American Eagle Outfitters, which carry sportier and preppier looks.

Other firms are trying to do the sexy looks of Britney Spears without going too far.

"We try to keep some sort of balance," said Maria De'Angelo, designer at Star City, a junior company. "We want to get the sexy looks without getting skintight. A lot of girls can't fit into those looks."

She said her company offers plenty of Lycra spandex, which clings to the body, but draws the line at super-short or extra-clingy items.

"You can't stop kids," De'Angelo noted. "They are always going to wear sexy things."

Atoosa Rubinstein, the editor in chief of CosmoGirl, said her magazine doesn't just feature what teen icons like Spears wear, but tries to show fashions worn by "real teens."

"We are very conscious of the way teens really want to dress," she said. "Most of our readers don't embrace what Britney and Christina wear. Our slogan is 'If you can't wear it to school, it's not cool.'"

DISCUSSION QUESTIONS

Racy School Fashions under Fire

1. Immodest fashions have prompted schools to institute dress codes. Do you feel this trend promotes a stronger environment for learning? How?

2. This article examines the increased popularity of sexier and more immodest clothing. What social situations are okay for such an appearance and which are not?

36 All That's Bare Is Fit to Wear, So Why the Stares?

Jenny Lyn Bader

Blame HBO's "Sex and the City" or blame the decline of the ozone layer, but skin is in. American women are showing more of it than ever before.

Summer itself is hotter. And over the last decade, the proliferation of the Wonderbra coincided with global warming so that just as cleavages became more pronounced, shorts became shorter.

The stock market, always synchronized with hemlines, has reached crazy new heights and so has the slip dress. Some of the skirts, like some of the stocks, have since plunged down again. Other skirts, like other stocks, have reached these new heights without having much to them in the way of visible material: They're so sheer, they're almost transparent.

With the triumph of minimalism, the handkerchief has returned, not as a decoration in a man's pocket but as an entire piece of women's clothing, featured in handkerchief tops and hanky hemlines. Sleeves, once a staple of the workplace, have become optional. MTV's official anthem for its Spring Break 2000 was the "Thong Song," the R-and-B artist Sisqo's ode to revealing apparel.

A brief history of skimpy: When things from the lingerie or handkerchief category first became "clothes," they seemed like mistakes. The model wearing the bra top down the runway looked as if she had been interrupted while getting dressed. The woman arriving at the party in the camisole looked as if she had been awakened from a nap. Backless shoes and skirts appeared incomplete. But now everyone can tell that these things are not mistakes, because it has become O.K. to wear what was formerly considered underwear or handkerchiefs in most situations.

They're not fashion mistakes, at least. But following fashions can lead to other mistakes. Just as tight corsets put Victorian women into severe physical discomfort, so today's scarf tops and cropped tanks can bring stylish dressers to new levels of personal discomfort. As women have embraced the empowerment and comfort of wearing less, they have also been punished by those who can't see past naked skin. As Erin Brockovich discovered, and as Julia Roberts learned when she played Ms. Brockovich in the recent movie, if women need to work twice as hard as men to prove they're as good, scantily clad women need to work three times as hard.

Female exposure has been attacked by the puritanical and the macho alike. At the George Washington Middle School in Alexandria, Va., 12-year-old girls wearing shorts of the lengths recommended by Seventeen magazine were accused of violating the school dress code, lined up and subjected to humiliating inspections. Last season, even the trend-setting sitcom character Ally McBeal was held in contempt of court for wearing a micro-mini.

On the day of the recent Puerto Rican Day parade in New York City's Central Park, women wearing the latest fashions were mauled by young men less interested in the pages of Vogue than in the violent imagery of traditional skin magazines.

It's a shame that plunging necklines and ascending midriffs have become identified with pornographic fantasies, because they do reflect an improved reality. Women of all sizes, shapes and ages wear the tie-backs and halters once seen only on the young and slim, partly thanks to better self-image and the increased acceptance of different body types. Designers have even made tube tops for the visibly pregnant.

While it seems generous of designers to want women to feel better about themselves, clothing makers do profit from skimpy fashions:

they can charge more and more for items that are tinier and tinier.

Less is simple, and simplicity especially delights the low-end retailers who copy and mass-produce couture. The popularity of the George label sold in England's Asda chain, which was just purchased by Wal-Mart, demonstrates that consumers like cheap versions of designer fashions so much that they will buy them in the supermarket. The American discount warehouse Sam's Club now sells clothes. Why go elsewhere? these non-clothing clothing stores seem to be asking. Wouldn't it be nice to wear less, pay less and think about the whole thing less?

It would be nice, if the judgments and gazes that followed weren't quite so judgmental and gazing. Those who dare to show the flesh and the confidence celebrated by current styles may find themselves in a zone of discomfort. Women who dress provocatively have traditionally been accused of sending a mixed message. But now that provocative is chic, women are the ones receiving the mixed message: Everyone's wearing it, but wear it at your own risk.

DISCUSSION QUESTIONS

All That's Bare Is Fit to Wear

1. In this article the author states: "As women have embraced the empowerment and comfort of wearing less, they have also been punished by those who can't see past naked skin." Explain and give some examples of why American women's liberty of clothing themselves as they choose has also created some problems for them.

2. What social and cultural factors encourage or discourage women from dressing provocatively? What do you feel is the current trend and why?

37 Reveal or Conceal? Examining the Meaning of Modesty in Postmodern America

Susan O. Michelman
University of Kentucky

This paper examines some of the contradictions and complexities associated with the meanings of modesty and immodesty of dress in contemporary American culture. American television, movies, music videos, and fashion have increasingly shown more and more skin (Thompson, 2000). Recent movies (such as *Charlie's Angels: Full Throttle*, starring Cameron Diaz, Drew Barrymore, and Lucy Liu; and *Gigli*, with Ben Affleck and the notorious Jennifer Lopez, who bared a lot at the Academy Awards ceremony several years ago in a revealing dress that challenged the boundaries of decorum) present

---

Original for this text.

---

contradictions to those who feel dress can be modest and still be fashionable. Some of the current reality television shows, including *Fear Factor*, *Survivor*, and *Dog Eat Dog*, create advertised excitement by using scantily clad women and men who perform acts of physical danger while the audience is taunted by the possibility that their very minimal attire will fall off while they are on camera.

Britney Spears, a leading pop icon to millions of young girls, has in four years gone from the cute girl next door to posing practically naked for the cover of *Rolling Stone* magazine (see Figure 6.1). On the fashion runway, nudity is commonplace and a quick way for a designer to get a little extra attention in the press. Baring of breasts is not a new or recent phenomenon in fashion. For example, Rudi Gernreich designed a topless bathing suit in the 1960s. However, designers of American swimwear for women are testing new waters by revealing more of the body in mainstream pop culture. Immodesty is certainly more than just showing more and more skin. It can also be the actual act of being immodest, including the "attitude" or shock value of such behavior. It is also about how the behavior is read by the viewer and the corresponding response. A recent article in *The New York Times* illustrates how the bikini, an immodest clothing item, is now associated with aggressive behavior of some women in movies.

> …the bikini has undergone a transition from a symbol of languorous sexuality…to a symbol of tough, bloodletting, physical showmanship. In movies like "Charlie's Angels: Full Throttle," and television series like "Boarding House: North Shore" on the WB and "Surf Girls" on MTV, the tiny, triangle-topped bikini is the millennial equivalent of the power suit—the costume for women who ride 20-foot waves or smash foreheads of evildoers, thus proving they are just as combative as men. (Bellafante, 2003)

American consumers of pop culture view the increasing immodesty that has become more and more commonplace and seemingly accepted and assimilated into mainstream American culture. One needs only to go to the local shopping mall to see how these fashions have filtered into all retail, from Nordstrom to the Gap. Abercrombie & Fitch has been censored for their use of nudity in their advertising campaign, and Victoria's Secret posts oversized ads in malls and on billboards of women in scanty underwear who dwarf the viewer with their well-endowed physical attributes.

CURRENT DISCOURSE ON MODESTY

In the midst of all this body-baring, there is an increasing backlash in American society advocating a return to a more conservative appearance. In *A Return to Modesty*, Shalit (1999) explores the broader topic of contemporary modesty for young women that speaks of innocence, mystery, sexual reticence, protection of hope, and vulnerability. She examines immodesty in dress as part of a larger issue that encompasses behaviors associated with the way one appears. The author agrees that talking about modesty or immodesty in dress is a complex issue, because revealing clothing does not always signify immodesty as exemplified in the dress of other cultures:

> In Western societies modesty in dress will manifest itself differently from that among the Andamanese, and within Western society different things will be immodest at different times. But that doesn't mean we can't establish what immodesty in dress is. When a culture becomes immodest, it is immodest with respect to the conventions that have gone before. (p. 67)

Shalit looks at the problems of appearance within the context of what she describes as the "normalization of pornography" (pp. 49–54). The contemporary debate volleys between conservative censorship and civil libertarians with, as she describes, ordinary men and women suffering the nonresolution of this conflict. The looseness of contemporary sexual mores for unmarried young adults is at the heart of Shalit's concerns, and she addresses women's immodest dress as an important component of the problem. In an effort to find a way back to a more modest approach to sexuality, she turns to religious themes taken from her own Jewish background. She observes that, almost unanimously, religions view modesty as inextricably linked to spirituality and holiness.

In *Secret Keeper: The Delicate Power of Modesty*, Gresh (2002) appeals to teenage girls from a conservative Christian perspective to examine how immodesty in dress works against them to create a social environment that promotes sexual promiscuity. She uses the Gestalt Theory of visual design to explain how a plunging neckline or a short skirt creates a response of sexual arousal in men through the visual and psychological completion of a body-revealing appearance. In Gresh's view, this is not just fashion, it is a sin. Likewise, Pollard (2001), in *Christian Modesty and the Public Undressing of America*, evaluates the significance of the increasingly revealing bathing suit for women during the twentieth century and the acceptance of immodesty and, more importantly, a weakening of Christian morality. Pollard, as well as the other authors cited, is particularly concerned with the proliferation of barer images in the American media and the increasing acceptance of their existence by the majority of the American public.

The proliferation of Web sites on the topic of modesty is another way to view the current and increasing interest in this topic, primarily from religious groups such as conservative Jews and fundamental Christians, Mormons, and Muslims, as well as neo-conservative interest groups who feel that the degree of immodesty in American culture has gone too far.

Why has tension over this issue surfaced at this time in America? And why is a fundamental religious viewpoint now gaining rapid acceptability? In the current social environment, the interest in modesty is much more than a shift in fashion from immodest to modest or a predictable change in the continuous cycle of fashion that discards something old for something new and trendy. The increased interest in modesty is more than an attempt to renew or distance ourselves from our former immodest selves. Rather, I believe we are witnessing the ascendance and assertion of religious views on fashion and the body. Currently in America, the act of being modest

and fashionable are not two mutually exclusive behaviors.

It is important to examine how and why religious groups are entering the fashion discourse, contesting the idea that modest dress is incompatible with being fashionable. The concerns of fundamental religions are being mainstreamed into the larger popular culture of fashion, particularly among the adolescent and postadolescent age group of young women who spend more on fashion than other age groups of women. Current changes in Americans' perception of religion create a social environment open to a re-examination of issues of modesty and immodesty.

CURRENT RELIGIOUS TRENDS IN AMERICA AND MODESTY

A current Gallup survey discloses that roughly four out of ten Americans identify themselves as evangelical or born-again Christians (Tolson, 2003). Evangelical colleges across the United States are gaining broader acceptance and moving closer to the academic mainstream (Silverstein & Olsen, 2003). According to the Council for Christian Colleges and Universities, U.S. enrollment at its schools climbed 26.6 percent from 1997 to 2002. Although evangelical schools account for only 3.1 percent of students in U.S. four-year colleges, the schools' enrollment growth has outpaced that of public and other private institutions. Wolfe (2003) argues that religion in the United States is being transformed in radically new directions. Evangelicalism dominates the culture. For example, President Bush, whose conversion experience reportedly launched him onto the road of politics, is only one of many American political leaders who are self-proclaimed evangelicals. This identity permeates the language, concerns, and faith-based social initiatives in contemporary American society. Americans are highly influenced by this evangelical milieu in high places:

> ...many characteristics of the evangelical style—its strongly personalist and therapeutic tendencies, its market-savvy approaches to expanding the flock and even a certain

theological fuzziness—have permeated other faith traditions in America, including Roman Catholicism and Judaism. Wolfe says, only half facetiously, "We are all evangelicals now." (Tolson, 2003)

The current evangelical following is differentiated from fundamentalism, a hypermoralistic, biblically literalist, and antiintellectual viewpoint. Evangelicalism dominates the culture and is "personalist, therapeutic, entrepreneurial" (Tolson, 2003).

Evangelicals, like fundamentalists, are concerned with feminist trends toward gender equality, which they believe are symptomatic of a declining moral order (Ferrante, 1995). Evangelicals and other fundamental religious groups believe that female sexuality is dangerous if left unharnessed and uncontrolled (Fernea & Fernea, 1995). This belief leads to the religious practice of proscribing modest and proper dress for female members. Modest dress for women includes covering the body in an attempt to obliterate body curves and avoid exposure of too much skin through plunging necklines and short skirts or shorts. Muslim and Orthodox Jewish women practice covering their heads in public, as hair is interpreted as a sexual sign for these groups (Miller & Michelman, 1997).

Covering body curves appears to be somewhat less of an issue for Christian evangelical, Mennonite, and Orthodox Jewish women than for Islamic women. Thinness is the ideal body shape for Mennonite men and women. Their religious view defines thinness as an expression of self-denial and control. Sensory enjoyment such as eating is considered sinful; therefore, a properly dressed Mennonite woman is both modest and thin (Arthur, 1997).

In 1986, Concerned Women of America, a group of female religious advocates drawn from both the fundamentalist and evangelical movements, wrote of the "supernaturalism" inherent in a woman's beauty and its potential for good or evil in the workplace (Edwards, 1993). However, since the 1980s, fundamental and evangelical women have had to adapt to the new economic realities of entering corporate America. For example, at Bob Jones University in South Carolina, classes begin with prayer but also teach young women to be Christian, competitive, and fashionable:

> In a classroom where 20 female students sat recently, Bibles and notebooks stacked neatly before them, facing half a dozen headless dress forms draped in deft knockoffs of Todd Oldham and Donna Karan, Prof. Diane Hay of the home economics department was teaching one of her popular safe beauty classes. (Edwards, 1993)

For years, many evangelical and fundamental women were directed to find work at home or in low-wage jobs at Christian hospitals and schools. Since the 1980s, these women have successfully entered the more competitive business world and have learned how to dress fashionably to both fit in and move ahead. The trend in the 1980s set the stage for fundamental women's current interest in dressing in a more mainstream and also fashionable way to fit in and compete. Today, the evangelical trend encompasses a broad swath of society and is thus having an increasingly influential impact on consumer America—more specifically, the fashion industry.

THE MODESTY DISCOURSE WITH FASHION

During the spring semester of 2002, while I was teaching a class titled "Dress, Gender, and Culture" to undergraduate students at the University of Massachusetts, I devoted a section of the course to the topic of modesty. I was frankly surprised at the high level of interest and discussion on this topic. I thought that these students, who had been raised on a steady diet of Madonna and more recently Britney Spears, would have some reluctance to engage in topics of modesty. Despite relentless marketing techniques pushing young women toward more provocative appearances, these students were anxious to discuss modesty and the general lack of it in American popular culture and fashion.

The Internet is a good place to examine grassroots interests in topics. When I first began

exploring the topic of modesty in the late 1990s, there were a few Web sites devoted to modest dress. Today, there is a proliferation from varying perspectives, still largely religious in orientation but conveying the visual message that this is not just a fringe movement in American society. For example, the Web site www.modestprom.com gives directions to young women on how to "fill in" strapless prom gowns. From the perspective of the creator of this Web site, the dress can be transformed to give it "more glamour and personality." They state that "strapless gowns are so common, you just might be able to get a used one very inexpensively—then with the purchase of just a little material, you can transform it into a modest gown." Figure 6.4 shows how a low-front neckline considered too revealing can be transformed to a more modest and yet fashionable presentation. In these illustrations, the point is well taken that the modest presentation is fashionable.

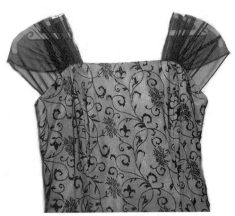

FIGURE 6.4 *A strapless and body-baring prom gown undergoes a makeover on www.modestprom.com.*

A group of young women in Kansas City, Missouri, generated enough interest in the modest prom dress issue to get the attention of a Nordstrom buyer, who was convinced to purchase a selection of more modest dresses. They now have a Web site (www.goodworks.net) and have generated 10,000 signatures on a petition they want to take to stores to show how important this issue is to them (see "The Pared-Down Prom Dress" in this chapter). They are hoping for 200,000 signatures. *Inside Edition*, an American television news show, aired a segment about these young women in contrast to a high school prom in Los Angeles where the dress was very revealing. This action indicates the growing interest and demand for more modest clothing and the impact its supporters can have on the retail market.

One of the great spokeswomen for the modesty movement is Danah Gresh (2002), a guest columnist on the Christian Broadcasting Network (www.cbn.com). In an article dated December 4, 2003, "The Fashion Battle: Is It One Worth Fighting?," you can watch and listen to her being interviewed on this topic. What you see is a very attractive and well-spoken young woman who advocates for purity and what she describes as "pure freedom," the title of her Web site. She appeals to the positive power of modesty for young women and argues that the end result of today's immodest fashion is sexual promiscuity:

> We believe that the temptation to fail sexually comes in different forms for girls and for boys. We also believe that they will one day enjoy God's gift of sex within the confines of marriage for different reasons. Whereas the girls are primarily emotionally driven, the guys are primarily driven by sight. Because of this dichotomy, it is vital that we educate them separately and emphasize different areas of temptation. (www.purefreedom.org)

This Web site is designed to appeal to young women. Gresh is using trendy and fashion-conscious marketing techniques to promote her message. She advertises that her first book, *And the Bride Wore White: Seven Secrets to Sexual Purity*, is the basis for a girls retreat in over 2,000 churches in different countries, reaching over 60,000 teenage girls.

This consumer group of evangelical young women is gaining a larger voice in mainstream consumer culture; likewise, they are demanding a greater influence in the design and production of modest fashions.

Conclusion

A sociological trend of changes in American religion is having a profound impact on consumer culture, specifically fashion for young women. Religious values can lead fashion, as demonstrated in the increasing interest in more modest fashion and the movement against immodesty. Ironically, this backlash against the fashion industry and subsequently popular culture, which historically came from feminists, is not led by them at the current moment, but rather by evangelical young women who are opposing the rampant immodesty in consumer culture and, based on their religious beliefs, are saying no to bare fashion.

A review of the literature on modesty and anthropological research demonstrates that views on modesty vary historically and also with cultural beliefs. Despite highly media-hyped immodest style, often aimed directly at young women, an increasing number of modesty-seeking consumers, often linked by strong religious values, are influencing the consumption of fashion. Through a proliferation of Web sites and campaigns directed at retail, these young women, choosing to buy modest clothes, have created an assertive discourse with fashion.

References

Arthur, L. (1997). Clothing, control, and women's agency: The mitigation of patriarchal power. In M. L. Damhorst, K. Miller, & S. Michelman (Eds.), *The Meanings of Dress*. New York: Fairchild.

Bellafante, G. (2003). More itsy-bitsy teeny-weeny than ever. *The New York Times*. Accessed July 15, 2003, at www.nyt.com.

Edwards, L. (1993, May 30). Worldly lessons. *The New York Times*, C1, C9.

Fernea, E. W., & Fernea, R. A. (1995). Symbolizing roles: Behind the veil. In M. E. Roach-Higgins, J. B. Eicher, & K. K. P. Johnson (Eds.), *Dress and Identity*. New York: Fairchild.

Ferrante, J. (1995). *Sociology: A Global Perspective*. Belmont, CA: Wadsworth Publishing Co.

Gresh, D. (1999). *And the Bride Wore White: Seven Secrets to Sexual Purity*. Chicago: Moody Press.

Gresh, D. (2002). *Secret Keeper: The Delicate Power of Modesty*. Chicago: Moody Press.

Gresh, D. (2003, December 4). The fashion battle: Is it one worth fighting? Christian Broadcasting Network. Accessed January 15, 2004, at www.cbn.com.

Michelman, S. (2003). Reveal or conceal: American religious discourse with fashion. *Etnofoor*, XVI(2):76–87.

Miller, K., & Michelman, S. (1997). Dress and world religions. In M. L. Damhorst, K. Miller, & S. Michelman (Eds.), *The Meanings of Dress*. New York: Fairchild.

Pollard, J. (2001). *Christian Modesty and the Public Undressing of America*. San Antonio, TX: Vision Forum, Inc.

Shalit, W. (1999). *A Return to Modesty*. New York: Free Press.

Silverstein, S., & Olsen, A. (2003, December 14). Evangelical colleges gaining wider acceptance in academia. *Lexington Herald-Leader*, A23.

Thompson, M. (2000). Gender in magazine advertising: Skin sells best. *Clothing and Textiles Research Journal*, 18(3):178–181.

Tolson, J. (2003, December 8). The new old-time religion. *U.S. News and World Report*. Accessed February 16, 2004, at www.usnews.com.

Wolfe, A. (2003). *The Transformation of American Religion*. New York: Free Press.

DISCUSSION QUESTIONS

Reveal or Conceal?

1. How influential are conservative religious groups on mainstream fashion? Do you feel that the current political environment would encourage more modesty?

2. When Janet Jackson bared her breast at the Super Bowl, why do you feel there was such a strong public reaction?

CHAPTER 7

Dress in the Workplace

Kimberly A. Miller-Spillman

AFTER YOU HAVE READ THIS CHAPTER, YOU WILL UNDERSTAND:

- How dress facilitates or hinders human interaction in the workplace.

- Why dress helps individuals acquire, learn, and perform job roles.

- How dress affects and reflects specific jobs in business, sports, medicine, service professions, and entertainment.

- How male and female interviewers view dress for women interviewing for a middle management position.

- How to present oneself in a professional setting to the best advantage.

Working takes up a large portion of adult life. Spending 40 to 60 hours a week at work, in addition to commuting time and getting ready for work (including getting dressed), make our time spent on work-related activities substantial. Work dress becomes one of the most frequently used parts of the wardrobe and, for many individuals, is the part of the wardrobe on which they spend the most money. Because work provides money for family and self-support, work tends to be highly valued by most individuals. In addition, many people prepare for careers through long years of education, training, and building a professional reputation and accomplishments. For many adults, work roles define much of one's self-identity.

This chapter describes how dress affects relationships at work. Dress is a powerful communicator, especially when people interact at work. Clothing researchers have attempted to unravel the role that dress plays in the work environment, but more research is needed to fully understand this phenomenon. For instance, Johnson and Roach-Higgins (1987) have studied the effect women's dress and appearance have during job interviews. More recently, clothing researchers have examined the effect of masculine dress (Johnson, Crutsinger, & Workman, 1994), body type (Thurston, Lennon, & Clayton, 1990), and the ideal business image (Kimle & Damhorst, 1997) on a woman's success in the workplace. Articles in this chapter will address both men's and women's dress at work to demonstrate the importance of appropriateness of work dress.

In the late 1990s, casual dress received attention from business executives and clothing scholars. The casual dress trend was interesting from several perspectives. One explanation for the casual dress phenomenon is that following the turbulent late 1980s/early 1990s, when downsizing was so prevalent in business, employers wanted to give employees a perk, especially one that did not cost employers money. So casual dress days became a cost-effective way to raise morale among apprehensive employees. In 2004, the trend in business wear is moving away from casual dress. Many took casual dress to an extreme, and employers got tired of employees showing up for work looking as though they had just rolled out of bed. As a result, the pendulum appears to be swinging back toward more formal dress in the workplace; however, it is not likely to return to suit-and-tie formality. More likely, a new category of dress will be defined somewhere between the extremes of formal and casual dress.

DRESS AND HUMAN INTERACTION AT WORK

In Chapter 1, we learned that roles are positions that people occupy in a group or society. Work roles typically require a specific type of dress. For example, a farmer needs overalls, a lawyer needs a business suit, and a judge needs a robe. To a large extent, one who looks the part through appropriate dress can be confident that others will assume that he or she legitimately holds the claimed position. Because dress is such a powerful communicator, appropriate work dress conveys that individuals not only understand their work roles but can perform them effectively.

Roles within a society can be either achieved or ascribed. **Achieved roles** are those that we work to earn. College degrees, work skills, even marriages, are roles that individuals must strive to attain. A wedding band and an academic robe are examples of achieved roles expressed through dress. An **ascribed role** is a position that people acquire through no fault or virtue of their own. Age, gender, skin color, and birth order are examples of ascribed roles. Ascribed roles have an immense impact on individuals because they are so visible and, with the exception of gender, they can rarely be changed. Age, gender, and skin color are difficult to hide in everyday interactions with others, and therefore their impact is very great. Both achieved and ascribed roles are expressed through dress at work.

If roles are the special tasks that a person performs in a society, **status** or **prestige** is the social stratification in which groups and individuals are ranked and organized by legal, political, and cultural criteria (Marshall, 1994, p. 510). In addition, a status hierarchy reflects the value society places on certain roles or groups of roles (Storm, 1987). The presence (or absence) of a status symbol is one way that perceptions regarding status are formed. A Rolex watch, for example, is a major status symbol in U.S. culture. If a doctor or lawyer wears a Rolex watch, others may assume that he or she has not only the financial means to purchase such an item, but the skills required to achieve occupational success in his or her field as well. Height in men is another example of a status symbol. Tall men are judged to be more attractive than short men, and because attractiveness equates to higher prestige, tall men are afforded more status than their shorter counterparts. For example, adding a hat to a police officer's uniform not only adds inches to his or her height, but can also enhance perceptions of authority and status (Volpp & Lennon, 1988). Dress at work functions to visually express status distinctions in the workplace.

Social class is a concept that is related to, and greatly defined by, one's occupation. Although social class distinctions are blurry, in the United States, individuals are generally divided into three classes: upper, middle, and lower. Social class is a complex issue involving a person's social background, education, and occupation. When social class and dress become a concern in the workplace, it is typically because an individual does not adopt dress appropriate to the position. For example, a woman who is promoted to management but continues to wear dress similar to what secretaries wear in her firm may hit the "glass ceiling," preventing further promotion or even causing demotion (cf. Form & Stone, 1957). An employee is expected to look the part that he or she plays, and when that does not occur, that person may be labeled as someone who does not have the right image and therefore, the right qualifications for the job. Social class expressed through dress at work can create problems when an employee's social class does not correspond to the job held.

The terms **white-collar dress** and **blue-collar dress** refer to types of occupations. These terms imply the social classes historically associated with white-collar and blue-collar occupations. Management and labor jobs were symbolized by dress typically worn for these roles: a man's white dress shirt worn with a suit for a management role and denim and a darker-colored shirt or uniform worn by a laborer (see Figure 7.1). Some presidential candidates have borrowed the traditional symbolism of blue-collar and white-collar dress. These candidates have worn a blue shirt while campaigning in parts of the country that have organized labor unions. The message of the blue shirt is, "I may be running for President, but I know what it means to physically work hard." Wearing a blue shirt is meant to establish connections with constituents and gain voter support. Conversely, the candidate will adopt a white shirt for general campaigning and official duties. Wearers of white-collar dress are perceived as professional, conservative, and credible. Awareness of different environments and expected dress is often half the battle when dressing for work. One way to ensure appropriate work dress is to observe others at work and adopt their dress codes.

FIGURE 7.1 *Carhartt manufactures apparel for those who work and play outdoors and identify their primary market as blue-collar males aged 18–55. Carhartt is often referred to as the "Cadillac" of workmen's clothing.*

RESEARCH ON DRESS IN THE WORKPLACE

People often make judgments about others in just a few seconds. The term **person perception** refers to the way we learn and think about others and their characteristics, intentions, and inner states (Taguiri & Petrullo, 1958). Forming a first impression is the first step in person perception. A job interview is one situation in which a first impression can determine one's future earning capacity; therefore, appropriate dress for an interview is crucial (see "How Personnel Interviewers See Women's Job Interview Dress"). Not surprisingly, clothing researchers have studied the effect of dress during a job interview (Rucker, Taber, & Harrison, 1981; Damhorst & Pinaire Reed, 1986; Damhorst & Fiore, 1999).

Physical attractiveness has also been studied in relation to job interviews. In general, we know from research studies that attractive people have several advantages over those who are perceived as unattractive. Attractive people have advantages over unattractive people in the classroom, the courtroom, and in asking for and obtaining help (see Kaiser, 1997, for a summary of research on physical attractiveness). In a job interview setting, attractiveness is an advantage for men; however, women who are moderately attractive have advantages over women who are unattractive or highly attractive (Heilman & Saruwatari, 1979).

Susan Watkins (1984) studies and designs clothing for specific needs, that is, a bulletproof vest for a police officer, protective clothing for an agricultural worker who sprays chemicals, and clothing that is easily donned and doffed for physically handicapped individuals. As jobs become more specialized and as the population grows older, clothing for specific needs becomes important. Hockey players need a specialized type of dress to protect them from injury while engaging in a physically demanding occupation, just as construction workers need specialized dress items that enable them to work on rooftops efficiently and without injury. With the advancement of technology, some workers are required to wear clothing that protects the product (e.g., sensitive computer equipment, electronics) from the worker (e.g., hair, lint, tobacco smoke). And as baby boomers approach retirement age, their needs must be addressed by the clothing industry. By now it should be obvious that dress at work is multifaceted. Next, we will look at some specific examples of work dress.

Dress and Ascribed Roles

Because ascribed roles can rarely be changed, using dress to offset stereotypes becomes a useful tool in the workplace. Age, gender, and skin color—in certain situations—may be perceived as a negative (think female cop, female firefighter, or young-looking college professor). Presenting one's self appropriately through dress can often help to offset negative stereotypes. For example, one might be perceived as too young to do a job. A youthful appearance may be read as too inexperienced, too naive, or too avant-garde to be trusted to do a good job. The reverse is also true. An older appearance may be read as too old-fashioned, too conservative, or possessing a skill set that is too outdated. Dressing "older" or "younger" might help to overcome these common perceptions.

Gender becomes an issue in the workplace when a professional woman is pregnant. It can be difficult to convince bosses and colleagues that her work will not suffer, or that she doesn't secretly plan to quit her job soon after the baby is born. Although many women are now postponing pregnancy until careers are well-established, negative perceptions about pregnant women in the workplace still persist. Maternity career apparel (see Figure 2.5) is one way to visually—and subconsciously—combat those stereotypes (see Belleau et al., 1990). Expectations that a woman will be back to her prepregnancy size 12 weeks after giving birth, even if nursing, is causing stress for some employees (see "Casino Gives Workers Look They Can, Must Live With"). But as industries become more service-oriented and image-conscious, this trend may continue to grow.

Just getting a job for some women may be difficult. Management positions in the past typically went to white men. Being female or black may lower the chances of landing a management position. In "How Personnel Interviewers See Women's Job Interview Dress: A 2002 Update," Damhorst and her coauthors give women some pointers on how to dress for a job interview when applying for middle management jobs. The authors also report that the interviewers surveyed in this study were slightly more conservative than those in 1991 when judging the appropriateness of interview dress. The authors suggest that "when in doubt" about how to dress for an interview, go conservative. On the other hand, women in top positions have more leeway in choosing dress than those who are just starting out (see "Female Executives Use Fashion to Send a Business Message").

Skin color can exclude a person from a position or make it difficult to move up in the corporate hierarchy. Edwards, in "How Black Can You Be?," describes how dress can increase the comfort factor for whites—one of the main challenges blacks have to face when working in an executive position. Edwards makes a good point when reminding black professionals that others in the office (often white coworkers) may wonder if black culture is more important to you than corporate culture. All professionals must assume responsibility for the work culture they have chosen to inhabit. There are many behaviors (e.g., sexual harassment) and dress items (e.g., dirty T-shirts) that are not acceptable at work, and if your workplace looks down on cornrows (see "Casino Gives Workers Look They Can, Must Live With"), perhaps you should take note and dress accordingly or move on to another industry.

Dress and Specific Occupations

Whereas it might be difficult to describe the dress of a mother in U.S. society (a role that has undergone significant changes), most people have a clear picture of what a police officer should be wearing. A police uniform is an example of **role-related dress,** that is, dress that has become inextricably tied to a particular occupation. Legitimacy, power, and authority are characteristics communicated by police uniforms. Research confirms that such clothing as uniforms can legitimize and convey power (Bickman, 1974). In order for police officers to successfully do their job, they must be perceived as legitimate and authoritative. The appropriate clothing symbols make this perception possible.

In the article "Just Playing Doctor?," author Calmetta Coleman follows a controversy between some medical residents and their veteran counterparts. The controversy is over the length of the doctor's coat. Should a resident, who has earned a medical degree, be forced to wear a shorter coat while more experienced doctors wear longer coats? The more experienced doctors believe that the shorter coat communicates that the resident, although a *real* doctor, should not mislead a patient into believing that he or she is a seasoned medical doctor. Clearly a marker of status in American culture, the white doctor's coat is another example of role-related dress. Hospitals can be confusing places with everyone from janitors to surgeons wearing scrubs (see suggested reading Seabrook, 2002). Instead, wearing dress that clearly identifies the wearer to patients and their families would be beneficial.

There is uniform agreement as to what a jockey should wear, but the issue here is body weight. Jockeys face a weight limit each time they ride (see "Health to Pay"). There has been media attention lately about weight loss practices of some fashion models and celebrities (see Chapter 2), but there has been less attention on jockeys and their battle with weight. Although some jockeys are naturally small, most practice methods that are dangerous to their health. The book *Seabiscuit* has shed some light on the chances jockeys take to meet their weight limit.

Low-income women come in all body weights, shapes, and sizes (see "A Clothing Gift Program for Low-Income Women"). The problem is a lack of appropriate clothing as they move from job training programs to full-time jobs. Damhorst and McLeod describe the effect a program has on women who receive two sets of brand new clothing, shoes, handbags, and accessories. Although women in the program did not have a measurable difference in self-esteem after the giveaway event, the participants all reported feeling more confident about attending job interviews with the clothing they now had.

Summary

Dress in the workplace is important because most working people spend 40 to 60 hours a week at their job. That is a lot of time and a lot of human interaction to consider. Appropriate dress can make the difference in receiving a job offer, appearing effective in a job role, and receiving a promotion. Understanding how dress can facilitate or hinder human interaction in the workplace can give employees a head start on making favorable impressions at work. Most importantly, dress is a powerful communicator—especially in the workplace.

Suggested Readings

Kimle, P. A., & Damhorst, M. L. (1997). A grounded theory model of the ideal business image for women. *Symbolic Interaction*, 20:45–68.

Prud'homme, A. (1999, March 28). From unemployed to interview-ready: A nonprofit offers clothes, haircuts and hope. *The New York Times*, BU10.

Seabrook, J. (2000, March 18). The white dress. *The New Yorker*, 122–127.

LEARNING ACTIVITY

Interview a Professional

Objectives: To observe and interview a professional about his or her work dress, including casual dress policies and personal preferences. To form an opinion about dress in the workplace based on an interview with a professional in a field of personal interest.

Procedure

Choose a profession in which you have an interest. Talk to a professional in that field for a minimum of 20 minutes about his or her dress for work. Ask the person if you can meet him or her at work, so you can see that person in a professional setting.

Ask as many of the following questions as time allows:

1. Does your company have a dress code? Formal or informal? If so, what is it?
2. What do you wear to work on most days? Do you vary your dress according to activities you have planned for that day?
3. How much time and energy do you spend on dress for work?
4. Does your company allow casual dress? If so, why? If not, why not?
5. Is casual dress allowed every day or just on certain days of the week or month?
6. How do you feel about the company's casual dress policy? Do you like it? Why or why not?
7. How do you prefer to dress at work?
8. Have you seen a difference in your performance when dressed in formal dress versus casual dress?

Discussion Questions

What did you learn about dress at work that surprised you? Are you still interested in this profession after completing this assignment? If so, why? If not, why not? How do you want to dress when you begin your career?

Writing Activity

Write two or three paragraphs about your thoughts on the direction of casual dress in business. Do you think that casual dress was a fad that has passed? Or do you think that casual dress will be a part of business dress in the future? What effect (if any) do you think that dress that emphasizes status distinctions will have on the effectiveness of teamwork? Explain the reasons behind your position.

References

Belleau, B. D., Miller, K. A., Elliot, P., & Church, G. E. (1990). Apparel preferences of pregnant employed women. *Journal of Consumer Studies and Home Economics,* 14:291–301.

Bickman, L. (1974). The social power of a uniform. *Journal of Applied Social Psychology,* 4:47–61.

Damhorst, M. L., & Fiore, A. M. (1999). Women's job interview dress: How personnel interviewers see it. In M. L. Damhorst, K. A. Miller, & S. O. Michelman (Eds.), *The Meanings of Dress,* pp. 92–97. New York: Fairchild.

Damhorst, M. L., & Pinaire Reed, J. A. (1986). Clothing color value and facial expression: Effects on evaluations of female job applicants. *Social Behavior and Personality,* 14:89–98.

Form, W. H., & Stone, G. P. (1957). *The Social Significance of Clothing in Occupational Life* (Technical Bulletin 262). East Lansing: Michigan State University, Agricultural Experiment Station.

Heilman, M. E., & Saruwatari, L. R. (1979). When beauty is beastly: The effects of appearance and sex on evaluations of job applicants for managerial and nonmanagerial jobs. *Organizational Behavior and Human Performance,* 23:360–372.

Johnson, K., Crutsinger, C., & Workman, J. (1994). Can professional women appear too masculine? The case of the necktie. *Clothing and Textiles Research Journal*, 12: 27–31.

Johnson, K., & Roach-Higgins, M. E. (1987). Dress and physical attractiveness of women in job interviews. *Clothing and Textiles Research Journal*, 5:1–8.

Kaiser, S. B. (1997). *The Social Psychology of Clothing: Symbolic Appearances in Context* (2nd ed. rev.). New York: Fairchild.

Kimle, P. A., & Damhorst, M. L. (1997). A grounded theory model of the ideal business image for women. *Symbolic Interaction*, 20(1):45–68.

Marshall, G. (Ed.). (1994). *The Concise Oxford Dictionary of Sociology*. Oxford: Oxford University Press.

Rafaeli, A., Dutton, J., Harquali, C. V., & Mackie-Lewis, S. (1997). Navigating by attire: The use of dress by female administrative employees. *Academy of Management Journal*, 40:9–45.

Rucker, M., Taber, D., & Harrison, A. (1981). The effect of clothing variation on first impressions of female job applicants: What to wear when. *Social Behavior and Personality*, 9:53–64.

Storm, P. (1987). *Functions of Dress: Tool of Culture and the Individual*. Englewood Cliffs, NJ: Prentice Hall.

Taguiri, R., & Petrullo, L. (1958). *Person Perception and Interpersonal Behavior*. Stanford, CA: Stanford University Press.

Thurston, J., Lennon, S., & Clayton, R. (1990). Influence of age, body type, fashion and garment type on women's professional image. *Home Economics Research Journal*, 19:139–150.

Volpp, J. M., & Lennon, S. J. (1988). Perceived police authority as a function of uniform hat and sex. *Perceptual and Motor Skills*, 67:815–824.

Watkins, S. M. (1984). *Clothing: The Portable Environment*. Ames: Iowa State University Press.

38   How Personnel Interviewers See Women's Job Interview Dress: A 2002 Update

Mary Lynn Damhorst, Kelly Jondle, and Kristi Youngberg
Iowa State University

Sarah, graduating with a bachelor's degree in three months, is preparing for a job interview and wants to make a good impression. She worries that her basic gray suit might be too conservative for an interview and that the recruiter will think she is too bland and dull for a management job. She's seen lots of pantsuits sold in stores; should she wear a pair of dress pants with her jacket or not? In dozens of television shows, such as *Ally McBeal* and *Sex and the City*, women revealed cleavage and wore very short skirts to work. Should Sarah dress like they do on TV?

It is no wonder that Sarah might have questions about what to wear to a job interview. Appearance has been estimated to influence up to 70 percent of employment interviewers' judgments (Springbett, 1958), and clothing has been found to have even more influence on hiring decisions than does physical attractiveness (Johnson & Roach-Higgins, 1987; Riggio & Throckmorton, 1988).

In addition, women have moved into management and administrative roles in unprecedented numbers since the 1970s. Their growing appearance in management roles has lent some confusion as to how women should dress for the office. To gauge just part of the growth, in 1970 women in the United States held 16.7 percent of managerial and administrative roles, other than farm managers (U.S. Department of Commerce, 1974). By 2001, women held 46 percent of the similar category of executive, administrative, and managerial roles (U.S. Department of Labor, 2003). The 30 percent increase of women in management and administration over 30 years of time is quite remarkable.

As individuals and groups take on new roles, they tend to adopt symbols, including dress, to help them learn and carry off their new roles (Solomon, 1983). Has clothing considered appropriate for business and administrative roles changed now that women are more commonly seen in those roles? We know that casual dress became more acceptable in many businesses during the 1990s (Adler, 1995; Janus, Kaiser, & Gray, 1999; Kimle & Damhorst, 1999), but is casual dress now appropriate for high-performance situations, such as an employment interview? And some press reports indicate that many younger women actually are emphasizing their sexual attractiveness in business dress today and feel that they are successful in business because of their boldness in dress (Pollock, 2000). Great variety in recommendations for women's business dress is found in the popular press (Ogle & Damhorst, 1999), perhaps as a reflection of shifting norms.

In 1991, we examined how personnel interviewers evaluated appropriateness of skirted suit ensembles for middle management job interviews (Damhorst & Fiore, 1999). We report here a repeat of that study during 2002 to see if evaluations had changed 11 years later. This time we added pantsuits to the study, because women wearing pants to work became more common during the 1990s (Patteson, 1997).

The purpose of the study, then, was to identify aesthetic components of women's apparel that are appropriate in the business employment interview situation for management-level female applicants. Findings from this 2002 study were compared to the 1991 findings to see if rules for interview dress have changed.

METHOD

The respondents included 42 female and 27 male human resource managers, recruiters, and employment interviewers for 69 businesses. The respon-

Original for this text.

dents were either recruiting for their firms at a state university (n = 34) or worked for businesses (n = 35) in cities within 40 miles of the state capitol of Iowa. Headquarters of the recruiting firms were located throughout the United States. Firms ranged in size from four to 130,000 employees, with the median size around 51 employees. Age of respondents ranged from 21 to 64 years. We excluded businesses primarily selling clothing, just in case there might be expectations for more fashion-forward appearances in job applicants for those firms.

The data collector asked each respondent to sort through 113 color photographs of women's suits (skirts or pants included) and a few dresses. Ensembles were selected to represent the wide variety of style variations appearing in mail-order catalogs during 2001 and early 2002. Each full-color photo included a full-length, frontal view of a standing model. Hair and facial features, as well as background, were cut away to eliminate contribution of those cues. Posture of models could not be controlled, but models with highly active or unusual stances were eliminated. Pictures were mounted on separate sheets of neutral gray paper and encased in clear film folders.

The respondents sorted the pictures into piles differing in level of appropriateness for a middle-management employment interview with their firm. After sorting, the respondents described their reasons for ranking the outfits. We scored the piles designated as least appropriate or inappropriate as "1," as appropriate for an interview as "3," and as maybe appropriate or unsure as "2." Rankings across the 69 respondents were tallied for each suit. We also conducted a statistical cluster analysis that identified suits more often grouped together by the respondents.

RESULTS

Guidelines for Appropriateness

Eight suits ranked as most appropriate, with average rankings of 2.77 to 2.67. Cluster analysis showed that the top eight suits and 38 more suits, with average rankings of 2.61 to 2.17, were often grouped together as appropriate for a job inter-view. From the rankings it is clear that not all of these suits were seen as equally appropriate by the recruiters and personnel interviewers, however.

The very top-ranked group of eight suits was highly similar in its characteristics (see Figure 7.2). Classic tailoring characterized the suits that all echoed style characteristics of men's business suits. Pants and skirts were equally represented (four suits each). We will call the top eight suits the *safe suits*—safest for job interviews with a wide variety of interviewers.

The safe suits fit most of the rules for appropriate job interview attire in 1991 (Damhorst & Fiore, 1999). But in contrast to the top-ranked suits in 1991, the 2002 safe suits strayed hardly at all from the characteristics defining appropriateness. The characteristics of the top-ranked safe suits are listed below. We present these as guidelines or rules for "ideal" interview suits—ideal at least from the standpoint of the employment interviewers. An "(Absolute)" follows a rule that was absolute or never broken among all 46 appropriate suits:

- The overall design was highly symmetric; only a small pin or button might give limited asymmetry.

- Necklines were completely covered or only revealed 2 or 3 inches of bare skin; a turtle-neck, scarf, or necklace could help to fill in the neckline area. No hint of cleavage was allowed. (Absolute)

- The neckline and upper body were the focal emphasis of designs. Accessories, if any, should be placed there.

- Sleeves were full length, set-in, or fitted at the shoulder (Absolute) and tailored.

- Jacket lengths fell to upper hip or mid-hip area. Jackets at waist or higher were seen as too casual.

- Jackets were worn open or completely buttoned (except the top button at the neck, if any).

- Jackets had a convertible collar with lapels, similar to collars on men's suit jackets, or a simple partial roll shirt-style collar without lapels and worn open only at the top neckline button.

FIGURE 7.2 *Most Appropriate: The three top-ranked suits for middle-management job interviews.*

- Skirts and pant legs were not tight or full. (Absolute)

- Pant legs and skirt silhouettes were straight or slightly tapered to the hem.

- All pants were full length and ended at the upper foot (Absolute); all skirts either just covered the knee or were long and about 3 to 4 inches above the ankle. (Absolute)

- Solid-colored fabrics were most common, and jacket and skirt or pants matched.

- Colors were all dark or middle in value and were classic "neutrals"—navy, gray, brown, black, beige, or tan.

- Fabrics were smooth and simple dense structures, not complex laces, knits, or boucles. (Absolute) Menswear gabardines and wool-look flannels were common. No denims or casual cotton fabrics were allowed. Shiny satin fabrics, furs, and leather were also not appropriate.

- Hosiery was required, in nude or sheer dark colors rather than opaque. (Absolute) No textured hose was allowed. (Absolute)

- Shoes had heels (1-1/2 to 3 inches high) and a closed toe. Boots were not appropriate unless covered by a pant leg.

- One accessory was allowed beyond earrings (which were not visible in the pictures); all accessories were simple in style, including a small-scale print scarf, short strands of gold chain or pearls, or a small pin. Watches were probably allowed but were rarely visible in the pictures.

- Waistlines were indicated by slight fitting in the jacket or by belts at the waistline shown under an open jacket. (Absolute)

- Garments did not envelope the body with great volume of material, but were also not skin tight. (Absolute)

- Forms were "crisp" and structured rather than draped and droopy or gathered and puffy. (Absolute)

- Styles were not highly casual or formal (in a shiny, lacy, or sparkling manner).

The few deviations among the safe suits were that one of the safe suit jackets exposed a bare neckline, but not very deep and with a necklace partially covering the neck. Also, one safe suit was worn with shoes that had a small, round toe opening, but with little toe exposure.

The remaining 38 suits in the appropriate cluster included more variations from the safe suit rules; but, with each additional variation from the rules, an increasing number of interviewers rated the suits as "maybe" or "inappropriate." Only the lowest-ranked suits in the group incorporated more than two violations of the rules. It is likely that many of the lower-ranked suits might be at least marginally appropriate in an interview, but the wearer would take more risks with the image she conveyed.

There were many suits in the appropriate grouping or cluster because there was quite a bit of disagreement among respondents. And sometimes a respondent ranked a suit as appropriate even though he or she noted there was a small feature that was not appropriate. Some of the deviations from the rules mentioned by respondents as problematic included: (1) deeper neckline exposure or shirt left open at the neck with collar casually rumpled to expose a narrow view of the neck and upper chest; (2) three-quarter length sleeves; (3) high contrast trim, large buttons, or unusual collars that brought too much visual interest to the outfit; (4) open-toe shoes or sandals; (5) a one-piece "coat" dress; (6) a knee-length jacket; and (7) large jewelry, such as a large pearl necklace.

Although appearing among the appropriate suits, boot-cut pants and A-line skirts may have been a bit trendy in styling and not yet classic enough for top rankings. Collarless jackets worn buttoned to the neck were always lower in rankings. Double-breasted jackets introduced more asymmetry to a few outfits, but designs were still very balanced.

Two bright-red suits, a magenta suit, and some very-light-beige suits added color options, but any suits in the pink or purple color families were rated among the lower half of the appropriate group. The only plaids or checks were very classic black-and-white or black-and-red patterns; no prints were found in the appropriate cluster. Absolutely no skirt was shorter than the knee. Only one very classic red suit included a narrow slit to about 4 inches above the knee.

A very few interviewers mentioned that some suits seemed too formal for a middle-management interview, such as the skirted suit in Figure 7.2. They rated these suits as "maybes," as they felt they would be more appropriate for an executive level interview.

The Maybe Suits

Suits that clustered together in the middle range group often featured two or three deviations from the safe suit guidelines. (See Figure 7.3 for examples.) More often seen in this group were:

- Wider exposure of bare skin in upper chest area.

- Long jackets, a few inches above the knee to midcalf.

- Short sleeves (three-quarter and mid-upper-arm length).

- Multicolored stripes in the jacket.

- Jackets and pants or skirts of coordinated but not matching fabrics.

- Printed or plaid skirts or shirts worn with a solid-colored jacket.

- Pleated skirts.

- Leather or suede jackets or pants.

- Satin, velvet, or fur as a trim or garment fabric.

- Backless, casual shoes.

- Toes completely visible.

- Boots worn with skirts.

FIGURE 7.3 *Middle-range suits: These three suits were ranked appropriate by some interviewers, but rated as questionable or inappropriate by others. The satiny, draped fabrics, short skirt, and multichain necklace were key components that lowered their appropriateness.*

A simple black sheath dress with long sleeves was also in the maybe group. The one dress ranked as appropriate had a convertible collar and lapels to make it look more like a suit.

The Most Inappropriate Suits

Fifteen highly varied suits were most often sorted together as inappropriate for job interviews. Average rankings were lowest of all suits, ranging from 1.68 to 1.17. Characteristics that helped to relegate these outfits to the inappropriate pile were:

- Very low-cut neckline.
- Skirts several inches above the knee.
- Capri pants.

- Busy texture or bold stripes or print in jacket and/or skirt fabric.
- Matching leather jacket and pants.
- Embroidery highly contrasting with the base fabric.
- High-contrast trim on pant legs.
- Slits in pant legs or skirts slit up to midthigh.

Often, a combination of many factors worked together to relegate a suit to the worst pile. For example, one white pantsuit had shiny gold rhinestones and studded trim, making it look more appropriate for an evening event. A low-ranked three-piece knit velvet outfit with a coat to midcalf would probably work better for entertainment at home. In Figure 7.4, the wide-legged,

FIGURE 7.4 *Very Inappropriate: Short jackets were seen as too casual; plaid pants and the printed jacket were too distracting; and the very short skirt, opaque hose, and boots were considered completely wrong for an interview.*

plaid pants with a short, casual suede jacket and bright pink shirt moved it too far from appropriateness standards.

Male vs. Female Evaluations

Men and women rated many of the suits similarly. However, men found only 22 suits to be appropriate, while women included 41 suits in the appropriate group. Men were less accepting of deviations from the rules.

Women were more accepting of tweed fabrics and also white and black plaids, even when visually dynamic. Women were more accepting of A-line knee-length skirts—a newer silhouette at the time. They also were more positive about collarless jackets and variety in collar styling. They ranked a tailored tweed dress with convertible collar far more highly than did the men. Men also ranked suits as only middle range in appropriateness when the outfit was asymmetric; was purple, maroon, or in the yellow color family; or had a longer than midthigh jacket. Men were actually more positive than were the women about suits with pants and the color brown.

The men overall were slightly more positive than were the women toward traditionally tailored suits that included slits into the thigh area. Some of the men were apparently more tolerant of leg display, but most were not. For instance, a short-skirted, pale blue suit with cleavage visible was ranked very low by both men and women. Sexual display may attract many male interviewers, but will not necessarily impress them of the wearer's business acumen. And a sexy outfit may substantially repel female interviewers. Several respondents mentioned that interview attire should not make the applicant look as though she is on her way to a bar.

Recruiters vs. Iowa Respondents

The difference in evaluations of suits between college recruiters and human resource managers working for Iowa firms is difficult to assess. The differences are similar to gender differences, and this is likely because more Iowa human resource managers were female (24 vs. 11 male).

Two of the female recruiters felt that when recruiting on the coasts they had to accept greater variety (i.e., more violations of the "safe suit" rules) in what applicants wore. They admitted that they used a stricter standard when recruiting in the Midwest, because they felt that job seekers tended to be more conservative in appearance in the central states. Whether this is actually true or not needs more study. But, apparently, at least some recruiters do have expectations, even stereotypes, for job applicants based on where the applicant resides. Though this seems a bit unfair, it is probably a good idea to learn about local or geographic differences in expectations when interviewing for jobs, especially if the applicant insists on dressing in violation of the safe suit rules.

CONCLUSIONS

From the rankings of appropriateness of the 113 outfits, it is apparent that pants and skirts can both be highly acceptable attire for women to wear to job interviews. (But beware: Two of the interviewers mentioned that they thought that skirts were still more appropriate.) In general, the most acceptable styles for job interviews included some similarities to men's traditional business suits and an overall impression of business formal styling. The employment interview is a ritualized situation, with tacit expectations that the applicant display a highly formalized and polished version of the self. Adherence to conservative business styling is more important than wearing the latest fashions.

2002 vs. 1991

Overall, the most appropriate suits in 2002 were more conservative in style detail and colors than were the suits selected as most appropriate in 1991. Back then, green and gold colors were found in highly appropriate suits, not just subdued neutrals. Low-contrast, "quiet" plaids were found in some highly ranked suits in 1991. Skirt and jacket could be coordinated separates, not necessarily made of the exact same material. And not all top-ranked jackets had collars and lapels in 1991, while the 2002 top-ranked suits almost all had a tailored convertible collar and lapels. Some skirts were pleated in 1991, adding to style variety of top-ranked suits.

In the 1991 appropriate cluster, suits were perhaps more formal overall than appropriate 2002 suits; the latter included some pantsuits worn with more casual knit tops among the top 46 suits. And the outfits in 2002 tended to incorporate even less jewelry and accessories than the already sparely accessorized 1991 suits.

One main difference in 2002 suits was that a bit more of the upper chest area could be revealed. Suits could be worn with no apparent blouse, shirt, or scarf underneath, as long as neckline exposure was not too deep. That degree of neck exposure was rarely seen in appropriate 1991 suits. It seems that modesty requirements have relaxed ever so slightly, but only in necklines and not in skirt lengths.

A Return to Conservatism?

The researchers cannot help but ask the question, "Why so conservative in 2002?" We quite frankly expected that there would be more variety acceptable in interview dress for women as we move closer to 50/50 parity of men and women in administrative and managerial roles. We assumed that a more "feminized" appearance that allowed a more elaborated aesthetic code—a code that incorporated more play with styling and color (Michelman, 1999)—would now be common and acceptable in business dress.

Perhaps the economic recession in the early years of the twenty-first century and a limited job market had something to do with standards that job interviewers used for judging applicant dress.

A tight job market results in more competition for jobs, so applicants have to conform to more exacting expectations in all types of behaviors. But 1991 was not a great time for job hunting either. The economy was in a downturn then, too. Recession cannot be the only answer for the conservatism in dress.

It could be that women in business are now more accustomed to simplifying their appearances to make it easier to dress for work, and the simplified code applies to interview attire as well. Following simplified codes for tailored and conservative appearances might help the time-stressed businesswoman to cope. The variety featured in women's business dress during the mid-1990s and earlier was probably confusing to some women (Ogle & Damhorst, 1999). Simplified codes, such as our "rules" for safe suits, inevitably make it easier to get dressed, as long as one has a closet full of conservative suits.

In addition, the current generation of female recruiters and human resource managers could be more conservative or, and this is more likely, more socialized to business norms. Interviewers are used to seeing how women can borrow and adjust simplified dress codes based on menswear norms, and they now seem to expect this in interview dress. Add to this the "minimalist" fashion trends of the last six or seven years—trends that frequently featured fitted jackets, mostly in black, with collars and details that resembled men's business jackets. These trends easily interpreted into business wear for women.

And finally, note that we asked respondents to consider the suits for a middle-management interview. For jobs as a designer or in fields that are highly fashion-oriented, the codes for appropriate interview dress could be quite different. And, of course, some small firms in the computer software industry are likely to have a more relaxed code for interviewing.

What's a Fashion-Oriented Person to Do?

The women who take the first author's classes tend to be fairly interested in fashion. Many of them hated the appropriate styles back in 1991 (they could not believe that they needed to wear skirts down to their knees), and students now are appalled at the conservatism of the top-ranked suits in the latest data collection. Most of the appropriate suits are not something many young and fashion-oriented women want to wear.

But recall that the job interview is a ritualistic situation in which the job applicant makes a symbolic performance. Many of the outfits in the maybe or inappropriate groups might be perfectly acceptable on the job. In many firms, one does not need to appear quite so conservative on the job every day. But the interview situation seems to require more conformity and conservatism, less aesthetic variety and play. Projection of a sensible, professional, and business-committed appearance seemed to be expected by the recruiters and employment interviewers. One male respondent stated: "Their idea of what's appropriate, not appropriate is kind of a signal." Employment interviewers clearly use dress as information about the applicant.

So, we suggest having at least two fairly conservative suits for job interviews. The great number of suits in the appropriate cluster indicate that there is some leeway in style choices. But we recommend leaning toward the safer suit side, unless the applicant is a highly confident risk-taker. The pieces can always be mixed and matched and given more fashion flair with accessories once one gets the job. Of course, the degree of flair always needs to be adjusted to the particular firm and occupation within which an individual works (Kimle & Damhorst, 1997).

Will men and women be wearing nearly identical styles in the not-too-distant future? Only time will tell. But the degree of menswear tailoring incorporated in the most appropriate women's suits indicates that right now a surprising degree of conservatism is perceived as appropriate by a substantial number of employment recruiters and interviewers for that very symbolic form of dress—the job interview suit.

References

Adler, J. (1995, February 20). Have we become a nation of slobs? *Newsweek*, 56–62.

Damhorst, M. L., & Fiore, A. M. (1999). Women's job interview dress: How the personnel interviewers see it. In M. L. Damhorst, K. A. Miller, & S. O. Michelman (Eds.), *The Meanings of Dress*, pp. 92–97. New York: Fairchild.

Janus, T., Kaiser, S. B., & Gray, G. (1999). Negotiations @ work: The casual businesswear trend. In M. L. Damhorst, K. A. Miller, & S. O. Michelman (Eds.), *The Meanings of Dress*, pp. 264–268. New York: Fairchild.

Johnson, K. K., & Roach-Higgins, M. W. (1987). The influence of physical attractiveness and dress on campus recruiters' impressions of female job applicants. *Clothing and Textiles Research Journal*, 6:87–95.

Kimle, P. A., & Damhorst, M. L. (1997). A grounded theory model of the ideal business image for women. *Symbolic Interaction*, 20:45–68.

Kimle, P. A., & Damhorst, M. L. (1999). Women's images in corporate culture: The case of casual day. In M. L. Damhorst, K. A. Miller, & S. O. Michelman (Eds.), *The Meanings of Dress*, pp. 269–271. New York: Fairchild.

Michelman, S. O. (1999). Appearance for gender and sexuality. In M. L. Damhorst, K. A. Miller, & S. O. Michelman (Eds.), *The Meanings of Dress*, pp. 168–175. New York: Fairchild.

Ogle, J. P., & Damhorst, M. L. (1999). Dress for success in the popular press. In K. K. P. Johnson & S. J. Lennon (Eds.), *Appearance and Power*, pp. 79–101. New York: Berg.

Patteson, J. (1997, January 13). Dress for success, '90s style. *The Des Moines Register*, 1T–2T.

Pollock, E. J. (2000, February 7). Deportment gap: In today's workplace, women feel freer to be, well, women. *The Wall Street Journal*, A1, A20.

Riggio, R. E., & Throckmorton, B. (1988). The relative effects of verbal and nonverbal behavior, appearance, and social skills on evaluations made in hiring interviews. *Journal of Applied Social Psychology*, 18:331–348.

Scherbaum, C., & Shepherd, D. (1987). Dressing for success: Effects of color and layering on perceptions of women in business. *Sex Roles*, 16(7/8):391–399.

Solomon, M. R. (1983). The role of products as social stimuli: A symbolic interactionism perspective. *Journal of Consumer Research*, 10:319–329.

Springbett, B. M. (1958). Factors affecting the final decision in the employment interview. *Canadian Journal of Psychology*, 12(1):13–22.

U.S. Department of Commerce, Social and Economic Statistics Administration. (1974). *Statistical Abstract of the United States 1974*. Washington, DC: U.S. Bureau of the Census.

U.S. Department of Labor, Bureau of Labor Statistics. (2003). *Household Data Annual Averages: Employed Persons by Occupations, Sex, and Age*. Accessed January 22, 2003, at www.bls.gov/cps/home.htm#empstat.

DISCUSSION QUESTIONS

How Personnel Interviewers See Women's Job Interview Dress

1. Why do you think male interviewers preferred slits in conservative-skirted suits more than female interviewers did?

2. How would you explain the more conservative preferences of interviewers in 2002 as compared to the interviewers in 1991?

3. What is your reaction to the findings of this study? Do you think that national politics play a part in what interviewers believe is appropriate interview dress?

39   Casino Gives Workers Look They Can, Must Live With

Darlene Gavron Stevens

Laura Moore thought she already had all that it took to be a good cocktail waitress at Harrah's Casino in Joliet.

But beginning this month, long-wearing lipstick and buttery hair highlights will be as vital to Moore's job as remembering customer orders and showing up to work on time. Every workday, she will have to look just as she does in a photograph taken after she was given a makeover by the company's image consultants.

"I was appalled," said Moore, a seven-year Harrah's veteran. "What if I don't want to keep my highlights up? I have to get it approved? I don't even know how they can do this legally. It seems like we are jogging back 50 years."

Mandatory makeovers, "personal best" photos and unprecedented new appearance standards are part of the Las Vegas-based company's Beverage Department Image Transformation Initiative, a program officials say is needed as an antidote to the anything-goes attitude of the '90s.

It goes so far as to say a woman who gives birth is expected to fit into her old uniform by the time the baby is 12 weeks old.

"In some ways, it's like being in the military," said spokesman Gary Thompson of Harrah's Entertainment, which hopes the policy will unify its 21 casinos and distinguish the brand. "There's a certain standard you have to meet before you come to work."

The move is drawing double-takes from workplace activists who last decade cheered the downfall of rigid weight requirements and mandatory makeup for flight attendants, five-inch heels and skimpy outfits for Atlantic City cocktail waitresses.

Harrah's action also comes at a time when more employers are relaxing dress codes. Even Walt Disney World, which since 1957 has been known for stringent standards, recently began allowing men to wear mustaches and beards after it became more difficult to recruit workers.

Although it may seem like a throwback, Harrah's contends that the carefully constructed policy is legal, in part because it applies equally to women and men.

The policy appears to be legal, unless it discriminates on the basis of age or religion, according to legal experts interviewed Friday. Companies are permitted to set fairly strict standards of appearance for employees, the legal experts say. They can ban jewelry, require men to wear suits, mandate a certain hair length and even discriminate based on weight, to a degree.

"They have broad latitude in prescribing how you look and appear on the job," said Bill Gould, a law professor at Stanford University and former chairman of the National Labor Relations Board.

If an employer wants to create an atmosphere through employee appearance, it is perfectly within the employer's right, said Sheribel Rothenberg, an employment attorney in Chicago. "Basically, employers can ask a lot," she said.

Harrah's prefers to view the program as a perk for its 1,400 beverage servers. Thompson estimates that it costs $3,000 per person for all the personal, professional attention given by its handpicked team of makeup, hair and image consultants, plus new uniforms.

And Harrah's is betting that workers will be lining up to take advantage of the new program, which spells out grooming "requirements" with the detail of a women's magazine.

For female servers, hair "must be teased, curled or styled every day you work. Hair must be worn down at all times, no exceptions."

Men cannot wear ponytails, and hair must not extend below the top of their shirt collars.

Workers may get a new hairstyle—but only if it is approved and a new photo is taken. Generally speaking, extreme changes will be frowned on, Thompson said.

Women must wear face powder, blush and mascara, and "lip color must be worn at all times." Men are not allowed to wear makeup.

As for the new uniforms, a seam can't be touched for a year—unless the alteration is for medical reasons or "positive body enhancements," which the company says is self-explanatory.

Even women returning from maternity leave are expected to zip into their old, form-fitting costumes within 12 weeks, nursing or not. But the company will "work with" employees who need help trimming post-baby fat, Thompson said.

"If someone was a size 8 and they come back (from leave) a size 12, that's not acceptable," said Charlotte Rogers, food and beverage manager of the Lake Tahoe Harrah's. "They should be coming back as a size 8, but we can help them along."

Workers are expected to look like their "personal best" photo every day or risk being disciplined for insubordination, according to the policy. Updated photos will be taken each year to account for "subtle body changes," it states.

Corporate managers, Thompson said, are not undergoing the makeovers.

"Seems like someone is pushing the envelope," said Paul Paz of the National Waiters Association. "They're going to have a heck of a time finding someone to work there."

It is one thing to have standards, noted Anne Ladky, executive director of Women Employed, "but to require a certain look for a year sounds fundamentally intrusive."

Harrah's says it is simply attempting to raise the bar for dress codes by giving workers—men and women, equally—the tools to look and feel better.

Joliet is the 12th property in 75 days to be introduced to the program, said Reimi Marden, the Las Vegas consultant and coach hired by Harrah's. Her pitch has spread like glitter to the Bellagio, Desert Inn and other image-minded hotels.

Marden oversaw last week's training and makeover sessions for about 150 Joliet beverage workers, and she helped hire local hair and makeup artists who carried out the makeovers.

"This is a gift for you guys, an opportunity for you to do and be your personal best," a perky Marden told the generally subdued gathering of Harrah's servers, some of whom wore ponytails and hair clips—styles strictly banned under the new policy.

"What is it our players connect to?" Marden asked before plowing through grooming tips such as the importance of tongue brushing and why men should wear socks that cover the calves. "Our image, from the inside out."

While some Harrah's have embraced the dress code or gone along ("We wanted to bring some class back," said Lake Tahoe server Barbara Campbell, 43), others said it was a waste of time.

"I'm OK with myself," said Tracey Drewniany, a Harrah's Joliet server for a year. "It doesn't make me feel better to put lipstick on. If you don't have self-esteem it doesn't matter how much lipstick you put on."

Moore, who is seven months' pregnant, worries about being able to keep up her approved image in the final weeks of her pregnancy.

"If it wasn't mandatory, it might be nice," said Moore of the makeovers. "A lot of people were insulted."

Some employees, she added, left an information meeting in tears.

Over the years, a sensitivity to gender issues in the workplace—and fear of lawsuits—has prompted many employers to allow workers more leeway in what they wear to work.

"This controversy disappeared off the road as dress codes loosened up and as women in general were less willing to take jobs that have costumes," said Ladky of Women Employed.

Companies also may be less inclined to require revealing outfits because "more employers understand now that they have a responsibility to maintain a workplace free of sexual harassment," she added.

Employers have every right to establish a dress code and portray a certain image to customers, but federal law requires that men and women be treated equally, said Reginald Welch, a spokesman for the Equal Employment Opportunity Commission.

"Of course it sounds odd," he said of the Harrah's initiative. "Our question would be, is it easier for men to meet the standards than the women?"

Thompson said Harrah's policy is not discriminatory.

"It's not a case of forcing them to look like models," he said. The company wants the employees to be "clean and well-groomed."

"We are trying to say, 'This is the way you look now. We expect you to maintain (that look)," he said. "We will work with you on it, but we expect you to maintain these standards."

In the past, employees have waged some successful battles against rigid dress codes. A 1992 lawsuit by a Sands Casino waitress who thought it was unfair that male servers got to wear pants and low shoes while women had to wear scanty clothes and 5-inch heels was settled after the Atlantic City casino agreed to give female servers the option of wearing slacks and lower shoes.

Hyatt Hotels Corp. in 1998 cracked down on local hotel policies that prohibited cornrow hairstyles after several women filed complaints with the EEOC.

In 1991, Continental Airlines dropped a policy that required makeup on flight attendants after a former employee charged she was fired for complaining about the standard. That same year, American Airlines settled a 17-year-old legal fight by agreeing to relax its weight standards for flight attendants by taking into account the worker's age as well as height.

So far, there have been no reported complaints at Harrah's in Lake Tahoe, which gave the staff makeovers in February, said Rogers, the food and beverage manager.

Rogers said she has not had to discipline anyone for not looking like the photos in a Rolodex on her desk.

"We had some who liked that 'oatmeal' look," she said, referring to employees who didn't wear makeup before the new policy. "Now, they don't look like they just rolled out of bed."

DISCUSSION QUESTIONS

Casino Gives Workers Look They Can, Must Live With

1. Do you think that an employer, such as Harrah's, should be allowed to make their employees live up to a picture taken after a makeover for one year?

2. Is it legal to tell an employee how he or she must look when on the job? When is it illegal?

3. Other large corporations have dress policies similar to the one described in this article. For instance, Walt Disney has a booklet devoted to appropriate dress styles, hairstyles, and so on, for their employees. What about an individual's personal rights?

40 Female Executives Use Fashion to Send a Business Message

Carol Hymowitz

As Janet Clarke prepared to travel to Houston last week for a board meeting at Express Jet, she pondered what outfit to wear to project a polished look. The director of the airline company and of Cox Communications eventually selected a tailored pantsuit—and paired it with Manolo Blahnik heels and a tangerine-colored handbag.

"I bought a lot of blue suits and bow ties when I started my career, but now there's so much pluralism in dress—and it's fine to put flair and color into a business wardrobe," says the former Citibank marketing executive.

As the nation's fashion designers show their latest collections on New York runways this week, executive women will be looking for new business styles that reflect their individual tastes. Male executives continue to alternate between classic suits and casual khakis, but women shun a uniform look.

The younger generation of working women, in particular, favors trendy styles, rejecting even the notion that they should be judged by their clothes. Women in top positions are more likely to use fashion to convey a particular image or to send a business message.

Carly Fiorina, Hewlett-Packard's chairman and CEO, projects power and authority in black-and-tan designer pantsuits, but wore a purple suit to convey the merger of H-P (which has a blue logo) and Compaq (red logo).

Andrea Jung, CEO at Avon, the cosmetics maker, could walk a runway herself in her sleek, high-style, Chanel and Armani suits and strappy high heels—and serves as an advertisement for the beauty industry. Meg Whitman, eBay's CEO, wore khakis and a blue button-down shirt with an eBay logo when she addressed 10,000 customers in Orlando, Fla., in June. It was the same outfit every employee at the conference was wearing and fit Ms. Whitman's image as an accessible boss.

The choices signal women's greater confidence to express themselves as they gain more clout at work. But the corporate dress code is still confusing to many, especially to those making their way to the top. Ms. Clarke has purged boxy suits from her wardrobe in favor of a more feminine, narrow cut, but debates what is appropriate for a business meeting. Fur is politically incorrect, she says, and leather is too faddish. "And there's no way I'd wear a mid-thigh skirt," she says. "You still have to dress for success and avoid anything provocative or too revealing, especially when you are surrounded by men in white shirts."

Karen Kaplowitz, a lawyer and consultant in Princeton, N.J., who owns half a dozen black suits, shuns most designer creations. "A lot of it is geared toward looking sexy, and that can detract from being effective at work," she says. "I want to look attractive, but I dress to create trust and credibility with my clients." Lately, however, she is shopping with her 14-year-old daughter, looking for stylish shoes to spruce up her conservative wardrobe.

Women who work in creative industries, such as advertising or entertainment, have always had more license to wear funky fashions than those in, say, manufacturing. When Sunny Bates, a New York executive recruiter, recently interviewed two 30-something women for a job at a media company, neither wore a suit. One wore black cargo pants, a black knit top and a woven belt, the other a tailored skirt and sleeveless shell—and a tattoo on her hand. Neither would be seen as extreme at the company. "I don't know any women who wear hose in the summer anymore," adds Ms. Bates.

But could bare legs, or jeans and sneakers, derail a corporate career? A 33-year-old manager, who last year moved from a job in television in New York to a corporate post at a Connecticut company, says she's in wardrobe culture shock. When she showed up at work in open-toe shoes, several women colleagues asked her how she could walk in them, and a few told her they were inappropriate for the office.

"They still have these old-school stereotypes about business attire," she says. Determined to introduce a less conservative dress code, she wore her open-toe shoes almost every day this summer and plans to wear a leather skirt this winter.

Marianne Spraggins, CEO of Alic Investment Advisers, a unit of Atlanta Life Insurance in Atlanta, gravitates toward clothes that express her love of edgy design, but project a professional demeanor. "You don't have to look like a man, but you have to look serious if you want to be taken seriously," she says.

When she launched her career in finance more than 20 years ago, she realized that as one of the few African-American women on Wall Street at the time, "I was going to stand out no matter what I wore, so I might as well be myself."

She wears her hair in a twist with a braid, also favors Chanel and Armani suits, and doesn't shy away from red and other bright colors. And she takes fashion cues from other successful women. After she saw Ms. Jung wearing open-toe high heels with no hose, she says, "I decided that look, which I'd been afraid to try, was OK."

Executive coach Dee Soder recently surveyed male CEOs about perceived barriers to female advancement. They said women who had weak handshakes or who couldn't wear stiletto heels without wobbling weren't seen as strong leaders.

DISCUSSION QUESTIONS

Female Executives Use Fashion to Send a Business Message

1. Many believe that a woman's sexuality is a powerful tool that can be used at work to "get ahead." What do you think about this issue? How might this opinion be expressed through dress?

2. Professional women have these two extremes for dress: either (1) dress like a man, in boxy, dark colored suits, or (2) dress in brightly colored clothes that accentuate her figure. There are many possible choices between these extremes. List several examples.

3. If you were an image consultant, how would you advise women just beginning their professional careers to dress? How would you advise women in top executive positions to dress?

41 How Black Can You Be?
Audrey Edwards

Affirmative action. Equal opportunity. Multiculturalism. Diversity. Sensitivity training. Workforce 2000. A whole new language has sprung up in the last 30 years attempting to account for a new phenomenon in the corporate workplace: the entrance of African-Americans [see Figure 7.5]. Of course we've been in other American workplaces since the very beginning: in the fields and the big house, the kitchens and factories, civil-service posts and self-employed enterprises. But it's only been within this civil-rights generation that we've landed in any great numbers in what's been called the corporate arena, that bastion of Europower and privilege where companies and nations are run—and fortunes made—by a group still largely White and male.

The fact that so many African-Americans now sit at the head of the table in corporate boardrooms is the surest sign of just how much things have changed. We have Kenneth I. Chenault running American Express; Lloyd Ward heading Maytag; Ann M. Fudge ruling at Maxwell House; Mark Whitaker the editor at *Newsweek*; Sylvia Rhone calling the shots at Elektra Records.

The list goes on, at big and small companies. The phenomenon, however, has also given rise to a sticky new question: Can you run White and remain Black? Can you succeed in White, corporate, private-sector America, a culture that at times seems the very antithesis of Black culture, without selling out your own culture?

The questions speak to the "dual consciousness" W.E.B. Du Bois first observed at the beginning of the last century, a conflict still stirring in the souls of Black folks. We're a people in perpetual unrest because we still feel forced to choose: between identifying Black or American; acting Black or White; siding Black or female; thinking Black or corporate, as if the two must be separate. We are the only people known to say things like "I'm a manager who happens to be Black," or "I'm a woman first and Black second." The trouble with this is that whenever we try to deny, make incidental or compartmentalize the defining feature of our race in the workplace (or any other place, for that matter), we tend to be less effective.

The most successful corporate Blacks don't consciously decide to be Black. They just never

FIGURE 7.5 *Black male executive.*

Reprinted by permission of Audrey Edwards.

forget they are Black. Race is one of the things that defines them, but not a thing that limits them. There is no dual, schizoid war raging in their souls, for they are clear about who and what they are. And while they don't necessarily lead with their Blackness in the workplace, the acknowledgment of its reality is a part of what gives them their power.

It's one thing, though, to embrace a Black identity; it can be quite another to express that identity at work—to literally wear our ethnicity on our sleeve, in how we dress, speak or (perhaps most significant for us as Black women) wear our hair. The issue here usually gets down to what makes Whites comfortable.

Sharon Davis (not her real name), a television news reporter in the local market of a major city, let her hair go natural a few years ago and now wears it in twists. But she knows her bosses are more comfortable with female broadcasters having straight hair. So when she's on the air, she puts on what she calls "my hat"—a straight-haired wig—to cover the twists.

Is Davis a sellout or just strategic? "Wearing a wig works for me," she says without apology. "It's cheaper and easier than always getting my hair done and saves my hair from the damage of relaxers. To me the wig just goes along with the makeup and other props you use for TV." Davis is not only clear about *why* she wears a wig on air but also clear on why she *should*, given the folks she works with. "As long as they [Whites] have a problem with your just being here," she says wearily, "why should you give them something else to have a problem with?"

Like other Black veterans in the corporate culture, Davis knows how much race still fuels the work environment. As Blacks in the White-run workplace, we still too often have to prove ourselves, if not legitimize our very presence. Whether in the boardroom or the newsroom, we can be made to feel we must alter, contort or even deny who we are in order to make it. As a successful news reporter for more than 20 years, Davis is clearly making it, and at this point in her career feels she no longer has to prove herself. Or at least no longer has to contort, damage or deny her hair to prove she can do her job.

DRESS PUMPS AND DREADLOCKS

Hair, like skin color, has always been a defining feature of Black culture. It is the striking thing that sets us apart from other cultures. It shouldn't be surprising, then, that in the workplace where our hair can be kinky, curly, permed, locked, twisted, braided, cornrowed, relaxed, weaved or wigged, it is the one thing most likely to make Whites least comfortable. "For Black women, one of the issues around corporate image has to do with the difference in hairstyles," says psychologist Ronald Brown, Ph.D., president of Banks Brown, a management-consulting firm in San Francisco. "For instance, when a woman wears dreadlocks in a corporate environment, the core message others receive is that you are probably more involved with your own culture than the corporate culture. There may be the sense that you're rejecting the very culture that's made the rest of us successful."

But what really makes Whites uncomfortable, argues Davis, is that "they just don't know what we do with our hair, and they think they should know, which is why they never ask. I really think they feel that not knowing might somehow make them racist. And it's the more astute, liberal-minded ones who feel this way. Conservative Whites don't think their ignorance makes them racist, so they will come right on out and ask about our hair."

Yet deeper than any discomfort Whites may have about hair is their great distress when they can't categorize, label or identify at all, contends another television reporter, Lloyd Gite, of Fox News in Houston. "Nothing trips up White folks more than not being able to tell who you are when they look at you," says Gite, 48, a light-skinned Black man who shaved his head a few years ago. Gite says that before his head was shaven, people mistook him for anything from Puerto Rican to Chinese to Greek when they saw him on TV. There has been much more comfort with his shaved head, the look Michael Jordan made distinctly Black. The television news business, says Gite, basically wants its Black men to look Black, and its Black women to look a little closer to White.

What's appropriate in any given corporate culture is a function of the culture itself: Who sets the policy at the top—someone fair-minded? Or someone closed and rigid? What are the rules? What product is the culture producing? How much in the way of conformity is necessary to get the product out? In the culture of television news, where the image is as important as the message, there is more pressure to adhere to a certain look. Blacks who make it in such "show" businesses come in understanding that and are willing to play by those rules. "I learned very early in my career not to do anything to change my look without letting them [her White bosses] know," says Davis.

NEW BATTLEFIELD, SAME OLD STRUGGLE

If the culture in one industry rewards "sticking to a look," other industries, technology, for one, reward innovation and improvisation. There's more room for mavericks and Lone Rangers in Silicon Valley's Wild West tech culture. There's room for Zandra Conway, who works at Hewlett-Packard's Atlanta office as a technology-solutions specialist. In the old days, Conway, 43, would have been called a militant or an activist. These days, with her locked twists, colorful head wraps, Black posters, calendars and photos displayed in her office cubicle and her in-your-face ethnic pride, she is in the corporate workplace to *represent*. "Embracing who you are is what gives you power and strength," she says.

It was natural, then, that Conway would help start an Atlanta chapter of Hewlett-Packard's Black Employees Forum when she arrived in the city from San Jose, California, three years ago. It makes sense that she invites Black experts like diversity trainer Roosevelt Thomas and business author Dennis Kimbro to come in to speak to both Black and White employees. It's a given that she makes sure there is a Black History Month program at the company every year and ongoing professional and educational workshops. "White males are still trying to understand things like diversity, quotas and affirmative action," she explains. "Once they sit

down and talk—and they see we can talk—it helps break down stereotypes. We have to be the key in sensitizing Whites to our presence. If we don't, they will just ignore it and keep going. They should know about the wonderful things we've done in our history and know why we're proud of our heritage."

But it hasn't always been easy getting other company Blacks involved. "That's one of the struggles," Conway says. "Some don't want their White coworkers to know they're going to a Black Forum program. They're afraid there'll be backlash. And there has been some. But nobody's ever said anything to me."

Conway's up-front activist style has proven to be a natural fit at Hewlett-Packard, which is why she's been there 19 years. Like every other cutting-edge company, Hewlett-Packard wants to make profits and stay ahead of the competition. But it also knows that the companies most likely to have the winning edge in the future will have to have all sorts of people and points of view contributing to the bottom line. As Conway points out, Hewlett-Packard is aware that the American workforce will be increasingly made up of people of color in this new century. "They know they need to make sure they can retain African-American employees," she says. "So they look to me when it comes to diversity issues. They understand that diversity has got to be an important part of the corporate aim."

And Conway understands, indeed relishes, her role as corporate conscience. What makes all the difference is that the company she works for supports that role. Zandra Conway is successful expressing her full, Black self because she works in a corporate environment that values her full, Black self. But even at such politically correct companies, it can take a minute for the policies mandated by headquarters to filter down to the troops. "This is the South, and there's still some Jim Crow mentality," Conway says of the Black resistance to diversity she encounters. That resistance, that Jim Crow mentality, is expressed every time Blacks think they shouldn't talk too much or too long to other Blacks at work or join Black employee groups (don't want Whites to think you're not a "team player"). It's expressed every time they refuse to hang socially with Whites, be it during or after work (don't want them to think you're going to be their friend!); or feel they have to make a point to high-five the brothers in the mail room (don't want them to think you ain't down); or wish that sister from accounting would stop trying to talk to them (doesn't she know you're a department head and can't socialize with the clerks?). It's expressed every time Blacks in the corporate workplace think or act along separate, conflicted and segregated racial lines on the job.

It should go without saying that just about the worst thing you can do as a Black person in the workplace is act as if race is incidental to who you are. Whites may appear to be more comfortable with such self- and race-denial on your part, but they never really respect it and don't really trust it either. A corporate player who thinks of herself as a manager who "happens to be Black," or as a company woman but not a race woman, or as a smart and talented young sister who will always be rewarded on merit and not ever tripped up by race comes across as naive. And naïveté makes you vulnerable.

So does not forming alliances across the board—with Whites, Blacks and others—since such alliances can benefit you. "When you segregate and leave yourself out of forming friendships with people, it's very limiting, professionally and personally," says Jerri DeVard, vice-president of customer acquisition and new business development at Citibank in New York City. "Why would you want to do that? If you perceive there is going to be some negative impact on claiming and expressing who you are as a Black person, then there will be. The thing is to just be yourself. I wear who I am on my sleeve. I don't happen to be Black. I am."

Yet DeVard, the epitome of corporate chic, with her soothing but authoritative voice and friendly style, does not make the Whites she works with uncomfortable. The Black-American art and African sculpture that adorn her office, the Black causes she gets her company to support and the personal time she takes to make sure younger Blacks coming up avoid the "land mines" still littering the corporate landscape all say she is a race woman. Her vice-president's title says she is an officer at one of the largest banks in the world. The fact that she manages to integrate both into one smooth-running Black corporate whole is perhaps the truest measure of her success—and her power.

BLACK AS YOU WANNA BE?

Like DeVard, many high-profile corporate Blacks are quite comfortable being who they are. They've learned not only how to be themselves but also to express an authentic ethnic self and make it work for them. Take Mae Watts Brown, 47, sales manager for radio station WAIT in Chicago, who will occasionally lapse into Black colloquialisms to lighten things up. "The biggest challenge Blacks have in the corporation is in how we speak," she contends, recalling a White-female coworker at another job who took a "huge account" from her after she'd made it profitable. Brown said the colleague would refer to her as "Mae Ax Brown."

"Now, I've never said *ax* for *ask*," Brown says, still miffed by the memory, "but that was her way of trying to put me down as a Black person." Brown eventually sued over the stolen account and they settled. Interestingly, though, she now uses Black slang herself in one-on-one interactions with Whites when she wants to ease up. "I might say something like 'Girl, please!' or 'I know that's right!' It's my way of cutting Whites some slack. Plus, it makes me more comfortable."

This is the ultimate challenge: to find what makes us comfortable in the workplace without making Whites uncomfortable working with us. Now sometimes this is a no-win proposition. Some work environments, no matter what we do, are just hostile, even dangerous to Black emotional health. Think Texaco or Denny's before both were exposed and sued. In such arenas the best move may be simply to split.

For the most part, however, the workplace is not particularly dangerous, even when it's not being especially welcoming. What it really is, says psychologist Ron Brown, is artificial. We spend much of our waking lives interacting with people who have nothing to do with our lives after work. We may do work that has no intrinsic meaning to us beyond a paycheck. We may have to act nice when we don't feel like it or cooperate when we'd rather tell you where to go. The thing is, this is true for everybody in the workplace. This is the nature of work.

Like Mae Brown, we have to learn to cut everybody some slack. "Black women don't realize they enter the corporate workplace with what's viewed as very confident styles," says Brown. "What's normal in African-American culture—dressing in vibrant colors, gesturing to make a point, speaking in voices that tend to be deeper, louder, with more power and resonance—comes across as confident. That can be very startling to Whites who are used to thinking of Black people as being disadvantaged. They aren't used to seeing self-possessed Black women who may be just one of a few [Blacks] in a sea of many [Whites]. And if that woman dresses well, speaks well and seems to fit in very well, some Whites are subtly intimidated." Much of the time Black women at work are just "coping," Brown says, but that's not the perception.

As a result, there are times we may, indeed, have to tone it down. Not deny who we are, but soften who we are if it is keeping us from being heard or understood. This may mean anything from not wearing a kente-cloth suit if the corporate look is button-down Brooks Brothers to refraining from doing a gooseneck or rolling your eyes the next time a coworker gets on your nerves. It is ultimately up to you to figure out what will work and not work in the corporate culture you've chosen to do business in, just as

you must, in the first place, choose a work environment that's likely to be compatible with who you are. "Part of our self-care involves choosing a workplace in which we're comfortable," says Linda Anderson, Ph.D., a New York City psychotherapist and corporate coach. "The ideal corporate environment acknowledges our differences without making the mistake of either exaggerating or minimizing those differences. On the other hand, we've become savvy enough to understand that if we choose to work in corporate America, the cultural workplace can't be what affirms us."

Affirmation is more likely to come in afterwork activities through Black professional organizations or outreach programs involving the company you work for and the community you live in. And for many, the corporate work experience is just the temporary means to a larger end: attaining the skills needed for entrepreneurship or for working in a Black-owned business.

Finding a comfortable corporate fit isn't really all that difficult, when you think about it. "This is not hard at all, compared with our foremothers picking cotton," says Zandra Conway. We at least now have the freedom to choose the line of work we do. And if the ancestors could figure out how to make it when there was no choice, how can we do any less in an era that certainly has more, if not always equal, opportunity?

DISCUSSION QUESTIONS

How Black Can You Be?

1. One TV news reporter states that wearing a straight wig on the air is just another prop needed to do her job. How does this compare to the articles "Black Hair—Black Times" in Chapter 10 and "To Apu, with Love" in Chapter 2?

2. What do you think about the idea that those who deny their race are less effective?

3. What is "the nature of work" that Edwards refers to in her article? Does this idea apply only to African Americans? Why or why not?

42   Just Playing Doctor? Shorter Coats Make Residents Feel Naked

Calmetta Y. Coleman

What distinguishes a doctor most? The stethoscope? The fees? Or is it that long, white coat?

That's been the burning question here at Duke University Medical Center ever since a young doctor dared to ask if residents could start wearing long coats.

Jamy Ard, 28 years old, popped the question last summer at a monthly breakfast for internal-medicine residents with the chairman of their department, Barton Haynes. A three-decade-old department policy restricted the use of knee-length white coats to veteran doctors. Internal-medicine residents had to wear blazer-length white coats—though residents in other departments, including surgery and pediatrics, had recently switched to the longer coats.

BUTCHER-WEAR

Nowadays, very few hospitals maintain such sartorial distinctions (Massachusetts General in Boston is a notable holdout, though some attending physicians there also wear short coats). Anyone arguing that medical residents haven't earned a knee-length white coat must answer—or dodge—the question of what butchers, barbers and cosmetics clerks did to earn them. "At Duke, sometimes even managers in environmental services wear long coats," says resident Michael Mullowney, 30. Environmental services is the custodial department.

Dr. Haynes, 52, declined to rule on the issue. Any change in coat-length policy, he announced at the breakfast, should be considered by the Graduate Medical Education committee, which oversees the residency program and is composed entirely of full-fledged—that is to say, long-coated—physicians. Dr. Haynes told Dr. Ard to poll his fellow residents and submit a request to the committee.

Among the department's 150 residents, Dr. Ard found substantial support for his campaign to abolish the short-coat rule. Residents boast medical degrees. They work longer hours and spend more time with patients than do veteran physicians. Why should residents wear a coat that causes some patients to mistake them for students or nurses?

"YOU'RE A DOCTOR?"

When first-year resident M. Angelyn Bethel, 28, went to take care of a patient and the woman got a look at her short coat, "she said, 'Are you certain you're a doctor?' I told her I was, but she would have none of it. I eventually had to leave the room to find someone in a long coat to tell her I was OK."

The blazer-length white coat, in conjunction with the white pants that traditionally go with it, makes doctors "look like they're going to serve ice cream," says fellow resident Dr. Mullowney.

The policy could even turn away some residency candidates, short-coat opponents have warned: Resident Gina Vaccaro, 27, says the short-coat requirement "almost deterred" her from coming to Duke.

That argument doesn't impress veteran physicians. "If you're basing a career choice on a hemline, you don't need to be here," says Dan Nikcevich of the Graduate Medical Education committee.

To other traditionalists, the long-coat envy seems adolescent. "If you're a teenager, you're going to want to dress like the people older than you," says Russel Kaufman, 53, who went through Duke's residency program about 20 years ago and is now vice dean of education for the medical school.

White coats aren't all about status, of course. They protect a doctor's regular clothes—typically shirts, ties, blouses and such—from blood and other stains and germs in general. Their deep pockets are handy for carrying prescription pads, stethoscopes and other small tools.

But as long ago as the 17th century, length of coat was used to make distinctions. British and American physicians wore long coats, for instance, surgeons short ones. By the early 20th century, it was common in medical America for residents and interns to wear short white coats, while veteran doctors donned long ones.

About 90 residents responded to Dr. Ard's poll, and a "clear majority" favored ditching the short-coat policy, he says. Some took emphatic positions, such as third-year resident Mallory McClure, 29. She was prepared "to walk around in circles and picket," she says. "I have paid my dues. I have my M.D. And that's it."

GOING TO GREAT LENGTHS

A minority of residents voted in favor of wearing short coats until their residency is completed. "We all have a ways to go before we reach that landmark," says Cheryl Russo, 31, a second-year resident.

After receiving Dr. Ard's formal request and the results of his poll, the Graduate Medical Education committee met last fall and repealed the short-coat requirement.

In announcing the change in policy, however, the committee warned residents not to let patients think they are veteran physicians. "We had a long talk with our house staff and told

them that what really matters is that they explain to the patients who they are within the hierarchy of learning," Dr. Haynes says.

The hospital, which typically supplies the coats, already had bought short ones for residents this year. But at least half of the 150 residents went out and bought their own long coats, at about $30 each.

Some residents say a foot or so of fabric can make an amazing difference. Dr. McClure, the third-year resident, says a neurosurgeon whom she declines to name never acknowledged her when she wore a short coat. But the first day she wore a long one, the neurosurgeon said hello. "I said, 'Oh, you see me now,'" Dr. McClure recalls. "He knew what I meant."

SELF-ESTEEM ISSUES

But traditionalists say that behind the whole brouhaha is resident insecurity. Those residents "who didn't have any concern about their self-image didn't seem to change to a long coat," says William Yarger, 62, chief of medical services for the Veterans Affairs Medical Center, which is staffed by Duke physicians.

The battle isn't necessarily over. In repealing the short-coat policy, the Graduate Medical Education committee made an exception: Knee-length coats remain off-limits to first-year residents, known as interns. "I have strong feelings that interns should wear short white coats," says Dr. Nikcevich, 38.

This policy, which many other hospitals also follow, doesn't sit well with some interns. "The long coats are more comfortable, they're more slimming, and they command more respect," says intern Peter Kamilakis, 27.

The new policy bothers even some senior residents. "I think it kind of puts the interns down," says Dr. Vaccaro, a second-year resident. As a show of solidarity with interns, she continues to wear a short coat.

Just Playing Doctor?

1. The author makes the point that if cosmetics counter employees can wear long white coats, why can't those who have recently earned a medical degree wear one? What is your opinion on this issue?

2. This article is about status distinctions in the workplace, giving senior doctors longer coats while restricting residents to shorter coats. Do you think this is a silly concern? A self-esteem issue on the part of insecure residents? Or a legitimate battle for recognition of an earned degree?

3. Do you think the person who brought the issue to light is an astute reader of cultural signs? Or someone who has nothing better to do?

4. What purposes (other than status distinctions) do the white coats serve?

43 Health to Pay: Pressures Push Jockeys to Extremes for Weight Loss

Maryjean Wall

As a 9-year-old boy, Randy Romero rode races where the jockeys were really light. Sometimes the "jockey" was no more than a few strips of plastic substituting for a rider on a horse.

A horse can run a hole through the wind when you take the weight off its back. And there's nothing like plastic flapping in the breeze to scare a horse into running fast. Romero grew up in the bayou country of Southwest Louisiana observing strange ways for racing horses "light."

The boys he rode against were also light. But Romero was not. He starved himself to 70 pounds. Later he learned to "flip" his meals by sticking a finger down his throat, forcing himself to vomit. At 16 he started taking the diuretic Lasix. Now he says those habits have ruined his health.

At 44, Romero has become an outspoken advocate of raising the minimum weights to benefit jockeys [see Figure 7.6]. Although he's been retired four years from riding, Romero has raised a timely topic among jockeys.

The world's top money-winning jockey, Chris McCarron, said when he retired last month that he is "absolutely" behind a growing momentum to see jockeys riding at least a few pounds heavier than the average 111 to 113.

McCarron also said that jockeys need to understand the damage they inflict on their bodies by using extreme weight-loss techniques.

Romero, in fact, has blamed his need for a liver and kidney transplant on his lifelong battle with weight.

On closer reflection, however, he says his kidney and liver problems probably did not result from radical weight-loss techniques but from other hazards he encountered during his jockey career.

He now says his diseased liver might have resulted from a blood transfusion received after severe burns he suffered in a weight-loss "box" years ago at Oaklawn Park.

He says his failing kidneys might have resulted from the large number of anti-inflammatory medications he says he had to take after 22 surgeries.

Nonetheless Romero and retired jockey Shane Sellers have seized on Romero's illness to seek a forum for the weight-loss plight of jockeys.

© Lexington Herald-Leader.

McCarron, who plans to keep up his leadership in The Jockey's Guild even in retirement, said from California that Romero's plea should not be taken lightly. According to McCarron, traditionally low riding weights and radical weight-loss methods are for many riders a very real problem.

FIGURE 7.6 *Jockeys must weigh in prior to racing. Some jockeys adopt dangerous habits to make the weight standard.*

EVALUATING SCALE OF WEIGHTS

Romero estimates that "out of 10 riders, two do not reduce at all." California-based Kent Desormeaux, who won the Kentucky Derby with Real Quiet and then with Fusaichi Pegasus, said that "98 percent of us have to reduce."

Their estimates, while unscientific, are validated by the empirical findings of a study conducted in Australia and published in March. Australian scientists discovered what professional jockeys already knew too well. Their conclusion was that "the majority" are forced to practice at least one radical technique to meet the sport's weight requirements. The study was published in a journal called "Sport Nutrition and Exercise Metabolism."

Significant to racing authorities was the scientists' conclusion that dehydration resulting from these rapid weight-loss techniques "increases the risk of accident and injury to both horse and jockey."

Yet racing authorities have paid little attention to this danger through the years. Jockeys continue to ride at weights that have not changed radically since the late 19th century, when The Jockey Club's Scale of Weights was devised. The scale represents the weights to be assigned to horses according to the time of year, the sex of the animal, its age and the distance of the race.

The Scale of Weights has been raised by about 20 pounds in some categories through the years, according to racing steward Pete Pederson, in California. Still, he said, "some of it's antiquated."

The Jockey Club no longer controls the Scale of Weights, which now falls under the jurisdiction of individual racing commissions. The jockey's dilemma remains the same, however. Either he meets his horses' weight assignments or he soon finds himself out of work.

That's not a problem for Pat Day, who maintains an average weight of about 103 pounds. He's naturally light and does not have to reduce.

That gives Day an edge even beyond his extraordinary talent. Other jockeys say that Day probably rides with more strength than a rider who spends hours in the sauna, sweating his strength away.

All the same, Day does not think that clearing the way for jockeys to ride at heavier weights will solve the big problems.

"It's a short-term answer to a long-term problem," said Day, the third-winningest rider in history. Raise the window of opportunity, according to Day, and you'll see the same scenario only with larger people trying to make the weight.

Carl Nafzger, who trained Kentucky Derby winner Unbridled, said higher weights won't hurt horses—as long as the spread between highest and lowest weights in a race is not too great. The heavily-weighted horse is forced to race harder. That's how breakdowns can occur, according to Nafzger.

But Hall of Fame trainer D. Wayne Lukas sees the weight-loss cycle only continuing if jockey weights go higher. Like Day, he sees heavier people trying to become riders if that window opens.

Yet for the safety of horses, Lukas said, it's "most important" to have them ridden by the lightest possible people.

"We race year-round," Lukas said, "which means more stress on the horses. Speed and weight are the detrimental things to a horse's longevity."

DOING WHATEVER IT TAKES

Many concur that weight is detrimental to a horse's speed. That's why jockeys have to keep their weight low however they can. No one wants the jockey checking in at a couple of pounds overweight.

Before the Civil War, when many jockeys were slaves, their owners reportedly kept the small boys from eating too much to keep them from getting too big.

Reducing has taken some creative twists since then. Readers of Laura Hillenbrand's *Seabiscuit* will recall Eddie Arcaro's comment: "Some riders will all but saw their legs off to get within the limit."

The book mentioned a few other old-time methods, including swallowing a pill containing the egg of a tapeworm. Then there were the bottles of "bowel scourer" that surely must have been fairly potent, if not effective—a few of them spontaneously exploded in the jockeys' room in Tijuana.

Chick Lang, a former jockeys' agent and former general manager of Pimlico Racecourse, can recall riders donning rubber sweat suits and burying themselves up to their necks in horse manure piles, to induce more heat.

"In the meantime, the racing secretaries (who assign weights, according to the Scale of Weights) sit back and eat a double hamburger," opined jockey Craig Perret.

Perret made that comment tongue-in-cheek. He said it wasn't intended as criticism. He's not even actively campaigning for adjusting the Scale of Weights. But every day he rides, he has to reduce. He fears that someday he will suffer consequences to his health.

Reducing strategies cover every ground from flipping to swallowing diuretics to taking diet pills and sweating in the sauna.

"We don't have two months to reduce," Perret said. "We play with minutes. We've got hours to take it off."

Perret says he loses a pound to $1\frac{1}{2}$ pounds daily, but on rare days he might have to lose up to five pounds.

Flipping is perhaps the most controversial practice, one that jockeys and racetrack managements are not keen to discuss. Some observers have even compared flipping to bulimia.

"I see it every day," said Pederson, the steward in California. "I see top riders coming out of the (sauna) or flipping. These are really bad things that should be addressed."

Dr. David Richardson, a surgeon in Louisville who has owned racehorses and is familiar with the racetrack lifestyle, said he does not believe the majority of jockeys are suffering severe problems as a result of reducing.

But he also said that flipping has side effects, including irritation of the stomach or esophagus.

Veteran jockeys also tell how their teeth enamel becomes eroded after years of flipping. Some even lose their teeth.

Romero said his body got so accustomed to years of flipping that when he retired from riding, his body needed another "$1\frac{1}{2}$ years to quit flipping."

It's racing's dirty secret. Yet racetrack managements accommodate the practice of flipping by providing jockeys with a special "heaving bowl." The porcelain bowl is larger than a toilet but smaller than a washtub. It can be found in any jockeys' locker room among the toilet stalls.

Fifteen years ago, UPI reporter Pohla Smith began a provocative series on jockeys and weight with an observation about the widespread practice of flipping.

"At the core of horse racing lies a self-imposed misery," Smith wrote, "that racing's owners and trainers do not want to see, fans are largely unaware of, and most jockeys cannot escape.

"It is represented by a sound better suited to back alleys and washrooms than to a sport known for its riches, beauty and power.

"It is the sound of someone vomiting."

SWEATING AWAY THE WEIGHT

The other popular weight-loss strategy, more suited to polite conversation, is the sauna that jockeys still call the "hot box." The term is a holdover from days when the box was a one-man contraption that enclosed the jockey up to his neck. A multitude of light bulbs inside the box generated the heat that made the jockey sweat. The sweating removed fluids and reduced the rider's weight.

Romero suffered severe burns in such a box years ago. He'd rubbed himself down with alcohol and oil before tightening the hatch on the hot box. Then his arm hit a lighted bulb. "The combustion blew me out of there," he said. Three of his 22 surgeries resulted from that inci-

dent. Romero said that 10 years after the burn incident, he got a $1.8 million settlement that comes to him in installments.

The modern-day hot box is actually a system of three rooms: a dry heat room, a steam room and a "cooling down" room which is still warm, but cooler than the other rooms. Temperatures in the dry heat and steam rooms might be between 150 and 160 degrees.

Desormeaux, at Hollywood Park, said the hot box routine is "very difficult." Sometimes he sits in the steam room for 30 minutes. Sometimes he incorporates calisthenics into his sweating regimen.

SAFER ALTERNATIVES

Raising weights likely will be discussed in Kentucky, in the opinion of Bernie Hettel, the Executive Director of the Kentucky Racing Commission. He says it might be time to reexamine the Scale of Weights, as some states already have.

But as talk heats up, Lukas and Day both wonder why more jockeys can't follow Laffit Pincay's lead.

Pincay, 55, the winningest jockey ever, has fought weight throughout his career. Lukas often told the story of how he flew cross-country with Pincay—and watched him eat only a single peanut the entire way, after slicing it into tiny bits.

Then Pincay found relief. He'd refined what he'd learned from nutritionists until he formulated a diet that allowed him some fruit, oil and salt.

At 52 he became the winningest rider ever in 1999 passing Bill Shoemaker's 8,830 wins.

At the same time, Pincay told how he felt far better than he'd had before his new diet. Using this regimen, he maintains a weight of 115 pounds.

In Lukas' view, the weight question always has and will revolve around one premise:

"If you want to be a rider," Lukas said, "you're going to have to make sacrifices."

"Laffit Pincay," he said, "is living proof it can be done."

1. Do you agree that raising weight limits will only increase the number of people using extreme weight-loss techniques to "make the weight"? Why or why not?

2. Did you know about the extreme measures that jockeys use to make their weight limit? How does it compare to wrestling? To body building? To runway modeling?

3. List the ways that jockeys reduce their weight before a race. What are some of the consequences of these methods?

4. Should there be a "heaving bowl" at fashion runway shows for models?

44 A Clothing Gift Program for Low-Income Women: Corporate Giving with an Impact

Mary Lynn Damhorst and Harriet McLeod
Iowa State University and University of Nebraska, Lincoln

It was a gala event. The five guests of honor were treated to midmorning breakfast. Each was paired with a local fashion expert for a friendly chat over breakfast about the woman's color and style preferences and current wardrobe. Then the experts personally escorted each guest during a shopping experience in the host department store. With helpful advice from their experts, each guest selected two complete work-appropriate outfits, two pairs of shoes, and two handbags from the store's current inventory. Sales personnel gave endless attention to the guests, running to get correct sizes and alternative garments to try out. The guests also received a mini-makeover and skin care consultation from the cosmetics personnel. The guests received a selection of makeup products and were able to keep their outfits, shoes, and bags—compliments of the retailer. Each guest also received a watch from the jewelry counter. Professional photographers took photos of the women in one of their selected outfits and as a group with their personal shoppers. There were oohs and ahs as the women showed off their new looks. A local TV station covered the event. After selecting out-

fits, lunch was served and each guest received gift bags containing various products. It was quite a day!

The five guests of honor had not won a prize from a drawing. They weren't wealthy customers being treated like queens by the store. They were, instead, women who had been achieving success in educational programs to work themselves out of low-paying jobs or unemployment. They were women in transition—women from a wide array of circumstances, including displaced homemakers, welfare recipients, ex-convicts, and victims of spousal abuse—who shared a common need to find employment that would provide them with a living wage. Some of these women had been out of the workforce for an extended period of time; others had never worked outside the home. Some had held only jobs that paid minimum wage.

Sears Roebuck & Co. conducted this event and many like it for their Fashion Takes Action (FTA) program. The philanthropic program was

Original for this text.

designed to give women in transition work-appropriate attire to help them in job interviews and on the job. From 1998 through 2001,[1] Sears partnered with a variety of organizations that work with low-income women to identify potential participants for the FTA program.

In 2000 (the year we conducted a study of FTA), Women Work! was the philanthropic partner for the FTA program. Women Work!, the National Network for Women's Employment, is a national nonprofit organization "dedicated to empowering women from diverse backgrounds and assisting them to achieve economic self-sufficiency through job readiness, education, training and employment" ("Honoring Our Past," n.d., back cover). Women Work! is an outgrowth of the Displaced Homemakers Movement that began in the 1970s. The organization provides local affiliates with training and technical assistance to prepare women to enter, reenter, or train for the workforce. Through a collaborative effort the organization strives to create and strengthen policies and programs for women ("Honoring Our Past," n.d.).

Sears developed the FTA program to provide physical appearance products and a psychological boost that might help move women to the next step in their employment activities. Women chosen for this program were in the latter stages of their academic or work training programs; they were women who needed and were ready to use this particular aid. Sears believed that the FTA program helped circumvent the "Catch 22" situations that low-income women could experience—that is, the lack of appropriate clothing serving as an impediment to getting or keeping a job.

The assumption underlying Sears' program was its belief that work-appropriate clothing may positively affect women's self-esteem and self-confidence. This belief does have some grounding in academic research, albeit not direct. Solomon and Douglas (1985) described clothing as a "tactical weapon" in job role performance that can help to establish credibility of the role player. They proposed that appropriate work dress can give a worker greater confidence in a new job or in employment interviews by symbolically compensating for lack of experience in a job field. Fiore and DeLong (1990)

found evidence that self-esteem can be positively affected by therapy sessions in which women learn how to modify their appearance. Turner-Bowker (2001) asserted, "Attractive apparel is a sign of privilege, yet it is a necessity for those expecting to enter and succeed in the workforce" (p. 314). However, low-income women may have little left from their earnings after satisfying other basic needs in their families. Buying clothing for themselves that is appropriate for the workplace is often a necessity that cannot be met.

A number of volunteer organizations provide an array of services to low-income women to enhance their appearance and sense of well-being as they prepare to enter or reenter the workplace. For example, at Hype & Humble, a nonprofit organization focused on empowering women and children in crisis, the women receive massages, facials, and makeovers given by a celebrity stylist and listen to motivational speakers ("Helping Hands," 2001). Other groups such as Bottomless Closet, Eve's Closet, and Dress for Success provide the women with "gently used" professional clothing (Johnson-Elie, 2001; "Program Seeking Business," 2001; Whitehead, 2001; Zanos, 2002).

Founders of these organizations believe that helping a woman feel better about herself, due to an internal or external source, is an important step toward self-sufficiency. Another commonality is that the beneficiaries of these organizations are referrals from other agencies. Oftentimes, the women may be involved in a job training program or enrolled in an academic program at these referring agencies. Many of the clothing giveaway organizations were started after recognizing that some women, recently prepared for the work world, did not know what appropriate office attire was and/or did not have the money to purchase an appropriate wardrobe.

The FTA program differed from other clothing gift programs because it allowed the women to select from current seasonal clothing offered to the general population, paired the women with fashion experts with professional training as stylists or trend watchers, and conducted the shopping event in a retail store in a celebratory manner. The number of locations where the FTA program was conducted expanded from one city in 1998 to five cities in 1999 and 10 cities in 2000 and 2001. At each location, four or five participants were usually treated to the shopping event. The events take approximately four hours.

The FTA program was in its third year in 2000 when data were collected for this research. Sears Corporate encourages its employees to participate in community projects through its Good Life Alliance program. The FTA program was one opportunity that employees had for earning their volunteer hours.

Sears Corporate supported the FTA program financially and with human resources. The gift items that the women received during the shopping event were paid for through the Corporate Office. In conjunction with the FTA event, the local Sears stores sponsored a seven- to 10-day used clothing drive. Items received during that time period were given to the local affiliate of Women Work! that participated in the shopping event. Sears also contributed $100,000 during 2000 to be shared between Women Work! and its local affiliates.

AN OPPORTUNITY TO STUDY FTA

The 2000 FTA program was conducted in 10 cities in the United States—Chicago, Dallas, Denver, Los Angeles, Pittsburgh, Baltimore, Atlanta, Miami, District of Columbia, and New York. We were invited by Sears, through the PR firm 2wo-One-2wo that coordinated FTA, to conduct a study of the program and its impact on the women participants. The study was funded by Sears. Our observations and data collection were conducted at eight of the 10 shopping sites.

The Women Beneficiaries

The women selected by the Women Work! Affiliate programs to participate in the FTA events are the major focus of this research. They were identified by the program coordinators as women ready for the job market or women who needed a psychological boost while participating in job training (see Box 1).

A total of 51 women participated in the FTA program in 2000. Thirty-six women shopped in the cities visited by the data collector for the FTA event, and all but three of these women participated to some extent in the research. We could not collect data at the New York shopping events, but six of the 10 women who experienced the FTA program there agreed to participate at some level in the research. A total of 39 women, or 76 percent of the women who experienced the FTA event in 2000, participated in some aspect of this study.

There were two ways that the FTA shopping was conducted: In all cities except for New York and Los Angeles, four to five women were invited to a local Sears store to shop for work-appropriate clothing while accompanied by a fashion expert. These shopping sessions took place in late spring and the fall of 2000. In Los Angeles, a total of seven women participated. In New York City, women shopped at various times during the year rather than as one group.

Among the 39 women completing some phase of the research, demographics were collected from 37 (see Table 1). The average age was 34, but more of the women were in their 20s and 40s. Ethnic diversity of the participants was far greater than that of the U.S. population, with 61 percent of ethnic minority background (see Table 2).

All but four women were single parents at the time of the study. The women as a group were raising a total of 86 children. Profiles of five of the participants are presented in Box 1 to give more insight into the lives of some of the women.

Procedures

Questionnaires assessed participants' confidence, knowledge, and sense of adequacy of their work wardrobe, work-related confidence and efficacy, general confidence and self-efficacy, self-esteem, and evaluation of the FTA program. Questionnaire data were collected before and after the women participated in FTA. Prior to the shopping events, the data collector contacted the Women Work! affiliate program coordinators by phone to explain the study and to ask for their help in administering the pretest questionnaire to

BOX 1
A Look at the Participants

Five short profiles give a sense of some of the women who were beneficiaries of the Sears FTA program. These women were selected to reflect the diversity of the clients served. Their lives are described as they were at the time of the FTA program. Their names have been changed to protect the privacy of the individuals.

Theresa is a 55-year-old, European-American mother of six children, who had recently adopted her granddaughter and has been a foster mother for 27 children. Theresa and her husband have been married for 43 years. Her husband suffered a series of strokes approximately 10 months prior to her participation in the FTA shopping event. Theresa's husband was the primary wage earner in the family, so she turned to social services for support after his illness. The social services program that Theresa enrolled in required her to look for employment. Theresa has a high school diploma and never worked outside her home prior to her husband's illness.

Theresa and her family live approximately three hours away from the city where she partici-pated in the shopping event. Theresa and one other woman (see Francois below) chosen to participate in the event traveled to the city the day before the event. Their overnight accommo-dations were at the expense of Sears. Theresa's husband and granddaughter were also pres-ent at the FTA event.

Octavia is a 44-year-old Latin-American, mother of five chil-dren, and grandmother of three. Octavia is separated from her husband. She has completed some college and is enrolled in a program to earn a childcare center director's license. She plans to open up her own day-care center and to that end is preparing a business plan. Octavia was previously em-ployed for 11 years but was laid off. After being laid off for one year, she enrolled in the training program.

Lois is a 39-year-old, Euro-pean-American mother of two children. She is divorced, and she and her children have re-turned to her parents' home to live. Lois attends a community college, is pursuing a nursing career, and has plans to eventu-ally get her Ph.D. in a related area. Lois was previously em-ployed in a large city in an office setting.

Dorothy is a 34-year-old, African-American mother of two children. She is separated from her husband. Dorothy has train-ing in cosmetology, is attending college, and just prior to the FTA shopping event was employed in a career service department at the college she is attending.

Francois is a 26-year-old, African-American mother of one child. She has never married. Francois is currently employed full-time in a health-related field. Francois completed a job train-ing program at a community col-lege, has taken a series of job placement tests through a so-cial services office, and had been involved with her educa-tion program for about one and a half years.

Francois was the second woman who traveled several hours to attend the shopping event. She and Theresa, whom she was introduced to the day before the shopping event, shared a hotel room the night before the shopping event at the expense of Sears.

TABLE 1

Age	#	Education	#	Ethnicity	#
18–19	3	Some high school	1	African-American	18
20–29	11	Completed high school	7	European-American	13
30–39	8	Vo/tech	1	Latin-American	7
40–45	11	Some college	25	Native American	1
48–57	4	Associate degree	2	College degree (4 yr.)	1

the women beneficiaries. The coordinators brought the confidential pretests to the shopping events in envelopes sealed by the participants. The posttest or follow-up questionnaire was given to the women immediately after the shopping event. Some women completed the posttest at the Sears store before they departed; others returned it in a self-addressed, stamped envelope.

Interviews were conducted with participants during the shopping event and approximately three weeks later by telephone. The in-depth telephone interviews comprised the bulk of the findings for this study.

Findings

SELF-ESTEEM AND SELF-CONFIDENCE.
Self-esteem scores and the various work and general self-confidence scores did not differ significantly before and after the FTA sessions. This may be due to the initially strong self-esteem and confidence scores among the women. The average pretest score for self-esteem, for example,

was 2 on a scale of 1–5, with lower scores indicating more positive feelings about the self. The women selected to participate in the program were clearly women who had taken charge of their lives to put themselves on the path to self-support and who were having some success achieving their goals. With initial scores so strong, it is hard to detect if these women became more positive about themselves.

However, several of the women reported that they *felt* more self-confident after taking part in Fashion Takes Action. Throughout the nine interviews, the women continually talked about how the FTA session increased their readiness to go to job interviews, improved their morale, and generally made them feel happy. On her second questionnaire, one woman wrote:

> Fashion Takes Action helped give me the confidence and security I needed to enter the work force and distinguish myself from others. I immediately found a great job after the experience.

TABLE 2

Marital Status	#	Children	#
Married	3	0	0
Never married	12	1	11
Divorced or separated	21	2	13
	1	3	4
		4	3
		5	3
		6	0
		7	1

CONFIDENCE IN WORK CLOTHING.
Both the interview content and the questionnaire scores indicated that the FTA session made the women more confident that they had clothing that was appropriate to wear to work and job interviews. Their mastery of knowledge of what was appropriate for work increased. The work clothing confidence/knowledge scores became significantly more positive after the sessions. Before the FTA program, the women had an average of 3.8 on a scale of 5 for clothing confidence/knowledge, but after the sessions the average score was 2.4

(a lower score is more positive). Many of the women contended that they now had a better sense of what to wear for interviews and on the job because of the advice they received from their personal shopping partner. One woman noted: "The advice was just as important as the clothing."

The connection between feelings that they had appropriate clothing with feelings of self-confidence was evident in the interviews of most of the women. Three of the women explained the relationship between self-confidence and dress:

> . . . clothes don't make a person, but they help a whole lot. . . . help a lot of women gain just that little bit, enough of confidence to go out and feel good about sitting down in front of that interviewer. And knowing that she's got the right clothes on and that she looks good in what she's got on.

> And you have to feel confident in yourself before you can give the impression that you are a confident person.

> It is really nice that they are doing it. It is a great help. And it just like makes your confidence go through the roof. It is just such a confidence builder. You feel so proud. [Q: What do you feel proud about?] Just, I guess, looking good will automatically bring anybody's confidence level up, and it helped you with that part. It brings you, you can walk in there proud. You have on an outfit that is not ... raggedy, it is [not] old. If your outfit is not the way you want it to be, you are thinking about that. Or let's say, if you had a messed up shirt on and you couldn't get the stain out, you are worried if that stain is showing, [or worried] if the person that you are interviewing with or that you are talking to can see the stain. You have those distractions on your mind. When you have fresh, nice wardrobe or nice clothes, things like that can just be avoided and put out of the way.

The women recognized that clothing would not get them a job, but that clothing and grooming were tools that they needed to acquire in their preparation for entering the workforce and for career development. In four hours' time, the fashion experts shared lessons with the women on how to build a basic work wardrobe. When asked if she had received enough tips from her fashion expert to put together an outfit by herself, one woman replied: "I think I could do better than what I was doing." Another noted that her new clothing might help her climb the ladder of success in her job:

> To me in the atmosphere where I was working, ... all the people and the department heads and the people that had positions dressed professional, and that is where I'm trying to go. And I knew as long as I stayed in jeans and T-shirts that I wasn't going to be taken seriously. So by me changing my attire, it seems like people have changed the way they think about me and react to me. . . . 'Cause it gives me confidence to speak up where I would be quiet normally because you don't want people focusing on you because of how you look.

Related to their wardrobe confidence, the women's ratings of their own attractiveness also significantly increased as a result of the FTA sessions. The increase was substantial: average ratings went from 3 before the sessions to 1.6 after (a lower score is more positive). Perhaps the positive feedback from the fashion experts, the makeup consultation, and the substantial positive attention from store personnel and photographer enhanced feelings of attractiveness:

> Besides feeling like a queen for the day, and I've never had as much attention paid to me, I don't think in my whole life as I did that day. And it just, you feel real bubbly inside, and when you come out of there with those new clothes and the new makeup and everything, you really feel pretty. I actually felt pretty that day when we were making those pictures. That is why I really got into it with the flipping the jacket out [playful gesture made when her picture was being taken]. I was really into [laughs]. I actually felt pretty that day when we were making those pictures.

> [Q. Do you see clothing or the cosmetics directly tied to how you feel about yourself?] No, I think a lot of it had to do with some of

the pampering I felt and the direct attention to me. I didn't have to share anybody's attention to me. I had my own personal person that more or less guided me by my hand to shopping.

One woman who wore plus sizes also felt that the attention she received at her FTA session made her feel better about herself:

I feel better about myself [after FTA]. When you are a large woman, you won't know anything about that because you are not large. But when you are a large woman, you automatically feel like everything is wrong when you walk in a room. And that people feel that they've got to move over against the far wall for you to come by, you know. At least I feel that way. So the better I can dress, the better I feel. Because you can be fat, as long as you are classy fat you are OK. If you are poor fat, you've got a problem and everybody is going to put you down. And I've experienced both sides of it. [Q: So with the new makeup, the new look, you feel better?] Yes. I feel like I have a little bit of class or pizzazz or whatever you want to call it that makes me feel like that maybe I'm as good as the next person even though I'm still fat.

OVERALL IMPACT. All of the women who were interviewed expressed emphatically that the FTA session was "wonderful," "cool," "grand," and "beautiful" and that they were deeply grateful for the experience. They were very satisfied with the clothing, makeup, and gifts they received, and all felt that the items would be highly useful and appropriate for job interviews and work. Two of the women had already worn Sears' outfits to job interviews by the time of the follow-up interview, and three had worn their outfits to work.

Those who received watches were surprised that Sears would include such an essential and expensive item. Two women did not own any watches before the sessions, so the gift of a watch was precious to them.

Several of the women emphasized that it was nice to get attention for themselves, some-

thing they felt they rarely received. As single mothers, they are always buying things for their children and doing without to make ends meet. Two women stated:

. . . when they are single parents, they don't do anything for themselves because you need to buy things for the children all the time. So either way, this was like "Wow!"; this was a day for us, and it was just nice.

I had never had a day that was that special that I could go and enjoy myself and have that many people there encouraging and being just so wonderful. It was wonderful!

That so many of the women felt they never received much positive attention gives a hint of the difficult circumstances that many of them have experienced.

WHAT THE PROGRAM DOES FOR SEARS. Though the items they received were useful, the women unanimously implied that the manner in which Sears conducted the program was as important or more important than the gifts. They could not believe that someone would spend so much time and attention on them. The Sears and PR firm personnel were highly praised by the women. The women noted that the Sears staff seemed to be happy to help them during the sessions. As described by two participants:

Every department that we went to, I think they just did everything they could to make us feel special. . . . They all seemed to be on top of everything and ready to do whatever they needed to do.

Yes, the people that I met there also was [sic] very special for me. They gave us a lot of confidence.

The women also talked about the fashion experts whom the participants were thrilled and honored to meet. Many of the women mentioned that they felt very comfortable with their expert shopping advisors. The women were amazed that these busy professionals acted as though the participants were worthwhile individuals who deserved time and attention.

. . . and they did all of this and they took their time of their day to come out there, and they didn't have their noses in the air, and they were very helpful, and they were very friendly.

The fact that they were treated as valued individuals who had earned a reward was surprising to them and greatly impressed all the participants. That Sears did not conduct the program as a charity giveaway was greatly appreciated by the women. The feeling that they were important and valued guests seemed to do as much or more for the women's feeling of self-confidence and self-worth as receiving free clothing and gifts. A number of the women hoped that Sears would continue this program for many more women who are working their way toward employment and self-support. They felt that the program was so valuable that they hoped others could benefit, too:

> . . . it is like someone taking a chance on you, you know. And you know she doesn't have this or that, but she deserves it because she is working as hard as she can to do what she wants to do.

The Fashion Takes Action program had deeply impressed them and was intricately remembered even weeks after the event. Overall, the program made the women feel good about themselves, to an extent that an observer of the program might not realize. One of the women in her interview said:

> I am just in awe of what they have done. . . . sometimes you just can't put into words how thankful you are for something.

According to the women who participated, Sears can bask in pride over the FTA program. Many women mentioned that they are telling their family and friends about the event, and recognized that their glowing reports will be effective word-of-mouth advertising for Sears. When asked if they plan to shop at Sears in the future, all replied "yes" or stated they would like to, but that their limited incomes might prevent them from shopping at Sears. (Of course, their incomes may improve as they complete their schooling/job training and enter the full-time workforce.)

Overall, the women in the program had nothing but praise for Sears and the Fashion Takes Action program: "Sears just really outdid themselves. I was really impressed with them."

Suggestions for Improvements

All of the women interviewed were reluctant to make any suggestions for improvement because they thought the program was so successful. Most had no suggestions. From the interviews and questionnaires, here are a few suggestions meekly given:

- More time needed! (This seems to reflect how much fun the women were having rather than a critique of the program.)

- Include underwear as part of the offerings, as underwear can be essential in how outerwear looks and fits. (In the fall sessions, Sears included underwear among the gifts.)

- Include hairstyling as part of the program. (Only one of the Sears stores hosting the FTA shopping had a hairstyling salon.)

- Professional styles for plus size and very small sizes were limited. This may have been due to the limited offerings near the end of season or may reflect limited offerings in those sizes. Attractiveness and appropriateness of some styles carried for larger-sized bodies also may need careful analysis by Sears buyers.

Indeed, two of the larger-sized women had trouble getting clothing gifts. One store had to send the outfits after the session from another store. In addition, one plus size woman reported that she felt uncomfortable in the dressing rooms with so many people coming and going to help her. She felt embarrassed around the other skinny women. Sears soon realized that they needed to check on availability of clothing in the sizes of the women before the FTA event. And great care is needed to sense comfort zones of all the women while trying on garments.

While most of the fashion experts did a great job, one had projected an unpleasant critical stance and had left the event early. Another expert at that session stepped in to take care of the abandoned guest. The wardrobe advice across experts also varied greatly. The fashion experts were a great feature of FTA, but an individual occasionally and unexpectedly could cause problems.

The Sears FTA program is a philanthropic program that may be conducted as much to provide positive promotion for the corporation as to help the women beneficiaries. Many of the participants seemed aware of this possibility, but expressed hope that Sears did get good press from the event. Critics may question whether the women were being exploited by Sears or whether the program served to encourage consumerism among the women who would return to shop at Sears. These criticisms may be valid, but from the beneficiaries' perspectives, Sears had done a wonderful thing for them. When a person has lived with little, consumer power seems to be a good rather than evil thing. Sears' effort at philanthropy may be judged through several lenses or perspectives. We have focused on the women's evaluations and comments about the program here.

Note

1. In 2002, Sears shifted focus to the Sears American Dream Campaign, a $100 million community commitment that will help American families to outfit and maintain their homes (see www.searsamericandream .com/).

References

Fiore, A. M., & DeLong, M. R. (1990). A personal appearance program for displaced homemakers. *Journal of Career Development*, 16(3):219–226.

Helping Hands: An L.A. program nurtures homeless women. (2001, December). *Essence*, 32(8):50.

Honoring Our Past, Shaping Our Future. (n.d.). Washington, DC: Women Work!

Johnson-Elie, T. (2001, April 3). Clothes help make the new worker: Non-profits supply dresses for success. *Milwaukee Journal Sentinel*. Accessed March 5, 2002, at web.lexis-nexis.com/universe/document.

Program seeking business apparel and volunteers. (2001, March 24). *The State Journal Register* (Springfield, IL). Accessed March 5, 2002, at web.lexis-nexis.com/universe/document.

Solomon, M. R., & Douglas, S. P. (1985). The female clotheshorse: From aesthetics or tactics? In M. R. Solomon (Ed.), *The Psychology of Fashion*, pp. 387–401. Lexington, MA: Lexington Books.

Turner-Bowker, D. M. (2001). How can you pull yourself up by your bootstraps, if you don't have boots? Work-appropriate clothing for poor women. *Journal of Social Issues*, 57(2):311–322.

Whitehead, C. (2001, May 19). Dressing for success: Program suits up women in workplace. *The Florida Times-Union*, K1.

Zanos, Y. (2002, February 12). Dressing and assessing. *Pittsburg Post-Gazette*, B4.

A Clothing Gift Program for Low-Income Women

1. Do you think that Sears is exploiting disadvantaged women for positive media attention? Does it matter if they are?

2. Why do you think that there wasn't a measurable difference in self-esteem scores before and after the event?

3. If a Sears store in your city were to sponsor this type of event, how might you volunteer to be involved?

4. Identify other efforts in your home or college community that assist low-income individuals with dress for work. How could you individually (or your favorite organization) assist in these efforts?

5. What are the advantages of having low-income women select clothing from current fashion offerings versus selecting clothing that is gently-used? If business dress is mostly conservative, why would current fashionable dress be a necessity to make the program successful?

CHAPTER 8

Dress from Infancy to Adolescence

Mary Lynn Damhorst

AFTER YOU HAVE READ THIS CHAPTER, YOU WILL COMPREHEND:

- The many ways in which dress and appearance are an important part of childhood and adolescence.

- The physical, cognitive, emotional, and social aspects of dress and human development.

- How both the family and society invest identities in children through dress.

- How conformity and similarity in appearance can be positive experiences during childhood and adolescent development.

As we age, human lifespan stages shape the types of roles we take on in society. At each stage, important developments occur in physical characteristics, thinking and knowledge, and social skills. Cognitive, social, emotional, and physical developments at each stage also influence needs for dress and how the individual becomes involved with appearance. We will take a quick tour through lifespan stages in the next two chapters. In this chapter we look at childhood through adolescent stages of life. Chapter 9 considers adult life stages through the elder years. Our focus tends to be on individuals in U.S. society because of limited comparable information from other cultures.

CHILDHOOD

Dress and appearance are pertinent components in child development. We will consider how involvement with dress progresses at each major developmental stage. Approximate age divisions or "stages" within which major physical, cognitive, and socialization changes occur help to map development in relation to dress. The age divisions for major developmental changes vary by authority and focus of analysis; we will consider the following:

- **Infancy** from birth to 6 months.
- **Toddler stage** from 6 months to 2 years.
- **Early childhood** from 2 to 6 years.
- **Middle childhood** from 6 to 10 years.

All children go through developmental stages in the order given, but the exact age at which each event happens varies (Flavell, 1977). Disabilities may prevent some individuals from reaching all stages. We will trace some of the major features of a child's developmental changes during all stages.

Physical Coordination

Infants are constantly moving when awake, though their movements have a small range as infants cannot yet walk or crawl. Clothing should not be too binding, so as to allow small motor movements that facilitate an infant's exploration of the surrounding environment and development of such skills as reaching and grasping. During the toddler stage, large motor coordination progresses as the toddler learns to crawl and walk. The fit of clothing (i.e., loose but not too bulky) should not impede these activities and thus becomes more vital at this stage (Ryan, 1966; Stone & Sternweis, 1994). The transition from diapers to training pants usually begins during the toddler stage; this is an important step toward building a feeling of independence in the child.

Skills at physical activities increase as muscular coordination advances during early childhood. Fit, flexibility of materials, and comfort continue to be crucial for the child. Durability and safety (e.g., flame retardance, no swallowable or removable objects) of clothing and materials are important purchasing criteria. Fine motor skill coordination also develops during early childhood. Clothing, dolls, and toys with large buttons, zippers, laces, and other fasteners can help children practice dressing skills (see Figure 8.1). During the early childhood years, many dressing skills are mastered, giving the child a sense of independence (Allen & Marotz, 1999). However, it may take until age nine or later that the child can handle more complex hair care and other grooming regimens.

The elementary schoolchild may enjoy sports activities, including the prestige that comes from accomplishments and involvement in sports. The child may like clothing that represents those sports (e.g., a soccer shirt, Nike brand clothing) or that associates the wearer with well-known sports figures (e.g., Air Jordan shoes).

Cognitive Development and Symbol Usage

During the infant months, sensory skills and memory structures develop. Clothing and blankets are part of the infant's tactile and visible environment. Textures and colors may be interesting and stimulating to an infant.

By the toddler stage, the child recognizes people and objects and begins to develop a sense of ownership of clothing items (Allen & Marotz, 1999). Verbal skills also emerge

FIGURE 8.1 *Shoe Shuffling Sam has many shoes: one ties, one closes with Velcro, one has buttons, and one snaps to provide practice with clothing openers.*

during the toddler years. The child often learns names of colors, garment pieces, and recognizable figures in prints and embroidery, making clothing one of many tools in the process of learning how to talk.

By the end of early childhood, the child moves into what Piaget called **concrete operations,** the stage during which the child develops, among other skills, basic math reasoning and the ability to generalize (Schickedanz et al., 1998). Children can learn some cultural stereotypes, many triggered by appearance stigmas such as obesity, physical unattractiveness, and old age (Brylinsky & Moore, 1994). This is an important time for parents to be aware that peer groups and media may introduce negative and limiting stereotypes; parents need to talk openly with children about these stereotypes and their dangers.

Depending upon peer and family purchase patterns and a child's exposure to media, apparel brand names and logos may become familiar symbols during early and middle childhood and may be highly desired by a child (Derscheid, Kwon, & Fang, 1996; Mayer & Belk, 1985). Brands are symbols that can develop meanings of acceptance and prestige and may help the child feel associated with a particular group or admired person. Children's apparel brands purchased by some families are challenging our sense of what should be spent on children's clothing (Bellafante, 2003; Langley, 2000). However, about 18 percent of children live in poverty in the United States today (National Center for Children in Poverty, 2002). Their families often have trouble supplying all their clothing needs. Poverty levels in the United States are higher among children than among any other age group.

Socialization

Taking on the role of the other, that is, imagining how another person thinks, requires advanced cognitive development. Imagining the other's perspective is a crucial foundation for communication and socialization into society. Children start developing role-taking skills at an early age (Schickedanz et al., 1998). During the early childhood years, it is not unusual for children to **play with dress** to help them "put on a role" and experiment with identities, whether it be the identity of Wonder Woman, Darth Vader, a mother, or an elephant (Stone, 1962). During middle childhood, play with dress and enjoyment of fantasy through Halloween and other costumes continues. Kim Miller-Spillman reports in "Playing Dress-Up" that adults have many memories of costumes they wore during childhood. Play with dress, whether specific character costumes, handed-down adult clothes, or pieces of fabric that can be worn as capes, skirts, and the like, can be very beneficial and enjoyable for children. Play with dress facilitates creative activity and encourages practice at taking on the role of the other (Schickedanz et al., 1998; Stone, 1962). Children may play at roles they might take on in adult life (anticipatory socialization) and may engage in play at fantasy roles (fantastic socialization) (Stone, 1962).

During middle childhood, dressing for games also becomes common. Gregory Stone (1962) defined **game dress** as uniforms and team emblems that help the child identify and take on roles of self and other players in a game. Taking on the role of multiple others in a game is a complex cognitive task; game activity helps the child develop skills at thinking about perspectives of multiple others.

Throughout childhood, parents and guardians are continually dressing their children to conform to socioeconomic, gender, religious, and other role expectations. In addition, conformity in appearance becomes increasingly important to the child as she or he ages (Schickedanz et al., 1998). The toddler frequently mimics dress of others and begins to learn meanings of dress through adults' often bemused responses to imitations (Cahill, 1989). During early childhood, a garment similar to that of an admired parent, adult, or older sibling may make the child feel grown-up and similar to the admired person. Also, dressing like friends in preschool and in the neighborhood becomes increasingly important, and by middle childhood, fitting in with neighborhood friends and at school is highly valued (Ryan, 1966). Conformity fosters a feeling of belonging; similarity helps the child feel socially comfortable. Uniforms may be well liked by a child, especially if the uniform links the child to a desired group such as a sports team or other youth groups such as the Boy Scouts. Even school uniforms may be liked if the child likes school.

In "Taking a New Look at Uniforms and Their Impact on Schools," Sterngold reports that school administrators in California adopted student uniform policies in efforts to enhance children's safety, decrease emphasis on socioeconomic class differences, and control children's inappropriate behaviors and truancy. Some administrators suggest that school uniforms even improve student grades. Adoption of school uniforms usually occurs when a number of policies and practices are modified during school reform efforts; therefore, the real impact that dress has on school child behavior is difficult to assess. The research of uniform effects on school children and adolescents is inconclusive (Coffman & Jurta, 1996). (See Figure 8.2.)

Gender is learned through socialization and is expressed through dress as well as other behaviors. Infants and toddlers do not make independent choices for apparel, so purchase agents such as parents play a dominant role in "investing" gender in the child through selection of gender-specific apparel (Stone, 1962). Cahill (1989) noticed that day-care personnel and parents tend to reward both boys and girls for appearing in

FIGURE 8.2 *Preschool kids in Seoul, Korea, line up during a field trip. Their colorful uniforms provide a cheerful display.*

gender-specific clothing. (See Figure 8.3.) By early childhood, play with dress also helps the child learn gender roles. Cahill described how preschool children up through age 3 seem quite comfortable playing with opposite gender roles. Play with clothing and makeup may be encouraged more among girls who are being socialized to develop greater interest in dress and the hedonic aspects of appearance. But around age 4, boys in particular start to become increasingly sensitive to teasing and criticism from peers if they stray from the restricted code of menswear. As we saw in "Day-Care Dress Up Not Amusing to Boy's Dad" in Chapter 5, some parents are disturbed to see cross-dressing in their children. However, there is no evidence that cross-dressing during childhood necessarily leads to transvestism or homosexuality in adult life. By middle childhood, codes for gender appropriateness of dress are well learned (Kaiser, 1989), and are often believed more rigidly than is apparent from the way the child actually dresses (Allen & Marotz, 1999).

Appearance Concerns

The multitude of memories of dress that adults in Miller-Spillman's study ("Playing Dress-Up") could recall clearly highlight the importance of dress in childhood. Dressing up for holidays, religious events, parties, and visiting beloved grandparents was remembered. Dress clearly marks special events and helps to make the events special. Memories of school and everyday dress and also costumes and play dress indicate that dress is a pervasive part of childhood experience.

Engaging in dressing activities can be fun, and the gaudier and frillier the dress, the more fun it can be for many toddlers (Ryan, 1966). The toddler also learns that cute or new garments and clothing patterned with well-known cartoon characters and logos can generate positive responses from adults. The link of appearance to social rewards is established early in life. The intriguing world of beauty pageants for young girls in the United States is described in "The High Cost of Beauty." This article describes the extreme engrossment in appearance that has become an "occupation" for some children; beauty pageants for children are often criticized for putting too much emphasis on appearance.

In addition, children are not immune to ideal images of thinness as attractive. Researchers are finding girls as young as 4 years old who express concerns about their weight and who mimic dieting behaviors and restrict their food

FIGURE 8.3 *Hannah celebrates her first birthday. Her outfit includes bows, ruffles, and gathers that would not be likely on boys' apparel.*

intake (e.g., Smolek & Levine, 1994). Many girls in middle childhood talk about their need to diet, indicating that socialization to weight control is well learned at an early age. Mothers in particular have a notable impact on how their daughters think about the body. Parents train their children how to care for and present their physical selves (Shilling, 1993), and mothers are more likely to be the caretakers and guardians of family norms of appearance (Smetana, 1988). In addition, parents have influence on children's eating behaviors and attitudes toward thinness. For example, parents who diet are more likely than nonrecent dieters to try to help their children lose weight (Striegel-Moore & Kearney-Cook, 1994). In this era when child obesity is on the rise, some parents may become overly concerned about their children's weight, while some are not making enough effort to see that their children maintain healthy diets and exercise patterns. During the early 1990s, 11.4 percent of children ages 6 to 11 were overweight; only 6.5 percent were reported to be overweight in the late 1970s (Kolata, 2000).

By age 9 or earlier in the United States, children become independent purchasers of some clothing and grooming products and are becoming socialized to shopping skills. In a Youth Monitor study of children as consumers conducted in the 1980s, researchers were surprised to find the degree to which children were involved in shopping (Greene & Greene, 1990). Over half of girls ages 9 to 11 were buying hair conditioner, nail polish, and deodorant, and about a third bought their own perfume. About one-fifth were purchasing various types of makeup. Almost half of boys ages 9 to 11 purchased deodorant for themselves, and about one-fourth were buying various hair care products and cologne.

Some businesses look at children as a lucrative target market, while critics have questioned whether the independence children have in selecting and purchasing adult grooming products is appropriate. Are children growing up too fast? Do children's appearances reflect more maturity than they can handle during childhood? These are questions that, at present, have no clear-cut answers.

ADOLESCENCE

Girls aged 8 to 12 are sometimes informally referred to as "tweens," referring to a transition stage from childhood to adolescence (see "T'ween Spirit"). More often in research, adolescence is divided into the following two periods:

- **Early adolescence**: 11 to 14 years for girls and 12 to 15 years for boys.
- **Late adolescence**: 15 or 16 to 20 years.

Physical, cognitive, and social developments continue throughout adolescence. Many of these changes influence adolescent interests and needs in regard to dress.

Physical Changes and Self-Perceptions

Dramatic changes occur in the body during adolescence. Adult height is reached during these years, and growth spurts may cause some adolescents to go through phases of being physically awkward. Complexion problems are not uncommon among teens, leading to purchases of an array of products designed to control and camouflage pimples and acne.

Primary and secondary sex characteristics develop, further increasing body awareness. Boys and girls reach sexual maturity, and concern about sexual attractiveness and defining sexuality also increases. Because of growing interest in looking like an adult, both boys and girls start to prefer styles that, to them, do not look too childish. Increasing conflicts between adolescents and parents are common as the offspring, who seemed to be children "just yesterday," attempt to experiment with adult appearances. Girls in particular are given cultural encouragement through media images, fashion trends, and certain peer groups to dress in a sexually provocative manner, often despite the objections of protective parents. Of course, individual differences abound. Some mothers register concern that their daughters do not spend much time on their appearance and do not use makeup as soon as other teens do.

Body satisfaction among girls tends to increase slightly in later adolescence, probably resulting from greater satisfaction with the body as it more fully matures and develops (Damhorst, Littrell, & Littrell, 1987). As boys mature they may become more involved in bodybuilding to develop upper body muscles for a culturally ideal male physique (see "Measuring Up" in Chapter 5). Emphasis on priming the body for various sport activities may also occur. Deaths among adolescent boys who were starving themselves and exercising excessively to reach weight goals for wrestling raised questions during the 1990s about the pressures put on young men training for sports (Naughton, 1998). Boys, and increasingly girls, are often encouraged by coaches, family members, and peers to endanger personal health and safety through extremes of weight management and drug abuse for the sake of sports achievements.

FIGURE 8.4 *April won't admit that her outfit might be a bit uncomfortable in Canada's fall weather. Zipping her jacket would take time, wouldn't look cool, and would make her mother right.*

Socialization

Stephen Hall in "The Bully in the Mirror" reports that adolescent boys are under increasing pressure to build muscle mass and spend time on their appearance. Use of supplements and steroids to take shortcuts to bodybuilding is increasing. The boys interviewed reported endless teasing and physical harassment if they were smaller or fatter than other boys. Becoming "buff" is seen as a ticket to having girls and boys pay positive attention. Hall contends that men's bodies are now becoming as objectified as women's, leading to increasing body dissatisfaction and related disorders among boys. During adolescence, socialization to body norms occurs as much or more through peer interactions as it does through parents.

Parents still have an influence, however. For example, Bonnell and Satran (1985) found that mothers who frequently criticized or were uninterested in their early adolescent daughters' appearance had lasting negative effects on their daughters' appearance satisfaction well into adulthood. Mothers who were positive had long-term positive effects on daughters' appearance satisfaction. Mothers' influence outweighed fathers' effects on how daughters felt about their appearance. Of course, parents do need to intervene sometimes when adolescent dress is offensive or not appropriate for weather or other situations (see Figure 8.4).

Girls in the United States are culturally encouraged to diet and exercise to pursue a thin body. Parker and colleagues (1995) found that ethnic background can shape how the adolescent feels about her body. African American girls grow up in a cultural tradition that encourages making the best of one's appearance and openly praising others for looking good, regardless of physical size or shape. In contrast, white girls seem to feel there is only one option for attractiveness—thinness. The Caucasian girls in the study described substantial dissatisfaction with appearance and extensive criticism of themselves and others in measuring up to thinness standards. The obsession with thinness and weight control has made white adolescent females in the United States a population at risk for poor nutritional status and unhealthful eating behaviors (Adams & Shafer, 1988).

Cognitive and Socioemotional Development

In addition to body changes, cognitive changes lead many adolescents to feel that everyone notices everything about how they look. The adolescent still has some of the concreteness in thinking and egocentrism of childhood while moving on to development of more complex hypothetical thinking skills of **formal operations** (Schickedanz et al., 1998). The adolescent becomes increasingly adept at taking on the role of the other, but sometimes over-interprets and over-imagines reviews from others.

Adolescents who are overweight or have appearance impairments truly suffer during this phase of development. In "Pony Party," Lucy Grealy describes the burdens of living with substantial facial disfigurement caused by cancer when she was 9. Continual procedures of facial reconstruction surgery failed to repair her appearance. She describes feeling like a "freak" during adolescence as she witnessed young children staring at her in amazement and adults turning away and trying not to notice. Her distorted face became the center of her identity.

Conformity through appearance may be more common in adolescence, particularly early adolescence, than at any other stage in life. Rather than passive acquiescence to others, adolescents use conformity for actively trying out identities. Many teenagers seem almost to "graze" through new looks in a very dynamic search of self-identity (Kaiser & Damhorst, 1995). Rebecca Mead describes the recent teen and college student shopping scene in Japan in "Shopping Rebellion." The speed of moving from look to look, the postmodern play with rules, the amount of money spent on teen clothing, and the complex symbolic messages sent through dress by teens illustrate the grazing for identities that can occur during adolescence.

Creekmore (1980) found that high school students strongly believed that the most popular students are apt to be attractive and well dressed. They tend to believe they can judge people on the basis of appearance. Many teens become preoccupied with appearance in their search for identity. They use dress as one of many tactics to achieve belonging in peer groups and success in dating relationships. These social supports may help to ratify the self and strengthen self-esteem (Daters, 1990). In "Reading, Writing and Body Waxing," Healy examines the enormous effort and money that some adolescent girls spend on appearance during the end of summer back-to-school rush. In affluent New York City suburbs, girls were convinced that manicuring their total look for the first week back in school was essential to securing a spot in the social hierarchy and presenting their new and improved identity for the semester to come. Of course, their family income levels probably allow for the extreme expenditures on clothing, hair styling, manicures, tanning beds, and cosmetic surgery.

Shopping becomes an enjoyable socializing activity for many teenagers. Now that so many parents are working outside the home, adolescents are often allowed more independence in shopping (Walsh, 1985). Adolescent boys also are more involved in shopping for their own clothes than in prior generations. Teens prefer to shop with friends: they need social consensus to help in making purchase decisions. Tracy Bulla describes the recent focus on the tween-aged market in "T'ween Spirit." That market has expanded in development due to greater shopping independence of 8- to 12-year-olds and increased focus on fashion among that age group.

Media Use and Impacts

Teens today are also more skilled at using computer technology than were prior generations. Retailers popular with adolescents, such as Delia's Inc., have been able to reach a broad market through their online catalogs ("For Clueless Grown-Ups," 1998).

FIGURE 8.5 Girl Zone *magazine on the Web is committed to helping adolescent girls develop a realistic and positive sense of their bodies.*

Website stores offer instantaneous access to latest trend ideas, regardless of where the teenager lives. As Web access continues to increase in households across the United States and around the world, adolescents may increasingly use the Internet as a source of fashion information and product access. But for now, about 94 percent of girls and 74 percent of boys say they prefer shopping in the physical and social space of malls (Gardyn, 2003).

Adolescents also use media imagery to learn about possibilities for self-expression and self-image. Early adolescents seem to use media to learn about adult life, even though they may realize that many of the appearances they see are not appropriate for themselves during early adolescence (Kaiser & Damhorst, 1995). Adolescents are also surrounded by media images of thin and perfect bodies and tend to be more susceptible to believing that those impossible norms are attainable. The list in Chapter 2 of media effects on girls' body image and gender identity outlines recent research that found that greater involvement with visual media such as TV and fashion magazines correlates with greater body dissatisfaction and desire to achieve thinness norms.

There is hope, however. Ogle and Thornburg (2003) analyzed *Girl Zone* (Figure 8.5), an online teen magazine that takes a socially responsible approach to encourage girls to accept and have healthy attitudes and practices toward their bodies. Ogle and Thornburg note the increase of positive body-related articles in magazines such as *Seventeen*. In addition, not all teenagers are helplessly sucked into accepting the impossible standards presented in media, particularly as they move into later adolescence (see "Young and Chubby" in Chapter 2). Lisa Duke studied African American and European American girls' assessments of their favorite teen magazines. She reports in "Just Because It's a White Magazine . . ." that the African American girls were often critical of the lack of representation of real girls like themselves in the magazines. Even though they often liked the articles in mainstream teen magazines, they wanted to see more representation of girls who weren't so thin, so perfectly and unrealistically made up, and so white. The white girls in the study did not tend to notice the limited representation of diversity and were less critical consumers of the magazines.

Summary

Dress and appearance are critical components of child and adolescent development. Physical skills and coordination increase throughout childhood, allowing the child to increase independence and mastery over the physical actions involved in dressing. Sport dress facilitates participation in physical activities during childhood and adolescence.

By early and middle childhood, cognitive and social developments lead to skills that may result in stereotypical thinking triggered by appearance cues. Children use dress to form impressions of others and by adolescence may move to more complex and hypothetical thinking about appearances and what they mean. Adolescents may become convinced that appropriate and attractive dress and appearance are crucial to popularity and successful dating relationships.

Conformity to peers begins to become important by early childhood and increases in importance through early adolescence. Dress plays an important role in helping the individual feel a sense of belonging and acceptance and to help in searching for self-identity. Shopping for dress also increases as a social activity for many individuals during middle childhood and adolescence. Learning to dress and manage appearance are key components of socialization to societal norms.

Suggested Readings

Brumberg, J. J. (1997). *The Body Project: An Intimate History of American Girls.* New York: Random House.

Cahill, S. E. (1989). Fashioning males and females: Appearance management and the social reproduction of gender. *Symbolic Interaction,* 12:281–298.

Grealy, L. (1994). *Autobiography of a Face.* Boston: Houghton Mifflin.

Ogle, J. P., & Thornburg, E. (2003). An alternative voice amid teen 'zines: An analysis of body-related content in *Girl Zone. Journal of Family and Consumer Sciences,* 95(1):7–56.

Parker, S., Nichter, M., Nichter, M., Vuckovic, N., Sims, C., & Ritenbaugh, C. (1995). Body image and weight concerns among African American and white adolescent females: Differences that make a difference. *Human Organization,* 54(2):103–114.

Roach, M. E. (1969). Adolescent dress. *Journal of Home Economics,* 61(9):693–697.

Rudd, N. A., & Lennon, S. (1995). Body image: Eating, substance abuse, and appearance disorders. In *Invest in Youth: Build the Future,* pp. 41–57. Alexandria, VA: American Association of Family and Consumer Sciences.

LEARNING ACTIVITY

Memories of Childhood and Adolescent Dress[1]

Objectives: Analyze examples from your own childhood or adolescence to understand how stages of human physical and mental development influence feelings about and use of dress.

Procedure

In small groups, recall and share memories from childhood or early adolescence. Try to think of memories that involve some aspect of dress (e.g., wearing a favorite costume, a hated suit, or shoes on the wrong feet; trying on Mom's or Dad's clothes; ruining a favorite piece of clothing). If you cannot remember any incidents with dress, try to recall an event for which you remember what a sibling, cousin, or friend was wearing at the time.

Then, identify the stage of development that you or the person you remember were in at the time. Was it infancy, toddler years, early childhood, middle childhood, or early adolescence? Remembering the approximate age at which the event took place will help you identify the stage of development.

Finally, examine how the examples of dress in each memory illustrate concepts and principles of development. Search through the introduction to the chapter to see if concepts such as motor coordination, family economics, play, formal operations, and the like help to explain what happened in the memory. Work with your group to identify concepts involved. Then, share an example with the whole class.

Note

1. Adapted from a class exercise by Hazel A. Lutz.

References

Adams, L. B., & Shafer, M. B. (1988). Early manifestations of eating disorders in adolescents: Defining those at risk. *Journal of Nutrition Education*, 20(6):307–313.

Allen, K. E., & Marotz, L. R. (1999). *Developmental Profiles* (3rd ed.). Albany, NY: Delmar Publishers.

Bellafante, G. (2003, November 4). The littlest clotheshorse. *The New York Times*, B11.

Bonnell, K., & Satran, P. (1985, February). Out of the closet! 13,000 women reveal their attitudes, priorities, feelings about clothes. *Glamour*, 189–192.

Brylinsky, J., & Moore, J. (1994). The identification of body build stereotypes in young children. *Journal of Research in Personality*, 28:170–181.

Cahill, S. E. (1989). Fashioning males and females: Appearance management and the social reproduction of gender. *Symbolic Interaction*, 12:281–298.

Coffman, C., & Jurta, A. (1996, December). Do school uniforms make the grade? *Textiles and Apparel News*, 11(3):3–4.

Creekmore, A. M. (1980). Clothing and personal attractiveness of adolescents related to conformity to clothing mode, peer acceptance, and leadership potential. *Home Economics Research Journal*, 8:203–215.

Damhorst, M. L., Littrell, J. M., & Littrell, M. A. (1987). Age differences in adolescent body satisfaction. *Journal of Psychology*, 121:553–562.

Daters, C. M. (1990). Importance of clothing and self esteem among adolescents. *Clothing and Textiles Research Journal*, 8(3):45–50.

Derscheid, L. E., Kwon, Y. H., & Fang, S. R. (1996). Preschoolers' socialization as consumers of clothing and recognition of symbolism. *Perceptual and Motor Skills*, 82:1171–1181.

Flavell, J. H. (1975). *The Development of Role-Taking and Communication Skills in Children*. Huntington, NY: Robert E. Krieger.

Flavell, J. H. (1977). *Cognitive Development*. Englewood Cliffs, NJ: Prentice Hall.

For clueless grown-ups: A retailing field guide. (1998, December 9). *The Wall Street Journal*, B1.

Gardyn, R. (2003, April). Born to be wired. *American Demographics*, 25(3):14–15.

Greene, K., & Greene, R. (1990, March). The shocking statistics. *Redbook*, 174:93.

Kaiser, S. B. (1989). Clothing and the social organization of gender perception: A developmental approach. *Clothing and Textiles Research Journal*, 7(2):46–56.

Kaiser, S. B., & Damhorst, M. L. (1995). Youth and media culture: Research and policy issues. In *Invest in Youth: Build the Future*, pp.153–169. Alexandria, VA: American Association of Family and Consumer Sciences.

Kolata, G. (2000, October 19). As children grow fatter, researchers try to find solutions. *The New York Times*, A1.

Langley, M. (2000, August 24). Italian firm fashions a look tailor-made for indulgent parents. *The Wall Street Journal*, A1, A8.

Mayer, R. N., & Belk, R. W. (1985). Fashion and impression formation among children. In M. R. Solomon (Ed.), *The Psychology of Fashion*, pp. 293–308. Lexington, MA: Lexington Books.

National Center for Children in Poverty. (2002, March). *Early Childhood Poverty: A Statistical Profile*. Accessed March 8, 2004, at www.nccp.org/media/ecp02-text.pdf.

Naughton, J. (1998, March 18). The weighting game: High schools taking action for wrestlers. *The Des Moines Register*, 1S, 5S.

Ogle, J. P., & Thornburg, E. (2003). An alternative voice amid teen 'zines: An analysis of body-related content in *Girl Zone*. *Journal of Family and Consumer Sciences*, 95(1):7–56.

Parker, S., Nichter, M., Nichter, M., Vuckovic, N., Sims, C., & Ritenbaugh, C. (1995). Body image and weight concerns among African American and white adolescent females: Differences that make a difference. *Human Organization*, 54(2):103–114.

Ryan, M. S. (1966). *Clothing: A Study in Human Behavior*. New York: Holt, Rinehart and Winston.

Schickedanz, J. A., Schickedanz, D. I., Forsyth, P. D., & Forsyth, G. A. (1998). *Understanding Children and Adolescents* (3rd ed.). Boston, MA: Allyn & Bacon.

Shilling, C. (1993). *The Body and Social Theory*. Thousand Oaks, CA: Sage.

Smetana, J. G. (1988). Concepts of self and social convention: Adolescents' and parents' reasoning about hypothetical and actual family conflicts. In M. R. Gunnar & W. A.

Collins (Eds.), *Development during the Transition to Adolescence*, pp. 79–122. Hillsdale, NJ: Lawrence Erlbaum.

Smolek, L., & Levine, M. (1994). Toward an empirical basis for primary prevention of eating problems with elementary school children. *Eating Disorders*, 2(4):293–307.

Stone, G. (1962). Appearance and the self. In A. Rose (Ed.), *Human Behavior and Social Processes*, pp. 86–118. Boston, MA: Houghton Mifflin.

Stone, J., & Sternweis, L. (1994, September). *Consumer Choices: Selecting Clothes for Toddlers, Ages 1 to 3*. University Extension Bulletin Pm-1105. Ames: Iowa State University, Cooperative Extension Service.

Striegel-Moore, R. H., & Kearney-Cook, A. (1994). Exploring parents' attitudes and behaviors about their children's physical appearance. *International Journal of Eating Disorders*, 15:377–385.

Walsh, D. L. (1985, February). Targeting teens. *American Demographics*, 21–25, 41.

45 Playing Dress-Up: Childhood Memories of Dress

Kimberly A. Miller-Spillman
University of Kentucky

Why do some people avoid dressing in costume with something close to embarrassment while others avidly seek opportunities to dress in costume? Is enjoyment of dress-up as a child a precursor to enjoyment of costume dress as an adult? Do adults avoid costume dress if they did not play dress-up as children? Is it possible that those who dress in costume are comfortable expressing different parts of the self through dress while those who do not dress in costume are not? To tackle these questions, I used the concept of childhood memories of dress. Already intrigued by the prospect of dress (including costume) symbolizing parts of the self, I became equally fascinated by the possibility that childhood memories of dress might reveal some insight as to why some embrace costuming while others do not. In general, I wondered if dress was an important part of childhood memories. If given the opportunity, how would adults describe dress worn during a particular childhood memory?

To address these questions, I surveyed people who enjoy costume dress as adults and asked them to describe dress worn during a particular childhood memory. From 223 historic, ethnic, and science fiction reenactors (see Table 1), I received responses about both childhood memories of dress and current dress. Both responses are included in my analysis to present a full picture of how these reenactors think about dress and parts of the self. The reenactors' responses were read multiple times, then coded into one or more analytical categories (Strauss & Corbin, 1990) within the Public, Private, and Secret Self (PPSS) Model.

Eicher (1981) developed the PPSS Model by building on Stone's (1965) idea of appearance and the self.[1] Later, Eicher and I collaborated on an expanded version (Eicher & Miller, 1994) of her original model. The PPSS Model connects types of dress (reality, fun/leisure, fantasy) with parts of the self (public, private, and secret) (see Table 2). Reality dress is the dress that is seen in public for work, school, or church; fun/leisure dress is for relaxing after work and on weekends with family and friends; and fantasy dress expresses our fantasies and secret desires. The public part of the self is what we let everyone see. The private part of the self is the part we let family members and friends see. And the secret part of the self we let no one or only close intimates see.[2]

Based on surveys of college students and adults between 1978 and 1982 and in 1990, I know that:

- There are significant associations between the perception of one's role and identity at Halloween and dressing in costume (Public Self), and college women are less likely than men to disguise their identity (Secret Self), to believe they had new identities with their costumes, or to believe they could play different roles at Halloween (Miller, Jasper, & Hill, 1991).

- College students dressed in Halloween costumes were more likely to drink alcohol than were their noncostumed counterparts, and college students who masqueraded with a group were less likely to use marijuana and other drugs (Public Self) (Miller, Jasper, & Hill, 1993).

- Women who dress in costume reported more sexual fantasies (Secret Self) about dress and more childhood memories of dress (Private Self) than reported by men who costume (Miller, 1997).

- Men who dress in costume do so mainly because they love history (Private Self); women who costume do so mainly to assume another persona (Secret Self) (Miller, 1998).

Original for this text.

TABLE 1

Respondents included in the sample by organization.

Organization	Number of Questionnaires Distributed	Number of Questionnaires Returned
Actors Guild	7	7
English Country Dancers	12	10
Heritage Hill Foundation, Civil War Reenactment Group, Buckskinners (Fur Traders), 60th Regiment (British) Reenactors	157	71
Morris Dancers	12	9
Renaissance Festival Group	20	15
Science Fiction Convention	178	53
Scottish Country Dancers	24	22
Society for Creative Anachronism	41	36
TOTALS	451	223

However, I am still uncertain what role dress plays in childhood memories. Is dress as significant to men's childhood memories as to women's? How much detail can adults remember about dress in their childhood memories? How intense or emotionally charged are childhood memories of dress?

Questionnaires were distributed to 451 reenactors, people who dress in costume as adults. I received 223 questionnaires that included 92 written responses (representing 41 percent of respondents). Written responses from women ($n = 68$) outnumbered those from men ($n = 24$) almost three to one. On average,

TABLE 2

The Public, Private, and Secret Self Model.

	Reality Dress	**Fun/Leisure Dress**	**Fantasy Dress**
Public Self	Gender Uniforms Businesswear (1)	Office parties Dating Sports (2)	Halloween Living history Festivals (3)
Private Self	Housework Gardening Novelty items (4)	Home Exercise (5)	Childhood memories Sensual lingerie (6)
Secret Self	Tight Underwear (7)	Some tattoos Novelty underwear (8)	Sexual fantasies Assume another persona (9)

Source: Eicher, J. B., & Miller, K. A. (1994). Dress and the public, private, and secret self: Revisiting a model. *Proceedings of the International Textiles and Apparel Association,* p. 145. Reprinted by permission of the International Textiles and Apparel Association.

women used about eight descriptive words to describe dress worn during a childhood memory (M = 7.6), while men used about three words (M = 3.1). In this article I will analyze 56 quotes (more than half of total responses received) with particular interest in how these quotes fit within the PPSS Model.

The largest number of quotes describing childhood dress depicts public situations. The cell for Reality Dress and the Public Self (see cell #1 in Table 2) includes memories of Easter Sunday (see Figure 8.6), Confirmation/First Holy Communion, regular "worship/church" dress, school/community dress, and everyday work dress. These quotes are examples of Public dress in which one represents his or her family or where there is a connection to a family member (e.g., mother) or significant other (e.g., babysitter). These quotes often illustrate social situations of heightened importance, that is, one is only confirmed once and there is only one first day of school. Here are several examples:

FIGURE 8.6 *Three sisters—2, 4, and 9 years old—pose for a picture in 1964 in their all-white Easter Sunday outfits.*

Easter Sunday Dress

- Having to wear pink every Easter—I still hate pink! (#1304, female, 35 years old)

- Easter esp[ecially] four years [old]—dress with pink skirt and lots and lots of petticoats, white top with pleats and buttons down the front and short sleeves, patent leather shoes and white gloves. (#1380, female, 33 years old)

- Ten years old—this one [is] the best because my mother didn't like the dress and I loved it—Linen dress, navy and white—navy skirt—straight cut and rather severe—at least to mother's concept of what was appropriate for Easter. (#1380, female, 33 years old)

- When I was in the second grade my mother made me an Easter dress, as usual; but on Palm Sunday one of my friends wore a dress to church that I thought was the most beautiful dress ever made. Of course, I had to have one just like it, and my mother's feelings were hurt. She bought me the dress but I felt so guilty about hurting her feelings that I never enjoyed [wearing] it. (#4K, female, 31 years old)

- Easter with a new hat each year, one flat hat with a feather across it. (#1202, female, 48 years old)

- Easter dress, [I had] matching [clothes] with my sister. Floral top, white pleated skirt. (#1227, female, 37 years old)

- For my Easter outfit when I was 7 my mother made me a coat from one that had been my grandmother's. I remember it as a lightweight, beige wool, and she made a real velvet navy blue collar and velvet covered buttons. I loved the feel of the velvet, and I had a yellow straw hat too. (#1036, female, 44 years old)

- A long white Easter dress made with Swiss dot material and eyelet trim with an embroidered panel on the bodice of blue flowers tied with pink ribbon that my mother made—I was about 7. (#1202, female, 23 years old)

- I remember a particular Easter when my whole family (all eight of my siblings) and I were all home. I was 4 years old, my sister Susan and I both wore navy blue and white polka dot dresses with white collars. We also wore white knee high "fashion" boots. (#1057, female, 26 years old)

- I also remember several of my Easter outfits. Lots of crinolines and patent leather shoes. (#5K, female, 36 years old)

Confirmation/First Holy Communion Dress

- Fell down in slush in my first communion suit. (#1044, male, 37 years old)

- My First Holy Communion and that beautiful white dress. I still remember how happy I was that day. (#1311, female, 36 years old)

- First communion—my mother made my white dress. (#1015, female, 40 years old)

- Confirmation—white dress, shoes, veil. (#1212, female, 33 years old)

- My confirmation dress. (#1192, female, 45 years old)

- I wore a white dress for my confirmation, and both high school and college graduations. (#1022, female, 31 years old)

- My confirmation dress—I wore a blue dress with white tights and white sandals. I also had a pearl necklace. (#1205, female, 28 years old)

Regular Worship/Church Dress

- I remember as a teenager or preteen—had a white, pleated, "flapper" dress. I wore it with blue stockings and long beads to church—horrified my mother (but also amused her). (#1224, female, 47 years old)

- White hat with ribbon streamers and two fake daisies on the end of the ribbons. Black and white saddle shoes and gloves. Sunday mass "uniform" for girls in our family. (#1324, female, 35 years old)

School/Community Activity Dress

- My favorite dress in first and second grade was a blue dress with the planets (e.g. Saturn and its rings) in the print pattern. It had "secret" pockets and white piquet trim. I can remember wearing it on the playground on a hot September day. (#1194, female, 42 years old)

- I had a red sweater that Mother always had me wear to the State Fair and I called it my "Fair Sweater." (#2K, female, 35 years old)

- First day of kindergarten—dress made out of brown plaid material by the mother of a babysitter of mine—my favorite babysitter. She had a matching shirt. (#1380, female, 33 years old)

- I tore a red dress at school one day. It was not a particularly good dress, but I felt very embarrassed. (#5K, female, 36 years old)

- As a child, I was expected to look "right" so dressing up gave me an opportunity not to. My memory is of refusing to wear shoes to school when I was little because none of my mother's friends wore shoes. (#1230, female, 24 years old)

- Fifth grade banquet—red and black dress with ruffles and black hat. (#1030, female, 13 years old)

- Last day of school, fourth grade. A dress of blue and black big plaid cotton with a black vest-type top with shiny buttons. A big wide shiny black belt. White socks with lace, black shiny shoes. (#1042, female, 30 years old)

Everyday Work Dress

- Any one of several disasters that landed me in the hospital; I was always wearing jeans or work clothes. (#1018, male, 29 years old)

- Being allowed to do "man's" work on the farm for the first time—wearing bib overalls and t-shirt. (#1169, male, 45 years old)

Three themes emerge from the quotes in the Reality Dress/Public Self cell: (1) mother's influence, (2) formal dress occasions, and (3) gender dress. The first theme is reactions to mother's influence (similar to Stone's [1965] ubiquitous mother[3]). Rebellion against mother's expectations of dress seemed to generate enduring memories, such as *not* wearing shoes to school or wearing garments considered by mother to be *too severe* for Easter. Adults also remembered feeling proud because mother made or bought a garment for a special occasion. The second theme is formal dress occasions that include prescribed dress such as a white dress or a suit for Confirmation Sunday or having dressy clothes for Easter Sunday. Most of the quotes refer to gendered dress, the third theme, that is, fancy dresses with lace and bows for girls and suits or work clothes for boys. Notable are two memories about soiling (i.e., fell down in slush) or damaging dress (i.e., tore a red dress). Probably remembered because of failure to live up to a middle-class standard of clean, spotless dress.

Weddings

Several of the respondents remembered dress worn to weddings as flower girls. I placed these quotes in the cell of Reality Dress and the Private Self (see cell #4 in Table 2) because weddings, though held in public places, are often attended by those who receive personal invitations, making them more private than public occasions. Here are two examples:

- I was about 6 years old and a flower girl for my uncle's wedding in Biloxi, Mississippi (we lived in Boston). I had grass-green patent leather Mary Janes, my first "dressy" shoes, and I couldn't take my eyes off them. (#1039, female, 30 years old)

- I was 4 years of age when my brother married and I was "volunteered" as a flower girl. The inducement was [a] pink chiffon and taffeta dress with a can-can slip, patent leather slippers, white lace socks, and a floral headpiece…. (#3K, female, 34 years old)

Feeling Different

Also in the cell of Reality Dress and the Private Self were memories of feeling different, that is, having dress choices restricted because of a physical condition or class differences. Here are two examples:

- Association a painful one—I had bad eczema as a child—covered with bandages—other children wore shorts and I couldn't—wore long white cotton stockings almost year round. My girl cousins wore frilly sundresses—I couldn't—*hated it!!* Felt like a freak because I couldn't dress "normally." (#1284, female, 55 years old)

- Someone pointing out that my clothes came from Goodwill. (#1297, male, 34 years old)

Themes for Reality Dress and the Private Self include formal dress that was almost certainly the antithesis of everyday dress for these girls, that is, taffeta, chiffon, can-can slip, and patent leather shoes, and feelings about dress from those who couldn't wear "normal" clothes because of a physical condition or lack of financial resources.

Included in the cell of Reality Dress and the Secret Self (see cell #7 in Table 2) is this quote about presenting one's alter ego (Secret Self) at work (reality dress). Although not a childhood memory, this quote is an excellent example of Reality Dress/Secret Self:

Back in the days when I could afford to buy clothes, I would wake up in the morning and decide who I wanted to be that day and dress accordingly. Sometimes it was merely a matter of attitude—what I wished to project, sometimes I would dress out the personas of characters—both my own and sometimes media characters. If I had to cope with something during the day I really didn't want to have to deal with I would decide which character would handle the situation best and go "in character." Nobody but me knew I was in costume. (#1380, female, 33 years old)

Dressing for work places this quote in Reality Dress. "Nobody but me knew I was in costume" places this quote as part of the Secret Self. Her description is similar to putting one's "game face on" for a challenging situation.

Included in the cell for Fun/Leisure Dress and the Private Self (see cell #5 in Table 2) are memories of birthday parties, family celebrations, family vacations, and visiting grandparents:

Birthday Parties

- My mother persuaded me to wear a pair of pants I did not want to, to my birthday party. It upset me. I was 8 or 9 [years old] at the time. (#1008, male, 24 years old)

- A birthday party—my own, but I was too sick to be dressed or have other children [over]. One of my presents was a pink, quilted robe with blue birds and flowers. Wrapped in it, I felt happy and "up" for the family celebration, and I'm still grateful to the thoughtful relative who had bought it the day before. (#1422, female, 51 years old)

Family Celebrations

- Christmas mornings opening presents in our pajamas and going to church with our white turtleneck[s] and blue blazers. (#1197, male, 32 years old)

- Xmas '78—Green (dark) turtleneck or green jeans. (#1328, female, 24 years old)

- I remember one Christmas when I was about 5 [years old] that I wore a gray wool jumper with poodles on a full, flaring skirt. (#1315, female, 38 years old)

- Christmas—A special outfit for each year until this year. (#1212, female, 33 years old)

Family Vacations

- I can remember wearing a favorite shirt on a trip to Canada with my family and friends. I think it was my favorite because it was extremely comfortable. (#1218, female, 25 years old)

Visiting Grandparents

- I wore a red and white striped sundress and matching parasol (mitered) to visit my Grandmother's gardener's family on their farm…when I was about 5. We picked green corn. I had a good time. (#1243, female, age withheld)

Although not a childhood memory, I included the following quote in Fun/Leisure Dress/Private Self, because most of us have forgotten a special event or arrived somewhere unprepared. This quote is from a 23-year-old woman who belongs to a dance group:

> I am completing this [survey] during our Valentine's dance. I forgot that it was tonight so I came dressed for class rather than a dance. I felt very uncomfortable and out of place— even considered leaving immediately. Then I thought about it for a minute and realized these people don't care. And we're all here just to have fun. (#1202)

Themes for Fun/Leisure Dress/Private Self include a memory of being grateful for a dress gift that mended a disappointment, wearing pajamas to open Christmas presents, colors of clothing and special outfits associated with Christmas or a special visit, and sentiments such as "these people don't care" that I forgot to dress for the dance and "we're all here just to have fun."

Included in the cell for Fun/Leisure Dress and the Secret Self (see cell #8 in Table 2) is a quote about hiding one's identity (Secret Self) at a party (Fun/Leisure Dress). This quote is not a childhood memory, but it does illustrate cell #8 of the grid model:

> I like it if people at a party do not recognize me. (#1311, female, 36 years old)

Costuming

Included in the cell for Fantasy Dress and the Public Self (see cell #3 in Table 2) are quotes about costuming in public settings. These quotes, while not childhood memories, illustrate Fantasy Dress/Public Self:

- It's amazing what you can get away with when you dress alike. People assume that those in uniform—even if clearly unofficial—have a right to be where they are and do what they are doing. They are in a sense official because they represent an organization rather than just a group of individuals. (#1232, male, 38 years old)

- I attribute my interest in costuming to my desire for public notoriety. (#1216, male, 30 years old)

- I costume to show my individuality. (#1281, male, 41 years old)

- With historical costuming there is a great investment, and I would like to get greater usage from my investment…this hobby is a great escape from everything and with today's pressures everyone needs an escape valve of some sort. (#3K, female, 34 years old)

These quotes illustrate the unwarranted power of dressing uniformly, the desire for public notoriety, expression of individuality, and the need for an escape valve provided by costuming.

Military/Ethnic/Fantasy Play

Included in the cell for Fantasy Dress and the Private Self (see cell #6 in Table 2) are memories of playing dress-up as kids for family plays and gifts of military and ethnic clothing.

- Dressed in army dress uniform my uncle gave me while in service during World War II. (#1067, male, 55 years old)

- When I was about 5 years old I was given a plaid blazer and pants from Scotland. I was quite fond of these, as an aunt had brought them back from a visit. My background is German, so I found them exciting. (#1181, female, 34 years old)

- Putting on impromptu "quick change" plays for my parents—a wide variety of old clothes, including some from the "old country." (#1004, male, 20 years old)

- Playing pirates with my sisters and brothers. Newspaper pirate hats, ripped sweat shirt, vest, cutoffs, eye patch, and cardboard sword. (#1009, male, 27 years old)

- Dress-up—a lot—old 50s prom dress, hats…. (#1212, female, 33 years old)

- My grandmother made me a shirt and trouser of tan denim and put red fringe across the yoke and down the outside seams (to play Indian while wearing). (#1240, female, 36 years old)

Fantasy Dress among these quotes includes a WWII uniform, dress from other countries that was exciting, dress from the "old country," pirates' dress, and dressing like "Indians." The quotes refer to the Private Self because they mention parents, siblings, an aunt, an uncle, and a grandmother.

Included in the cell for Fantasy Dress and the Secret Self (see cell #9 in Table 2) is a memory of a young boy's fantasy:

I was 7 or 8 years old and we lived in a big house on top of a hill in a small…town…. I distinctly remember standing on that hill wearing a navy blue detective style coat. The wind was blowing just right and I made a wish with my hands in my coat pockets, spread my coat out behind me and spread my arms. I charged down the hill into the wind expecting to fly. And through the magic of a young boy's imagination, I did fly. Ever after, that was my flying coat but it never lifted me to the sky again. Never again was the wind just right. (#1K, male, 38 years old)

This is an excellent example of Fantasy Dress because people cannot fly even with the help of a coat and the wind. It is unclear which part of the self this quote illustrates. We don't know if he was alone during this incident or if he told anyone about his experience. Therefore, I placed this quote in the Secret Self because it is unclear whether or not he shared this fantasy previously.

The following quote also fits in the Fantasy Dress/Secret Self cell because of the reference to dress used in an intimate situation. Not a childhood memory, this quote is about a fantasy projected for some time in the future:

> I have put together a set (eight bags) of yet unused clothes for an intimacy dress-in. (#1281, male, 41 years old)

Lastly, some respondents thought the event of their memory was more important than dress, while others thought dress was more important than the event. Here are several examples:

Event Most Important

- Many memories of people, places, but nothing about clothing. (#1215, male, 30 years old, not included in analysis)

- Many [occasions], but clothes not remembered, just the experiences. (#1376, female, 28 years old, not included in analysis)

- Hmmm.... No, the dress seems unimportant compared to the situations themselves, unless directly affected. For example, I remember a science experiment at school when I accidentally spilled bleach and ruined a brand new pair of green corduroy overalls...I think I remember the dress so well because it was actually the focal point of the conflict. I caught hell from my mom! (#1355, female, 23 years old, included in Reality Dress/Public Self, cell #1)

Dress Most Important

- I wore a yellow knee-length dress with white flowers to my mother and stepfather's wedding. I was 4 years old. The odd part about this memory is that until I asked my sister, I didn't remember where I wore the dress; I just remembered the dress. (#1312, female, 23 years old, included in Reality Dress/Private Self, cell #4)

- In most of my memories, I can remember what I wore. (#1024, male, 28 years old, not included in analysis)

- I remember what I was wearing on many occasions. Especially things like birthdays, weddings that I attended, and the first day of school. (#1282, female, 25 years old, included in Reality Dress/Private Self, cell #4)

As a result of my analysis of childhood memories of dress and the Public, Private, and Secret Self Model, I'd like to make several observations: The first is that some cells have more memories than others (see Table 3). The largest number of childhood memories ($n = 37$) reflected Reality Dress and the Public Self (cell #1), outnumbering quotes in any other cell. It is not surprising that the most public situations are also the most memorable. The cell with the second largest number of quotes ($n = 16$) was Fantasy Dress and the Private

TABLE 3

Number of responses analyzed for the current article and the total number of responses received.

	Reality Dress	Fun/Leisure Dress	Fantasy Dress
Public Self	28 analyzed 37 received (1)	0 analyzed 7 received (2)	4 analyzed 7 received (3)
Private Self	4 analyzed 4 received (4)	10 analyzed 14 received (5)	6 analyzed 16 received (6)
Secret Self	1 analyzed 2 received (7)	1 analyzed 3 received (8)	2 analyzed 2 received (9)
TOTALS (Received)	43	24	25

FIGURE 8.7 A 7-year-old girl poses after being "made up" by her older sister in August 1967.

Self (cell #6). I would not have predicted this cell to be the second-largest prior to this study, but now that the results are in, I can see how playing dress-up with brothers and sisters can create lasting memories (see Figure 8.7). The cell with the third largest number of quotes ($n = 14$) was Fun/Leisure Dress and the Private Self (cell #5). I would have predicted this cell to outnumber the Fantasy Dress/Private Self ($n = 16$) cell, but actually, the numbers in these two cells are very similar.

The second observation occurred when I examined the three categories of dress, Reality, Fun/Leisure, and Fantasy (column totals as opposed to row totals); I found that memories of Reality Dress ($n = 43$) outnumbered memories of Fun/Leisure Dress ($n = 24$) and Fantasy Dress ($n = 25$). Of the 43 memories about Reality Dress (includes all three parts of the self), 26 dealt with religious or school events. This was not surprising, because most of a child's public time is spent at school and/or church. The remaining memories were about participating in weddings and feeling different from others. Memories of Fun/Leisure Dress ($n = 24$) focused on family celebrations, birthday parties, and visiting grandparents. This isn't surprising either, because most adults have memories of Christmas celebrations and birthday parties with family. In addition, most adults over the age of 40 can also remember the deadly Family Vacation—those 10-hour car trips with little or no air conditioning and having to sit quietly in a crowded backseat with siblings. Fantasy Dress quotes ($n = 25$) focus on what children would consider "the exotic," such as war uniforms, clothing from other countries, pirates' dress, and "Indian" dress. These memories fit Stone's (1965) ideas of childhood fantastic socialization.[4]

The third observation is that there are differences among men and women regarding their descriptions of dress during childhood memories. Overall, there were more quotes from women ($n = 43$) analyzed than from men ($n = 14$). Women in the study used about eight words to describe dress during a significant childhood memory, while men used about three. However, not every woman was descriptive (i.e., "My confirmation dress."). But what women provide in number of descriptive terms, men seem to make up for in emotional intensity (i.e., "Fell down in slush in first communion suit."). Finally, of the 12 Fantasy Dress quotes analyzed, male fantasy quotes ($n = 8$) outnumbered female fantasy quotes ($n = 4$), supporting Stone's (1965) finding that boys participate more in fantastic socialization and girls participate more in anticipatory socialization.

As the quotes demonstrate, for the adults surveyed, strong connections exist between dress and a particular life event. Do reenactors dress in costume to recapture the excitement associated with childhood events? Future research is needed to compare childhood memories of dress between those who "costume" to those who do not. Additional research on the Public, Private, and Secret Self Model will tell us more about the significance of dress to different parts of the self.

Notes

1. Stone (1965) wrote a critical article about appearance and the self using symbolic interaction theory. Included in the article

were descriptions of dress-related behaviors such as program and review, anticipatory and fantastic socialization, and the ubiquitous mother.

2. See Eicher (1981), Miller (1990), and Eicher and Miller (1994) for more details about the PPSS Model.

3. Stone (1965) described the ubiquitous mother as the prime agent of socialization for children. This socialization included dressing both male and female children in dresses, a common practice at the beginning of the twentieth century. According to Stone, being socialized by a woman caused men problems in developing strong sexual identities.

4. Childhood fantastic socialization, according to Stone (1965), includes dressing out roles that could never realistically be assumed later in life, such as Superman, Superwoman, or Spiderman. Anticipatory socialization includes dressing out roles that can be adopted later in life, such as mother, father, or teacher.

References

Eicher, J. B. (1981). Influences of changing resources on clothing, textiles, and the quality of life: Dressing for reality, fun, and fantasy. *Combined Proceedings, Easter, Central, and Western Regional Meetings of Association of College Professors of Textiles and Clothing,* 36–41.

Eicher, J. B., & Miller, K. A. (1994). Dress and the public, private, and secret self: Revisiting a model. *Proceedings of the International Textile & Apparel Association,* p. 145.

Miller, K. A. (1990). Dress as a symbol of the self and its relationship to selected behaviors. Unpublished doctoral dissertation, University of Wisconsin, Madison.

Miller, K. A. (1997). Dress: Private and secret self-expression. *Clothing and Textiles Research Journal,* 15(4):223–234.

Miller, K. A. (1998). Gender comparisons within reenactment costume: Theoretical interpretations. *Family and Consumer Sciences Research Journal,* 27(1):35–61.

Miller, K. A., Jasper, C. R., & Hill, D. R. (1991). Costume and the perception of identity and role. *Perceptual and Motor Skills,* 72:807–813.

Miller, K. A., Jasper, C. R., & Hill, D. R. (1993). Dressing in costume and the use of alcohol, marijuana and other drugs by college students. *Adolescence,* 28(109):189–198.

Stone, G. P. (1965). Appearance and the self. In M. E. Roach & J. B. Eicher (Eds.), *Dress, Adornment and the Social Order,* pp. 216–245. New York: John Wiley & Sons.

Strauss, A., & Corbin, J. (1990). *Basics of Qualitative Research: Grounded Theory Procedures and Techniques.* Newbury Park, CA: Sage.

DISCUSSION QUESTIONS

Playing Dress-Up

1. Do you have significant memories of dress as a child? If so, do they relate to the Public, Private, or Secret Self?

2. Do you remember playing with dress as a child? If not, did you ever wear costumes for Halloween or other events? What did you wear for play and Halloween? Did you like the costumes and play dress? Why?

3. Why do you think that men tend to have fewer childhood memories of dress than do women?

46 Taking a New Look at Uniforms and Their Impact on Schools

James Sterngold

For Carl Cohn, the path to educational innovation began a decade ago on a gritty Long Beach street when a few dozen children, caught in the middle of a gang shootout, were forced to the floor of a school bus.

Mr. Cohn was a former truant officer in this heavily industrialized port city adjacent to Los Angeles, and in the wake of that lawlessness he was asked to head an antigang task force. Its principal aim was, like that of some United Nations peacekeeping missions, to protect noncombatants, known elsewhere as primary school students.

"We needed to give safe passage for students through some very tricky terrain," said Mr. Cohn, now the superintendent of schools here. "We realized the way to make it visible who the students were was clothing, uniforms. We didn't think about all the other issues. It was safety, pure and simple."

It was an unusual start for what came to be hailed as a major step in helping to reinvigorate public education, not just here but across the country.

In 1994, Long Beach mandated uniforms at all its elementary schools after trials at a couple of schools. Test scores and grades rose. Absenteeism, failures and discipline problems declined. Schools in more than 35 states have now adopted uniforms policies, with Philadelphia set to adopt such a policy this fall.

But it is worth recalling the sobering origins of that success as Long Beach takes the next step, completing the introduction of uniforms at its first high school. The school district that helped push school uniforms to the front lines has now pulled them back, if slightly, as a tool.

Woodrow Wilson High School, to which students must apply for entry, has phased uniforms in one year at a time, and next year, students in all grades will be wearing khaki bottoms and burgundy or white collared shirts. But a visit to the school and conversations with administrators, parents and students reveal a subtle appreciation for the limitations as well as the merits of uniforms.

For one thing, if uniforms mean uniformity, these are a failure. The school allows the students to fulfill the requirements in many ways. They can wear trousers, skirts, baggy shorts or capri pants on the bottom and a range of tops on condition they are white or burgundy and have collars.

Jon Meyer, the school's co-principal, said the administrators chose loose standards to allow older students to express themselves while minimizing the potentially divisive effects of dress, like designating gang affiliation or economic differences. He is even toying with eliminating a rule requiring students to keep their shirts tucked in in the classrooms.

The point, Mr. Meyer said, is that they have found uniforms just one of several tools for refocusing the school, and, he insisted, they require complete support by parents and students.

"It's not the answer, but it contributes," he said. "I don't think that the uniform alone does a whole lot, actually."

Nonetheless, there have been improvements. Three years ago, the school had 861 suspensions. This past year, there were 280.

And that is not just because the school began a policy three years ago that students apply to get in. Despite that, the student body still represents a cross section of the city. Well over a half of the students come from families with incomes below the poverty line, said Keith Hansen, the assistant principal, and 350 of the students speak English as a second language.

But the real issue is that uniforms were just the most visible of several reforms introduced. Students are required to take more credits, including four years of a foreign language, math, science and English. They must maintain a C average.

Noelle Ebright, who will begin her senior year at Wilson in the fall and was the student government president last year, said of uniforms, "They aggravate me more than they help me." But she added that they appeared to have cut down on the number of fights.

Richard Flanary, a senior administrator at the National Association of Secondary School Principals, in Arlington, Va., said the limited amount of research on the subject had placed only modest emphasis on uniforms as a way of turning around a troubled high school.

"There is no direct link between uniforms and performance," Mr. Flanary said, "but we know there is a link between the school, environment and performance. Uniforms might be one way of affecting the environment, but just one."

Still, even with their expectations moderated, Long Beach officials are believers, if well-informed believers.

"Frankly, it's a very good question as to whether 5 or 7 years from now uniforms will still be a priority," Mr. Cohn said. "There is a part of me that says if we really want to grow these young people into young adults, it is, in fact, their behavior that will really mark them, not what they wear.

"Having said that, these are difficult times. And there is the reality that there is something to be gained if these young people spend less time paying attention to their dress."

DISCUSSION QUESTIONS

Taking a New Look at Uniforms and Their Impact on Schools

1. What do you think of wearing uniforms to school?

2. Have you ever worn a school uniform regularly? What did you think of your uniform? If you never wore school uniforms, find someone who has and interview them about the experience and their attitudes toward uniforms.

3. What reasons have educators given for implementing uniform policies?

47   The High Cost of Beauty: Inside the World of Baby Pageants, Where Kids Get Early Lessons in Selling Themselves

Jeannie Ralston

The atrium of the Embassy Suites off Interstate 35 in Austin, Texas, looks like a casting call for extras in a Cinderella movie. Tiny girls prance in beaded, lacy gowns, their hair fluffed and beribboned, their lips pink and dewy.

It's Saturday evening, and Deborah Tushnet is quickly finishing dinner with her husband, Marc, her 4-year-old son, Jeremy, and her daughter, Lacy Rose, 14 months. Lacy Rose is vying for a title in the 0-to-23-months division of the Universal Royalty National Pageant, and the crowning ceremony will take place in 30 minutes. "The judges emphasize what the director tells them to," Tushnet says. "This year, I can tell, they want blondes, they want glitz." She gets up to change her light-brown-haired daughter into her "crowning dress."

Filing into the ballroom for the announcement of winners, Kimberly Goralewicz is considering her daughter Courtney's chances to win in the 2-to-3-year-old division. "We have some serious competition, so I don't know! It's not just who's the prettiest. They're looking for the total package: the clothes, the hair, the makeup, the modeling."

Nearby, Deanne Westbrook is jiggling her 10-month-old, Zarian, already a veteran of 18 pageants, on her lap. "She's done the best she's ever done," she says. "We came to have fun, and we have."

It's been almost five years since child beauty pageants gained national attention after the murder of 6-year-old JonBenet Ramsey, a regular contestant. While her death has dried up the pageant network in some areas of the country, such as Colorado and South Carolina, elsewhere it still thrives. There are an estimated 25,000 pageants across the country, mostly in the South, according to the International Pageant Association.

Annette Hill of Austin started the Universal Royalty Pageant system a year before the Ramsey murder. She says she wanted an event with a fun, family atmosphere, where every child felt special. "Everyone gets something," says Hill, an enthusiastic pageant promoter. "I give out a little gift bag to everyone so the children still feel like they won something. At their age, they don't know, really." The pageant has divisions for boys and girls, newborn up to adult—most of whom pay $600 to enter (some get discounts)—with the under-5 categories having the most entrants. The vast majority of contestants are girls. Entry fees for some pageants can be as high as $2,000.

"Once you do a pageant and win, it's like a drug—you can't wait to do another one," says Griff O'Neil, founder and president of the International Pageant Association. But pageants have benefits too, says Hill, such as promoting mother-daughter bonding and, as she and other pageant fans stress repeatedly, building self-esteem. "Pageants teach kids how to speak in public," she says. "Pageant kids take charge a little more than other kids." Hill compares the competitions to sporting events, adding that Little League could be harmful if parents put too much pressure on kids. She admits that there are demanding "pageant moms" but claims that most have a healthy perspective.

"This is the cowboy hat I wore when I won World," Deborah Tushnet says as she lovingly handles a tiny red hat. "See, it has my name on the band." Tushnet, who lives and teaches music in Houston, won the World's Miss LaPetite title when she was 5. She notes that her winnings helped put her through college.

Reprinted by permission of The Parenting Group.

She's in her room at the Embassy Suites on Friday evening, the first night of the two-day event, getting her daughter ready for the western-wear competition. "It's so different from when I was competing," she says. She's nursing Lacy Rose, whose outfit—white hot pants and a red-and-white blouse, like a miniature Dallas Cowboys cheerleader costume—hangs at the ready. She drops her voice. "One woman said she saw a girl at the last pageant with brown hair, and now she's a blonde! Dyeing girls' hair at this age? Come on! That's what I'm competing against."

The only extra help Lacy Rose gets are curlers and blush on her cheeks. And some cover-up on any bruises on her legs. Tushnet also puts "a little Dippity-Do on her hair, but no hairspray."

Deanne Westbrook is in line along the wall of the ballroom, holding Zarian in her arms. She's with about 20 other mother-daughter pairs waiting to go up on the makeshift stage at the front of the room. "We've been doing this since she was two weeks old," says Westbrook, a bubbly blonde from Sherman, Texas, whose two older children are boys. "I always wanted a girl. So far she likes it." Zarian recently won Baby Miss Graceland County, wearing the same turquoise hat-and-short set covered with silver fringe and stars that she's got on tonight. "We bought [this outfit] off the Internet from a lady in Ohio. It was too expensive [$500]," Westbrook says, cringing. She bends over to pick up Zarian's pacifier, also turquoise.

Soon it's Westbrook's turn to take her daughter onstage. She holds Zarian in front of her chest and waves the baby's arm at the judges as she walks from one masking tape "X" on the stage to another. Other pairs follow the Westbrooks. Some babies lumber along in heavy cowboy boots, holding their mother's or father's hand. Their parents whisper in their ears, cajoling them to wave, smile, walk this way or that. In the audience, grandmas or friends call out the girls' names or jump around, trying to make them smile or laugh for the judges.

Madelyn Chapa, 23 months, has won four pageants this year, including Texas State Queen. She gallops onstage like a horse and kisses the back of her hand, as if she's throwing a backward kiss. "Can you give a pretty face?" her mother, Olivia, whispers in her ear, prompting her daughter to smile. The Chapa family has traveled here from Mission, Texas, to go for the crown. Modeling moves are considered surefire judge pleasers, so Madelyn's mother undoes the Velcro on the purple satin-and-rhinestone-trimmed skirt that she made herself, revealing the one-piece outfit underneath. The judges smile approvingly and jot notes on their pads.

The 2-to-3-year-old division follows the babies'. Two-year-old Britney Williams, wearing a lime-green outfit with white mink at the shoulders and cuffs, stares into the stage lights and blinks her mascara-laden lashes. With her mother guiding her from behind and her grandmother shouting encouragement in the audience, Britney walks to the different marks onstage and poses. Next comes 3-year-old Shyanna Kenner, who whips off her fur-trimmed royal-blue jacket and throws it over her shoulder, prompting cheers from the audience. Head to toe in fuchsia, Ashley Jacobs, 3, walks onstage without her mom and poses with her arms beside her and her hands out to her sides, parallel to the floor (a posture called "pretty hands"). She turns around and looks over her shoulder coquettishly at the judges.

"We do about six or seven a year," says Tammie Kenner, Shyanna's mother, after her daughter is offstage. "This year we haven't lost one. We're usually a division winner." Kenner realizes that a win this time might be more difficult. "We're paying someone to do her hair and makeup," she says. "The competition is tough. There's a lot of great little girls here." For the western-wear competition, Shyanna is wearing only a bit of light lip gloss. Her hair is pulled to one side into a fat braid; her bangs are curled and sprayed. "It's not all hers," Kenner says with a guilty smile as she touches her daughter's braid.

Only a handful of girls compete in the talent competition (it's not required). Zarian Westbrook is dressed in a blue bird outfit, feathers covering her hair. She sits in a faux nest and shakes her hands to the beat of "Rockin' Robin." Meanwhile, Madelyn Chapa's father, Mario, is running after her in the back of the ballroom, "trying to get her hyper," her mother says. Madelyn, who's in platform shoes and an acid-green pantsuit, will do a disco dance to "Shake Your Groove Thang." In her hand, Olivia Chapa holds a homemade cardboard microphone; it's glitter-covered, with a hole in the top. "That's where we put candy," Chapa explains. "Sometimes she'll chew on it and it looks like she's singing."

It's 7:30 A.M. on Saturday morning, and the hotel is already buzzing. Three makeup artists and hairstylists have clients stacked in their rooms, like planes waiting for takeoff at a busy airport. These women charge $100 to $300 for their work, according to Annette Hill. One of them, Karen Hutter, is asking 5-year-old Rheagan Carroll to pick a lipstick. As Hutter puts makeup on Rheagan's unblemished young face, Hutter's husband suggests clear mascara rather than dark brown. "Not today," declares Rheagan's mom, Rebecca Carroll, a reading teacher from Tyler, Texas. "Today we're pulling out the big guns. There are lots of kids here." Rheagan has already won 51 trophies and a car since she started to enter pageants at the age of 1.

One floor up, Susan Gosney is working on 3-year-old Shyanna Kenner's hair while Tammie Kenner holds her in her arms. Shyanna is nose to nose with her mother, who's trying to distract her. "I don't have too much hair to cover up the extensions," Gosney is saying as she combs and teases. "I'm hiding them the best I can." Shyanna is fidgeting and squirming unhappily. "When she sees what she looks like, she'll be happy," Gosney says. Actually, Shyanna, who's already in her makeup—foundation, streaks of blush, eye shadow, mascara—is on the verge of tears. "Don't cry," her mother says urgently. "Please don't cry." Gosney finishes the cascade of curls, and Kenner takes her daughter's hand. "Don't touch your face. Don't touch your face," she says.

In the darkened ballroom, contestants and moms are lining up once again for their promenades across the stage. This time they are competing in the beauty portion of the pageant, in which most of the girls wear ornate dresses that can cost up to $1,000, according to Hill.

"I want to remind everyone how important it is to applaud for each and every contestant," proclaims the emcee before the pageant begins. "It's important that we build their self-esteem."

When Madelyn Chapa's turn comes, her father is onstage with her. Her mother is behind the judges, blowing kisses, but Madelyn doesn't seem to want to cooperate. Her father slips her a piece of candy, and she heads toward the center of the stage to face the judges. "Say hi," her father, kneeling beside her, whispers in her ear.

Next, the contestants prepare for the sportswear competition. The girls wear glittery pantsuits and jackets, to demonstrate modeling skills. Courtney Goralewicz, 3, is in her room, changing into a hot-pink Lycra jumpsuit and a jacket with sequins and pink fur trim.

Courtney loves pageants, her mother reports. At 5 months, she won the first pageant she entered, in their hometown of Killeen, Texas. "After that, we were hooked," says Goralewicz.

Courtney has been in 25 pageants, some as far away as Ohio. She's gotten so that she can walk up on the stage and do her modeling moves without her mom—one of the only girls in her age group who goes onstage alone. "She's really good about hair and makeup," says Goralewicz. "This one," she says, nodding toward Courtney's older sister, 5-year-old Kayla, who sits slumped on the floor, "hated having makeup on and having her hair done. And if they're fighting you the whole time they're getting dressed, they're not going to do well onstage. You spend five hundred dollars on an entrance fee, five hundred dollars on airline tickets, and then they cry onstage and you've lost everything."

During the sportswear competition, it's easy to tell who's had coaching—the tiny models who know to shift positions, to do something cute, such as pretend to shoot a gun, then blow on their finger. Several girls—even the coached ones—break out of their routines and head for the prize tables behind the stage, which are piled with gifts for the winners: bicycles, a mini-beauty salon, shiny trophies.

Any girl who expects to score big points will take off her jacket and throw it over her shoulder, a move that always generates the loudest cheers. The older, more accomplished girls make it look like a dance number, and none is better at this than Rheagan Carroll. She almost skips across the stage, performing a choreographed and seamless routine.

During Rheagan's performance, Denell Powell stands behind the judges, holding her 2-year-old daughter, Jour'Ney, in her arms. Because Jour'Ney won at the last national pageant, she can't compete this year. But she can learn. "Look at that beautiful winning smile," Powell whispers to her daughter. "Look how she's focused only on her judges. She's so poised, so controlled. She's only got her winning smile for her judges." Powell strokes Jour'Ney's face. "Always have that winning smile for your judges when you get onstage."

"I'm sorry, I couldn't get my jacket off," Rheagan Carroll tells her mother after she finishes her sportswear competition. One jacket sleeve had gotten awkwardly stuck during her routine. Rheagan seems distressed as she changes out of her pink pantsuit. "It wasn't my fault; it was the jacket's fault." "It doesn't matter. The judges loved you," says her mom as she helps the little girl with the anchorwoman's hair and makeup take off her clothes.

When making their decision on winners, the judges consider facial beauty, overall appearance, and personality, says Hill: "For overall appearance, they're looking at the total package." That includes hair, makeup, and the caliber of clothes. "Because I like the glitz and the makeup, I emphasize that." Hill says she doesn't approve of makeup on babies—except for blush. And she likes what she calls minimal makeup on toddlers: "a little bit of mascara, a little bit of lipstick, maybe a tad of eye shadow, a tad of base."

At the Universal Royalty National Pageant, winners are named in every age category, with each one collecting $175. Though this doesn't come close to covering the entrance fee, it doesn't deter parents. Indeed, O'Neil of the International Pageant Association reports that many pageants don't award any prize money at all. The Universal Royalty pageant offers a comparatively substantial payout for the two overall winners at the national contest: $1,000 each.

In the 2-to-3-year-old division, Shyanna Kenner is named third runner-up. A girl from Colorado wins the category, while Courtney Goralewicz wins Miss Congeniality of the whole pageant. Lacy Rose Tushnet, Zarian Westbrook, and Madelyn Chapa are crowned "Future Winners," a title for those who don't place. ("She didn't do as well as usual; I don't know why," says Olivia Chapa of Madelyn. "Maybe because she has a cold.")

One crying mother of a Future Winner, Stephanie Gray of Tulsa, soon returns to the ballroom with red eyes. "I at least expected her to place," she says. She wipes her eyes with both hands. "I thought she looked good. She did her modeling. She made all her turns." She sniffles. "I'm used to her being at the top—I just want to ask the judges what we need to improve on."

Finally, it's time to announce the biggest award of the night for the age group: the 0-to-5-year-old National Grand Supreme. "And the winner is," the emcee says breathlessly, "Rheagan Carroll." Rheagan sprints to the stage, where she's showered with flowers. Rebecca Carroll watches in rapture with her fists clenched beneath her chin. Rheagan gets her picture taken holding ten $100 bills spread out like a hand of poker.

Outside the ballroom, Ashley Jacobs, wearing a pink confection of an outfit, is alone, leaning against a glass case. "I didn't win any toys," she pouts, sliding down so that the side of her face is pressed against the glass. "I didn't win a trophy."

In some ways, pageants do resemble sporting events: They encourage competition and emphasize winning. But sporting events are ultimately decided by the participants' skill, a byproduct of practice and hard work, while at a pageant, all the practice in the world doesn't matter if your dress, hairdo, and makeup—to say nothing of your face and build—don't meet certain elusive standards of physical perfection. As a result, both triumphant Rheagan and sad little Ashley have been offered a very clear, and very adult, lesson: At a beauty pageant, looks aren't everything. They're the only thing.

The High Cost of Beauty

1. What positive effects might participation in beauty pageants have on a child?

2. What negative effects might beauty pageant competitions have on children?

3. If you have or will someday have an attractive child, will you be interested in having your child compete in beauty pageants? Why or why not?

48   T'ween Spirit

Tracy Bulla

WHO'S THAT GIRL?

She's 8 to 12 years old. She watches MTV and the WB, surfs the Internet, and reads teen magazines. But even if she doesn't do any of these things, she goes to school where fashion meets its harshest critic—another discerning 10-year-old girl. She may very well be your best customer.

"She's very savvy, very smart, very receptive to newness. She knows how she wants to look, and she influences the purchase," explains Patricia Welman, merchandiser for the Los Angeles-based I.L.U. Girls line, which debuted for Spring 2000. "The tween trend is by far the strongest trend in any apparel division right now." The tweens represent a lucrative category, according to Jody Schwartz, designer of the New York-based XOXO Girls line, an offshoot of the popular XOXO junior collection. "The pre-teen market is the largest growing segment of consumers in the world today," Schwartz says. "If anyone follows trends, it's the pre-teens. They're on the pulse of what's cool, trendy and forward."

Just think of these forward young ladies as tinier versions of juniors, minus the plunging necklines and backless halters. "Tweens are where teens were 25 years ago," says R. Fulton Macdonald, president of International Business Development Corp. in New York. "With approximately 78 percent of mothers working at least part-time and many families without two parents at home, these young people are neces-

sarily more self-reliant—they dress themselves. They define the clothes they want, and they don't want 'kids' clothes." Furthermore, he adds, "In an era of casualization among adults, tweens don't want to dress up, but they do want to dress savvy, with *savoir faire*."

Britt Bivens, a New York-based consultant for Promostyl, the worldwide trend forecasting service, notes that this age group has both a new look and a new mindset. "We have to think of 11 year olds like they are not 11 anymore—they're older [acting] than they used to be." She adds that this is in part due to brand placement in movies and television shows. For example, American Eagle outfits the cast of *Dawson's Creek*.

"They're the most intelligent shoppers you will find," agrees Stefano Lawani, buyer for Moushka Bambino, a hip children's specialty boutique in Scottsdale, Ariz. "They hit the malls every weekend, and they know where the good deals are. They know if they—and their mothers—are getting ripped off."

After surveying which apparel categories generated the most profits, Moushka Bambino decided to reduce its infant selections while deepening its 7 to 16 offerings. Currently, about 48 percent of the store's profits are drawn from the tween category. "Pre-teens are your most dif-

---

Reprinted by permission of Earnshaw Publications, Inc.

ficult audience to please, but once you have mastered it they are your most loyal client," Lawani emphasizes. They know if a salesperson is appeasing them or talking down to them, and they want to be treated like an adult. "My best advice is don't think of them as children anymore."

Lawani says that his store will continue to focus on the pre-teen shopper. "This generation is what's going to keep these children's stores in business. They're the driving force behind their parents' wallets," he says and gently warns retailers: "If you don't catch this trend, you're going to be in for some economical heartache."

PROFIT POTENTIAL

While the tween market appears to be ripe for growth, vendors and storeowners need to consider several factors. First, and foremost, the fashion element must exist to please this intelligent young consumer—not an easy task, considering the fine line that children's designs must walk to fulfill the needs of a girl who is both innocent and hip. "We're trendy but not trashy," says Stephanie Trinidad, sales manager for Sugar XX in New York, a girls' 7 to 16 line that debuted for Holiday 1999. Second, kids this age still want comfortable clothes that are easy to care for—no matter how grown-up they may wish to be. Jodi Werner, national sales manager for Rampage Girls in New York, summarized the complexity of the design issue: "It's got to be fun, it's got to have a twist, but it still has to be salable, and that's very hard to do sometimes." Jamie Delaney, fashion director and owner of New York-based Rocket Girl, aims to strike a balance by keeping the styling young. "I'm not promoting an older look—I'm promoting more fashion for this customer."

Monah Li, designer of the Los Angeles-based children's and women's lines bearing her name, says that her line does not feature bra straps or any other styles bordering on "Little Lolita" looks. She acknowledges that her own daughter favors jeans and T-shirts and hints at the tween peer pressure: "I don't know what I would do if she wanted to wear that. That's the problem, when everyone else does it."

And while most designers agree that they err on the side of caution for this age group,

buying too conservatively can also pose risks. "My biggest fear is that if you get too safe, then you will be taken over by someone else who shows what can't be gotten anywhere else," says Moushka Bambino's Lawani.

A third factor is that since tween category is relatively undeveloped area of the market, it's difficult to predict what lies ahead. Sales are solid and steadily increasing at many companies, but the majority of vendors are young, just like the market itself. At trendy Jane Doe Kids in Los Angeles, the one-year-old children's line pulls in about 25 percent of the profits with the rest from its women's division, according to president Henry Abeger. "It's a very competitive business, especially if you don't have a women's company. [Because of that], it was easier for us to get in." But Abeger is optimistic because of the shift away from generic looks and toward fashion. "People in the basics business are going to feel the difference next year," he says. "We can't give our basics away."

With more and more companies getting into the tween business, the question remains: who is going to buy all of this? Trousers Up, a mainstay junior label from the '70s, introduced a children's line in Spring 1999 that is sold in both children's stores and shops catering to juniors. "The growth potential is enormous, but what will actually happen depends on the department stores," explains Richard Bag, president of the New York-based vendor. He says that the percentage of sales for the Trousers Up line have increased to double digits. He predicts that "if department stores move away from their matrix resources and open an expansion for new and upcoming resources, there will be tremendous growth taking place."

TAILORED RETAILING

Tweens want trendy but comfortable duds, and they want to buy them in places tailored to their idea of what's hip. Be it an in-store boutique or a separate department, tweens want to feel that they are shopping in their own special store—without being reminded that it's for kids.

"Retailers need to be aware that it's not just about the clothes," says Jolyn Stockton, girls' 7 to

16 designer for Esprit in San Francisco. She says that the success of specialty chain Limited Too, is in part due to the fact that the inside of the store looks like a kids' bedroom. "That's what kids respond to," Stockton says. "It's the whole nine yards [of merchandising]."

So extras such as makeup stations, accessory areas, mini lounges, bedroom accessories and fun fixtures appeal to this age group and keep them coming back for more. "[When] signs are written in crayon to make it cute, the merchandise doesn't reflect that," says Stockton. "It's all about what their friends wear, and the goal is to appeal to them so the kids can go shopping together."

At the 19-year-old Space Kiddets in New York, owner Cynthia Radocy tried unsuccessfully to sell infant through 14 in one store. "It never really clicked. The (7 to 16) girls didn't want to be in that environment with little kids in the store." So a year ago, Radocy opened a tween Space Kiddet directly above her children's store on the second floor. She carried brands such as Juicy, Groove Camp, Paul Frank (a junior brand), Petit Bateau, Tiki, Les Tout Petits and Monkey Wear, Radocy's first-year total reached half of her sales of the downstairs children's shop. "When the girls come upstairs, they think, 'Ooh, I'm a big girl now. I'm in my own department store.'"

To add to the fun, she lets her young shoppers pick the CDs that are played in the store and stocks up on jewelry and accessories, much of which she buys from women's vendors. Radocy also stocks junior apparel, which crosses over for the tweens, too, in the smaller sizes and hires a young sales staff who range in age from 19 to 23. She notes that the tween sales often generate a solid volume during a single mother-daughter shopping trip. "The sales are quite healthy upstairs for one mother buying for one girl. The Mom is so happy if the girl likes what she sees, so the Mom will be more indulgent."

HERE TO STAY

While there's a great deal of hype surrounding the tween trend, the fact is that fashion has truly arrived to the children's market. "It's a change in styling," Promostyl's Bivens explains. "We're talking about everything [women's, juniors, girls'] moving toward a more sophisticated look. Denim is a perfect example, because it's not just jeans anymore," she says. "The days of the little pink dresses—they're not necessarily drawing to a close—but they're definitely being challenged by pure fashion."

DISCUSSION QUESTIONS

T'ween Spirit

1. Do you remember clothes shopping when you were a tween? What was it like?

2. How can tween girls be most effectively reached by a retailer?

49 The Bully in the Mirror

Stephen S. Hall

On an insufferably muggy afternoon in July, with the thermometer pushing 90 degrees and ozone alerts filling the airwaves, Alexander Bregstein was in a foul mood. He was furious, in fact, for reasons that would become clear only later. Working on just three hours of sleep, and having spent the last eight hours minding a bunch of preschool kids in his summer job as a camp counselor, Alexander was itching to kick back and relax. So there he was, lying on his back in the weight room of his gym, head down on an incline bench, earphones pitching three-figure decibels of the rock band Finger Eleven into his ears as he gripped an 85-pound weight in each hand and then, after a brief pause to gather himself, muscled them into the air with focused bursts of energy. Each lift was accompanied by a sharp exhalation, like the quick, short stroke of a piston.

The first thing you need to know about Alexander is that he is 16 years old, bright, articulate and funny in that self-deprecating and almost wise teen-age way. However, about a year ago, Alexander made a conscious decision that those weren't the qualities he wanted people to recognize in him, at least not at first. He wanted people to *see* him first, and what they see these days are thick neck muscles, shoulders so massive that he can't scratch his back, a powerful bulge in his arms and a chest that has been deliberately chiseled for the two-button look—what Alexander now calls "my most endearing feature." He walks with a kind of cocky gravity-testing bounce in his step that derives in part from his muscular build but also from the confidence of knowing he looks good in his tank top and baggy shorts.

As his spotter, Aaron Anavim, looked on, Alexander lifted the 85-pound weights three more times, arms quivering, face reddening with effort. Each dumbbell, I realized as I watched, weighed more than I did when I entered high school. Another half-dozen teen-agers milled around the weight room, casting glances at themselves and one another in the mirror. They talked of looking "cut," with sharp definition to their muscles, and of developing "six-packs," crisp divisions of the abdominals, but of all the muscles that get a workout in rooms like these, the most important may be the ones that move the eyes in restless sweeping arcs of comparison and appraisal. "Once you're in this game to manipulate your body," Alexander said, "you want to be the best," likening the friendly competition in the room to a form of "whipping out the ruler." While we talked between sets of Alexander's 90-minute routine, his eyes wandered to the mirror again and again, searching for flaws, looking for areas of improvement. "The more you lift," he admitted, "the more you look in the mirror."

In this weight room, in a gym in a northern New Jersey suburb, the gym rats have a nickname for Alexander: Mirror Boy. That's a vast improvement over the nicknames he endured at school not long ago. "I know it sounds kind of odd to have favorite insults," he told me with a wry smile, munching on a protein bar before moving on to his next set of lifts, "but Chunk Style always was kind of funny." And kind of appropriate. Until recently, Alexander carried nearly 210 pounds on a 5-foot-6 frame, and when I asked if he was teased about his weight, he practically dropped a dumbbell on my feet. "Oh! Oh, man, was I *teased*? Are you kidding?" he said in his rapid, agreeable patter. "When I was fat, people must have gone home and thought of nothing else except coming in with new material the next day. They must have had *study groups* just to make fun of people who were overweight." He even got an earful at home. "My parents—God bless them, but they would make comments *all the time*. My father would say, 'If you eat all that, you'll be as big as a house.' And I'm, like: 'Dad, it's a little late for that. What am I now? A mobile home?'"

The day of reckoning came in April 1998, during a spring-break vacation in Boca Raton, Fla. As his family was about to leave its hotel room to go to the beach, Alexander, then 15, stood in front of a mirror and just stared at the spectacle of his shirtless torso. "I remember the exact, like, *moment* in my mind," he said. "Everything about that room is burned into my head, every little thing. I can tell you where every lamp was, where my father was standing, my mother was sitting. We were about to go out, and I'm looking in this mirror—me, with my gut hanging over my bathing suit—and it was, like: Who would want to look at this? It's part of me, and *I'm* disgusted! That moment, I realized that nobody was giving me a chance to find out who I was because of the way I looked."

And so Alexander decided to do something about it, something drastic.

There is a kind of timeless, archetypal trajectory to a teen-ager's battle with body image, but in most accounts the teen-ager is female and the issue is anorexia or bulimia. As any psychologist knows, however, and as any sufficiently evolved adult male could tell you, boys have body-image problems, too. Traditionally, they have felt pressure to look not thin, but rather strong and virile, which increasingly seems to mean looking bulked up and muscular, and that is why I was interested in talking to Alexander.

Although more than 30 years in age separates us, hearing him give voice to his insecurities, to imagined physical flaws, reminded me all over again of my own tortured passage through adolescence, my own dissatisfaction with a body that seemed punitively untouched by any growth spurt and my own reluctant accommodation with certain inalienable facts of nature. Like me, Alexander had been teased and harassed about being short in stature. Like me, he had struggled to overcome his physical shortcomings as a member of the high-school wrestling team. Unlike me, he also battled a severe weight problem, but at a similar moment in life, we had both looked in the mirror and hadn't liked what we'd seen.

Still, a lot has changed since I was 15. Consider the current batch of cold messages from the culture at large. The new anabolic Tarzan.

"Chicks dig the long ball." Littleton. (Buried beneath a ton of prose about gun control was the report that Eric Harris apparently felt dissatisfied with his height, repeatedly complaining that he was smaller than his brother.) Aggressive advertising campaigns showing half-naked men in which the Obsession could just as easily be about your own very toned body as about someone else's. Even a lawsuit at the higher echelons of American business peeled away the pretense of adult civility to show that the classic junior-high body-image put-down—Michael Eisner dissing Jeffrey Katzenberg as a "little midget"—is alive and well in the boardroom, as it has been in the locker room for decades. You would never know that for the past quarter-century, feminist thought and conversation has created room for alternatives to traditional masculinity, in which toughness is equated with self-worth and physical stature is equated with moral stature.

No one can quite cite any data, any scientific studies proving that things are different, but a number of psychologists with whom I spoke returned to the same point again and again: the cultural messages about an ideal male body, if not new, have grown more insistent, more aggressive, more widespread and more explicit in recent years.

Since roughly 90 percent of teen-agers who are treated for eating disorders are female, boys still have a way to go. Young girls have suffered greatly from insecurity about appearance and body image, and the scientific literature on anorexia and related body-image disorders depicts a widespread and serious health problem in adolescent females. But to hear some psychologists tell it, boys may be catching up in terms of insecurity and even psychological pathology. An avalanche of recent books on men and boys underlines the precarious nature of contemporary boyhood in America. A number of studies in the past decade—of men, not boys—have suggested that "body-image disturbances," as researchers sometimes call them, may be more prevalent in men than previously believed and almost always begin in the teen-age years. Katharine Phillips, a psychiatrist at the Brown University School of Medicine, has specialized in "body dysmorphic disorder," a psychiatric illness in which patients become obsessively preoccupied with perceived flaws in their appearance—receding hairlines, facial imperfections, small penises, inadequate musculature. In a study on "30 cases of imagined ugliness," Phillips and colleagues described a surprisingly common condition in males whose symptoms include excessive checking of mirrors and attempts to camouflage imagined deformities, most often of the hair, nose and skin. The average age of onset, Phillips says, is 15.

Two years ago, Harrison G. Pope Jr., of Harvard Medical School, and his colleagues published a modest paper called "Muscle Dysmorphia: An Underrecognized Form of Body Dysmorphic Disorder" in a relatively obscure journal called Psychosomatics. The study described a group of men and women who had become "pathologically preoccupied" by their body image and were convinced that they looked small and puny, even though they were bulging with muscles. The paper got a lot of attention, and it led to an even more widely publicized study earlier this year from the same lab reporting how male action-figure toys like G.I. Joe and the "Star Wars" characters have bulked up over the years.

Recent figures on cosmetic surgery indirectly confirm the anecdotal sense that men are going to greater extremes to improve their appearances. Women still account for about 90 percent of all procedures, but the number of men undergoing cosmetic surgery rose about 34 percent between 1996 and 1998, with liposuction being the most sought service. "Basically, men in general are getting the same medicine that women have had to put up with for years, which was trying to match an unattainable ideal in terms of body image," says Pope, who has focused his studies on college-age men just past adolescence. "Boys are much more prone at this point to worry about being beefed up, about having muscles," says Mary Pipher, a psychologist and the author of "Reviving Ophelia," a book about adolescent girls. "As we've commodified boys' bodies to sell products, with advertisements that show boys as bodies without heads, we've had this whole business about focusing on the body." And, she adds, families move so often that teen-agers "don't really know each other very

well, so the only piece of information that's really accessible is your appearance."

There is one trenchant piece of research that justifies the sudden new focus on male development. Inspired by the AIDS epidemic, Government-sponsored researchers began an enormous survey of sexual attitudes in teen-age boys called the 1988 National Survey of Adolescent Males. Joseph H. Pleck, a psychologist at the University of Illinois at Urbana-Champaign and one of the principal investigators of the study, reported in 1993 a factor called "masculinity ideology," which indicates the degree to which boys subscribe to the more traditional standards of male comportment: the need for respect from peers and spouses, a reliance on physical toughness, a reluctance to talk about problems, even a reluctance to do housework. "The more traditional the attitude about masculinity in adolescent males," Pleck found, "the higher their risk for risky sexual behavior, substance use, educational problems and problems with the law."

"This one variable is a really powerful predictor of behavior," says Dan Kindlon, a researcher at the School of Public Health at Harvard and co-author, with Michael Thompson, of "Raising Cain." "When you look at the kinds of kids who are in trouble in terms of—you name it—drugs and alcohol, suicide, attention-deficit disorder and learning disabilities, the prevalence statistics are so skewed toward boys that it's enough to knock you over. And when they looked at kids over time, the kids who had the highest risk were the highest in terms of this masculinity ideology." Since this ideology is so pervasive in boys, Kindlon says, it creates a kind of social pecking order based on physical size and the *appearance* of toughness.

The confusions that arise in young males as they try to reconcile the traditional masculine values of their fathers, for example, with a post-feminist culture that celebrates sensitivity and openness have created a "national crisis of boyhood," according to some psychologists—as well as a boomlet of academic interest in boys and a burst of popular literature on the subject. In addition to "Raising Cain," there is William S. Pollack's "Real Boys," Michael Gurian's "Wonder of Boys" and James Garbarino's "Lost Boys," as well as a spate of books and magazines about male fitness. Many of these books were inspired by the groundbreaking research in the 1970's and 80's by Carol Gilligan, of Harvard's Graduate School of Education, who charted the psychological and moral development of adolescent girls. Now Gilligan and Judy Chu, her research associate, are listening to boys' voices too. And one of the most eagerly awaited books this fall is "Stiffed," an account of the "masculinity crisis," by Susan Faludi, author of "Backlash."

Some academics claim to have seen the crisis coming for years. After the recent outbreaks of school violence in Littleton, Jonesboro and Springfield, Pollack said, "It's boys who are doing this, because of this code about what they can say and can't say, how they feel about their body self, how they feel about their self-image, how they feel about themselves in school." There's "no coincidence," he added, that boys are unleashing this violence in school.

You don't have to buy the alarmism implicit in Pollack's point to appreciate that body-image concerns form part of a larger, more complex and in some ways changeless ethos of male adolescence that would be trite and obvious if it weren't so true: boys, like girls, are keenly aware of, and insecure about, their physical appearance. Boys, unlike some girls, do not talk about it with their parents, other adults or even among themselves, at least in part for fear of being perceived as "sensitive," a code word for "weak." Indeed, they tease each other, on a scale from casually nasty to obsessively cruel, about any perceived flaws, many of which involve some physical difference—size, shape, complexion, coordination—and since adolescent teasing begs for an audience, much of this physical ridicule occurs in school. If you don't change the "culture of cruelty," as Kindlon and Thompson put it in their book, you'll never defuse the self-consciousness and concerns about body image in boys.

"When you go to ask men questions about psychological issues," Kindlon says, "you've got two things going against you. One is emotional literacy. They're not even in touch with their emotions, and they're doing things for reasons of which they're not even aware. You're not getting

the real story because *they* don't even know the whole story. And even if they did, a lot of them would underrepresent what the problem was, because you're not supposed to ask for help. If you can't ask for directions when you're lost in a foreign city, how are you going to ask for help about something that's really personal? Especially if you're an eighth grader."

Getting boys to talk about their bodies is not an easy thing to do, as I learned when I met with several groups of teen-agers. On one occasion, six middle-school boys and I sat around a table on a warm afternoon very close to the end of the school year at a Manhattan public school in Chelsea. I asked them to describe the feelings they have when they look at themselves alone in the mirror, and for its sheer confused candor, it was tough to top the remark of Mickey, a 13-year-old who begins the ninth grade in a public school early next month.

"I don't know," he said at first. "I can't even tell what stage of puberty I'm in. Some parts, I'm sure about, but"—he added with an impish smile—"other parts, I'm not so sure."

We went around the table. Dwayne, mentioning that he appeared younger than his 13 years, looked forward to the effect this would have later in life. Bernie, lean and a little more satisfied than the others, said he didn't want muscles and would never use steroids. James saw a chubby 13-year-old in his mirror. ("I just want to be skinnier," he said plaintively.) Adel, who shot up six inches and gained 24 pounds in the last 14 months, monitored acne outbreaks with the avidity of a D.E.A. agent. Willie, a powerfully built 15-year-old with impressive biceps, derived no solace from his solid athletic build. "When I look in the mirror, I wish my ears were bigger and my feet were smaller. I wear size $11^1/_2$ shoes. My behind is big, too. But," he added, "girls like it." In retrospect, the most interesting thing about the conversation was how the older, bigger boys dominated the discussion while the younger, smaller boys deferred: size cued the communication.

Take any half-dozen boys and you'll probably get close to hitting the same cross section: the fat one, the skinny one, the one who's self-conscious about being tall and the one who's self-conscious about being short, the jock and the kid who plays in the band. No one here looked like Mark Wahlberg. They slouched in the body language of feigned boredom, although that may just have been another way of expressing wary curiosity, as if body image is something they think about *all the time* and talk about almost never.

Mickey, the eighth grader, captured the problem well. "When you're at this stage," he observed, "it's all about fitting in to something, cliques and stuff. And when you're not at the same stage of life as other kids, it's harder to fit in." He was using "fit," of course, in its metaphorical sense, but it was exceptionally apt: the essence of the word is physical, of shapes and interactions and congruence. For boys in the midst of the exotic and uncontrollable incongruence of puberty, growing up in an internal world flooded with hormones and an external world flooded with idealized male images, the fit may be tighter than ever before.

In seventh and eighth grades, Alexander Bregstein didn't fit in at all. "I was picked on in every single class," he recalled, "every single day, walking the hallways. It was beyond belief. They would do things like hide your bag, turn your bag inside out, tie your shoelaces together. Some of the stuff I just can't repeat, it was so awful." They called him Fat Boy. They thought he was lazy, that something was wrong with him. He knew it wasn't true, but he also realized that his physical appearance made him a social outcast and a target—neither of which is a good thing to be in early adolescence.

When you visit the office of Harrison (Skip) Pope, in a grim institutional building on the rolling grounds of McLean Hospital in Belmont, Mass., the first thing you notice are the calipers hanging on the wall—partly as objets d'art, but partly as a reminder that what we subjectively consider attractive can sometimes yield to objective measurement. Pope, after all, was one of the scientists who devised what might be called the Buff Equation, or: FFMI = W x (1 − BF/100) x h^{-2} + 6.1 x (1.8 − H).

The formula is ostensibly used to calculate a person's Fat-free Mass Index; it has sniffed out presumed steroid use by Mr. America winners, professional bodybuilders and men whose unhealthy preoccupation with looking muscular has induced them to use drugs.

Pope is a wiry, compact psychiatrist who can squat 400 pounds in his spare time. ("You can reach me pretty much all day except from 11 A.M. to 2 P.M.," he told me, "when I'm at the gym.") I had gone to see him and his colleague Roberto Olivardia not only because they were the lead authors on the G.I. Joe study, but also because their studies of body-image disorders in slightly older postadolescent men may be the best indicator yet of where male body-image issues are headed.

Shortly after I arrived, Olivardia emptied a shopping bag full of male action dolls onto a coffee table in the office. The loot lay in a heap, a plastic orgy of superhero beefcake—three versions of G.I. Joe (Hasbro's original 1964 version plus two others) and one G.I. Joe Extreme, Luke Skywalker and Han Solo in their 1978 and mid-90's versions, Mighty Morphin Power Rangers, Batman, Superman, Iron Man and Wolverine. The inspiration for the whole study came from . . .an adolescent girl. Pope's 13-year-old daughter, Courtney, was surfing the Web one night, working on a school project on how Barbie's body had radically changed over the years, and Pope thought to himself, There's got to be the male equivalent of that.

Once Pope and Olivardia gathered new and "vintage" action figures, they measured their waist, chest and biceps dimensions and projected them onto a 5-foot-10 male. Where the original G.I. Joe projected to a man of average height with a 32-inch waist, 44-inch chest and 12-inch biceps, the more recent figures have not only bulked up, but also show much more definition. Batman has the equivalent of a 30-inch waist, 57-inch chest and 27-inch biceps. "If he was your height," Pope told me, holding up Wolverine, "he would have 32-inch biceps." Larger, that is, than any bodybuilder in history.

Now let it be said that measuring the styrene hamstrings of G.I. Joe does not represent

20th-century science at its most glorious. But Pope says it's a way to get at what he calls "evolving American cultural ideals of male body image." Those ideals, he maintains, create "cultural expectations" that may contribute to body-image disorders in men. "People misinterpreted our findings to assume that playing with toys, in and of itself, caused kids to develop into neurotic people as they grew up who abused anabolic steroids," Pope said. "Of course that was not our conclusion. We simply chose the toys because they were symptomatic of what we think is a much more general trend in our society."

Since the early 1990's, evidence has emerged suggesting that a small number of adult males suffer from extreme body-image disorders. In 1993, in a study of steroid use among male weight lifters, Pope discovered that 10 percent of the subjects "perceived themselves as physically small and weak, even though they were in fact large and muscular." Researchers termed this syndrome "reverse anorexia nervosa" and started looking for more cases. Two years ago, the Pope group renamed this disorder "muscle dysmorphia," the more specialized condition that involves an obsessive preoccupation with muscularity. Men who were clearly well developed and, by anyone's standards, exceedingly muscular, repeatedly expressed the feeling that they were too small, too skinny and too weak, to the point that their obsessive quest to build up their bodies began to interfere with work and relationships—in short, their entire lives.

"It's very hard to document trends like this in quantitative terms," Pope said, "because people who are insecure about their body appearance are unlikely to come out of the woodwork to confess that they're insecure about their body appearance. And so it is an epidemic which by definition is covert. But it clearly has become a much more widespread concern among men in the United States."

Alexander said he felt that insecurity at a visceral level. He was not only overweight, but also undersize. "I've been called short umpteen times," he said during a pause in his routine, and the only time I saw a hint of visible anger in his face was when he talked about being discriminated against because of being short.

"Kids are *so* self-conscious," Kindlon says. "One of the reasons that this body-image stuff is so powerful is because there's such an increase in self-consciousness as you move into puberty. I don't know anybody who has a good neurological explanation for it, but clearly there's real egocentricity, especially in early adolescence. Everything revolves around *you*. You walk into a room and you think everybody is looking at you. These kids are petrified because they always feel like they're onstage. Clothes at least are something that you can change. Fat kids and short kids are the ones who get it the most."

Another factor tends to complicate the sense of feeling like an outsider. Girls usually reach puberty earlier than boys, and the starting line is starkly marked by menstruation. Boys, by contrast, beginning around the age of 11, suddenly find themselves awash in hormones, but without any navigational landmarks. The amount of testosterone in the bloodstream rises roughly 100-fold in boys during puberty. (It also rises in girls, though not nearly so much.) And yet biology is not behavioral destiny, according to the research of Richard Tremblay, director of the Research Unit on Children's Psychosocial Maladjustment at the University of Montreal. In a long-term study that has followed boys from kindergarten through high school, Tremblay's group has shown that the most aggressive boys at age 13 actually had *lower* than average levels of testosterone, although the most socially dominant boys had the highest levels of the hormone.

"The real damage gets done in middle school," Pollack says, "when boys and girls are most out of sync with each other in their development." He tells of a group of mothers, including feminists, who yanked their sons out of public school and put them in single-sex schools because they were getting harassed by girls. "They weren't physically harassing them. But they were calling them on the phone, wanting to talk to them. They were wanting to be romantic, and some of them wanting to be sexual. In an assertive way, not in an aggressive way. And these were little shrimp boys, as I call them, who wanted to play Nintendo and basketball and weren't ready for this level of development. They were two years behind. When this goes on for two or three years at the middle school and then you're throwing them into the environment of high school, then you've got this revved-up negative experience from middle school that gets over-aggressified in high school. And it just gets worse."

I can vouch for that. In 1965, just shy of 14, I was not only the shortest kid in my freshman gym class, but also the new kid in school, my family having just moved to a suburb west of Chicago. It had rained heavily the day before, and there were huge puddles on the fields around which we were ordered to take the obligatory lap at the end of calisthenics. As I was running along, two larger boys—football players, it turned out—came up behind me, knocked me down and then, each taking a leg as if grabbing a wishbone, dragged my 4-foot-9, 82-pound frame along the ground and through several pond-size puddles. It is part of the dynamic of stoic boyhood, of suffering the routine bullying and hazing in resentful silence, that my parents will learn of this incident for the first time when they read this article.

As I spoke with adolescent boys and psychologists, it became clear that of all body-image issues, size is the most important, in part because it leads to a kind of involuntary self-definition. One morning I met with a group of boys attending a summer session at the Chelsea Center of the McBurney Y.M.C.A. in Manhattan. I asked them if they had nicknames, and almost every name referred to a physical quality. Mouse. String Bean. Little J. Leprechaun. Shortie. Half Pint. Spaghetti.

These insults, even the benign ones, seem to have the half-life of nuclear waste for kids. Adel, now a hulking and self-confident 6-foot-2 10th grader at the public school in Chelsea, recalled specific insults about his size and clumsiness dating back to the 4th grade. Another boy, who will attend Friends Seminary, in Manhattan, this fall, told me he has always been teased about being tall; he recalled with painful precision what was said, when and by whom—eight years earlier. Rob, who will begin boarding school in the fall, was the shortest in his class, and he could barely contain a fidgety, amusingly self-aware impatience. "Can I talk about feeling insecure about being short?" he piped up at one point. "I'm insecure about being short, because all the bigger kids think, correctly, that they can beat me up."

Harmless teasing? Psychologists have begun to suggest that the stress of all this taunting and hazing may have significant biological effects on boys during puberty. Kindlon, for example, cites the research of Bruce McEwen, a Rockefeller University neuroscientist who has shown in animal studies that prolonged and chronic stress leads to biochemical and structural changes in the brain that compromise the development of cognitive functions like memory. And Katharine Phillips, the Brown University psychiatrist who specializes in body dysmorphic disorder, says that some adolescent boys may have a biological susceptibility to teasing, which in extreme cases can lead to psychiatric illness. Men who suffer from B.D.D. may believe they are so ugly or unattractive that they refuse to leave their homes—they become, in effect, body-image agoraphobics, and they almost always date the onset of this insecurity to adolescence.

Leaving such extreme pathology aside, the point remains that a boy's body image is shaped, if not determined, by the cruelest, most unforgiving and meanest group of judges imaginable: other boys. And even if you outgrow, physically and emotionally, the body image that oppressed you as an adolescent, it stays with you in adult life as a kind of subdermal emotional skin that can never be shed, only incorporated into the larger person you try to become. I think that's what Garry Trudeau, the formerly small cartoonist, had in mind when he described life as a tall adult as that of a "recovering short person."

It was during his sophomore year, getting "the daylights pounded out of him" in wrestling and gaining even more weight, that Alexander began what he calls, with justification, his "drastic transformation." He started by losing 30 pounds in one month. For a time, he consumed only 900 calories a day, and ultimately got down to 152 pounds. He began to lift weights seriously, every day for three months straight. He started to read magazines like Flex and Men's Fitness. He briefly dabbled with muscle-building supplements like creatine. He got buff, and then beyond buff.

By the time his sophomore year in high school began, Alexander had packaged his old self in a phenomenally new body, and it has had the desired effect. "My quality of social life changed dramatically when I changed my image," he said. He still maintained friendships with the guys in the computer lab, still programmed, still played Quake with dozens of others. But he worked out at the gym at least five times a week. He shifted his diet to heavy protein. He pushed himself to lift ever-heavier weights. Until an injury curtailed his season, he brought new strength to his wrestling. Still, he wasn't satisfied. When I asked him if he ever felt tempted to try steroids during his effort to remake his physical image, he denied using them, and I believe him. But he wasn't coy about the temptation. "When someone offers you a shortcut," he replied, "and it's a shortcut you want so bad, you're willing to ignore what it might be doing to your insides. I wanted to look better. Who cares if it's going to clog up my kidneys? Who cares if it'll destroy my liver? There was so much peer pressure that I didn't care."

Alexander was especially pleased by the good shape he was in—although he didn't care for aerobics, his resting heart rate was low, he ran a mile under six minutes and seemed to have boundless energy. But fitness was only part of what he was after. As he put it: "No one's looking for a natural look, of being thin and in shape. It's more of looking toward a level beyond that." He added that "guys who work out, especially guys who have six-packs and are really cut up, are the ones girls go after."

To be honest, I was a little dubious about this until I spoke with an admittedly unscientific sampling of teen-age girls. It turned out that they not only agreed with the sentiment, but also spoke the same lingo. "If you're going swimming or something like that, girls like the stomach best," said Elizabeth, a 14-year old. "Girls like it if they have a six-pack, or if they're really ripped, as they say. That's the most important thing. And arms too."

"But not too much," added her friend Kate, also 14. "You don't like it if the muscles are too huge."

"It changes your perspective on them if they have a flabby stomach," Elizabeth continued. "And the chest is important too."

There is nothing inherently dangerous about weight lifting. "It's great exercise," says Dr. Linn Goldberg, professor of medicine at Oregon Health Sciences University and an authority on muscle-enhancing substances in high-school athletes, who lifts weights with his 18-year-old son. "Here's the problem, though. Our studies show that supplements are gateway substances to steroid use, and kids who use them are at greater risk for using anabolic steroids." Goldberg noted that 50 percent of males participate in athletics at some point between the 9th and 12th grades, and a recent study of more than 3,000 boys in Oregon and Washington by Goldberg and his colleagues showed that 78 percent of high-school athletes use supplements, which include creatine, ginseng, ma-huang and androstenedione, the supplement made famous by Mark McGwire, who recently renounced its use.

Many of the kids with whom I spoke were well aware of the health risks associated with the use of anabolic steroids, especially the fact that the testicles shrink with prolonged use. (Steroids also increase the risk of cardiovascular diseases and some forms of cancer.) Despite a great deal more scientific uncertainty about the risks—and benefits—of the supplements, however, Charles Yesalis, an expert on steroid abuse at Penn State University, estimated that "creatine use is epidemic at the junior-high-school level, and ubiquitous at the high-school level."

In my conversations with boys, it began to dawn on me that male adolescents pass through two distinct stages. During the early phase, when self-consciousness is at its peak, boys tend to look inward, think asexually and act like, well, boys. As they get older, their field of view enlarges, and they start to pay more sophisticated attention to cultural images and their own sexuality. And they become very interested in whatever their objects of romantic attraction are interested in.

So if you ask 13-year-old boys what catches their eyes, they'll say "The Simpsons" and "Revenge of the Nerds" and ads for Mountain Dew. If you ask 16-year-olds the same question, they tend to mention "Dawson's Creek" and "American Pie" and fashion advertising.

"When you hear girls gawking at Abercrombie & Fitch about how hot the guy is on the bag—that makes an impression," Alexander told me one night on the phone. The "guy on the bag" turned out to be an exceptionally cut youth not wearing a shirt. "If I look this way," Alexander said, "I've got my foot in the door." This very heterosexual impulse, however, was elicited by a school of advertising whose genealogy follows a risqué and decidedly homoerotic lineage.

In the slow male striptease known as men's fashion advertising, there have been plenty of landmark cultural images in recent years. Calvin Klein, which until recently developed all of its advertising in-house, has been pushing the boundary of taste navel-ward and beyond ever since 1980, when a 15-year-old Brooke Shields teasingly announced that nothing came between her and her Calvins. There was Bruce Weber's photo of the model Jeff Aquilon splayed on a boulder for Calvin Klein in 1982 and Mark Wahlberg (then known as Marky Mark) prancing in Calvin Klein underwear in 1992. But the ad that made sociologically explicit what had been implicit all along is what detractors have called Calvin Klein's "basement porn" campaign of 1995.

These television spots—they were, almost incidentally, for jeans—featured a deliberately cheesy, amateurishly lighted basementlike setting with cheap wall paneling. They began with an adult male voice posing questions to youthful and shirtless boys. The models were, of course, beautiful, but only in retrospect do you realize how toned and buff their bodies were—and how the ads made sure you noticed. In one commercial, the off-camera voice says: "You have a lovely body. Do you like your body?" In another, a boy who has both the looks and indifferent demeanor of a young James Dean sits on a ladder, wearing jeans and a white T-shirt.

"You got a real nice look," an adult male voice says off-camera. "How old are you?"

"Twenty-one," the boy says.

"What's your name?"

"August."

"Why don't you stand up?"

When the boy complies, the man continues, "Are you strong?"

"I like to think so."

"You think you could rip that shirt off of you?" The boy pulls down on the T-shirt with both hands and suddenly rips it off his body, revealing an extremely lean and well-developed chest. "It's a nice body!" the man exclaims. "Do you work out?"

"Uh-huh." The boy nods again.

"Yeah, I can tell."

I don't think of myself as culturally squeamish, but the ad struck me as so creepy that when I screened it at home recently, I became concerned that my 15-month-old son, toddling around the room, might be paying attention. "The style, the look, the leering tone, even the 'chicken hawk' voice-over—Klein mimicked, closely, the style and tone of cheap basement gay pornography," says Bob Garfield, a columnist at Advertising Age and a longtime critic of what he calls Klein's "shockvertising" approach. If it is true, Garfield adds, that these commercials influence how boys think about their bodies, it reflects in part "the opening up of gay culture, where male objectification has almost nearly the effect that the objectification of females has had for time immemorial for women."

This point is not lost on researchers. "The feminist complaint all along has been that women get treated as objects, that they internalize this and that it damages their self-esteem," says Kelly D. Brownell, director of the Yale Center for Eating and Weight Disorders. "And more and more, guys are falling into that same thing. They're getting judged not by who they are, but how they look."

There is no way to plug popular culture into an equation and see what effect it has on mass psychology, of course, but there is widespread sentiment that these provocative images of buff males have really upped the ante for boys.

Writing of both men and women in her new book, "The Male Body," Susan Bordo notes that "in an era characterized by some as 'postfeminist,' beauty seems to count more than it ever did before, and the standards for achieving it have become more stringent, more rigorous, than ever." Some of the research on body-image disorders in males indirectly makes the connection to cultural images.

Olivardia, who conducted extensive interviews with men suffering from body dysmorphic disorder, says the patients bring up Hollywood movie stars all the time. "Arnold Schwarzenegger, Stallone, Jean-Claude Van Damme. And Calvin Klein—that name has been brought up quite a lot of times." If you pick up an issue of Gentleman's Quarterly or Men's Health or Teen People (or even this magazine), you'll see the trickle-down effect: a boy removes a tank top for Guess jeans. Firemen drop trou for Jockey shorts. Even the recent ads for "Smart Start" cereals by Kellogg's feature a naked torso. Consider: a six-pack in a cereal ad!

Indeed, the bare, hairless, ripped chest has become so ubiquitous as a cultural icon that it occurred to me that contemporary advertising may have completely reinvented—or at least relocated—the physiological epicenter of male insecurity. Once, the defining moment of terror in a boy's life came in the locker room at shower time—the place, as a boy at the Chelsea school put it, "where there's nowhere to hide." There's still plenty of angst about penis size; many boys simply don't take showers after gym class these days, but I heard genuine fear in the voices of older boys when they spoke about the impending horror of going to camp or the beach and having to appear in public *without a shirt.*

After Alexander finished his workout that hot July day, we stopped to get something to drink at the gym's cafe. "I feel pretty good right now," Alexander admitted, "and I was furious when I went in there." It turned out that the night before, he had a conversation with a girl that took a decidedly unsatisfying turn at the end.

At a time when the collective amount of American body fat is enough to stretch the jaws of Skip Pope's calipers from coast to coast, when so many adults amble about like fatted calves

and so many children are little more than couch potatoes in training, it's hard to find fault with disciplined, drug-free efforts by teen-age boys to add a bit of muscle; weight lifting is not a sport with shortcuts, and it has become an essential adjunct to contemporary athletic performance. But there is a psychological side to all this heavy lifting that may be as unhealthy and undermining on the inside as it seems fit on the outside. And it resides not in that telltale mirror, but in how we see ourselves.

"I look in the mirror and I don't see what other people see," Alexander told me. "I look in the mirror, and I see my flaws. People go, 'Oh, you're narcissistic.' I go, 'No, I was looking at how uneven my pecs are,' although I know that in reality, they're, like, a nanometer off. And I have three friends who do exactly the same thing. They look and they go, 'Look how uneven I am, man!' And I go: '*What* are you talking about! They look pretty even to me.' It's not narcissism—it's lack of self-esteem."

I'm not so worried about kids like Alexander—he clearly has demonstrated both the discipline to remake his appearance and the psychological distance not to take it, or himself, too seriously. But there will be many other boys out there who cannot hope to match the impossibly raised bar of idealized male body image without resorting to the physically corrosive effects of steroids or the psychologically corrosive effects of self-doubt. Either way, the majority of boys will be diminished by chasing after the golden few.

Moreover, this male preoccupation with appearance seems to herald a dubious, regressive form of equality—now boys can become as psychologically and physically debilitated by body-image concerns as girls have been for decades. After all, this vast expenditure of teen-age male energy, both psychic and kinetic, is based on the premise that members of the opposite sex are attracted to a retro, rough-hewn, muscular look, and it's a premise that psychologists who study boys have noticed, too. "While girls and women say one thing, some of them continue to do another," Pollack says. "Some of them are still intrigued by the old male images, and are attracted to them."

Because he's a perceptive kid, Alexander recognizes how feckless, how disturbing, how *crazy* this all is. "I tell you, it's definitely distressing," he said, "the fact that as much as girls get this anorexic thing and they're going through these image things with dolls and stuff, guys are definitely doing the same." True, he admitted, his social life has never been better. "But in a way it depresses me," he said, before heading off to a party, "that I had to do this for people to get to know me."

The Bully in the Mirror

1. Were boys you knew in high school (including yourself if you are male) involved in working out and pumping iron? How about men in college? What effect does working out have on their body image?

2. Do you think that a washboard abdomen and huge biceps are attractive to high school girls, so much so that they don't pay attention to boys who are less built?

3. Teasing is getting national notice as a serious problem in middle schools and high schools. Were you teased or did you tease other kids in school? Was the teasing about physical characteristics? Who was teased less at school and why?

 ## 50   Pony Party

Lucy Grealy

I had finished chemotherapy only a few months before I started looking in the Yellow Pages for stables where I might work. Just fourteen and still unclear about the exact details of my surgery, I made my way down the listings. It was the July Fourth weekend, and Mrs. Daniels, typically overbooked, said I had called at exactly the right moment. Overjoyed, I went into the kitchen to tell my mother I had a job at a stable. She looked at me dubiously.

"Did you tell them about yourself?"

I hesitated, and lied. "Yes, of course I did."

"Are you sure they know you were sick? Will you be up for this?"

"Of *course* I am," I replied in my most petulant adolescent tone.

In actuality it hadn't even occurred to me to mention cancer, or my face, to Mrs. Daniels. I was still blissfully unaware, somehow believing that the only reason people stared at me was because my hair was still growing in. So my mother obligingly drove all sixty-odd pounds of me down to Diamond D, where my pale and misshapen face seemed to surprise all of us. They let me water a few horses, imagining I wouldn't last more than a day. I stayed for four years.

That first day I walked a small pinto in circle after circle, practically drunk with the aroma of the horses. But with each circle, each new child lifted into the tiny saddle, I became more and more uncomfortable, and with each circuit my head dropped just a little bit further in shame. With time I became adept at handling the horses, and even more adept at avoiding the direct stares of the children.

When our trailer pulled into the driveway for a pony party, I would briefly remember my own excitement at being around ponies for the first time. But I also knew that these children lived apart from me. Through them I learned the language of paranoia: every whisper I heard was a comment about the way I looked, every laugh a joke at my expense.

Partly I was honing my self-consciousness into a torture device, sharp and efficient enough to last me the rest of my life. Partly I was right: they *were* staring at me, laughing at me. The cruelty of children is immense, almost startling in its precision. The kids at the parties were fairly young and, surrounded by adults, they rarely made cruel remarks outright. But their open, uncensored stares were more painful than the deliberate taunts of my peers at school, where insecurities drove everything and everyone like some looming, evil presence in a haunted machine. But in those back yards, where the grass was mown so short and sharp it would have hurt to walk on it, there was only the fact of me, my face, my ugliness.

This singularity of meaning—I *was* my face, I *was* ugliness—though sometimes unbearable, also offered a possible point of escape. It became the launching pad from which to lift off, the one immediately recognizable place to point to when asked what was wrong with my life. Everything led to it, everything receded from it—my face as personal vanishing point. The pain these children brought with their stares engulfed every other pain in my life. Yet occasionally, just as that vast ocean threatened to swallow me whole, some greater force would lift me out and enable me to walk among them easily and carelessly, as alien as the pony that trotted beside me, his tail held high in excitement, his nostrils wide in anticipation of a brief encounter with a world beyond his comprehension.

The parents would trail behind the kids, iced drinks clinking, making their own, more practical comments about the fresh horse manure in their driveway. If Stephen and I liked their looks (all our judgments were instantaneous), we'd shovel it up; if not, we'd tell them cleanup wasn't included in the fee. Stephen came from a large, all-American family, but for me these grownups provided a secret fascination. The mothers had frosted lipstick and long bright fingernails; the fathers sported gold watches and smelled of too much aftershave.

This was the late seventies, and a number of corporate headquarters had sprung up across the border in New Jersey. Complete with duck ponds and fountains, these "industrial parks" looked more like fancy hotels than office buildings. The newly planted suburban lawns I found myself parading ponies on were a direct result of their proliferation.

My feelings of being an outsider were strengthened by the reminder of what my own family didn't have: money. We *should* have had money: this was true in practical terms, for my father was a successful journalist, and it was also true within my family mythology, which conjured up images of Fallen Aristocracy. We were displaced foreigners, Europeans newly arrived in an alien landscape. If we had had the money we felt entitled to, we would never have spent it on anything as mundane as a house in Spring Valley or as silly and trivial as a pony party.

Unfortunately, the mythologically endowed money didn't materialize. Despite my father's good job with a major television network, we were barraged by collection agencies, and our house was falling apart around us. Either unwilling or unable, I'm not sure which, to spend money on plumbers and electricians and general handymen, my father kept our house barely together by a complex system of odd bits of wire, duct tape, and putty, which he applied rather haphazardly and good-naturedly on weekend afternoons. He sang when he worked. Bits of opera, slapped together jauntily with the current top forty and ancient ditties from his childhood, were periodically interrupted as he patiently explained his work to the dog, who always listened attentively.

Anything my father fixed usually did not stay fixed for more than a few months. Flushing our toilets when it rained required coaxing with a Zenlike ritual of jiggles to avoid spilling the entire contents of the septic tank onto the basement floor. One walked by the oven door with a sense of near reverence, lest it fall open with an operatic crash. Pantheism ruled.

Similarly, when dealing with my mother, one always had to act in a delicate and prescribed way, though the exact rules of protocol seemed to shift frequently and without advance notice. One day, running out of milk was a problem easily dealt with, but on the next it was a symbol of her children's selfishness, our father's failure, and her tragic, wasted life. Lack of money, it was driven into us, was the root of all our unhappiness. So as Stephen and I drove through those "bourgeois" suburbs (my radical older brothers had taught me to identify them as such), I genuinely believed that if our family were as well-off as those families, the extra carton of milk would not have been an issue, and my mother would have been more than delighted to buy gallon after gallon until the house fairly spilled over with fresh milk.

Though our whole family shared the burdens of my mother's anger, in my heart I suspected that part of it was my fault and my fault alone. Cancer is an obscenely expensive illness; I saw the bills, I heard their fights. There was no doubt that I was personally responsible for a great deal of my family's money problems: ergo, I was responsible for my mother's unhappy life. During my parents' many fights over money, I would sit in the kitchen in silence, unable to move even after my brothers and sisters had fled to their bedrooms. I sat listening as some kind of penance.

The parents who presided over the pony parties never fought, or at least not about anything significant, of this I felt sure. Resentment made me scorn them, their gauche houses, their spoiled children. These feelings might have been purely political, like those of my left-wing brothers (whose philosophies I understood very little of), if it weren't for the painfully personal detail of my face.

"What's wrong with her face?"

The mothers bent down to hear this question and, still bent over, they'd look over at me, their glances refracting away as quickly and predictably as light through a prism. I couldn't always hear their response, but I knew from experience that vague pleas for politeness would hardly satisfy a child's curiosity.

While the eyes of these perfectly formed children swiftly and deftly bored into the deepest part of me, the glances from their parents provided me with an exotic sense of power as I watched them inexpertly pretend not to notice me. After I passed the swing sets and looped around to pick up the next child waiting near the picnic table littered with cake plates, juice bottles, and party favors, I'd pause confrontationally, like some Dickensian ghost, imagining that my presence served as an uneasy reminder of what might be. What had happened to me was any parent's nightmare, and I allowed myself to believe that I was dangerous to them. The parents obliged me in this: they brushed past me, around me, sometimes even smiled at me. But not once in the three or so years that I worked pony parties did anyone ask me directly what had happened.

They were uncomfortable because of my face. I ignored the deep hurt by allowing the side of me that was desperate for any kind of definition to staunchly act out, if not exactly relish, this macabre status.

Zoom lenses, fancy flash systems, perfect focus—these cameras probably were worth more than the ponies instigating the pictures. A physical sense of dread came over me as soon as I spotted the thickly padded case, heard the sound of the zipper, noted the ridiculous, almost surgical protection provided by the fitted foam compartment. I'd automatically hold the pony's halter, careful to keep his head tight and high in case he suddenly decided to pull down for a bite of lawn. I'd expertly turn my own head away, pretending I was only just then aware of something more important off to the side. I'd tilt away at exactly the same angle each time, my hair falling in a perfect sheet of camouflage between me and the camera.

I stood there perfectly still, just as I had sat for countless medical photographs: full face, turn to the left, the right, now a three-quarter shot to the left. I took a certain pride in knowing the routine so well. I've even seen some of these medical photographs in publications. Curiously, those sterile, bright photos are easy for me to look at. For one thing, I know that only doctors look at them, and perhaps I'm even slightly proud that I'm such an interesting case, worthy of documentation. Or maybe I do not really think it is me sitting there, *Case 3, figure 6-A*.

Once, when my doctor left me waiting too long in his examining room, I leafed through my file, which I knew was strictly off-limits. I was thrilled to find a whole section of slides housed in a clear plastic folder. Removing one, I lifted it up to the fluorescent light, stared for a moment, then carefully, calmly replaced it. It was a photograph taken of me on the operating table. Most of the skin of the right side of my face had been pulled over and back, exposing something with the general shape of a face and neck but with the color and consistency of raw steak. A clamp gleamed off to the side, holding something unidentifiable in place. I wasn't particularly bothered; I've always had a fascination with gore, and had it been someone else I'd have stared endlessly. But I simply put the slide in its slot and made a mental note not to look at slides from my file again, ever.

With the same numbed yet cavalier stance, I waited for a father to click the shutter. At least these were photographs I'd never have to see, though to this day I fantasize about meeting someone who eventually shows me their photo album and there, inexplicably, in the middle of a page, is me holding a pony. I have seen one pony party photo of me. In it I'm holding on to a small dark bay pony whose name I don't remember. I look frail and thin and certainly peculiar, but I don't look anywhere near as repulsive as I then believed I did. There's a gaggle of children around me, waiting for their turn on the pony. My stomach was always in knots then, surrounded by so many children, but I can tell by my expression that I'm convincing myself I don't care as I point to the back of the line. The children look older than most of the kids at the backyard parties: some of them are even older than nine, the age I was when I got sick. I'm probably thinking about this, too, as I order them into line.

I can still hear the rubbery, metallic thud of hooves on the trailer's ramp as we loaded the ponies back into the hot and smelly box for the ride back to Diamond D. Fifteen years later, when I see that photo, I am filled with questions I rarely allow myself, such as, how do we go about turning into the people we are meant to be? What relation do the human beings in that picture have to the people they are now? How is it that all of us were caught together in that brief moment of time, me standing there pretending I wasn't hurt by a single thing in this world while they lined up for their turn on the pony, some of them excited and some of them scared, but all of them neatly, at my insistence, one in front of the other, like all the days ahead.

DISCUSSION QUESTIONS
Pony Party

1. How did Lucy Grealy's facial disfigurement as a result of cancer influence her relationships with others?

2. How did her face affect her self-identity?

51   Shopping Rebellion: What the Kids Want
Rebecca Mead

Takeshita Street, in the Harajuku district of Tokyo, is the equivalent of Eighth Street in New York: it is a narrow commercial passageway, crammed with stores selling imported Levi's, baby-doll T-shirts, and platform boots that have all the charm of medical appliances. Such attributes naturally make it a favorite resort of Japanese teenagers, who are the most avid consumers in a country where, since the end of the Second World War and in spite of a ten-year recession, consuming is a crucial part of the national identity. On the weekends, Takeshita Street is mobbed by thousands of fashion-conscious Japanese youths: boys who parade around in slouchy hip-hop clothes, and girls who wear thrift-store-style dresses layered over bluejeans, a look that really works only if you weigh less than ninety pounds, which most of them seem to.

It would be easy, while squeezing through the crowds on a Saturday afternoon, to miss a store called Brand Select Recycle, which is marked only by a blue sign pointing up a narrow staircase, painted with the names of designer labels—Under Cover, Bathing Ape, Gucci, Prada, and, spelled incorrectly, Martin Margaiela. The store is about six hundred and fifty feet square, its peeling paintwork illuminated by fluorescent light; it is crammed with rack upon rack of secondhand clothing, with hand-lettered, improbably high price tags pinned on. A black hooded sweatshirt bearing an image of Mickey Mouse holding a microphone and striking a rock-star pose, made by a company called Number Nine, sells for a hundred and twenty-eight thousand yen, which is close to a thousand dollars. A T-shirt with the same Mickey Mouse image goes for more than four hundred dollars. Even in a society as affluent as Japan, where there's no poverty to speak of, these prices are enough to make a visitor wonder whether the yen underwent a catastrophic devaluation in the time it took to climb the stairs.

A thousand-dollar secondhand sweatshirt is, however, just an expression of market forces.

"Six months ago, Number Nine was not as expensive as it is now, and probably next year it will go down in price," the store's owner, Akihiko Takeuchi, explained to me when I visited in November. Takeuchi is thirty-nine years old, which, in the world of Japanese youth culture, is decidedly middle-aged. His thinning hair bears all the signs of having been barbered rather than styled; he wears loose plaid shirts and gray flannel trousers and black sneakers, and even though he gets his shirts and sneakers from Hermès and his pants from Comme des Garçons, he wears them with all the aplomb of a man who shops at Sears.

He doesn't set most of the prices at Brand Select Recycle, he explained to me; they are established by the individual consigners of the items, who pay him a commission. By watching the buying and selling practices of his customers, who are mostly high-school and college students, Takeuchi has an unrivalled perspective on the fluctuating indices of Tokyo street fashion: the week I visited, for example, he'd found that boys were seeking out items from Head Porter, a Japanese luggage brand whose nylon snakeskin-patterned wallet was selling for a hundred and fifty dollars—twice its original retail value. I found sixteen-year-old Koudai Matsuhita, who was wearing a school blazer and had shaved eyebrows, intently pawing through the Number Nine Mickey Mouse T-shirts; he explained that they had a "rock-and-roll feel" that he liked. Another hot label was Bathing Ape, a Japanese skatewear brand whose signature is a distinctive camouflage pattern; a Bathing Ape nylon blouson jacket was selling for ninety-eight thousand yen, or seven hundred and forty dollars.

But Takeuchi explained that his customers weren't simply slaves to a label: he showed me a Bathing Ape chunky knit cardigan, its wooden buttons carved with images of apes; the style hadn't taken off when it was first released to stores, and now Brand Select Recycle was offering it for just a hundred and ninety-four dollars, much less than its original cost. And a mainstream designer label like Comme des Garçons had little heat in the Brand Select Recycle marketplace; you could buy a secondhand Comme shirt for fifty-eight hundred yen, or forty-four dollars. Even after years of watching his clients' purchasing patterns, Takeuchi said that he was still unable to predict when one brand would surge in popularity while another fell out of favor. "It's kind of like the image of the capitalist economy—the more desired it is, the more expensive it is," he said. "It cannot be accounted for rationally."

What is known in Japan as the bubble economy—the economic boom of the nineteen-eighties—provoked massive speculation in the markets and in real estate, and Japan is still experiencing the prolonged, low-level hangover that has persisted since the bubble burst, in the early nineteen-nineties. But you wouldn't know that the country is in recession from the way young people spend money. Because of the recession and the inflation of real-estate prices, many young Japanese continue to live at home well into their twenties; buying clothes is one of the things that living rent-free in a small apartment with your parents permits you to do. One young Japanese curator, Koji Yoshida, explained to me that the phenomenon of the free-spending Japanese youth is a product of paternal guilt. "In Japanese families, the ascendance of the father is the usual phenomenon, but after the bubble burst fathers lost their rights and respect," he told me over coffee one afternoon. "Fathers had to appease their children by giving them lots of gifts and money." Whether or not you accept the idea that Japan's youth-oriented consumer culture is sustained by a kind of commercial Oedipal agon, the swarming shopping districts of Tokyo on weekends do resemble a world in which adults have been more or less dispensed with. It's as if the streets had been cleansed of anyone over the age of thirty.

The crucial element that is being sold at shops like Brand Select Recycle is scarcity. In spite of the parallels with the financial markets, Takeuchi's customers aren't buying four-hundred-dollar T-shirts as investments. They want to be seen wearing an item that hardly anyone else owns but that everyone will recognize as exclusive. Scarcity, of course, is an integral part of high fashion, but it often has a basis in the practical difficulties of supplying consumer demand: customers will wait months for a Birkin bag from Hermès not just because the company knows the marketing value of making a product hard to get but because the bags are painstakingly created by a small number of highly skilled craftsmen.

In Japan, however, all the skill goes into engineering the scarcity: designers produce only limited editions of T-shirts or jackets, items of the sort that can be easily mass-produced. This means that shopping in Tokyo feels a little like a bizarre parody of grocery shopping in Soviet Russia: you might want to buy a bunch of bananas, but the only thing for sale is pickled cabbage. At the Bathing Ape store just off Takeshita Street, where T-shirts are displayed like prints in an art gallery, sandwiched between sheets of clear plastic, half the display cases are empty, since the company might produce only five hundred of any particular T-shirt design. At certain popular stores, like Silas & Maria, a British skatewear brand, would-be shoppers are required to wait in orderly file in the street, as if they were on a bread line, before being permitted, twenty or so at a time, to rush in and scour the sparsely stocked shelves for any new merchandise. The next twenty customers aren't allowed in until the last of the previous group has left and meticulous sales assistants have restored the shelves and racks to their unmolested condition. The whole cycle can take half an hour or more. This is what Japanese teen-agers do for fun.

One of the striking things about spending any time among fashion-conscious Japanese kids is how utterly nerdy they can be in their pursuit of cool. In Europe and the United States fashion falls decisively into the category of the frivolous and playful; in Japan the right T-shirt or cap is sought with a kind of dogged intensity, and not just by a fringe group of fanatics. Japanese boys in particular seem to treat fashion in a manner appropriate to stamp collecting or train spotting. Entire magazines are dedicated to the subject of teen boys' haircuts. The look of the moment is to have it bleached to a coppery color, cut into spiky peaks on top, and left shaggy around the ears and neck. The style is called "the wolf," although the boys look less lupine than feline, as if they were chorus members from "Cats."

"What looks dishevelled is highly calculated," John Jay, a creative director of the Tokyo branch of Wieden & Kennedy, the advertising company, explained to me when I visited his company's penthouse office. Jay's main client is Nike. "There is a word here, *otaku*, which is about being focussed and almost obsessed with something you like," he said. *Otaku* originally referred to a category of young Japanese men who were fixated on *manga*—the distinctive cartoon art that is popular reading material for adults in Japan. The word is now used to describe someone with a fanatical interest in computers or fashion. One designer, Hiroaki Ohya, drew upon the Japanese obsession with technology to produce, in his spring collection, a sporty woman's blouse that was shaped like a computer, with a screen printed on the breast, a keyboard at the waist, and a curved panel on the back which bulged out, like an iMac.

In the past two decades, Japan's contribution to fashion has been twofold. In the early eighties, a trio of designers—Yohji Yamamoto, Issey Miyake, and Rei Kawakubo, of Comme des Garçons—started teaching Japanese and Westerners alike that wearing layers of oddly shaped black garments could be terrifically stylish. In the late eighties and into the nineties, it was Japanese consumers who drove an international mania for luxury brands that resulted in all kinds of musty old labels—the Burberry raincoat, the Louis Vuitton suitcase—being dragged out of mothballs and transformed, improbably, into trendy items. Those two phenomena continue: in 2001, the Japan market accounted for fifteen per cent of all sales for the LVMH Moët Hennessy Louis Vuitton group, and the opening of a huge Louis Vuitton store in the Ginza district of Tokyo in late

2000 drew four thousand customers a day. No younger Japanese designers have challenged the creative dominance of the big three; new designers who have emerged, such as Junya Watanabe, have done so as protégés of the established designers, not as their revolutionary offspring.

Over the last ten years, though, Tokyo has also witnessed a metastasis of street fashion: you see styles that originated in the West, often associated with a particular musical category such as punk, or rap, or hip-hop. Hip-hop style is as prevalent among Japanese boys as it is on the C train, although in the absence of an actual ghetto, where they might hone their look, Japanese boys turn to hip-hop life-style stores such as Real Mad Hectic, where they can not only buy work boots and triple-fat goose-down jackets of the sort favored by American rap fans but also watch a videotape of highlights from the N.B.A. on a flat-screen TV while nodding along to the Jay-Z album playing over the sound system.

Many of the most popular Japanese brands aren't available in Europe or the United States, because there's little economic incentive for the designers to undergo an expensive expansion into foreign markets when the domestic market is so strong and so easily accommodated. (Bathing Ape, for example, has only one store outside Japan, in Hong Kong. You need an appointment to get in.) Because the Japanese are fanatical about fashion in the way that the Brazilians are about soccer or the Germans are about cleanliness, walking around Tokyo can feel like being trapped in an endless Halloween party where everyone but you has come as a member of the Beastie Boys, the Cure, or TLC.

The past couple of years saw the flourishing of the *yamamba*, or "mountain witch" girls, who tanned their skin dark brown, teased their bleached hair into silver snarls, and wore pale pearlized lipstick of the sort not seen since Dusty Springfield; they appear mostly to have retreated back to the mountains, though there are still a substantial number of tanned-and-blonded girls to be seen who model themselves on the look of Ayumi Hamazaki, one of Japan's several Britney Spears derivatives. These girls can usually be found hanging around a store called Egoist, which for a time was so trendy that the salesgirls themselves became icons. They appeared in the company's catalogue, and some of them established their own Web sites to dispense advice to their followers. One of the Egoist girls, a twenty-three-year-old named Shizue Nohara, told me that she'd worked at Egoist for three years. "I like to be the leader and have other people follow me," she said. She was dressed in a gray rabbit-fur jacket and bluejeans, Egoist's theme for the season being "Rodeo Girl." The previous season had been "Sexy and Boyish."

Another recent trend was wearing boots with twenty-centimeter platform heels. There have been at least five reported shoe-related fatalities, one involving a twenty-five-year-old who died after tumbling off her own footwear, and another who lost control of her car's brake pedal and crashed into a pole, thereby killing her passenger. Among the teen fashion avant-garde, platforms are over: one day in the shopping district of Shibuya I met two fashion students from Bunka, Tokyo's equivalent of F.I.T., who were both wearing white lace dresses layered over pants, and crocheted shawls tied around their shoulders, granny style, and who assured me that "comfortable shoes" were now in vogue. Given that they were wearing gold-and-silver ballet slippers in heavy rain, though, "comfort" was clearly a relative term.

For a Westerner, distinguishing between clothes and costume can be difficult. Every weekend, on a bridge near the train station in the Harajuku district, dozens of suburban teen-age girls and a few boys stand around all day wearing gothic drag: black vinyl kimonos or full punk bondage gear, with whitened faces and blackened eyes. The kids on the bridge are misfits of a sort. There was one unusually fat girl with a white-painted face, wearing her school uniform: short skirt, thick cream-colored leg warmers rumpled around her ankles like the skin of an ancient elephant. (Many Japanese girls wear their school uniforms even when they're not in school. There is, not coincidentally, a Japanese word, *rorikon*, a loose transliteration of "Lolita complex," referring to the fondness among Japanese men for little girls.) "I come here to have a relationship with other people and to see my friends," she told me, and it

was hard to imagine another fashion scene into which someone of her size would fit.

And yet their rebellion is a kind of performance which is grounded on a thriving commercial foundation: entire stores are devoted to selling the "gothic Lolita" outfits; and the inspiration for most of their looks comes from what are known as *bijuaru-kei rokku bando*, "visual-type rock bands": groups like Dir En Grey, five heavily made-up young Japanese men whose music is little more than an excuse for their often changing costumes, which can be ordered from special catalogues. Lately, those costumes have included white doctors' coats spattered with fake bloodstains, worn with bloodstained bandages wrapped around the wrist. As a result, the bridge at Harajuku looks like an emergency medical site staffed by the suicidal, bastard offspring of Boy George.

Given the influence of Western street style, Japanese boys have to work hard to create an identity that feels original. It's significant, in this regard, that the most admired figures in Japanese youth culture are not, as they might be in the United States, musicians or actors or athletes but d.j.s. John Jay, the Weiden & Kennedy ad man, told me, "D.j.s represent the ability to create something yourself. They're very international. Japanese have a place on the international d.j. circuit. They give Japanese youth a sense of self-confidence, and they represent something that doesn't have to apologize for the past."

A number of the most popular streetwear labels in Japan are created by former d.j.s, who produce their collections much as they produce records, by taking bits of inspiration from fashions that already exist, repackaging them, and then selling them in a limited edition. The most celebrated d.j.-turned-designer in Tokyo is a thirty-seven-year-old named Hiroshi Fujiwara, whose name is spoken with something like reverence by Japanese fashion sorts. I first heard of him from the owner of Brand Select Recycle, who told me that the designers of Bathing Ape and Number Nine were "disciples" of Fujiwara.

Fujiwara travelled to clubs like Heaven in London or Paradise Garage in New York in the eighties, and then introduced Japanese audiences not just to Western club music but to fashion labels like Stüssy. These days, he helps Nike out with marketing ideas (he prefers not to call himself a consultant, just a friend, but he is the kind of friend who has flown in the company's private jet) and writes a column of fashion recommendations for a magazine called *Men's Non-No*. Fujiwara recently held an Internet auction of his possessions, in which a nylon jacket with a fabric insert on one sleeve, a piece he had both designed and worn, sold for 1.1 million yen, nearly eight and a half thousand dollars.

"Ten years ago, nobody thought about making their own clothes," Fujiwara told me, when I visited him in his office above the Nike store. "But you don't need a fashion background to make T-shirts. I would work with designers and say, 'I want a zipper here,' and they would say, 'You can't have a zipper here,' and we would have big fights." He says that one of his favorite new brands is a label called Unsqueaky, which a former salesgirl from Ready Made, a store he used to run, has started. "We wanted to call it Squeaky," Fujiwara said, "but someone already had that name, so we called it Unsqueaky."

For Japanese girls, the main fashion choice is between being *kawaii*, or cute—which means you wear girlish pastel-colored clothes that might have pictures of furry animals on them, and sometimes you actually carry a toy furry animal with you [see Figure 8.8]—and *bodikon*, or body-conscious—which means you dress like a cross between Lil' Kim and a *manga* character. Japanese concepts of female sexiness are about as easy for an outsider to decipher as a Japanese newspaper, but they go something like this: men find *kawaii* girls sexy because they're pretty and decorative and unthreatening, but a girl can't be too committed to the *kawaii* aesthetic because men will think she's a freak. In some cases, the men will be right about this: at a store called Milk, which didn't seem to sell anything without pink pom-poms attached, I met a young woman who had her hair in two bunches high on her head, and was wearing a short, white fake-fur coat with teddy-bear faces appliquéd onto the pockets and matching teddy bears on a scarf around her neck, and who stood pigeon-toed with her belly sticking out, like a preschooler. She said that her boyfriend had been

embarrassed to be seen with her at first, but he'd got used to it. She was thirty-one years old.

The cute look is said to signify an assertion of independence on the part of the young women who adopt it, since, rather than simply putting on an ensemble presented to them by a designer, they are creating their own whimsical outfits and giving their inventiveness free rein. There's a popular magazine in Japan called *Cutie*, which offers hints on how to make one's person and environment more cute: a recent feature suggests sticking red heart-shaped cutouts all over your toilet seat, and coating all but the screen of your television set with a layer of white, furry fabric.

Confusingly enough, the *bodikon* look, which is all skimpy skirts and plunging necklines and high-heeled boots and other signifiers of hooker wear, is also understood to be an assertion of female independence. "Body-consciousness" is associated in the Japanese imagination with black women; and black culture is, among Japanese youth, taken to represent a kind of strength and sexuality, in a manner that would make an American reach for the sensitivity-training manual. Thus you find stores like Shoop, a boutique in a department store called 109 Building, where, as well as buying fake dreadlocks, girls can purchase what are known as "B-style" clothes: form-fitting dresses with athletic stripes down the side seams, and jackets bearing the slogan, in English, "Strong Black Woman" or "Black For Life." One day I met Kaori Ohta, a nineteen-year-old high-school student who was shopping at Shoop. She wore a fitted denim jacket, a short denim skirt, and high heels, had bronzed skin, and wore a long auburn wig. She'd been black for about three months, she explained; prior to that she'd been *kawaii*, but had decided that the *bodikon* look was a more appropriate expression of her strength and sexiness. However, she explained, expressing her sexiness did not amount to being a sex object. "I don't have a boyfriend, but if I did he would have to appreciate me for who I am inside, for my soul," she told me, batting her eyelashes. Ohta hoped to become a psychologist when she finished school.

Given the exaggerated femininity of girls' fashion in Japan, you might imagine that the country is being swept with a wave of ironic, post-feminist Girl Power. In Japan, though, feminism is still a new idea. It was only sixteen years ago that women were granted equal rights in the workplace, and young women who wish to have a serious career still find that acquiring a husband, not to mention having a child, can be a quick route to professional decline.

A popular figure among would-be unconventional Japanese girls is a twenty-seven-year-old photographer named Hiromix, who became famous for pioneering what is known as "girls' photography," images of herself and her friends hanging out. I visited Hiromix in her studio and listened to her views on Japanese gender relations, which were very bleak. "Almost all Japanese men suffer from a Lolita complex," she said. "Basically, Japanese guys feel they are threatened by these capable women, and would like them to be a little more stupid." Girls capitulated to boys by choosing cuteness over beauty, she said. "Beauty indicates a distance which is not reachable, whereas something cute is something that is accessible."

The Japanese tendency to detach style from content can be perplexing to an outsider: the kids hanging out on the Harajuku bridge might resemble the British punks who loitered on the

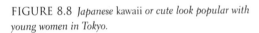
FIGURE 8.8 *Japanese* kawaii *or cute look popular with young women in Tokyo.*

King's Road twenty-five years ago, but rather than sniffing glue and snarling at passersby the Tokyo punks are polite and accommodating, happily posing for the tourists and doing nothing even as self-destructive as smoking a cigarette.

But local observers will explain that, although the semiotics are different from those of the West, Japanese youth fashion is not without meaning. Masanobu Sugatsuke, who is the editor of *Composite*, a fashion-and-culture magazine, said he believes that the fact that Japan is essentially a classless society means that young people have no way to distinguish themselves from one another except by adopting Western-derived tribal identities—surfer, skater, biker, punk, raver—even if they've never been near a surfboard in their lives. These outfits are, however, an expression of an authentic Japanese experience: that of belonging to a society that until recently was extremely ordered and disciplined, but which, over the past decade, has grown more uncertain and unpredictable. Rather than becoming company workers like their fathers, young Japanese people are increasingly becoming what are known as *furita*, people who work part-time and without job security, either because they choose to remain independent or because companies aren't hiring permanent staff workers.

"Japanese people don't want to be growing up so quickly," Sugatsuke told me. "They would like to stay young mentally and socially." In Japan, living at home with your parents and going shopping every weekend is a form of rebellion. Outsiders have described this devotion to fashion as self-indulgent and amoral; Oliviero Toscani, the former creative director of Benetton, told the *Asahi Shimbun* a few years ago that the girls who gathered in Harajuku every weekend in their oversized romper-room dresses and their silly shoes and their weird makeup were "tragic angels," living "the only existence in the world that is alien to the problems of the contemporary world, such as poverty, war, class discrimination, or joblessness." Toscani's view of the flawed youth of Tokyo did not, however, prevent Benetton from using the Harajuku girls in a worldwide advertising campaign.

It's not quite true to say that Japanese fashion exists without any view of the wider world or a political consciousness; it's just that the consciousness expressed is peculiarly Japanese. A designer who goes by the name Nakagawa Sochi, whose brand is called 20471120, is known for clothes that explicitly respond to Tokyo's overwhelming consumer culture. I met Nakagawa late one evening in a bar—he showed up with his brother and a friend, and, over several beers, he explained the epiphany he had undergone when he moved to Tokyo from Osaka. "Tokyo is free, but you don't have freedom here," he said. He is thirty-four, has spiky hair, and was wearing a Yankees baseball shirt. "When I came here, I found I couldn't schedule my time properly. There were all these cable television channels, and so I would watch television all the time. Even when there was a program I wanted to watch, I would get distracted by the other channels and miss the program I intended to see. Of course it is capitalism: when there are demands there are supplies to meet them. But in Tokyo we have too many supplies." From this insight, Nakagawa created the Tokyo Recycle Project, in which he proposes that fashion followers, rather than buying a new item, bring him their old clothes, which he will recycle into a new garment. It's as much an art project as it is a commercial fashion enterprise, and his work has been showcased at P.S. 1 in New York. The recycled item that Nakagawa shows in his publicity material—a baseball jacket which has been turned into a pair of pants, its sleeves having become below-the-knee pantaloons and its front having been transformed into what looks like a very sturdy pair of felt underwear—seems hardly likely to take off on the high-street level, even in Tokyo.

Other Japanese designers address international affairs, including Kosuke Tsumura, the creator of a line called Final Home. For the past few years, a mainstay of the Final Home collection has been a long coat made from transparent nylon which looks like a quilted down coat with all the down removed. The coat is designed to serve as a final home in the case of a natural or man-made disaster, Tsumura explained to me when I went to his studio, in a far-flung commercial district of

Tokyo. For warmth, you can stuff its many pockets with newspapers, or with the floppy nylon teddy bears which Final Home also sells.

"Each customer customizes the number of bears, according to the weather," Tsumura told me. "In my own coat, I wear maybe ten bears. And if you have children, they can also play with the bears and not be scared of the disaster." After the Kobe earthquake, Tsumura sent ten of his coats to the disaster-relief efforts. When I saw him in November he was contemplating making a coat-and-bear donation to the Afghan refugees. Another item available from the Final Home store is a peculiar toy machine gun, made from floppy stuffed nylon. "It is a criticism of war, because the gun is not usable," Tsumura told me. "It is an expression of a yearning for peace."

Pacifist appropriations of militaristic chic were everywhere in Tokyo this fall, as if fashion designers had anticipated what turned out to be a widespread Japanese unease with the American war in Afghanistan. At the stores of Under Cover, another of Tokyo's trendiest brands, customers could buy a brightly patterned umbrella with a machine-gun-shaped handle, and the centerpiece of Under Cover's fall collection for women was a dramatic ball gown made from camouflage material; on the bodice, hundreds of large, pink rhinestones had been appliquéd. "The message is anti-war," the label's designer, Jun Takahashi, told me. "Of course, if your clothes are covered with jewels you can't go to war."

Takahashi works in a recently-constructed studio, a hangarlike space with exposed-brick walls; there is a cozy arrangement of Eames chairs and other modern furniture, and, custom-built into the panels of three desks at which Takahashi and his colleagues sit, oversized lettering reading, in English, "Fuck the Design." Takahashi is thirty-two, and when I visited he was wearing a baggy gray-and-black sweater, messed-up combat pants, a denim worker's cap, and fabric sneakers covered with images of hamburgers with eyes. Of all the young designers currently working in Tokyo, Takahashi is the one thought most likely to succeed on the international stage, thanks to his ability to blend the energy of contemporary Tokyo street fashion with the conceptual high-fashion artistry of Comme des Garçons or Yohji Yamamoto. Takahashi is an acolyte of Rei Kawakubo's, who says of him, "I like his attitude, his politeness, his rebel spirit, and the fact that he is always looking for new and strong ways of doing things, like me." Kawakubo and Takahashi are collaborating for the first time on a line for a new store which will open in Tokyo later this month.

Takahashi's latest collection was entitled "The Illusion of Haze," and consisted of a series of ruffled and embroidered dresses and blouses in tulle and floral cotton prints, and carefully tailored jackets and pants in pastel colors; a layer of black gauze netting had been artfully sewn or stapled over each garment, so that the flounces beneath were interestingly squashed, the sunny innocence of their contours rendered slightly menacing. The collection, which was generally considered the highlight of last November's Tokyo fashion shows, was, Takahashi explained, a critique of "cute" style.

For his part, Takahashi professes not to understand what drives *otaku* fashion followers to pay four hundred dollars for his T-shirts and those of the other young designers. "It's a very Japanese phenomenon," he said, shaking his head. "Japanese people read magazines as their bibles, and when they see images in them they have to have them and will pay anything. Generally, Japanese people can't make up their own minds and have to have an example to follow." Takahashi will be offering something new for young consumers to become fanatical about, when he opens a new Under Cover store in which he intends to sell one-of-a-kind, hand-sewn items. "I want to communicate with the customers with a kind of warm feeling," he said. The prices these clothes will fetch if they ever make it to the racks of Brand Select Recycle just don't bear thinking about.

Shopping Rebellion

1. How is shopping and style for young people in Japan different or similar to shopping in the United States?

2. How are conformity and individuality a part of adolescent fashion involvement in Tokyo?

3. Does the Japanese shopping scene for young people fit with components of postmodernism (described in Chapter 3)? Which postmodern characteristics are evident?

52   Reading, Writing and Body Waxing
Patrick Healy

Surrounded by throbbing dance music and heads shrouded in foil, Samantha Friedman, 15, sat inside the Aqua Salon and ran through her back-to-school agenda.

Her haircut was already out of the way. (Her stylist had lopped off six inches.) That left a manicure and pedicure at Diva Nails, then an eyebrow wax. Samantha is starting her sophomore year at Hewlett High School, and she planned to look just right for the occasion.

The back-to-school rush has reached a feverish pitch here and across the region. But increasingly, especially for teenagers in affluent suburbs like this where reputations and cliques solidify faster than cold gravy, it is less about pencils and notebooks and more about the high-gloss, high-expense business of personal appearance.

"It's like the new start of everything," Samantha said. "Everyone will say they don't care, but they do. Everyone's trying so hard. Everyone's at the tanning salon. Like seven kids I know got nose jobs just this week."

Teenagers across cultures and income levels buff themselves before school, but in affluent enclaves like Long Island's Five Towns, Scarsdale in Westchester County or Wyckoff, N.J., the preening is lavish and elaborate, and a force in the local service economies.

So what's on the menu? According to Irma Zandl, a Manhattan consultant who studies trends among teenagers, this year, it's Japanese hair straightening, Brazilian bikini waxing, teeth whitening at a dental day spa and eyebrow sculpturing.

"These girls are going to school with girls just like them who have a very discerning eye," Ms. Zandl said. "Everything has to be perfect. The school is where the drama is, and the more perfect you are, the smoother your way will be."

Here in Hewlett, south of Valley Stream in Nassau County, where the mean family income is $96,100, according to the 2000 census, and high school students cruise the neighborhood in leased BMW's, businesses are deep into the back-to-school frenzy. At the Aqua Salon, one of Hewlett's most popular among teenagers, the owners said the back-to-school crowd had increased their business by 20 to 30 percent.

"It's an image transformation time," said Perry Golino, 38, a co-owner of the salon who does only coloring, no cuts, and has a three-week waiting list. "I see the pattern. A lot of kids every summer go through a transition. It's a stage performance, the first week of school."

Some were returning to high school, while others, like Lauren Hanono, were going back to college. In a day and a half, Ms. Hanono, 19, of Lawrence, N.Y., crammed in a hair coloring, a haircut, a manicure and body wax and an eyebrow wax. It's service she said she couldn't find in Bloomington, Ind., where she is a junior at Indiana University.

"It's like roughing it," said Ms. Hanono, a communications major.

Holly Green, who owns the Infinity Boutique, a specialized clothing shop in Cedarhurst, N.Y., said that besides Christmas, this was her busiest season. Teenagers flock to Ms. Green's store, raving about her talents in altering jeans.

Ms. Green, 52, who was once sent home from high school for wearing a miniskirt, now finds herself working 6 a.m. to midnight making similar fashions. The back-to-school clientele spends about $20,000 to $30,000 there each week, she said.

"We're totally booked," Ms. Green said. "Everyone just comes in. Some people are a little nuts, some people are compulsive, some are neurotic. It's like a bakery. We're practically taking numbers."

Summer was a lull, but around the second week of August, the teenagers began pouring back from summer camps, group sightseeing tours and college prep programs. In different ways, they begin to focus on that first day of school. Last year, Lauren Zeluck, now 15, was so nervous that she cried for five hours the night before. Sam Berg, a sophomore, has already planned her outfit: striped jeans, a pink collared shirt and a tank top with spaghetti straps.

"You want to look different every year," said Stevania Williams, 16, as she ran her tongue back and forth across her teeth. "With me, I got my braces taken off today. It felt weird; it felt smooth."

Wednesday afternoon, Stevania, a junior at Uniondale High School, was waiting for her father to pick her up from her orthodontist's office. She'd had the braces on for two years, and she had timed their removal just right.

Stevania was one of 90 patients who visited Dr. Seth Kleinrock's office that day, and 140 were scheduled the next day for tightenings, or to replace a retainer lost or bracket broken over the summer. At dentists' and physicians' offices in the area, appointment books were filled, as parents had scheduled checkups months in advance.

At the beach or beside her backyard pool in Wyckoff, Amanda Katz, 15, operated under the simple principle of the darker the tan, the better it looks. Her friends, too. School means six to eight hours of drawn shades and fluorescent lights, so they are flocking to the shore for midriffs the color of stained oak.

"You want everyone to be like, 'She looks good or different,'" Amanda said.

The beauty curve began around fourth grade with mother-daughter trips to the nail salon and ramped up fast, said a group of teenage girls who got together on a recent evening for one of many end-of-summer parties. They go to the salons alone now, or with one another, but their parents still pay for the visits, through credit cards or allowances.

"They don't care about school—they care about getting primped," said Jody Linsky, who lives in Hewlett and has two teenage daughters. "It's good to live now, right?"

At the party, different sides of the girls emerge as they talk. They have already lost a best friend, who died of an aneurysm last summer. They fawn over new cellphones and Von Dutch hats, but they speak with a steely knowingness about boys in their grade who get drunk a lot and violent sometimes. They hug one another constantly, and one of them chats breezily while a male friend gives her a hickey on the neck.

"I feel like high school changes you so much," said Samantha Chaplin, 15. Earlier that day, her brown hair had received rivers of blond highlights, and a slight man named Sid had plucked her eyebrows with a piece of twisted thread. "When we were in middle school, it was the outfit," she said. "Now, it's the whole package."

On Wednesday night, Marissa Fuchs, a sophomore, and two of her friends were hanging out in an upstairs bedroom of a friend's house, considering their reasons for going to all the effort.

Perched on a double bed, they contemplated the options: were they preening for their friends, for the older guys at school, or maybe, just to feel good, just for themselves?

No, Marissa said. It's all about giving a good first impression to your teachers.

At that, her friends fell back onto the bed like rag dolls, laughing and laughing.

DISCUSSION QUESTIONS

Reading, Writing and Body Waxing

1. Is extensive involvement in dress before starting school in the fall characteristic only of upper class high school girls? Did this happen at your high school?

2. What does all this primping indicate about high school girls? How does this fit with the adolescent stage of social and emotional development?

53 "Just Because It's a White Magazine… Doesn't Make It a Bad Magazine:" African American Readers and "Mainstream" Teen Magazines

Lisa Duke
University of Florida

The most popular magazines targeted to American girls, that is, *Teen, YM,* and *Seventeen,* are filled with advertising and editorial touting the latest personal care products, cosmetics, fashions, exercise programs, and weight-loss systems. Teen magazines inform or remind readers of the newest products and looks available on the beauty market and instruct girls on the value and proper use of these goods (Evans et al., 1991). The advertising for these products and services is presented in a most favorable environment, with text that presents the consumption of fashion/beauty products as a natural part of being female, integral to achieving an ideal version of femininity, and key to a girl's social success (Budgeon, 1994, p. 64). Critics of the teen-magazine genre have claimed the "fashion discourses" that are the mainstay of these publications "indoctrinate consumers into an ideology of consumption . . . immers[ing] consumers' self-

Adapted from "Get Real!: Cultural Relevance and Resistance to the Mediated Feminine Ideal" by Lisa Duke in *Psychology & Marketing* (2002), 19(2):211–233. Copyright © 2002 John Wiley & Sons, Inc. This material is used by permission of John Wiley & Sons, Inc.

perceptions in cultural meanings and social ideals that foster depthless, materialistic outlooks, and a perpetual state of dissatisfaction over one's current lifestyle and physical appearance" (Thompson & Haytko, 1997, p. 16).

In what is perhaps the first, most influential textual analysis of a magazine targeted to girls (the British publication, *Jackie!*), McRobbie (1978) identified "codes of femininity" (p. 2); among these were codes of romance, personal and domestic life, fashion and beauty, and pop music (p. 36). McRobbie argued that these codes were the essential elements of scripts the magazine provided for girls to use in the exercise of their everyday lives. All girls were presumed to have identical interests and an equal need and desire for such scripts. In a content analysis of American teen magazines 15 years later, Evans et al. (1991) came to a similar conclusion: "Articles and advertisements mutually reinforced an underlying value that the road to happiness is attracting males for a successful heterosexual life by way of physical beautification" (p. 110).

Media critics have routinely maintained that the magazines' pressure on girls to "make up and slim down" is unhealthy and ostensibly unavoidable; the implication has been that this pressure is keenly felt by all girls and the effects are strong (e.g., Currie, 1996). Further, Jackson and Kelly (1991) have claimed that the effects of mediated standards of beauty might be even more detrimental to Black females, who are "underrepresented and/or portrayed differently than are White females" (p. 68). However, there is a growing literature that indicates that African American girls may be more resistant to messages regarding ideal beauty as it is routinely presented by mainstream media (Duke, 2000; Frisby, 2000; Milkie, 1999).

This research addresses a gap in the literature on audiences of fashion/beauty media by introducing themes of opposition and anti-consumption that have not previously been explored. These findings are part of a longitudinal study initiated in 1994, on how White and African American adolescent girls interpret and use the material in the top teen magazines: *'Teen, Seventeen, YM* (Duke, 2000).[1]

AFRICAN AMERICAN READERS OF TEEN FASHION/BEAUTY TEXTS

Teen magazines are an impressive force in the print world. In a national ranking of 300 top U.S. magazines (ranked by estimated gross revenue), *Seventeen* ranked 4th, *YM* was 77th, and *Teen* 88th (Endicott, 2000). All three magazines posted growth of total revenues from 3–7.4% in '98–'99, and each of the publications has paid circulations in excess of 2,000,000. Of the 14 million girls between the ages of 12 and 19 in the United States, it is estimated that over half read *Seventeen* (1997 MRI Teenmark, Mediamark Research database).

African American girls make up a substantial percentage of the audience for the top three mainstream teen magazines. *Seventeen* reaches 44% of "ethnic females 12–19" (defined as African American, other race, or from a Spanish-speaking household); *'Teen* and *YM* each reach 34% of these same girls. African American girls ages 12–19 make up the single largest non-White group of readers—they comprise, on average, about 12% of the readership for each of the three major teen titles (1997 MRI Teenmark). The 1997 MRI TwelvePlus notes that although only 12% of people over the age of 12 identify themselves as Black, 16% of *Seventeen*'s readers do, meaning that magazine draws a greater percentage of African American readers than are represented in the population.

Content analyses of mainstream magazines, including but not exclusively fashion magazines, show that African Americans have had gradually increasing representation in the text and advertisements (Bowen & Schmid, 1997; Stevenson & Stevenson, 1988; Zinkhan, Qualls, & Biswas, 1990). However, the Black representation in mainstream magazines lags behind the percentage of Blacks in the population (Atkin, 1992). One study of fashion advertising found African American women represented in just 2.4% of ads in magazines whose subscribers were 15% Black (Jackson & Kelly, 1991, p. 69). Among the explanations offered most often for scant minority representation in mainstream magazines and the use of minority models who closely mimic the Anglo/American ideal are marketers' fears that the larger contingent of White consumers may not identify with and therefore may not buy products represented by people of color (Gitlin, 1983). Also, marketers may believe they more effectively reach minority markets by placing advertising in media vehicles specifically intended for minorities (Bowen & Schmid, 1997). Critical theorists argue that the real issue at stake is the continued control and subordination of Blacks, who are positioned through media texts and images as a group responsible for and deserving of their relative social powerlessness (Bourne, 1990; Ukadike, 1990).

If teen magazines imply any girl can be beautiful and socially successful with their help, what does the relative absence of Black girls say—that ideals of femininity do not apply to them? How do African American girls negotiate those messages?

The Culturally Situated, Adolescent Media Audience and Racial Identity Theory

Because of researchers' focus on White youth, the unique adolescent experience of African American girls has seldom been addressed (Smith, 1982). "The net result has been . . . that little attention has been given to either how a Black girl perceives herself as a female or how she is perceived by others as a female" (p. 262). In fact, race has profound implications for studies of what it means to be an American female; it is one of the most important indicators of girls' self-image. Prendergast, Zdep, and Sepulveda (1974) found that Black girls rated themselves consistently higher than White girls did on several dimensions of self-esteem (e.g., being good looking, being athletically adept). These results have been supported by later studies, which have found that African American girls rate their overall attractiveness much higher than White girls (Parker et al., 1995). Smith (1982) has noted, "Despite the evidence that Black girls and

women are faced with the prospects of being devalued by both Black and the general White society in favor of White women, Black females have been able to maintain a positive sense of self against what appear to be overwhelming odds" (p. 281).

Bell-Scott and McKenry (1986) have argued that African Americans do not turn to the larger society to meet their esteem needs. Rather, it is the African American family and community that give their youth the emotional sustenance needed to maintain esteem. The role of families—in particular, mothers—in nurturing the Black adolescent female's self-esteem is evident in the literature (Duke, 2000; Leeds, 1994). In a theme that recurs throughout the literature on how Black girls negotiate demands of all-pervasive, White-dominated fashion and beauty texts, a supportive minority culture successfully mitigates the more damaging messages of the society at large.

METHODS AND PROCEDURES

This article is part of a longitudinal study that uses in-depth interviews to trace the magazine interpretations of girls as they age from early to late adolescence. The data discussed in this article are drawn from a group of 16 African American girls—8 in early adolescence, ages 12–14, and 8 who are 17 and 18, and 10 White girls, ages 16–18. Participants are from middle-class suburbs of Atlanta, Savannah, and Chicago, and were chosen via the snowball method after the researcher met a core group of girls through acquaintances.

After agreeing to participate in this study, girls were provided with money to purchase a teen magazine, which they were asked to read before their scheduled interviews. The teen magazine of a girl's choice was used as a stimulus device during the interview.

Interviews began with a grand-tour question (Crabtree & Miller, 1992, p. 81), "Tell me, and show me, how you read this magazine." This allowed the participant to talk at length, with the magazine serving as a prompt. Although an interview guide was used in initial exchanges with participants, the conversation was allowed to flow naturally and the guide was referred to only to ensure all the issues had been covered.

FINDINGS
How Girls Read

Girls read the same teen magazine differently as they age, and, eventually, many "graduate" to reading women's service and adult fashion magazines. But even at the time of girls' peak interest, early adolescence, reading a teen magazine is, for the most part, an activity to fill in time between important activities. For most girls in this study, most of the time, the teen magazine was an abiding companion in times of boredom, entertaining their eyes and minds on long car trips and during interminable study halls. They turned pages to the magazine in time to music on the radio, or with eyes that shifted steadily from written page to television screen and back again. Girls read in the bathroom, in school classrooms, and, more often than not, in their bedrooms before nodding off to sleep.

Often, girls read in tandem with some other activity that did not require their full attention, like talking on the phone. They seldom read the whole magazine at one sitting, nor did they even read entire stories or articles, especially if they had to turn a page to do so. Girls read in stages, usually scanning the magazine first for brightly colored pictures or the headlines of particularly relevant articles. Later, they would return to the magazines to revisit images and articles they found compelling. Girls described keeping the magazines for years, picking them up several times over great spans of time, seeing new things each time they read.

Magazines build loyalty with their readers by presenting the same kinds of material, in a similar form, month after month. This consistency engages the novice, but irritates the more worldly wise. Older girls identified formulae in the text not evident to younger girls. The predictability of the content initially lends authority to the ideas and concepts common to all the major teen titles. These texts speak in one voice about girls and their place in the world. As girls become familiar with the content and format of teen magazines, it becomes less pressing to examine each issue closely; one blends into another, with the same ads, with different pictures of the same kind of girl, worrying over the same issues, pursuing the same kinds of boys. At some point, around age 17, the lessons of teen magazines have been embraced or ignored, but they have certainly been *learned*.

Race Matters: Reading in Black and White

> Kenya, 13 (on teen magazine fashions): I don't know anybody who would wear this.
> Interviewer: How about the makeup? . . .
> Kenya: I don't wear makeup.
> Interviewer: Okay. And how about the shampoo and stuff like that?
> Kenya: Un uh. 'Cause . . . my beautician washes my hair.

The big three teen magazines, 'Teen, Seventeen, and YM, position themselves in the market as magazines for Everygirl—regardless of race. But Black girls seemed to understand that in this category, every girl was White—White models, White products, a White perspective. White dominance is naturalized, an accepted and unspoken truth of mainstream media consumption.

Black girls detected bias in almost every aspect of the text: the images, the products featured, the behaviors portrayed, the topics covered. The breadth of the magazines' bias remained invisible to White girls, but was all too clear to many Black girls—the mainstream teen magazine ignores or overlooks their most fundamental concerns and interests as African Americans:

> Tonya, 17: And I was looking at (the calendar page) because . . . wanted to see if they mentioned anything about . . . African

American History Month. And it didn't. So, I flipped on. . . . They're limiting their scope . . . just including silly little things and not things that are relevant to the outside world.

Although older White girls recognized relatively few models of color in teen magazines, they argued that somehow this was less important than that the text was appropriate for all girls. The dearth of minority images was attributed to demands of the market ("Black girls don't read these magazines") and oversight ("There are usually a lot more pictures of Black girls—this is not a good issue"). White girls had no conception of how the text might change to reflect more closely the needs and concerns of Black girls; they were unaware that the world created in teen magazines was seen by older Black girls as a White one. The inclusion of more pictures of people of color would make the magazines' treatment of all girls equal in White girls' minds.

Younger Black girls, too, were generally less aware of the bias older Black girls detected; this may be due to their greater desire to fit in to the dominant picture and be addressed as a teen girl rather than a Black teen girl, as predicted by racial identity theory. Older Black girls were more interested in being recognized as African Americans. Such recognition would go beyond a superficial inclusion of more photos of people of color; girls also noted the absence of text that addressed their unique experiences, perspectives, and needs as Black people:

> Nicole, 17 (from focus group): Some stuff is universal. But then there's the makeup and stuff you can't relate to, and it's like, you know, we live in a White world. . . . I try not to think about stuff like that, but basically, yeah, it is.

Cultural Relevance: The Real vs. the Ideal

Real content was what many African American girls looked and yearned for in the text—a way of thinking about and seeing the world consistent with their experience as members of a particular minority culture. For example, some of the girls saw the problem pages, with letters from girls looking for answers they could find nowhere else, as more real than other kinds of content:

> Shawn, 17: "Sex and Body Talk.". . . The cool thing about that is that people are asking real questions in here . . . Like people who are scared to ask questions to other people and you can find the answer in the magazine. I always look at that.

Few other kinds of content were described as real. In fact, Black girls consistently criticized teen magazines for departures from what they thought of as real. *Not real* was seen as expected content oriented to Anglo/Americans. It was material that presented a literally monochrome picture of youth, without nuance, texture, and color:

> Kira, 17 (from focus group): I know it's a majority White clientele, but (the magazine) goes to all types of people and it's not realistic these days to have a whole magazine full of White people and the token Black girl . . . 'Cause they know that more than only White people subscribe to this magazine. They just get one Black person—you have no Latinos, no Asian Americans, nothing. Stupid.

Not real were formulaic stories with predictable endings that came too soon and too easily:

> Tonya, 17: [This is a story about] the girl who's . . . gonna be on this Lifetime Special . . . "Fifteen and Pregnant." . . . I just wanted to see how they portrayed it . . .
> Interviewer: Do you have any friends that are pregnant or were pregnant?
> Tonya: Yeah . . . they're just as immature now as when they got pregnant. I can see [the Lifetime Special] . . . making her have this transformation, like she's this woman now and knows all.

Not real was presenting minor setbacks as tragedies, written from a perspective that routinely put relatively simple problems center stage:

> Interviewer: Did anything in "Romance" pertain to you?

Shelly, 17: No, it was actually corny. . . . She had tryouts, everybody thought she made it, but she didn't. Her boyfriend brought her roses. Her family took her shopping. I'm thinking, "Oh, this isn't reality. I know that wouldn't happen to me." . . . My family would be like—"Go get a job now!"

Not real was not affordable to the typical middle-class girl:

Focus Group Voice 1: You wish you had the money to buy all this stuff.
    Voice 2: . . . Or if you do buy them, where are you going to wear them?

Not real was assuming an image that was perhaps socially advantageous, but directly opposed to the real you or the you others have come to know. For example, by taking on a new, more mainstream persona, singer/actress Courtney Love was seen by one Black girl as abandoning a core group of people with whom she had been strongly associated—an alliance based strongly on contrary aesthetic and cultural ideals. She also saw that the result of Love's transformation was fawning encouragement and idealization by the media:

Nicole, 17: Courtney Love . . . she's all over every fashion magazine . . . how she is so beautiful and wonderful. . . . I feel like if this was her, she would have been that way all along . . . Because she's not Cindy Crawford or anything. She's the lead singer for Hole . . . A pure grunge person like herself walking around in pastel colors and high heel, strappy shoes? . . . If I was like a hardcore fan, I probably wouldn't listen to her music anymore. . . . You'd be like "No, she used to be like me, jeans and a T-shirt. Now look."

Not real was the way the fashion and beauty industry (mis)understands or (mis)represents itself as serving all women. Not real was only showing Black women at the extreme ends of the color continuum and then placing those women in culturally incongruent places, situations, and product endorsements:

Nicole, 17: I just don't think Black people use Paul Mitchell myself, so that (ad featuring a Black model) is just a lie. My God, . . . Paul Mitchell would ruin my hair.

Not real was a recurring group of unfamiliar yet purportedly famous, beautiful, but disconcertingly homogeneous faces:

Tonya, 17: I like reading the magazine, but it doesn't have any African American or Hispanic or Asian models. . . . So even though I like reading it, sometimes I can't relate to all the things that they put inside. They could make it more realistic, with more culture.

Not real was the magazines' propensity to make interaction with boys seem intimidating or, at the very least, uncomfortable. It was magazines' implication that spending time with a boy is the most important thing a girl can do:

Tonya, 17: The theme of it (fashion spread) was the girl met a guy at some beach house and suddenly things got a lot more interesting. Like she couldn't just have a good time with her family or be realistic . . .
    Interviewer: How would you have shot it if it were your spread? . . .
    Tonya: . . . Not necessarily having to have some guy involved . . . they make it seem like boys are oxygen . . . like you have to have a guy to be a teenager.

Whereas White girls occasionally mentioned that models in the magazines were artificially made up and therefore not real, Black girls regularly commented on the lack of realism in multiple aspects of the magazine. In short, unrealistic material was that which ran contrary to African American girls' culturally situated viewpoint.

In general, African American girls felt White magazine models who were very thin or made up were not attractive; that diet products and cosmetics were not essential or even desirable for Black girls to look their best. In their eyes, personality, attitude, character, and style were the primary elements of real beauty (Duke, 2000; Parker et al., 1995). African American girls were aware of but did not accept the preferred reading, that is, the reading intended by the texts' producers. Nor did they find the unrealistic nature of the text particularly pleasurable as fantasy material.

The realism the African American girls spoke of was not the difference between the real and the imagined. After all, most girls, Black and White, recognize that mediated images routinely alter reality. White girls often spoke of wanting to see more real girls in their magazines—girls who did not look like models. But they usually passed over the occasional image of real girls in the text. White girls knew to say reality is better, but their eyes led them back to the ideal—a reality only for the limited few who work hard enough for the look. Englis (1995) has argued that, "for many who aspire to this quasi-mythical lifestyle," advertising fantasy can be perceived as real (p. 14). African American girls compared the fictional work to their real-world experience and not only denied the veracity of the ideal, but *preferred their reality* to it.

A New Class of Beauty

Within the pages of the magazine, girls saw three distinctly different classes of models. Rated on a continuum of inaccessibility, the supermodel is at the top—older than other females in the magazine, heavily made up and retouched to present an almost otherworldly beauty, usually seen only in pages financed by major national advertisers. Well-known singers, actresses, and other performers may also fall into this category. They were women the girls knew by name and by reputation; girls saw some of them on multiple pages in every magazine, every month, for years. The frequency with which this handful of women appear make their images indelible in the minds of girls—every girl in the study knew who Tyra and Claudia and Cindy are, what they look like from head to toe, and even details of their personal lives. These are the models with most power to influence how nonreaders view the ideal, because they cut across magazines and media; their images are ubiquitous.

Next on the continuum are the fresh new faces, the lesser known advertising models and models appearing in the magazines' editorial sections. These girls appear younger than the supermodels and they work in relative anonymity. Although they are seldom seen in successive magazines, they seemed vaguely similar to girls who say they all look the same. The magazines seek to personalize some of these models by offering information about them, but girls seemed most interested in learning their ages. To many of the girls in this study, Black and White, these models were a departure from supermodels in that they are more like Everygirl: beautiful, but not exceptionally so. However, most Black girls paid very little attention to the appearance of models. For example, Kira was a reticent reader; she only looked at *Seventeen* because her fashion and beauty magazine of choice, *YSB* (oriented to young, single, black girls), was no longer being published. Kira never commented on the models. When asked about the White model wearing a bathing suit she liked, she said, "I didn't even notice her." She turned great clumps of pages when she came to the articles containing beauty advice. "Yeah, because, to tell you the truth, they have nothing to do with me. 'Cause I don't have that kind of hair, so I have no use to look at them."

In 1994, these two levels of models—well-known supermodels and celebrities and anonymous professional models—dominated the pages of teen magazines. Virtually none of these were women of color, but the few who appeared were said by Black participants to conform closely to Anglo/American beauty standards. In recent years, however, the magazines have introduced a new level of model: real girls who, though attractive, find their ways into magazines because of their style and accomplishments and because they exemplify a particular regional appeal. Last on the continuum from supermodel to nonmodel, and closest to the reader, these girls are most frequently seen in "School Zone," a recurring *Seventeen* feature in which students from a specific high school are highlighted for their unique styles. This feature was intriguing to most participants in this study—Black and White—because School Zone was populated with girls who were real (in contrast to fake professional models) and diverse.

Black girls looked at the real girls in features like School Zone and saw people like themselves and their friends. They liked what they saw. If she could be anyone in the magazine, Tonya, an African American girl, said she would not choose a model but a girl in the School Zone feature because "she seems pretty cool." With features like School Zone, girls were given the chance to look beyond appearance to know more about the faces on the pages—where the featured teens live, what they think, how they coexist with others different from themselves. School Zone teens are often pictured naturally, in groups of friends, in actual school settings. Girls seemed to be attracted to this feature, its models, and their presentations because they are so distinctly different from the typical magazine fare.

For example, Shawn, a Black girl, prided herself on being able to blend with different groups of students at her school. When she read, she sought out *Seventeen*'s School Zone feature with black-and-white photos of real best friends from different schools across the country. She said she would like her best friends to be featured in a story. She pointed to people who are physically dissimilar with particular interest, "I think that they have totally different personalities and it's cool they go together."

School Zone was influential on a number of levels, not least as a source of fashion ideas. The clothes worn in this section are chosen not by advertisers and magazine stylists, but by teens. Girls seemed to be able to tell the difference. Another Black girl, Faith, was drawn to the School Zone feature because, "All that other stuff (fashions) . . . it don't look like something I would wear. And much of this stuff . . . looks okay."

School Zone gave girls an opportunity to see how teens in other parts of the country and world negotiate some of the same appearance and personal style issues with which they struggle. School Zone was one of the most favorably mentioned features in all the magazines, but it is but a small part of a single title. The use of real girls in teen magazines gave the text greater relevance to the African American girls in this study, even when the real girls were White.

Black girls consistently responded favorably to images that reflected the naturalism and greater variety of facial features and body types that they embrace as beautiful.

Reading against the Mainstream: Why Girls Persist

With the exception of the rare feature like School Zone, Black girls were excluded from mainstream teen magazines in a number of ways—looking past a bevy of White models to the text, Black girls still failed to see representation of their lives or the lives of the majority of Black people. Black girls saw advertised products and ways of interrelating as race specific. Even characters in a story were ascribed a race based on cultural clues: One girl said she knew a story was about a White woman because it was about adoption and she did not know many Black people who adopt babies. The same girl noted that certain clothing brands mentioned in the text were White brands. Even girls whose lives were comfortably middle-class identified the affluent lifestyles portrayed in fashion/beauty magazines as "White":

> Nicole, 17: . . . Black people in general, they don't buy Gucci pants . . . They buy what's affordable . . . I'm sure like Oprah probably is like that . . . but not like the average Black woman.

For comparison, a copy of an all-Black teen magazine, *Sisters In Style*, was introduced during the interviews. Although some of the Black girls responded favorably to the publication, especially to the boys it featured, an equal number rated the magazine negatively or said it was not for them. Older girls took issue with what they saw as the shoddy production values and shallow content of *Sisters in Style*. Tonya, 17, who defined herself as a reader, was unimpressed by the magazine. "At least with *Seventeen* . . . you go into a little depth." *Sisters In Style*, she says, "is a lot of pictures, very little words." At the postinterview focus group, even Kira, 17, who initially favored the all-Black publication, questioned its quality standards: "I need more than pretty pictures of (male music star). At least, *Seventeen*, you've got a variety of things you can read about. I wouldn't spend my money for some pictures and maybe two articles." Nicole, 17, also disliked that the publication was printed on a low quality stock that made for poor photographic reproduction; in addition, she objected to the magazine's idealization of young Black girls lacking the sophistication she exemplified and sought:

> Nicole, 17: The little Black teenagers they have in there just look cheesy . . . I'm not like that! . . . They're the little Black girls with the braids and little funky haircuts . . . Or they're still in the baggy pants . . . It's like you look at that and think, "Hmm, I'm a young Black teenage person and that's how I'm supposed to look." And you don't think about what *you* like anymore. It's based on what you see. And . . . I don't want to be like that.

Most African American girls in this study were generally dissatisfied with being segregated into a niche magazine audience. Over and over, Black girls stressed their desire for greater inclusion in the well-produced, widely available teen magazines read by the majority of teen girls. But they also expressed a desire to include more people of all ethnic and racial backgrounds in mainstream publications. When asked what they might include if they edited a magazine just for Black girls, African American participants frequently rejected the notion that their magazine should serve an exclusive target:

> Melissa, 13: I wouldn't make a magazine just for Black girls . . . It would have an equal amount of Black and White people . . . All different kinds of colors . . . Asian guys and Black guys and White guys.

To achieve fairer representation, Black girls say magazines need to consider not only the color of the models they use, but also editorial and advertising. The Black girls in this study want greater diversity in the types of beauty products teen magazines feature, the images of success they portray, and the breadth of cultural experience they address.

DISCUSSION

Englis (1995) has noted marketers' tendency to "assume all consumers are attracted by alluring images of young, urban upscale Caucasian success" (p. 16) and has underscored the need for research that focuses on the marketing implications of consumers' group memberships. Fiske (1988) has preferred Altman's (1986) conception of the text as a menu, from which the audience selects items and creates meanings relevant to their social and cultural perspectives. Participants in this study exemplify this view; in some instances, they demonstrated their agency through "partial consumption," that is, they took from teen magazines the material they judged to be truly "generic," or that meshed with their views as African Americans. Black girls in this study also routinely assumed an anticonsumption attitude by ignoring or negatively critiquing material that they felt reflected an unalloyed Anglo/American focus and an ideology of *White* femininity. Indeed, critique of the limited and idealized presentations of femininity in mainstream teen magazines constituted a large part of Black girls' interpretative act.

The middle-class African American girls in this study make up what Fish (1980) would call an "interpretive community" in that, by virtue of their membership in a marginalized group, they voiced similar interpretations of much of the material in mainstream teen magazines. Although these girls did not speak as a univocal mass, they did share assumptions about the nature and purpose of the text and developed strategies for constructing meanings that differ from the audience majority. Although the African American girls in this study read mainstream teen magazines regularly, they did not engage the texts as fully as did White girls, for simple reasons: They did not see their values in the magazines. They did not see products they can use. Their tastes and attitudes were watered down or ignored. Their family and friends were nominally visible. They did not see *themselves*. And yet, teen magazines claim African American girls as part of their target audience and these girls represent a significant percentage of the readership.

Especially for older Black girls, a primary gratification for reading these magazines was not aspiration to, but critique of, the ideals reflected in the text. Thus, these girls gain a greater sense of solidarity with other Black girls and affirm the value of a more inclusive African American beauty culture. In this sense, then, mainstream teen magazines are more than mere commodities—"they are goods to think with, goods to speak with" (Fiske, 1989, p. 30); what is said and thought, however, may be diametrically opposed to the text producer's preferred reading, depending on the cultural context of the reader.

In mainstream teen magazines, White girls are presented with material that largely reflects, reinforces, or amplifies their individual and cultural ideals. Black girls, on the other hand, recognize that the bulk of material in these magazines conflicts with the interests and ideals of most African Americans. When girls in this study noticed a disparity between their lived reality and the reality presented in teen magazines, they typically moved toward resolution of this difference in one of two ways: White girls were more likely to adjust their sense of reality in order to accommodate ideas and images presented in teen magazines. For example, one White participant commented that real teenage girls didn't look like the models in *Seventeen*. A few moments later, she reversed herself, saying some girls *must* look like the models, "People are born like that . . . they don't all get pimples." The feminine ideal presented in mainstream teen magazines is just close enough to White girls' reality to appear attainable—all a girl need do is master the diet, exercise, fashion, and makeup regimens promoted by the magazines. Pursuit of excellence in these four areas of appearance enhancement frequently enticed White girls into the marketplace in search of the newest and best tools available for replicating the feminine ideal presented in the text. Month after month, White girls who buy into the ritual of beautification through consumption end up back at the table of contents of their favorite teen magazine, seeking the latest information on beauty by the book.

African American girls are not oblivious to beauty standards; they do, for example, enjoy fashion, purchase hair products, and have their nails done, as do many White girls. However, African American girls were far less likely to embrace the idea perpetuated by teen magazines that beauty can be bought; they resisted the notion that a girl's attractiveness, her social standing, her very identity, are inextricably linked with commodity consumption (Agger, 1992, and Pringle, 1983, cited in Duke & Kreshel, 1998, p. 50). For example, most African American girls in this study used no cosmetics and saw no need for them. In mainstream fashion/beauty texts, White girls see and strive for "better" versions of themselves. For the Black girls, however, exclusion from these publications seemed to bolster anticonsumption attitudes, leading them to reject the magazines' central premise that their looks, their lives, their reality, could be improved if they conformed more closely to the mediated feminine ideal.

Black girls easily perceived the teen magazines they read as targeting White girls—however, they were able to take what was useful from the text nonetheless. As one African American girl pointed out, "Just because it's a White magazine doesn't necessarily make it a bad magazine." Black girls' response to exclusion was simply to continue reading until they found material to which they could relate—as Bobo (1995) has noted, "we have learned to ferret out the beneficial and put up blinders against the rest" (p. 55). Unlike White girls, who frequently consume teen magazines in search of transformation, African American girls sought information, for example, about social issues, relationships, and health. Material such as issue-oriented features (e.g., on abortion or drug use), some of the fashion articles, problem pages, horoscopes, quizzes, and venues where readers share their most embarrassing moments were of interest to girls of all races, but Black girls were interested in little else teen magazines had to offer.

This study demonstrates the power of interpretive communities to resist the dominant culture's "generic" consumer appeals. Indeed, Fiske (1989) has argued "semiotic resistance"—one example of which is African American girls' denigration of Eurocentric beauty messages in mainstream teen magazines as *not real*—"results from the desire for the subordinate to exert control over the meanings of their lives" (p. 10). Thus, the Black girls in this study derived a sense of power and indeed, pleasure, from critiquing beauty images that did not reflect their ideals. Rather than subvert their identities to an unattainable mediated standard, they used the text to help consolidate self- and racial identities.

In this study, younger African American girls (ages 13 and 14) did not consciously engage the text with as strong a racial orientation as older girls (ages 17 and 18). They did not seem as conscious of the racial bias older African American girls said was inherent in the magazines. Older Black girls consistently self-identified positively and in opposition to "White" standards; for example, several girls commented on the overemphasis they believed White girls and teen magazines put on looks and male/female relationships, and declared that Black girls were too sensible to act similarly.

Media critics who worry that texts such as teen magazines present girls with a false sense of reality and unrealistic ideals need to qualify their statements. Asking which girls and whose reality may lead to new avenues of inquiry as researchers continue to explore how patterns of consumption are used to differentiate groups and mark social boundaries (Englis, 1995).

Even if minority girls judge teen magazine images of girls of color as inauthentic, what might the long-term effect of exposure be—greater assimilation into the dominant view, passive resistance, or ongoing anticonsumption and ideological opposition? These are questions that can only be addressed by more research that accommodates the culturally situated responses of girls, and by researchers who approach participants as active, engaged members of increasingly challenging markets.

Note

1. Participants are described as African American or Black, interchangeably, or White, as participants used these terms.

References

Agger, B. (1992). *Cultural Studies as Critical Theory.* London: Falmer.

Altman, R. (1986). Television/sound. In T. Modleski (Ed.), *Studies in Entertainment: Critical Approaches to Mass Culture*, pp. 39–54. Bloomington: Indiana University Press.

Atkin, D. (1992). An analysis of television series with minority-lead characters. *Critical Studies in Mass Communication*, 9:337–350.

Bell-Scott, P., & McKenry, P. C. (1986). Black adolescents and their families. In G. K. Leigh & G. W. Peterson (Eds.), *Adolescents in Families*, pp. 410–432. Mason, OH: South-Western Publishing.

Bobo, J. (1995). The color purple: Black women as cultural readers. In G. Dines & J. M. Humez (Eds.), *Gender, Race, and Class in Media: A Text Reader.* Thousand Oaks, CA: Sage.

Bourne, S. C. (1990). The African American image in American cinema. *Black Scholar*, 21:12–19.

Bowen, L., & Schmid, J. (1997). Minority presence and portrayal in mainstream magazine advertising: An update. *Journalism and Mass Communication Quarterly*, 74:134–146.

Budgeon, S. (1994). Fashion magazine advertising: Constructing "femininity" in the "postfeminist" era. In L. Manca & A. Manca (Eds.), *Gender and Utopia in Advertising: A Critical Reader.* Lisle, IL: Precopian Press.

Crabtree, B. F., & Miller, W. L. (1992). *Doing Qualitative Research.* Newbury Park, CA: Sage.

Currie, D. H. (1996). Decoding femininity: Advertisements and their teenage readers. *Gender and Society*, 11:453–478.

Duke, L. L. (2000). Black in a blonde world: Race and girls' interpretations of the feminine ideal in teen magazines. *Journalism and Mass Communication Quarterly*, 77: 367–392.

Duke, L. L., & Kreshel, P. (1998). Negotiating femininity: Girls in early adolescence read teen magazines. *Journal of Communication Inquiry*, 22:48–71.

Endicott, R. C. (2000, June 12). Ad Age 300. *Advertising Age*, 51–60.

Englis, B. G. (1995). To be or not to be: Lifestyle imagery, reference groups, and the clustering of America. *Journal of Advertising*, 24: 13–16.

Evans, E. D., Rutberg, J., Sather, C., & Turner, C. (1991). Content analysis of contemporary teen magazines for adolescent females. *Youth and Society*, 23:99–120.

Fish, S. (1980). *Is There a Text in This Class? The Authority of Interpretive Communities*. Cambridge, MA: Harvard University Press.

Fiske, J. (1988). Critical response: Meaningful moments. *Critical Studies in Mass Communication*, 5:246–250.

Fiske, J. (1989). *Reading the Popular*. Boston: Unwin Hyman.

Frisby, C. M. (2000, August). Black like me: How idealized images of Caucasian women affect body esteem and mood states of African American females. Paper presented at the Association for Education in Journalism and Mass Communications, Phoenix.

Gitlin, T. (1983). *Inside Prime Time*. New York: Pantheon.

Jackson, L. A., & Kelly, S. E. (1991). The frequency and portrayal of black females in fashion advertisements. *The Journal of Black Psychology*, 18:67–70.

Leeds, M. (1994). Young African American women and the language of beauty. In K. I. Callaghan (Ed.), *Ideals of Feminine Beauty: Philosophical, Social and Cultural Dimensions*. Westport, CT: Greenwood Press.

McRobbie, A. (1978). *Jackie!: An Ideology of Adolescent Femininity*. Birmingham, England: The Centre for Contemporary Cultural Studies.

Milkie, M. A. (1999). Social comparisons, reflected appraisals, and mass media: The impact of pervasive beauty images on black and white girls' self-concepts. *Social Psychology Quarterly*, 62:190–192.

Parker, S., Nichter, M., Nichter, M., & Vuckovic, N. (1995). Body image and weight concerns among African American and White adolescent females: Differences that make a difference. *Human Organization*, 54:103–114.

Prendergast, P., Zdep, S. M., & Sepulveda, P. (1974). Self image among a national probability sample of girls. *Child Study Journal*, 4:103–114.

Pringle, R. (1983). Women and consumer capitalism. In C. V. Bladock & B. Cass (Eds.), *Women, Social Welfare and the State in Australia*, pp. 85–103. Sydney, Australia: Allen & Unwin.

Smith, E. J. (1982). The Black female adolescent: A review of the educational, career and psychological literature. *Psychology of Women Quarterly*, 6:261–288.

Stevenson, T. H., & Stevenson, W. J. (1988). A longitudinal study of Blacks in magazine advertising: 1946–1986. In *Proceedings of the Annual Meeting of the Southern Marketing Association*, pp. 75–78. Carbondale, IL: Southern Marketing Association.

Thompson, C. J., & Haytko, D. L. (1997). Speaking of fashion: Consumers' uses of fashion discourses and the appropriation of countervailing cultural meanings. *Journal of Consumer Research*, 24:15–28.

Ukadike, N. E. (1990). Western film images of Africa: Genealogy of an ideological formulation. *Black Scholar*, 21:30–48.

Zinkhan, G. M., Qualls, W. J., & Biswas, A. (1990). The use of Blacks in magazine and television advertising: 1946–1986. *Journalism Quarterly*, 67:547–553.

"Just Because It's a White Magazine..."

1. There are a few African-American models in teen magazines today. Why, then, did the African-American girls detect ethnic bias in the mainstream teen magazines?

2. Why did the African-American girls read *Seventeen*, *YM*, or *Teen* magazines? There are a few teen magazines targeted to African-Americans, so why don't they prefer them? What gratifications do they get from the mainstream magazines?

3. What long-term effects would seeing a lack of representation of people like the self in the media have on an individual?

4. Ethnic minorities are underrepresented in advertising. Yet, despite limited appearance role models in mainstream media, African-American girls tend to have higher body satisfaction than do European-American girls. Why is this the case?

CHAPTER 9

Dressing throughout Adulthood

Mary Lynn Damhorst

AFTER YOU HAVE READ THIS CHAPTER, YOU WILL COMPREHEND:

- The many ways in which dress and appearance are an important part of adulthood.

- The physical and social aspects of dress and adult development.

- How identity and appearance change throughout adult life.

- How personal history is reflected in dress and the body.

- That experiences and life history of a generation may be reflected in dress.

If we were trying to describe adulthood back before the 1960s, we would find greater regularities and predictability of lifespan trends across age categories. But today, trends linked to adult ages are blurring in the United States. For example, in the first half of the twentieth century during peacetime periods, most people tended to marry and begin families by their early 20s. Now, many individuals experience first marriage during their 30s and 40s. Levinson (1986) suggested that adults go through similar developmental stages, but individuals may experience those stages at varying ages. Order of major life events is becoming less predictable. The impact of this variety of consumer life-styles upon needs and preferences for apparel and other appearance-related products is substantial.

Three general stages of adulthood, which have been defined by Levinson (1986), are:

- **Early adulthood,** ages 17 to 44 years.
- **Middle adulthood,** ages 45 to 64 years.
- **Late adulthood,** ages 65 and older.

Some characteristics of life in these age ranges are examined in this chapter, and generational differences are discussed.

EARLY ADULTHOOD (17 TO 44 YEARS)

About 44 percent of the U.S. population is currently in the broad age group of early adulthood (U.S. Census Bureau, 2000). Tremendous **variety** characterizes the lives of early adults. Some individuals marry and have children soon after high school. They begin adult lives while still in adolescence. Others continue with education all the way through graduate school. Still others vacillate through periods of work and college education, resulting in a complex patchwork of roles throughout much of early adulthood. The span between the ages of 17 and 44 is a time of important decisions about marriage, divorce, home life, occupational life, and personal life. Important experiences related to family formation, occupational success, love, definition of sexuality, and realization of life goals occur for many individuals during this age span (Levinson, 1986). Clothing and appearance certainly mirror these experiences in life.

At some time during early adulthood, many individuals marry and begin to have children. Most individuals also begin careers during this age span. Because more women are working outside the home than ever before (65 percent of women aged 16 to 44, according to the Census Bureau) and a great number of single-parent households occur, family members have less time to shop. These trends are resulting in more traditionally "male" shopping patterns among adult women who are frustrated by the inefficiencies of retailers that do not cater to their time-poor lives (Vandeventer, 1993). More adult consumers now opt for mail-order and Internet purchases of apparel or shop with only a limited number of retailers who give service and styles they can depend upon. Some adults, harried by time demands, simply buy a reduced amount of goods. Shopping was an enjoyable leisure-time activity for fewer and fewer adults in the 1990s (Vandeventer, 1993).

Aging of the body begins during this time of life, though many individuals still look relatively young. Great variety occurs among individuals as to when they will start noticing changes in hair, skin, and weight. With a **double standard** still in force in society—that as men age they develop an attractive "patina," while women who age lose attractiveness—many women feel that their worth as women deteriorates with aging of the body. Nevertheless, an increasing proportion of men are now getting cosmetic surgery (Kalb, 1999). This age group in general has included active consumers of surgeries to enhance appearance. Over 35 percent of cosmetic surgery patients are under the age of 50 (Hamilton & Weingarden, 1998).

Individuals certainly approach aging in a variety of ways. Mithers, in "A New Look at Beauty, Aging and Power," examines the general fear that many women in early adulthood have about aging. She found that some women felt great terror and self-repulsion at the first signs of aging, some experienced a feeling of power in work roles and sexual relationships as they began to look older, and others talked of how they were beginning to redefine beauty among older women. Giesen (1989) found that single adult women were less apt than married women to define their attractiveness and sexual appeal on the basis of physical characteristics. Perhaps marital status and experiences influence how one thinks about the aging body. Jamie Lee Curtis exposes in "True Thighs" what is happening to her body shape now that she is in her 40s. Not many years ago she was considered a role model for thinness and fitness. As she moves toward middle age, she has developed fat patterning that does not fit Hollywood notions of beauty and glamour. Jamie now writes children's books and is developing a new career for herself that does not require a youthful appearance. She is convinced that basing one's whole sense of identity and achievement on physical beauty is a losing battle.

And what about men? Researchers have found that men are more positively biased toward youthful appearances in others (Kogan & Mills, 1992). How do men feel about themselves as they begin to age? More research would be helpful in understanding men (and women) in early adulthood.

MIDDLE ADULTHOOD (45 TO 64 YEARS)

About 22 percent of the U.S. population today is 45 to 64 years old (U.S. Census Bureau, 2000), and by the year 2020 this age group will comprise 25 percent of the United States (The Kiplinger Washington Letter, 1995). During middle age, adults tend to reach their **peak income earning years** in addition to the highest career levels they will experience (Vandeventer, 1993). That gives this group substantial consumer power in society, not to mention political and economic clout. Middle-aged individuals are more apt to take leadership roles in their professions and communities, and serve as mentors for younger adults at earlier stages of development. Middle-agers also are likely to need appropriate work clothing. Because of career and income accomplishments, they may be willing to spend more for quality in apparel than they were at earlier life-span stages.

Life hardly settles into a routine of sameness for all persons in middle age. Some individuals decide during this time to redefine career and self through shifts in responsibilities, such as moving into higher-level administrative roles in their organizations or professions or pursuing totally new careers. New job roles often require new wardrobes. Family roles change, too. Some individuals are involved in raising young families as a result of late starts on having children, while many others finally experience the "**empty nest syndrome,**" when children leave home and become self-supporting. Empty-nest parents have more money and time to spend on themselves. Apparel for travel and leisure pursuits may become a greater part of purchase patterns for empty-nest couples. During middle age, many women begin careers, start new businesses, or go back to college—pursuits delayed because of child care roles earlier in adulthood. Divorce also throws many men and women into the singles' scene, with renewed concerns about managing appearance to attract a mate. Also during middle age, adults increasingly need to take on caretaker roles for their aging parents, a role that often changes living situations, time, and income expenditures. Overall, a variety of changes in lifestyle experiences and consequent clothing needs of middle-aged individuals happens during these years.

The body also changes during middle age. During their 40s, if not sooner, men are apt to experience loss and thinning of hair if they are genetically inclined toward baldness. Graying of hair also becomes more noticeable during middle age. Interest in hair color products increases among both men and women. A decline in basal metabolism occurs in the 40s for most men and women, resulting in weight gain if the individual does not substantially increase exercise and decrease food intake (Garner, 1997). Most people cannot sustain their thinner early adult body size, in many cases because of lack of time for increased exercise and an unwillingness to go hungry all the time. Wrinkles and facial lines start to appear, making the market for moisturizers and "age-defying" cosmetics increase for this age group. Tanning, if still pursued, takes an ever-greater toll on skin texture and dryness. In essence, aging and its effects on the body become more apparent during middle age.

North America, in particular, has a **culture obsessed with youthfulness.** Signs of aging do not fit with cultural ideals for attractiveness. Victoria Secunda (1984) suggested that the United States is so obsessed with the physical self that we feel that as aging deteriorates the body, the self also degrades and "depreciates." The fear of physical obsolescence associated with aging leads increasing numbers of men and women during middle age to resort to body modifications that restore youthfulness or delay the appearance of aging. Most middle-aged individuals want to look younger and increasingly feel that it is acceptable to try to look younger (Harris, 1994). Many adopt hair, skin, and cosmetic surgery treatments to delay signs of aging. In "Move Over, Tupperware," Creager describes the recently developing trend of using Botox injections to temporarily erase facial creases and wrinkles. Just a few years ago, the combination of the words *Botox* and *parties* in one sentence would have seemed absurd, due to the deadly nature of the poison. But careful injection in tiny quantities can make a face appear more youthful.

We should expect in a youth-oriented society that many men and women would experiment with a variety of products and processes to deal with their aging bodies. It could also be logically deduced that body dissatisfaction during middle aging should increase at substantial rates. Surprisingly, studies do not find a substantial increase in body dissatisfaction among middle-aged men and women in comparison to younger age groups (Garner, 1997). Perhaps as the individual ages, new standards for attractiveness are personally devised, and impossibly young media images are rejected as role models. Or maybe by middle age, the importance of appearance begins to decrease as individuals find themselves engrossed in work, family, and personal accomplishments that they feel are more important indicators of the self. Ogle and Damhorst (in press) found that women in their 40s developed new notions of identity grounded in aspects of the self other than appearance. These redefinitions probably help middle-aging women to maintain a positive sense of self. Further research is needed to uncover the strategies middle-aged individuals use to psychologically cope with the aging body.

By middle age, individuals have lived and dressed themselves through decades of fashion changes. It seems intuitively logical that many would have defined and settled into a preferred personal style by this age (cf. Eckman, 1997). This phenomenon deserves further research. However, many middle-aged consumers still want to look current and do not reject all fashion changes. The fashion industry seems to hold the general stereotype that middle-aged individuals are boring and uninterested in fashion and that fashion is really defined and led by the young. If fashion is only what is new, hot, and cutting-edge, perhaps the industry should focus only on the young. But recall our definition of fashion in Chapter 1: Fashion is a collectivity, that is, what is seen as appropriate and attractive within a group. With middle-agers so numerous in the population and with greater spending power than at prior stages of life, firms who listen carefully to market segments in this age group could do very well in profits (Waldrop, 1990). With so many individuals above the age of 40, does a relentless emphasis on youthfulness and thinness in fashion make good business sense? The advertisement in Figure 9.1 shows a recent effort to target an older market segment. Such

FIGURE 9.1 *Older model for Linda Allard for Ellen Tracy. Models who appear 60 and above are rare in the fashion press.*

efforts are slowly becoming more common. Nevertheless, relative invisibility of older individuals in media still pervades.

LATE ADULTHOOD (65 YEARS AND OLDER)

It is difficult to know what label to use when discussing late adulthood. Such terms as *elderly, elder, mature,* and *older* are somehow imprecise or laden with negative connotations. Perhaps only in a culture so youth-obsessed as is the United States do we find ourselves in such a quandary to use politically correct terms when referring to the aging population. The aging American knows far too well, however, that the appearance of old age can serve as a **stigma.** The media often stereotype older persons as fragile, helpless, incompetent, ugly, unproductive, and even silly (Kaiser & Chandler, 1985). And many institutions and individuals act as if they believe the stereotype is generally true. Cynthia Rich, in "Ageism and the Politics of Beauty," discusses the revulsion we have toward the aging body. In myriad ways, older people, particularly women, are told that they are ugly, asexual, and "out to pasture." Older persons are underrepresented in the media and are often degraded as foolish or incompetent (Greco, 1989; Vesperi, 2001). With about 12 percent of the U.S. population in this age group now and a projected 16 percent or more of the population in late adulthood by 2020, can we afford to pigeonhole so many people so narrowly and negatively (U.S. Census Bureau, 2000)?

As among other adult age stages, individuals in late adulthood lead quite varied lives and place different importance on appearance and fashion (Greco, 1986). Joy Kozar (see "Older Women's Attitudes toward Aging, Appearance Changes, and Clothing") interviewed older women and found that they were interested in clothing and concerned with appearance, despite stereotypes that older people don't care about how they look. The women who were interested in appearance when they were younger carried those interests on into their older years.

George Moschis (1996) found that state of **health** and degree of interest in **social activity** were major variables distinguishing older consumer segments. He divided older consumers into four market segments: (1) healthy indulgers, (2) ailing outgoers, (3) healthy hermits, and (4) frail recluses. These segments, although oversimplified, give some sense of diversity among this age group. An individual may move in and out of more than one of these segments during the elder years.

The "healthy indulgers" segment includes retired individuals who focus on enjoying life and doing things they always wanted to do when they were younger, such as travel, attending community events, and socializing with friends and extended family. This group tends to be in good health and is financially better off than many middle-agers. They need clothing for active lifestyles, but may shift their expenditures to leisure rather than work-related apparel (Lee et al., 1997). "Ailing outgoers" are also a socially active group. Despite having experienced major health problems, they want to get the most out of life and keep as active as possible. This group is interested in looking socially acceptable, but are a prime market segment for mail-order purchases, probably because of the physical demands of in-store shopping. This group also expresses a desire for functional clothing with easy dressing features.

Not all older persons are quite so outgoing. Moschis found a sizeable number of "healthy hermits," individuals whose health is good but who withdraw psychologically and socially to some extent. Many in this segment have experienced challenging life events such as the loss of a spouse. Despite their more limited socializing, healthy hermits emphasize conformity in clothing and will pay more for well-known brands that give confidence in quality and acceptability.

"Frail recluses" have experienced greater levels of physical decline, which reduces their ability to go out and be socially active. They are more apt to accept old age status. The numbers of individuals with serious health problems become greater as age increases. This is, in part, why expenditures for apparel tend to peak around age 68 and steadily decrease with increasing age (Lee et al., 1997). Other possible reasons for decreasing expenditures include such factors as reduced wear and tear put on clothing as activity decreases, reduced interest in buying clothing as concerns about limits of retirement income increase, and less need for more expensive work and formal clothing.

As aging progresses, all individuals are apt to experience many common physical changes, as illustrated for aging women in Figure 9.2. Tierney (1987) describes changes in the aging body. Both men and women lose an inch or more in height as a result of wearing down of cartilage between the bones. Gravity takes its toll via sagging and wrinkling of skin, and aging

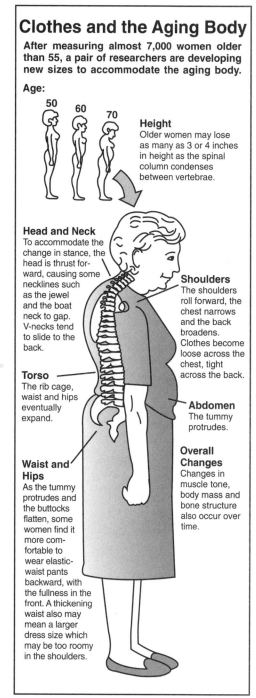

Clothes and the Aging Body

After measuring almost 7,000 women older than 55, a pair of researchers are developing new sizes to accommodate the aging body.

Age:

50   60   70

Height
Older women may lose as many as 3 or 4 inches in height as the spinal column condenses between vertebrae.

Head and Neck
To accommodate the change in stance, the head is thrust forward, causing some necklines such as the jewel and the boat neck to gap. V-necks tend to slide to the back.

Shoulders
The shoulders roll forward, the chest narrows and the back broadens. Clothes become loose across the chest, tight across the back.

Torso
The rib cage, waist and hips eventually expand.

Abdomen
The tummy protrudes.

Overall Changes
Changes in muscle tone, body mass and bone structure also occur over time.

Waist and Hips
As the tummy protrudes and the buttocks flatten, some women find it more comfortable to wear elastic-waist pants backward, with the fullness in the front. A thickening waist also may mean a larger dress size which may be too roomy in the shoulders.

FIGURE 9.2 *Many changes occur as the body ages.*

spots and other pigmentation problems will probably also occur. Clothing designs that hide wrinkled and discolored areas are often preferred by this age segment. Although weight gains tend to slow down after age 60, gravity resettles body weight downward. The waist thickens in men and women, and chest muscles and bustlines tend to sag. As muscles weaken, many individuals stand less erect. Loss of muscle control for urinary elimination requires some older people to use adult diapers, an embarrassing adjustment for some individuals (Dychtwald & Flower, 1989).

Joint and skeletal problems become more common, in some cases requiring special fitting of clothing to adjust to curvature of the spine. Arthritis is more common in late adulthood and can reduce a person's ability to reach and to manipulate fingers; easy dressing features such as front zippers and larger buttons may be helpful. The skin thins and dries out as it grows older, making aging individuals more sensitive to rough textures, heat, and cold. Further decline in basal metabolism also increases cooling of the body (Dychtwald & Flower, 1989). Layering of clothing can give flexibility in dealing with sensitivity to temperature. Need for moisturizers, skin care products, and protection from the sun increases. Sallow skin and gray hair may change an individual's choice of color in apparel and makeup.

Despite all of the probable body changes, aging adults have not been found to have lower levels of body satisfaction than individuals in younger adult groups (Garner, 1997). As they age, women often become more content with their bodies (Oberg & Tornstam, 2001). As among middle-agers, women in late adulthood may readjust their standards for what is satisfactory. Kaiser and Chandler (1985) found that men who were judged attractive by older adults were neat and well-dressed. Appearing healthy also may have high importance in assessments of attractiveness. In addition, more emphasis may be put on attractiveness of men among older married couples. Peterson and Miller (1980) found that couples who thought that the husband was attractive tended to have more positive marital relationships. The wife's level of attractiveness was not a factor in marital satisfaction. Do older couples simply ignore the wife's appearance because of the societal notion that older women cannot be attractive? That is a frightening thought!

Marital status also has an influence on expenditures for dress among older persons. Single women in this age group spend more on clothing (Lee et al., 1997), possibly as a result of independence in spending patterns, but also in part because of renewed interest in dating and attracting a new mate after losing a spouse. Romance does not necessarily end with retirement.

THE FLOW OF SELF-HISTORY

Adulthood, just like childhood and adolescence, is a time of continuing changes and developments (Secunda, 1984). Dress and feelings about the body reflect the **dynamic lifespan process** at any age. Clothing and the body have **histories**—histories that remind us of critical and valuable moments and experiences in life. "Integral to a sense of who we are is a sense of our past" (Belk, 1988, p. 148).

Our body histories very much shape our identities. The way we look in childhood and adolescence perhaps never fully leaves our sense of self. Hanan al-Shaykh ("Inside a Moroccan Bath") tells the cross-cultural history of her body. As a young woman in Beirut, she experienced great disappointment and constant taunting by others that she was too thin. Women in Arabic cultures are perceived as more attractive if they have fuller, rounded bodies. Her adult life spent in Europe helped her to redefine her thinness as attractive because of the Western preference for thinness. She is surprised, however, to have feelings of deficiency flood back to herself when she visits a North African culture later in her adulthood.

Our identities are shaped by responses from others (see Chapter 4). Even through adulthood, appearance expresses our identity, and responses from others toward appearance help us to assess who we are among others. We compare ourselves to others throughout life in the fluid process that is the self.

GENERATION EFFECTS

People born during the same era in time within a culture experience the same historic events and share many life experiences. Patterns of consumer behavior, including dress, emerge to reflect the times in which people live. And **generations,** or **age cohort** groups, shape the times in which they live. We will take a look at characteristics of most adult generations living today. Their characteristics are grossly generalized when talking about generations. Divisions between generations are, of course, not as clear as the division by years implies.

Older Generations

Americans in late adulthood include individuals described by Strauss and Howe (1991) as born during the **Great Power era** in the United States. All of the G.I. generation (born between 1901 and 1924) and most of the so-called Silent generation (born between 1925 and 1942) lived through the challenges of the Great Depression and World War II (Strauss & Howe, 1991). They lived and worked during an era when great programs were undertaken to expand science, technology, medicine, and industry. Government also undertook huge programs in social services such as Social Security and welfare.

These generations grew up in times when fashion trends were shaped to a great extent by Paris and top designers. Conformity and formality in dress were common in everyday life. Men wore suits to work, and women would dress up to go shopping. Gender roles were traditionally oriented to men in the workplace and women taking care of the home; the norm of wearing skirts for going out of the home, trim and defined waistlines, and bustline focus in women's fashions helped to emphasize gender differences. Their early life experiences still seem to shape clothing attitudes of the older generations to some extent. The Depression years experience seemed to instill a sense of frugalness in many and an aversion to spending too lavishly on a wardrobe, though the sense of what is frugal varies with socioeconomic status. The appreciation of science and technical progress helped make this generation highly positive about synthetic fibers and durable press finishes—attitudes that may shape purchase preferences still today.

Middle-Aging Baby Boomers

A phenomenal increase in the birth rate in the United States occurred between 1946 and 1964. People born during those years are often called the **Baby Boom generation** (Light, 1988). This huge population group has dominated fashion trends and consumer behavior greatly during the last half of the twentieth century, due to their market power and visibility. This generation has fundamentally shaped the times in which it has lived (Strauss & Howe, 1991).

The baby boom is actually two generations: (1) 1946–1954 (early boomers) and (2) 1955–1964 (later boomers). Both groups are characterized by great diversity (Light, 1988). Yet, all baby boomers have lived through a time when:

- A revolution in social values occurred. The boomers ushered in the postmodern era with their questioning of the Vietnam War and anything "establishment." Nontraditional thinking about the meaning and stability of marriage, women's roles, and sexual freedom became commonplace during the boomers' adolescence and young adulthood. New norms of modesty and expanded options for women's dress came along with those changes.

- More baby boomers completed high school and went on to some college than was ever seen in earlier generations. The overall higher level of education may be why boomers have more appreciation of the importance of style in consumer products than did their parents.

- This is the first TV generation, so it has been able to learn about fashion trends faster than did previous generations.

- Boomers grew up in an age when federal antidiscrimination laws were under expansion. The diverse group hates labeling and stereotyping. They also see status distinctions as formalities that put up obstacles to close, meaningful interaction. Their lack of tolerance of great formality lead to boomer managers implementing casual dress codes for businesses in the '90s. Society in general has moved toward increasing casualness of manners, rules, and dress during their lifetime (Adler, 1995).

- Among boomers, there are more singles who never married and more divorced (almost one-half of their marriages failed) than found in previous generations. This generation includes many who don't rely on a mate for development of self-identity. Some suggest that this makes a generation of consumers who are more independent about developing personal style.

- This generation, which idolizes diversity, demands more choices in product availability. Hence, mail and now Internet and TV shopping have provided more options and less reliance on limited local sources.

(see Light, 1988).

Older and younger baby boomers differ in some ways. For example, older boomers may be more politically idealistic, having participated in protests of the Vietnam War and other political turmoil in the 1960s and early 1970s. Younger boomers experienced greater levels of divorce among their own parents and also a number of economic recessions as they were entering the workforce. Paul Light (1988) suggested that younger boomers have substituted greater levels of materialism over idealism, due to greater instabilities during their younger lives.

Young Adult Xers

Generation X (born between 1965 and 1976) dominates early adulthood today. This generation is more cynical than the baby boomers and has questioned many of their norms (Strauss & Howe, 1991). They marry later, start families later, and have exhibited even greater variety in living patterns than did the boomers as young adults (Paul, 2002). But now, they have settled into worklife and, for over 50 percent, parenthood, making them a strong market for work dress and children's clothing (Paul, 2002).

Some analysts suggest that this generation, relatively small in numbers in the population, has had to work harder to get noticed. Hence, some extreme fashion and in-your-face appearance statements have emerged with Xers. For example, tattooing and piercing grew in popularity with this generation. Punk and new wave styles adopted by this generation in the 1970s and 1980s reflected a sense of aimlessness and meaninglessness that contrasted with the boomers' endless search for meanings in life. However, Generation X eagerly adopted and expanded on some of the boomers' innovations, such as jeans and casual dress trends, postmodern questioning of traditional rules for aesthetic combinations, acceptance of diversity in appearance, and expression of sexuality in dress. The increased influence of ethnic minority groups (i.e., rap styles) on fashion changes emerged with Generation X. Men in this generation adopted earrings and increasing use of a wide array of grooming products to exhibit greater androgyny in dress (see "Turning Boys into Girls" in Chapter 5). At the same time, Xer men more often worked out and sometimes used steroids to pump up muscles, and women wore revealing short skirts and low-cut tops, sometimes to work. Androgyny and sex differentiation have been displayed simultaneously.

Newbee Adults

Though some would argue that they are part of Generation X, the older members of **Generation Y** (born 1977 to 1994) have moved into adulthood (Weiss, 2003). They are almost as numerous as baby boomers, but are so far more stylistically similar to Gen Xers. Their numbers should lend them tremendous influence on fashion and lifestyle changes in society.

Whereas many boomer parents talk a lot about the importance of tolerance of diversity, Gen Ys live diversity. About one in three 21-year-olds is not European-American (Weiss, 2003). Their fashion influences frequently come from ethnic minority groups (see "Generación Latino" in Chapter 10).

When they were young, boomers rebelled noticeably against their parents, but Yers feel connected to theirs (Strauss & Howe, 1991). They are wearing styles such as boot-cut jeans introduced by their parents in the 1960s.

Unlike previous generations of young people, Gen Yers are skeptical consumers of traditional advertising (Weiss, 2003). They are much less brand-loyal and are willing to mix discount brands with expensive brands in clothing. But they are also more willing to purchase exclusive, expensive, and designer brand clothing than their parents were as young people. Could this in part be facilitated by the fact that they have access to credit more than any previous generation of young-young adults? The average 21-year-old is carrying almost $3,000 in credit card debt (Weiss, 2003). Also, young men and women are equally interested in shopping (Weiss, 2003), in contrast to previous generations

Computer technologies and cell phones are ubiquitous in their lives; Yers often train their parents on new equipment. They often multitask using multiple media at one time. This generation gets more fashion information through the Web.

Generation Y has a strong sense of independence that may influence their approach to appearance in the future. Their approach to adulthood is yet to unfold.

Summary

In this chapter, we examine three general life stages—early, middle, and late adulthood. During each stage, a variety of life experiences occur, and individuals experience these in varied orders. However, general trends in life stages create dress needs and consumer wants at each stage. For example, in early and middle adulthood, career and work dress needs are stronger. Older consumers are more apt to need special adjustments in clothing because of the physical changes of aging. The aging body becomes increasingly evident as the stages progress. Our youth-oriented culture may be influencing a greater number of middle-aged men and women to get cosmetic surgery as they try to maintain younger appearances. Surprisingly, body satisfaction does not substantially decrease as the signs of aging increase. More research is needed on how individuals cope with the aging body. The era in time during which people live affects dress trends of the generation. Lifespans and dress trends were examined for multiple generations living today.

Suggested Readings

Foster, P. (Ed.) (1994). *Minding the Body: Women Writers on Body and Soul.* New York: Bantam Doubleday Dell Publishing Group.

Harris, M. B. (1994). Growing old gracefully: Age concealment and gender. *Journal of Gerontology*, 49(4):149–158.

Melinkoff, E. (1984). *What We Wore: An Offbeat Social History of Women's Clothing, 1950 to 1980.* New York: Quill.

Moschis, G. P. (1996, September). Life stages of the mature market. *American Demographics*, 44–47, 50.

Secunda, V. (1984). *By Youth Possessed: The Denial of Age in America.* Indianapolis, IN: Bobbs-Merrill.

LEARNING ACTIVITY

Market Segment Analysis: Targeting Your Grandparents

Objective: Compare older individuals you know to previously identified market segments to understand how their dress may reflect their social life, activities, and health situations.

Procedure

Choose one of your grandparents or a person 65 years or older whom you know well. If you do not have a grandparent or if your grandparents are not 65 or older, choose another older person whom you know.

Record the age and gender of the person you have chosen.

Consider the four market segments of older Americans found in research by Moschis (1996) and described briefly in the chapter introduction. Identify one or more of the four market segments to which your grandparent/older person fits best. It is possible that a person has characteristics of more than one segment. Consider health situation, activities, and socializing habits of the person. The segments are:

- Healthy indulgers
- Healthy hermits
- Ailing outgoers
- Frail recluses

Describe the lifestyle and dress patterns of the individual. What is the person's wardrobe like? What are their attitudes toward dress? What are their shopping preferences and behaviors?

Do the dress and lifestyle patterns fit the general descriptions of the market segment to which you have assigned your older person? Do the person's wardrobe and shopping patterns make sense with his or her lifestyle and health situation?

References

Adler, J. (1995, February 20). Have we become a nation of slobs? *Newsweek*, 56–62.

Belk, R. W. (1988). Possessions and the extended self. *Journal of Consumer Research*, 15:139–168.

Csikszentmihalyi, M., & Rochberg-Halton, E. (1981). *The Meaning of Things: Domestic Symbols and the Self*. New York: Cambridge University Press.

Darling, L. (1994, January 23). Age, beauty and truth. *New York Times*, 1, 5.

Dychtwald, K., & Flower, J. (1989). *Age Wave: The Challenges and Opportunities of an Aging America*. Los Angeles: Jeremy P. Tarcher, Inc.

Eckman, M. (1997). Attractiveness of men's suits: The effect of aesthetic attributes and consumer characteristics. *Clothing and Textiles Research Journal*, 15(4):193–202.

Garner, D. M. (1997, January/February). The 1997 body image survey results. *Psychology Today*, 30(1):30–44, 75–76, 78, 80, 84.

Giesen, C. B. (1989). Aging and attractiveness: Marriage makes a difference. *International Journal of Aging and Human Development*, 29(2):83–94.

Greco, A. J. (1986). The fashion-conscious elderly: A viable, but neglected market segment. *Journal of Consumer Marketing*, 3(4):71–74.

Greco, A. J. (1989). Representation of the elderly in advertising: Crisis or inconsequence? *Journal of Consumer Marketing*, 6(1):37–44.

Hamilton, K., & Weingarden, J. (1998, June 15). Lifts, lasers and liposuction: The cosmetic surgery boom. *Newsweek*, 131(24):14.

Harris, M. B. (1994). Growing old gracefully: Age concealment and gender. *Journal of Gerontology*, 49(4):149–158.

Kaiser, S. B., & Chandler, J. L. (1985). Older consumers' use of media for fashion information. *Journal of Broadcasting & Electronic Media*, 29:201–207.

Kalb, C. (1999, August 9). Our quest to be perfect. *Newsweek*, 134(6):52–59.

The Kiplinger Washington Letter. (1995, December 22). *2000 and Beyond*. Washington, DC: The Kiplinger Washington Editors.

Kogan, N., & Mills, M. (1992). Gender influences on age cognitions and preferences: Sociocultural or sociobiological? *Psychology and Aging*, 4:73–78.

Lee, J., Hanna, S. D., Mok, C. F. J., & Wang, H. (1997). Apparel expenditure patterns of elderly consumers: A life-cycle consumption model. *Family and Consumer Sciences Research Journal*, 26:109–140.

Levinson, D. J. (1986). A conception of adult development. *American Psychologist*, 41:3–13.

Light, P. C. (1988). *Baby Boomers*. New York: Norton.

Moschis, G. P. (1996, September). Life stages of the mature market. *American Demographics*, 44–47, 50.

Oberg, P., & Tornstam, L. (1999). Body images among men and women of different ages. *Ageing and Society*, 19(5):629–644.

Ogle, J. P., & Damhorst, M. L. (in press). Critical reflections on the body and related socio-cultural discourses at the midlife transition: An interpretive study of women's experiences. *Journal of Adult Development*.

Paul, P. (2002, January). Meet the parents. *American Demographics*, 24:42–47.

Peterson, J. L., & Miller, C. (1980). Physical attractiveness and marriage adjustment in older American couples. *The Journal of Psychology*, 105:247–252.

Secunda, V. (1984). *By Youth Possessed: The Denial of Age in America*. Indianapolis, IN: Bobbs-Merrill.

Strauss, W., & Howe, N. (1991). *Generations: The History of America's Future, 1584 to 2069*. New York: William Morrow and Company.

Tierney, J. (1987). The aging body. In H. Cox (Ed.), *Aging* (5th ed.), pp. 42–47. Sluice Dock, CT: Dushkin Publishing Group.

U.S. Census Bureau. (2000). *American Fact Finder*. Accessed March 8, 2004, at factfinder.census.gov.

Vandeventer, E. (1993, March 18). Demographics drive buying trends. *Standard & Poor's Industry Surveys*, 161(11, Sec. 1):T61–T65.

Vesperi, M. D. (2001). Media, marketing, and images of the older person in the information age. *Generations*, 25(3):5–9.

Waldrop, J. (1990, August). The fashion harvest. *American Demographics*, 4.

Weiss, M. J. (2003, September). To be about to be. *American Demographics*, 25(7): 28–36.

54   A New Look at Beauty, Aging and Power
Carol Lynn Mithers

I laughed when I found my first gray hair. I was 26 and mourning the end of a relationship with a man of 38 who had often told me I was too young for him. The well-timed appearance of that silver strand was like my body making an inside joke.

A few more years went by and the hairs slowly but relentlessly multiplied. I stopped laughing and started experimenting with hair dyes. Then I started worrying about wrinkles. The last summer I got a tan I found tiny white marks under my eyes and realized with astonishment that these were under-eye creases that the sun couldn't reach. After that, I noticed deep brackets growing around my mouth. The amused, almost incredulous response I'd had to that first touch of gray—look! on me!—gave way to a muted panic: Something was happening that I was entirely powerless to stop. On the afternoon of my thirty-fifth birthday, I had what can only be described as a tantrum. My lover of many years was taking me to dinner, and I spent hours in front of the mirror frantically trying on and rejecting clothes, for none of them turned my reflection into the one I wanted to see. "Nothing looks good!" I whimpered over and over. "My hair, my face, these pants….Nothing looks right."

My lover watched, upset and perplexed. "What exactly is going on here?" he asked. The answer, of course, was that I was terrified. The first time you find it impossible to deny that you're aging—whether the evidence is the appearance of a wrinkle or the arrival of a particular birthday—is the first time you confront the melancholy fact of your own mortality. And if you're female, it is also the first time you face the truth that before long you will be an "older" woman. That the former frightened me seemed perfectly natural; that the latter did just as much was embarrassing.

As a child I'd learned not to ask the age of my mother's friends, for apparently the question was one that shamed any woman over 29. But that had been a different time, one in which a woman's main source of power was her physical appeal, and her main job the bearing and raising of children—which meant that she was "used up" by her forties, when the kids left home, or her fifties, when she entered menopause. By the time of my thirty-fifth birthday, everything had changed. Women had a choice of professions, of when and whether to bear children; they held a real measure of political and economic clout. Even the look of female maturity I recalled from childhood—"sensible" short hair, a thick body with a shelf-like bosom clothed in a frumpy pastel housedress—was nowhere to be seen. Instead, even women in their sixties and beyond were as trim, fit and vibrantly stylish as their much younger sisters. My feelings seemed so hopelessly retro that I felt stupid just for having them. At a time when there was no shortage of older female "role models"—including, soon, a sleekly confident 45-year-old who would redefine the role of first lady—surely no one but me faced the idea of aging with such confusion and terror.

Wrong. Women are obsessed, as we are about nothing else—except, perhaps, weight—with the physical fact of growing older; our feelings are a contradictory tangle of reason and blind emotion, exhilaration and despair, old and new beliefs. In 1900, the average female life expectancy was 48. Today it is 79, which means many of us will be "older" women almost half our lives. All of us are wrestling with that fact, struggling to define what it means to age—how we want to act, look and be seen, how aging makes us feel.

Intellectually, every woman knows that she'll eventually get—and look and feel—old. Emotionally, no one believes it. So when the first real sign of aging appears, usually around the late twenties, it creates a shock so intense that women remember it in vivid detail long afterward. "Last year, I looked at pictures of myself at 22 or 23 and saw that then I'd had round cheeks and soft-looking skin and now I didn't," says Ariel,[1] 30, an editor. "Suddenly my face looked very thin to me, angular in a way it hadn't before. A little drawn. There seemed to be some sort of freshness of life that was missing. Suddenly I realized I didn't look young anymore."

A very few women—often those raised in places or cultures that hold elderly people in high esteem—can accept such a realization with relative ease. "I grew up in Santa Fe, New Mexico, when it was a city of only around 45,000 people and everyone had known each other's families for generations," recalls Carmella Garcia, 30, an insurance broker. "Good looks were nice, but looks didn't define who you were. I live in L.A. now and most of my friends are really neurotic about aging—they're always talking about their wrinkles and sagging knees. My mother raised 13 children and I never heard her complain about getting older. She's 69 and has these wrinkles that are really lovely—crow's-feet around her eyes and smile wrinkles on her cheeks. She has wonderful salt-and-pepper hair. I wouldn't mind looking like that."

Other women's responses are more stereotypical, with all the denial and hysteria of a "Not Another Birthday!" card. Faced with a body that no longer burns off burgers and chocolate milk shakes, Georgia, a 31-year-old bank teller, rises at five to go running, swims in the evening and does aerobics on her lunch hour. Jean, a 35-year-old store manager, is fixated on her incipient crow's-feet, cutting out every magazine article about face-lifts, collagen shots and chemical peels; "By 40, I'm going to do something serious about my skin," she swears. At 30, Hayley, an accountant, so mourns the loss of her youthful looks that it casts a pall over her life. "I wish I'd never lain out in the sun," she says. "I have wrinkles everywhere, from my hands to my face. I hate being this old. Women in their twenties have the world in their hands. Men of any age like them. They like themselves. In your thirties, you're at the mercy of society. There's a desperate feeling, like time's running out."

Certainly such extreme responses are most common among those who have always received attention for their looks. But large numbers of average-looking women also find themselves thrown badly by the first signs of age. "All of a sudden," says one otherwise pragmatic 27-year-old, "I'm spending big money on creams that I know are just triumphs of packaging." At one level, such reactions are a predictable human response to the essential strangeness of physical alteration. We do so much growing and changing through childhood and adolescence that reaching adulthood feels like arrival: What we look like in our early twenties—how we feel and what we can do—is who we *are*. When that reality shifts—when a face that was full becomes thin, when a customary evening cup of coffee suddenly causes insomnia—it feels strange, wrong. "It's as if you don't know your own body anymore," says Ella, 31, a reporter.

In addition, the truth is that many physical changes associated with aging aren't improvements. Eyes that start to need reading glasses or once-tireless legs that now turn stiff after a single day of skiing are undeniable evidence that one's body is weakening, a warning that the coming years may impose genuine limitations—of physical ability, of choice. "I've had this self-protective attitude that people can be fit when they get older if they want to be," says Marla, 33, a graphic artist. "But this year, my grandmother, who's in her eighties and has always been very active, didn't make it to my wedding because she felt too sick. It made me think that maybe having a good attitude isn't going to save me. I'm no longer so sure that you can be terrific until you drop dead. And I've started to get some early arthritis symptoms in my knees. Sometimes in the morning I have trouble walking. It's frightening, and it's made me focus intensely on physical fragility. And *that's* brought up the question of what I'm doing with my life. There's a part of me that feels I haven't pursued things closest to my heart. I've always dreamed of being a serious painter, traveling and living in foreign cities, and my body's changes made me realize that if I really want to do that, I don't have forever. If I become a semicripple, I can't decide to suddenly change careers and go all over the world."

But human fears of mortality and physical breakdown are only part of the story. It's their changing appearance that causes many women to face aging with at best ambivalence and at worst dread. Despite the broadening of women's roles (and despite reassurances from individual men), a double standard about aging remains very much alive. In our culture, men may be considered attractive whatever their age—wrinkles make their faces "interesting"; gray hair makes them "distinguished." The attributes that make women attractive are invariably youthful qualities such as a "fresh" face and "taut" body; in fact, female attractiveness and youth are so linked that descriptions of a nonyouthful appearance almost invariably involve negative adjectives. Older breasts aren't soft, they're "sagging"; an older female face isn't just thin but, as Ariel put it, "drawn."

As a result, most women feel deep in their being that getting older makes them less desirable. Debra, a 36-year-old social worker whose clients are elderly, erupts in protest whenever she hears a remark she considers ageist—yet she admits that she finds it difficult to accept aging in herself. "There's a difference between thinking someone else is an attractive older woman and seeing your own aging as attractive," she says. "I'm obsessed with my wrinkles. I don't see them as a sign that I'm washed up, but they mean not being as pretty." Feeling "not as pretty" is no small matter: Because looks and desirability have traditionally been the foundation of a woman's power, such a change threatens a loss of status and influence.

The equation between aging and loss of power is one that many women have learned from their own mothers. Susan, a 27-year-old broker, says she first began to worry about growing older when she was 22 and her mother reached her early fifties. "She started quietly making disparaging noises about how old she was looking," Susan remembers. "One time while we were shopping I noticed that when she was trying on an outfit she was pulling on her face in an unconscious effort to make it look younger. I found that such a sad gesture. It was the first time it struck me that aging was a tough process to deal with—that it had obviously snagged my mother and it would probably get to me as well. Looking good has been important

most of my life; I credit a certain amount of the attention I've gotten to my appearance. When I expect to feel worst is that middle time—you're not yet old, but you're no longer young. My 80-year-old grandmother seems very beautiful to me. Where you see the struggle between youth and age is in the faces of *middle-age* women."

There's nothing new about the double standard in aging, or about how deeply women internalize it and how bad it makes them feel. What *is* new, however, is that these feelings, once accepted with sad or bitter resignation, now evoke overt rebellion. "I feel what I feel," Susan says fiercely. "But I'm fighting it every step of the way." It's a fight that takes several forms. As they look toward the future, women are reaching out, in a kind of hunger, for a new, more appealing image of older women. Some have embraced the ideal of the woman whose face and body actively deny her age—the woman who works out, dyes her hair, lifts her face, and looks, at 45 or 55, as conventionally attractive as someone years younger. Others vehemently object to this equation of artificial youth with attractiveness. Mary, a 41-year-old nurse, derides "women I see at my gym—50- and 60-year-olds with too much makeup, lifted faces and thong leotards." Her wish is for an expanded standard of female beauty, so that a woman who looks her age can still be considered appealing. "I want to look sexy no matter how old I am," Mary says. "But I'm not sure how a sexy 41-year-old looks. I don't want to make a fool of myself."

A few others, like Anne, 40, an educational programs analyst, argue against both positions. Either way, she says, women are judged too much on their appearance. Emphasizing that women can—or should—look great at any age denies the reality and circumstances of many women's lives. "My weight has become a big deal between my husband and me," she says. "There's this notion that women should remain thin and sexy and gorgeous forever, but when you're working, raising a child and running a house, you can't always pull it off. I can't look like a little tootsie—and I don't even want to—I'm not one."

Fortunately, many women are finding that their most negative reactions to getting older are challenged by the actual experience of aging. Age is not, they say, simply about loss. Judith, a

37-year-old teacher who reports being raised on "stories of women who get old and used up and then their husbands dump them for younger women," learned during a yearlong affair with a 26-year-old man that age could bring an unexpected sexual power. "It was great," she says. "Yes, in part I enjoyed it for the wrong reason—because I felt like if a younger man wanted me, it must mean I was still OK. But it wasn't just that. He looked up to me because I was older, and he was always a little worried about whether I'd find him interesting. Having someone worry about keeping *my* interest rather than the other way around was an amazing experience. It made me feel intellectually powerful in a way I never had before in a relationship. I wasn't afraid to let loose with what I thought. And I wasn't afraid to let loose sexually, either. You know all the publicity about how women reach their sexual capacity in their thirties? That's how he saw me—as the incarnation of this erotic, multiorgasmic creature. It was very exciting."

Thirty-six-year-old Debra acknowledges that despite her "obsession" with her wrinkles, her new face has brought her a professional respect she never enjoyed before. "When I first started working, I was 23, probably looked 19, and everyone around me was much older," she says. "They treated me like a cute little girl rather than a professional. I had to just go quietly about my job until they saw I could do it—I later had people tell me they never expected me to be competent. I once had a run-in with a colleague who was in her late thirties, and afterward she remarked to someone, 'Go tell the little girl....' Those things don't happen anymore. I don't have to struggle to get people to believe I know what I'm doing. I can be more relaxed in how I act at work, even in how I dress." It's not, she points out, that gaining professional respect cancels out her sadness at feeling she looks "less pretty"; none of the women I spoke to said that job success completely overshadowed their concerns about aging. "How I want to get treated at work and how I want to look are two separate things," Debra says. "But at least I have the chance to trade one strength for another."

Similarly, many women reported that having a good love relationship eased, but did not eradicate, their fear of growing older. "There's no respect for age in my business," says Linda, 42, who works in the film industry. "But I'm happily married and still in love, and my husband still thinks I'm beautiful and desirable. Because of him, it's harder to make me feel I'm getting fat or used up. I never lie to people in my profession about my age."

Sharon, 34, a homemaker, points out that motherhood can make the signs of aging seem less important. "My rear end is floppy, and there's not much nice that I can say about it. The minute I heard you could use Retin A to make stretch marks disappear, I meant to go out and get some. But I haven't. I guess I figure that if you let yourself get obsessed about these things, they'll take over your life. Besides, I have two wonderful kids to show for those marks. Would you want to go through something as life-changing as pregnancy without having it show?"

Forty-two-year-old Marty, who owns a temporary-employment agency, points out—as did a number of women in their forties—that being forced to face the physical imperfections that come with age can, ironically, lead to feeling at ease with one's body for the first time. "Since I was 35 I've worked out almost every day, and I'm very proud of how I feel and look," she says. "In college, I could barely make it around the track—I'm far stronger now than I was. And I'm happier with what I have. I've never had what you'd call a great body, and it really used to grieve me. But now when I see some perfect creature, I don't feel bad anymore. It's because I've had to let that wish go. I know I'm never going to look like that—I'm too old, it's impossible. In some ways that's a little sad. But it also frees me from the old envy and compulsion."

"I wish I were less tired and more fit, but in general, I like the way I look now," says Leslie Spanier-Wyant, 42, an executive at a child-care-management company and mother of a five-year-old. "Ten years ago, whether or not I looked perfect was always at the forefront of my mind. But who has time for that anymore? Besides, it turns out that it doesn't matter. It doesn't matter in terms of doing well at my job, it doesn't matter to my daughter, it doesn't even matter to my husband. In everything that's important to me, perfect looks just don't matter."

What one hears most in women's voices is that a rebellion against negative images of the "older woman" and a discovery of the gains that come with age have begun to alter the way we feel about getting older. There are signs that the old cultural double standard may be crumbling a bit, too. It's no longer taboo to talk about menopause, for example, and here and there one hears the adjective "beautiful" applied to a woman in her fifties or sixties—and not just a Gloria Steinem or a Jacqueline Onassis. For the first time ever, photos of over-40 models in sexy, glamorous poses are appearing in major magazines—a step forward even when you acknowledge the inevitable airbrushing. Last year, sultry, sensual photos of Hillary Rodham Clinton were published in *Vogue*. The photos acknowledged something revolutionary: A woman who was not conventionally beautiful could become physically alluring through her power. Increasing female visibility in business and government has brought nearer the advent of the woman whose appeal is ageless because it is based on her strength and ability. "You don't look at Janet Reno or Pat Schroeder and think 'Gee, they're looking old,'" says Karen, a 31-year-old union organizer. "These are women of substance."

Full change will require more. Women, insists 27-year-old Susan, must learn to be kinder to each other. "Some of this we do to ourselves," she says. "We go to reunions with nothing more pressing on our minds than seeing who'll look ten years older and who won't. I've heard the pleasure in my mother's voice when she talks about how old her sister looks. Even if those words aren't aimed at you, you feel their brutality. We make each other feel diminished, and we've got to stop it."

A deep transformation of culture is needed too. It's unrealistic to expect that we'll ever lose our profound attraction to youthful beauty, for such beauty symbolizes a time in life when everything is new and full of promise. But in large part we have prized youth in women because the qualities we most valued in women *were* those of youth: innocence, guilelessness, malleability. As that changes, and as more and more women occupy positions of importance, prestige, power, and respect, the chances increase that women, like men, may be considered beautiful by virtue of our sophistication, wit, talent, and accomplishments, for who we are and what we have done rather than how old we happen to be. We may finally understand that we can praise "taut" faces and bodies and also celebrate those that are "ripe," "plush," or "soft," that enjoying images of young women doesn't mean that we can't also enjoy the beauty of older women—a beauty that is unlifted, unretouched, *real*.

Note

1. When only a first name is used, it is a pseudonym, and some other identifying details may also have been changed.

A New Look at Beauty, Aging and Power

DISCUSSION QUESTIONS

1. What were the various images and ideas that women had about getting older?

2. How do the negative fears that some women had about aging reflect current U.S. societal myths about aging?

3. Are the positive images of getting older that some women had rare and unrepresentative?

Or do the positive images foretell a changing societal notion of women, aging, and beauty?

4. How do you feel about becoming middle-aged and then elderly?

55 True Thighs

Amy Wallace

Jamie Lee Curtis wants to expose herself to you. It is, she says, the only way to make things right.

Look at her, traipsing around a white-washed Los Angeles photo studio in nothing but a sports bra and tight spandex briefs. When she strikes a pose, her dark blue eyes stare unabashedly into the camera lens. But don't let the swagger fool you: She knows she's taking a risk. The 43-year-old movie star, who bared her breasts in *Trading Places* and did a bawdy strip-tease in *True Lies*, has certainly shown more skin in the past than she's flashing right now. But in a very real way, she's never been more naked.

At her insistence, the photographer, Andrew Eccles, is shooting her with no makeup, no manicure, no professional coif, no diamond jewelry and no high couture. The lighting is unforgiving. So is the full-body camera angle and Curtis' straightforward stance. But everything is just as the actress wants it. She says it's the least she can do.

"There's a reality to the way I look without my clothes on," she says. "I don't have great thighs. I have very big breasts and a soft, fatty little tummy. And I've got back fat. People assume that I'm walking around in little spaghetti-strap dresses. It's insidious—Glam Jamie, the Perfect Jamie, the great figure, blah, blah, blah. And I don't want the unsuspecting forty-year-old women of the world to think that I've got it going on. It's such a fraud. And I'm the one perpetuating it."

But not anymore. In an age when divas often use their clout to nix unflattering photos in magazines, Curtis has demanded the opposite: Glam Jamie will pose only if Real Jamie gets equal time. See that worry line between her eyebrows? It exists, she earned it and she wants it to show.

She even knows what this article should be titled. "True Thighs," she declares.

You might think that the Scream Queen—as she's been known since her star turns in a string of horror films, starting with 1978's *Hal-*loween—has lost her marbles. She hasn't. Quite intentionally, Curtis is reinventing herself. It's a process that started ten years ago, when she began writing books for children and discovered something more gratifying—she likes to say more "authentic"—than the pretending for which she gets paid millions. Her first four children's books, which are not only smart but also tend to land on best-seller lists, have dealt with issues as varied as adoption and mood swings. But they all share a common thread: It's okay to be you. The fifth, which hits bookstores this month, is the most directly self-affirming so far. Its title? *I'm Gonna Like Me: Letting Off a Little Self-Esteem* (HarperCollins).

Which, in a roundabout way, is how Curtis ended up here, in this airy photo studio, wearing unflattering undies, not a smudge of eyeliner and a big fat smile on her face. She knows that her body, held up as an icon of female perfection in movies such as, well, *Perfect*, has made some women think that they don't measure up. She knows how that feels—not being good enough. The daughter of two members of Hollywood royalty, Janet Leigh and Tony Curtis, this actress has struggled with feelings of inadequacy all her life. So while she knows that part of her still clings to her bodacious physical image, she is enjoying the hell out of poking a hole in it.

"You know, a G-string would make me look a lot better because G-strings make your legs look longer," she says, clearly pleased. "This underwear, it cuts you off. It's not good." When the "before" photos, complete with worry lines and exposed midriff, are in the can, Curtis looks radiant. "I love you people!" she yells at Eccles, be-

Amy Wallace is a senior writer at *Los Angeles Magazine*. Her work has also appeared in *The New Yorker*, *The New York Times Magazine*, *Details*, *Elle*, *The Nation*, and other magazines. Reprinted by permission.

a

b

FIGURE 9.3 *(a) Jamie Lee as she really is—no lights, no makeup, no retouching. (b) To achieve the glam Jamie, it takes a village and a fat checkbook—the cast of 13 primping and prepping for three hours.*

fore ducking into a back room, where a makeup artist and manicurist await. Only now, with Curtis' blessing, can the transformation to Glam Jamie begin.

In youth-obsessed Hollywood, where the dearth of good roles for women over 28 is a constant lament, it's a ballsy move to admit your age at all—let alone revel in it. But Curtis is seeking something bigger than her next acting job. She wants to feel at peace with her flaws, her genes. "Demystifying has been a real goal for me," she says. "For myself, as well as on a public level."

To be sure, her acting career has slowed down. Last year, she got good reviews for her role in *The Tailor of Panama*, with Pierce Brosnan; she also appears in Billy Bob Thornton's *Daddy and Them*, set for release next year. Since then, however, she's been absent from the big screen, save for a cameo in this summer's *Halloween: Resurrection*, the series' eighth installment. In this film, her character is finally killed off—a plot point that seems to fill Curtis with relief. "Laurie Strode is dead," she says happily. "And I never have to be in another sequel again."

The timing couldn't be better. As the Scream Queen exits, the Self-Esteem Queen is poised for her entrance. And Curtis has chosen this magazine as the place to reveal herself. Literally.

"I'm trying really hard to take the veil off the fraud, to be real, to start with me," she tells me over lunch the day before she will pose in her skivvies. We are in the dining room of the sunny, comfortable four-bedroom Spanish-style home that the actress shares with her husband, satirist and film director Christopher Guest, and their two children. It is, Curtis points out, a house that she and Guest bought with their own money. Contrary to what many people assume, she's never received financial support from her famous family.

"In the recovery program I'm in [for addiction problems], they talk about peeling an onion, exposing more layers," she says. The myth of the perfect Jamie is, she confides, something she "actively participated in—and, by the way, profited from. Now, I'm sitting here high on my hill, debunking the very foundation that I sit on. Don't think I'm not afraid of it. I'm not financially independent enough that I don't rely on outside income still."

"But it's just money. It isn't love," she continues, observing that not one of the many close girlfriends who make up her "Estrogen Posse" works in the movie industry. "That's what I have to remember," she explains. "I don't have any dear friends from the movie business. It's my job. I do it well, I worked hard, I made some money, I saved some money. You know, I didn't let it go to my head. I knew that it was going to have an end point."

This is not the first time that Curtis' work has led her to make changes in her life. In 1999, after writing her third book, *Today I Feel Silly & Other Moods That Make My Day*, it occurred to her that, even as she was urging kids to pay attention to their feelings, she had difficulty expressing her own. The result: She quit drinking and ended a lengthy addiction to painkillers that she said began when she was recovering from plastic surgery. Yes, that's right: Curtis is a veteran of the nip-and-tuck.

"I've done it all," she says, breaking yet another unwritten Hollywood rule: Never fess up. "I've had a little plastic surgery. I've had a little lipo. I've had a little Botox. And you know what? None of it works. None of it."

Curtis leans forward in her chair. "Ten years ago, before anybody did that, I had fat taken from underneath my eyes because I was on a movie and I was puffy," she says. "And I re- member the cameraman saying, 'I can't shoot her now.' I remember being mortified. And yet, you know what? Nobody tells you if you take fat from your body in one place, it comes back in another place. All of these 'bettering' experiences are not without risk. And there is this illusion that once you do it, then you'll be fine. And that's just horseshit. I looked worse. *Worse.* Am I right?"

Her question is directed to Annie, her 15-year-old daughter, who has joined us at the table and is munching a falafel burrito. The girl tries to answer, but she is laughing too hard, which makes Curtis look at her fondly, and then point at me. "She's going to write, 'Her daughter laughed knowingly,'" she warns. Annie keeps giggling. "What did you say?" Curtis presses. "You're allowed to tell me now. Totally allowed."

"I said," Annie says finally, "you're neurotic."

"I am neurotic," Curtis agrees, smiling.

There's a lot of laughter in the Curtis/Guest household. It's a place where visitors are sometimes greeted with the cheerful salutation, "Welcome to hell!" and where for years there was no dishwasher because—to her family's amusement—Curtis insisted that housework made you feel good about yourself. It's a place where, even in summer, there are holiday gifts hidden away on top of bookshelves ("I buy Christmas presents in April," she says), and where a framed *New Yorker* cartoon depicts a bearded man in a carriage drawn by two cheetahs ("Amish Midlife Crisis," the caption reads). It's also a place where, in the middle of an interview, Curtis will suddenly dash out of the room, retrieve a camera and start taking your picture.

"Stop," she commands when I protest. "The light is pretty."

Curtis loves photographs. They're all over her house—ones she took, plus others by such famous photographers as Sally Mann and Dorothea Lange. Upstairs, in the hallway outside her children's bedrooms, every class picture from each year of their upbringing is displayed. In a drawer in her study, she keeps a greeting card of her mother, screaming in the shower in

Psycho. Beneath it is a 1971 school portrait of Curtis, age 12, with feathered hair, braces and a floral print dress ("That's attractive," she says sarcastically. "That was actually the dress I got felt up in first.") There's also an unusually geeky Polaroid she took of her husband of 18 years, his head partially shaved for a role in his upcoming comedy about folk singers. Curtis loves to get it out, roll her eyes and say, delightedly, "Here's the guy I married!"

The actress has taken a series of self-portraits, too, all of which play with her famous image. Using a mirror, she's photographed her back, the way the soft skin folds into creases when she twists around. She's examined her own feet. But her favorite seems to be a black-and-white shot of another mirror, broken into shards on the ground. "You have to find me," she says as I search for her face reflected in one tiny sliver. "I'm in there."

"I'm tremendously immature," Curtis announces. We're back in the dining room, which looks out at one of Santa Monica's windswept canyons. "I'm still the type of person who will chew my food and open my mouth." She glances down, only to discover that her black Jil Sander jeans are inexplicably unbuttoned. She shoots me a look as if to say: See? Annie agrees with her mother's self-assessment: "She's the four-year-old in the family."

But now, the actress' immaturity—which served her well in such comedies as *A Fish Called Wanda*—is really paying off. She loves to get down on the floor with children. She loves the way they talk, urgently and without self-doubt. "I hear them and I think, 'Oh, that's just poetry,'" she says. When she goes on her book tours, she gets a charge out of talking to other parents. It feels important, she confesses, in a way that acting never has.

Curtis isn't finished with acting. Not yet. She has optioned a memoir by a fellow children's-book author, Leah Komaiko, about Komaiko's friendship with a 93-year-old blind woman. Playwright Wendy Wasserstein, whom the actress got to know when she did *The Heidi Chronicles* on TV, is adapting it for the screen. Meanwhile, though, she has no movie roles lined up.

Annie likes to tease her mother about being retired. "I think what's happening is that the more I like me, the less I want to pretend to be other people," Curtis says. "I would like to say I'm retired. I'm not sure I can afford to be retired. But if I could, I'd retire in a heartbeat. A lot of people stay at the party too long." She stops, suddenly sure of what she intends to say. "I think there's a point where you become a caricature of yourself. And it would be very easy for me to become that. For ten years there, you would draw the caricature of me in some leotard with my breasts hanging out. I don't think that would be the case now."

Or at least, that's what she's hoping. Already, Curtis regrets that when her six-year-old son, Tom, hits adolescence, his friends will be able to rent a movie that shows her topless. "I have to hope that I'll be so far out of show business by then. I hope they're like, 'Jamie who? Oh, yeah, she writes kiddie books, huh?'"

The photographs on these pages are Curtis' effort to jumpstart that transition. To have a life beyond the movie business, she figures, you've got to find out who you are without the stylists, the Harry Winston jewels and the fancy borrowed outfits. You've got to be able to look in the mirror and recognize yourself.

"Hopefully, in two years, when I promote my next book, I will literally be able to look like just me," she says. "There is a me that I will get to that will say to the editors of magazines, 'This is what I wear, this is how I wear my hair, this is the color I wear on my toes, this is how my hands look.' I want to do my part, as I develop the consciousness for it, to stop perpetuating the myth."

She glances down at her feet, shod in designer sandals, and smiles. "I'm going to look the way God intends me to look," she says. "With a little help from Manolo Blahnik."

True Thighs

1. Why did Jamie Lee Curtis pose without makeup and in her underwear for *More* magazine? What does she intend to do by showing what happens even to glamorous movie stars as they move into middle age?

2. Should Jamie just work out a little more and go on a diet? (This is a woman who is fairly athletic.) What happens to the body as it ages?

3. How is Jamie dealing with her changing body?

56 Move Over, Tupperware: Botox Parties Sweep the Country

Ellen Creager

Drink Chardonnay, nibble hors d'oeuvres, get needles poked in your face.

This lovely evening is brought to you by Dr. Gregory Roche, a Bloomfield Hills, Mich., facial cosmetic surgeon who is trying hard to popularize in the sensible Midwest the fad of Botox parties.

If you haven't heard, a Botox party is where people who hate their wrinkles can get injected with muscle-paralyzing botulism toxin in the forehead, crow's feet or eye furrows in a festive atmosphere.

"It's the hot new thing, like a Tupperware party," says Barbara DiMaria, 55, of Bloomfield Hills, standing in Roche's enormous kitchen along with 12 others intrigued by the nosh and needles. "None of us needs Tupperware. A lot of us need this."

Even Roche's wife, Bonnie, is involved. She made the guacamole, salsa and beef tenderloin. She got the flowers and made the family dogs, cats, parrot and pet raccoons behave.

A few months ago, her husband experimented on her, injecting her lip with a tiny dose of Botox to see what would happen. She couldn't whistle or sip through a straw for three months until it wore off.

Last week, she had three doses of Botox to smooth out eye lines.

Tonight, only three people want to be Botoxed: DiMaria, her friend Nina Brooks and Debbie Murphy, a surgical assistant in Roche's office.

Murphy, 37, has a forehead as taut as a new calfskin wallet. She can't move it or wrinkle her brow anymore, but her face is line-free. The worry furrows between her eyes are gone, too. This is her fourth Botoxing.

"People before told me I looked tired and unhappy," says Murphy, who wanted the drug after she saw patients' results. "Now, I like it. It's great."

Nina Brooks, 54, is here to get her furrows filled, too. "I've had this guy for 30 years," she says, pointing to a vertical crease between her eyes.

She and her crease will have to part ways without family support. "My husband wouldn't even come to watch," says Brooks. "He asked, 'Are they going to be poking someone?' He wouldn't have anything to do with it."

Brooks' husband's attitude is what Roche aims to change. Botox, he says, might be a fad, but he does not want to miss the opportunity.

"I think it's an entry-level drug. It gets people in the door," says the surgeon.

On his Web site—http://www.drroche.com/—Roche advertises that if you get 10 friends together for a Botox party, the host or hostess gets a discount, paying $350 per area instead of the normal $425 to $750. It's a way to drum up interest in a fad popular on the West and East coasts. Everyone else at the party pays full price.

"The Midwest is always slow to catch on," says Roche, who sees Botox as a loss leader for his office. He estimates half his Botox patients will eventually opt for one of seven face-lifts, laser resurfacing or other procedures he offers.

Insurance won't pay for Botox or any cosmetic procedure. A vial of Botox costs the manufacturer $40. The markup to doctors is 1,000 percent, to $400. Doctors mark it up about 700 percent, to about $2,800, and can treat three or four patients per vial.

DiMaria and Brooks don't know how much their Botox treatments will cost tonight. "Their office will send a bill," Brooks says, not appearing to worry.

Roche sees nothing wrong with doing a medical procedure in his kitchen. Heck, he once stitched up an Isiah Thomas injury right here after a Pistons game. A Botox treatment involves three things: the toxin, saline solution and a short needle the diameter of a hair—smaller than a tattoo needle. Patients don't even need to wash their faces before treatment.

The party revs up, with everyone standing around the black marble island, nibbling and sipping and chatting. Someone cuts into the white chocolate cake, putting slices on festive red and orange plates.

FIGURE 9.4 *Botox ad, 2004.*

Over in the corner, Roche, still in purple scrubs from the office, injects Murphy near the eyes and nose. Then he seats DiMaria in a chair hand-decorated with glued-on pencils. Bruce the Shih-Tzu, one of four Roche dogs, wags his little shaggy body and bobs his little head with the bow on top. DiMaria picks up the wriggly dog and plops him in her lap.

"See how easy this is? You can even hold a dog," she says, looking serene.

Bruce wriggles around, watching as Roche, in sterile gloves, draws 25 units of Botox into the tiny needle. DiMaria sits still. Roche pokes the needle into the center of her forehead and injects some of the clear liquid.

Then Roche makes her scrunch her eyes. On the top of her crow's feet he injects two tiny bits more. Then he puts two more injections near the furrows between her eyes. She gasps ever so slightly. A drop of blood oozes from one injection, but it's quickly patted down. Each spot is slightly swollen with toxin, but that will disappear within an hour. In two days the Botox will kick in, paralyze the tiny muscles and relax the skin above to make the creases vanish.

Moments after her injections, DiMaria is back chatting with the group.

Then it's Brooks' turn. Roche injects her in nearly the same spots. Nobody else really pays attention, their conversation turning to the Red Wings and Formula One racing. But Brooks is so fair-skinned that when she rejoins the group, the outer corner of her left eye is beginning to bruise.

Somebody gets a Ziploc bag of ice. She holds it to her eye.

"Don't tell anyone you got Botox," Roche kids.

"I won't," she says with a grin. "I'll tell them you hit me."

Although it is made of the poison that causes the food poisoning botulism, Botox is safe, Roche says, because it is so diluted. The drug has been used for more than a decade to treat excessive sweating, migraines and other medical problems. A single injection for cosmetic reasons uses five units. A unit is about a drop. One reason Botox parties are cost-effective for doctors is that once a vial is open, it must be used within four hours.

Because it paralyzes muscles, Botox has to be used only on specific spots. Used around the mouth, it can cause drooling or trouble with talking. It is not good on frown lines around the mouth, because then only the smile muscles work, "And sometimes you end up looking like the Joker," Roche says.

Too much Botox in your face, and you can get an expressionless look. Too much Botox too close to the eyebrow, and you can get a droopy eyelid.

Botox given on the wrong forehead muscles can cause the eyebrows to rise in a constantly surprised look.

"You need to find a doctor familiar with the muscles of facial animation," Roche says. Of course, Botox wears off in three to five months, so nothing, even a mistake, is permanent.

Tonight, the needles now are only a memory. The party coasts along, brief pain forgotten. Nobody has had to sign a consent form, pay a bill, change into a sterile gown. The party is a hit.

"I'm real private, but this doesn't have the same stigma as other medical procedures," DiMaria says. "It's not a big deal. Besides, if you get all your friends to do it, there is security in numbers, then nobody can talk!"

Move Over, Tupperware

1. When you start to develop wrinkles and aging creases in the facial area, do you think you will opt for Botox treatments? Why or why not?

57 Ageism and the Politics of Beauty
Cynthia Rich

If you are a younger woman, try to imagine what everything in society tells you not to imagine: that you are a woman in your seventies, eighties, nineties, or older, and yet you are still you. Even your body is yours. It is not, however, in the language of the embalmers, "well-preserved," and though the male world gives you troubles for it, you like it that way. Apart from those troubles, you find sometimes a mysterious integrity, a deep connection to life, that comes to you from having belonged to a body that has been large and small, thin and fat, with breasts and hips of many different sizes and shapes, and skin of different textures.

In your fifties and sixties when your eyebrows and pubic hair and the hair on your head began to thin, it bothered you at first. But then you remembered times when you tweezed your eyebrows, shaved your pubic hair and legs and underarms, or took thinning shears to your head. "Too much" hair, "too little" hair—now you know that both are male messages.

One day you pick up a book that you find rich and nourishing—for example, *Getting Home Alive* by Aurelia and Rosario Morales, published by a feminist press. It is a political book and a sensuous book, and you like the way its politics and its sensuality seem merged. One of the authors, Rosario, is a younger woman, in her fifties, with a warmth of connection to other people, especially women. It is when you come to a section about aging that abruptly the connection—with you—is broken. You find the poet writing with dread and loathing at the thought that one day she must live inside the body of a woman who looks like you:[1]

> Stop!
> I don't want my scalp
> shining through a few thin hairs.
> Don't want my neck skin to hang—
> neglected cobweb—in the corner of my chin.
> Stop!

It shouldn't take this guided tour for any of us to recognize that an old woman must find it insulting, painful, personally humiliating, to be told in print that other women in her community find her body disgusting.

What you—the old woman—find especially painful is that the feminist newspaper where this excerpt was first printed, the feminist publisher, the poet herself, would surely protest if Jewish features, Black features, or the feature of any other marginalized group were described—whether in the form of the outsider's contempt or the insider's self-hatred—with this kind of revulsion. They would not think of their protest as censorship of literary expression. They would know that such attitudes do deep damage to a work artistically, as well as humanly and politically.

Yet clearly they are not the same standards when speaking with disgust about the bodies of old women. So the message has a double sting. The "ugliness" of your physical being is not a cruel opinion but an accepted fact; you have not even had the right to be insulted. How is it that you, the old woman, find yourself in this place?

I believe the revulsion toward old bodies is only in part a fear of death, as the poet suggests—she ends the poem, "No quiero morir." (Of course there is no reason why women over 60 should have to hear such insults whether they remind us of death or not.) Or else everybody would find soldiers going to battle repugnant, young women with leukemia disgusting, the tubercular Violetta in *La Traviata* loathsome. This is a death-obsessed and death-fearing society, that's true enough. But the dying young woman has always been a turn-on.

Reprinted by permission of Spinsters Ink, Denver, CO.

No, there is another more deeply anti-woman source for this disgust. Once again it is men who have defined our consciousness and, as Susan Sontag noted ten years ago, in aging as in so much else a double standard reigns. True, old men who are quite powerless are sometimes viewed by younger men as if they were old women. But older men routinely seek out much younger women for exotic companions and usually find them. In white Western society, the older woman is distasteful to men because she is such a long way from their ideal of flattering virginal inexperience. But also she outlives them, persists in living when she no longer serves them as wife and mother, and if they cannot make her into Grandma, she is—like the lesbian—that monstrous woman who has her own private reasons for living apart from pleasing men. On the one hand she is a throwaway, on the other a threat.

White men have provided the world with little literature, sculpture, or painting in which the old woman's body is seen through the eyes of desire, admiration, love, wonder, playfulness, tenderness. Instead they have filled our minds with an extensive literature and imagery of disgust, which includes a kind of voyeuristic fascination with what they see as the obscurity of female aging. Men's disgust for old women's bodies, with its language of contempt (shriveled, sagging, drooping, wizened, ravaged, liver spots, crow's feet, old bag, etc.) is so familiar to us that it feels like home.

Still, if this were all, how is it that twenty years of ground-breaking feminism have not led us to rise up to challenge such a transparent, gross form of woman-hating? An honest answer to that question is painful but essential, and Barbara Macdonald has named the key to our resistance. Younger women can no longer afford to ignore the fact that we learned early on to pride ourselves on our distance from, and our superiority to, old women.

While I was thinking about this article, the picture of an old woman caught my eye from the comic pages. The three frames of "The Wizard of Id" show an old woman with thin hair pulled to a tiny topknot on her head, her breasts and hips a single balloon. The wizard, her jaunty old husband, hand debonairly on hip, legs crossed with a flair, has bragged: "The king and I are judging a beauty contest tonight." She wags her finger. "That's degrading!" she exclaims through her down-turned toothless mouth. "My lady friends and I will picket!" The Wizard gets in the last word, which of course leaves her speechless: "That'll make a nice contrast."

This slice of mainstream media is jammed with political messages. Old women are ugly. Their view of things can be dismissed as just a way of venting their envy of young women. The old men, who have status and power, and therefore are the judges who matter, prize the young women's beauty and judge old women's bodies to be contemptible. The old woman has no defense since she, too, knows old women are ugly. And: the young woman's body in fact gains in value when set beside that of an old woman.

Images like this accustom younger women to unthinkingly adopting an ageist stance and woman-hating language from men. But also the old woman's low currency temporarily drives up our own. Just as the "plain" white woman is at least not Black, the "plainest" younger woman is at least not old. The system gives us a vested interest in maintaining the politics of beauty and in joining in the oppression of old women.

The principal source of the distaste for old women's bodies should be perfectly familiar. It is very similar to the distaste anti-Semites feel toward Jews, homophobes feel toward lesbians and gays, racists toward Blacks—the drawing back of the oppressor from the physical being of the oppressed. This physical revulsion travels deep; it is like fear. It feels entirely "natural" to the oppressor; he/she believes that everybody who claims to feel differently is simply hiding it out of politeness or cowardice.

When I was twelve, I had an argument with my grandmother. (Because of ageism, I feel a need to point out that she was no more racist than most white Baltimoreans of all ages in the 1940s.) It was probably my first political argument, and I felt both shaky and strong. Buttressed by a book on what in the '40s was called "tolerance," I didn't see why little Black girls couldn't go to my school. I can still remember her voice as she bypassed the intelligence argument. "But just think—would you want one to come to your house and spend the night!" Yes, *but would you want to marry one?* Physical revulsion is an ideal tool for maintaining oppressive systems, an instant check whenever reason or simple fairness starts to lead us onto more liberal paths.

To treat old women's minds as inconsequential or unstable is in one sense more serious, more dangerous, than disgust for their bodies. But most women find that the more our bodies are perceived as old, the more our minds are dismissed as irrelevant. And if we are more than our bodies (whatever that means), we also are our bodies. If you find my body disgusting, no promises that you admire or love my mind can assure me that I can trust you.

No, the issue of "beauty" and "ugliness" is not frivolous. I think of two white women who are in their sixties. One, a lesbian psychologist from a working-class, radical home, has written about the compelling urge she felt to have a facelift—until she became aware that what she was dealing with was not her own ugliness but the ugly projections of others, and became instead an activist against ageism. The other, a former airplane pilot and now a powerful photographer, has made a series of self-portraits that document, mercilessly, the bruises and scars of her own facelift. These are not conforming Nancy Reagans. These are creative, independent, gutsy women, and they heard the message of society quite accurately: the pain of an operation for passing is less than the pain of enduring other people's withdrawal.

One example of how the danger increases when an old woman's body is seen as less valuable than a younger woman's is that the old woman is unlikely to receive equal treatment from medical practitioners, male or female. Old women attest to this fact. Recent research agrees: a UCLA study confirms that old women with breast cancer are treated less thoroughly than younger women, so that their lives are "needlessly shortened."

In her pamphlet, *Ageism in the Lesbian Community* (Crossing Press), Baba Copper points to the daily erosions of "ugly." She observes that the withdrawal of eroticism between women "which takes place after middle age (or at the point when a woman no longer passes for young) *includes withdrawal of the emotional work which women do to keep the flow of social interaction going:* teasing, touching, remembering details, checking back, supporting" (emphasis mine).

I hear a voice, "All of this may be true. But aren't you trying to place the heavy boot of political correctness on the mysteries of attraction?" No. But obviously the fewer women we can be drawn to because they are "too" Jewish or fat or Asian or old, the more impoverished our lives. And also: if we can never feel that mysterious attraction bubbling up towards an old woman, a disabled woman, an Hispanic woman, we can pretty well suspect that we are oppressive to such women in other ways.

Sometimes I sense a presumption that the fact that each of us is growing older gives us all license to speak of old women's bodies in insulting and degrading ways—or even makes this particular form of woman-hating somehow admirable and honest. Yet the fact that one of us may well in the next twenty years become disabled or fat doesn't make feminist editors eager to hear the details of any "honest" loathing we may feel for the bodies of disabled or fat women.

It does not surprise me that ageism is still with us, since eradicating oppressive attitudes is hard, ongoing, embarrassing, painful, gut work. But as a movement feminism has developed many sensitivities that are at least well beyond those of the mainstream. And we are quite familiar by now with the basic dynamics that almost all oppressions have in common (most of which we learned from the insights of the civil rights movement and applied to feminism and other liberation movements). Erasure. Stereotyping. Internalized self-hatred including passing when possible. The attempt to prove the oppression is "natural." Impugning of the mental and emotional capacities. Blame-the-victim. Patronizing. Tokenizing. Segregation. Contempt mingled with fear. And physical revulsion. So it seems almost incredible that we have not learned to identify these most flagrant signals of ageism.

How can we begin to change? We—especially those of us in our forties and fifties—can stop the trend of examining in public how disgusted we are at the thought of the bodily changes of growing old. Such examinations do not display our moral courage. They reveal our insensitivity to old women who have to hear once more that we think their bodies are the pits. We can recognize that ideas of beauty are socialized into us and that yes, Virginia, we *can* begin to move in the direction of re-socializing ourselves. We can work for ourselves and for any revolution we might imagine, to develop a deeper and more resonant—dare I say more *mature?*—concept of beauty.

I am looking at two photographs. One is of Septima Clark, on the back of the book she wrote in her late eighties about her early and ongoing work in the civil rights movement. The other is a postcard of Georgia O'Keeffe from a photo taken twenty years before her death. The hairs on their scalps are no longer a mass, but stand out singly. O'Keeffe's nose is "too" strong, Clark's is "too" broad. O'Keeffe's skin is "wizened," Clark's is "too" dark. Our task is to learn not to look insultingly beyond these features to souls we can celebrate, but instead to take in these bodies as part of these souls—exciting, individual, beautiful.

Note

1. The poem excerpted here is "Old," by Rosario Morales, from *Getting Home Alive* by Aurora Levins Morales and Rosario Morales (Firebrand Books, 141 The Commons, Ithaca, NY 14850, 1986), p. 186.

DISCUSSION QUESTIONS

Ageism and the Politics of Beauty

1. What is ageism?
2. How is appearance a central part of fear and hatred of the aging process?
3. Do you agree that society is more ageist toward women than men? Why or why not?

58 Older Women's Attitudes toward Aging, Appearance Changes, and Clothing

Joy M. Kozar
University of Southern Mississippi

When I was in my younger days, I weighed a
few pounds less, I needn't hold my
tummy in to wear a belted dress.
But now that I am older, I've set my body free;
there's the comfort of elastic where once
my waist would be.
Inventor of those high-heeled shoes my feet
have not forgiven; I have to wear a nine
now, but used to wear a seven.
And how about those pantyhose—they're
sized by weight, you see, so how come
when I put them on the crotch is at my
knee?
I need to wear these glasses as the print's been
getting smaller; and it wasn't very long
ago I know that I was taller.
Though my hair has turned to gray and my
skin no longer fits, on the inside, I'm the
same old me, it's the outside's changed a
bit.

—Maya Angelou, 2003

As Maya Angelou explains, physical appearance
changes as we age. It is an unavoidable process
that we encounter as we get older. We all will experience transformations difficult to control, including wrinkling skin, weight gain, loss of muscle
mass, and graying hair. Throughout life, women
tend to worry more than men do about changes in
their appearance and are more likely to be dissatisfied with their bodies as a result of these changes
(Oberg & Tornstam, 1999). With age, however,
many women like Maya Angelou begin to accept
age-related transformations as natural (Hurd,
2000). Generally, older women are more comfortable with their bodies than are younger women.

Accepting and valuing our bodies as we get
older can become increasingly more difficult because of society's emphasis on being young and
physically fit. The media is filled with advertisements promoting and celebrating America's
youth and sexuality while degrading the older
population (Vesperi, 2001). Past researchers have
reported that older people are underrepresented
in the media and are especially ignored in advertisements for clothing and cosmetics (Carrigan & Szmigin, 1999; Greco, 1989). When seen
in advertisements, older people are usually depicted as disabled, frail, dependent on others,
poor, and lonely. These images are stereotypical
and outdated, however, as older Americans
today are healthier and more socially and physically active than previous generations (Greco,
1989).

The purpose of this study was to examine
the functions and meanings attributed to clothing and physical appearance by older women.
Of particular interest was whether the concern
with one's physical appearance changes over
time, as well as the importance of having new
and/or fashionable clothing. The value placed
on others' opinions regarding dress and appearance will be addressed and the similarities and
differences among women of different age
groups will be noted.

Findings regarding the apparel consumption patterns of older consumers are especially
useful to businesses targeting the mature market
segment. By identifying differences and similarities among older consumers, retailers can enhance their abilities at forecasting older consumers' behavior as related to clothing purchase
and acquisition. Additionally, by studying older

Original for this text.

consumers, marketers can explore and recognize the apparel purchasing characteristics and needs of this important market segment.

METHOD

Three focus groups were conducted with a total of nine women aged 65 and older in Ames, Iowa. To explore the differences and similarities of older female consumers, participants were asked to join one of the groups based on their age. In total, four participants aged 65–74 years (young-old), two participants aged 75–84 years (middle-old), and three participants aged 85 and above (old-old), were interviewed for this study.

During the focus groups, the women were asked to discuss both their past and present needs and wants for clothing, as well as their interests in fashions and purchasing of new apparel items. Examples of questions included:

- Does clothing have the same importance to you as it did in years past?

- As you have gotten older, are you concerned with your physical appearance?

- If you are concerned with your physical appearance, what are you most concerned about (big hips, wrinkles, height, thinning hair, etc.)?

- In past years, was looking fashionable important to you? If so, is looking fashionable still important to you?

- Does what you wear today differ from what you wore 10 years ago?

- Does what you wear today differ from what you wore 20 years ago?

Of those women who volunteered to participate in the study, four were widowed, three were never married, and two were married. All the participants had obtained a high school diploma, and most had received some form of post-secondary education or job training. The majority of the participants, particularly those widowed or never married, lived a lower-middle-class lifestyle.

RESULTS

In the narratives of the interviews, five major themes emerged. Sample statements made by participants are included to illustrate their thinking about clothing and appearance. Fictitious names are provided to maintain anonymity.

Importance of Clothing Continues with Age

The women clearly stated that clothing has remained important to them over time. The women who had always felt that looking good and having attractive clothing is important generally still felt the same way. This attitude was expressed for a variety of reasons, including maintaining an active social life, caring about one's appearance, and concern about what other people think:

> Clothing has remained important to me as I've gotten older, because I'm still really active and have a social life. (Betty, young-old)

> Clothing is still very important to me. I get up and get dressed every morning even when I'm home all day by myself. I want to look good still. I want to project an image that I feel good and still care what I look like. I think it's important to look nice and attractive so that others will accept you. (Hilda, middle-old)

> It's important to keep yourself up. I wear makeup, fix my hair, and wear fresh clothing almost everyday. You need to be presentable to others. (Olive, middle-old)

Shift to Greater Independence of the Self over Time

While participants of all ages seemed to be concerned about their physical appearance, it was evident that with time, a greater sense of independence emerges as women become less preoccupied with the opinions of others. Although the oldest participants (aged 85 and above) still expressed a desire to maintain their image, these individuals were also more concerned about pleasing the self rather than worrying about how others view them. This indicated a difference in the functions and meanings for clothing among older versus younger participants:

> I don't care as much what anyone else thinks. I look as nice as I can when I'm around others. I don't want to look crummy, but I'm not in the public eye very much. I dress to please myself.... That attitude changes as a person grows older you know.... You just worry less about pleasing other people. (Mary, old-old)

> I was more worried about my image when I was younger and working. I was a grade school teacher, and back then I wore a different outfit each day of the week. I am still active and I still care about my appearance. Not as much though as the past. (Faye, old-old)

> I wear anything when I'm at home. I care more about my appearance when I'm out. I like to feel good about my appearance, but I'm not so worried with that anymore. (Dorothy, old-old)

Looking fashionable seemed to be important to the younger participants. However, keeping up with the latest trends appeared to be less of a priority than it was in earlier years for these women:

> I still value people's opinion of my appearance and choices of clothing. It is important to me to have the new styles, fashions, and colors of clothing.... I just feel younger in new clothing. (Louise, young-old)

> Looking fashionable or stylish is still important to me, but not as much now as past. When you get older, you don't have to always keep up with everything [in terms of latest trends]. But, I still love to wear trendy styles.... I think they look good on me. (Hilda, middle-old)

Concerns over changes in mobility and physical balance also seemed to affect the choices of shoes:

> A lot of the things that I like to wear, I can't anymore...like higher heels or other really cute shoes.... I'm afraid of falling now. (Olive, middle-old)

Concern over Appearance Maintains with Age

Participants in all the age categories reported a need for good hygiene and concern about their overall physical appearance. Similar to past studies (Hurd, 2000; Tunaley et al., 1999), weight was identified as the hardest age-related change to control:

> I always maintain proper hygiene and I worry some about my weight. Losing weight is getting harder and harder as I get older. I have a difficult time finding clothes that fit right and look nice. (Betty, young-old)

Likewise, the respondents in the oldest age category communicated more specific concerns over their physical appearance than the two younger age groups:

> I am still concerned about my physical appearance. Wrinkles and thinning hair are my biggest concerns now. Especially, too, this "turkey neck." (Mary, old-old)

Attitudes toward Clothing and Appearance Remain Steady over Time

An unexpected finding was that the value placed on clothing during one's childhood and adolescent years seemed to carry over into adulthood. Taking a lifespan perspective, it is possible that attitudes learned about prioritizing purchase decisions remain virtually unchanged over time.

In this study, the availability of resources emerged as an issue for some of the participants.

Those individuals who were raised with more money and could afford the latest fashion styles were the participants who indicated that they still place a great deal of importance on their physical appearance and wearing stylish, attractive clothing. Those participants who discussed living with tight resources while growing up had to learn at an early age to place importance on having more basic items as compared to the newest styles and latest fashions:

> Having new clothing was never a priority because we needed money for more essential things. Money was tight.... We had to buy clothing on sale.... That's why I still do that now. (Alice, young-old)

Moreover, women, regardless of age, who indicated that expensive clothing always has been important to them, still maintained that belief. These individuals perceived higher-priced garments and brand-name apparel to be higher in quality:

> Expensive clothing is better and worth more for your money.... Cheaper clothing is not as durable and is less quality.... Brand named clothing lasts longer, too. (Hilda, middle-old)

Preference in Clothing Changes with Age

Regarding preferences in clothing, the women commented that they wear comfortable clothing more frequently, including more T-shirts instead of blouses and more slacks instead of skirts. The majority of the women indicated purchasing more "wash and wear," easy-to-care-for clothing that requires no ironing. The young-old age group reported that clothing that is more modest in design is not necessarily preferred, but is sometimes chosen for warmth. However, the women in the old-old age group mentioned that more modest clothing has become increasingly important over time due to changes in physical appearance, including wrinkling and loss of muscle tone. Another difference between the oldest age group and the younger participants was that these respondents also indicated that their clothing needs have altered more with age. The participants in the oldest age group indicated a greater liking for fabrics with stretch and elasticity and softer, cozier fabrics. Furthermore, these women expressed a more pronounced need to wear vibrant colors to offset the yellowing of the skin that occurs with age:

> I wear a lot of clothes that cover my neck, arms, and legs. I don't wear shorts anymore. I choose clothing with vibrant colors so that I don't seem so bland. I just feel washed out if I don't wear bright colors. My typical outfit is mainly slacks and a pretty blouse.... This is more comfortable.... I don't need to be so dressed up anyways. (Mary, old-old)

Conclusions

As a result of this study, five major themes emerged relating to older women's attitudes toward dress, appearance, and age-related changes. It was found that clothing remains important to women over time, and participants of all ages were found to be concerned about changes in their appearance resulting from the aging process. However, as they aged, women seemed to become less worried about the perceptions of others and more interested in pleasing the self. Preferences in clothing also seemed to change with age, as participants aged 85 and older indicated a need for more modest clothing, with stretch, elasticity, and brighter colors.

Marketers in the apparel industry should be aware of these findings, as using stereotypical images of older women in advertisements today, or ignoring them altogether, could offend this market segment. Furthermore, identifying with older consumers is vital to a firm's success in today's competitive marketplace. Understanding the strong interests in appearance that many older women hold and particular product needs and wants of older consumers will enhance service of this growing market segment.

References

Angelou, M. (2003). *Growing Older*. Accessed June 11, 2003, at www.vibrantuniverse.com /growing_older.html.

Carrigan, M., & Szmigin, I. (1999). The representation of older people in advertisements. *Journal of the Market Research Society*, 41(3):311–325.

Greco, A. (1989). Representation of the elderly in advertising: Crisis or inconsequence? *The Journal of Consumer Marketing*, 6(1):37–44.

Hurd, L. C. (2000). Older women's body image and embodied experience: An exploration. *Journal of Women & Aging*, 12(3/4):77–97.

Oberg, P., & Tornstam, L. (1999). Body images among men and women of different ages. *Ageing and Society*, 19(5):629–644.

Tunaley, J. R., Walsh, S., & Nicolson, P. (1999). "I'm not bad for my age:" The meaning of body size and eating in the lives of older women. *Ageing and Society*, 19(6):741–759.

Vesperi, M. D. (2001). Media, marketing, and images of the older person in the information age. *Generations*, 25(3):5–9.

DISCUSSION QUESTIONS

Older Women's Attitudes

1. Was clothing still as important to these women as when they were younger or did they no longer care how they looked?

2. How had their preferences for clothing changed since they were younger?

3. How did attitudes they had toward clothing in their younger years carry over?

59   Inside a Moroccan Bath

Hanan al-Shaykh

The steam rises. It ascends like clouds drifting upward from the earth to the sky, brushing the naked bodies as gently as butterflies or eyelashes closing in sleep. But it spoils eye makeup, robs hair of its shine, dissolves the red on lips and cheeks, and erases penciled eyebrows. I'd be glad if it engulfed me completely and turned me into a ghost. I am hesitant, embarrassed, unsure of myself. I want to rush and hide away in a corner, or just leave altogether.

I didn't expect to react like this. When I undressed and entered the baths, the throb of noise and heaving female flesh took me completely by surprise. What's happening to me, the emancipated woman who writes about frustration, passion, lust, ecstasy, and describes thighs and breasts in minute detail? Why am I staring as if I've never seen a woman's body before, overwhelmed by the sight of them all, even those I know, and shyly clasp my arms across my front, clutching my armpits as if I'm desperate to hide my breasts? This means I'm still suffering from the same complex I always had about my body, which I thought was dead and buried once I dared to wear a two-piece bathing suit, fell in love, married, had children, lived in the West.

The steam increases, rising from the tiles, soapy, sweaty, smelling of henna and perfume, bearing the gossip exchanged by the bathers in spite of the shrieking and yelling of the children. The baths are for washing but also for caring for the body on a grand scale. Bodies that are not laid aside after fulfilling their functions in marriage, sex, and childbirth to become merely factories swallowing and excreting food can continue to expect this fate. I see women descending on their bodies like furies, flaying them with loofahs and stones as if they want to exchange their existing skins for new ones. I've never seen a shop in Europe with half the bath products that they have on offer here: country-style soap, cleansing mud the color of petrol, dried rose petals ground to a powder, ghassoul for the hair, artificial loofahs with bristles that look as if they're for washing the dishes or sweeping the floor, natural loofahs, pumice stones, manufactured stones. Bathing and massaging the body is supposed to be the main point of visiting the public baths, even though most houses have their own bathrooms. From what I've seen of these small, cold rooms, they are mainly used for washing the clothes, while here the women are dotted about the vast space singly and in clumps, intent on pulling and pummeling their flesh, pouring water over themselves, rinsing their hair, embracing the steam as it enters every pore, and sitting in silence from time to time. It's as if the desire to be alone with their bodies as they wait for the heat to strike them has killed the wish to talk with the others. So all this activity is for the sake of being alone with

the body released from its prison of constricting undergarments, thick outer garments, headcover and shoes, and cleansed from the dust of the streets, the clinging smells of food, and the sweat running under the arms, between the breasts, and down the forehead with the effort of scrubbing tiles in dim rooms, washing children's heads, rubbing chickens with lemon and cumin.

I look at the women sitting, standing, bending, squatting, stretching, some silent, some shouting and laughing. I gaze at their plump, plump bodies, their hanging breasts, the numerous folds of skin on their stomachs, the fat that makes the flesh around their thighs pucker into circles like fans. And there are bodies disfigured by burn marks, scars, surgery, old age. However, it seems to me as I watch them move gracefully around the baths, floating, ethereal, that they are preparing to make love to freedom and will soon be in ecstasy. I stand here totally confused in the heat. I am in Shoufshawen in Morocco with my Moroccan friend, who has begun scrubbing a patch of the tiled floor with her loofah and soap, muttering to herself for forgetting the extra towels to sit on, then raising her voice to a shrill cry to answer back to an old woman who's accused her of stealing her place.

I would like to sit down in the heart of the muggy warmth and close my eyes so that all I can hear is the slop and smack of the water as it rinses bodies clean of the dust of the outside world, but I can't bring myself to. I am still shocked by my discovery that I am not completely at ease with the shape of my body, having thought I'd gone beyond that stage long ago. It doesn't help when the masseuse remarks laughingly to my friend that she will only charge me half price since she is only going to have to massage half a body.

From the time I first began to have a mental picture of my face and figure without needing to look in a mirror, I understood that I was suffering from an incurable illness: the disease of thinness, with its accompanying symptoms of pallor and weakness. No, I didn't discover this for myself. I heard it constantly on the lips of others, adults and children, and saw it in the way they looked at me. They not only made comments and throwaway remarks, confirming what I already knew, but were out to criticize and reproach me. "Why are you so thin?" "Why are you letting yourself fade away?" Some went to great lengths to stress the defect they had been kind enough to draw my attention to, and I was known as the skinny girl, kibbeh on a stick (i.e., my head was the kibbeh and my body the stick), bamboo cane, cornstalk. They would put their thumbs and forefingers round my forearm and if they met (and they always did) there would be roars of laughter and a general feeling of satisfaction that the magic test had worked. When the teacher wanted to describe the backbone in nature study, she made me take off my overall and turn my back so that she could point with her ruler to each vertebra.

Being thin meant that I was branded as sickly and physically weak, and so I was never encouraged in sports periods or picked for teams. Instead they would call out, "Hey, skinny! If they rolled you up in the gym mat no one would notice!" So the idea that I was different from my peers began to preoccupy me and make me keep to myself, unsmiling and with none of a child's spontaneity. I think now that my reluctance to concentrate in class might have been a product of this feeling of terror that overcame me every time I thought I might have to leave my cozy lair and stand up by the board in front of the whole class.

As soon as I was old enough to know what I was doing, I began to take cod liver oil capsules and make my family buy fresh milk, for I had made up my mind to gain weight by any means possible. When my efforts came to nothing I forced myself to get used to my bony shoulders and my protruding collarbone, which formed a necklace each time I raised my shoulders, although I don't suppose anyone was entertained by this but me.

I used to envy the ripe, round cheeks of the other girls, and their chubby arms and legs. I was jealous of the fattest girl in our class, with her many chins, thick forearms, and her huge bottom that shook at the tiniest movement. I envied swellings of any kind: swollen eyes, cheeks inflamed with toothache, thighs that were red and angry following injections. I welcomed anything that would allow me to enjoy an increase in flesh, to prove that I was not a barren wasteland, had a normal body that reacted to illnesses and external influences. I was so envious, and I withdrew from my fellows and drew pictures of myself looking like a balloon on a couple of matchsticks. I was jealous, jealous and turned inward, convincing myself that I was different. I pretended not to enjoy belly dancing like the rest of the girls because it was old-fashioned, and so I sat out at weddings, my jealous eye observing the swaying breasts and buttocks of the girls who were dancing, and the perfect control they had over their waists and stomachs so that their whole bodies writhed and coiled like serpents in venomous harmony. My other eye tried to pretend it wasn't there, terrified that it would meet the eyes of the dancers and they would insist that I join them on the floor, as was the custom, whereupon I would fall into the snares of shame and humiliation. I was quite certain that if I danced and tried to twist and sway I would bend stiffly like a wooden plank and if I squirmed sensuously I would look as if I'd suffered an electric shock.

I kept apart, in mixed gatherings as well as all-female occasions, persuaded that I was different because of my passion for words and stories, and that I was going to be a writer. I used to retire into a corner with pen and paper, and pretend to be writing poetry, off in another world far removed from my companions' ephemeral preoccupations, knowing in advance with absolute conviction that nobody would ever ask me to dance, or marry me, and that I would never have children. My periods didn't come because I was so thin, and the proof was that I was almost fourteen and therefore well past the age when they should have arrived. So as soon as I saw the long-awaited brownish spots in my knickers, I flew to announce it to the women of the house, then rushed to the neighbors to give them the news, or rather to make them acknowledge that I was normal. However, reaching puberty did nothing to alleviate my anxiety about my scrawny shoulders, the nonexistence of my chest and bottom, and my thin wrists and arms. I used to shut my eyes attempting to push away the recurring image of a boy holding me in his arms, because a schoolfriend had said I was like a soup made of bones when she embraced me one day, and after that I had always imagined that as soon as a boy touched me my bones would stick into him so sharply that this would be his abiding image of the encounter.

I created an image of pure fantasy for myself, a girl sitting staring distractedly at the horizon or up into the sky, alone day and night, a girl who had abandoned her body and become a specter, or a spirit, pale and solemn like one of Dracula's victims. I convinced myself that I had been made of different clay from those plump, fleshy girls who won the hearts of boys with humdrum tastes and greedy appetites. God had created me without bumps or curves to flutter gracefully through life like a butterfly. To my surprise, this self-made persona attracted a boy who used to call me the Virgin Mary, or the nun, and who got out of dancing with me by saying he was afraid I'd break or be contaminated. He sent me Khalil Gibran's books and pictures of sunrises and sunsets.

I did nothing to change my image until I saw a poster of Audrey Hepburn that stuck in my mind. I felt she had come to take revenge on Brigitte Bardot for me.

I saw her closing her eyes and yielding to a kiss. I saw her encircled by two strong arms. I saw her, and I saw myself for the first time: long neck, pale skin, dark eyes, black hair and eyebrows. I bought a copy of *Breakfast at Tiffany's* and a pair of dark glasses with round frames, and borrowed a long black cigarette holder. I followed her news on and off screen. Was she in love? Married? Did she have any children? Was she planning to? I went to see all her films two or three times to observe and register everything that passed between her and the hero and try to detect whether he really wanted to kiss her even though she was so thin. Did he hold her fragile body as if she was any other actress,

or was he scared that he would break one of her ribs? Would he reach out to feel her breast or deliberately ignore it to avoid causing embarrassment? I gazed at the relevant scenes to learn by heart the position of her arms and the manner of her response, and eventually made the discovery that with her thin body she had exploded preconceived notions of what a woman ought to be like. I remember writing after I'd seen one of her films, "She isn't the woman everyone falls in love with, or a flirt, or a woman with problems. She's a child, personifying innocence. She's untamed love, a fragrant fruit, graceful as a willow. Her face talks, laughs, cries, lives, captivating the hero and the audience and leaving them satisfied."

By imitating Audrey Hepburn and her hairstyle when I was seventeen, I attracted the attention of assorted poets, journalists, and cinema buffs of the opposite sex in my city, Beirut. First I had prepared the ground and redirected their ideas and enthusiasms along a particular course, feeding them with the notion that I belonged to a new breed of women who were attractive in a special, different way, by virtue of being thin and delicate in contrast to the male's brute strength. As this new-style woman was discussed and the connection made between me and her, I began to gain in confidence and self-esteem, although I put myself in a special category, which separated me from conventional femininity. A poet who was responsible for the cultural page of a daily newspaper began contacting me every time he came across a news item relating to Audrey Hepburn or a photo of her. I felt he was flirting with me via her, especially when he got his hands on the first photos of her in a bathing suit. He said she was like a swan or Lolita. Hope grew in me that I would become an object of desire even if it meant copying Audrey Hepburn's style. I pictured that anyone sitting across a table from me would be enchanted by my slender body and my innocent, childlike gestures, until one day I was sitting in a café with the poet just as she would have sat, confused and lost in the bustle and smoke and loneliness. I inhabited a different world from my family. I had been born and brought up in the heart of a noisy city in a house where they preferred the call to prayer and the sound of the Quran to singing and music. The clash between the city, with the clamor of its cinemas and cafés and universities, and my restricted home environment with my family's subdued voices and monotonous daily routine was almost killing me. Uncertain where I stood, I longed to retreat into a corner and write of the sorrow and despair that gripped me whenever I thought about death and loneliness, or about getting away from home and recreating myself on my own terms. So I cried tears of bewilderment in front of the poet, wondering what it was I wanted. I cried like Audrey Hepburn when she stood in the rain calling her cat: "Cat! Cat!" The poet reached out a hand to me, squeezed my arm, and patted me on the shoulder. I knew he couldn't take me in his arms like the hero when he was trying to ease Audrey Hepburn's loneliness and confusion in the face of the turbulent world. I was reassured by the warmth of his touch even though I was worried that people would notice. I clung to his hand as if it was my temporary life line, a compass that would help me find my way to the ends of the earth. Within me I carried this image of woman as fragile, delicate, and passionate beside man's overwhelming strength. Then the poet spoke hesitantly, full of sympathy and understanding: "I know what your problem is. It's because you're thin. That's what's responsible for all this grief. This uncertainty. You have to put on weight. A few kilos and you'll see, you'll be a different person. I used to have exactly the same problem."

After this episode I was no longer surprised by the way others viewed me, or how their ideas and perceptions regarding my thinness acted upon each other. I attached myself to an imaginary raft and rode the waves, rising and falling but never losing my grip. When I went to Egypt to study I wrote to a journalist friend who had his own arts and gossip page in a magazine, describing my experiences abroad and enclosing a recent photograph, and I was only mildly annoyed when a poem by him appeared in the magazine a few weeks later that

included the line "My love's put on about two kilos and I love her almost twice as much." While I was in Egypt an Egyptian student used to follow me around the university saying "You're pretty. I love you. If only you weren't so skinny. Try and put on a bit of weight. You'd be a really beautiful woman. I'll tell you how to make me fall in love with you. If you do as I say you'll become like a big ripe peach. You have to eat macaroni. Blancmange. Rice. Beef marrow." And I wasn't really hurt when they told me that his girlfriend didn't care when she saw him pursuing me because she was sure that he couldn't fall in love with a woman whose arms and legs were practically nonexistent. Meanwhile his mother took pity on me, totally convinced that being away from my family and my country had affected my health and reduced me to this weakened state.

The poet's words, which had robbed me of my confidence and happiness, made me able, eventually, to stick my tongue out in response to a remark I heard as I walked proudly past a café: "What a pity! That face and a body like a sparrow!" They also made me tolerant with the dressmaker when she suggested putting a double lining in my dress especially at the shoulders and hips. I blocked my ears and remained attached to my imaginary raft, swinging between the heights and the depths, but never falling off. I calmed down and took a hold of myself, reminding myself that I hadn't come to Egypt because I was desperate to find love, but for the sense of freedom I could enjoy there. I remembered the mother of one of my friends back in Lebanon. She weighed over two hundred kilos, and how her eyes had sparkled when she found out I was going to Cairo! Her hand had flown to her throat in a thoroughly feminine gesture. "You're so lucky! Cairo! Only in Cairo do I feel that I'm really beautiful." Meanwhile her husband, who was a gynecologist, remarked that I should massage my breasts with olive oil every day to make them grow.

The steam rises from my body and the bodies around me. I realize why I am sad. The moment I entered the baths I saw myself as thin again, imperfect next to the plump ripeness of the other women. I am filled with sadness for the years that should have been like Aladdin's lamp or a magic carpet, transporting me away to discover the color of music or the heart of an ant, while instead I had been crammed into a rigid, gloomy mold with only a tiny chink to breathe through. Now I am demanding of myself, of the steam, of the women, why I had been denied this kernel of joy and security, this chance to explore, all because of a handful of flesh that wasn't there. I'd felt poverty-stricken and embarrassed hearing people say all the time that I was thin because I hadn't been fed properly. I'd stopped having the heart to look for emotional attachments, and felt inhibited when I moved and spoke. Sometimes I would rush into the café limping, pretending I'd hurt my foot to distract attention from my thin legs, and also just to confuse things. In my attempts to convince myself that I was desirable, I would be drawn into playing games with men, even those I didn't care about at all. For the sake of this absent flesh I had begun hiding my body under yards of material so that I looked like a cabbage with a human head, and inhabiting dark chambers of anxiety, fearful that I would never be able to have children. A neighbor of mine used to encourage her daughters to eat up food they didn't like by saying "Look at Hanan! If you don't eat up, you'll get like her!" And when one of them shouted, "I like Hanan! I want to be like her!" her mother said, to shut her up, "But Hanan will live all by herself. She'll never have children and nobody will ever call her Mama." How could I carry a child? Would the fetus have room, or would it be squashed up against my pelvis? How would it get its nourishment, seeing that the food I ate didn't seem to put any flesh on me?

I feel that the bodies around me, the hills and mountains of flesh observing me, have themselves nailed the conditions of entry over the door to happiness, by setting the standards of strength and beauty and decreeing what is acceptable and desirable. For these women still stick to the rule that says that the male eye is the only mirror where they can see their true reflection.

In the past, mothers, grandmothers, aunts, and neighbors were equipped with microscopic eyes for seeking out and examining future brides for the sons of the family in the public baths. They preferred to make their inspection there because the steam removed penciled eyebrows, made fine hair cling limply to the scalp, revealed whether the woman's body was firm or not. It had to be rounded, even if this meant there was no waist to speak of, have broad hips and a gently curved stomach sloping down to the thighs, uninterrupted by any bony protrusions. A woman's body was for bearing children, providing them with nourishment, giving them all the milk they wanted, and keeping them warm in the folds of its flesh. It was also for feeding and satisfying man's greedy lust. This is why the famous poets of the pre-Islamic era did not sing about thin women. Their poems about love and beauty are always concerned with curvaceous bodies, and even modern literature glorifies solid, voluptuous flesh and connects it with sexual desire.

But do the standards of the past still apply? Have Arab women not been affected by the West, where the revolutions not just against fat but any surplus flesh have resulted in illnesses, the coining of terms like anorexia and bulimia to designate them, and widespread recourse to cosmetic surgery, sometimes with unfortunate or even disastrous results?

Although it's hard to generalize, I think thinness is still considered undesirable in the Arab world, even among young women and adolescents. By this I don't mean they'd choose to be fat these days, but they like a shapely, athletic figure, combining grace and energy with femininity: prominent bust, slender waist, flat stomach, then curving buttocks and nicely rounded but firm bottom and thighs. They have a keen sense of what men find attractive, but at the same time have their own clearly defined criteria of what is desirable in a man: an athletic, well-proportioned body, "someone who fills his clothes," as they say, for a thin man, according to the conventional wisdom, is weak, has low self-esteem, and lacks personality, the exact opposite of what a woman wants in a man.

Inside the bath, the women's eyes never leave me and I am certain they are wondering where I am from. It must be the color of my skin. Am I from Fez, where the women delight in white skin and black hair? From the way they look I guess they approve of my fair skin, apparently still desirable because the dominant skin color in the Arab world is brown. Nevertheless, brown skin features in all the popular songs, but when I remarked on this to my mother, who was lamenting over the way my skin had changed color that summer, she replied, "Don't let these songs fool you. They're purely to reassure brown-skinned women."

It's my white skin that saves me now. It is a mark of femininity and fragility because it contrasts with the darker skin of men. It inspires poetic comparisons like "pearly white," "white as snow," "white as the surface of a jug of milk." But even whiteness has its conditions: There must be a tinge of crimson on the cheeks, otherwise it represents purity, chastity, and coldness.

The looks and whispers are giving way to laughter, or barely suppressed sniggers. I have the uneasy feeling this time that they are thinking about my thinness in connection with sex, trying to picture me with a man. I'm used to provoking such reactions in other women fatter than me. Several years ago an elderly relation had picked me up and lifted me high in the air, exclaiming "You poor thing! You're as light as a feather! Does your husband squash you flat?" A friend asked me where my bottom had gone, and there are people who commiserate with my husband, saying there's nothing for him to hold on to.

I return their stares, wishing they knew what I am thinking: They will leave here buried under mounds of cloth to protect themselves from the shock of the cool air outside and perhaps also from the wounding glances of men, but when they reach home they will throw it all

off and prance and sway before their husbands. Some will dress up in belly dancers' costumes, like a woman I know, or in underwear so clearly designed to be crudely seductive that it ends up with a surreal quality: I once saw a pair of battery-powered panties with a light that flashed on and off at the crotch. I know these women are scared of their husbands being prey to other women and want to keep them at home at any price, so they attract them at the level of lust and purely physical satisfaction, discounting the idea, on behalf of both themselves and their men, that love is also the desire to possess and delight in beauty.

I am boiling hot and move into one of the baths' cool rooms. Suddenly I think of my daughter, who is eighteen, and feel myself returning to normal. I see her slender figure in my mind's eye, and people complimenting her on being so tall and slim. I recall a photo of myself in my adolescence and decide that my thinness wasn't sickly but attractive: I look exactly like my daughter in it, except that I am seven centimeters shorter than her. I laugh involuntarily at the memory of another photo taken around the same time of me with my stomach sticking out. I used to take deep breaths and inflate it so that I looked fatter, even though I knew it gave me a distorted shape.

I retreat into myself. I will try to give this quietness to the one I love. I am perfectly content to be leaving and going back to the European city where I live, where people compliment me on keeping my figure. But I am still weighed down by these old-new feelings, which bring back to me a picture of my friend's father, the gynecologist, stamping on his brakes in the middle of a Beirut street indifferent to the stream of cars behind him, and shouting through the window as if there was no one else for miles around, "Hanan al-Shaykh! So you're married at last! Are your tits any bigger these days?"

Inside a Moroccan Bath

1. How did Hanan al-Shaykh's feelings about her body evolve when she was a young woman?

2. What kind of reviews shaped her feelings about her body? Who gave her feedback?

3. What change in her life brought her a marked change in body satisfaction?

4. Why does she return to adolescent feelings about her body in the Moroccan baths?

CHAPTER 10

Race and Ethnicity

Susan O. Michelman

AFTER YOU HAVE READ THIS CHAPTER, YOU WILL COMPREHEND:

- That people have culturally constructed categories of race and ethnicity affecting social issues and problems regarding appearance.

- The relationship of race and ethnicity—particularly as they affect issues of appearance—to gain an appreciation for the experience of those in the minority in American society.

- The impact that issues of race and ethnicity have on American consumer culture.

In this chapter, we will consider how race and ethnicity affect issues of dress and appearance. Although these concepts will be considered and discussed individually, it is important to understand that these issues have an impact on appearance and must be considered collectively as they intersect and interact with one another within every society.

RACE AND APPEARANCE

Race is a term that refers to certain visible and distinctive characteristics that are determined by biology. Along with gender, it is the first thing we notice about another person. The challenge, however, lies in identifying the physical traits that distinguish one race from another. By convention, people are assigned to one of three racial categories—Caucasoid, Mongoloid, or Negroid. Many of the world's population of 6.3 billion people do not fit neatly into one racial category in which there are sharp dividing lines distinguished by features such as black skin versus white or curly hair versus straight (Ferrante, 1994). For example, most Australian Aboriginals have black skin and Negroid facial features, but they also may have blond, wavy hair (Newman, 1995). (See Figure 10.1.)

Race is a social construction. The physical characteristics that distinguish one group from another are determined less by physical characteristics than by what a particular culture defines as socially significant. Consider the diversity of being "black" in the following statements:

> Brazil historically has not had a rigid conception of race and thus has a variety of "intermediate" races. In fact, the designation of race is so fluid that parents, children, brothers, and sisters are sometimes accepted as representatives of very different races. (Harris, 1964)

In South Africa there are four legally defined races—black, white, colored, and Indian—but in Great Britain the term *black* is used to refer to all people who are not white. An African-American visiting Tanzania is likely to be considered white by the African blacks there (Newman, 1995).

FIGURE 10.1 *Physique and dress of this gentleman of 1860 are indicators of his status in society.*

In American society we tend to see race in categorical terms: black or white, red or yellow, brown or black. Even when there are mixed-race children, we still tend to place them in categories. The United States still adheres to the **one-drop rule** for blacks, but not for any other racial group. The term comes from a common law in the South during slavery that a "single drop of black blood" made a person black. According to the U.S. Census, to be considered black one needs only to have any known African black ancestry. Anthropologists call this a hypodescent rule, meaning that racially mixed people are always assigned the status of the subordinate group. Hence, a person with seven out of eight great-grandparents who are white and only one who is black is still considered black (Davis, 1991). Trice, in the article "Complex Issues of Complexion Still Haunt Blacks," looks at the issue of skin color, which can be linked to perceptions of self-worth.

People have created categories of race, and therein lies the source of some of the social issues and problems regarding appearance that will be addressed in articles in this chapter. Yamanaka, in "When Asian Eyes Are Smiling," reflects on how she, as a Japanese-American girl growing up in Hawaii, manipulated her eyes with a thin strip of transparent tape. This changed the look of her eyes from what she describes as "slant eyes, seeing-through-venetian-blinds eyes" to a more mainstream, and to her acceptable, appearance. As she matured, she gained greater acceptance with her natural appearance.

Racial injustices have their basis in equating the social value of individuals with their physical appearance. **Racism** is a belief that something in the biological makeup of an ethnic or racial group explains and justifies its subordinate or superior status (Ferrante, 1994). A hundred years ago in the United States, there were churches that "had a pinewood slab on the outside door . . . and a fine-tooth comb hanging on a string . . ." (Angelou, 1987). You could attend the church if your skin was no darker than the pinewood and if you could comb your hair without any snags. In "Complex Issues of Complexion Still Haunt Blacks," Trice discusses the implications, sometimes within the African-American community itself, of varying shades of skin tones. She contends that there is a value system going back to slavery days when light skin was preferable to dark. Under apartheid in South Africa, a state board oversaw the racial classification of everyone in the country. One test was to place a pencil in a person's hair; if it fell out, the person was classified as white (Finnegan, 1986). Wickliffe, in the article "Black Hair—Black Times," examines how African-American hair and styling are an expression of self and individuality. Frequently, some of these styles make a strong connection to African ancestry. Other readings in this chapter will challenge you to examine social constructions of race as they relate to issues of appearance.

ETHNICITY AND APPEARANCE

Ethnicity is a learned cultural heritage shared by a category of people that can include common national origin, ancestry, style of dress, language, dietary habits, and ideology, to name just a few characteristics. Race and ethnicity are separate concepts, yet are frequently used incorrectly as interchangeable in meaning. For example, Chinese-Americans are quite different ethnically from Chinese people born in China, although their racial background may be identical. One's ethnicity plays a major role in others' perceptions of a person's appearance. The sociologist Paul Starr (1982) found that, in the absence of a distinctive skin color and other physical characteristics, ethnicity is judged by others on the basis of many imprecise attributes such as language, residence, type of jewelry, tattoos or other body markings, and, of course, dress. The article "My Jewish Nose" by Jervis is a personal reflection on being Jewish in a California community that she considers to be not so Jewish. She specifically focuses on why many Jews dislike their noses and have "nose jobs" as a way of physically fitting in and not standing out as an ethnic minority. This particular author affirms that she wants to retain her Jewish nose as well as her ethnic identity.

Racial and ethnic classification schemes may contain false assumptions that specific abilities (e.g., athletic talent, intelligence), social traits (e.g., criminal tendencies, aggressiveness), and cultural practices (e.g., dress, language) are transmitted genetically. Therefore, the experience of being a minority person in a predominantly white culture such as the United States is one where individuals may be denied access to important resources such as education, health care, and higher levels of income based on the false assumption that their race or ethnicity is inferior. Consumer research groups have confirmed that blacks often speak of being watched too closely, or, on the other extreme, ignored in retail settings. This is a good example of how a behavior of minority groups may be stereotyped on the basis of race and ethnicity. In the article "Generación Latino," Stapinski examines the growth of the Hispanic market and explains why so many companies are targeting this demographic section of American society. By 2005, Hispanic youth will be the largest ethnic youth population in the country, and they are having a broad impact on consumer issues in the mainstream marketplace, including everything from food to fashion.

Ethnic dress and ethnicity are linked to each other (Eicher, 1995). Much has been written about both the history and present-day practice of the meaning of ethnic dress. It remains a tangible and visible way that many hold on to their own backgrounds within the context of rapid social change and shifting identities. Frequently, ethnic clothing, by its symbolic nature, has become the piece of material culture that remains part of the unwritten history of certain groups. For example, some Hmong quilts made by women who experienced the Cambodian conflict in the 1960s are a pictorial history of their lives before, during, and after the war that was infrequently recorded in words.

Author Annette Lynch explores similar issues in the article "Hmong American New Year's Dress: The Display of Ethnicity." Currently, changing demographics, particularly in urban areas, have created a new interest in what it means to be a member of an ethnic minority, particularly if the person is white and from the dominant culture. Many popular clothing styles are **trickling up** from the media, street culture, and styles formerly reserved for ethnic minorities. Consequently, what was "out" in terms of ethnic dress style in the past may be very "in" today, particularly for adolescents. Lynch examines how Hmong refugees from Laos have experienced radical changes in all aspects of the social life as they have moved from their life in isolated and traditional hill tribes to crowded, technologically sophisticated lives in the United States. The effects of American culture have similarly had an impact on the modification or abandonment of traditional dress, particularly among the younger Hmong not born in Laos. The article provides an example of **cultural assimilation,** a process that occurs when one group moves to or integrates with another group.

Summary

By examining the relationship of race and ethnicity, particularly the impact they have on issues of appearance, we can gain an appreciation for the experience of those in the minority in American society. The articles presented in this chapter will challenge critical thinking skills that relate to the multiple realities and perspectives of "appearing" in the minority. This is helpful in order to develop a framework to evaluate our social system, to question it, and to understand how a person's perspectives, life chances, options, and opportunities, as well as those of others, are shaped by it.

Suggested Readings

Holloman, L. (1990). Clothing symbolism in African American Greek letter organizations. In B. Starke, L. Holloman, & B. Nordquist (Eds.), *African American Dress and Adornment: A Cultural Perspective*, pp. 140–150. Dubuque, IA: Kendal Hunt Publishing Co.

hooks, b. (1992). *Black Looks: Race and Representation*. Boston: South End Press.

Mercer, K. (1991). Black hair/style politics. In *Out There: Marginalization and Contemporary Cultures*, pp. 247–264. Cambridge, MA: MIT Press.

O'Neal, G. S. (1998, Spring). African American women's professional dress as expression of ethnicity. *Journal of Family and Consumer Sciences*, 28–33.

LEARNING ACTIVITY

Ethnic Stereotypes and Their Consequences

Mary Lynn Damhorst, Harriet McLeod, and Cassie Moon
Iowa State University and University of Nebraska

Objective: This exercise is a challenging in-class group activity that helps participants dissect a stereotype, consider the relationships of component parts of a multifaceted phenomenon, and understand consequences of labeling minority groups in the United States.

A stereotype is a classification or typing of a group of people that results in applying a set of generalized characteristics to them. Even though the stereotype usually does not completely fit any one individual, all members of the group are typed the same. In this exercise, each student in class will be asked to verbalize a stereotype in society. Do not be afraid to "speak the unspeakable" and list highly controversial ideas. You are not saying that you hold this stereotype, but that these ideas are held by some people in the United States. We will examine the dangers of stereotypical thinking as we move through the exercise.

Procedure

Form groups of four to seven people.

Think of a group of Americans (i.e., Native, Asian, African, or Hispanic) that is stereotyped in United States society. List the label given to the group.

Next, work as a group to write down a list of characteristics commonly assigned to that group when stereotyped. As you list items, put a star next to those that relate to appearance.

Next, identify those parts of the stereotype that are either negative or positive.

Ground Rules

Some essential ground rules when working on this exercise are:

1. It is okay to feel uncomfortable about writing down a stereotype; we all can learn valuable lessons from the discomfort.

2. It is okay to write socially and politically incorrect thoughts and words during this exercise. You will need to verbalize and understand the components of a stereotype that may seem ugly or even absurd. Laughing about the stereotypes is permissible, as this helps relieve tensions about the stereotypes.

3. It is important that no one gets angry at stereotypes that other groups construct; no one in class should be accused of actually holding the verbalized stereotypes. This is a learning exercise, not a statement of personal beliefs. An atmosphere of tolerance and openness is essential for learning.

Discussion

When class groups are through recording the stereotypes and noting positive and negative components, each group should:

1. Read the stereotype their group devised to the whole class.
2. Consider whether the appearance components of the stereotype help to trigger the labeling.
3. Read what they think is negative about the stereotype and think about what consequences those negative components may have for the people to whom the stereotype is applied.
4. Read what they think is positive about the stereotype and think what consequences those positive components may have for the people so labeled.

Discuss whether any two or more individuals can have all the components of any of the stereotypes. Is it fair to apply the stereotype before knowing a person, even if the stereotype fits somewhat?

References

Angelou, M. (1987). Intra-racism. Interview on the Oprah Winfrey Show. Journal Graphics transcript #W172:2.

Davis, F. J. (1991). *Who Is Black?* University Park: Pennsylvania State University Press.

Eicher, J. (1995). Dress as expression of ethnic identity. In J. Eicher (Ed.), *Dress and Ethnicity*. Oxford: Berg Publishers.

Ferrante, J. (1994). *Sociology: A Global Perspective*. Belmont, CA: Wadsworth Publishing Co.

Finnegan, W. (1986). *Crossing the Line: A Year in the Land of Apartheid*. New York: Harper & Row.

Harris, M. (1964). *Patterns of Race in the Americas*. New York: Norton.

Mercer, K. (1991). Black hair/style politics. In *Out There: Marginalization and Contemporary Cultures*. Cambridge, MA: MIT Press.

Newman, D. (1995). *Sociology: Exploring the Architecture of Everyday Life*. Thousand Oaks, CA: Pine Forge Press.

Sproles, G., & Burns, L. (1994). *Changing Appearances: Understanding Dress in Contemporary Society*. New York: Fairchild.

Starr, P. (1982). *The Social Transformation of American Medicine*. New York: Basic Books.

60   When Asian Eyes Are Smiling

Lois-Ann Yamanaka

Kala's got droopy eyes. She's been stretching out the skin with Scotch tape and Duo eyelash glue since the seventh grade. As a Japanese-American girl growing up in Hawaii, Kala, my sister, learned early to hate the way she looked—her eyes especially, slanty and rice-y in her mirrored reflection.

She has what we call single eyes: the piece of skin that hangs from the brow is smooth and taut, and very different from the *haoles*, or whites, who have deeper-set eyes with a distinct fold above the lid. Double eyes, in other words. Kala wasn't alone in her quest to look more like a white girl. We all longed for eyes like those of Cheryl Tiegs, Cheryl Ladd, or Natalie Wood, whom we watched in late-night reruns of *This Property Is Condemned.* And we would get those eyes by stretching and pulling and then taping and gluing the skin of our lids back into a self-made fold.

Now, 12 years later, Kala and I are in a plastic surgeon's office in Honolulu, where I live. The doctor looks at me first, and I wonder if he's thinking, "Does this one want the fatty tissue from her chin removed?" Then he looks at Kala. "Hmmm. Sagging eyelids. . . ." He sees. He's heard the tragic Oriental-eye story a hundred times before.

When we were teenagers, Kala would give her three sisters the haole eyes that all Oriental girls wanted. (And we were Orientals back then, though we've come to be defined as Asian Americans, another neat category for all of us. We were Orientals with our own aisle called Oriental Foods in every supermarket in town, as though every other aisle was Occidental Foods.) She would put a dab of Duo eyelash glue on a toothpick, make a thin line over my lid, then lift the skin slightly into the glue. "Don't blink," she would warn, "or you'll get an uneven, bumpy line." And in a minute, I had double eyes.

On our sisters, Melba and Claire, she used pieces of Scotch tape and would carefully place a thin strip in a well-formed arch right over their lids. When the skin folded over the tape, their double eyes rivaled Donna Mills's: Where God didn't, Kala did. She made visible creases (medically known as the supratarsal folds) for all of us.

And then we'd have *haole* eyes. No more Oriental eyes, dammit—slant eyes, seeing-through-venetian-blinds eyes, kamikaze eyes, your-ancestors-started-World-War-II eyes, Nip eyes. We had double eyes, thank you very much, even if we couldn't wet our faces when we went to the beach, lest we emerge, eyelids sagging, glue white and bumpy, and pieces of Scotch tape floating like shiny dead minnows in the tide.

In school, my friend Melanie stretched her skin out so much that she was forced to pull more and more of it into the tuck, until the red veins under her eyelids were exposed. Her eyelashes stood straight up, and all the way through high school she never got a really good blink during daylight hours. Then there was Nina, who explained to us the uselessness of curling our eyelashes after we had glued our eyelids unless we wanted to pinch the meat in the process and risk an eye infection. And Suzanne, Nancy, and Debbie, whose parents financed clandestine trips to Japan for eye operations the summer of my junior year in high school. The three rich and popular girls returned with the puffy surprised look of double eyes for a fabulously tapeless and glueless senior year free of supratarsal oppression.

"So you need blepharoplasty surgery?" the doctor asks Kala.

"Yes."

"Both eyes need some work," he says. He hands my sister a photo album of his bletharoplasty successes. We gaze at all the Asian faces in the album, a lineup of *haole* wannabes, page after page of beautiful "before" faces without smiles. Why did they do it? And then the "after"—women smiling for the camera with their eyes healed but still slightly swollen six months after surgery. So many faces: a classic Japanese, a porcelain Korean, flawless Chinese features.

A sad realization came over me as we flipped through the doctor's book. We were all Oriental girls who had never seen our faces in a magazine, on TV, or in the movies, unless you're talking Suzie Wong, Fan Tan Fanny, or Mrs. Livingston. The only roles available to beautiful Asian actresses were riddled with Charlie Chang-chop-suey talk and stereotypes; Juanita Hall as Madame Liang in *Flower Drum Song* was African-American. Agnes Moorehead, Katharine Hepburn, and Shirley MacLaine were *haole* with heavy eyeliner. They didn't count.

When Kala was home in Honolulu last Christmas, we counted the blepharoplastics in our aerobics class (mostly Japanese nationals), on interisland flights, and the streets of Chinatown. (And contrary to what *haole* America thinks, we don't all look alike, and we can tell a Japanese from a Chinese from a Korean from a Filipina from an Indian). We can also tell who couldn't afford a top-notch surgeon like the one Kala went to see and was forced to go to the butcher Korean doctor. He flies in twice a year and lines up hordes of Asian women who all suspiciously begin to have the same surprised expressions.

Kala earned a cosmetology degree a few years back in San Francisco and learned how to contour her nose with brown and white eye shadow—her own Japanese nose, she thought, was too flat. She learned to draw dark eyeliner on top of the glue on her eyelid, creating the illusion of even more of a fold. Now in the doctor's office, she sees my reflection in the plastic sheet-ing covering the photos, and it's almost identical to her own. She closes the photo album. The look she gives me makes me sad. In her eyes, I see all the Asian girls and women who have mutilated themselves in the hopes of looking white. "I think I'll treat Mommy to Las Vegas with this money instead," Kala finally says, deciding against the surgery.

"Scotch tape was made for wrapping Christmas presents," I say.

Kala really doesn't look as droopy as she thinks. She's Japanese-American beautiful, and her face alone gets us a good table at a crowded restaurant or into the faster lane on the freeway during rush-hour traffic.

She grimaces. "That's the magic of Scotch tape," she muses. We get up to leave the building. "The transparency."

She's right about the whole notion of our feeling invisible in the eyes of others. For us, it was the lack of images of ourselves in magazines, literature, movies, and pop culture that made us want to be otherwise, Orient to Occident, yet we were so utterly visible and transparent in our attempts.

Kala, who's now back in San Francisco, sends me magazine articles on Josie Natori, Tina Chow, Gemma Kahng, Naomi Campbell, Anna Sui, Jenny Shimizu—every one an affirmation. I send her copies of books by Maxine Hong Kingston, Chitra Divakaruni, Nora Okja Keller, Cathy Song, Jessica Hagedorn, Gish Jen, Cynthia Kadohata, where we see our own faces.

We recognize our lives in movies, television, and plays because of actresses such as Ming-Na Wen, Gong Li, Joan Chen, Margaret Cho, Tia Carrere, Lea Salonga, Tamlyn Tomita.

Our Asian-American eyes, open now and knowing, are fixed on images and words that mirror and help shape our definition of self. Kala and me, we're starting to like what we see.

When Asian Eyes Are Smiling

1. Why was this title picked for the article? How do you feel the author is addressing the complexities of ethnicity and appearance?

2. Do you feel the author is addressing her conflicted issues over her appearance in a more positive and healthy way? How?

61   Generación Latino

Helene Stapinski

Every weekend, 21-year-old Jovan Flores drives his black Volkswagen Jetta—with oversize, shining chrome tailpipe—from his house in Norwalk, Connecticut, to the tony town of Ridgefield. On this particular Saturday, with hip hop bleeding from his tinted windows, Flores is driving to the town's new skate park to meet some of his clients—30 little white boys who are learning to be just like him.

Flores, known as Face in hip hop circles, is one of the premiere break dancers in the New York area. In its second coming, the nationwide break dancing charge is being led by Latino youth. Flores, whose family hails from Puerto Rico, teaches break dancing to Ridgefield teens with the help of his friends Juni from Chile, Hydro from Colombia, and Double, an Anglo from Connecticut.

"When you're Latin, you're taught to dance differently because of the different rhythms," says Guillermo Perez, a 19-year-old trend watcher from San Francisco who's seen Latin-style break dancing spread to the West Coast. "There's different hip movement, different leg movement. You're moving so much that it's easy to just throw yourself on the floor and continue."

As Flores cruises into the Ridgefield skate park, it's easy to spot the nervous looks on the faces of many of the adults observing the scene. Clearly, the kids feel differently about his arrival.

"Face!" they yell, gathering around and practically breathing him in, molecule by molecule. Like Face, they wear their baseball caps turned backward, plus beaded necklaces, Esco and Puma shirts, and big Nikes.

In Ridgefield and across the country, it's not just dancing the white kids are picking up on. Young Latinos like Flores and his crew are redefining the way teens talk, walk, and dress.

"The music I used to listen to was lame," says 14-year-old Matt. "I listened to what was on MTV. I was into rock—Metallica, Rage Against the Machine." Now he and his friends prefer Nas, the rapper who endorses the hugely popular Latin-flavored Esco clothing line. "My mom was like, 'Don't get too much into that rap stuff.' But we break it out."

One 19-year-old of Norwegian extraction searches a mix tape for "that Mexican thing"—a song peppered with horn blasts. Another boy, wearing a colorful, South American-style woven hat, practices his head spin.

Flores shakes his head and smiles at the Spanish slang like "moms" and "pops" that colors his students' vocabulary. "If you talk to them now, you'd think they were one of us," he says, shrugging. "And the transformation only took six months."

According to Juan Faura of Cheskin Research, it was just a matter of time before Latino youth began to change the mainstream cultural landscape. "I've been screaming my head off for quite a while that Hispanic teens are the future of marketing," says Faura, director of transcultural research for the California-based market research company. Currently 4.3 million strong, Hispanic youth ages 12 to 19 account for more than 14 percent of the total Hispanic population in the United States, and 13.6 percent of all teens. By the year 2020, the number of Hispanic teens will grow by 62 percent, according to Census bureau projections, to 7 million, compared with a 10 percent growth in the number of teens overall.

When it comes to spending money, Hispanic teens don't hold back. They blow an average of $320 a month, 4 percent more than the average teen does, according to Teenage Research Unlimited. Overall teen spending was a whopping $141 billion in 1998, and Hispanics contributed $19 billion, or 13.4 percent of the total.

Already, because of their growing numbers, Latino teens are no longer a minority group in some areas of the country. "They don't view themselves as minorities, so their influences kind of rule the school," says Faura. "They're saying, 'You know, there are a lot of us here.' So they're mainstreaming their customs."

In fact, by 2005, Hispanic youth will be the largest ethnic youth population in the country. And the trend will only keep growing. By 2001, 18 percent of all babies born in the United States will be of Hispanic origin.

Even slow-to-change, whitewashed places like Hollywood are beginning to acknowledge the existence of the Latino community—at least when it comes to how much they spend on entertainment. According to a recent report by the Tomás Rivera Policy Institute in Claremont, California, Latinos spend 6.5 percent of their entertainment budget on movies, theater, opera, and ballet, compared with 4.7 for Caucasians. That economic power is finally beginning to translate into starring roles for young Latino actors, although the gains are still relatively small. A May report by the

Screen Actors Guild on Latino employment in Hollywood found that the number of film and television acting jobs going to Hispanics has actually declined since 1997. But it's no longer acceptable for someone like Madonna to play a famous Latina on screen, like she did in *Evita* just three years ago.

Though she wanted the role of Frida Kahlo in the upcoming film on the fabled painter's life, Madonna lost the part to Salma Hayek, who is also starring in one of the summer's biggest releases, *Wild, Wild West*. And Broadway star John Leguizamo, whose one-man show *Freak!* drew thousands of Latino and Anglo fans, has a starring role in Spike Lee's summer blockbuster, *Summer of Sam*. Hayek and Leguizamo are further proof to Latino kids that they are part of the big picture and part of the mainstream.

That's a far cry from just a few decades ago, when Puerto Rican Americans like Christina Benitez were barely accepted in peer groups. "People wouldn't know where I was coming from," says Benitez, now president of Lazos Latinos, a Hispanic marketing company. "They expected Puerto Ricans to have greasy hair and be slashing people's tires."

Anglo kids these days are much more accepting of multicultural ethnic groups. In a recent survey, 53 percent of teens said they have at least one close friend who is of a different race or ethnic group. Benitez credits increased communication and easier travel with helping Latinos hold on to their cultural heritage. "We're free to bring information over and enjoy it more than when I was a kid," Benitez says.

That information and the customs that translate along with it are not only acceptable to Anglo teens, but are now appealing to those in search of some cultural identity. An identity that may not necessarily be their own. The latest installment of MTV's cinema verité soap opera *Road Rules*, for instance, features six Gen-Y kids driving around Central America in a Fleetwood RV—dubbed "The Woodie"—decorated with Mexican tiles, a picture of Our Lady of Guadalupe, and rosary beads. They even have a Chihuahua along for the ride.

Trend analysts like Marian Salzman, head of the Brand Futures group at Young & Rubicam, have been predicting for the past year that American teens in general are putting a premium on refurbished culture. They're also in search of spirituality, stronger family ties, and a splash of color in their lives—three things that Latino youth culture already embrace.

"One of the reasons Latino culture is crossing over is because it's based on family values," says Benitez. "This is what the country is hungry for. What it's dying for. The stabilization of the home. But at the same time, the culture is fun and infused with emotion. You can have fun with your family—God, what a concept!"

Like most large cultural waves, the music is the first to break through. In the 1940s, for instance, it was Desi Arnaz and Carmen Miranda who made it cool to be Hispanic.

"What's going to be real hot is the emergence of Latino music," says LaRon Batchelor, a partner at Starpower, which leverages brand power for corporate and entertainment properties. "It always begins with the music."

Ricky Martin, the former Menudo member and *General Hospital* star who stole the Grammy awards show this year with his Spanglish performance, and whose video, "Livin' La Vida Loca," is in the Buzz bin on MTV, is becoming the crossover king. In May, he made the cover of *Time* magazine, when the English version of his album was released and a new duet with Madonna just hit the airwaves.

"Ricky Martin blew everyone away at the Grammys," says Perez of San Francisco, who has worked on Levi's trend advisory panel. "When they scanned the audience, I swore I saw Puff Daddy sitting there, thinking, 'Oh no. What am I going to do now?'"

Martin is just the tip of the iceberg for Latino music, says Batchelor. Party crews in northern California, young Latin trendsetters who deejay, are often brought in by white kids who want to "have a really tight party," says Faura.

Rappers like Big Pun, the first Latino hip hop artist to go platinum, and C-Note, the new boy-group, are on their turntables. Both of Julio Iglesias' young sons are starting to cross over, as is Selena's brother, A.B. Quintanilla, who just came out with a hip hop-tinged album. Then

there's Marc Anthony, the new Menudo, and Chayanne, who are all appealing not only to Latino teens, but to the Anglos as well.

"I believe it'll catch on," says Batchelor of the trend. "Latino music is a music of passion."

Helping to spread the Latino beat is the variety of musical styles available. If you don't like one style, you're bound to like another that suits your tastes. In Southern California, mariachi, banda, and norteño music rule. Cumbia sounds—like tejano, which uses polka beats and accordion—are hot in Texas. But in Miami, Caribbean salsa is big. New York's clubs play a mix of merengue from the Dominican Republic and rock en español, not to mention hip hop.

"It's absolutely happening," says John "Gungie" Rivera, New York's biggest Latin party promoter. "It's just cool now. Common sense tells you with so many Latinos in the world and in the U.S., it was bound to happen."

He not only sees Anglos crowding the dance floors of the Conga Room and the Latin Quarter, but fighting for reservations to restaurants like Patria in New York, Topo La Bamba in Chicago, and Cha Cha Cha in Los Angeles. Latin food has always been popular in the United States, but now it's ultra-trendy. Latinos and Latino wannabes alike can be found washing down their fancy $14 lobster-filled empanadas with expensive tequilas and the newest round of imported beers.

In fact, Mexican beer is the fastest-growing import category in the beer industry, says Benitez. "Corona was just leading the way," she says. The newest addition to the market is a beer called Tequiza, which includes the tequila base, agave, and is being marketed by the grandaddy of all brewers, Anheuser-Busch.

Following on the heels of the Latin beat is Latin-influenced fashion. Willie Escobar Montañez, a New York City-based Latino designer, believes that designers like Tommy Hilfiger oversaturated the urban black line. "People are looking for a fresh look from hip hop," he says, "like the Latin look. Our voice is out there now."

Escobar Montañez has added guayabera shirts to his Esco line this year. The boxy, short-sleeved, lightweight shirts were once only popular with old Cuban men because they're extremely comfortable and because of the big breast pocket, perfect for storing cigars. But now kids everywhere, from Miami's South Beach to New York's hip Lower East Side, are sporting the shirts.

Esco isn't the only company making money from the traditional guayabera. In Los Angeles, a young designer named Mario Melendez is making a killing. And down in South Florida, Rene La Villa of Miami Cool Wear has seen his 20-year guayabera business spike by nearly 25 percent in the past two years. Over the Internet, La Villa sells mostly to Anglos. "The guayabera is cool," he says.

Even Donna Karan has added the shirt to her line for women, retailing at a not-so-cool $95.

Other Latin-influenced fashions include baseball shirts with the number 77 printed on them—the former area code for Puerto Rico, explains Escobar Montañez. "The Latin customer immediately identifies with it," he says. "They're not scared of putting something on the garment that says, 'I'm Puerto Rican.' We're no longer refugees."

Straw hats are cropping up in the showrooms of Versace, Dolce and Gabana, and even the Gap. And Che Guevara T-shirts are showing up on college campuses, making the revolutionary the newer, hipper Malcolm X, says one trend watcher.

On the feminine side, embroidered clothes are all the rage. At the national chain retailers Urban Outfitters and Bebe, the Latin theme is big this summer. "I have a friend who works at Bebe who said, 'I think they hired me because I'm Mexican,'" laughs Perez. "I told her, 'Honey, you got that stuff in your closet already.'"

Tighter-fitting, Jennifer Lopez-inspired dresses and pants are also hitting the runways, says Christy Haubegger, president and publisher of *Latina* magazine. "You're seeing different body types, curvier body types that don't look like Kate Moss," she says. Body art like henna tattoos also started with the Latina culture, as did long, brightly colored, airbrushed nails. "Nail art is moving into the Midwest," says Haubegger. "We did that years ago."

Strong eye make-up, darker lined lips, and liquid eyeliner are other fashion trends that are crossing over from the Latina community. "Latinas never stopped using liquid eyeliner," boasts Haubegger. "But now it's like, 'Oh wow! Gwyneth Paltrow is doing it.'"

Hispanic girls spend 60 percent more on make-up than all female teens; 50 percent more on acne products; and more than twice as much on hair products. That's a lot of eyeliner.

Clothes and makeup aren't the only aspects of the culture that white girls are embracing. From the upscale town of Weehawken, New Jersey, to the more laid-back streets of San Francisco, young Anglo girls can be seen doing the Rosie Perez head wag, talking Spanglish, and smoking Newport cigarettes—a Latino brand of choice.

"They talk fast and wag their head," says Perez (Guillermo, not Rosie). "Half the time, I'm like, 'Girl, what *are* you saying?'"

Though some companies, like Anheuser-Busch and DKNY, are already riding the Latino wave, many more are still ignorant of the hip crossover trends, barely even marketing to Latinos themselves, let alone the wannabes, says Faura. They've ignored the fact that the Hispanic population is 30 million strong and is growing four times faster than the general population. Projected Hispanic buying power has increased by 67 percent since 1990, to $356 billion.

"Marketers have to understand that the new majority is going to be people of color," says Salzman of Young & Rubicam. "The new minority is going to be your white, 'all-American' kind of kid."

"The sooner the corporations catch wind of it, the better," says Phil Colon, marketing and sales director of *Urban Latino* magazine. "Companies who are behind the curve on this thing might just miss it." A Tommy Hilfiger-like fashion explosion drawing on Latino trends is in America's forecast, says Colon. He believes using the Hispanic community to sell to the wider Anglo audience is inevitable, and a very smart move.

Because the Latin community is so brand loyal, marketing to them pays off in more than just the crossover connection. Once you solidify your support in the Latin community, you have it for years, says Faura. "If you can connect, you've got consumers for life."

However, reaching the target—the young Latin community and their Anglo wannabes—calls for some alternative advertising. "Companies have to start using more nonconventional means," says Colon. "Kids are not hanging out in front of the television. They're not home. They're playing ball or are outside hanging out. Television is not the medium to reach youth. It never was and never will be."

Instead, radio, billboards, stickers, and bus wrapping are both effective and cost-effective, he says.

Faura agrees that marketing to a mass audience using Latino youth culture is not only inevitable but could be hugely successful—more successful than even the recent African American hip hop crossover. "Part of being Hispanic is being authentic and real," says Faura. "There's the soul of it. And if you can capture that in your fashions and in the way you position them, you'll make a bigger splash than Tommy Hilfiger did."

In some ways, it may be harder to market the Latino look than it was the hip hop trend because of the diversity inherent in the Latin culture.

"It's hard to capture the essence of Hispanic teens in one product in terms of clothing and music," explains Angelo Figueroa, editor of the fast-growing *People en Español*, whose circulation rose 25 percent from 1998 to 1999. "Hispanic teens are culturally all very, very different, unlike African American teens in the U.S. who are basically listening to the same kind of music. You have to walk this fine line to make sure it appeals equally to all these groups."

But, he says, branding from Latino trends is not impossible. Just a lot more tricky. Because the population is so huge and is home grown, the ultimate crossover appeal of Latino teen culture could be wider and even more hard hitting than any cultural crossover in the past.

"It'll be harder to do," says Colon, "but the rewards are a lot bigger."

DISCUSSION QUESTIONS

Generación Latino

1. Discuss how Latino culture has influenced fashion, including dress and other aspects of popular culture. Who are some of the influential trendsetters?

2. Discuss why Latino culture is having an impact on mainstream culture.

62 My Jewish Nose
Lisa Jervis

I'm a Jew. I'm not even slightly religious. Aside from attending friends' *bat mitzvahs*, I've been to temple maybe twice. I don't know Hebrew; when given the option of religious education, my junior-high self easily chose to sleep in on Sunday mornings. My family skips around the Passover Haggadah to get to the food faster. Before having dated someone from an observant family, I wouldn't have known a *mezuzah* if it bit me on the butt. I was born assimilated.

But still, I'm a Jew—even though my Jewish identity has very little to do with religion, organized or otherwise. I'm an ethnic Jew of a very specific variety: a godless, New York City–raised, neurotic middle-class girl from a solidly liberal Democrat family, who attended largely Jewish, "progressive" schools that thought they were integrated and nonracist. Growing up, almost everyone around me was Jewish; I was stunned when I found out that Jews make up only two percent of the American population. But what being Jewish meant to me was that on Christmas day my family went out for Chinese food (some years, Indian) and took in the new Woody Allen movie. It also meant that I had a big honkin' nose.

And I still do. By virtue of my class and its sociopolitical trappings, the option of having my nose surgically altered was ever-present. From adolescence on, I've had a standing offer from my mother to get a nose job.

"It's not such a big deal." "Doctors do such individual-looking noses these days, it'll look really natural." "It's not too late, you know," she would say to me for years after I flat-out refused to let someone break my nose, scrape part of it out and reposition it into a smaller, less obtrusive shape. "I'll still pay." As if money were the reason I was resisting.

My mother thought a nose job was a good idea. See, she hadn't wanted one either. But when she was sixteen, her parents demanded that she get that honker "fixed," and they didn't take no for an answer. She insists that she's been glad ever since, although she usually rationalizes that it was good for her social life. (She even briefly dated a guy she met in the surgeon's waiting room: a boxer having his deviated septum corrected.)

Even my father is a believer. He says that without my mother's nose job, my sister and I wouldn't exist, because he never would have gone out with Mom. But I take this with an entire salt lick. My father's a guy who thinks that dressing up means wearing dark sneakers; that pants should be purchased every twenty years, and only if the old ones are literally falling apart at the seams; and that haircuts should cost ten dollars and take as many minutes. The only thing he notices about appearances is to say, "You have some crud . . ." as he picks a piece of lint off your sleeve. But he cared about the nose? Whatever.

Even though my mother was happy with her tidy little surgically altered nose, she wasn't going to put me through the same thing, and for that I am truly grateful. I'm also unspeakably glad that her comments stayed far from the "you'd just be so pretty if you did" angle. ("Yours isn't as big as mine was," she would say. "You don't *need* it.") I know a few people who weren't so lucky. Not that they were dragged kicking and screaming to the doctor's office; no, they were coerced and shamed into it. Seems it was their family's decision more than their own—usually older Jewish female relatives: mothers, grandmothers, aunts.

What's the motivation for that kind of pressure? Can it be that for all the strides made against racism and anti-Semitism, Americans still want to expunge their ethnicity from their looks as much as possible? Were these mothers and grandmothers trying to fit their offspring into a more white, gentile mode? Possibly. Well, definitely. But on purpose? Probably not. Their lust for the button nose is probably more a desire for a typical, "pretty" femininity than for any specific de-ethnicizing. But given the society in which we live, the proximity of white features to the ideal of beauty is no coincidence. I think that anyone who opts for a nose job today (or who pressured her daughter to do so) would say that the reason is to look "better" or "prettier." But when we scratch the surface of what "prettier" means, we find that we might as well be saying "whiter" or "more gentile" (I would add "bland," but that's my personal opinion).

Or perhaps the reason is to become unobtrusive. The stereotypical Jewish woman is loud, pushy—qualities that girls really aren't supposed to have. So is it possible that the nose job is supposed to usher in not only physical femininity but a psychological, traditional femininity as well? Ditch the physical and emotional ties to your ethnicity in one simple procedure: Bob your nose, and become feminine in both mind and body. (This certainly seems to be the way it has worked with someone like Courtney Love, although her issue is class more than ethnicity. But it's undeniable that her new nose comes on a Versace-shilling, largely silent persona, in stark contrast to her old messy, outspoken self.)

Thankfully, none of the women I know have become meek and submissive from their nose jobs. But *damn*, do they have regrets. One told me it was the biggest mistake of her life; another confessed to wanting her old nose back just a few short years after the surgery. They wish they'd stood up to their families and kept their natural features.

Even though I know plenty of women with their genetically determined schnozzes still intact, women who either refused or never considered surgery, sometimes I still feel like an oddity. From what my mother tells me, nose jobs were as compulsory a rite of passage for her peers as multiple ear-piercings are for mine. Once, when I was still in high school, I went with my mother to a Planned Parenthood fundraiser. It was a cocktail party–type thang in some lovely apartment, with lovely food and drink and a lovely short speech by Wendy Wasserstein. But I was confused: We were at a lefty charity event in Manhattan, and all the women in attendance had little WASP noses. (Most of them were blond, too, but that didn't really register. I guess hair dye is a more universal ritual.)

"Why are there no Jewish women here?" I whispered to my mother. She laughed, but I think she was genuinely shocked. "What do you mean? All of these women are Jewish." And then it hit me: We were wall-to-wall rhinoplasties. And worse, there was no reason to be surprised. These were women my mother's age or older who came of age in the late '50s or before, when anti-Semitism in this country was much more overt than it is today. That kind of surface assimilation was practically the norm for Jews back then, and those honkers were way too, ahem, big a liability on the dating and social scenes. Nose jobs have declined since then. They're no longer in the top five plastic surgery procedures performed, edged out by liposuction and laser skin resurfacing. (I guess now it's more important to be young and trim than gentile, what with societal forces of youth-and-beauty worship replacing post–World War II fear and hatred . . .)

I don't think it's a coincidence that I didn't consider my nose an ethnic feature growing up in New York. I didn't have to, because almost everyone around me had that feature (and that ethnicity) too. It wasn't until I graduated from college and moved to California that I realized how marked I was by my nose and my vaguely ethnic, certainly Jewish appearance. I also then realized how much I liked being marked that way, being instantly recognizable to anyone who knew how to look. I once met another Jewish woman at a conference in California. In the middle of our conversation, she randomly popped out with, "You're Jewish, right?" I replied, "With this nose and this hair, you gotta ask?" We both laughed. I was right: The question was just a formality, and we both knew it.

Living in California, I'm particularly in need of those little moments of recognition. I know that a Jew living in, say, Tennessee might laugh at me for saying this, but there are no Jews in California. I feel conspicuously Semitic here in a way that I never did anywhere else (not even at my small Ohio liberal arts college—after all, that place was filled with New York Jews). Few of my friends are Jewish, and those random "bagel and lox" references just don't get understood the way I'm used to.

Only once did I feel uneasy about being "identified." At my first job out of college, my boss asked, after I mentioned an upcoming trip to see my family in New York, "So, are your parents just like people in Woody Allen movies?" I wondered if I had a big sign on my forehead reading, "Big Yid Here." His comment brought up all those insecurities American Jews can have about our ethnicity that, not coincidentally, Woody Allen loves to play on—and overemphasize for comic effect: Am I *that* Jewish? Is it *that* obvious? I felt conspicuous, exposed. But regardless of that incident, I'm glad I have the sign on my face, even it it's located a tad lower than my forehead.

See, I don't have a whole lot of Jewish heritage to hold on to. My family's name was changed—it's not as if "Jervis" is particularly gentile, but it sure is a lot less obvious than "Jersowitz," which my grandfather jettisoned before my father can remember. Temple was never a part of my life—I'm an atheist. I don't know what Purim is about. Hell, it takes me a minute to remember how many candles go in the menorah—and last week I used mine for a candlelight dinner with my husband-to-be, a half-Christian, half-Buddhist Japanese American whose thoughts on God's existence are along the lines of "I don't know, and I don't really care."

But in a larger sense, Judaism is the only identity in which culture and religion are supposedly bound closely: If you're Irish and aren't a practicing Catholic, you can still be fully Irish; being Buddhist doesn't specify a race or an ethnic identity. African Americans can practice any religion, and it doesn't make them any less black. But "Jewish" is a funny ethnicity. Is it a race; is it a set of beliefs? Color doesn't have much to do with it. In fact, the question of whether or not Jews are white can be answered in as many different ways as there are people who have an opinion on the topic.

To me, being a Jew is cultural. But for me it's a culture tied only marginally—even hypothetically—to religion, and mostly to geography (New York Jews are different from California Jews, lemme tell ya) and sensibility/temperament (hyperintellectual, food-lovin', neurotic, worrywartish, perfectionistic). So the question for me is: What happens when Jewish identity becomes untied from religion? I don't know for sure. And that means I'll grab onto anything I need to keep that identity—including my nose.

DISCUSSION QUESTIONS

My Jewish Nose

1. The author discusses how her appearance is tied to both her cultural and religious beliefs. Cite examples from other religious groups that tie appearance to cultural and religious beliefs.

2. Why do you feel this author's mother was so much in favor of her having cosmetic surgery? What message(s) did that send to the daughter?

63 Complex Issues of Complexion Still Haunt Blacks

Dawn Turner Trice

A story in The Wall Street Journal last week on a harassment lawsuit caught my attention.

It was about a dark-skinned African-American restaurant worker at an Applebee's restaurant in Georgia who said his boss called him awful and derogatory names, including "black monkey" and "tar baby."

Dwight Burch said the name-calling continued from Jan. 1, 2001, until March 26, 2001, the day he allegedly was fired for threatening to report the comments to the restaurant's headquarters.

Burch took his case to the Equal Employment Opportunity Commission but not as a racial discrimination suit. The case was considered "color discrimination" because the boss was a light-skinned African-American man. Last week, Applebee's settled the lawsuit and paid Burch $40,000.

Since the mid-1990s, intrarace complaints to the EEOC have increased from 413 to 1,382 nationally. To be clear, racial discrimination accusations are by far the majority of complaints to the EEOC, said Robert Royal, an EEOC attorney who handled the Burch case.

One reason for the increase in color bias complaints is awareness. Workers are learning that they don't have to grin and bear insults from anyone, including people from the same race.

Though the numbers are interesting, what I found even more interesting, if not more distressing, was that this is just more evidence that skin tone is something that still trips up some of us black folks.

How much is it an issue? I'm not sure numbers from the EEOC or any other agency can really bear that out.

This is about a value system that goes way back to slavery days and said light skin was preferable to dark skin. Another facet of this insanity suggested straight hair was better than nappy or kinky hair. Keen facial features were preferable to broad noses and thick lips (collagen lip injections notwithstanding).

Way before the Journal article, I was talking to a friend who is a hair stylist about this issue and I mentioned that our generation isn't as color conscious as our parents' generation. More of us are wearing our hair in natural styles. We're better at appreciating our spectrum of skin tones.

He rolled his eyes.

I told him about an older family member who has always refused to use "black" as a race designator. To this day, she considers herself "colored," despite having lived through the humiliation of "Colored Only" and "White Only."

When I was growing up, she would point to her caramel-colored arm and say: "Look at my skin, I'm not black." And I would say, "Well, white people aren't really white either." But that never changed her line of reasoning.

If you were pretty and dark brown, to her you were "pretty for a dark-skinned girl." There was always some caveat, some mental brown paper-bag test that you had to pass for her to consider you beautiful.

But, I told my friend, I don't blame her. She was subject to that whole systematic brainwashing to make blacks feel inferior. But we're moving beyond that, right?

My friend sucked his teeth: "If we are, it's slowly. Very slowly."

He said it's true that you can flip through major fashion magazines these days and see African-Americans of every hue and hairstyle.

But we're also the generation—and he knows this from his salon—that buys hair weave at a furious clip. We can get colored contact lenses to change our eye color. We can afford skin lightening systems, if we choose to go the route of, say, Michael Jackson, who prefers that ghastly, ghostly hue.

Sure, women and men of all races make similar cosmetic changes. Those with so-called ethnic features reconfigure their "Italian" noses or change the slant of their Asian eyes. (Hispanics have their own issues with light skin versus dark skin.)

But the difference for African-Americans is how much we're still haunted by slavery.

Back to the restaurant case: I would guess that if the boss had insulted any other feature on Burch, the comments would not have stung as badly.

Skin color still carries with it so much of our self-worth. It's complicated, I know.

It's also tiring, and after a while, the only color it makes you feel is blue.

Complex Issues of Complexion Still Haunt Blacks

1. Cite individuals who are positive role models for blacks in fashion, television, movies, and music. How does their appearance play a role in their popularity?

2. Discuss why skin color and self-esteem are related. How have blacks addressed these issues in a positive and constructive way?

64   Hmong American New Year's Dress: The Display of Ethnicity

Annette Lynch
University of Northern Iowa

Hmong Americans are refugees from Laos who settled in the United States as a result of the Vietnam conflict. The Lao Hmong living in the United States originally migrated out of China in the early nineteenth century into northern Lao hill country. During the Vietnam War, Hmong were recruited by the American forces to fight against the Laotian communists. Immigration to the United States began in 1975 after the withdrawal of the American army and the assumption of political power by the Laotian communists. Fieldwork (Lynch 1992) supporting this article

was conducted in St. Paul and Minneapolis, Minnesota, in a community of approximately 18,000 Hmong Americans.

Within the Hmong American community, textile arts and dress have continued to play a traditional role in structuring social life and marking significance. *Paj ntaub* (flower cloth) is the general term used to refer to all the varied textile arts created by Hmong women. Techniques used include embroidery, appliqué, reverse appliqué and batik as well as the additive arts of assemblage. These arts, like other *kev cai* (customs) discussed by Tapp (1988), have been self-consciously practiced by Hmong Americans as they have used the customs of the past to fashion meaningful lives in the diaspora.

Drawing generally from the academic literature on the expression of cultural difference within modern nation states (Moerman 1964; Barth 1969; Cohen 1973; Glazer and Moynihan 1975; Epstein 1978; Roosens 1989 and Glick-Schiller and Fouron 1990) and specifically upon the work of Sarna (1978) and Comaroff (1987), I will focus upon Hmong American use of New Year's dress as a marker of ethnic identity and pride. I present this Hmong American case study as an argument for a definition of ethnic dress based on its descriptive role in identifying conceptually distinct types of social boundaries marked by the dressed body.

THE CONCEPT OF ETHNICITY

Sarna (1978), writing on the American immigrant experience, argued that American immigrant groups identify themselves by region, village, or family when they enter the United States but are labeled and treated as a homogenous ethnic group by American institutions and power structures. He goes on to argue that ethnic groups use cultural content to construct symbols of cohesiveness and pride as a defensive response to discrimination based on ethnic identity. In this way fragmented clusters of immigrants become cohesive ethnic groups by accepting and eventually symbolizing externally drawn ethnic boundary lines. Cultural content, which is often an eclectic mix of cultural elements drawn from throughout the ethnic group membership, is used both to accommodate and resist dominant American power structures.

Comaroff (1987) posited that the "marking of contrasting identities—of the opposition of self and other, we and they—'is primordial'"

(p. 306). He argues that, despite social and cultural differences, all human groups classify themselves in relationship to others. His argument offers a conceptually distinct definition of ethnicity premised on the fact that the substance underlying boundary lines between groups differs depending upon social and cultural circumstances. Using Comaroff's distinctions, totemic (as opposed to ethnic) boundary lines are established between equally powerful and structurally similar groups. In contrast ethnic boundaries are asymmetrical power-based relationships between structurally dissimilar groups.

In the following analysis I will show that as the Hmong people experienced social and cultural upheaval, they moved from using dress to mark totemic boundaries to using dress to display ethnic identity.

LAO HMONG DRESS

Different Hmong dress styles were historically associated with different regions of Laos and Thailand and with different linguistic sub-groups of Hmong. The clearest distinctions existed between the two broad categories of Green and White Hmong dress, which in turn corresponded to two major linguistic subgroups. Green Hmong handwork can be most simply identified by the use of blue batik to produce pattern. White Hmong handwork used the reverse appliqué technique to produce intricate white patterns.

The dress of White Hmong women included a white pleated skirt with black leggings worn with a black shirt with blue cuffs and front edging. A rectangular collar at the back of the shirt was heavily decorated with handwork. The ensemble included a black apron and was worn with belts adorned with silver coins. In contrast, the dress of a Green Hmong woman customarily included a pleated skirt dominated visually by a wide central panel of blue batik work and decorated with appliqué and embroidery. They wore dark shirts similar to the White Hmong women, but their collars were worn face down. Both groups of women wore a version of a dark wrapped turban form, which generally featured a black and white striped turban tie.

White Hmong men wore black shirts with blue cuffs and black flared pants. Accessories included a dramatic pink or red waist sash, narrow coined belts and black skullcaps with red topknots. Green Hmong men's pants were also black but were cut large with a low crotch and fitted ankles. They also wore dark cuffed shirts and black skullcaps (Cubbs 1986).

Scholars trace the roots of the Lao Hmong subgroups which are marked by corresponding differences in dress styles to China where the Han Chinese ascribed separate status to various sub-categories of Miao (Geddes 1976; Dewhurst and MacDowell 1983; Cubbs 1986). Sub-styles of dress in the Lao context were internally perceived and understood categories. Peterson (1990) pointed out the extensive information that was carried by dress in Lao Hmong communities:

> the individual is recognized as Hmong by other Hmong, who with a glance will know if the stranger they meet shares their dialect, marriage customs, house style, spiritual offerings, standards of beauty in clothing and song, and other cultural facets that distinguish one subgroup from another. They mutually recognize, in a twinkling, what kinds of limits might structure their future relationship. (p. 118)

Dress thus immediately sets up a relationship between the Hmong individual wearing the dress and the Hmong individual perceiving the dress. The two individuals knew how to respond socially to one another and what relationships were possible based upon internally understood visual cues.

Lao Hmong dress marked what Comaroff (1987) would call a totemic boundary between the related subgroups. The bounded groups were structurally similar and had roughly the same amount of power. The subgroups of Lao Hmong spoke different versions of the same language and tended to perform rituals in slightly different ways. These cultural differences, while internally perceived, were often not externally appreciated. Dress as a visible sign was more often noticed and commented upon by outsiders, thus perhaps accounting for the use of dress by the outside world to label the differing subgroups.

HMONG AMERICAN NEW YEAR

Hmong-style dress, worn on an everyday basis in Laos, is reserved for special occasions in the United States. Hmong American women are typically married in Hmong-style dress and families dress up for family photographs in the summer. The largest public display of Hmong American dress is the annual public celebration of New Year, generally held in St. Paul over the Thanksgiving weekend. My research focused specifically upon the meaning of dress worn within the context of the public celebration of the New Year.

Hmong New Year as celebrated in the Lao village context was the single annual holiday celebrated at the close of a busy agricultural season. It was an opportunity for families and friends to gather and renew the bonds tying the community and family together. Clan leaders and shamans performed rituals of renewal to usher in the New Year, banish the cares of the old year, and make peace with the spirit world in order to safeguard the community for the coming year. Women sewed throughout the year to prepare new clothing to be worn first for the New Year celebration and subsequently throughout the year for everyday attire. Treasured and costly clothing not worn on a daily basis was taken out of the storage baskets to add additional pomp to the newly sewn ensembles. A ball toss courtship ritual was played throughout the holiday season and provided an opportunity for young Hmong men and women to meet and get to know each other. Many marriages followed the holiday season.

The New Year as celebrated in the United States is a rare opportunity for public display of ethnic pride. While for much of the year community members try hard to fit into American culture, the New Year is an opportunity to be Hmong again in a supportive environment. Lao Hmong who relocated to the United States arrived relatively unprepared for life in the industrialized West. Most (92%) came from rural backgrounds and many (72%) were not able to read or write in their native language (Mallinson, Donnelly, and Hang 1988: 21). Resulting high rates of welfare dependency have made it difficult for youth to be proud of their heritage and families. Teenagers enrolled in public schools are particularly sensitive to the judgments of their peers. For example, one young man attempted to mask his ethnic identity by claiming to be a member of the more culturally assimilated Vietnamese community. For these teenagers and for the community at large, the New Year provides an arena in which ethnic identity is affirmed and displayed.

The public celebrations of Hmong New Year held in St. Paul in the late 1980s, like comparable nineteenth century immigrant celebrations discussed by Bodnar (1985), drew upon long-standing practices yet were adapted to the new American context. Focusing primarily on youth, the public celebrations in St. Paul juxtaposed ancient Hmong ritual and American popular culture. The auditorium floor was dominated by a ball toss courtship ritual by day and a rock and roll dance by night. The stage featured spectacles ranging from shamanistic rituals to heavy metal rock and roll performed by punk Hmong teenagers. The conflicts inherent in the position of Hmong teens as the generation between Hmong and American cultures were acted out in plays written in local schools, in speeches delivered by Hmong teenage leaders, and in the structure of the celebration, which in 1989 moved from an opening day focused on the Hmong past to a closing day focused on the Hmong future in America.

Dress styles derived from Lao Hmong prototypes were worn to the public celebration by many Hmong American teenagers and some Hmong American children and adults [see Figure 10.2]. Hmong American teenagers used

FIGURE 10.2 *Young women dressed in New Year finery playing ball toss.*

dress throughout the two-day festival to mark movement from one cultural world into the other. One Hmong teenager explained the use of clothing by saying that "at the New Year if we do something Hmong we wear Hmong clothes, and if we do something American we wear American clothes" (AL-F-03),[1] thereby indicating a conscious association of dress with cultural identity.

While Hmong style dress was most typically worn by youth at the New Year celebration, it was generally designed by older women in the community. Older styles of Lao Hmong dress were transformed through the process of cultural authentication[2] to reflect American as well as Hmong culture. Teenagers and the older women who sewed the garments drew inspiration from the range of cloth and trims available in American fabric stores to create ensembles that, while rooted in Lao Hmong prototypes, were a creative blend of both Hmong and American influences. As will be outlined, the transformation of Lao Hmong dress marking subgroup membership into Hmong American dress marking cohesive group identity is an apt illustration of Sarna's concept of ethnic group formation and Comaroff's distinction between totemic and ethnic boundary lines.

DRESS: THE DISPLAY OF ETHNICITY

At my first Hmong American New Year in November of 1988, I naively assumed that teenagers were wearing distinct substyles of dress associated with their family and region of origin. I was therefore surprised when a girl told me to be sure to watch for her the next day as she would be wearing a costume associated with a different subgroup. Teenage girls typically owned and wore a variety of substyles of dress. When I interviewed the winner of the 1989 Teen of the Year contest, she proudly showed me photographs of her taken in four different substyles of dress.

Teenagers were perplexed when I asked them why they wore the substyles of other groups and generally attributed little meaning to the practice. Most teenagers simply told me it was the new style, the American way. But importantly,

being a Hmong American rather than a Lao Hmong was often associated with the freedom to wear other subgroups' styles. For example, the following is drawn from an interview with a Hmong American female Teen of the Year contestant:

> See, that is the change now. Now we can wear any one—any kind. I could be a Green Hmong, I could wear White Hmong clothes, it doesn't really matter. It doesn't really matter in Laos too, but in Laos you wear what you are. But now it is the style—if you like it you wear it. We are becoming more Americanized in that way. (AL-F-01)

It was typical that the teenagers discussed the impulse to wear the other styles or to mix the styles as a fashion impulse or as an aesthetic choice. "It looks good" and "it is the new style" were often the words used by the teenagers. The following response concerns the practice of mixing the different substyles within a single ensemble: "I usually mix them up. I wear the hat with the White, and the hat doesn't go with the White dress. It doesn't really matter but it surely looks good so why not?" (AL-F-05).

The practice of mixing the substyles together and wearing those of groups other than one's own was documented throughout the United States. Sally Peterson (1990) commented that "there are not many Green Hmong families in Philadelphia, but almost every family with daughters owns a Green Hmong skirt—particularly if it is made in the new style."[3] (p. 94). In Missoula, Montana, Susan Lindbergh's (1990) research compared how Hmong American teenage girls dressed for the New Year with the way their mothers dressed in Laos:

> Transition is evident in the costumes that the girls wear. Whereas their mothers dressed for the New Year's in Sam Neua (White Hmong substyle) or Xieng Khouang costumes, depending on the subgroup into which they were born, the young women in this study each own costumes representative of at least two, if not three, different subgroups from which they select one to wear, depending upon personal preference. Wealthy girls may wear a different costume for each night of the

New Year celebration to display their riches. Frequently subgroup garments are mixed, creating a hybrid costume. (p. 45)

In a similar vein, Joanne Cubbs (1986) reported that new style ensembles worn by teenagers at the New Year in Sheboygan, Wisconsin combined elements of White Hmong and Green Hmong dress (p. 71). The pattern of mixing sub-styles I discovered at the New Year in St. Paul was thus a national trend moving toward the use of dress to express shared group (ethnic) identity rather than distinct subgroup (totemic) identity.

Lindbergh (1990) discussed the possibility of the above interpretation, but in the end dismissed it as an outsider's perception without internal validity. She provided an example of a response she received when she asked a young woman about the meaning of the blurring of the lines between the subgroup styles:

> When asked whether the blurring of lines between costume subgroups meant that the Hmong were beginning to identify with all Hmong rather than with their individual subgroups, a conclusion an outsider might draw, one young woman seemed confused by the question. Ties with her family, her husband's family, their places of origin and shared experiences within their lineages are still more important to her than any general sense of being Hmong. She feels tremendous loyalty to being from Sam Neua (a White Hmong subgroup), even though in the United States as a teenager she chose to wear a variety of different costumes, and though as an adult she continues to collect them for herself and for her daughters. (p. 50)

In contradiction to Lindbergh, I hold that the outsider sometimes sees the bigger picture missed by insiders who tend to offer more personalized interpretations centered upon their own individual experiences rather than the ethnic group as a whole. The fact that the woman quoted above both values her own substyle of dress and collects a variety of other substyles likely indicates that Hmong-style dress has a myriad of meanings to her, some of which are perhaps more easily articulated than others. The nationwide trend to mix the substyles together into hybrid ensembles and to wear the substyles of other groups indicates that Hmong-style dress had group as well as individual significance, an insight that is perhaps more easily perceived by a more objective outsider's eye.

While most forms of new style dress worn to the New Year were tied by their wearers to Lao Hmong prototypes, the popular rooster style women's New Year hat, a highly decorated cloth hat topped with dramatic coxcomb, was consistently classified as Hmong American despite evidence that similar hat styles did exist in historical Green Hmong dress (Cubbs 1986; Peterson 1990; AL-F-03; Lynch, Detzner, and Eicher, 1995). Early versions of the American-style New Year hat combined White Hmong handwork with a Green Hmong children's hat style. The dramatic mixing of the two major substyles of dress within a single form makes the hat a prime example of dress expressive of a cohesive ethnic identity. The more contemporary versions of the hat integrated elements of American material culture into the design. Sequins, lace, and American trims were borrowed and creatively integrated through the process of cultural authentication into striking symbols of Hmong American identity.

Summary and Conclusions

Hmong Americans entered the Thai refugee camps and later the United States in fragmented groups and continued to categorize themselves by what I would label a totemic classification. However as the integrity of their world was threatened by outside forces they became defensive and thus more conscious of their ethnic as opposed to totemic identity. While allegiance to the White or Green Hmong subgroup or to a specific clan was of fundamental importance in the Lao village context, it became progressively less important as the Hmong were threatened and discriminated against on the basis of their more inclusive ethnic identity.

Sarna posits that as ethnic groups endure discrimination based upon an externally ascribed ethnic boundary line, that line becomes important internally as well. When the Lao Hmong were targeted for extermination by the communists based upon their ethnic identity, the Hmong themselves began to assign more salience to their ethnic as opposed to totemic identity. Allegiances to totemic classifications became less important as the once separate Hmong subgroups became vulnerable to outsiders based upon their more inclusive ethnic identity. As Hmong refugees were moved into camps in Thailand and later relocated to the United States, they continued to be treated as a cohesive ethnic group and received both positive and negative treatment based upon that identity.

The transformation of regional substyles of Lao Hmong dress into a cohesive Hmong American style can be interpreted as symbolic of Hmong American ethnicity. As the generation most acutely experiencing discrimination based on their ascribed ethnic identity, teenagers wear dress which expresses Hmong cohesiveness and pride. By wearing a mix of Hmong substyles teenagers visibly accept and celebrate their ascribed ethnic identity both as individuals and as corporate representatives of their families and community.

In conclusion, I propose a classification system for dress that marks opposing cultural identities. My classification system differentiates between dress expressing symmetrical totemic relationships between structurally similar groups, and dress expressing asymmetrical ethnic relationships between structurally dissimilar groups. I propose that regionally distinct Hmong dress styles worn in Lao villages marked totemic differences between similar and equally powerful Hmong subgroups. In contrast, Hmong American style dress worn at New Year marks an ethnic boundary between the Hmong and what they perceive to be more politically and economically powerful groups.

The term ethnic is often used as a convenient substitute for academically dated terms such as tribal and primitive (see Chapman, McDonald and Tonkin 1989: 14). Because of this convenient quality, ethnicity (and the related term, ethnic dress) is a slippery concept that has been used in many different ways in many different places. The use of the term "ethnic dress" to refer to defined characteristics of a specific type of social boundary, as suggested in this chapter, transforms it from a convenient label into a useful concept. Further, it begins to build necessary linkages between academic literature focused upon defining ethnic identity and research on dress.

Notes

1. Interview data is coded according to the author's initials and subject number through the manuscript.

2. Cultural authentication is a process by which a borrowed cultural element works its way into the culture through language (being assigned a specific name), patterns of significant use, and aesthetic transformation (Ereksomia and Eicher 1981).

3. New style Green Hmong skirts are more heavily embroidered and appliquéd than the older style skirts—the more heavily embellished the better is an underlying aesthetic criteria of the new style.

References

Barth, F. (1969). *Ethnic Groups and Boundaries: The Social Organization of Cultural Difference.* Boston: Little Brown.

Bodnar, J. (1985). *The Transplanted.* Bloomington: Indiana University Press.

Chapman, M., McDonald, M., & Tonkin, E. (1989). Introduction of *History and Ethnicity.* London: Routledge.

Cohen, A. (1973). *Urban Ethnicity.* London: Tavistock Publications.

Comaroff, J. L. (1987). Of totemism and ethnicity: Consciousness, practice and the signs of inequality. *Ethnos,* 52(3/4):301–323.

Cubbs, J. (1986). Hmong art: Tradition and change. In *Hmong Art: Tradition and Change.* Sheboygan, WI: John Michael Kohler Arts Center.

Dewhurst, C. K., & MacDowell, M. (1983). Michigan Hmong Arts. Publications of the Museum, Michigan State University Folk Culture Series, 3(2).

Epstein, A. L. (1978). *Ethos and Identity*. London: Tavistock.

Erekosima, T., & Eicher, J. (1981). Kalabari cut-thread and pulled-thread cloth. *African Arts*, 14(2):48–51, 87.

Geddes, W. P. (1976). *Migrants of the Mountains: The Cultural Ecology of the Blue Miao of Thailand*. Oxford: Clarendon Press.

Glazer, N., & Moynihan, D. P. (1975). *Ethnicity, Theory and Experience*. Cambridge, MA: Harvard University Press.

Glick-Schiller, N., & Fouron, G. (1990). Everywhere we go, we are in danger: Ti Manno and the emergence of a Haitian transnational identity. *American Ethnologist*, 17(2): 329–348.

Lindbergh, S. M. (1988). Traditional costumes of Lao Hmong refugees in Montana: A study of cultural continuity and change. Unpublished master's thesis, University of Montana, Minneapolis.

Lynch, A. (1992). Hmong American New Year's dress: A material culture approach. Unpublished doctoral dissertation, University of Montana, Minneapolis (Dissertation Abstracts International, 53, 228B).

Lynch, A., Detzer, D., & Eicher, J. (1995). Hmong American New Year rituals: Generational bonds through dress. *Clothing and Textiles Research Journal*, 13(2):111–120.

Mallinson, J., Donnelly, N., & Hang, L. (1988). *Hmong Batik: A Textile Technique from Laos*. Seattle, WA: Mallison/Information Services.

Moerman, M. (1964). Ethnic identification in a complex society: Who are the Lue? *American Anthropologist*, 67:1215–1230.

Peterson, S. N. (1990). From the heart and the mind: Creating *paj ntaub* in the context of community. Unpublished doctoral dissertation, University of Pennsylvania (Dissertation Abstracts International, 51, 1724A).

Roosens, E. E. (1989). *Creating Ethnicity: The Process of Ethnogenesis*. Newbury Park, CA: Sage.

Sarna, J. (1978). From immigrants to ethnics: Towards a new theory of "ethnicization." *Ethnicity*, 5:370–378.

Tapp, N. (1988). The reformation of culture: Hmong refugees from Laos. *Journal of Refugee Studies*, I(I):20–37.

DISCUSSION QUESTION

Hmong American New Year's Dress

1. How is the roaster hat worn by Hmong teenagers on New Year's symbolic of both their ethnic identity and assimilation into American culture?

65　Black Hair—Black Times

Vanessa Wickliffe
University of Kentucky

The use of hair as an expression of self or "who am I" began a long time ago. As early as the fifteenth century, hair functioned as an indicator of a person's marital status, age, religion, ethnic identity, wealth, geographic origin, and rank within a community (Byrd & Tharps, 2001; Peters, 1992). For example, religious vows, significant events, and symbols were represented in braid work and transmitted cultural values (Peters, 1992). Boone (1986) examines the importance of hair in fifteenth-century West African communities. She suggests that in those communities, "merely to be presentable, a woman's hair must be clean, oiled, and plaited" (Boone, 1986, pp. 143–144). Disheveled hair meant insanity and loose morals. Boone further pointed out that Mende cultures found it morally unfitting to leave the hair unarranged, and they equated unkempt hair with wild behavior. Men and women would spend hours and hours grooming their hair into braids and plaits. Ornate combs were used to arrange and decorate the braids and hairstyles, and herbal ointments and palm oil were used to make the hair shiny and manageable.

Hair grooming continued to be important to Africans until between 1619 and 1808, when approximately 400,000 Africans were forcibly removed to British Mainland America or, as it later became, the United States (White & White, 1998). The West Africans who filled the slave ships to the "New World" included the Wolof, Mende, Mandingo, and Yoruba Africans (Byrd & Tharps, 2001). Once in this land, dominated by pale skin and straight hair, African hair was deemed unattractive and inferior by Europeans. This brought about the use of terms such as *kinky* and *wool* to describe the hair of black slaves, exemplifying negative character traits (i.e., ugliness) and low social positions (Craig, 2002). Slave children were taught by their white masters to refer to their hair as "wool." The slave owners knew that hair was important to slaves and therefore would shave their heads or crop their hair as a form of punishment (Buchman, 2001; White & White, 1995).

Although slave owners saw black hair as unappealing, they still allowed slaves to comb and style their hair as they pleased. Because the hair was hard to manage, many would use wool cards to arrange it in the absence of combs. Wool cards were implements used to prepare washed fleece for spinning to make the fibers lie evenly in one direction (Byrd & Tharps, 2001). The slaves spent Sundays grooming and shaping their hair in ways that were familiar to them from their home countries.

By the 1830s, African Americans began to give in to the persistence of white norms to straighten their hair. According to Rooks (1996), blacks fell prey to the idea that black hair was messy, hard to care for, and too coarse to behave the way "regular" hair should, and therefore that they should "fix" their hair to look like white hair. Without the combs, herbal ointments, and palm oils used in Africa for hairdressing, the slaves were forced to depend on:

> . . . oil-based products like bacon grease and butter to condition and soften the hair, prepare it for straightening, and make it shine. Cornmeal and kerosene were used as scalp cleaners, and coffee became a natural dye for women. Men used axle grease meant for wagon wheels over their hair for a combination dye job and straightener. Women would slather the hair with butter, bacon fat, or goose grease and then used a butter knife heated in a can over a fire as a crude curling iron. Sometimes a piece of cloth warmed over a flame would be pulled across the head and worn for a short while to stretch the curls out.

Original for this text.

Women also wrapped their hair in strings, strips of nylon, cotton, or eel skin to decrease the kink and leave looser curls. Lye mixed with potatoes (decrease caustic nature) would be used to straighten the hair, but it would sometimes eat the skin right off a person's head. (Byrd & Tharps, 2001)

A NEW CENTURY

By the beginning of the 1900s, blacks had survived slavery, a Civil War, and an emancipation that left them economically and politically disadvantaged as compared to whites (Byrd & Tharps, 2001). Blacks still tried hard to make themselves more acceptable as compared to whites by continuing some of the discussed techniques to copy white hairstyles. I conducted an informal survey among friends, coworkers, and family members regarding their feelings about African-American hair. Ages of those surveyed ranged from 30 to 58 years. Occupations of those surveyed included a college student, a chemist, an accountant, housewives, professional hair stylists, and retailers of black hair products. These people represented each era beginning in the early to mid-1900s through the present and either experienced the importance of hair, were knowledgeable of the periods discussed, worked in the hair industry, or had discussed the importance of hair with other African-Americans. One of the respondents, Donald Prier, an African-American from Louisiana, talked about processed hair. He stated:

> From the 1920s through the 1950s, black entertainers like Cab Calloway, Lena Horn, Red Foxx, and athletes like Joe Louis and Sugar Ray Robinson were black role models who sported "processed hair."

The "conk," or straightened hair, was one of the methods used to emulate white hair. The conk was the straightening of the hair using a lye and potato mixture. In 1954, George E. Johnson introduced a safe, "permanent" straightening system that could be purchased at retail stores and applied at home (Byrd & Tharps, 2001). My Aunt Bernell said, "You could tell when a man had gotten his hair done using this mixture, because it would turn the hair red."

Madame C. J. Walker and Annie Malone made their fortunes producing pomades, miracle growths, and straightening combs to help accomplish the straight hair look. A straightening (hot) comb is a metal comb that is heated on a stove or burner and then pulled through the hair to straighten it temporarily (Byrd & Tharps, 2001).

Straightening the hair was and still is a painful and time-consuming project. To straighten the hair using a hot comb required sitting in a hot kitchen near a hot stove, heating the comb, oiling, pressing, and pulling the hair. Mary Ruth Kelley remembers those days with four sisters:

> When we had no money for pomades and hair grease, my mother would use the fat from hogs or old bacon grease to oil and straighten your hair. Your hair would look really good and shiny, but when you went out in the sun, the flies would come near you or your hair would start to smell. The downside to this hair straightening process is that if you went swimming, or got wet in the rain, your hair would draw up and become kinky again. Black folks today, even with their perms, worry about their hair, because when it rain, you see 'em running for cover.

During the '60s and '70s, as white society continued to constantly devalue the natural state of black hair, people like Angela Davis, Jesse Jackson, and many others sported the "Afro." The Afro was a symbol used to connect to Africa and to enforce the idea that blacks were beautiful and thus demanded respect. For a few years in the 1960s, a black woman could feel exhilarated just by walking down the street wearing unstraightened hair, her glorious Afro style exemplifying beauty, defiance, and pride (Craig, 2002). Some of my friends (Brenda, Sandra, and Betty) were reminiscing about Afros:

> Your hair said something about you.

> I remember washing all that hair and then oiling it with some form of hair grease. Then I would plait it up at night, put lotion on the

ends so that it would not be frizzy, and then I would roll up the plaits on rollers so that my Afro would be fluffy. Then when you got up in the morning, you had to unplait all that hair and use a pick to comb it out and shape it up.

You could tell which guys had girlfriends, 'cause they would be seen sitting on the floor while the girl greased his scalp and plaited his hair for him, and sometimes you would see them when the girl would be taking it loose and combing it with a big rake.

You could tell who took pains with their Afro and who didn't. And then when you went to parties, you didn't want to slow drag because your 'fro would get mashed on one side.

Yeah, we would use some of that pomade or royal crown to grease that hair and make it shine. You had to oil it or it would break out. You were in the mix then, but you just prayed the wind didn't blow real hard, or all your hard work would be gone.

FIGURE 10.3 *Afro hairstyle, worn by the author in the 1970s, is popular again today.*

Back then, whew!! It wasn't anything finer than a brother with a well put together 'fro.

During the time of the Afro, there were still those who chose to straighten their hair, because the Afro was thought by some blacks and most whites to be unruly, lack an appearance of the importance of good grooming, and created an image of defiance. Many thought that the unruly Afro accentuated the negative aspects of the black race. Young children were taught that a well-behaved child or an attractive, young black lady with pressed hair was an asset to her race (Craig, 2002). So, many worked hard to accommodate what was considered good grooming and appropriate representation of the black race:

> Even in the '60s and '70s, entertainers like James Brown, The Temptations, and The Supremes, all wore unnatural hair. These were supposed to be our role models.

> Hey, you had the brothers with the conks. Man, they would use lye mixed with other concoctions to straighten their hair, and then they would put plenty of grease on it to make it lay down.

> Then you had the sister with the straight hair who sat by the stove in the heat to straighten that stuff. Boy, that was a job, but if the rain caught you, it just kinked right back up.

WHERE ARE WE NOW?

One of the noticeable things about black hairstyles today is their sheer variety (Buchman, 2001). On any given day on any busy street of any American city, you will find beautiful black women sporting a vast array of hairstyles, colors, lengths, and textures (Norment, 1996). Today, black women freely choose from silky straight hair, very short naturals, braids and dreads, and much more. Whatever the design, the hair is arranged as an expression of self-love and acceptance, individuality, and self-expression, as well as liberation and freedom ("Hair Today," 1998; O'Keefe & McNeal, 1997; Buchman, 2001). Many hairstyles are also chosen based on aesthetics, cost of constructing and maintaining the "do," and the amount of time needed for maintenance ("Hair Today," 1998; O'Keefe & McNeal, 1997; Buchman, 2001). Carol Richardson, a stylist from Charleston, South Carolina, said that, "Styles are also chosen to achieve a particular image or personality, and to correct damaged hair that has been over-processed or has started to thin in places."

Black women who choose to wear braids, naturals, dreads, and cornrows are still portraying self-love and individuality, but some choose to wear their hair as such because of a connection to the past. Braids are synthetic or human hair that is braided into an individual's real hair. Cornrows are braiding and twisting in various forms attached to the scalp (O'Keefe & McNeal, 1997).

Another reason for the choice of these styles is the ease and convenience of having well-groomed hair that does not have to be washed regularly or styled on a daily basis. As a result, mornings are not spent curling and styling hair before starting the day. Although braids, dreads, and cornrows do not require a great deal of attention on a daily basis, the time spent and cost

of getting one's hair styled as such is an issue. For example, depending on the type of braids (mini or micro), a person could spend up to 25 hours sitting in a chair getting his or her hair braided.

Human or synthetic hair is the choice, but the cost increases as the quality of the hair gets better. Synthetic hair can cost 99¢ a package and higher depending on the quality or brand (such as Beverly Johnson). Human hair can range from as low as $6.99 to up to $19.99 a package or more, depending on the texture (wet and wavy, permed, and so on). The cost to get hair braided depends on the style and ranges from under $100 (cornrows) to $200 or more, depending on the style of braids (mini or micro). Carol Richardson indicated that the cost of getting hair braided can vary by geographic location. She recommended that you tie the braids up with a silk scarf at night to keep them from getting frizzy and oil the scalp regularly.

Some black women have long hair, but there are some with very short hair who would like long hair. A conversation with a few prominent African-Americans revealed that a great number of people believe that white society promotes and sets the standards for beauty. After our

FIGURE 10.4 *Braided hair done using the crochet method.*

discussion, Marcus Prier, a graduate of Southern University, stated:

> After watching television for a period of 4 hours, I noted that numerous images of entertainers such as Beyoncé Knowles, Jennifer Lopez, Janet Jackson, Sallie Richardson, and other female entertainers. The music video channels (MTV, VH1, and BET) all had music videos that displayed images of Afro-American women whose physical appearance composed of fair skin complexions. Coincidentally, all of the aforementioned women had hair that was long in length and or possessed a smooth ('good') texture. The following day, I noticed that several prominent daytime soap operas also have Afro-American women who possess the all important 'long-flowing' locks. I am inclined to believe that these images only help to uphold the notion that society's concept of beauty is still being held to European standards. (Marcus Prier, personal communication, 2003)

Prior decided to ask ten African-American women about the use of the product that we call the "weave" in order to verify or refute the idea that its use is based on a learned stereotypic image of beauty. He randomly picked women from different geographic regions who had various levels of income and education. Marcus found that:

> Four of the Afro-American women whom I interviewed said that they sometimes find it necessary to use a weave in order to 'enhance' their beauty. Several Afro-American women expressed that they felt the societal pressure of not having long hair. One individual expressed that she used weaves because she felt that the professional, Afro-American men in her circle often use women of Latin decent [sic] as the standard of comparison. She went on to say that the use of the weave, in conjunction with hazel colored contact lenses, gives her a sense of confidence when it comes to competing with 'exotic/Latin video' girls.

> Five of the women did indicate that they were inclined to use weaves in order to provide themselves with a means of aesthetic variety. These individuals said that they found

it to be fashionable to use weaves in order to accent their wardrobes.

Others who participated in the discussion stated:

> You can look at those that are in the media and on BET and other television stations. A great majority of the women have long straight hair, and some of the men have wavy hair. Some of that hair is real, but a great deal of it is not real.

> Not only that, but most of the blacks in the media are very fair skin. Sometimes you can't even tell what they are.

> And how much weave do you see on the celebrities? You got bleach blond, two-toned, and wet and wavy.

> Tyra Banks, Iman, Naomi Campbell, Janet Jackson, Diana Ross, Toni Brackston [sic], just to name a few, all wear or have worn weave.

WEAVE: HOW IS IT DONE?

In earlier years, women bought what were called "falsies" and "attachments" to replace hair loss due to straightening and relaxing and/or to keep up with trends in hairstyles that relate to acceptance (Byrd & Tharps, 2001). Today, these hairpieces are called "extensions" and "weaves" and are still used for the same reasons. Those who choose to get extensions will spend a great deal of time and money getting it done.

The type of hair used for extensions, braids, and other styles includes synthetic and human hair. The hair comes in lengths of 8 to 20 inches and sometimes longer. The price of human hair can range from $6.99 to more than $100 for a one-pound package. The cost of synthetic hair may start at $6.99 and higher for a one-pound package. Applying and designing the hairstyle can be very expensive. Usually, the stylist may charge as much as $10 per track to put the hair on the client's head, and then there is an overall cost for the stylist's time. That could start at under $100 to as much as $200 or more. This, again, depends on geographic location and the reputation of the stylist. Celebrities have been known to spend hundreds and thousands of dollars on their "do."

The amount of time involved in getting your "do" done is dependent on how the hair is attached. If it is all glued in, it could take up to two or more hours; but if it is sewn in, then it could take two to four or more hours to complete the process.

Joyce Jones, an experienced hair stylist from Houston, Texas, describes the process of getting extensions. For the look of straight hair, the individual must get a relaxer to straighten the hair. This should be done early on so that the hair is not weakened by the application of the extensions. The determining factors as to how the hair is to be applied to the head are the length of time the hair is going to be kept and what purpose it will serve. Sometimes the extensions are just for a prom or other special event. In that case, a temporary technique would be used. If the hair is to be kept for a longer period or is being attached to cover balding, then another technique would be used. For temporary attachments, the hair is glued to the head using glue made especially for that purpose. The individual will have decided and discussed with the stylist how she wants her hair styled. The hair comes on what is called a track and can be cut to whatever length needed. The individual's hair is parted for positioning of the track. Glue is then placed on the edge of the track and pressed to the head in the parted area of the hair. Using a curling iron, heat is applied to the area where glued to hasten the setting of the glue. Then the individual's hair is brushed and blended to cover the track and style the hair.

If the hair is to be sewn in, then the customer's hair is either cornrowed or braided close to the scalp in a circular style. If the hairstyle is to be used to cover balding, sometimes a small piece of netting is stitched to the individual's hair, then the tracks are sewn to the netting with needle and thread. In some cases the tracks are sewn directly to the customer's hair.

Conclusion

As early as the fifteenth century, Africans braided and plaited, twisted and decorated their hair to communicate messages of status, age, and much more. From the time of slavery onward, blacks fought to keep their attachment to Africa through something as simple as hairstyles. Even throughout the beginning of the twentieth century, well-kept hair was a symbol among blacks of self-respect for the race they represented. Rebellion by some and resistance by others to emulate white hairstyles appeared during the 1960s and 1970s with the introduction of the Afro. This hairstyle served as a symbolic connection to Africa and also a way to say that "black is beautiful." Today, the importance of hair goes beyond the realm of attachment to ancestry, and also serves as a symbolic connection to politics, culture, and social meanings, as well as a visual statement about individuality in the black community.

References

Boone, S. (1986). *Radiance from the Waters: Ideals of Feminine Beauty in Mende Art.* New Haven, CT: Yale University Press.

Boyd, V. (1993). The ritual. *African American Review,* 27(1):43–46.

Buchman, R. (2001). The search for good hair: Styling black womanhood in America. *World and I,* 16(2):190.

Byrd, A. D., & Tharps, L. L. (2001). *Hair Story.* New York: St. Martin's Press.

Craig, M. L. (2002). *Ain't I a Beauty Queen?* New York: Oxford University Press.

Hair today, hair tomorrow: Are the new hairstyles right for you? (1998, May). *Ebony,* 53(7):70–73.

Norment, L. (1996). The new hair freedom: With variety in color, length and texture, black women of the 90's enjoy coiffure choices from traditional to Afro centric. *Ebony,* 51(12):106–110.

O'Keefe, K., & McNeal, D. (1997). Hair as an art form: Self expression and African history shape today's popular styles. Accessed May 7, 2003, at www.burr.kent.edu/archives/1997/fall/Hair.html.

Peters, J. C. (1992). Braids, cornrows, dreadlocks, and hair wraps: An African continuum. Accessed May 7, 2003, at www.accad
.ohio-state.edu/~dkrug/367online/
ethnicarts4/r_resources/reading/Peters.asp.

Rooks, N. (1996). *Hair Raising Beauty, Culture,
and African American Women.* New Brunswick, NJ: Rutgers University Press.

White, S., & White, G. (1995). Slave hair and
African American culture in the eighteenth
and nineteenth centuries. *Journal of Southern History,* 61(1):45–76.

White, S., & White, G. (1998). *Stylin' African
American Expressive Culture: From Its Beginnings to the Zoot Suit.* Ithaca, NY: Cor-
nell University Press.

DISCUSSION QUESTIONS

Black Hair—Black Times

1. According to the article, what drastic steps
   would African-Americans use to make their
   hair similar to white Americans during earlier times?

2. Describe the various reasons for differences
   in hairstyle selection today for African-
   Americans.

3. How do social and economic factors influence the choice of hairstyles among
   African-Americans?

CHAPTER 11

Fashion as Social Process

Mary Lynn Damhorst

AFTER YOU HAVE READ THIS CHAPTER, YOU WILL COMPREHEND:

- Why fashion is a social process requiring human interaction.

- The complex interaction of cultural, industry, group, and individual factors that fuel fashion change.

- That many theories are useful for explaining the fashion change process.

- How fashion change has continual impact on meanings of styles.

- That not all styles are fashion and that some cultures, groups, and individuals opt not to participate in the larger fashion system.

Cargo pants, everywhere in 1998. Ralph Lauren cargo pants in suede—$2,295. Abercrombie & Fitch cargo pants—$58. Arizona private-label cargo pants at JCPenney—$25. For fall 1998, Old Navy corduroy overalls with cargo pockets for babies. In spring 2004, cargo pocket pants were still everywhere. The style continued to be featured in the marketplace. (See Figure 11.1.)

How do trends get started, and how do they spread? *The Wall Street Journal* (Ono & Bounds, 1998) credited hip-hop group Goodie Mob with starting the cargo pants trend in 1995. European kids in army-surplus cargo pants were another purported

a   b

FIGURE 11.1 *Cargo pants came in many styles and prices during 1998–1999 and again in 2004. Here are examples targeted for two different markets: (a) Ralph Lauren in 1999 and (b) cargo pants featured in 2004.*

innovator, while an ad campaign by retailer Old Navy in 1997 may have spread awareness of the trend in the United States (Ono & Bounds, 1998). The style was originally developed as functional wear for British military men in the early twentieth century. But why has the style recycled into fashion now?

Initial innovation of a trend is often impossible to trace. In this chapter, we will consider a number of cultural, social, and personal factors that can influence fashion trends. These factors shape meanings of fashion. Marcia Morgado outlines the re-emergence of Hawaiian shirts as fashionable attire in "Refashioning the Hawaiian Shirt." She uses **rubbish theory** to explain the process of how a style of shirt developed in Hawaii two centuries ago was transformed to souvenir status and a sign of a tacky tourist during the twentieth century, then re-emerged recently as desirable and fashionable attire worn throughout the world. Similarly, the re-emergence of cargo pants as fashion wear could be explained in part by rubbish theory.

The term **fashion** has many meanings to many individuals. It might imply slavish conformity to some, styles that are new and exciting to others, a threat to tradition to yet another group, or merely products to sell in the open marketplace for economic gain. Although it means many things to many people, fashion most definitely is a social process. As was stated in Chapter 1, fashion is a way of behaving that is temporarily adopted by a discernible proportion of members of a social group as socially appropriate for the time and situation (Sproles & Burns, 1994). Fashion is a complex process that cannot be explained by any one theory, so we will take many perspectives to understand the process.

Jean Hamilton (1997) organized influences of fashion on a continuum from **micro-level** personal or individual factors to larger **macro-level** cultural influences (Table 1). Hamilton emphasized that fashion results from:

1. Individual action (negotiation with self) within...
2. Social groups (negotiation with others) that choose (or do not choose) products and style ideas offered by...
3. The fashion industry (fashion system) that is, in turn, influenced by...
4. Larger trends and forces of the surrounding culture (cultural system).

These four levels in the continuum are interconnected in that fashion is influenced by all components of the system working together simultaneously. We will examine each level, starting with the macro level first.

TABLE 1
*Hamilton's Micro–Macro Continuum**

Level		Influencing Factors
Macro-level		
M	**Cultural system**	• Cultural values and ideology
A		• Tradition versus change
C		• Media, arts, economy, religion, politics
R		• Generation and population trends
O		
•	**Fashion system**	• Retail buyers, fashion designers
		• Fashion media and promotions
•		• Global production system
•	**Negotiation with others**	• Conformity
		• Fashion leaders and innovators
•		• Trickle-down theory
		• Trickle-across diffusion
M		• Trickle-up theory
I		
C	**Negotiation with self**	• Individual choice, tastes
R		• Aesthetic learning
O		• Ambivalence
Micro-level		

*Table expanded from Hamilton (1997).

CULTURAL SYSTEM

The culture of a society will determine whether a fashion system exists. Fashion change is found most frequently in cultures that value technological progress, individual expression, and capitalistic free-market exchange (Sproles & Burns, 1994; Kaiser, Nagasawa, & Hutton, 1995). Cultures that allow youthful experimentation and search for identity are also conducive to rapid changes in fashion (Horn & Gurel, 1981). An economic situation in which notable numbers in the population have discretionary income to spend on extras is also necessary, as fashion change requires expenditure on new styles before clothing is completely worn out.

Herbert Blumer (1969) proposed that a new style is most likely to be adopted as fashion when the style fits with the **Zeitgeist** or spirit of the times. Large population groups can shape lifestyles in a society and can have substantial influence on fashion changes, largely as the result of economic rewards that can be gained from catering to a huge market segment. Behling (1985) demonstrated how the baby boomer generation influenced U.S. fashions during their adolescence in the 1960s through early adulthood in the 1980s. By the late 1980s, however, it was clear that the baby boomers were losing hold on fashion trends, at least those featured in fashion media. Short skirts and narrow silhouettes became fashionable at the same time many boomers were developing middle-aged bodies. Clearly, more than numbers and economic clout is required to shape fashion trends in U.S. culture where youthfulness is so adored.

Teri Agins in "What Happened to Fashion?" presents four **megatrends** in U.S. culture that phenomenally changed the fashion system at the end of the twentieth century. A complex shift of a variety of cultural patterns changed consumer lifestyles and employment situations, and restructured consumer values and consequent purchases of clothing. Within the postmodern climate of questioning authority, consumers stopped looking to top designers to dictate what was fashionable. Tradition-oriented retailers and design firms have lost strong impact, and new forces of fashion leadership are emerging.

As we saw in Chapter 3, a larger trend in society, such as postmodernism, may be reflected in dress. Part of that present-day trend is pluralism or acceptance of diversity (see Chapter 1). Perhaps the increasing trend toward recognition of diversity in the population has encouraged the U.S. fashion industry to pay attention to more diverse markets. Interest in ethnic minority consumer markets began rapidly expanding in the 1990s after U.S. census results indicated substantial and future increases in those populations. Rafael Jimenez (see "Urban Tactics") is a young entrepreneur who saw a unique market for T-shirts among consumers who had roots in the Dominican Republic. His T-shirt lines have grown to clothing lines that sell to broader consumer markets at Bloomingdale's and other retailers. What may start as a **niche market** product may eventually capture the interest of a wider array of consumers (see Figure 11.2).

Brecca Farr explains in "Plus-Size Modeling" that possibilities for employment as a petite women's plus-size model were almost nonexistent before the early 1990s because that **target market** was generally unrecognized by the fashion industry. The industry found that it could make money by focusing on women who need larger sizes. In 2000, for example, 16 percent of unit sales of women's apparel was in the plus-size range (Fetto, 2001).

In a highly traditional culture, however, styles rich in historical meaning change slowly over time. Dressing to represent membership and role in a group, tribe, or clan is emphasized over individual expression (see Figure 11.3). This type of dress is **traditional,** and styles do not change substantially with each season or year.

In some groups or nations, modern fashion systems are rejected to make political or ideological statements. Mainland China had rejected fashion for political reasons after the Communist takeover in 1949. The Communist political system of the People's Republic of China systematically repressed individual expression through dress and other behaviors during the 1950s through the 1970s. The good of the many was emphasized over the individual and was expressed through overt conformity. However, China began to relax its repressive policies and opened its doors to the outside world in the late 1970s. By 1985, political leaders declared that fashion would be good for China's textile industry and opened up markets to supply changing styles to the people of China ("Peking's Designer Diplomacy," 1985). That change in political opinion about fashion may reflect deeper changes in ideology of the Chinese Communist system, as it has moved from an idealistic form of Communism to a pragmatic policy of involvement in world markets. Cris Prystay, in "As China's Women

FIGURE 11.2 *Giorgio Armani claimed Latina inspiration for part of his Fall 2002 collection.*

Change, Marketers Notice," describes the change in how today's young Chinese women think about and present themselves in a society that now embraces fashion as appropriate consumer expression.

FASHION SYSTEM

The **fashion system** today is a globally based set of business establishments, small entrepreneurs, industry and government institutions, trade unions, and other agencies that have an impact on what products the consumer has to choose in the marketplace. Economic interests drive most fashion system decisions, though government interests (e.g., a boycott of a disfavored nation's products or raw materials) can put limits on choices, too. Rita Kean (1997) pointed out that consumer choice is dramatically limited by the industry as it makes many fashion and style decisions based on such matters as cost, production feasibility, government import quotas, and gut-level guesses about what will sell. Many design features such as diamond-shaped godets and bound buttonholes rarely appear in moderately priced ready-to-wear apparel today because of the high cost of labor for sewing those details. Only in designer lines and custom-made apparel do these details appear, usually at a very high price.

No single agency or occupation has complete control over product offerings. A channel of interrelated decisions about colors, materials, and style details is made by

FIGURE 11.3 *Cuna women of the San Blas Islands incorporate unique expressions in their reverse appliqué molas, jewelry, and waist sashes, but display an overall conformity to traditions of form and color.*

textile manufacturers, design firms, producers, promoters, and retailers. The overall system tends to simplify the range of offerings to control complexity (Kean, 1997). For instance, simplification of offerings is reflected in sleeve stylings offered in shirts and jackets today. Very few apparel lines include anything but simple set-in, raglan, and drop-shoulder sleeve cuts. Color choices are also simplified. If a U.S. consumer wanted to buy brown pants back in 1988, his or her search probably would have been futile. In 2004, brown was readily available as a fashion "neutral," resulting from color trends followed by industry.

Style decisions are also substantially influenced by retail buyers. In "The Shadow Designer," Lubow provides an in-depth look at a Saks department store buyer and her influence on the designers whose lines are sold by the upscale retailer. The buyer directly passes along information to designers about what is selling and what the retailer is unwilling to order. Retail buyers are one type of **gatekeeper** for the fashion industry, making choices for their stores that further limit and simplify the range of style offerings. The fashion buyer directly attempts to interpret societal trends in its merchandise to capture the *Zeitgeist* and consumer dollars.

The fashion system works simultaneously with the cultural system. Some cultural systems may put unique restraints on the fashion system. Since 1979, when the Shah of Iran was overthrown and fundamentalist Islamic clerics took over the country, women's attire in public has been carefully monitored and controlled. Fassihi, in "In Tehran, Boutiques Stock Hot Outerwear under the Counter," explains that although the Iranian government occasionally eases social restrictions, strong limitations are put on tightness and body exposure in women's clothing styles, as well as on how much of their hair is allowed to show in public. The limits have not stopped fashion change, however. During times of greater constraints, retailers often keep "hotter" fashions behind the counters or in back rooms for adventurous customers. And designers such as Ms. Alf continually create new designs that push in small ways beyond the limits of government rules. Fashion change continues despite the restrictive system.

NEGOTIATION WITH OTHERS

Ultimately, it is consumer choice that makes a style fashion. Retail buyers and fashion designers may limit product offerings, but consumers do not buy all of what is offered, as Agins points out in "What Happened to Fashion?" Fashion magazines feature a limited selection of designs each season, but these are fashion "proposals" that become fashions only if a substantial number of consumers adopt the new looks. The mass of consumers determines the dominant styles that are popular for the season or year.

The **diffusion** of a style or look across a great number of consumers is a process of style adoption and change involving face-to-face interactions of individuals, strangers seeing each other on the street, and mass media and retail display of styles (Sproles & Burns, 1994). **Innovative consumers,** always a small proportion of a population, first sport new ideas in hairstyles, clothing, and other aspects of dress. **Early adopters** then select from the innovative looks and help to make the chosen styles visible to the wider population. If early adopters include fashion opinion leaders who are successful in making the new look acceptable or legitimate to friends and acquaintances, greater conformity and mass adoption will probably follow. As the look spreads in acceptance and use, innovators are apt to become bored by the look and move on to something new and challenging. The diffusion process shifts to new style introduction and continues to cycle onward. The older looks tend over time to become so familiar that they are adopted less frequently. Their use goes into decline and the style virtually disappears—until it is revived 25 or more years later as new and "cool." During the late 1990s, flared leg jeans, previously fashionable in the late 1960s and early 1970s, reappeared as fashionable.

Consumer adoption across leaders and followers involves complex processes of **negotiation** of meanings. Leaders and innovators must be individualistic and willing to take risks, as others may not like many of their choices. Opinion leaders have been found to talk a lot about new trends, helping to introduce new styles to friends and discuss attractiveness and benefits of the style (Reynolds & Darden, 1972).

Much of the negotiation about "what is fashion" occurs through observation and not direct discussion, however. Most of us watch what others in our communities are wearing and adopt or reject accordingly. If something is seen on others around us, it is easier to get comfortable with the new look and to think of it as fashionable and attractive. If we start to notice that a style we bought a few years ago is now rarely worn by others, we begin to redefine the meaning of the old style as out-of-date or "dowdy."

A number of theories have been proposed to explain the reasons fashion change occurs. There are alternative theories to rubbish theory, described in "Refashioning the Hawaiian Shirt." Each theory focuses on different components of the change process.

Some of the earliest theories emphasized social class emulation. The **trickle-down theory** of fashion proposed that the upper classes introduce new styles (Simmel, 1904; Veblen, 1912). Style ideas are copied, in cheaper versions, by the middle and lower classes who want to mimic the upper classes. When they see themselves copied, the upper classes move on to new styles that haven't been worn by the "unchic" in middle and lower classes. This theory may have worked fairly well when class divisions were highly emphasized in the United States. However, it is now difficult to identify many fashion trends that start with the upper classes. Each social class in the United States may be doing its own thing or all may adopt their own versions of the same look in a sort of horizontal or **trickle-across diffusion** (King, 1963), just as we have seen with cargo pants. Our upper-class leaders today are often celebrities such as singer Britney Spears or David Beckham, the British soccer star. Emulation by the public may help to sell their endorsements, CDs, or tickets for their games, thereby helping to diminish any immediate rush to differentiate the star from fans.

Herbert Blumer (1969) contended in **collective selection theory** that social class was not the main driver of fashion change. Any group that captures the spirit of the

times can have an influence on fashion. During the 1990s, rap groups had a phenomenal influence on adolescent male fashion (Spiegler, 1996). A combination of the tough inner-city living situation they came from, their creative music, their rebelliousness, and their active and bold manipulation of style gave rap groups a cachet that captured the interests of many adolescents. In this case, the celebrities who helped to introduce the styles from the streets were the rap performers themselves, rather than unrelated fashion leaders who picked up ideas from lower socioeconomic groups to serve as **gap-bridgers** to the mass public. This example fits to some extent with subcultural innovation or **trickle up theories** of fashion (Hebdidge, 1979; Sproles, 1985). Interestingly, some rap groups did not let the mainstream fashion industry solely profit from borrowing (some call it stealing) their style ideas. Some groups have started their own alternative apparel design firms. And now that many rap performers have become maturing successful stars, the clothing lines they offer are in some cases featuring suits and dressier apparel (Trebay, 2004).

Subgroups that want to distinguish themselves from mainstream society may put together unique looks to express their group identity. Conformity within groups may be substantial to show identification with the group, but deviation and differentiation from mainstream consumers is emphasized (Polhemus, 1994). A great deal of innovation and diversity is expressed through appearance among diverse subgroups in many societies today. Such groups may arise to express religious ideas, interests in hobbies or lifestyles (e.g., biker groups, quilting enthusiasts), commitment to political statements, or feelings of isolation from society (e.g., Modern Primitives discussed in Chapter 4). (See Figure 11.4.)

FIGURE 11.4 *Native American girl in powwow costume. Unique markets for dress arise to accommodate religious, ethnic, and special interest groups.*

NEGOTIATION WITH SELF

Of course, an individual's unique tastes will also shape adoption of new styles. Economic circumstances and lifestyles place limits on what consumers can afford and use. Each individual also has his or her own speed at becoming accustomed to and accepting (or rejecting) new aesthetic combinations and forms (Sproles, 1985).

Kaiser and coauthors (1995) proposed that a decision process fueled by psychological **ambivalence**—a feeling of tension or unease—moves consumers to adopt or reject new style ideas. Individuals are constantly assessing and reassessing their appearance choices every day. Is a look too young or too mature, too formal or too casual, too straight or too questioning of norms? We carry on inner dialogues with ourselves as we decide what to buy, what to wear, and what to discard. Ambivalence arises from uncertainty as a person considers the many style options from which to choose. An individual's interaction and negotiation with others and the fashion system within the larger cultural system create ambivalences, but also help him or her to resolve ambivalence about what to wear.

Summary

Macro-level and micro-level factors and influences help shape individual choices for dress. We look to others around us, to industry offerings, and to cultural themes and trends to help in deciding what to wear or not wear. Even an individual who decides not to fit with the mainstream uses many levels in making that decision. Fashion systems require social interaction. Individuals who are innovative and consumers who are conforming are both necessary for the process of fashion diffusion. Industry marketers or famous designers alone cannot make fashion trends happen without consumer acceptance and adoption of styles.

Characteristics of culture are reflected in the fashion trends of a society. Trends in the arts, technology, and popular culture shape style trends. Large population groups sometimes shape fashion trends because of their vast market potential. Smaller groups—such as segments of the upper class, punk rockers, or rap groups—may inspire fashion trends if they capture the spirit of the times. In order to express political, religious, or other values, some cultural groups do not engage in rapidly changing fashions. In cultures dominated by value in tradition, fashion systems may not develop or may have limits imposed. Even within fashion-oriented cultures, subcultural groups and nonconforming individuals may reject popular looks and dress to express their lack of fit with mainstream values and lifestyles. The processes of fashion change and individual adoption or rejection of fashion are tremendously complex and involve all levels of a society.

Suggested Readings

Agins, T. (1999). *The End of Fashion: How Marketing Changed the Clothing Business Forever.* New York: HarperCollins.

Behling, D. (1985). Fashion change and demographics: A model. *Clothing and Textiles Research Journal*, 4(1):18–24.

Hamilton, J. A. (1997). The macro–micro interface in the construction of individual fashion forms and meanings. *Clothing and Textiles Research Journal*, 15(3):164–171.

Hebdige, D. (1979). *Subculture: The Meaning of Style.* London: Methuen.

Kaiser, S. B., Nagasawa, R., & Hutton, S. (1995). Construction of an SI theory of fashion part 1: Ambivalence and change. *Clothing and Textiles Research Journal*, 13(3):172–183.

Kean, R. C. (1997). The role of the fashion system in fashion change: A response to the Kaiser, Nagasawa and Hutton model. *Clothing and Textiles Research Journal*, 15(3): 172–177.

Spiegler, M. (1996, November). Marketing street culture: Bringing hip-hop style to the mainstream. *American Demographics*, 18(11):29–34.

Sproles, G. B. (1985). Behavioral science theories of fashion. In M. R. Solomon (Ed.), *The Psychology of Fashion*, pp. 55–70. Lexington, MA: Lexington Books.

LEARNING ACTIVITY

Marketing Morality

Objective: Recent advertising and marketing strategies help us consider ethical responsibilities of the fashion industry. Perspectives of many groups and individuals are important in assessing ethical and moral issues.

Procedure

The apparel retailer Abercrombie & Fitch has for years been criticized by parents and social critics for what seems to be promotion of college student and underage drinking and sexual behavior as fun and fashionable (Coleman, 1998). In April of 2002, Abercrombie & Fitch introduced a line of T-shirts that instigated a series of protests against the retailer as a promoter of ethnic slurs (see Figure 11.5).

The five T-shirts included graphic designs reminiscent of signage used for Asian-American businesses during the 1950s and earlier. The slanty-eyed, cartoonish characters wearing coolie hats were accompanied by slogans such as "Wong Brothers Laundry Service: Two Wongs Can Make It White" and "Wok-N-Bowl: Chinese Food and Bowling." Many Asian-Americans today consider such signs as racist and insulting.

The appearance of the T-shirts in the stores unleashed a torrent of e-mail and phone complaints, as well as picketing groups outside stores. Multiple Web sites were set up to broadcast the problem and the boycott campaign.

The retailer immediately recalled the new line of shirts. A spokesperson for Abercrombie & Fitch immediately issued a statement apologizing that the shirts were found offensive. He stated that it was never the intention of the firm to offend anyone and that the product designers and marketers did not realize that the shirts would be seen as disrespectful.

FIGURE 11.5 *Protests started within a day after Abercrombie & Fitch introduced T-shirts offending Asian-Americans.*

Discussion

In a small group in class, discuss the protests against the Abercrombie & Fitch T-shirts. Include and consider diversity of opinions if they occur. Consider the following issues:

- Were the protests an appropriate reaction to the line of T-shirts featured by the company, or were they an overreaction based on political correctness?

- Should Abercrombie & Fitch have recalled the T-shirt lines, or should they have left them in stores? What would the consequences have been if they had continued to sell the shirts?
- Should the retailer be excused because it removed the offending products and apologized? Or should further action be taken against the company?
- Why do you think the T-shirts got beyond the product development team? Were the staff truly ignorant? Or did the retailer purposely release the shirts knowing that they would be offensive? Such a devious move might help to maintain the "bad boy" image of Abercrombie & Fitch.

References

Behling, D. (1985). Fashion change and demographics: A model. *Clothing and Textiles Research Journal*, 4(1):18–24.

Blumer, H. (1969). Fashion: From class differentiation to collective selection. *Sociology Quarterly*, 10:275–291.

Coleman, M. S. (1998, August 7). Course canceled: "Drinking 101." *The Des Moines Register*, 11A.

Fetto, J. (2001, June). More is more. *American Demographics*, 23:8.

Hamilton, J. A. (1997). The macro–micro interface in the construction of individual fashion forms and meanings. *Clothing and Textiles Research Journal*, 15(3): 164–171.

Hebdige, D. (1979). *Subculture: The Meaning of Style*. London: Methuen.

Horn, M. J., & Gurel, L. M. (1981). *The Second Skin* (3rd ed.). Boston: Houghton Mifflin.

Kaiser, S. B., Nagasawa, R., & Hutton, S. (1995). Construction of an SI theory of fashion part 1: Ambivalence and change. *Clothing and Textiles Research Journal*, 13(3):172–183.

Kean, R. C. (1997). The role of the fashion system in fashion change: A response to the Kaiser, Nagasawa and Hutton model. *Clothing and Textiles Research Journal*, 15(3): 172–177.

King, C. W. (1963). Fashion adoption: A rebuttal to the "trickle-down" theory. In S. A. Greyser (Ed.), *Toward Scientific Marketing*, pp. 108–125. Chicago: American Marketing Association.

Ono, Y., & Bounds, W. (1998, July 9). Army pants with pouchy pockets storm fashion world. *The Wall Street Journal*, B1, B7.

Peking's designer diplomacy. (1985, May 20). *Newsweek*, 46.

Polhemus, T. (1994). *Tribal Styles*. New York: Thames and Hudson.

Reynolds, F. D., & Darden, W. R. (1972). Why the midi failed. *Journal of Advertising Research*, 12:51–62.

Simmel, G. (1904). Fashion. *International Quarterly*, 10:130–155.

Spiegler, M. (1996, November). Marketing street culture: Bringing hip-hop style to the mainstream. *American Demographics*, 18(11):29–34.

Sproles, G. B. (1985). Behavioral science theories of fashion. In M. R. Solomon (Ed.), *The Psychology of Fashion*, pp. 55–70. Lexington, MA: Lexington Books.

Sproles, G. B., & Burns, L. D. (1994). *Changing Appearances.* New York: Fairchild.

Trebay, G. (2004, February 6). Maturing rappers try a new uniform: Yo, a suit! *The New York Times,* A1.

Veblen, T. (1912). *The Theory of the Leisure Class.* New York: Macmillan.

66 Refashioning the Hawaiian Shirt

Marcia A. Morgado
University of Hawaii

Examine the individual depicted in Figure 11.6. Who is this person? What elements in the illustration provide clues to his identity?

Chances are you guessed that the figure is intended to represent a tourist, and you based your guess on appearance-related elements in-cluding his apparent age and body type, the cameras, hat and sunglasses, the sandals and long socks, and the Hawaiian shirt worn with mismatched shorts. These clues form a coherent system of *signs*, or visual cues, that lead us to recognize a classic stereotype: the tourist as fashion nerd. Some writers (e.g., Shindler, 1979) suggest that the image of the clueless tourist garbed in an outrageous Hawaiian shirt has near-universal recognition as a comic stereotype. Central to both the stereotype and its humorous nature is the assumption that Hawaiian shirts, with their corny tropical print motifs, garish color combinations, and pajama-like styling, represent the epitome of bad taste in dress.

A peculiar discrepancy becomes evident if we move away from cartoon images to consider the Hawaiian shirt in the context of contemporary fashion, commerce, and social life. Those who follow fashion know that Hawaiian shirts have recently and repeatedly appeared in the runway shows and ready-to-wear lines of such big-name designers as Giorgio Armani, Tommy Hilfiger, and Ralph Lauren, and that they are *hot items* (i.e., strong sellers) in the merchandise offerings of popular labels like Abercrombie & Fitch, Nautica, Roxy, and Quiksilver. There are large markets for expensive Hawaiian shirts in Tokyo; inexpensive shirts are in demand from street vendors in Singapore; and moderately priced Hawaiian shirts are prominent in the shops and on the backs of consumers in Amsterdam, London, Munich, Paris, New York, and Los Angeles. The Hawaiian shirt has clearly become a global fashion phenomenon.

FIGURE 11.6 *Who is this person? What clues do you have to his identity?*

Adapted from "From Kitsch to Chic: The Transformation of Hawaiian Shirt Aesthetics" by Marcia A. Morgado in *Clothing and Textiles Research Journal* (2003), 21(2):75–88.

This raises some interesting questions. How can we explain the contradiction between the pervasive stereotype of the Hawaiian shirt as a symbol of a trashy, tasteless, tourist aesthetic and the reality of the shirt's popular appeal? How can we account for what appears to be a curious shift in aesthetic sensibility that has refashioned this hokey joke into an attractive, desirable, and highly marketable commodity?

THE SEARCH FOR SATISFYING ANSWERS

One approach to questions such as these is to search for a fit between the observed phenomena and theories designed to explain similar conditions. The purpose of the approach is not only to make sense of the issues in question, but also to test theories for their ability to provide satisfying answers.

Many theories have been proposed to explain how cultures guide the beliefs, values, and behaviors of their members. Among these is one called *rubbish theory* (Thompson, 1979). Rubbish theory is based on the idea that cultures provide the *conceptual tools* (or ways of thinking) that govern how meanings are attached to objects and ideas and how those meanings undergo change.

RUBBISH THEORY

According to rubbish theory, an important component of the system of ideas that guides Western culture is that all objects are assigned to one of two categories: either the *transient* or the *durable*. Objects assigned to the transient category have short lives: their social, economic, and aesthetic value decreases over time. Objects assigned to the durable category have infinite lives, and their value increases over time. As examples, consider two types of products: fashion apparel and oil paintings. Fashion apparel, by definition, is short-lived. We expect it to become less fashionable and less desirable

over time, and we anticipate that today's fashions will be tomorrow's retail markdowns. On the other hand, we are inclined to think of paintings as enduring art forms, to appreciate their potential value as investments, and to assume that over time their market value will increase. Our expectations and behaviors suggest that fashion apparel is assigned to the transient category, while paintings are often assigned as durable.

Category assignments serve an important social purpose. Because objects in the durable category are more valuable and more desirable than transient objects, it is in the interest of the wealthy and powerful to try to keep the objects they own in the durable category (where they continue to increase in value) and to keep others' objects in the transient category (where they continually become worthless). This insures that the status quo is maintained, that power does not change hands, and that the social and economic systems continue to work in the interests of the powerful. The term *hegemony* refers to circumstances that appear to support entrenched systems of wealth and power. Assignments to the transient and durable categories preserve hegemony.

Sometimes, however, objects that begin life as transients do become durables. For example, discarded items found at garage sales or flea markets and purchased for next to nothing may suddenly be revealed as valuable antique collectibles. The purpose of rubbish theory is to explain how this happens.

Between the transient category and the durable category is a third category called *rubbish*. Its purpose is to account for the discarded items. Objects assigned to the rubbish category have no life span and no economic value, and thus they are more or less invisible. That is, no one pays attention to them. Like the transient and durable categories, the rubbish category is only a mental construct, but we can imagine it as a trash heap, a place where objects are dumped once they become worthless. The backs of our closets and bottoms of dresser drawers may serve as literal equivalents, for fashion apparel is often stashed there when we tire of it.

According to the theory, the rubbish category makes it possible for worthless objects to be rescued and transformed into durables. Certain conditions govern possible transformations:

1. **Objects enter the market as transient.** A group of objects begins life assigned to the transient category. The objects are priced for mass markets and they have broad appeal.

2. **The objects gradually slide into rubbish.** Over time the objects become increasingly less interesting and less attractive. Their market value declines, and eventually most are discarded. Some wind up in thrift stores; many go out with the garbage. A long period ensues during which there is no interest in the objects and they have no market value. This renders them invisible. They are now consigned to the rubbish category.

3. **Catastrophic circumstances limit the supply.** A catastrophe occurs that makes it impossible for more of the objects to be made. For example, an artist dies, a secret formula is lost, or a resource is exhausted. The remaining objects are now scarce.

4. **The objects are rescued.** A few enterprising individuals rediscover the objects and find subtle variations and complex details that went unnoticed during the transient stage. The discoveries initiate renewed interest in the objects. Their market value begins to climb.

5. **The objects are reassigned to the durable category.** As market values rise, the aesthetic value of the objects is reassessed, and it becomes increasingly clear that their intrinsic beauty has been overlooked. Prices for the objects reach astronomical heights, far beyond the reach of ordinary people. They are now available only in high-priced collectors' markets and are recognized as timeless classics. The objects are added to museum collections. Figure 11.7 illustrates the path of possible transfer between categories.

THE HAWAIIAN SHIRT AS TRANSIENT

Accounts of the origin of the Hawaiian shirt are as varied and colorful as the shirts themselves. Some trace it to a plain muslin garment introduced in the early 1800s by Christian missionaries who insisted that naked Hawaiians wear it to cover themselves. Others say it developed from a colorful, patterned work shirt worn by American pioneers in the mid-1800s and that the first to wear the shirts were Chinese immigrants. Still others claim that its origins are in silk shirts hand-painted with traditional Polynesian patterns and that these originated in the Hawaiian Islands in the 1920s as custom-made souvenirs for wealthy tourists. What can be substantiated is that ready-made Hawaiian-style shirts were designed, manufactured, and sold in the Hawaiian Islands by the mid- to late 1930s, that they were intended as souvenir commodities for the tourist market, and that they were absolutely bizarre relative to the standards of the time.

Multiple elements in the shirt's design rendered it unique. The boxy silhouettes, pajama-like collars, and square-cut hems were novel, but the most unusual features were aspects of the textiles. The print designs involved crazy combinations of flowers, trees, musical instruments, fish, birds, words, boats, hula dancers, fruit, maps,

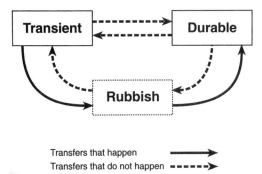

FIGURE 11.7 *Transfers that can and cannot happen between the transient and durable categories.*

tourist sites, and warriors, often rendered in caricature, printed on silky rayon fabrics, and dyed in vibrant hues and unfamiliar color combinations. These features made the shirt instantly recognizable and contributed to its status as both an essential souvenir purchase and the key element in the stereotype of the tourist as the ultimate fashion nerd. A typical shirt from the 1940s appears in Figure 11.8.

During the 1950s, Hollywood films offered audiences romantic and exotic images of Hawaii and spurred the growth of tourism to the Islands. They popularized island fashion as well. By mid-century, Hawaii was a popular tourist destination and the design, manufacture, and sale of Hawaiian shirts was big business. Later studies would show that nearly 100 percent of visitors to the Islands purchased at least one Hawaiian shirt. Thus, the tacky tourist stereotype was reinforced by the fact that many tourists bought and wore Hawaiian shirts. Cartoons, jokes, and amusing songs about tourists in dreadful Hawaiian shirts worn with black socks, and/or mismatched shorts, and/or in the company of a woman in an equally tacky mu`umu`u, proliferated.

According to rubbish theory, goods assigned to the transient category are characterized by popularity, moderate prices, and short lives. The status of the Hawaiian shirt at mid-

FIGURE 11.8 *Hawaiian shirt, dated early 1940s.*

century matched the popularity and price criteria. The life span criterion would soon be met as well.

THE HAWAIIAN SHIRT AS RUBBISH

Over time, the styling characteristics of the shirt underwent change. Silhouettes narrowed and standard shirt collars, often in button-down form, replaced the floppy ones. The new shirts looked crisp and business-like, were easily tucked into the trousers, and more closely resembled the standard sport shirt. Sophisticated prints and modern color schemes that represented more general fashion trends replaced the earlier wild patterns. The fabric changed as well, for easy-care fabrics had rendered rayon obsolete. And, because many of the new shirts were constructed with the textiles turned wrong side out, the print designs were softened and the colors subdued. Influential firms in Hawaii's apparel industry began to consider themselves in the fashion and resort-wear business, rather than in the Hawaiian shirt trade.

From the early 1960s through the mid-1980s, the original form of the Hawaiian shirt was effectively dismissed from mainstream marketplace transactions. By 1970, discarded shirts from the 1940s and 1950s could be found in thrift stores for as little as 25¢. This signaled the Hawaiian shirt's descent into the rubbish category. It would remain there—invisible—for some 20 years.

THE HAWAIIAN SHIRT AS DURABLE

Meanwhile, reports of a little-known fire at the DuPont textile mill in New York began to circulate. Rumor had it that DuPont was the principal supplier of the silky rayon fabrics used in the original Hawaiian shirts and that a fire in the late 1940s or early 1950s had consumed the company's entire rayon production facility. Like the whisper game Secret, where messages are altered as they pass from one source to another, the story was embellished as it moved from one reporter to the next. By the time the story appeared in *The New York Times* (Loomis, 1988, p. 12), all reserve inventories of the fabric were exhausted, and not only the rayon production plant but also the chemical formula for the rayon fiber had gone up in flames.

There is no evidence to support the story of the fire or the loss of the formula. DuPont's rayon facilities shut down as newer fibers were developed and the demand for rayon declined. However, the fabricated story established the essential scarcity factor on which subsequent reevaluations of the value and aesthetic merits of the Hawaiian shirt would depend.

By the early 1990s, a strong collectors' market for vintage Hawaiian shirts was evident, and magnificent coffee table books filled with colored pictures of vintage shirts, stories of their history, and details of their design and manufacture were available. Collectors, dealers, and museum curators wrote of their discoveries of subtle nuance and artistry in the construction of the shirts, the fabrications, and especially, in the prints. Their discoveries revealed that the shirts were not just jokes at the expense of the tourist. Rather, they were relics of a rare and irreplaceable form of folk art. Collectors revealed, for example, that expert craftsmanship preserved pattern motifs which were carefully matched across pockets and seams; that hidden messages were worked into some of the textile designs; that the names of textile artists were often hidden along the selvage edge of Hawaiian shirt fabrics; and that an examination of labels attached to the necklines revealed an array of miniature images that were art forms in themselves. Even the buttons were revealed as significant details, highly varied and unique in design. Reports indicate that serious collectors paid as much as $3,000 to $5,000 for a single shirt (e.g., Kitchen, 1999, p. 43). Several art museums mounted vintage Hawaiian shirt exhibitions.

According to rubbish theory, goods can be reassigned from the transient to the durable category only through prescribed circumstances that insure that the objects are: (1) removed from general circulation; (2) rendered scarce; (3) reevaluated as rare, beautiful, and highly desirable status symbols; and (4) made available only to the wealthy. The circumstances surrounding the Hawaiian shirt thus far appear to support the theory.

On the other hand, rubbish theory does not allow for the possibility that goods in the durable category can be reassigned to the transient category. How, then, can we account for the fact that Hawaiian shirts are considered valuable art objects concurrent with their visibility as fashion apparel? We can extrapolate from rubbish theory to explain this circumstance as well.

REFASHIONING THE HAWAIIAN SHIRT

As the last decade of the twentieth century drew to a close, the fashion press revealed that some manufacturers had invested tens of thousands of dollars in vintage Hawaiian shirts, presumably to serve as inspiration for their new sportswear collections. The press also reported that Hawaiian shirts were about to burst onto the fashion scene (e.g., *Daily News Record*, 1997, p. 1). And indeed, they did, and consumers around the world bought them. The transformation of the Hawaiian shirt from rubbish to durable had successfully altered the meaning of the shirt, refashioning an object of derision into an elite status symbol. Elite validation made Hawaiian shirts desirable and paved the way for their acceptance as global fashion.

Like all fashion goods, the new shirts have been assigned to the transient category. Even those that replicate details of the original models are transient. Rubbish theory tells us that all of these new shirts will experience short life spans, and that their aesthetic, social, and economic value will decline. Meanwhile, vintage shirts in the hands of collectors and dealers and those in museum collections will continue to increase in value.

THE TACKY TOURIST STEREOTYPE: MEANING IS MAINTAINED THROUGH CATEGORIES OF IDEAS

Despite its current status as a global fashion, connections between the Hawaiian shirt, the tourist, and excruciatingly bad taste remain intact. In a recent edition of the *New York Post* (and subsequently repeated in *The New York Times*), a reporter suggests that "Arnold Schwarzenegger's stylist should be terminated for allowing the action hero to leave the house wearing a shirt as ugly as the one he sported the other day...." The shirt was made up "in a cartoon-like print with a Hawaiian vibe. You know, the loose, untailored kind that makes you look like a tourist in your own backyard" (Norwich, 2003).

The extent to which actual tourists fit the stereotype is irrelevant. Rather, the significance lies in the idea of the clueless fashion nerd. The humorous stereotype serves a serious social purpose. It is a category assignment that supports the difference between *us* and *them*, *same* and *different*, and it persists because it facilitates the creation of meaning through comparisons between bad taste (theirs) and good taste (ours).

References

Hawaiian floral shirts, the tourists' favorite, are the 'in' print for spring. (1997, September 22). *Daily News Record*, 1.

Kitchen, J. (1999, July/August). Apparel that says aloha. *Hawaii*, 40–45.

Loomis, S. H. (1988, October 16). Hawaii's short-sleeved plumage. *The New York Times*, Sec. 5:12, 28.

Norwich, W. (2003, March 9). A shore thing. *New York Times Magazine*, Sec. 6:48.

Shindler, M. (1979, July 2). Aloha. *New West*, 48–53.

Thompson, M. (1979). *Rubbish Theory: The Creation and Destruction of Value*. Oxford: Oxford University Press.

DISCUSSION QUESTIONS

Refashioning the Hawaiian Shirt

1. The tacky American tourist stereotype emerged during the twentieth century. Is it still alive today? What characteristics make up stereotypes that people outside the United States have about American tourists? If you have no idea, find someone from another culture and ask him or her about stereotypes of American travelers.

2. Do you have a Hawaiian-style shirt? What do you think of them?

3. Can you think of other items of dress that are in fashion today that might be good examples of rubbish theory?

67 What Happened to Fashion?
Teri Agins

Supermodel Naomi Campbell has a killer body, a sassy strut, and a $10,000-a-day attitude. Famous for being fashionably late for work, she has left more than a few designers in the lurch right before a big show, wondering when—or if—she would appear. But the supermodel wasn't quite so cavalier when it came to Isaac Mizrahi, her buddy and the darling of America's designers. Nobody lit up a runway the way Isaac did during the 1990s. His witty, high-energy fashion shows were always the highlight of the New York collections.

On the evening of April 10, 1997, Mizrahi's fashion spectacle took place near Madison Square Garden, at the Manhattan Center on West 34th Street. At a quarter to six, with more than an hour to spare, the diva of the catwalks made her entrance, in sunglasses, $500 Manolo Blahnik stilettos, and a stunning spotted coat. On cue, bounding down the stage steps, emerged the man in black, Isaac Mizrahi, brandishing a Camel Light like a conductor's baton.

"There she is! *Na-o-mi!*" he exclaimed, swooping in to buss her on both cheeks. "Fab-u-lous." Mizrahi ooohed and ahhed, checking out her genuine leopard wrap. Evidently, the anti-fur era was over and out. Campbell was sporting the most politically incorrect of furs; leopards had been an endangered species since before she was born.

Naomi did a little pirouette, then swung open her vintage coat. The bronze satin lining was embroidered with the name of its famous original owner: Ann-Margret. "I got it in Los Angeles from this dealer," she explained in her girlish-British lilt. Suddenly, André Leon Talley, *Vogue*'s main man-about-Paris, stormed in to boom: "Girl, that coat is *major!*" The trio huddled for a dishy chat, then Mizrahi scooted her off backstage to get made up with the rest of the "girls," models like Kristen McMenamy and Shalom Harlow. As Campbell slipped away, her Hermès tote let out a "brrring," from her cellular phone. A cigarette ash fell to the floor as Mizrahi

spun around, his arms flying as he jabbered some directions to his backstage crew. "I just *love* this," he muttered to no one in particular.

This drive-by vignette from fashion's fast lane harked back to *Unzipped*, the lively 1995 documentary that followed Mizrahi through the exhilarating fits and starts during the months when he prepared his 1994 fall collection. *Unzipped*, which won the audience award at the Sundance Film Festival, captured all the hyperbole, razzle-dazzle, and parody of high fashion, juiced up by the ebullient Mizrahi, a showman so delicious you couldn't make him up.

Straight out of Brooklyn's well-to-do Jewish enclave, Mizrahi got fixed on fashion early in life. His elegant mother decked herself out in Norman Norell and Yves Saint Laurent, while his father, a children's-wear manufacturer, bought Isaac his first sewing machine when he was still in grade school.

By the time Mizrahi was fifteen, he was stitching up a storm, designing a collection called "IS New York" which he sold to friends and a few neighborhood boutiques. He was also an imp and a cutup who in the 1970s starred on-stage at the High School of Performing Arts and as an extra in the movie *Fame*. After studying fashion at New York's Parsons School of Design, he moved on to Seventh Avenue, where he became an assistant to designers Perry Ellis, Jeffrey Banks, and Calvin Klein.

Ambitious and fast-tracking, Mizrahi was ready to do his own thing by the time he reached twenty-five. He invested the $50,000 trust fund his late father had left him to launch his eponymous fashion house in a brick-walled loft in downtown SoHo. His March 1988 debut runway show was one of those rare and unforgettable moments that left fashion editors agog. They knew they had just witnessed the start of something big.

That spring, Bloomingdale's rushed to put Mizrahi's debut collection in its windows on Fifty-ninth Street and Lexington Avenue, where Mizrahi showed up in person to greet shoppers. The most enthusiastic fashionistas swallowed the hype and splurged on their first Mizrahis. Kal Ruttenstein, Bloomie's fashion director, remembered: "We sold Isaac to the customer who was aware of what he was doing."

What Mizrahi was doing was cool and high-concept. He had a sophisticated take on American sportswear, inspired by fashion's modern masters, Claire McCardell and Geoffrey Beene, with a nod to Mary Tyler Moore, Mizrahi's favorite TV muse. But he also pulled a few tricks from up his own sleeve.

Throughout the 1990s, Mizrahi stood out as America's most prolific idea man, turning out one innovation after another, in a splash of Technicolor delight: paper-bag-waist pants, a tartan kilt strapless dress, fur-trimmed parkas, and boxy jackets. He spiked his fashion-show programs with puns to describe fabrics and colors: "Burlapse," "Fantasy Eyelet," "Lorne Green," and "James Brown." The fashion editors lapped it up, with page after page of pictures and kudos. But among retail buyers, there was decidedly less of a consensus. Barneys New York and Ultimo in Chicago were among the handful of stores whose fashion-forward clientele craved the labels with the most buzz. Accordingly, such retailers could move a few racks of Mizrahi's $800 jackets and $350 pants most every season. But Mizrahi barely caused a blip at chains like Neiman Marcus and Saks Fifth Avenue, where his spirited fashions got buried in the broad mix of up-and-coming designer brands.

Gilding the Mizrahi mystique was his colorful, megawatt persona. With a bandanna headband taming his frizzy black hair, he was an adorable cartoon. Isaac was fashion's funniest Quotron, who chirped frothy declarations with the push of a button, just like Diana Vreeland, the legendary *Vogue* editor of the 1970s whose snappy sound bites ("Pink is the navy blue of India") have entered fashion's lexicon. "Le Miz"—as *WWD* dubbed fashion's wonder boy— once exclaimed about a chubby fake fur jacket: "It looks *divine* in beast." He held forth to *WWD* about his 1992 spring collection: "It will be all about irresistible clothes. The *only* kind that will sell."

But what merchandise actually sold was of little concern to the members of the Council of Fashion Designers of America and other fashion industry groups, who showered Isaac with a number of "best designer" awards during his first years. All Mizrahi needed now was solid capital backing to take his business to the next stage. "All my life, I dreamed of a design house like that of Calvin Klein, Armani or Yves Saint Laurent," Mizrahi once wrote in a pitch letter to potential financiers. His dream seemed like a foregone conclusion by 1992 when the venerable house of Chanel in Paris stepped in to help, signing on to become Mizrahi's financial partner. Chanel certainly had the expertise, having successfully staged its own renaissance in the 1980s, with management's deft handling of Chanel's perfumes and accessories, bolstered by the ingenious Karl Lagerfeld, who had become Chanel's couturier in 1982. Chanel was poised to parlay Mizrahi's marquee image into profits with the 1994 introduction of "Isaac," a bread-and-butter department store collection of $150 dresses and $300 jackets.

Meanwhile, Le Miz continued to reign as Mr. Fabulous on the high-fashion runways, as he mined his bottomless pit of creativity. And after his wacky performance in *Unzipped*, a star was born. Among his TV and movie credits, playing a fashion designer, naturally, was his bit part in the Michael J. Fox comedy *For Love or Money*. He was also a jovial guest on the TV game show *Celebrity Jeopardy!*, where he was the winner.

But while Isaac, the stylish personality, was in high demand, his clothes weren't. By 1996, Mizrahi's runway collections weren't wowing the fashionistas anymore, as Gucci and Prada were now the favorite flavors of the moment. Meanwhile, the Isaac collection on which Mizrahi banked his future just didn't click with shoppers, who were far too savvy to fork over $150 for a cotton shift designer dress when chains like Bebe and The Limited were turning out similar styles for as little as $49.99. As reality bit harder, Mizrahi had no choice but to close his Isaac division at the end of 1997, leaving his struggling fashion house hanging by a thread.

That's fashion. And that's the curious way success plays out in the fashion world. A designer can be deemed hot by buzz alone—as Mizrahi was from the start—even though the sales of his collections were barely tepid. But people outside the fashion loop would never be the wiser, because fashion coverage in newspapers and magazines was all about style, not substance.

The fact that Mizrahi's sportswear was thoroughly modern should have worked to his advantage, but his business habits were pretty old-fashioned. He saw himself as a latter-day couturier who designed for supermodels and the coolest fashionistas—but not ordinary women. Mizrahi couldn't connect with the critical masses because he didn't relate to them. For example, when retail buyers once begged him to repeat one of his few best-sellers—paper-bag-waist pants—Mizrahi couldn't bring himself to do a rerun. "I just got *bored* with them," he later recollected.

Flashing back to the final scene in *Unzipped*, Mizrahi showed what really mattered to him. There was Mizrahi, in post-fashion-show anxiety at a Manhattan newsstand, hovering over a copy of *WWD*, which applauded his latest collection, proclaiming "the man has a hit on his hands." The camera zoomed in on a giddy Mizrahi, who was bouncing down the street. But what was missing from this happy ending was the only review that counted in the real world: sales in stores.

Mizrahi, aloft in a cloud of chiffon, had yet to get serious about the bottom line. He was an artiste who refused to become another Seventh Avenue garmento. "Look, it is all I can do to make fabulous collections and fabulous clothes," he explained in July 1997. "That is *all* I can do. You know I can't imagine after all these years, *I can't imagine* how it will translate at retail."

On October 1, 1998, the curtain finally came down on Mizrahi's fashion show. Ten years of terrific reviews added up to little; the House of Mizrahi chalked up no more than an estimated $15 million at its peak in 1996—and zero in the profit column. The money men at Chanel, realizing that Mizrahi's moment had passed, slammed the door on America's most beloved Little Fashion House That Could. Mizrahi unzipped played like an obituary across the bottom of the front page of *The New York Times*. Out of fashion and headed toward a career in Hollywood, Mizrahi was sanguine—leaving the door open for his possible comeback. "I will always have a great love of fashion. I'll always be a fashion designer," he told *WWD*. [See Discussion Question 3 for an update.]

There's no better example than Mizrahi to show what has been happening lately in the real world of fashion. It's not only the end of the millennium, but the end of fashion as we once knew it.

Mizrahi is a direct descendant of the trickle-down school of fashion, the aspirational system in which high-fashion designers, their affluent clients buoyed by scads of publicity in *WWD* and *Vogue*, dictated the way everyone dressed. The old order was starting to unravel when Mizrahi first went into business in the 1987. But failing to read the shifts in the marketplace, Mizrahi became the quintessential fashion victim; he arrived on the scene just when fashion was changing. By the early 1990s, a confluence of phenomena arising from retailing, marketing, and feminism began transforming the ways of fashion forever.

For all of its glamour and frivolity, fashion happens to be a relevant and powerful force in our lives. At every level of society, people care greatly about the way they look, which affects both their self-esteem and the way other people interact with them. And it has been true since the beginning of time that people from all walks of life make the effort to dress in style.

Yet fashion, by definition, is ephemeral and elusive, a target that keeps moving. A clothing style becomes fashionable when enough people accept it at any given time. And conversely, fashions go out of style when people quit wearing them. Traditionally, the fashion system has revolved around the imperative of planned obsolescence—the most familiar examples being the rise and fall in skirt lengths, and for men the widening and narrowing of trousers and neckties. Every few years, when the silhouettes change, women and men have been compelled to go shopping and to rebuild their wardrobes to stay in style.

In America's consumer society, which burgeoned after World War II, apparel makers, designers, retailers, and their symbiotic agents, the fashion press, were the omnipotent forces pushing fashion's revolving door. They have been responsible for creating new fashion trends and inducing people to shop until they dropped, to scoop up the novelties the industry promoted. This order was a mighty mandate that prevailed throughout the 1980s, a system which established a consensus that kept millions of consumers moving in lockstep. Perhaps that's what William Shakespeare foresaw when he wrote: "Fashion wears out more apparel than the man."

But in recent years, a number of circumstances caused a revolutionary shift that upset the old order and wrested control away from the forces in the fashion industry. In 1987, designers missed the boat when they failed to sell women on short skirts. They misfired again, a few seasons later, with the somber "monastic" look and other fads, resulting in millions of dollars of losses to the industry. By the mid-1990s the forces of fashion had lost their ability to dictate trends. Increasingly, the roles have reversed. The power now belongs to us, the consumers, who decide what we want to wear, when we buy it, and how much we pay for it. And nowadays, consumers are a lot savvier and more skeptical when it comes to fashion.

Four megatrends sent fashion rolling in a new direction.

• *Women let go of fashion.* By the 1980s, millions of baby-boomer career women were moving up in the workplace and the impact of their professional mobility was monumental. As bank vice presidents, members of corporate boards, and partners at law firms, professional women became secure enough to ignore the foolish runway frippery that bore no connection to their lives. Women began to behave more like men in adopting their own uniform: skirts and blazers and pantsuits that gave them an authoritative, polished, power look.

Fashion's frothy propaganda no longer rallied the troops. The press beat the drums for a decade, but the name Isaac Mizrahi still drew a blank with millions of American women who hadn't bothered to notice.

A defining moment in high fashion occurred in 1992 with the closing of Martha, the venerable dress salon on Park Avenue. Starting in the 1930s, Martha Phillips, a feisty entrepreneur with impeccable taste, began her reign as one of America's leading standard-bearers for snob appeal and Paris originals. And for nearly six decades, elegant women beat a path to the pink-walled emporium on shopping trips that took hours as Phillips and her attentive staffers put their clients together in head-to-toe perfection. Such was the drill during an era when rich women derived much of their self-worth from wearing the best couture labels.

Martha's demise was the latest casualty in a rash of salon deaths, coming just months after the closing of such salons as Loretta Blum in Dallas, Amen Wardy in Beverly Hills, and Sara Fredericks in Boston. Martha Phillips and her exquisite counterparts couldn't hack it anymore because the pace-setting socialites who once spent a fortune on their wardrobes no longer devoted so much time and money to getting dressed up. Park Avenue style maven and decorator Chessy Rayner, who used to be a front-row regular at the Paris fashion shows, was among those who had made the conversion from clothes horse to fashion renegade. In 1992, she recalled: "Today my style is totally pared-down and non-glitz."

As such salons folded, many of their suppliers, namely the couture houses in Paris, faced a precarious future. For most of the twentieth century, Paris designers had set the standard, introducing the full-skirted "New Look" after World War II, the "sack" silhouette of the fifties, the "space age" sleek of the sixties, and the "pouf" party dress in the eighties. Such were the trends that Seventh Avenue manufacturers slavishly copied and adapted for the mass market. But by the 1990s, most Paris designers couldn't set the world's fashion agenda anymore. Styles were no longer trickling down from the couture to the masses. Instead, trends were bubbling up from the streets, from urban teenagers and the forces in pop music and counterculture with a new vital ingenuity that was infectious. The powers in Paris were taken aback when their captivated clients awoke from the spell of couture and defected in droves. And thus, the fortress of French fashion came tumbling down.

- *People stopped dressing up.* By the end of the 1980s, most Americans were wedded to jeans, loose knit tops, and Nike shoes, which became the acceptable standard of everyday dress even in offices. Leading the charge for informality were men, in their rejection of the business suit, which since the start of the industrial age had been the symbol of masculine authority and the uniform of the corporate workplace.

Starting in the 1980s, the bespectacled computer nerds at the helms of America's buoyant high-tech industries broke the pattern of stuffed-shirt formality in business. Microsoft Corp. founder Bill Gates emerged as the world's wealthiest man—and the personification of the Internet-set look, dressed for success in chinos and sports shirts.

In America's more traditional corporations, the men's fashion revolt first erupted in Pittsburgh, of all places. In the fall of 1991, Pittsburgh-based Alcoa, the giant aluminum concern, became the first major corporation to sanction casual office attire. The move came about after Alcoa had allowed employees who contributed to the United Way to dress casually during a two-week fund drive. The perk proved so popular that Alcoa decided to give its employees the option of never having to dress up again. Even Alcoa's top honchos stopped suiting up. One typical weekday morning in March 1992, Ronald Hoffman, an Alcoa executive vice president, was working in his suite on the thirty-seventh floor wearing a yellow V-neck sweater, an open-neck shirt, and slacks. "There

used to be a time when a white shirt went with your intelligence," Hoffman told *The Wall Street Journal.* "But now there's no reason to do this anymore."

Before long, the rest of corporate America had shifted into khakis and knit shirts at least one day of the week, which became known as "casual Friday." Computer giant IBM went so far as to go casual every day, starting in 1995. Levi Strauss & Co., the world's biggest apparel maker, caught the wave in the early 1990s with its loose-fitting Dockers casual pants, which quickly became a popular wardrobe staple for men. It took less than five years for Dockers to explode into a $1 billion-a-year business.

Without enough suit buyers to go around, many of America's fine haberdasheries and boutiques suffered the fate of Martha. Charivari, a flashy New York chain known for its dressy and expensive European designer imports for men and women during the 1980s, planned to ride out the dress-down trend. In 1991, Charivari plastered on billboards: "Ripped Jeans, Pocket Tees, Back to Basics. Wake us when it's over. Charivari." Instead, seven years later, it was Charivari that was over—and out of business.

Indeed, it seemed as though not only dress-up clothes, but good taste, had fallen by the wayside as millions of Americans sank into sloppiness, wedded to their fanny packs, T-shirts, jeans, and clunky athletic shoes. "Have We Become a Nation of Slobs?" blared the cover headline of *Newsweek,* February 20, 1995. The accompanying article provided a mountain of evidence that people were no longer dressing to impress, including a Boston funeral director who said that some families were now asking for their loved ones to be buried without a coat and tie.

- *People's values changed with regard to fashion.* Most people used to put "fashion" on a pedestal. There was a sharp delineation between ordinary clothes from Casual Corner and Sears and true "fashion" from Paris couturiers and boutiques like Charivari and Martha. But such a divide existed before so many options for fashion became widely available at every price level. Stores like Ann Taylor, The Limited, Gap, Banana Republic, and J. Crew turned out good-looking clothes that deflated the notion that fashion belonged exclusively to the elite. In effect, designer labels started to seem like a rip-off. Increasingly, it became a badge of honor to be a bargain hunter, even among the well-to-do. Discounter Target Stores struck the right chord with this tagline in its ads: "It's fashionable to pay less."

Many people like Deirdre Shaffer, a thirty-one-year-old part-time psychotherapist from a New Jersey suburb, learned this lesson quite by accident. In 1994, Shaffer and her husband attended a cocktail party at their local country club to which she wore a black dress from Ann Taylor and $12.99 black suede sandals that she had just purchased from Kmart. Earlier that day, Shaffer didn't have enough time to comb the upscale malls where she usually bought her clothes. So, while she was shopping in Kmart for paper towels and toothpaste, she wandered over to the shoe racks, where she found the sandals. That evening, Shaffer was feeling quite satisfied with her budget find. "I got more compliments on the shoes than my dress," she recalled, noting that her friends were "impressed when I told them they came from Kmart."

Indeed, seeing was believing for Shaffer and millions of folks who wised up. It was akin to a Wizard-of-Oz discovery: Behind the labels of many famous name brands was some pretty ordinary merchandise. Increasingly, the savviest shoppers started paying closer attention to details like fabric, workmanship, and value—and thus became less impressed with designer labels. *Consumer Reports*, which is best known for its evaluations of kitchen appliances and cars, helped millions of shoppers see the light when the magazine began testing different brands of clothes for durability, fiber content, and wear. The truism "You get what you pay for" was proven false. In a 1994 test of chenille sweaters, *Consumer Reports* concluded that a $340 rayon chenille sweater from the upscale Barneys New York "was only a bit higher in quality" than a $25 acrylic chenille sweater from Kmart. In another trial in 1997, the magazine gave its highest ranking for men's polo knit shirts to Honors, a store brand that sold for only $7 at Target, but whose quality scored well above those versions by Polo Ralph Lauren at $49, Tommy Hilfiger at $44, Nautica at $42, and Gap at $24.

Marketing analysts describe consumers' new embrace of the most functional and affordable clothes as the "commoditization" of fashion. Beginning in the 1980s, more apparel makers shifted most of their manufacturing from the U.S. to low-cost factories in the Far East, where they were able to provide more quality at an attractive price: good-looking polo shirts and other apparel that were perfectly acceptable to most people—with no sustainable difference between one brand or another. As more people had no reason or burning desire to dress up anymore, they had no qualms about buying their clothes wherever they could get the best deal—just as Deirdre Shaffer did at Kmart.

The commoditization of clothes coincided with the most popular clothing trends of the 1990s: the "classics," "simple chic," and "minimalism." This comes as no surprise. Such mainstream styles are far easier for designers to execute on a commercial scale, in that they are cheaper and safer to produce, with less margin for error in the far-flung factories in China, Hong Kong, Korea, and Mexico, where much of today's apparel is made.

Furthermore, there's a whole generation of people under forty who don't know how to discern quality in clothes. Generation X-ers born in the 1970s didn't grow up wearing dresses and pantyhose in high school, nor did they own much in the way of "Sunday clothes." These young people are largely ignorant of the hallmarks of fine tailoring and fit. Jeans, T-shirts, stretch fabrics, and clothes sized in small, medium, large, and extra-large are what this blow-dry, wash-and-wear generation have worn virtually all of their lives. While their mothers and grandmothers donned slips and girdles—and pulled out the ironing board before they got dressed—these young people had already formed the habit of wearing comfortable, carefree clothes.

• *Top designers stopped gambling on fashion.* Isaac Mizrahi mistakenly believed that there were enough fashion mavens still willing to put their trust in his taste level. But the best-selling designers nowadays know better. Liz Claiborne, Polo Ralph Lauren, and Tommy Hilfiger are among the fashion houses that grew into billion-dollar empires of apparel, handbags, cosmetics, and home furnishings. Such fashion houses just also happen to be publicly traded companies, which must maintain steady, predictable growth for their shareholders. The upshot: The big guns can't afford to gamble on fashion whims. Fashion as we have known it requires a certain degree of risk-taking and creativity that is impossible to explain to Wall Street. Even though the leading designers tart up their runways with outlandish, crowd-pleasing costumes, they are grounded in reality. The bulk of the actual merchandise that hits the sales floor is always palatable enough for millions of consumers around the world, thus generating the bottom line that Wall Street expects.

With so much consumer rejection of fanciful fashions, will the world turn into a sea of khakis and T-shirts? Will Paris couture and the likes of Mizrahi and Charivari ever rise again? And moreover, will fashion ever matter as it used to?

"The fact is that women are interested in clothes, but the average consumer isn't interested in the 'fashion world,'" observes Martha Nelson, the editor of *In Style* magazine. Women want attractive clothes that function in the real world, "not something that is impossible to walk and drive in. You know, clothes that fit into your life."

So, that's why we've come to the end of fashion. Today, a designer's creativity expresses itself more than ever in the marketing rather than in the actual clothes. Such marketing is complicated, full of nuance and innovation—requiring far more planning than what it takes to create a fabulous ballgown, as well as millions of dollars in advertising. In a sense, fashion has returned to its roots: selling image. Image is the form and marketing is the function.

Nowadays, a fashion house has to establish an image that resonates with enough people—an image so arresting that consumers will be compelled to buy whatever that designer has to

offer. The top designers use their images to turn themselves into mighty brands that stand for an attitude and a lifestyle that cuts across many cultures. Today's "branding" of fashion has taken on a critical role in an era when there's not much in the way of new styling going on—just about every store in the mall is peddling the same styles of clothes. That's why designer logos have become so popular; logos are the easiest way for each designer to impart a distinguishing characteristic on what amounts to some pretty ordinary apparel.

Having burnished his image through millions of dollars of advertising, Calvin Klein towers as a potent brand name and leverages his CK logo across a breadth of categories—$6.50 cotton briefs, $1,000 blazers, and $40 bath towels—even though there are plenty of cheaper options widely available.

Image, of course, works in conjunction with the intrinsics—the style, quality, and price of each actual item—and image comes from everywhere: the ambiance of the location where the clothes are sold, the advertising, the celebrities who wear the clothes, and so forth. Image is how the Gap sells a $12.50 pocket T-shirt, how Ralph Lauren pushes a $40 gallon of wall paint, and how Giorgio Armani moves $1,500 blazers.

These designers assault the American public with their ubiquitous advertising, most typically seen in the fashion press. But the roles have reversed there as well. Fashion publications like *WWD, Vogue, Harper's Bazaar, GQ,* and the rest have lost their power in their editorial pages to make or break fashion trends—the same power designers have lost to the consumer. Nowadays, the mightiest fashion brands, by virtue of their heavy-duty advertising, take their message directly to the public—unfiltered by the subjectivity of the editors: Ralph Lauren's ten-page advertising inserts in the front of *Vogue* and *Vanity Fair* are more arresting than any fashion spread featuring his clothes in the editorial pages of the magazine.

It was always confounding, this business of selling fashion. And now the industry has become fragmented into so many niches in which scores of companies churn out more and more merchandise at every price range, season after season. The fashion-industry powers at the head of the class prevail because they swear by retailing's golden rule: The consumer is king.

The following chapters [see Agins, T. (1999). *The End of Fashion*. New York: Quill] capture some of the industry's best-known players in recent years, as they've succeeded—and sputtered—in their quest to make fashion for profit, as well as for glory. Fashion, which began in the hallowed ateliers of Parisian couture, now emanates from designers and retailers from around the world, reaching the masses at every level. In today's high-strung, competitive marketplace, those who will survive the end of fashion will reinvent themselves enough times and with enough flexibility and resources to anticipate, not manipulate, the twenty-first-century customer. There's just no other way.

What Happened to Fashion?

1. Has fashion died, or has fashion become something other than it was back in the 1950s? Look at our definition of fashion. Think of how that definition fits with the four megatrends that Agins outlines. Is there still fashion out there? And if so, what is it?

2. Is "casual" the opposite of "fashion"? Explain.

3. For an update on designer Isaac Mizrahi, see "Movin' On Up" in *Vogue*, March 2003, pp. 554–561 and 593. Mizrahi now designs a line for Target while also reviving his upscale line. How might designing for Target help Mizrahi fit more successfully into today's fashion system?

68 Urban Tactics: And Bloomingdale's Returns His Calls

Seth Kugel

At 4:40 P.M. on Sept. 19, hours before Republica Trading Company introduced its spring 2004 clothing collection with a party at Barolo, a garden restaurant in SoHo, Rafael Jimenez was hunched over a computer in his garment district office, moving names from the R.S.V.P. list to the guest list and tacking on little notations— +1, +2, +3—indicating how many companions each guest could bring. Current total: 268 names down, 208 to go.

Six years after he incorporated Republica, the 35-year-old Washington Heights native is still the company's sole full-time employee. He is also the part-time secretary.

In an adjacent room, two of his old friends were describing how Mr. Jimenez's creations have made a splash in the Latino market without giving their creator a swelled head or tempting him to cash in on offers to buy the company.

"He's just the anti-rock star," said Neil Mossberg, a vice president of World Marketing, which sublets space to Republica. "He does it all on his own. He's just not into ego."

Phil Colon, a high school friend who handles advertising for Republica, through his company, Ruido Group, yelled across to Mr. Jimenez. "Do you have any enemies?" No answer; Mr. Jimenez was too busy sorting out the guest list.

By 11 that night, Mr. Jimenez had been transformed from secretary to public relations man, donning a Republica pinstripe newsboy cap and suede military-inspired shirt and mixing with the eclectic network of friends, associates and friends of associates that he has built up since he began selling Latino-themed T-shirts in 1995.

The first store to stock his wares was Corte Tropical, a Washington Heights barbershop a few blocks from where he grew up. The clothes caught the neighborhood's attention and sold fast. Earlier this year, his clothes landed in some far more impressive venues—11 of Bloomingdale's 31 stores, including stores on both coasts.

Much changed during the intervening years. Mr. Jimenez graduated from New York University, he incorporated his business as the Republica Trading Company, and retailers began to recognize the power and scope of the young Latino market. Republica expanded beyond T-shirts to caps, shirts, pants and jackets, in colors from muted to tropical, and fabrics from cottons and linens to cashmere and silk. But one thing remained the same: the T-shirts still flew off the rack.

Republica has yet to provide a steady income for Mr. Jimenez, who also works as a freelance television producer. But that may change: the company is on track to sell a half-million dollars of merchandise in 2003, up from $75,000 last year. The clothes, many by moonlighting designers from major houses, have captured the imagination and support of New York's growing network of young Latino professionals.

"We all kind of know each other," Mr. Jimenez said over a breakfast at El Malecon, a Dominican restaurant on the ground floor of the building where he grew up and where his mother still lives. "There's not a lot of college-educated Latinos, and there's even fewer that are working in any decision-making positions. When you meet someone, it's like, 'I respect what you do.'"

But it goes beyond respect. "When there's someone trying to do something, there's like a

code of ethics," said Mr. Colon, whose advertising company charges Republica what he calls a family rate for its services. "You've got to help the people who are trying to come up."

Mr. Jimenez's story, told so smoothly it is clear that he has recited it many times, goes like this. One day in 1995, when he was riding uptown on the A train and noticed someone wearing a Banana Republic T-shirt, he thought to himself, why not substitute the word Dominican for Banana and sell such a shirt in his neighborhood, where nearly everyone had roots in the Dominican Republic? The initial reaction? "People said: 'That's not going to work. Dominicans want tacky stuff.'"

But that summer, he printed 12 Dominican T-shirts, stuffed them in a backpack and started wandering through his neighborhood. The shirts sold out in 20 minutes, at $20 each. By the end of the summer, he had sold more than 300. Before long, he was also producing T-shirts for women, with logos that included "Dominican Baby," "Choco-Latina" for darker-skinned Latinas, and "Bizcocho," a term of endearment for Colombians. Mr. Jimenez eventually brought in professional designers and began selling through the company's Web site, www.Republicatrading.com.

Although the company's products remain rooted in Latino themes, the more recent T-shirts are subtler, giving a nod to Latin culture and the Spanish language but aiming for a broader appeal; as Mr. Jimenez put it, "When you go heavy-handed with Spanish stuff, it can be a little much." The 2004 line includes four T-shirts: one with roosters to evoke rural Latin America; another with the masked face of the Mexican wrestler, film star and cult figure Mil Mascaras; a third featuring words like "Freedom," "Culture" and "Peace" in English and Spanish; and a fourth with the Spanish word "Revolucion" superimposed on a tank with a quote from John F. Kennedy: "Those who make peaceful revolution impossible will make violent revolution inevitable." The collection also included casual shirts, some resembling guayaberas.

Republica's big break came when Mr. Jimenez shared a cab from the airport with a buyer for Federated Department Stores, Bloomingdale's parent company, that resulted in the chain's decision to include the T-shirts and hats across the country last April.

Sales have been so brisk that Bloomingdale's has agreed to buy 10 new T-shirt designs. "We've been constantly reordering," said Kevin Harter, men's fashion director for Bloomingdale's. "It absolutely has a great appeal on the floor."

Mr. Jimenez is not sure he wants fashion as his full-time gig. Although his interest in the field dates to his youth, when his father purchased cloth wholesale on Delancey Street and brought it to a Washington Heights tailor to make the family clothes, Mr. Jimenez sees himself as more entrepreneur than fashion-industry lifer.

It may not be quite the life his parents envisioned for him; their ambition was that he be a "professional."

"Doctor, lawyer, engineer, work in a business," Mr. Jimenez said. "Those are the four cornerstone careers in any Dominican family in order to be considered a professional." When he took five years off from college to work in the music industry, his father, who has since died, persuaded him to finish school. And his mother was often dubious about his fashion ventures, but seeing her son's clothes in Bloomingdale's didn't change her mind. Now she is a convert. "She sees me in El Diario," Mr. Jimenez said, "and then it's official."

DISCUSSION QUESTIONS

Urban Tactics

1. This article outlines the beginning success of an entrepreneur in the clothing industry. How does his story seem to differ from that of Isaac Mizrahi, described in the Agins article "What Happened to Fashion?"

2. How does Jimenez target his customers? How has he used ethnicity in his clothing lines?

69 Plus-Size Modeling: The Industry, the Market, and Reflections as a Professional in the Image Industry

Brecca A. Farr
Oklahoma State University

"Plus-size petite model."

Say that phrase and you'll likely hear, "What's that?" "You're kidding, right?" or "That's an oxymoron, like 'military intelligence.'"

Plus-size petites, also known as women's petites, is an apparel size range targeted for women between 5' and 5'4" tall and a size 14 or larger.

But wait, didn't I also say *model*? Yes, at 5'2" tall and a size 18 (approximately 195 pounds), I worked as a plus-size petite model and consultant. In this article I discuss my

<hr>

Original for this text.

work as a plus-size petite model and give an insider's perspective of the modeling industry, the plus-size market, and reflections on being a plus-size petite professional in the U.S. image industry.

THE MODELING INDUSTRY

Everyone in the modeling industry has his or her own story about how he or she began modeling. Many young women and men start off modeling part-time during their preteen or early teen years. Perhaps they entered a national contest and were among the winners. No one in his or her right mind graduates from college, works long enough in the apparel industry to advance into a well-paying job with a bright career ahead, just to quit for a two-week modeling gig with absolutely no guarantee of work afterward. But that's what I did. I don't recommend that as a common approach to career change. I was very lucky, literally being in the right place at the right time with the right height, size, and shape of body.

Most people don't realize that working as a model usually means you're self-employed. Being self-employed means no guaranteed salary and no benefits, such as medical insurance or a retirement plan. A few models are employed to work exclusively for one firm; often these are "fit models," and the firm attempts to create product differentiation based on the fit to that model's measurements. The vast majority of models are self-employed, however, be they freelance or under contract with an agency.

A reputable modeling agency, such as Ford Models, Inc., acts as a professional service. When my agent accepted bookings for me, Ford ran a credit check on the client. Additionally, Ford billed and collected my hourly fees. Modeling agencies also put together books of their models. Models usually pay for their pictures to be included in these books. The cost depends upon the agency, the number of pictures to be included, and the type of book being published. A full-color book highlighting all the agency's fashion models is more expensive than a black-and-white book featuring industry fit models (see Figure 11.9). For these services, I paid Ford a percentage of my fees, as is the practice in the industry.

As a model under contract with an agency, I capitalized on the reputation of my agency. Saying that I was a model with Ford initiated expectations for appearance and professionalism. When I walked into a prospective client's office, there was an expectation of attractiveness as well as knowledge about women's petites. The expectation of attractiveness included wearing stylish clothing of my own (including shoes and complete accessories), having my hair in a flattering style, and using makeup befitting my skin tone and ensemble. As do most new models, I worked with a professional makeup artist to learn how to appropriately apply my makeup when I first began to work.

FIGURE 11.9 *Brecca Farr as a women's petite fit model.*

There are two general types of models that I categorize as "fashion" and "closer-to-real-life." Fashion models include the supermodels, such as Cindy Crawford, Iman, or Christy Turlington, and the models seen on the haute couture runways of New York, Paris, Milan, and so forth. Also, these models are featured in fashion magazines such as *Vogue, Elle*, and *GQ*.

Fashion models represent idealized standards of beauty and attractiveness. Usually they are taller, thinner, and younger than the average woman or man. It is common for female fashion models to be over 5'10" tall and a size six or smaller. By comparison, when I worked in the New York City garment industry from the early to mid-1990s, industry statistics reported that the average woman in the United States was 5'3.8" tall, weighed 145 pounds, and wore either a size 12 or 14 dress. Within a group of fashion models, there may also be "body parts models." These models are women and men whose specific body part or parts, such as hands, chest, or legs, represent the ideal size and shape.

Compared to fashion models, closer-to-real-life models represent one or more target markets. These models still emphasize attractiveness, but they do not differ as greatly from the average person in their target market as do fashion models. Specialty size models are closer-to-real-life models and are often identified with apparel size ranges, such as petites, talls, or plus sizes.

Even within a group of plus-size models, there are degrees of how similar to real people a model may be. Many plus-size models featured in upscale clothing catalogs, such as *Spiegel For You*, wear sizes 12 or 14, because they are close to 5'11" or 6' tall. Often these models are sizes 12 or 14 because of their height, not because they are overweight. This is also true for many store or mall fashion show models who work in the plus-size range. Considering that plus sizes range from size 14 to 24, these models are on the small side of the scale.

Regardless of the type of model a person may be, there are body expectations. These expectations not only govern how the person will walk, talk, dress, and carry the self, but will also govern what the model must do to maintain her or his body and image. Critical expectations include the key body measurements that must be maintained, such as bust or chest, waist, high and low hip, thigh, and calf. Ongoing maintenance may be more difficult during a woman's menstrual cycle, when her breasts may swell or she retains more water and her body's measurements increase 1/2" or more.

Models constantly manipulate their bodies through a variety of methods, ranging from adjusting their caloric intake, exercising, surgery, smoking, or taking prescription or illegal drugs. The degree to which models manipulate their bodies depends on the individual, personal body chemistry, and what image or target market they are attempting to represent. Many of the models I knew had surgery—liposuction was most common.

Keeping the body in good condition may involve more than just exercising or eating healthy. Two hand models I knew wore gloves at all times to protect their hands. Dry skin or chipped nails could cost them jobs and income. Leg models I knew never shaved their legs with razors for fear of scratches. They also had to watch what types of exercises they did: too many repetitions on a StairMaster would increase the size of their calves. Any imperfections or blemishes could mean the difference between working and being unemployed.

For myself, I adjusted my diet and exercise routine to maintain the measurements I needed to work. I refused to have surgery to change my body's shape. I must state that I was never asked to have surgery. However, it was understood that if I wanted to extend the years I had to work in the industry and increase my client list, I would have to seriously consider cosmetic surgery at some point in the future.

THE PLUS-SIZE MARKET

My work as a women's petite model was only possible after the establishment of the plus-size market. I first worked as a women's petite model in 1992. It simply was not possible to earn a living as a women's petite model much before 1992 because the market didn't exist, according to the industry.

The plus-size market has been around for many years. Lane Bryant, one of the oldest plus-size retailers, has been in business for over 90 years. Traditionally, the plus-size market targeted older women, offering them dresses shaped like tents and bulletproof polyester pants. Only within the last 10 to 15 years has the apparel industry taken hold and pushed the boundaries of the plus-size market toward a more youthful and fashion-forward customer.

Why are these markets important? Estimates state that approximately 40 to 60 percent of all U.S. women are petite, specifically 5'4" and shorter (Shim & Kotsiopulos, 1990). In addition, 60 percent of U.S. women wear a size 12 or larger, and 31 percent of U.S. women wear size 16 or larger (Daria, 1993; "Why Is Size 8...," 1994). Table 1 presents the percent of the population classified as overweight. Erring on the conservative side, approximately 45 to 60 million U.S. women are represented in this special size market.

The women's apparel industry has been experiencing lackluster sales for the past several years. Retailers finally realized that opportunities for growth and increased sales were available in the plus-size market (Darnton, 1991; Feldman, 1992; Gill, 1991; Owens, 1997; "Sales of Women's Plus Sizes...," 1995; "Sizing Up Women's Apparel," 1994). One research organization stated that from June 1990 to June 1995, the plus-size apparel market increased 42 percent as compared to a 23 percent increase of total women's apparel during the same five years ("Sales of Women's Plus Sizes...," 1995). Many apparel retailers and manufacturers anticipate continued growth for this market. "The reason there's so much growth in this part of the industry is simple: there's a lot of money to be made" (Stiven, 1989). Phrased another way and often quoted in the market, "When looking at a firm's profit margin, there's no difference between skinny and fat dollars."

The recognition of the potential profits from the plus-size and plus-size petite markets challenged many beliefs about overweight women and men. Studies have documented a pervasive negative stereotype of large-size people.[1] Some of

TABLE 1

*Percentage of the U.S. population that is overweight**

Age Range	1976–1980		1988–1991	
	Men	Women	Men	Women
20–34	17.3	16.8	22.8	24.5
35–44	28.9	27.0	35.7	35.1
45–54	31.0	32.5	35.5	39.8
55–64	28.1	37.0	40.5	48.7
65–74	25.2	38.4	42.2	39.7
75 and older	n/a	n/a	26.0	31.5

n/a = data not available

*Overweight is defined for men as body mass index (BMI) greater than or equal to 27.8 kilograms per meter squared, and for women as BMI greater than or equal to 27.3 kilograms per meter squared. These points were used because they represent sex-specific 85th percentiles for persons 20 to 29 years of age in the 1976–1980 *National Health and Nutrition Examination Survey* (NHANES). Data are based on physical examinations of a sample of the civilian noninstitutional population in the NHANES. Pregnant women are also excluded (U.S. Bureau of the Census, 1997).

the attributes of the stereotype include laziness, lower socioeconomic status, weak-willed, blame-worthy, dirty, slow, unintelligent, withdrawn, un-attractive, and incompetent (Harris, Harris, & Bochner, 1982; Harris, Walters, & Waschull, 1991; Harris, Waschull, & Walters, 1990; Jasper & Klassen, 1990; Millman, 1980; Tiggemann & Rothblum, 1988). Apparel merchandisers and modeling agencies were not immune to these stereotypes.

Large-size women and men are assumed to be responsible for their condition, as if they all choose to be overweight. Society in the United States sanctions overtly hostile behavior toward plus-size women and men, unlike other stigmatized groups such as African-Americans (Crandall, 1994).

Millman (1980) states that large-size women are "mythologized"; that is, the issue of size goes beyond the reasons "normal" people cite for being offended by a large-size woman. Her size symbolizes deviant tendencies in rela-tion to societal norms. Large-size women are somehow seen as expressing rebellion against what society deems as appropriate. The reason-ing follows that if you accept the societal norm of beauty and attractiveness, you can't accept plus-size people.

Little sympathy or understanding of an in-dividual plus-size woman's situation is ac-corded (Millman, 1980). She is blamed for being fat. Furthermore, plus-size women may internalize this blame, thereby believing the myths and stereotypes (Harris, Waschull, & Walter, 1990). This belief may include self-fulfilling prophecies (Snyder, Tanke, & Ber-scheid, 1977). If a woman believes that she's unattractive and she can't find clothing that looks good or fits well, she is likely to project a message that says she doesn't care about how she looks. If people believe that she doesn't care how she looks, she'll be treated accord-ingly. And the cycle continues as she reacts to the way she's treated by others.

Millman (1980) puts it best when she states, "Being [a plus-size person] and the interpreta-tions made of it wind up affecting all of a per-son's life, pushing the fat person into a special,

marginal relationship to the world" (p. 72). This marginalization by society affects plus-size women in the way they interact with others. Withdrawing from society is not unusual for the plus-size woman (Millman, 1980), and, if she withdraws, her ability to develop social skills is hampered. Therefore, she withdraws further, promoting the image that she doesn't care about her appearance. This also continues to feed into the cycle of society's negative attitude and stereo-type of plus-size people.

When I worked in the modeling industry, at times public perceptions of the mere existence of a plus-size model were still that it was an oxy-moron. For example, I was discussing the new plus-size holiday line of a better price-point brand with a fashion consultant. An acquain-tance in the apparel industry joined our conver-sation, having overheard us discuss details such as "stylish," "contemporary," "greater comfort for a more shapely body without sacrificing aesthet-ics," "she [the consumer] can feel attractive and ready for a night out on the town." The new-comer to the conversation commented, "What are you talking about?" We replied with the name of the line and our excitement about its new offerings for the plus-size market. Her only comment was, "I never thought that company would produce clothes for fat women. I always thought they were concerned about their image."

These attitudes and stereotypes about over-weight people are also prevalent when you exam-ine the evolution of the women's plus-size market. At first, plus sizes were recognized as appropriate only for older women. The assumption was that these women, because they were older and over-weight, were not concerned about their appear-ance. If they weren't concerned about their ap-pearance, then they wouldn't spend a lot of money on their clothing. So, merchandise from budget-priced apparel firms comprised most of the market's offerings. Slowly, apparel firms rec-ognized that overweight women were not just 65 years of age and older, but that there were a lot of younger women as well. Furthermore, if the women were younger, then they were most likely to need clothes for work and leisure time. However, it has only been during the past 15 years that the plus-size market has begun to offer clothing for young women (under 30), as well as more contemporary styles at better to bridge price points (Wallach, 1985; Werner, 1987). Only published articles from the 1990s regularly state that plus-size consumers seek most of the same fashion trends as their smaller counterparts.

Very little scholarly research has focused on the plus-size market beyond documentation of stereotypes and potential social behaviors resulting from being overweight in the United States. Recent research includes a study that examined the relationship between a special-sized consumer's level of satisfaction toward her body and her level of satisfaction relating to apparel shopping and shopping behaviors (Shim & Kotsiopulos, 1990). Other research has focused on needs assessments of either the petite or the plus-size consumer (Chowdhary & Beale, 1988). No research has examined women's petites. The most consistent source of literature comes from trade press concerning recent market sales figures. Numerous articles also appear in popular periodicals, such as *Glamour, Essence,* and *The New York Times,* which discuss the difficulty plus-size consumers face when trying to find well-fitting and stylish clothing.

THE IMAGE INDUSTRY

When reflecting on my role as a professional in the image industry, three themes emerge: First is my perception that I was not a threat to other models in the industry. Second is enhancement of my self-esteem due to recognition and acceptance as an attractive woman. Third is development of plus-size markets and the fundamental challenge that development gives to the image industry.

As I mentioned earlier, many plus-size models featured in catalogs or on the runway were size 12 or 14 and very tall. Rarely were size 18 or larger models used, yet these sizes are closer to the midpoint of the plus-size range. If several models were hired for a particular photo shoot or modeling job, usually there was a specific look that was desired for each model. For example, if three plus-size models were to be featured, the client was likely to have a list of preferences—such as one blond model, one mature model, and one African-American model. If a plus-size petite model was also included on the list of preferences, at the time I worked that meant she would be myself or one of three other models working in New York.

When a general call for all plus-size models went out for a show or photographic work, most of the other models were surprised to see me. I was significantly shorter and larger than they were. Subsequently, I was not perceived as a competitor for their jobs. Because I was not a competitor, most of the models were very friendly and openly discussed how they maintained their body size and shape. We also swapped tips for makeup, hair styling, fixing shoes, and numerous other ways to change image and appearance.

When I was with other models or working with clients in the plus-size market, my status as a Ford model granted me instant acceptance. My education, professionalism, and personality were important with regard to maintaining that acceptance and earning their respect. That instant acceptance was, to me, a measure of my attractiveness; recognition and acceptance also gave me self-confidence. The Ford Modeling Agency doesn't offer contracts to unattractive women. When I worked, I played the role of a Ford model; therefore, I needed to capture some of the essence of being a model—my hair done, makeup just right, good clothes, nice shoes, and a very put together appearance. Additionally, I represented millions of women—regular women across the United States. And I wasn't the unattainable ideal standard of beauty.

The mere fact that I earned a nice living as a plus-size petite fit model and consultant validated the existence of the plus-size petite market. While Saks Fifth Avenue, Liz Claiborne, and Ellen Tracy, as well as other firms, produced, marketed, sold, and emphasized the continued development of plus-size clothing, the image industry made the statement that overweight women and men are acceptable. Yet, recognition and continued development of the plus-size market challenged a fundamental belief of the image industry—that thinner is better.

Since the time I left the market, the "thinner is better" belief continues to be challenged. Fashion magazines, such as *BBW* and the newly launched *Mode* ("Plus-Size 'Mode' Hits Stands," 1997), devoted to the plus-size woman and featuring models larger than size 14, continue to gain greater visibility on retailers' shelves. *Glamour* purports that each issue will include at least one ad or feature with a plus-size model. The Body Shop introduced an advertising campaign featuring Ruby, a redheaded rubenesque "Barbie-like" doll and accompanying caption: "There are 3 billion women who don't look like supermodels and only 8 who do" (Elliott, 1997). Recent health studies have stated that it is possible to be overweight and physically fit ("Experts Challenge Assertion," 1997).

Hopefully, the continued growth and development of the plus-size market will help women and men accept themselves and their bodies. From that acceptance, I wish everyone could feel the joy that self-confidence brings. I am still amazed at how much self-confidence I gained from working as a professional in the image industry and being well-paid because of the size and shape of my body.

Note

1. Many studies have examined the stereotypes associated with overweight or obese people (e.g., Crandall, 1994; Harris, Harris, & Bochner, 1982). The associated negative attributes were not found to be significantly different between overweight men versus overweight women.

References

Chowdhary, U., & Beale, N. V. (1988). Plus-size women's clothing interest, satisfactions and dissatisfactions with ready-to-wear apparel. *Perceptual and Motor Skills*, 66:783–788.

Crandall, C. S. (1994). Prejudice against fat people: Ideology and self-interest. *Journal of Personality and Social Psychology*, 66: 882–894.

Daria, I. (1993, February). Why more designers are designing large-size clothes—and why some still won't. *Glamour*, 91:149–150.

Darnton, N. (1991, February 25). Big women, big profits. *Newsweek*, 117:48, 50.

Elliott, S. (1997, August 26). The Body Shop's campaign offers reality, not miracles. *The New York Times*, C8.

Experts challenge assertion that thinner is always better. (1997, August 12). *The Washington Post*, Z13.

Feldman, A. (1992, March 16). Hello, Oprah, good-bye, Iman. *Forbes*, 142:116–117.

Gill, P. (1991, April). 141 niche: A perfect fit. *Stores*, 73:44–46.

Harris, M. B., Harris, R. J., & Bochner, S. (1982). Fat, four-eyed, and female: Stereotypes of obesity, glasses, and gender. *Journal of Applied Social Psychology*, 12:503–516.

Harris, M. B., Walters, L. C., & Waschull, S. (1991). Gender and ethnic differences in obesity-related behaviors and attitudes in a college sample. *Journal of Applied Social Psychology*, 21:1545–1566.

Harris, M. B., Waschull, S., & Walters, L. (1990). Feeling fat: Motivations, knowledge, and attitudes of overweight women and men. *Psychological Reports*, 67(Pt. 2):1191–1202.

Jasper, C. R., & Klassen, M. L. (1990). Stereotypical beliefs about appearance: Implications for retailing and consumer issues. *Perceptual and Motor Skills*, 71:519–528.

Millman, M. (1980). *Such a Pretty Face: Being Fat in America*. New York: W. W. Norton & Company.

Owens, J. (1997, April 30). Plus-size market is segmenting. *Women's Wear Daily*, 173:10.

Plus-size 'Mode' hits stands. (1997, February 17). *Mediaweek*, 7:3.

Sales of women's plus sizes outpace total apparel biz. (1995, November 6). *Discount Store News*, 34:25.

Shim, S., & Kotsiopulos, A. (1990). Women's physical sizes, body cathexis, and shopping for apparel. *Perceptual and Motor Skills*, 71: 1031–1042.

Sizing up women's apparel. (1994, May 16). *Discount Store News*, 33:A48.

Snyder, M., Tanke, E. D., & Berscheid, E. (1977). Social perception and interpersonal behavior: On the self-fulfilling nature of social stereotypes. *Journal of Personality and Social Psychology*, 35:656–666.

Stiven, K. (1989, April 24). Underserved market dresses up options. *Advertising Age*, 60:S-15.

Tiggemann, M., & Rothblum, E. D. (1988). Gender differences in social consequences of perceived overweight in the United States and Australia. *Sex Roles*, 18:75–76.

U.S. Bureau of the Census. (1997). *Statistical Abstract of the United States: 1997* (117th ed.). Washington, DC: U.S. Bureau of the Census.

Wallach, J. (1985, April). Strategies for selling large-size apparel…Who's doing it and how. *Stores*, 67:13–23.

Werner, T. (1987, March 9). Sizing up: Conston, apparel retailer, caters to larger customers. *Barron's*, 69.

Why is size 8 the industry standard? And where does that leave the rest of us? (1994, April). *Glamour*, 92:205–206.

DISCUSSION QUESTIONS

Plus-Size Modeling

1. Why was the plus-size market ignored and under-serviced until the 1990s?

2. What negative consequences does ignoring the plus-size market have for U.S. consumers?

3. How did Brecca's experience as a model affect her feelings about her body?

4. Since this article was written in 1999, the magazine *BBW* has gone out of print, yet estimates of the number of obese and overweight individuals in the U.S. population have increased for all age groups. The U.S. Surgeon General has also called on Americans to lose weight. Has the U.S. treatment of plus-size individuals changed since 1999?

70   As China's Women Change,
        Marketers Notice

Cris Prystay

On a recent visit to the Shanghai offices of a major toothpaste company, Linda Kovarik, associate director for strategic planning at ad agency Leo Burnett, noticed that many of the female employees kept framed glamour shots on their desks. The most frequent subject: themselves.

"I'm not talking about group hug with mom, dad and grandpa; it's just themselves," said Ms. Kovarik.

It was a telling portrait of the changing mindset of female consumers in China. "We are seeing a rise in materialism and ego. Women are expressing themselves in a way their mothers couldn't," she says. "Brands need to offer them room to be vain and to explain who they are."

Ms. Kovarik got a chance to gauge the mindset of Chinese women in a study of 64 consumers in Chengdu and Shanghai in May, the results of which she presented this week at a conference in Singapore. She recruited consumers to survey both men and women in their 30s and 50s about their perception of young Chinese women today. Half of those surveyed earned below the average income in their city, and half earned 60% above the average.

The myriad stereotypes of Chinese women—the exotic ingenue of the East, the filial traditionalist, the party stalwart—were entirely absent. Instead, one young woman wrote: "I am the center of the world, I am the [focal point]. Draw a circle and you can find me. I'm quite realistic, but sometimes I daydream. I'm a little bit selfish, but I'm always there for my friends."

"It sounds like Carrie Bradshaw, but this is a 22-year-old Shanghainese woman," says Ms. Kovarik, referring to the lead character in the TV show "Sex and the City." "One thing we learned was there's a lot of crossover, a lot of balancing acts. It's kind of 'Sex in the City' meets Martha Stewart."

To understand how much the economic clout of Chinese women has changed, consider the following figures. The average annual income in China's urban centers soared 315% between 1990 and 2000 to 6,317 yuan ($764), according to the China Statistical Yearbook. While Chinese officials don't break down income growth between sexes, women's slice of the pie has clearly grown. The portion of the female work force in managerial positions rose to 6.1% in 2000 from 2.9% in 1990, while the portion of women employed in professional or technical jobs rose to 22.8% from 17.4%, according to the National Bureau of Statistics of China.

Companies are taking note. In 1998, for example, Proctor & Gamble Co.'s marketing strategy for Rejoice shampoo, one of the country's top-selling brands, pulled an ad that featured an airline hostess and replaced it with one of a woman working as an airline mechanical engineer. The change was driven by consumer surveys that showed women had become more career focused, says P&G's Rejoice brand manager, Jacky Cheng.

Since then, women have again raised the bar, and Rejoice has tried to keep pace. The latest ad for Rejoice Refresh shampoo, running now on Chinese TV, features a girl playing beach volleyball. "You find a lot of these girls in China," says Mr. Cheng. "They're very demanding, they want to be better, but they also want to fulfill other aspirations. Previously, that was career fulfillment, but these days, it's 'I would also like myself to become a more beautiful lady.'"

A key driver of this new attitude, besides rising incomes, is the dramatic change in the retail landscape itself: Women are more fashion-focused because there's simply more fashion available to them. "The offerings have increased dramatically," said Jacques Penhirin, a partner at McKinsey & Co. in Shanghai. "For example, there was shampoo, but you had three or five to choose from. You've got 300 today." At the same time, quality has gone up and price has gone down.

During this period of rapid change, the income gap between women and men has actually grown. China's urban women make 62.7% of what men make for similar work, 7.4 percentage points lower than 1990, according to a July, 2001 survey by the All China Women Federation. Nonetheless, their attitudes are evolving at a breakneck pace. One-quarter of urban, unmarried women say they want to marry, but not have kids, according to a survey conducted by Sinofile Information Services. Another 11% of unmarried women say they would prefer to stay single.

"The traditional archetypes in China were the ingenue and the caregiver," says Ms. Kovarik. "As marketers, we can definitely explore more archetypes: woman as hero, woman as lover, woman as creator, explorer."

As China's Women Change, Marketers Notice

1. What factors have changed in China during the last ten years to make young women in China an important market for fashion?

2. What attitudes are young women in China expressing about themselves that seem inconsistent with Communism but consistent with fashion orientation?

71   The Shadow Designer

Arthur Lubow

Even without the Michael Kors "cashgora" poncho in pumpkin that was draped over her shoulders, June Horne would have stood out at the breast-cancer benefit held in late September at the flagship store of Saks Fifth Avenue. As she roamed around the Kors shop within Saks, chatting ebulliently with the designer, embracing old friends and glad-handing customers, her wattage surged to a fuse-blowing level. Horne is in her mid-40's, with a beautiful milk-chocolate complexion, brilliantined hair à la Josephine Baker and a full-bodied figure. She looks not like a waif who models designer clothes but like a customer who actually buys and wears them.

And she does, in fact, buy the clothes—for herself and, more significant, for thousands of others. Horne is one of eight buyers of American and European collections for Saks. She works

© Arthur Lubow. First published in *The New York Times Magazine*.

with 11 designers, including Kors (whose bulky brown turtleneck was under the poncho) and Zoran (the brown pants that coordinated with the sweater). A walking advertisement, Horne is also an effective saleswoman. When I asked about the cashmere-and-angora poncho, which seemed a little heavy for the overheated room, she said: "This is something that has sold better in brown than in this color, for some reason. So I thought I would wear this tonight. And I've already sold two." Afterward, I spoke to Kors about the poncho. "In the show, that was on a girl who was a size 2 and was 18 years old and had a braid down to her knees in hair extensions," he remarked. "You say, 'How am I going to translate that into the customer, into reality?' And June does that."

That is the role of the department-store buyer: to translate the look of the impossibly beautiful runway model into an outfit that a real-life woman can wear and (more to the point) purchase. In the two decades that Horne has been in the business, the role of buyers has swelled in importance. The most powerful will request revisions of finished designs, demanding everything from hemline adjustments to fabric changes. As many of the smaller specialty shops have closed their doors and the big stores have gotten bigger through mergers and acquisitions, the buyers for the few remaining titans in the upmarket apparel business—particularly Saks, Bergdorf Goodman, Neiman Marcus and Barneys—have become even more influential.

For the designers, the buyer is the earliest and most important reality check. Niche designers, whose clothes are as much art objects as garments, may refuse to hear a buyer's style suggestions. Stella Ishii, president of Staff USA, a distributor of such avant-garde designers as Susan Cianciolo and Martin Margiela, says: "I don't think they would change a neckline in response to a store's request. Such questions are never really posed." The longstanding maverick Geoffrey Beene also demurs, saying flatly, "I do not ask buyers what they want." But most designers do ask; they want to sell their clothes. And if they resent the creative interference, they aren't letting on.

Pushing her way through the throng at the Saks benefit, Horne schmoozed with the design-

ers she buys from. First stop was Richard Tyler. Horne had reviewed his spring 2000 collection at his showroom that morning.

"I know you didn't see many browns, but we could do more," Tyler said, after they had finished hugging.

"The pink was great," Horne said.

"We loved that you liked the blue jacket with the little shells," said Lisa Trafficante, who is Tyler's wife and business partner. In the Seventh Avenue lexicon, a "shell" is usually, as in this case, a simple scoop-necked shirt—not the calcareous covering of a mollusk. And the polite way of expressing your approval or gratification is to say, "I love it."

"I loved what you did today," Horne told them. "What my customers want from you is special sexy dresses. You know, the simple black dress we saw today."

Before leaving, Horne asked Trafficante to send along brown fabric swatches that might be made into dresses exclusive to Saks.

Across the floor, she spotted one of her younger designers, Victor Alfaro, who has made a name for himself with casual yet luxurious dresses and sportswear. "Victor has the ability to interpret a trend at an approachable price point," Horne said. "And he makes it wearable. With the low-cut pant, he gives you the same look, but he gives you more room in the seat."

As Horne swept over to greet Alfaro, Victor's assistant, Michelle Gerson, said to her boss, "Look at her, she doesn't miss a trend, with her Austrian crystal bracelets."

"She doesn't miss a trend," he agreed.

Alfaro and Horne discussed delivery dates. Then she fingered the cloth of some green pants.

"I've been walking through the store the last couple of weeks, and everyone says, 'Ms. Horne, Ms. Horne, we need lighter weights,'" she said.

"It's good to know now," Alfaro said. "Because I'm going to Milan in two weeks to choose fabrics. You don't want to do heavy fabrics for next fall if they're not selling. You don't want to repeat mistakes."

"I think we've seen enough sweaters," Horne said. "I see a difference in my sweater sales."

"They're not selling?" he asked.

"Only if they're in a set."

"Chunky's no good?" he asked. Thick sweaters are described in the business as chunky.

"No," Horne said firmly.

Horne and Alfaro would see each other the following morning in his showroom in a posh Fifth Avenue building, where a model would try on the clothes and Alfaro would hear what Saks loved and what Saks loved less. It would be an abbreviated, customized version of the runway show that Horne had attended the week before.

But before this appointment, and even before the runway show, Horne was granted a glimpse of Alfaro's spring 2000 collection. Like her counterparts at Nordstrom and Neiman Marcus, she had gone to a private showing of an early version of Alfaro's designs during the first week in August. "Before the fashion show, we had already an idea of what fabrics and colors the stores wanted," Alfaro explains. "We have to buy fabric way in advance and color it way in advance, so if we wait until the end of the show, we don't have time to get the fabrics and have them cut." Most designers follow this practice, to receive what is called an "early indication" of a store's preferences.

As a result, the major buyers privately have had their say before the collections are presented to the public. "My intention is to be in business and to grow the business," Alfaro says. "You're listening to people who are trying to sell your clothes. If you don't listen, you have to be out of your mind."

Alfaro's white showroom is lighted with overhead halogen bulbs that are tinted pink and cast a flattering light on all below. On the morning of Horne's appointment, the showroom was decorated with a large bouquet of white Casablanca lilies and shiny-leaved branches, in a glass cylinder that was wrapped in burlap and tied with rough cord. Large plates of cut fruit offered nourishment and complemented the decor. The clothes were hanging on a rack in the middle of the room.

Horne arrived accompanied by her associate buyer, Elizabeth Chin, and a contingent from Saks's flagship New York store. Alfaro and Linda Coffey—until this month his vice president for sales—had brought in a regulation-grade thin and beautiful model, Linda Quo, for the occasion. Quo came out from behind a screen in an aqua matte jersey shirt-dress with a leather-trimmed neckline that plummeted toward her navel.

"How is that going to close up?" Horne asked.

Alfaro was prepared for this question. He showed Quo where a clasp would go, and had her pinch the spot with her fingers. Horne then asked her to sit, watching carefully to see how much cleavage was exposed.

"And the slit?" she asked, pointing to the gash that went way up the side of the skirt.

"It's going to be lower," Coffey said.

"As fabulous as Linda is, she's not the normal customer," Horne emphasized. She then focused on the aqua belt that completed the look of the dress. It was being sold as a separate accessory. She thought it should be bundled with the dress. "Victor, anything you can put on the garment, the extra piece—if they don't have to go elsewhere to find it, the sale goes much faster," she said. "Where are they going to find a belt to coordinate with that color?"

A salesman from the New York store was still scrutinizing the slit that rode high up the skirt. "I just don't like it this high," he said.

"The slit will be lower," Coffey promised. "We have to make them sexy for the runway."

"You'll drop it," Horne said with a laugh. "And if you don't, we'll send it back."

As the New York sales team prepared to leave, Alfaro nodded in Horne's direction, and said: "She's very helpful. She always tells me what works and doesn't work."

The model next changed into a beaded suede halter top over white jeans. "My whole thing now is a casual bottom with a luxe top," Alfaro said. "Or the other way. To mix them."

"Items have become extremely important," Horne said.

"What?" Alfaro asked, looking puzzled.

"Items. The jean, the cutout jacket."

"Oh, items," Alfaro said, agreeing.

Alfaro walked to the other part of the show-room to meet with some magazine editors, leaving Horne and her associate to talk business with Coffey, in what is known in the trade as the writing appointment.

"So you have the classic pant," Coffey opened. "And then you have the jean."

"I think we need both," Horne said. "I think the statement this year is designer jeans. I'm loving the classic pant in the turquoise." She had momentarily forgotten that it was called aqua.

"And not the jean?" she was asked.

"I love the brown," Horne said, and then corrected herself. "I love the bark."

Coffey showed her color photocopies of looks in the runway show and urged her to see a belted dress in bark. Quo retired to put it on and soon returned. "Silk and wool shirt dress, 398 for 885," Coffey said. The first number was Saks's price, the second the retail price.

As she looped the belt in baroque curlicues, Coffey suddenly sensed Horne's response. "You don't like the dress?" she asked.

"I'm not loving it," Horne said.

"Well, then, it doesn't matter how I fix the belt," Coffey said, and she sent Quo back to change clothes.

"I think the other dress, which costs less and has the leather, is a better value," Horne said. That was the matte jersey shirt-dress (351 for 775) for which she had requested an attached belt, a lowered side slit and a buttoned neckline—simple changes that would make the garment more wearable for the average customer, without changing its silhouette.

Quo emerged from the makeshift dressing room in a white V-neck top. "These are all leather-trimmed," Coffey said.

"Great," Horne responded. "I love the extra details."

Returning to this part of his showroom, Alfaro overheard Horne's last comment. "In the beige and the aqua, you can see the leather better," he said.

Horne was taking notes in a spiral notebook that contained the designer's sketches of the collection. She crossed out a simple top in favor of a beaded one.

"No, you want that one, too," Coffey remonstrated.

"Why?" Horne asked.

"For layering. With jackets."

"Linda, let's stay with the novelty. I think the novelty is great."

Alfaro, who had disappeared again, re-emerged. "Victor, I love these details, the trim."

"The leather trim and the organza dresses up the jersey," he agreed. "And do you sell wool jersey in the winter? I was thinking of doing the leather trim again, continuing with what has been working."

"I think the trims, the details, are very important," Horne reiterated.

"Everyone reacts to it," Alfaro agreed.

Horne pointed to the leather-trimmed shirt-dress. "Why is this not being shipped with the belt?"

"She's right," Alfaro said to Coffey. "It looks flat without the belt." They made the decision to ship it to all stores with the belt.

Then Horne pointed to the low-cut neckline. "Snap?"

"Yes," Alfaro said. "It will go higher too. It won't be to the bellybutton."

"I love this dress," Horne said enthusiastically.

"It's a winner," Alfaro said.

Both Horne and the designers she covers emphasize that she would never dictate a design. "I want to know what people do not want," Michael Kors says. "I don't want to hear, 'Do that in purple.' If I do that, then I become a private-label resource. But if they say, 'Padded quilted skirts were an absolute disaster for three seasons,' I'm not going to go there."

Horne sees herself as a midwife to the creative process. She loves her job. As a girl growing up in Harlem, she had an aunt who worked in a bridal shop on Seventh Avenue. One day the aunt took Horne, who was then 13, to watch her work. "They were selling these beautiful big white dresses, and the buyers—I didn't know what they were called—were sitting there," Horne recounts. "During lunch, I asked, 'Who were those people you were selling these dresses to?'" From that moment, she knew what she wanted to be. She worked in retail clothing stores on her summer vacations; after graduating from high school, she earned a B.S. at the Laboratory Institute of Merchandising, and then won a place in the Saks Fifth Avenue executive-training program. That was in 1974, the same year she was married to Frank Horne, who is now a restaurant proprietor and consultant. Hired by Saks at the end of the course, she started as an assistant buyer in sweaters and swimwear. After two years, she was promoted to swimwear buyer. "I had very rarely been beyond 125th Street," she says. "And Saks was sending me to Israel and St. Tropez, to Greece and to Brazil for the bikinis."

Following a series of promotions, she was made associate divisional manager, on track for an executive position. But she wasn't loving it. "The title was great, but it kept me from buying," she says. "It's more financial—overseeing the buying. I wanted to talk with Calvin Klein, just to deal with the product line. I didn't want to be hidden behind an office. I got into the business because I enjoy working with creative people."

Not that financial exigencies are ever far from a buyer's mind. Before making the buy, Horne reviews the sales numbers at each store, to judge how to apportion the product. When making the buy for the Michael Kors line, she sat with an assistant buyer, Jason Tucker, in front of a cork bulletin board, to which he had tacked Polaroids of each outfit at the runway show.

"We are so regionally different that we have to look at each market," Horne said. "We'll do New York last, because that's easiest."

"They take everything," Tucker said with a chuckle.

"Exactly," Horne said. "Let's see what Greenwich is selling." She examined a sheet that listed the clothes of the various designers sold at the Saks store in Greenwich and their sales figures. "Relatively clean lines. I know what we're selling." By that she meant that she knew the numbers for the designers that she covers. But were those numbers consistent with those of other designers in the store? "I'm looking to see if she's still selling ensembles out there," Horne said.

Tucker understood that by "she," Horne was referring to the store manager in Greenwich. "No, she's not," he said.

"So our business is mainly in jackets and pants," Horne said. Tucker examined the figures. "Pants she's doing below the company," he said, meaning sales were weak. "Jackets she's doing very well."

Horne paused to consider how this information affected her buy. "I think in Greenwich we should put a lot of emphasis on the zebra jeans and on cotton sweaters in color," she said. "I like the leather jacket. How much does that go for?"

"$2,295."

"That's O.K. I notice with Jil Sander that they'll spend $3,000 for the jacket, but they'll balk at the pant. I think we should go with the expensive jacket but a less expensive pant. Eighteen-inch skirt, they're not interested, in that market. No miniskirts. They're a little conservative." She looked at the cork board. "We pick up the flamingo top. Flamingo-nude." Flamingo-nude is what Kors called his pink-and-orange fabric.

"That'll look great on anybody with a tan," Tucker said. "And everybody in Greenwich has got a tan, natural or not."

Horne next looked at a photograph of a zebra-print bikini top with a matching zebra-print skirt. "This is a Beverly Hills look. We bought that for Beverly Hills and maybe Palm Beach. They can wear that with a little jacket or a sweater around the neck." She rejected a beaded lace skirt with a cable cashmere sweater as "too urban" for Greenwich, then chose some floral-print jeans. "They should have a good range of sweaters, because that's what we're going to sell the jeans with."

"So what do we want to do with the lemon-lime patio pant?" Tucker asked. "Do we want a lime shirt? The basic shirt?"

"Nothing basic," Horne said, as if intoning a mantra. "Nothing basic."

They moved on to Balacynwyd, a suburb of Philadelphia on the Main Line. "This is a whole different thing," Horne said. "Bala. Bala." She half-closed her eyes, conjuring up her customer. "We need great novelty pieces, so they can see the newness of what he's doing. We should do double-face, and obviously the leather jacket."

"How about the leather pant? Will they do it?"

"Yeah. They just need the newest, hottest thing. Let's keep them in the hottest trends. Balacynwyd is not a miniskirt. But go into the whole jeans story. And we want to do more sleeves for Bala than in Philadelphia. Stay away from this." She pointed to a picture of a sleeveless cashmere sweater. "Save that for Beverly Hills. This is a store that should be doing the white palazzo pant."

"So they're going to have the white patio pant and the lemon-lime patio pant."

"Exactly."

"Do we want a car coat?"

"No," Horne said. "Sweaters. I see this as casual. This is her Gap."

Because she was traveling to Milan in two days, Horne stayed late at the office to finish the Kors buy, store by store. (Saks has Kors shops in 8 of its 59 stores.) The following afternoon she would complete the Alfaro buy. Her responsibility is to make sure that regional preferences are accounted for, and to check that the buy within each store is balanced. She then presents the numbers to her divisional manager, who must determine that the allocations jibe with the company's overall financial plan.

When the clothes are delivered in January, few will know that it was Horne who decided that Alfaro should add thread loops and a belt to his shirt-dress. Or that, having determined that the shell Alfaro showed under his cardigan was overly sexy ("The neckline was too low, you couldn't wear a bra and when you closed the cardigan you couldn't see it at all"), it was Horne who went back to the showroom, days after the writing appointment, and persuaded Alfaro to design a new shell that, she says, "we thought would help sell the cardigan." A designer concentrates on the collection, a buyer on the customer. "He can't be thinking about Neiman's and Bergdorf's," Horne says. "He's got to come out with a look. But I know who my client is for Victor Alfaro. And if that line doesn't have enough in one look or one classification for our client, we're going to have to ask for more."

Horne pointed to the slit that went way up the side of the Alfaro skirt. 'You'll drop it,' she said with a laugh. 'And if you don't, we'll send it back.'

DISCUSSION QUESTIONS

The Shadow Designer

1. How does a retail fashion buyer have an impact on designers?

2. How does a retail fashion buyer have an impact on consumers, or do they merely provide consumers with what they want?

3. Based on the description of June Horne, do you think that certain personality traits may help one to be a successful buyer?

72 In Tehran, Boutiques Stock Hot Outerwear under the Counter

Farnaz Fassihi

Katayoun Alf, a designer of Islamic outerwear in one of the world's strictest Islamic states, knows her customers. They are women such as Sepideh Karimi, a 28-year-old with golden highlights in her hair who strolled into a boutique here recently.

The racks in this store in a suburban mall were crammed with women's clothing that would shock the founding fathers of Iran's Islamic revolution.

Traditional Islamic women's wear is a long, loose and shapeless black or brown *hijab* that reaches the ankles. The garb's main purpose is to hide curves and smother all sexuality. But Ms. Karimi, like more and more young women in Iran's urban centers, wants something different.

"This is too loose," said Ms. Karimi as she modeled a blue coat, known as a "manteau," that hangs just below her hips, hugging her figure. "The sleeves are too long. I'm looking for something more sexy and see-through."

Women's wear has long been an Iranian social and political battleground, especially among the country's educated and relatively well-off urban elite. Millions of religious Iranian women still willingly wear hijab every day as part of their devotion to Islam. But for women who chafe at government-dictated religious rules, stretching the dress code has become a passion. And, try as it has, the conservative government hasn't been able to put a stop to it.

Hijab, a word that means veil, is an outgrowth of Islamic Sharia law, which requires all females over the age of 10 to conceal their hair under a scarf and wear a long, loose cloak that extends to the ankles. Reza Shah, founder of the Pahlavi dynasty in Iran and father of the Shah whom the Iranian revolution ousted in 1979, was keen on making Iran a secular, modern society. Headscarves, to him, were a sign of backwardness, and he ordered soldiers to rip them off women's heads. But when religious leader Ayatollah Khomeini came to power, Islamic revolutionary forces reversed the edict.

The hijab law written into Iran's constitution after the Islamic Republic's victory in 1979 made many Iranian women even more determined to bend the rules, an inch at a time, starting with the hemlines. The government pushed back. At first, stores and restaurants shunned women who weren't properly dressed, and a now-defunct police unit, known as "moral police," set up checkpoints to stop, fine and even arrest women who violated the rules. That didn't work, restrictions were eased, and women went wild.

"Everyone wants tight, tight, tight," said the salesman at the mall. "Let me show you Ms. Alf's most popular style," he told Ms. Karimi. "It's flying off the shelves."

With that, he pulled a definite no-no off the rack: a paper-thin beige tunic made of stretchy material with two slits on each side. It comes with a matching tank-top to wear underneath and sleeves decorated with brown Indian motifs. Ms. Karimi's eyes lit up. She quickly tried it on, then paid $35 to make the outfit her own.

Ms. Alf, a 46-year-old former computer engineer, is one of a handful of Iranian designers determined to transform hijab from shapeless to chic. These designers have a lot to do with the surprising, and to the conservative Iranian government, appalling, fashion display in the streets of Tehran and other big cities.

"The trend began two years ago when the government eased social restrictions. Suddenly we looked around us and said 'wow!'" said Ms. Alf, a tall, Iranian-born woman with layered brown hair and a round face, clad in one of her own designs: a black linen, knee-length coat with matching slacks. "Women are fed up," she continued. "They come to the shops and say, 'the sexier the better,' and we meet their demands or we won't sell a single item."

Soaring demand prompted the government, in late May, to attempt another of its periodic crackdowns on what it considers risqué women's outerwear. Its focus this time is on shop owners. For the first time, the government issued a written warning to stores and designers against making or selling "un-Islamic" manteaux and threatening heavy fines for shops that disobey.

A poster in the suburban mall where Ms. Karimi bought her Alf creation warns stores not to sell tight-fitting manteaux with slits longer than six inches and hemlines above the knee. Bright colors, such as red and pink, are also banned.

So shopkeepers are now keeping daring designs such as Ms. Alf's in out-of-the-way places and bring them out only when customers ask for them. The crackdown has merely increased demand among young Iranians tired of religious intrusions into their lives.

In the days after the 1979 revolution, Ms. Alf and others were already resisting. They let their hair stick out from under their scarves, wore red lipstick when they went shopping and decorated their loose outfits with gold appliqué and diamond studs. Ms. Alf, was fired from her computer job in part, she says, because the way she dressed was deemed un-Islamic. She decided to put her sewing skills and love of design to work making Islamic dress fashionable.

"I looked around me and saw that no one, including myself, enjoyed looking like a head-to-toe black blob. We all wanted to maintain our individuality while observing this hijab law. Plus, it's really boring to wear the same thing day after day," said Ms. Alf, sitting in her studio while a dozen workers cut cloth and sewed her summer collection.

Each season she designs and produces a collection of manteaux with the styles and colors derived from the latest European fashions. Her collection is sold at the well-known Malakouti boutique chain, which specializes in Islamic outerwear and has branches in Tehran and other major Iranian cities.

Ms. Alf, who is divorced and has a 21-year-old son, watches the Fashion Channel on satellite television religiously. She makes regular trips to Istanbul and Dubai in search of the latest trends. Last winter, all her coats were made of suede and trimmed in fur. This summer, she is pushing a figure-hugging linen tunic that hangs just below the hip and has long slits on the sides. Wide belts—and thin ones with beads hanging from the side—have been popular, as well. Light colors, including powder blue, beige and white, are selling well.

Given the new restrictions, Ms. Alf is thinking about next year. More clever than confrontational, she is planning a safari line: long, loose cloak manteaux that are stylish but technically within the restrictions. They will have zippered slits from hemline to waist, allowing women to adjust them at a moment's notice, and long sleeves that can be buttoned up to the shoulder.

Crackdowns just help business, Ms. Alf insists. She has been through them before. "The more they tighten the leash, the more resolve women get. It's one fight the clerics will never win."

In Tehran, Boutiques Stock Hot Outerwear under the Counter

1. Why, when they are required to keep so covered up, are many Iranian women interested in fashion?

2. Are the fashions that Iranian women buying the same as those people in the United States are buying? Why or why not?

3. Women in Iran are at great risk of punishment for wearing clothing that is too short, tight, or revealing in some way. Why would they risk pushing the rules just to wear new styles? Is fashion somehow subversive in a political system like Iran?

4. Why are Iranian retailers men?

CHAPTER 12
Dress and World Religions

Kimberly A. Miller-Spillman
and
Susan O. Michelman

AFTER YOU HAVE READ THIS CHAPTER, YOU WILL COMPREHEND:

- Examples of dress in different religions.
- How ideology in religion may be reflected through dress.
- How morality and sexuality are reflected through religious dress.
- Dress as a material artifact that mirrors change in religions.

This chapter focuses on the meaning of dress within world religions. Specifically, the articles in this chapter will consider issues of dress in the Orthodox sect of Judaism, Roman Catholic women religious (nuns), Islamic women who veil, fundamentalist Christians, and Mennonites. Membership in a religious group is not always associated with a particular style of dress. For example, in the United States, many Roman Catholics or Protestants wear the equivalent of work dress to worship at church. Other religious groups use dress to differentiate and set themselves apart from others in the larger society or surrounding world. The articles have been chosen to illustrate how and why religious dress symbolizes the values and beliefs of religious organizations. Dress will be examined for its ability to promote social stability within religious organizations and resist the rapid style changes associated with the contemporary fashion process of secular society.

IDEOLOGY AND DRESS

To understand religious dress, the cultural context of a religious group must be considered. Each of the major world religions included in this chapter—Islam, Judaism, and Christianity—has dominant ideologies that guide decisions about dress. **Ideology** is a set of ideas that do not hold up under the rigors of scientific investigation and that support the interest of dominant groups (Ferrante, 1995). For instance, dress within Christianity is based in large part on the story of Adam and Eve in the Garden of Eden; therefore, modesty should be a goal in dress. Judaism is based on the philosophy that individuals exist to glorify God; therefore, to be well-dressed is a religious duty—not one of personal preference. Islamic philosophy promotes the separation of the sexes, as do Mennonite beliefs. Women's bodies must be covered in public and their movements within society are highly restricted and carefully controlled by male family members.

WHAT IS RELIGION?

Religion is a set of beliefs, symbols, and practices that is based on the idea of the sacred and unites believers in a socioreligious community (Marshall, 1994). **Sacred** refers to that which people define as extraordinary, inspiring a sense of awe and reverence. Contrasted to the sacred is the profane or that which is considered an ordinary element of everyday life. **Monotheism** is a belief in a single God (e.g., Christianity, Islam, and Judaism), whereas **polytheism** is a belief in many gods (e.g., Buddhism, Hinduism, Confucianism, Taoism, and Shintoism) (Marshall, 1994).

Islam is based on the principal of submission to Allah or God. Its holy texts are the Koran and the Hadith (or sayings of the Prophet). Islam pays special attention to the status and clothing of women (Marshall, 1994). Although there are no specific injunctions or rules in the Koran regarding veiling, women are believed to have sexual powers that may tempt males (Ribeiro, 1986). Therefore, many Islamic women veil their faces and cover their heads, hair, necks, and bodies to a greater or lesser extent. Some Islamic women do not veil at all and are indistinguishable in a group of Western women. The type and extent of veiling of women varies greatly from one Islamic nation and from one group to another, depending on the nature of their beliefs and the political context in which they live. For example, Sciolino (1997) examines the veiling practices of women in Iran in 1997 and stresses the importance of women's hair and social status. Veiling can also be associated with expressing nationalism and/or anti-Western sentiment associated with rejecting Western fashion. For example, a number of years ago, under the Shah, most Iranian women did not veil and wore Western dress. When Ayatollah Khomeini, an archconservative ruler who desired a totally Islamic state, took power in 1978, women were mandated to veil. Currently, veiling is still in place but is less strictly enforced.

More recently, Lacayo reports in his article "About Face" on the status of veiling in Afghanistan in 2001. Women in Afghanistan, Lacayo reports, are caught between customs of the past and an uncertain future. The Taliban, who were very conservative regarding veiling practices, left power in 2001 and Afghani women await a new government's policy on the *burka*. Lacayo's article provides interesting contrasts between rural Afghani women and urban women in the city of Kabul.

In America, Muslim-Americans use a doll to teach girls the importance of veiling. Razanne, complete with head scarf *(hijab)* and long-sleeved dress, gives Muslim girls someone they can relate to (see "Muslim Doll Offers Image of Modesty and Self-Esteem"). There are several different types of Razanne dolls to emphasize that young girls can grow up to be whatever they like. There is now a Teacher Razanne, a Dr. Razanne, and a Muslim Girl Scout Razanne, and future dolls will include an Astronaut Razanne. Thus, Razanne teaches girls that veiling and modesty are not roadblocks to achieving personal goals.

Judaism originated in prophesies about the God Yahweh. Jewish religious knowledge is founded in the Torah, the first five books of the Hebrew Bible (corresponding to the Christian Old Testament; Macionis, 1996). As with other religions, Jewish beliefs vary from liberal to highly conservative interpretations. Hayt's article, "For Stylish Orthodox Women, Wigs That Aren't Wiggy," examines dress practices of Orthodox Jewish women who are part of a more fundamental sect of Judaism. "Conservative" Jews are actually less strict than Orthodox (although more so than reformed). Women who follow this tradition wear wigs in public from the time of their marriage. Covering their head with wigs ensures their modesty under Orthodox interpretation of Jewish law, while allowing them to visually fit into mainstream U.S. culture.

Kershaw's article, "The Skullcap as Fashion Statement," examines dress practices of Orthodox Jewish adolescent boys. The current fashion of wearing skullcaps with modern symbols has caused controversy among some parents and Jewish religious leaders. Because the purpose of wearing a skullcap is to symbolize humility before God, the commercialism of modern skullcaps is problematic for some Jews. Others are delighted that teenage Jewish boys have made a connection to a traditional practice and are quietly encouraging it.

Christianity, which includes sects of Catholicism, Protestantism, and the Anabaptists (including the Amish and Mennonites), from early times handed down a code of morals, including strict rules about clothing. Early Christian teachings stress the link between the outward appearance of the body and the state of the person's soul (Ribeiro, 1986). Several articles in this chapter examine the strong influence of Christian religious beliefs on appearance. For example, in "Clothing, Control, and Women's Agency," Boynton-Arthur discusses how compliance with group norms and more specifically control of women by male ministers within the community have left Mennonite women with few avenues for personal expression within the dictates of that church. The Mennonites are descendants of a seventeenth-century Swiss German Anabaptist sect who believed in the complete separation of church and state and asserted that contemporary society is corrupting. In all facets of life today, Mennonites strive for a simple existence, including plain dress for both men and women, based on nineteenth-century styles (Ribeiro, 1986).

Michelman's article, "From Habit to Fashion," examines how traditional habits or uniforms of nuns made their social identities more outwardly visible than their personal identities. When women take vows of religious life, they relinquish individuality in dress for social control of their bodies by the Church:

> Dress should reveal not just a humble state of mind, but show by its simplicity that the wearer spends little time on the adornment of the body, and is thus free to devote more—time and money—to the poor. This mixture of religious and personal morality is most evidenced in the habits of religious orders; their ample, loose robes of humble, often coarse fabrics, are both unprovocative and a protection against the temptations of the world. (Ribeiro, 1986)

From the time that women religious first wore religious attire as novices, they were instructed to view themselves not as individuals, but as representatives of a group. Michelman examines the personal and social conflicts that occurred when these women shed their habits but not their social roles in the 1960s.

DRESS AND RELIGIOUS FUNDAMENTALISM

Fundamentalism is a conservative religious doctrine that opposes intellectualism and worldly accommodation in favor of restoring traditional, otherworldly religion (Macionis, 1996). Fundamentalism is a more complex phenomenon than popular conceptions would lead people to believe. First, a fundamentalist cannot be stereotyped by gender, age, race, ethnicity, social class, or political ideology. Second, fundamentalists are characterized by a belief that a relationship with God, Allah, or some other supernatural force provides answers to personal and social problems (Ferrante, 1995). Third, fundamentalists do not differentiate between the sacred and the profane in their everyday lives. All areas of their lives, including work, family, and leisure, are governed by religious principles. Edwards, in her article "Worldly Lessons," discusses how female students at Bob Jones University, a Christian fundamentalist school, learn how to be "worldly" without denying their religious convictions.

Fourth, fundamentalists want to reverse the trend toward gender equality, which they believe is symptomatic of a declining moral order (Ferrante, 1995). Fundamentalists often believe the correct ordering of priorities in life requires subordinating women's rights to the concerns of the larger group and the well-being of the society, such as the "traditional" family.

Many of the articles in this chapter are about dress and religious fundamentalism. Why is control of dress, particularly for women, frequently a component of fundamentalist beliefs? Fundamentalist religious groups have often emerged after a perceived threat or crisis—real or imagined. Any discussion of a particular fundamentalist group must include some reference to an adversary. Dress, then, can be linked to a way of expressing group solidarity as well as indicating opposition to the general culture.

Dress acts as a visible symbol for the precepts of fundamentalism, including the fact that religious principles govern all aspects of the fundamentalists' lives (including dress) and that women's roles are frequently more "traditional" with individual needs and beliefs relinquished to the greater good of the family and religious group. This leaves fundamentalists open to criticism by feminists regarding the oppression of women by the patriarchal nature of many fundamentalist groups. **Patriarchy** refers to cultural beliefs and values that give higher prestige to men than to women (Newman, 1995). Women's roles as wives, mothers, and supporters of the faith may be seen as important, but men are given priority or exclusive rights to govern and take power in the group. Patriarchy has been regarded as a form of social organization and has been considered, particularly by feminists, as an undifferentiated theory to explain the whole of human history (Grimshaw, 1986):

> Patriarchy is itself the prevailing religion of the entire planet. . . All of the so-called religions legitimating patriarchy are mere sects subsumed under its vast umbrella/canopy. . . All— from buddhism and hinduism to islam, judaism, christianity—to secular derivatives such as freudianism, marxism and maoism—are infrastructures of the edifice of patriarchy. (Daly, 1990)

Agency is a concept used by feminists to describe the resistance women use to combat patriarchy. Boynton-Arthur describes, in her article "Clothing, Control, and Women's Agency," the agencies (i.e., the various forms of resistance) women in one Holdeman Mennonite community use in subverting the strict dress codes dictated by male ministers and deacons. Arthur describes the daily process of subtle changes in dress that give women an opportunity to express themselves creatively. Agency can also be found in Sciolino (1997), in which elite Islamic women work to affect political changes more favorable to women.

DRESS, RELIGION, AND MORALITY

Common themes can be identified among the articles included in this chapter. One such theme is modesty and its relationship to morality in religious beliefs. Some Christians, Jews, and Muslims have rules about covering parts of the body with sexual connotations such as hair, neck, breasts, arms, and legs. Women are frequently targets of modesty rules, and certain religious groups feel that **morality** is maintained through the behavior of women, including their dress (see Chapter 6, "Modesty and Immodesty"). Although not part of all religions, beliefs are held by some religions that regard female sexuality as dangerous if left unharnessed and uncontrolled (Fernea & Fernea, 1995). These beliefs lead to the religious practice of prescribing modest and proper dress for female members.

The result of modest dress is physical restriction on women. In "About Face" we learn that the burka can be dangerous, literally. Because the burka covers the head and face, it restricts vision of passing cars or carts in crowded areas. Peripheral vision was also restricted among women religious who wore full habit (see "From Habit to Fashion"), preventing nuns from driving cars and moving freely through their daily activities serving the poor and sick.

For an Orthodox Jewish woman to be properly dressed, she must cover her hair after marriage. This practice helps the woman to avoid expressing sexuality outside her marriage. As Hayt notes in "For Stylish Orthodox Women, Wigs That Aren't Wiggy," "women's hair exudes sensual energy" (p. 468). Holdeman Mennonite women must also cover their head and hair. The starched cap represents a Mennonite woman's humility to God and her resistance to worldly possessions. Submissiveness to her God, her community, and her husband is also symbolized by her head covering.

Among Iranian women, the chador covers the entire body (with the exception of the eyes). Sciolino (1997) reports that her informant mentioned twice that her hair was not to be described in the article. No mention of her hair color or length could be made. A description of an Islamic woman's hair is considered in that culture as "going too far."

Covering body curves appears to be somewhat less of an issue for Mennonite and Orthodox Jewish women than for Islamic women. Thinness is the ideal body shape for Mennonite men and women. Their culture defines thinness as an expression of self-denial and control. Sensory enjoyment such as eating is considered sinful; therefore, a "properly dressed" Mennonite woman is one who is thin.

A Muslim woman's modesty training begins early, as demonstrated by the article "Muslim Doll Offers Image of Modesty and Self-Esteem." Razanne is an alternative to Barbie for Muslim-Americans who want their daughters to feel comfortable within American popular culture. If Barbie's message to young girls is sex appeal, Razanne's message to young girls is modesty.

RELIGIOUS DRESS AND SOCIAL CHANGE

Although changes in religious dress occur with much less frequency than among those of the general population, forces of social, economic, and political change do influence sacred dress, as discussed in several articles in this chapter. For example, Michelman's study of women religious demonstrates the identity struggle Catholic nuns experienced when moving from full religious habit to secular dress after changes mandated by Vatican II in the 1960s. Her article, "From Habit to Fashion," examines how difficult it was for women religious to make the transition from a well-recognized and revered social identity as a Catholic nun in full habit to nonuniform, secular dress.

Sciolino's 1997 article "The Chanel under the Chador" supplies us with an excellent example of the differences between sacred and secular dress. The differences are in sharp contrast. The irony of wearing a Chanel-style suit (secular dress) under a chador (sacred dress) would prove baffling to most non-Islamics (see Figures 12.1a and b). Class differences among Islamic women were also noted by Sciolino. She describes the women she studied as the cultural elite, women who have both a Western education and growing political influence in their country. Sciolino compares the agendas of these well-educated women to those who are lower class and uneducated and who always

a   b

FIGURE 12.1 *Sciolino's 1997 article "The Chanel under the Chador" describes culturally elite women who wear Chanel suits (a) under a chador (b).*

wore the veil before and throughout Iran's troubled political times. Education and wealth provide social agency to individuals, so limits on movement and role-taking in society may seem more problematic to women in the cultural elite than to poorer women who lack access to political and social power.

Social class can be expressed through religious dress. For example, Bob Jones University students aspire to move among the cultural elite of American society, which is not a humble goal. Recognizing that dress can advance or retard professional goals, "safe beauty classes" prepare women for entry into professional and well-paying positions. *Style* is described by church-sanctioned teachers as a woman's armor, while *fashion* is characterized as "letting oneself go"—a description that is a clear condemnation of the evils of worldliness.

Similarly, Orthodox Jewish women who buy custom-made wigs that closely resemble their natural hair may be baffling to non-Jews. In Hayt's article, a rabbi states that there is a difference between immodest dress and stylish dress—and one does not necessarily preclude the other. Real hair that is covered with hair that is not the woman's own hair is perfectly modest to an Orthodox Jew. As frequently happens in cultures throughout the world, what might seem to be an illogical contradiction to outsiders may be completely sensible to an insider of the group.

Summary

This chapter covers examples of dress in different religions. In particular, we focus on dress in the Orthodox sect of Judaism and among Roman Catholic women religious, Islamic women who veil, fundamentalist Christians, and Mennonites. Ideology reflects the beliefs of a culture that justify particular social arrangements (Marshall, 1994), and these beliefs are reflected in religious dress. Several themes (i.e., morality, sexuality, patriarchy, and agency) were identified in our discussion of religious dress. Lastly, religious dress as a material artifact mirrors changes in religion that often coincide with changes in the greater society or culture. Dress within religious groups illustrates an apparent relationship between social stability and resistance to rapid style changes associated with fashion.

Suggested Readings

Dunbar, D. (1991, October 27). Everybody wants a piece of Africa now. *Los Angeles Times*, E5.

Polaneczky, R. (1995, December). You'll never guess who this woman works for. *Redbook*, 98–101, 119–120.

Sciolino, E. (1997, May 4). The Chanel under the chador. *New York Times Magazine*, 46–51.

LEARNING ACTIVITY

Religions' Rules for Dress

Objective: To learn about dress within a previously unfamiliar religion.

Interview

Interview someone who believes in a religious ideology with which you are unfamiliar. Consider religions (or faiths) of which you have little or no knowledge. Use the Yellow Pages of the telephone directory in your area to determine whom you could interview. Depending on your background, you may want to consider some of the following:

- Amish
- Buddhist
- Catholic priest or nun
- Greek Orthodox priest
- Hindu

- Jewish rabbi (or layperson)
- Mennonite
- Mormon
- Muslim

Develop five or six questions about religion and dress for your interview. You may want to know about specific dress items that you have seen in the media but did not understand. You may want to ask general questions about how dress is used during formal ceremonies (and by whom) compared to how a religious observer might dress on a daily basis. Other possible questions include: How is dress used in rituals of the faith? How does the dress of clergy (or religious leaders/teachers) compare to the dress of the worshipper?

After conducting the interview, share your information in small groups or during a class discussion. Or invite those interviewed to serve on a "religious panel" during class. Each speaker could be allowed 10 to 15 minutes to discuss dress within his or her own religion.

References

Daly, M. (1990). *Gyn/ecology: The Metaethics of Radical Feminism*. Boston: Beacon Press.

Fernea, E. W., & Fernea, R. A. (1995). Symbolizing roles: Behind the veil. In M. E. Roach-Higgins, J. B. Eicher, & K. K. P. Johnson (Eds.), *Dress and Identity*. New York: Fairchild.

Ferrante, J. (1995). *Sociology: A Global Perspective*. Belmont, CA: Wadsworth Publishing Co.

Grimshaw, J. (1986). *Philosophy and Feminist Thinking*. Minneapolis: University of Minnesota Press.

Macionis, J. J. (1996). *Society: The Basics* (3rd ed.). Upper Saddle River, NJ: Prentice Hall.

Marshall, G. (Ed.). (1994). *The Concise Oxford Dictionary of Sociology*. Oxford: Oxford University Press.

Newman, D. (1995). *Sociology: Exploring the Architecture of Everyday Life*. Thousand Oaks, CA: Pine Forge Press.

Ribeiro, A. (1986). *Dress and Morality*. London: Batsford Press.

Sciolino, E. (1997, May 4). The Chanel under the chador. *New York Times Magazine*, 46–51.

73   About Face: An Inside Look at How Women Fared under Taliban Oppression and What the Future Holds for Them Now

Richard Lacayo

In the streets of Kabul, you can see something these days that has not been glimpsed there for almost five years—women's faces. Now that the Taliban has fled the city, a few brave women have shed the burka—the head-to-toe garment, to Western eyes a kind of body bag for the living, made mandatory by the defeated religious leadership. Men sometimes look in astonishment at these faces, as if they were comets or solar eclipses. So do other women. From the moment in 1996 that the Taliban took power, it sought to make women not just obedient but nonexistent. Not just submissive but invisible. For five years, it almost succeeded.

The Taliban's ongoing collapse guarantees at least some improvement in the lives of Afghan women. They are emerging from the houses that they once could not leave except in the company of a male relative. Some are returning to the jobs they had to give up when the Taliban barred them from all employment except for a small number of health-care jobs dedicated to women. Even more remarkable, Kabul's sole television station now features a woman announcer. In a country where people were required to paint their windows black so that passersby could not see the face of any woman who might be at home, the announcer appears onscreen without a veil.

But just as the meltdown of Taliban military power has not brought real peace to Afghanistan, neither has the disappearance of its hated religious police brought women freedom overnight. Afghan society is tribal and conservative. Except for a small minority of educated professionals in Kabul, women have long been relegated to a subservient role. In rural areas of northern Afghanistan that are under the control of the Northern Alliance, the burka is still universal, though no law requires it. Even in Kabul, where Western-style skirts were not uncommon before the Taliban, many women say the burka is the least of their concerns. Dr. Rahima Zafar Staniczai, head of the Rabia Balkhi hospital for women, remembers how Taliban religious police would beat her in the street any time they caught her rushing to work uncovered: "They would hit us and spit on us, and then we would have to come in to the hospital to do our work." All the same, she says, what women wear is a secondary issue. She lists the real priorities. "First we need peace. Then we need a central government. Then we need education. After all that, we will be in a position to make a decision on the burka."

And even when something like peace and order returns to Afghanistan, just how sympathetic to the rights of women the next ruling order will be, no one can yet say. Women have not suffered the systematic oppression under the Northern Alliance that was the signature of Taliban rule. But the years the Alliance ruled all Afghanistan, 1992 to '96, are remembered by many Afghans for the brutality of the warlords. Some Alliance leaders are as hostile to notions of women's equality as any Taliban mullahs.

If the future is uncertain, the recent past is an all-too-well-substantiated fact. The Taliban made Afghanistan a laboratory for the systematic oppression of women. What it did will haunt that nation and the world for years to come.

THE WOMEN SPEAK

To Westerners, the most visible symbol of the Taliban's oppressive regime was the order that placed all women under the burka. Its long-standing place in Afghan culture is complicated. Many rural women, especially, claim to wear it willingly, at least when they speak in the presence of their husbands. There is even high fashion in burka wear. In Kabul, women allow a bit of lace trimming to show at the edge. The best burkas, from the Afghan city of Herat, have exquisite pleating that imparts a shimmering, watery feel but takes hours to iron.

But nearly any educated woman you speak to loathes the burka. So do many less educated ones—if you can question them where men cannot hear. The heavy cloth covering can induce panic, claustrophobia and headaches. It's a psychological hobbling of women that is akin to Chinese foot binding. It's also life threatening. Try negotiating a busy Kabul street—around donkey carts, careening buses and the Taliban roaring by in Datsun pickups—when your hearing is muffled and your vision is reduced to a narrow mesh grid.

What are Afghan women really like beneath the burka? Talk to three from Dasht-i-Qaleh, a tiny, impoverished village long held by the Northern Alliance. Though the Taliban's restrictions against women have no force here, nearly all the women wear the burka. Long-standing cultural tradition exercises its own police power. And though these women have agreed to speak to *Time* correspondent Hannah Beech, they will do so only through a female interpreter. They worry that their husbands might object if they learned that a man was present at the interview. During the conversation, a man does briefly enter the room. The women all hasten to cover their faces and turn toward the wall until he leaves.

On the streets, you would never know that these silent, shapeless forms, encased in these shrouds, have any views at all. But outside the earshot of men, the women are fierce, alive and opinionated. And when they shed their burkas, they turn out to be wearing brightly colored dresses. All three say they would prefer not to wear a burka or even a head scarf but fear they would be harassed. Zora, 28, says she has heard that when women go to Mecca on the hajj, the pilgrimage that all Muslims are enjoined to attempt at least once, they do so with faces uncovered. "If women can show their faces in Islam's most holy place, then why must we cover ourselves in Afghanistan?" she asks.

Like the others, Saida, 27, received no formal education, although her three daughters are enrolled in elementary school. Saida says her eldest daughter Nahid, 12, is getting ready for her betrothal to a 26-year-old farmer and does not have much time to spare for morning instruction. Besides, says Saida, Nahid tells her she learns at school that the Koran teaches her how to be a good wife and mother, instruction that exasperates Saida. "How can the Koran teach you how to live your life, how to take care of your children and your husband?" she asks. So Saida teaches her girls the really important things—how to cook, sew and soothe a husband's ego. "Teaching my daughters how to make their husbands comfortable is the most important thing," she says, "because if a husband is not comfortable, then the woman's life is hell."

"My husband says the Koran tells him he can control his wife however he wants," says Banaz, 32, a mother of seven. ("Five boys," she says, jubilantly. "Only two daughters.") "But I have read the Koran, and nowhere does it say this. He is lying to me." Still, Banaz can do nothing. If she disobeys her husband, he will beat her, as he has done many times before. Once, she claims, he hit her chest so hard that she could not breast-feed her daughter for a week.

The conversation turns to the routine brutalization of women in Afghanistan. Banaz says that four years ago her sister was raped by a soldier of the Northern Alliance, but only the women in the family know about it. Women in Dasht-i-Qaleh call rape "lying down" because it is so common that lying down quietly is the best way for a woman to cope. In a society that permits men several wives, the second or third wives, who tend to be younger and prettier, are vulnerable to rape by other males in the family.

Banaz says this happened to her sister, who was 14 when she was married off as the third wife of a local landowner. "It was a good marriage for the family," says Banaz. "But it was not a good marriage for her." She was raped by her husband's brother, a local mullah, whose prominence means that Banaz's sister has no hopes of retribution; it is her word against a holy man's. "In Afghanistan, the men go off to war," says Banaz, "but it is the women who fight their whole lives."

THE YEARS OF THE WHIPS

In the 1960s and '70s, Afghanistan was a typical developing country, poor and struggling, with a slowly expanding role for women. By 1964 they had been granted the vote. The cities had begun to produce a small élite of educated women, who entered the professions, wore Western skirts and mixed comfortably with men. The Soviet invasion in 1979 was a disaster for Afghanistan generally. But under the Russians, women's rights were protected—even advanced to a degree that alienated some in Afghanistan's tradition-bound society. More women were introduced into government, given an authority that many men found unnerving. Shaima Yunsi was a senior aide to the Interior Minister, Afghanistan's internal spymaster. "I was responsible for collecting information on the jihad warriors" who fought the Russians, she says. She likes to show a photo of herself from those days; in it she wears a green army uniform with a pistol tucked under her belt.

As bad as the Russians' occupation was, the chaos that followed their withdrawal in 1989 was worse, especially for women. Afghan warlords brought terror to the urban neighborhoods and villages they laid claim to. Young, undisciplined fighters treated women as plunder; rape became commonplace. Civil war broke out among factions of the victorious anti-Soviet resistance. With the triumph of the Taliban in 1996, conditions were in place for a final degradation of Afghan women.

The Taliban restored order to Afghan cities, but it was order of a sinister kind. Most of the leadership and the fighters were Pashtun tribesmen from rural areas of the south around Kandahar. In some respects, the harshness of their treatment of women was their attempt to extend across all Afghanistan the primitive social order of their villages at home. And it allowed the leadership to claim that Taliban rule had conferred on its male warriors a new degree of authority. The nation was a shambles, but at least the women were firmly under control.

The rules were enforced capriciously, sometimes ferociously, by religious police from the Orwellian-named Ministry for the Promotion of Virtue and the Prevention of Vice. Ministry thugs wielding lengths of steel cable would beat women in the street for infractions like wearing white socks. "If women are going outside with fashionable, ornamental, tight and charming clothes," an early decree from the ministry warned, they "should never expect to go to heaven."

It is hard to find a woman in Kabul now who does not remember a beating at the hands of the Taliban. As it consolidated power, its orders became increasingly bizarre and sadistic, based on its extreme interpretations of Koranic instructions. One of these demanded punishment for women who allowed their shoes to make noise when they walked down the street. But this surreal pettiness masked real misery. The ban on work for most women had a disastrous effect on schooling for both sexes, since as many as 70% of all Afghan teachers were women. Excluding them from the classroom meant that boys had few teachers to instruct them.

The work ban extended to widows, who were left no recourse but to beg. In a nation with as many as a million widows—out of a population of just 20 million—that decree alone produced a silent disaster. Sabza Gul, 32, now begs at the Kabul bus station and makes about 50¢ on a good day. Some years ago, when she was still living in a village north of the city, her husband went blind. The family became dependent on whatever money their son Humayoun, 17, could earn as a field worker. The fields were close to the occasional fighting between Taliban and

Northern Alliance forces. Eight months ago he was killed by a stray rocket. "There is no work for women," Sabza says. "We had nobody to look after the family, so I came to Kabul." Now that the Taliban is gone, she will try to find work cleaning offices or homes.

All schooling was forbidden to girls over the age of eight. A recent U.N. report estimated that at most 7% of Afghan girls were enrolled in school, compared with roughly half the boys. In Peshawar, the Pakistani city near the border to which many Afghan refugees have escaped, Masooda is a shy second-grade girl—but she is 16. She left school five years ago, on the day the Taliban entered her central Afghan town of Kota Sangi and beat her with a cane for not wearing a burka. When her family fled to Pakistan two weeks ago to escape U.S. bombing, she finally resumed lessons. "I once knew how to read, but I've forgotten everything," she says. "I'm ashamed to be so much older than everyone else."

For those who stayed home, determined mothers have found ways to get schooling for their daughters. Rawshan and Nasima, both 30, are married to the same man, Abdul Qadir, 55, a porter in a Kabul market who makes about $1 a day. Rawshan has one son and three daughters by Abdul. Nasima has one son and two daughters. Desperately poor, they live in a house peppered with bullet holes. For the past two years, Rawshan's eldest daughter Wahida, 10, has been going to a secret school in an abandoned building. She has only one hour of lessons a day, given by local women who volunteer their services, but she is slowly picking up the rudiments of math and learning how to read. "I would like my daughter to work outside the home," says Rawshan. "I stayed in the home, and I have had a terrible life."

Next to education, women's health suffered the worst consequences of religious rule. The life expectancy of Afghan women now is just 44 years. There are 17 maternal deaths per 1,000 live births, the second worst rate in the world, just behind war-ravaged Sierra Leone. The statistics only hint at what medical care for women is like in a nation where a male doctor is not al-lowed to give a thorough physical examination to a female patient. Women had to be examined wearing the full burka. Male doctors sometimes had to stand in a hallway shouting instructions to a female assistant. A doctor could be imprisoned for talking to a female patient who was not fully covered.

Dr. Sima Samar left Afghanistan in 1984 but runs two hospitals in Afghanistan as well as 10 clinics from her base in Quetta, Pakistan. "There was a lot of harassment from the Taliban," she says. "They would enter the hospital at 1 in the morning saying they had received a report that our female staff was not dressed properly or was talking with the male staff."

WHAT NEXT?

Even with the final defeat of the Taliban, when and if that occurs, Afghan women will remain in a vexed position. The forces vying to take the Taliban's place are not always friendly to women. Within the Northern Alliance, there is a fundamental split between Western-minded technocrats and conservative religious figures. Abdullah Abdullah, the Alliance's media-savvy Foreign Minister, is a technocrat. In his speeches he makes sure to point out that in Alliance-held areas women go to school. He goes so far as to support women's joining the government.

Not so Alliance President Burhanuddin Rabbani, once a foremost proponent of expanding the burka's reach across Afghanistan. More recently, Rabbani allowed to an interviewer that "wearing a head scarf is enough in the cities." But in the Northern Alliance stronghold of Faizabad, his acolytes make sure that all women are completely covered. "Rabbani is better than the Taliban," says Farahnaz Nazir, a women's rights activist in the Northern Alliance town of Khoja Bahauddin. "But he is still very conservative. He does not believe that women are equal."

That attitude extends into the rank and file. Zulmai is a Northern Alliance soldier lounging on a tank in the town of Farkhar. Ask him how many brothers he has, and he proudly tells you four, all soldiers. Ask how many sisters, and he says none. Press him repeatedly, and he finally admits to three. Why did he deny them? "Because girls are not important." He shrugs. "They do not count."

This helps explain why the signals being sent to women by Alliance forces in Kabul are so mixed. Though they reopened a movie theater there last week for the first time since the Taliban took power, women were not admitted. A brief street demonstration last week by women who wanted to march to the U.N. headquarters in Kabul to demand equal rights was blocked by the police, who claimed they could not guarantee the security of the protesters.

In recent weeks the Bush Administration, in cooperation with the British government of Prime Minister Tony Blair, has opened a public relations assault to point up the oppression of women under Taliban rule. Two weeks ago, Laura Bush delivered what is ordinarily the President's Saturday radio address to speak about the problem. "What this initiative has done is send a signal," says Jim Wilkinson, director of the Coalition Information Center, the White House office that coordinates the Administration's worldwide anti-Taliban message. "By talking about the problem, we're hopefully able to affect the solution as they set up the new Afghan government," he notes.

In Washington two weeks ago, National Security Adviser Condoleezza Rice and the President's Special Counselor, Karen Hughes, met with Eleanor Smeal, president of the Feminist Majority, and Mavis Leno, who has long worked to bring attention to the problems of Afghan women. "We asked the Administration to make returning women to equal status under the law a nonnegotiable issue in forming any new government," says Leno, wife of *Tonight Show* host Jay Leno. "That's pretty much the language Colin Powell used when he spoke at the State Department [last week], so it appears the government is going to do exactly that."

Or try to do. Afghanistan is famously resistant to outside interference. Ask the Russians. "When the Soviets came, they wanted to change

the country overnight, abandoning tribal codes that existed for centuries," says Nelofer Pazira, an exiled Afghan journalist and dedicated foe of the Taliban who stars in the film *Kandahar*. "People were appalled. They went completely in the opposite direction. Even more liberal families became very conservative."

No matter what other nations may think, in the end it will be up to the Afghans to find a new balance of genders in their society. Progress is likely to be slow, particularly outside the educated élites of Kabul. Even there it will be subject to the complex forces of coercion, family pressure and tradition. Mohammad Halim, who runs one of Kabul's best-known burka shops, says he has no plans to offer a wider variety of clothing. "It will only be in Kabul where women will take off their burkas. Elsewhere women will continue wearing them. This is a very old custom in Afghanistan." That very day, says Halim, more than a week after the Taliban fled the city, he sold 20.

Maybe Halim has not counted on the number of girls who think like Mashal. At 18, she wants to be a doctor. "I want to be freed from Allah," she says. "I don't want to wear a veil at all. I want to wear miniskirts." And he may not be counting on the determination of women like Fakhria, 35, a mother of four in Kabul. After the Taliban forced her from her job at a teacher-training college, she opened a secret beauty salon in her house in Kabul. A high wall shields her customers from prying eyes. Inside are pictures of female models torn from Pakistani magazines. On shelves beside a large mirror, she has a selection of lipsticks, eyeliners and hair sprays. In the West they would be commonplace. In a society that forbids them, they seem weirdly precious.

With the Taliban gone, Fakhria hopes to open a storefront salon. No blackened windows anymore to hide the forbidden faces. She also wants to go back to her teaching job. "I can make more money in a salon," she says. "But I want to pass on knowledge."

There is one kind of knowledge that all Afghan women can pass on now—what it was like to be trapped in a society that, however briefly, perfected their imprisonment.

About Face

1. Identify what aspects of wearing the burka reflect cultural tradition and what aspects reflect religious tradition.

2. Lacayo uses terms such as *tribal, primitive,* and *conservative* to describe the Northern Alliance's and the Taliban's rule concerning women and the burka. Do you agree with his use of those terms to describe the enforcement of wearing the burka? Why or why not?

3. Make comparisons to other articles in this text between the burka and the following:

   • Chinese foot binding ("The Enigma of Beauty")

   • Restricted vision ("From Habit to Fashion")

4. List some of the many meanings of the burka throughout its history in Afghanistan.

74 The Skullcap as Fashion Statement

Sarah Kershaw

Samuel Goldberg has 51 skullcaps—and counting. He has Knicks, Mets, Bulls, Michigan, Duke and Penn State. But for the month of March he wore Tar Heels and only Tar Heels, a blue suede number bearing the logo of his favorite college basketball team.

But that was last month. Now, his most treasured skullcap—kipa in Hebrew and yar-

FIGURE 12.2 *Skullcap with popular culture symbols.*

mulke in Yiddish—is the Nike one he recently picked up at a classmate's bar mitzvah, another blue suede one decorated with the trademark swoosh and an inscription inside, "Jason Katz Just Did it."

"I have more yarmulkes than socks," said Samuel, 13, a seventh grader at the Ramaz Middle School, a liberal Orthodox yeshiva on the Upper East Side of Manhattan.

Wild and weird skullcaps, adorned with everything from sports team logos to the Cookie Monster to the phrase "I drank 12 beers last night," have been popular among modern Orthodox Jewish boys for about a decade. But what was once a modest trend has become a full-blown craze inside the liberal yeshivas of New York City, where skullcap styles go in and out of fashion like hemlines.

With it all have come voices of dissent, the loudest from Jewish scholars and ultra-Orthodox leaders, including some yeshiva headmasters who have barred students from wearing anything but the traditional black velvet or suede kipa. After all, a kipa is worn by observant Jewish boys and men—and a growing number of women—as a sign of humility before God.

"We really feel the kipa symbolizes something," said Rabbi Yerachmeil Milstein, executive director of the Yeshiva Ketana, on the Upper West Side, where only traditional skullcaps are permitted. "It's a relationship with God, and somehow that message can get lost with all this brand noise. When it becomes this commercial, it loses its true symbolism."

The fad has also created potential legal problems for retailers. Companies, like Nike, trying to stamp out counterfeit logos have taken issue with some of the newest skullcaps, whose logos are sewn on by hand by mothers and grandmothers or produced as unlicensed products by designers who supply the Judaica shops.

Children's Television Workshop, for example, forced one Manhattan Judaica shop, the J. Levine Company in the garment district, to remove Sesame Street skullcaps from its shelves, said the store's owner, Daniel Levine.

A senior Nike official said that the company had recently confiscated a few adorned with swooshes, as part of a routine sweep in Manhattan of vendors selling unlicensed Nike merchandise. But the official, Vada O. Manager, director of global issues management, said Nike had no plans yet to focus on skullcaps because there are still relatively few available.

"The yarmulke, as venerable and noble an article of clothing it is, is not something we sell among our performance athletic line," he said. "But it's not something we plan to specifically enforce. That would be like trying to prosecute a kid who had a swoosh cut into his hair at the barber shop."

To many liberal Orthodox parents and educators, though, the kipa-collecting frenzy among 11- and 12-year-olds is a great development. It is not always easy to persuade adolescent city boys to wear a kipa, especially when their non-Jewish peers are wearing baseball caps and teasing them about the "beanies," a derogatory term for skullcaps.

"We are quietly encouraging it," said Rabbi Eliezer Rubin, headmaster of the Ramaz Middle School. "If the kids can find something positive to attach to ritual Judaism through their own personal choice, then we're only happy."

The fad, said Samuel's mother, Dale Goldberg, "takes something that has a religious aspect and makes it fun."

Samuel's father, Saul Goldberg, who owned four skullcaps growing up in Brooklyn, marveled at his son's collection. "I probably wore the same one every day," Mr. Goldberg said. "But Sam changes every day. A new one comes out, and it's his favorite."

Several boys at Ramaz, which is considered one of the most liberal yeshivas in the city, agreed that the new styles make wearing a skullcap more fun—or at least bearable. (A few admitted to covering them with baseball caps or removing them when they leave school grounds.)

Going back to the 1950's, when some boys, including Samuel's father, wore what were known as "ivy league" skullcaps, made of plaid and adorned with a belt buckle, Jewish boys and men have used their skullcaps to make statements about fashion, their political views or their own identity. In Israel the size and style of the kipa identifies its wearer's position on the ideological and religious spectrum. Some of the kipa decorations now popular in New York, including Pokémon and the Power Rangers, first appeared in that country.

But in New York City, the latest styles have come to symbolize an unprecedented assimilation of Jewish religious practice with American pop culture, several scholars said.

"It's a way of demonstrating that you share more than one culture," said Samuel Heilman, the Harold Proshansky professor of Jewish Studies at the City University of New York. "It says that I am—though I wear a kipa—very much in the mainstream of contemporary American culture."

The recent appearance of company logos on skullcaps has touched off some hand-wringing among other Jewish scholars, who say the trend that began with Sesame Street yarmulkes for toddlers has now gone too far.

Rabbi Andrew N. Bachman, director of the Edgar M. Bronfman Center for Jewish Student Life at New York University, said he was particularly disturbed by the Nike skullcaps because of what he says are the company's bad labor practices, which many Orthodox Jewish college students have protested. Nike says it is moving to improve working conditions at its factories overseas.

"There are so many Jewish kids involved in the anti-sweatshop movement on campus," Rabbi Bachman said. "There's some kind of disconnect between a religious symbol and a company emblem which, to me, symbolizes questionable ethical and labor practices."

By the time Orthodox boys reach high school, they tend to wear plainer styles, several parents and teenagers said.

Still, Rabbi Bachman said he had recently observed a few notable new kipa styles on campus, including what he described as rasta, hip-hop and "neo-Hasidic hippie" looks.

DISCUSSION QUESTIONS

The Skullcap as Fashion Statement

1. Prepare arguments on both sides of the issue of wearing skullcaps that reflect American popular culture. List reasons why this practice is a good idea; list reasons why this practice is not a good idea.

2. Identify in the article issues of conformity and individuality related to the fashionable skullcap.

3. How do you feel about the ethical issues presented in the article regarding unlicensed symbols? Regarding corporations who use bad labor practices?

75 For Stylish Orthodox Women, Wigs That Aren't Wiggy

Elizabeth Hayt

To express joy on a festive Jewish holiday, it is traditional to wear something new. Last week, for a Passover seder at her parents' home in Borough Park, Brooklyn, Suzy Berkowitz, 50, upheld tradition from head to toe. Exemplifying the Diana Vreeland dictum that elegance is restraint, she wore new Gucci pumps and a new Armani suit, hemmed discreetly just below the knee. She also wore a custom-made wig bought for the occasion.

Like many other Orthodox women who follow Halakha, Jewish law, Mrs. Berkowitz has worn a wig since her wedding day. Women's hair exudes sensual energy, the Talmud teaches, and covering it insures a married woman's modesty. But the Talmud also obliges a wife to care for her appearance, so though a hat or scarf will do, many Orthodox women favor wigs, the more natural looking the better.

In fact, it was impossible to tell that Mrs. Berkowitz's rich, auburn hair—bobbed chin length with soft bangs brushed off her face—was actually a wig. Stylish Orthodox women like Mrs. Berkowitz eschew synthetic ready-made wigs for custom ones of human hair that closely approximate their own tresses. And much attention is paid, from purchase to the cut and style (new high-end wigs come straight and uncut).

"We talk about wigs the way women who don't wear them talk about their hair," said Liba Noe, 45, of Borough Park, who with her husband owns Eshel Jewelry Manufacturing in Manhattan and who owns a Claire, called by its aficionados the Rolls-Royce of Orthodox wigs. "When women get together at a wedding or a party they ask, 'Where did you get your shoes, dress and wig?' They even ask, 'Who did it?'"

For Passover, Suzy Berkowitz chose a $2,000 Olga, made by Olga Berman, a Hungarian wig maker in Bensonhurst (Mrs. Berkowitz also owns a Claire and an equally high status Ralph). For that critical cut and style, she turned to Mark Garrison, whose Madison Avenue salon serves dozens of Orthodox clients who pay at least $600 to have their wigs transformed.

"Orthodox women want something contemporary and realistic, and don't want a wig to look like what it is," said Mr. Garrison as he began the slow, tedious process—three to four hours—required to shampoo, cut and style a wig. "It's a challenge. You can't rely on next time. There is no next time."

Most swank stylists, including Frederic Fekkai, John Barrett, Oribe, John Sahag and Oscar Blandi, do wigs for Orthodox women. They aim to make them modest but not matronly and definitely not wiggy, the word Orthodox women use to describe the heavy appearance of wigs.

Taking the idea of verisimilitude further, Mr. Fekkai suggested: "An Orthodox woman should have several wigs. A real haircut grows out at different lengths. You need more than one wig at different lengths."

Given the code of modesty that Orthodox women abide by, including clothes that must cover the knees, elbows and collar bone, is it a contradiction to wear a wig, especially a stylish one?

"When the practice of wearing a wig first emerged, there was quite a protest," said Rabbi Rafael Grossman, the president of the Rabbinical Council of America, the world's largest body of Orthodox rabbis. "There are those authorities who strongly object. A wig would seem to contradict the basic principle of avoiding incitement. But my personal view is that it is acceptable because the rudiments of Halakha only require women not to expose their hair, though a woman should avoid wearing a wig that could appear to be sensual."

Rabbi Avi Weiss, of the Hebrew Institute of Riverdale in the Bronx, agreed. "I would distinguish between being stylish and being immodest," he said. "Jewish law is not monolithic. There can be two views, and they can be both opposite and correct."

Wearing a wig is a fairly modern Jewish practice. Before the 19th century, proper Jewish women covered their hair with shawls or veils. In feudal times, some women actually shaved their heads to detract from their appearance and thwart rapacious landlords who had the right to claim a bride's virginity before the groom did. Today, some women who are Hasidic, an Orthodox sect, still shave their heads as an added measure of propriety. But by and large, women either pin their hair up or cut it short and wear a wig.

Many young Orthodox brides insist on wigs that match their hair in style, texture and color; which also helps ease the jitters when a newly-wed first dons a wig. "I want my wig to look exactly like my hair," said Elky Stern, 22 and a student at Touro College in Brooklyn, whose long blond hair will be covered when she gets married in June. "At college, everyone who is engaged discusses wigs. Even the guys talk about it because they know the girls are nervous."

Before she was married two years ago, Rifka Locker, 20, a fourth-grade teacher from Lakewood, N.J., had Mr. Garrison style her straight, red hair. He cut it above her shoulders, angled it around her face, and layered the top in a style that became the prototype for her straight, red wig. (Orthodox rabbis frown on male stylists working on a woman's real hair once she is married). Putting on the wig the morning after her wedding, Mrs. Locker remembered: "I was confident wearing it. No one could even tell I got married."

Mrs. Locker bought her two wigs—custom-made for special occasions, ready-made for everyday—at Claire's Accuhair in Midwood, Brooklyn.

Claire Grunewald, who is Zsa Zsa Gabor-like with her false eyelashes, rhinestone-rimmed glasses and strawberry blond bob with honey highlights, is an expert sheitel macher, or wig maker. A Holocaust survivor from Hungary, she spent three years after the war in a displaced people's camp, where she was an apprentice to a German wig maker. Mrs. Grunewald immigrated to the United States in 1949, at age 17, and has devoted most of her 65 years to Orthodox women.

"I had the most beautiful strawberry blond hair and didn't want it covered when I got married, but my religion dictated it," she said. "To make matters worse, no one could style my sheitel the way I liked it. At 19, it made me look 35. So I started making my own wigs. Then I had a dream to manufacture a beautiful wig for the Jewish community. I had a dream that when you walked down a street, you wouldn't be able to say, This young woman is wearing a wig."

The women who make up most of Claire's affluent clientele travel from as far away as California and Israel for the wigs made on the premises of her family-run shop, complete with private fitting rooms. Of the 15 female workers, many sit at banquet tables, ventilating, or tying, strands of hair into wig foundations. The three male workers, who are not permitted in the salon where women try on wigs, sort unrefined hair,

primarily imported from Eastern Europe, where a woman's braid sells for enough to feed a family for a month, Mrs. Grunewald said.

Six to eight braids per wig are woven into a lightweight, durable silk or lace-fitted cap. If styled, the process can take 40 to 60 hours. The cost is $1,700 for a Contessa, the ready-made style, and up to $4,000 for a custom design, depending on length and quality of hair. The expense, by tradition, falls on the bridegroom's parents.

"A Claire wig is a designer thing," said Chaya Nachsoni, the executive secretary of the company and one of Mrs. Grunewald's three daughters working at the shop. "People say to me, 'Oh, a Claire,' the wig everyone wants but no one can afford. It's the Rolls-Royce of wigs."

The status attached to a Claire wig is matched only by a Ralph, as in Raffaele Mollica, who works out of an atelier at 75th Street and York Avenue in Manhattan, where the floor is strewn with strands of hair and the walls lined with every variety of wig imaginable. There are long, dark Cher tresses, short, gray Geraldine Ferraro coifs, curly red Chelsea Clinton locks. Mr. Mollica, a native of Sicily, says he has had hundreds of Orthodox customers over the years, paying $2,700 to $3,500 for a wig that may take up to a year to make. Ralph devotees say it is well worth the wait.

Mr. Mollica got his start making wigs for Vidal Sassoon, who led the hair revolution of the 1960's, from set-and-tease to loose, flowing styles. Mr. Mollica has adapted his mentor's vision to wigs.

"He makes a wig cap which is white like my scalp," said Elisa Mermelstein, 29, a customer from Kew Gardens, Queens. "Also, the hair is thin, which prevents the wig from looking bulky. A white scalp and flat hair. Those are Ralph's trademarks. They make for a natural-looking wig."

With all the attention devoted to wigs, is there ever an opportunity for women to let down their real hair?

"Whatever the Torah prohibits the Torah permits," said Rabbi Mayer Fund, founder of the Flatbush Minyona, a synagogue in a largely Orthodox section of Brooklyn.

Since swimming is segregated by sex in Orthodox communities, women swim bareheaded, allowing their hair, which darkens from lack of sunlight, to have a fleeting chance to highlight naturally. And when Orthodox women are at home, where many wig-wearers don only a scarf lest an unexpected visitor appears, they will uncover their hair when ready for bed.

"You're keeping your hair for your husband," Mrs. Mermelstein explained. "He's the one who gets to see it."

For Stylish Orthodox Women, Wigs That Aren't Wiggy

1. Orthodox Jewish women must wear a wig after marriage to ensure modesty. Mennonite women and Islamic women are also required to cover their hair, especially when in public places. Why do you think covering a woman's hair is so important to these religious cultures?

2. Do you often think that religious dress and being fashionable are not compatible? How has this article affected your thinking on this issue?

3. What do you think of Mrs. Rifka Locker's statement that her wig matched her real hair so closely that "No one could even tell I got married"?

76   Worldly Lessons
Lynda Edwards

Bob Jones University, nestled here in the South Carolina hill country, is all butter-yellow buildings bordered by purple magnolia blossoms and a fountain sparkling with pink and blue-lighted spumes; the paint-box colors belie a serious house on serious earth. In a classroom where 20 female students sat recently, Bibles and notebooks stacked neatly before them, facing half a dozen headless dress forms draped in deft knockoffs of Todd Oldham and Donna Karan, Prof. Diane Hay of the home economics department was teaching one of her popular "safe beauty classes."

Like all B.J.U. classes, this one begins with prayer. Mrs. Hay—61, tall, slender and elegant—invoked God to help the girls absorb the lecture and guide them to ideal careers. Then she held up the image consultants' bible: "Dress for Success" by John T. Malloy. "I know you're familiar with this book," she said, "but what I want to talk about today is God's dress-for-success program."

She opened her Bible to I Corinthians 6:19: "…Ye are not your own. For ye are bought with a price; therefore glorify God in your body, and in your spirit, which are God's." The girls bowed their heads to take notes, then looked up.

Reprinted by permission of Lynda Edwards.

"Ye are bought with a price." Mrs. Hays repeated softly. "Your beauty, the talent and luck that will pave your way, have been paid for by your Lord. He must be your guide to the outside world." It was so quiet you could hear bees buzzing outside. "In the workplace," she went on, "it is wrong for any girl to wear a garment that rouses in any man desires that cannot be righteously fulfilled outside of marriage. The Bible also warns us not to be so masculine that we threaten men. If your talk is spiritual, but your look is cold, hard, carnal and calculating, the outside is what's believed."

Mrs. Hay rested a hand on a dress form clad in a chic cream wraparound blouse, slim brown skirt and leopard print belt. "I want you to look like you belong in the 1990's—your time—not the 1950's," she said smiling. "Style is your armor. Fashion says take off, forget your feelings, get used to this. Style comforts you, gives you confidence. Then, beauty serves you."

Like the feminist author Camille Paglia, fundamentalists (those who interpret the Bible literally, as opposed to evangelicals, who interpret it individually) have always believed that feminine beauty wields a nearly occult power, wreaking havoc if unharnessed, having a redemptive effect if properly cast. In 1986, Beverly LaHaye, president of Concerned Women of America, a group of female religious advocates drawn from both the fundamentalist and evangelical movements, wrote of the "supernaturalism" inherent in a woman's beauty, and its potential for good or evil in the workplace.

Such a belief made women's presence at work problematic. So for decades, fundamentalist women were directed to find safe harbors working in the home or in low-wage jobs at Christian hospitals or schools, said Paul Hetrick, the public affairs director of the Family Research Council, a Washington research organization that calls itself a "conservative pro-family advocate." The council is lobbying to alter the tax code to favor married couples with children, and mothers without paying jobs.

But since the late 1980's, fundamentalist women, like many other conservative American women, have had to adapt to the new economic realities and enter the workplace. In "Children at Risk," his 1990 book on family values, Gary Bauer, the president of the Family Research Council, extols working mothers who "believe in responsible living, the traditional standards of right and wrong, and in the God of our fathers." And last November, the child psychologist Dr. James Dobson, on his popular radio program, "Focus on Family," implored churches to show "respect, compassion and justice" to fundamentalist career women. Such women, Mr. Bauer and Dr. Dobson assert, are engaged in the "ministry of business."

At Bob Jones, besides professional skills, women learn to navigate a money-fueled culture that, when deconstructed, seems as ritualistically complex and socially treacherous as Edith Wharton's belle epoque. Through Bible-based lessons, female students learn how faith should inform their dress, deportment, conversational skills, etiquette and business ethics. If the lessons hold, they forge a lifelong spiritual cordon sanitaire around the fundamentalist as she encounters the snares of the secular office.

B.J.U., which has about 5,000 students, was founded in 1927 to combat liberalism, according to its recruiting brochure, and is influential enough to have snagged Presidents Ronald Reagan and George Bush as speakers. Although it is not accredited, it attracted recruiters from 40 corporations last year, including Dun & Bradstreet, Arthur Andersen and KPMG Peat Marwick. A CNN recruiter asked the career services director, Dave Williams, whether fundamentalists proselytize fellow workers. "I told him the stereotype of church ladies pushing leaflets in a parking lot is out of date," Mr. Williams said. "The best on-the job witness we can give is being the company's best employee."

Other fundamentalist Bible colleges do not trivialize the Bob Jones charm and beauty courses; in fact, schools like Liberty College, founded by the Rev. Jerry Falwell, have less elaborate versions. They are viewed as a smart way to tackle a public relations problem. When consumers hear I.B.M. they think of computers; say fundamentalism, and even some fundamentalists concede that people think of Jimmys—Swaggart and Bakker—and bad women with big hair.

In her book, "Beauty and the Best," Beneth Jones, the wife of the university's president, Bob Jones 3d, rebuts the myth that equates the fashions of the wholesome 50's with holiness: "The hold-on-to-the-death attitude of Christian women with bouffant hair is a case in point. All that backcombing and high-piling was so hopelessly outmoded by the blow-dry era that those who clung to it made spectacles of themselves."

Mrs. Hay was discussing legs. The students wore floral prints and pastel silks that swept their ankles; B.J.U. requires that skirts cover the knee whether a woman is standing or sitting.

"A man's eye travels from the floor up," Mrs. Hay said. "A Christian woman wants to do everything she can to draw his eye to her face because that is where her character is revealed. Accessories can guide his eye." She held silvery earrings up for the class to see. "An honest, brave, lovely face does more for your career than any dress can."

For most of the students, these classes, which are introduced to freshmen as an interdisciplinary orientation program, provide the first glimpse of the secular business world. "Most of our girls have college-educated parents earning low incomes—or nothing, if they're missionaries," said Bobbie Yearick, a drama professor. And, she theorized, upper-income managers, male and female, suspect working-class prettiness as being somehow insubordinate. She tells her students: "You're being scrutinized all the time. Be aware of what your face and voice are expressing at all times."

Since Proverbs 15:13 advises believers that "a merry heart maketh a cheerful countenance," and because even the grimmest of corporate cultures demand some measure of jollity and faux camaraderie, a happy face is a high priority. Mrs. Hay and Mrs. Yearick cited the perky countenance of Mary Hart on "Entertainment Tonight" as scripturally ideal.

"A woman must be sure her eyes inspire friendliness, not familiarity, in male co-workers," Mrs. Yearick said. No half-lowered lids or fluid gazes. "The voice should be bright, firm and free of all inflection. Men will claim to read anything in a tone."

But most female students at B.J.U. say they don't worry about inciting uncontrollable lust. What they do worry about is being mistaken for what fundamentalist preachers call "she-men": power-mad, humorless, Joan Crawford-y boss women who emasculate male, and backstab female subordinates. Erin Rodman, a red-haired education major who looks like a runway model, began working at 14 on a bean farm, then was a waitress at a pizza parlor to help pay family bills. "I was always very aloof, very professional to avoid harassment," she said. "But a man who wants to harass you will."

Mrs. Hay recounted this tale of one fraught encounter: A student was at her part-time job when a male co-worker made a pass at her. She told him to leave her alone and walked toward the door. He yanked her blouse collar and shouted, "Why do you advertise if you don't deliver?" She came to Mrs. Hay in tears. "We thought her dress might have caused him to misjudge a good book by a flashy cover," Mrs. Hay said, adding the skirt was "a little too short" and the blouse "a little too unbuttoned."

"We spent six months reforming her style," she said.

Later, Dave McQuaid, director of media relations at Bob Jones, having heard that Mrs. Hay had recounted the story, said: "Journalists rap us as saying women bring harassment on themselves when we don't think that. Understand that Mrs. Hay's expertise is esthetics."

Miss Rodman wants a career in public school administration. "Most of us going on to work in the real world worry about having to wear a tough shell," she said. "It's the emphasis on femininity, especially Mrs. Jones's lessons, that's most useful to us."

Mrs. Jones teaches on a stage before 500 freshmen in a sea-foam-green room ordinarily used for chamber music recitals. The stage, backed by an emerald scrim, is scattered with a few strangely numinous props—a podium, a chair, a coat rack, wooden steps. Mrs. Jones was once a B.J.U. drama major. On stage, she acts out what her book calls "Special Challenges to

Grace: Putting On or Removing a Coat; Exiting a Car; Sitting on Table-Attached Picnic Benches." The basics, too: walking and sitting in a chair.

For table-etiquette lessons, the students study diagrams, mapping the way from salad knife to shellfish fork. "I remind that in the real world, even if their business lunch is at McDonalds, they're representing not just their company but their faith," she said.

Students practice being an envoy for both at the university's "management house," a three-bedroom ranch house on campus built of lavender brick. It was originally intended to be a place for future homemakers to hone cooking and housekeeping skills. Now, it's also a laboratory for making parties and conversations. Students attend on-campus operatic and philharmonic productions to learn how to recognize arias, movements and au courant wear. Their aim is to be able to move among the cultural elite.

Four girls live at the house in four-week stints, during which a faculty member rates their progress as they plan and cook 56 meals, including a formal seven-course dinner. Faculty members are guests, simulating the roles of boss and boss's spouse. Students are graded on being hosts (giving the house tour, correctly matching dinner partners), culinary skills, presentation and conversation.

"I was shy and got an unfavorable critique for allowing long conversation pauses at the parties when I was hostess," said a business major and international banking aspirant who would not give her name because she had several job interviews lined up. "I also performed badly on icebreakers."

The faculty adviser gave her some pointers: Observe body language. Practice discussing stories in U.S. News & World Report, Fortune, the local paper and The New York Times. Quote The Times for the definitive secular view of the world. Ask the shyest person an open-ended question every 20 minutes. Keep any purpose to your social chat unstated, thus preserving the lightness of chance.

"I was so depressed I thought I'd never get it," the student said. "I thought maybe the Lord was pointing me to a job where I'd just deal with numbers."

The adviser made her the host of the formal dinner. She prayed for an hour before dawn. That evening, lulls occurred only when everyone was eating, wallflowers bloomed, and each guest exhibited his or her store of interesting shop talk. Two guests gave her business cards. "It was a sign," she said. "I'm not to be shy anymore."

In the business school, the hallways are dotted with Bible verses in calligraphy: "Servants, be obedient to them that are your masters...not with the eye-service as men-pleasers but doing the will of God from the heart," reads one; there are verses about quenching eternal thirst above the water fountains. All the classroom doors were open; a teacher could be heard drilling students on oil and soybean futures.

Alan Carper, 37, spent over a decade in the corporate world before coming here to teach B.J.U.'s senior management classes. One lesson focuses on the fundamentalist manager's dual responsibility to an H.I.V.-positive employee—defend his privacy and protect him from ostracism by colleagues—based on Christ's ministry to the sick. Another focuses on the Bible's exegesis of sexual harassment.

"And the bottom line is, no one asks for it," he said. "It's not a sexual crime. A harasser's aggression and rages would come out in other ways if the woman didn't exist. It's a crime of power. A female supervisor could harass a male subordinate, as in the story of Joseph and Potiphar's wife."

He follows the politically correct route of all American business schools till he hits a deadman's curve: whistleblowing. "If a Christian employee witnesses harassment of a co-worker, he or she must come to the co-worker's aid and corroborate her testimony," he said. "The Bible says not to give false witness, even if lying wins you favor with the powers that be." If a corporation sides with the harasser, the fundamentalist may have to resign. "We believe God will open up a path to an ethical corporation to replace the one that is lost," he explained.

It seems a hard fate for a young professional woman, especially after B.J.U. has invested so much time and energy in grooming her for the workplace. "But we don't want our career women to have their egos depend on some corporation," Mrs. Yearnick said. "Fundamentalism is our path. The only real power is the power to walk away.

"It's like soldiers: all you have for protection are the things you can carry. For a young woman, that is her faith, her grace and a lovely face."

1. Several of the readings on religion make reference to social class. Identify the social class issues in each of the readings and note how these issues are related to dress.

2. What is your opinion of "safe beauty classes" that prepare women at Bob Jones University for professional positions among the cultural elite of U.S. society?

3. Compare "Worldly Lessons" to articles in Chapter 7 on dress for work. For example, how does "Worldy Lessons" compare to "How Black Can You Be?" and "Casino Gives Workers Look They Can, Must Live With"?

77 Clothing, Control, and Women's Agency: The Mitigation of Patriarchal Power

Linda Boynton-Arthur

It is "part and parcel of daily experience to feel both free and enchained, capable of shaping our own future and yet confronted by towering, seemingly impersonal, constraints."
—M. Archer, *Culture and Agency*

In this chapter, by examining how clothing can simultaneously symbolize agency and constraint, I examine the ways women move between both. I do so in a particularly rigid social context which seems to offer little opportunity for resistance—a conservative Holdeman Mennonite community.[1] Holdeman Mennonite women live within but also negotiate the boundaries of their lives, and they do so in a tightly controlled and highly patriarchal world.[2] Meta-phorically referred to as "a mirror to the soul," women's clothing is considered by the Holdeman Mennonite community to be the external manifestation of inner attitudes. For Holdeman Mennonites, then, dress provides a visual display of religiosity.[3]

Sociologically speaking, it does more than this. Dress and, by extension, the body are the sites where different symbolic meanings are constructed and contested. This case substantiates Mary Douglas's thesis that the human body is a symbol for the social body, that is, that persons'

Reprinted by permission of Linda Boynton-Arthur.

bodies represent the values of the culture to which they belong. She explains that such symbols arise from pressures within a culture to create consonance between physiological and social experiences. The more value people give to social constraints, the more value they set on symbols of bodily control (Douglas 1970:67). Further, she argues that when social groups are threatened, they use the body in a symbolic manner to define and defend their boundaries (Douglas, 1982a:9).

Thus the control of women's clothing by Mennonite ministers as well as the ways women resist this contest represent a negotiation of symbolic meaning for their society at large. From this perspective, neither social control nor collective resistance is a clear-cut phenomenon. These issues are negotiated in everyday interaction in even the most tightly controlled communities.

While compliance with group norms or personal control is required for all Holdeman Mennonites, for women of the community, constraints involve both formal and informal controls that regulate almost every facet of life. The church community regulates social roles and social activities. If there is no specific rule, then usually a custom dictates the correct procedure for any activity. Diversity in any manner is frowned on. Following tradition is the rule which leads to homogeneity. Nevertheless, the women experience a measure of ambivalence. They find comfort in sameness but yearn for variety, especially in clothing.

Although Mennonites as a group feel threatened by the outside world, Holdeman Mennonite women in addition feel threatened by the men of the community. Because the women's need for variety and self-expression is expressed through subtle variations in their dress, clothing is a source of conflict between men and women. In this conflict men exercise control, with ministers having the most power. Women, however, walk a fine line between obedience to the norms and self-assertion when they react to the control exercised by men.

Plagued by anxiety, women nevertheless maneuver in a subtle manner. Through individual and group deviance from the norms, they attempt to change the details of their traditional

dress. In doing so they confront the established image and carefully fashion an alternative to the image defined by men, resisting what appear to be overwhelming constraints. Subtle changes in dress, then, function symbolically to establish solidarity among women and to circumvent patriarchal control.

Since resistance to change is characteristic of Holdeman Mennonite culture, the changes that do occur are, as we would expect, minute. Nevertheless the tension between agency and constraint, or power and resistance, becomes apparent in these subtle struggles over the symbolic meaning of woman's dress.

POWER AND RESISTANCE

Power and resistance are often examined in terms of their public impact. Control of women, however, is also an intensely personal matter tied to conceptions of self. Merten and Schwartz (1982) note that by transgressing the conventional boundaries between public and private, symbolic process in nonritual contexts acquires power to represent the self. They argue that by implicating the self in the constitution of new metaphors, symbolic process in everyday life gives meaning to normative conflict. Symbolic processes involved in normative conflict are frequently not investigated in depth in the social control literature.

Most research on social control tends to be macroscopic in nature and focuses on the use of formal/legal means of control. Goffman (1963, 1971) was among the first to remind us that there is an alternative: we could focus more microscopically in order to investigate symbolic processes. From this perspective, social control would be conceptualized as a social process which, while normatively governed, occurs in everyday interactions. The norms governing social behavior in any situation are implicit. They go unnoticed until they are violated. Then sanctions can be applied to bring behavior back into normative compliance. Here infractions are discouraged by others.

Goffman goes on to specify three forms that normative controls can take. First, there is *personal social control*. The individual refrains from improper behavior by self-regulation. If she or he has acted improperly, the offense is admitted and reparations are undertaken in order to reestablish the social norms. Second, there is *informal social control*. When the individual begins to offend, peers may warn that disapproval is imminent and that sanctions may be applied. Increasing pressure may be exerted until the offender is brought into line, which reaffirms social norms (Goffman, 1971:346–347). This feedback is one of the main mechanisms of socialization. Third, the threat that an offender introduces to the social order is managed through *formal social control*. These social sanctions are administered by specialized agents such as the police. Criminals break social rules and ideally are punished. In sum, personal, informal, and formal controls are the means by which conformity to social norms is effected. Deviation is inhibited or corrected, and compliance is assured (Goffman, 1971:347–348). Similarly, Douglas (1982a:5) has argued that "people who've banded together…will tend to coerce one another to develop the full implications of their style of life."

Further, Douglas (1982b) claims that all conflict within families, churches, and social groups is really about the boundaries of each institution. The dissent centers on how to deal with normative behavior that becomes encoded as rules. The rules may be as simple as dress codes or as complex as laws. Nonetheless, social control measures are used effectively by society to protect the institution's boundaries. The social body then, constrains the physical body. As a result, the body (including its care and grooming) is a highly restricted medium of expression.

One of the most significant boundaries in society is the line drawn between male and female. The gender system is defined by Schur (1984) as a pervasive network of interrelated norms and sanctions through which female (and male) behavior is evaluated and controlled. Gender-related norms maintain their dominance in society and influence the "micropolitics" of routine interactions (Emerson & Messinger, 1977).

In this chapter I take Goffman's recommendation to examine social control microscopically as my analytic starting place. From this position, and using an analysis of dress, I explore both the cultural constraints on Holdeman Mennonite women and their resistance to those constraints. I argue that even in the rigid structure of Holdeman Mennonite life, where men in general and ministers in particular have the power to exercise formal social controls, women resist. Since self-control is a basic requisite of life in Mennonite societies, individual women exercise personal control. In addition, women working together in groups exercise informal collective control. These controls both reinforce dress code norms and contest them.

Holdeman Mennonite women resist not through massive insurrection, but through the most minute everyday practices. By examining how social control is both exercised and resisted within their community, we not only get a picture of the women's never-ending creativity, but we add to the theoretical discourses on social control. Drawing on the insights of Douglas (1970) and Mauss (1936), we can understand women's bodies as an image of society, as giving visual expression to sociocultural values. In other words, women's bodies must be analyzed in conjunction with this social dimension.

Thus control of the Holdeman Mennonite women's clothing by their ministers and the women's resistance to it represent a negotiation of symbolic meanings about both women's bodies and the social body. Negotiations about women's dress are also negotiations about gender and power. As ministers and women struggle over dress codes, ministers symbolically reinscribe themselves as powerful and women as other. Women's bodies, clothed as they are, are symbolically marked and located on the margins. The social body is male. As women resist the dress code, they also restrict their otherness, their location on the margins of power. These struggles take place in the context of an ever-present historical past, which continues to have a great deal of influence on the Holdeman Mennonites' everyday life. History and tradition are used to maintain the status quo and prevent change.

SOME HISTORY

Branded in Europe as heretics, Mennonites migrated throughout the Continent from the sixteenth century on, hoping to escape religious persecution. Eventually some came to North America, where they established isolated communities required to "live and dress simply in avoidance of the world" (Boynton, 1986; Hiebert, 1973:25). This separation was facilitated by strict social control measures.

The theme that links social control and clothing norms is the historical pattern of "avoidance" or separation from the world. Mennonites believe that there are two kingdoms—the kingdom of God and the kingdom of the world. Separation from "the world" was a simple matter while the Mennonites were physically isolated in remote communities. However, as non-Mennonites moved in among these sectarians, Mennonites began to feel their influence, and many became acculturated. For conservative Mennonites who saw acculturation as a threat, separation from the world became a divisive issue that led to several schisms, including the Holdeman schism of 1859.

Alluding to acculturation and citing the loss of Mennonite distinctiveness, John Holdeman and his followers left the Old Mennonite church. For them, separation from the world was accomplished symbolically by retention of many of the old traditions, including plain dress,[4] formalized in both proscribed and prescribed dress codes. According to Hiebert (per. comm. 1980), in the early days of the sect Holdeman had prescribed a dress code for women which was characterized by a cape dress with a high neck, loose bodice, and fitted waist.

The historical pattern of modest and plain clothing has continued. Like other "plain people," the Holdemans believe that a lack of emphasis on external beauty leads to the expression of spirituality (Scott, 1986:15). Clothing, as all of life, has to be brought under the scrutiny of New Testament standards. The most salient symbol of a woman's Christianity is her black head-covering, worn to symbolize her submission to God, to men in general, and to her husband in particular.

Within Mennonite culture, women have always been subservient to the men. According to the Holdeman Mennonites, male power and female submission are divinely ordered and are rooted in the Bible, the authoritative word of God. This belief results in gender-based segregation within the sect. Men hold all positions of formal power. A group of ten to twelve ministers and deacons are expected to define and eliminate deviance in behavior and appearance. For these patriarchs, control of deviance seems a straightforward matter. Guidelines are based on tradition and the communal goal of living a good Christian life. Through consensus among themselves they determine where the boundaries of deviance are drawn—boundaries that make most change deviant.

If men have the formal power in the family and community, women have informal power rooted in their age-sets. Deliberately emphasizing the corporate nature of social groups, age-sets are a particular type of social organization, a permanent grouping of individuals by age and sex. The Holdemans are patrilocal, so as women marry into a congregation, they are accepted into an age-set.[5] Usually persons enter the set as children and pass through the age-grades as a group; as a consequence, "I" becomes "we" and suppresses individuality (Gulliver, 1968: 157–161).

In church and other social situations, such as picnics and dinners at the social hall, the sexes remain separate.[6] A Holdeman Mennonite woman, then, interacts primarily in a world of women organized by age-sets. These groups comprise not just a social network, but a working social organization whose complex function is devoted to affirming social norms. It monitors its own behavior in order to insure compliance to religious norms, while at the same time supporting some infractions of the norms. As a consequence, the age-set provides an informal female channel that subverts the formal channels of male control.

THE STUDY COMMUNITY

I studied a specific Holdeman Mennonite community called Bend in northern California, a farming community of 310 persons on the Sacramento River.[7] The community is comprised of sixty-five families. Because land is inherited patrilineally, it is common for several generations of a family to live on farms near each other. Most of the men in the community are farmers, and all of the married women are housewives. Large families are the norm (five children average), and raising children as good Christians is the central focus for all.

The community interacts extensively with the other West Coast Holdeman Mennonite congregations beyond Bend. These communities are linked through a national church conference, missionary work, and marriage. Since the Holdeman Mennonites are religiously endogamous, approximately half the young women leave to marry men from other congregations. The combination of endogamy, patrilocal residence, and few converts creates a community in which most people are related (at least distantly) to each other.

I collected data in two phases. During the first phase of fieldwork, which was intermittent and occurred over a forty-month period, I observed and conducted casual interviews with church members (1979–1984).[8] During the second phase, which occurred between 1985 and 1987, with follow-up interviews in 1991, I interviewed, in groups and individually, most of the local people who had left the church. Almost all of them had been formally expelled.[9] These interviews were tape-recorded and transcribed. Because these people had not returned to the church even under the intense pressure of shunning, they were acutely aware of the power of tradition, history, and social control in Mennonite society.

Tradition and control within the community overlap in the women's clothing. Dresses have changed little since the early days of the sect. Following the styles of their forebearers, women and girls wear shirtwaist dresses characterized by a wide, long skirt and a fitted bodice with buttons down the center to the waist [see Figure 12.3]. There is generally a small collar and belt. The uniform attire of Holdeman Mennonite women attests to separation from ex-

Orthodox   Married   Unmarried

FIGURE 12.3 *Dresses worn by Holdeman Mennonite women express both a religious affiliation and status (i.e., unmarried, married, and Orthodox) within the group.*

ternal society as well as separation of the sexes. Dress reflects the assumed natural gender differences that underlie patriarchal family and social systems.

A MIRROR TO THE SOUL: CONTROLLING THE IMAGE

Since nearly all members of the Holdeman Mennonite community attend every church activity, objective evaluation of a person's commitment to the faith is impossible, so symbolic measures such as dress codes are employed instead. The sexes have different standards as to proper Mennonite dress. While the women dress in a uniquely Mennonite style, the men dress in Levis and plaid shirts, much like outsiders. John and his wife were expelled for differing with the ministers over interpretation of doctrine. He explained: "It's always been that way. Women have always had to dress more carefully. It's a way of the men controlling the women. Holdeman men *need* to control women [because] they feel so controlled themselves." According to his wife, "The men feel like they're accomplishing something if they can get someone to do what they require of them. That is control—women's clothing shows they are being controlled—they have to dress plainer than the men."

A person's religious commitment is exhibited through personal control, so formal measures of social control are not often needed. However, cases such as those described below serve a preventative function in that they demonstrate to women the price they must pay for deviating from norms enforced by both informal and formal social control.

Formal Control

Ministers and deacons (all men) mete out in public formal measures of social control, including general displays of power, formal reprovals, denial of communion, a practice known as "church repentance," and expulsion. Most of their formal social control of women is related to

Mennonite men's particular image of a "proper" Mennonite woman. She should be sober in demeanor and appearance. She is expected to be thin and modestly dressed, visually testifying to her self-control over what are termed "lusts of the flesh." Sensory enjoyment is considered sinful; consequently, such pleasures as eating and sexual and emotional expressions are repressed. Any activity done solely for fun, or to excess, is prohibited. Self-denial is the rule in Mennonite life and is expected to be visible in appearance.

A woman's head covering is a potent symbol of her self-denial, submission, and acceptance of group norms. The following incident over such a head covering, related by an expelled woman, reflects conflict between women and ministers:

> We went through a period of time where we were having some trouble about the head covering. It is a three-cornered black flat scarf, which only becomes round when you shape and fold it around the bun. If you have a lot of hair, this is hard to do—you pin it on at the top, bring it down, fold in each side, tie it under, tuck the bottom tail around, and then it looks like a cap. What we began to do was to sew caps so we could just slap them on and pin them down. That wasn't allowed because the ministers said it wasn't traditional—but they only look at history if they can use it to their advantage.

Women often get into "church trouble," which usually starts with public reprovals. These typically began at a staff meeting (a weekly meeting of all the ministers and deacons), where the men discuss behavior considered deviant. And because rigid conformity is the norm for this sect, it does not take much to be labeled deviant. Women who are so labeled are continually watched by the staff for symbols that are perceived as deviations from established rules. An individual's behavior is interpreted in light of the deviance label, and this results in unequal enforcement of the rules. For example, Leah was in "church trouble" from the time she reached puberty until her midthirties, when she was expelled from the church. She recounted a reproval by the ministers:

I was eight-and-a-half months pregnant and overweight, and I had borrowed a maternity dress from my older sister Jane [an orthodox member], and I was sitting there and they were giving me the third degree—asking why I do this, or that—and I was crying and they asked why couldn't I please my husband. And one of the ministers said, "Just take for instance that dress you're wearing." It was a decent dress, but he said, "That dress is loud—a woman like you wearing such a dress is offensive." Jane wore it many times after I did, and never was reproved for it. I was the only one who was; it was because they saw me as a threat, because I have always been attractive and not ashamed of it. Ministers always kept their eyes on me.

This incident occurred at the church and involved only the ministers, Leah, and her husband. Formal reproval most often occurs in this manner. It is also common, however, for the errant member to be brought before the entire congregation for a public reproval. "Men do not get reproved very often: women are reproved by men in order to control them," Sharon reports during a group interview. As a member becomes more recalcitrant, the increasingly public and formal nature of the social control becomes evident.

Denial of communion and "church repentance" are formal declarations of deviant status. Leah stated: "The last few years they weren't allowing me to go to communion. They didn't really have anything on me except for my clothes, which was what they harped on. And my clothes were pretty much like everyone else's." "Church repentance" is a period of formal censure. According to an expelled woman, "repentance is like purgatory, like hell, like being shunned, but not quite. You're untouchable. People look at you and weep, because they know you're going to hell." In general these measures are effective in controlling deviance. Some women, however, are unable to accept the power of the ministers and are expelled.

The most drastic form of formal social control, expulsion, is followed by shunning (social ostracism). After appropriate deliberations, ministers expel people at a members' meeting. In Bend, 22 percent of members are expelled, which supports the national figure of 20 percent cited by Hiebert (1973:402). When expelled, a person is not allowed to eat at the same table with the family or have social or economic interactions with church members. The intense pressure generally is successful in returning the member to the fold.

Becky, who has been expelled five times, is one such member. She stated she could foretell her own impending church trouble when she began to experience an increasingly negative attitude toward Mennonite clothing:

> It felt suffocating, as though when I put on the clothes, I put on the church's rules. I was a different person in worldly [fashionable] clothing—I was uncontrolled. The church's rules didn't apply to me. As I got back into the frame of mind that is expected, I grew to appreciate that God wants me in the church; as that happened, I no longer wanted worldly clothes. Eventually, putting on the Mennonite clothes and head covering felt right.

Thus Becky's crisis was apparent visually in her appearance. This illustration points to the ability of clothing to symbolize not just group affiliation, but the construction and affirmation of both personal and cultural identity.

Informal Control

Maintaining group norms is the expressed purpose of informal social control measures. Using methods ranging from gossip to reproval (formal criticism), women insure conformity to norms and function as social control agents within their age-sets. They spend a great deal of time in the company of their friends, and the other members of the community are the main topic of conversation. Since intense scrutiny is considered a sign of Christian love, nothing goes unnoticed. When she breaks a norm, a woman knows the transgression will be noticed and become a current topic of conversation. If that threat is ineffective in redirecting her behavior, a woman's best friends will talk to her directly and express their concern for her spirituality. Members are continually aware of clothing and use it to gauge a person's submission of self to the group. Anna stated that "when Leah was expelled, it was so sudden. There were no signs that she was in trouble....Even her clothing was the same—I'd have expected to see some changes, like her dresses getting fancy or something, 'cause clothing was so important to her."

In the last months prior to her expulsion, Leah's conformity to clothing norms continued in spite of her ongoing difficulty with the ministers and deacons. This example illuminates a larger issue; women derive satisfaction from their social ties, and to retain them, the self is always subjugated to the will of the group. Deviation from the group standard is equated (negatively) with pride. Signs of individuality are seen as a rejection of group norms and values. Naturally, the expression of individuality in clothing is too obvious to be ignored. Charity, a minister's daughter who left the church in 1970 but still lives in Bend, concluded:

> If your clothes are straight down the lines as to the rules of the group, then everyone can see that you are submitting your will to the church. The Mennonite dress is like a uniform—it indicates that you're keeping everything under control. When you're having trouble with the rules, your clothing can show it. This is why everyone watches what everyone else is wearing and how they are wearing it, because clothing shows acceptance of all the rules of the church.

Some women resent the amount of control men exert over women, especially in regard to dress. Leah stated: "We have to conform to whatever the men want, whether it's the way we dress or our behavior. They think it's scriptural. I think it's just another way to *tame women down* [her emphasis]. The men say 'women, submit yourselves to your husbands.'" And submit they do to both formal public reprovals and informal private reprovals which generally occur between two women. One woman recalled: "On the first Sunday that my daughter wore little anklets with

lace around them, Rachael reproved me. She was really on her toes to catch that the first time they were worn!" Rachael's daughter explained: "In her heart, my mother despises confrontations. She comes from a long line of ministers, and will do anything to avoid getting into conflict with them." In order to prevent such conflict with the ministers, Rachael reproved other women out of sisterly concern.

It is in the best interest of all the women to keep each other committed to the social norms, in order to insulate themselves from formal control by the ministers. An expelled woman described reprovals she experienced while still a member:

> I was reproved for wearing a low-neck dress— it was a dress which was unbuttoned to just below the collarbone. The woman who reproved me was wearing a neckline lower than mine—but reproved me anyway....I was occasionally reproved for my daughter's dresses—I made her beautiful dresses which were a little bit on the fancy side. She loved them! Now that I've been expelled, the Mennonite women make ugly, plain dresses for her that she prefers to wear. She won't wear anything that I made anymore.[10]

Women are reproved for any number of infractions, but clothing is one of the more frequent topics. Katie said that "for instance, if my sister or a friend started wearing shorter skirts, I would worry that she was losing her spirituality. I would express my concern about this, and she would probably lower her hems." Holdeman women do not see this gesture as interference; instead they accept the informal reprovals as indicative of sisterly concern. The consensus is that women maintain vigilance over each other to keep themselves from straying too far from the norms and risking formal reprovals.

Through vigilance within their age-sets, women informally control their own dress, whereas men exert formal control over women and their appearance. These forms of control function quite differently. By enforcing a particular image of "proper" Mennonite dress for women and not allowing deviations from the clothing norms, the ministers exert a great deal of power and try to inhibit resistance. As they control women's dress, men both reflect and reinforce a particular image of women's bodies and the social body—an image that sustains their patriarchal power. By contrast, when women control women's dress, they provide some resistance to that power. They offer an alternative, no matter how minute—an alternative that mitigates against patriarchal power. They assert collective independence by using hyper-traditional dress in order to bring about changes in the less salient aspects of Holdeman Mennonite dress. Dressing more traditionally than men keeps women above male reproach. By informally enforcing dress codes among themselves, they actively deny men the opportunity to exert formal control. They actively deny men the opportunity to reinforce their patriarchal authority. Not only do women resist by depriving men of the opportunity to reinforce their definition, but they participate in shaping an alternative image of both women's bodies and the social body.

A MIRROR TO THE SOUL: SHAPING AN ALTERNATIVE IMAGE

By working together, Mennonite women are able to balance the restrictions imposed by ministers with some measure of individual expression. This process is empowering and results in some deviations from the usually explicit dress code. While not all the women approve of these variations, they stand together and do not interfere with the changes. The most obvious deviations occur among young women.

The community generally understands that adolescence is a period fraught with tension. Men defer to their wives in raising daughters, and the girls are given some leeway with the dress code. Girls exhibit rebellion by secretly wearing "worldly" clothing. Mary recalled that when she went to public high school (late 1960s), many of the Mennonite girls kept worldly clothing in their school lockers. Charity agreed: "I'd sneak them out of the house; I kept

some worldly things at school. I also wore two-inch-wide belts, so that when I rolled up the waistband to shorten the skirt, the roll wouldn't show. This way, dresses could be long around adults and short at school like the other [non-Mennonite] girls." Leah was in public school at about the same time as Charity and Mary and recalled that "It was in high school that I really wanted to dress different than the Mennonites.... My friends and I all dressed in worldly clothes when we got the chance. But they didn't have to sneak the clothes out as much as I did, 'cause my parents were so conservative. They could get by with fancier clothes...than I could."

Girls are not allowed to wear makeup, other than a medicinal foundation if they have acne. However, it is typical for Mennonite girls to use foundation and minimal makeup. According to Charity, "makeup has always been forbidden, but we used to sneak out mascara....I would dye my eyelashes with this stuff called Dark Eyes. Mom wondered why my lashes got so dark! The girls in the church now are wearing makeup, but they're sneaking it. They only wear enough that it barely shows." The ministers are apparently unable to discern subtle makeup from the absence of makeup. Leah stated that "the ministers would ask, 'do you wear eyebrow paint'? I'd say no. I wore mascara but I figured that if they didn't know the name for it, I wasn't gonna help them out. They didn't even know the difference."

In addition to using makeup, young women have more latitude with their wardrobes. The most overt instance of rule bending concerned Charity's sister-in-law who converted just before she married. Although "she's a total Mennonite today, she did rebel a little, for a while [just after she married] she left her hair down and wore jeans." Although this is generally unacceptable, the women in the congregation knew about it and looked the other way.

Similarly, the more conservative women overlook the tendency for young women to invest a great deal of time, energy, and money in their wardrobes. While Mennonite women agree that it is required that clothing be modest, single women wear dresses that fit snugly. Charity remarked: "If you're single, clothes are for sexual attraction, but you can't be too obvious. Once you've caught a man, there's no need to put so much time in extensive wardrobes.…When you have to wear one basic style, the only way to get variety is to have a lot of dresses. Many girls have extensive wardrobes." Becky concurred: "girls spend a lot of time designing dresses to be different from everyone else's. We find details to add that won't be objectionable. That's one reason why our dresses look different from the married ladies'—they don't have the time, or need to attract male attention!" The differences alluded to include such structural details as tucks, pleats, and yokes. Applied details are never acceptable, although details that could be considered functional are overlooked. There is an understanding that the rules of modesty can be bent during this short time in a woman's life, since marrying is of utmost importance.

A woman is not considered an adult until she has borne a child, so until then she is able to bend the rules somewhat. With motherhood, however, comes full adulthood and the expectation that a woman will become more settled and submissive. This expectation is apparent in the clothing of married women; they exhibit greater acceptance of the dress code, which reflects the corporate nature of the age-set. When deviations do occur, they are typically collective in nature.

Shoes (other than tennis shoes) must be black or brown, following tradition. They may not have heels smaller than a dime, and no open heels or toes are permitted. This effectively limits shoe selection to flat, unfashionable styles. Most Mennonite women, however, are short and want to appear taller, so when three-inch-high wedge-heeled shoes came into style in the 1970s, they were quickly bought by Mennonite women. Anna remembered that "the ministers complained that these were too worldly, but what could they do? We'd found the perfect solution to get around the rules!" Additionally, when black and brown shoes were no longer fashionable and became unavailable, Mennonite women dyed white shoes in an apparent attempt to get the acceptable colors. However, the accuracy of shoe dyes left much to be desired and some color variation came into the wardrobes of grateful Mennonite women. Katie remarked that "I used brown dye but got mauve—and I like it! [The minister] couldn't say anything, 'cause it'd be a waste to throw them out!"

Adherence to tradition, a major goal of the ministers, runs into conflict when it comes up against technological change. For example, women may not replace buttons with zippers. Nevertheless, the women found a way to circumvent the ministers' decision: "Changes happen that the ministers say don't follow tradition—we wanted to use zippers in the 1960s to save work. It takes a lot of time to make a dress that buttons," recalled Charity. (Several hours could be saved by constructing a garment that closes with a zipper rather than buttons.) However, the ministers sensed a redesign of the costume and could not be persuaded to accept the change, so the women agreed to keep the buttons and buttonholes down the front of the dress but to insert a zipper in the side seam to make getting dressed easier.

Traditionally, Mennonite women made their dresses out of printed cotton fabrics, but in the 1970s polyester knit fabrics were rapidly adopted when they became available. Not only is it quicker and easier to make dresses of polyester knit, but the fabric needs no ironing. Mennonite women consciously choose fabrics that resemble the old cotton calico prints they traditionally used in order to make a significant change without drawing the attention of the ministers.

Resistance to the image of the "proper" Mennonite woman as proscribed by the ministers is subtle. The most obvious examples of resistance are found in deviations from the clothing norms. In recent years, weight has also been a subject of quiet revolution. According to the local physician, in the early 1980s the obesity rate for adult Mennonite women was 15 percent, compared to thirty-five percent for women in the surrounding community (J. Bradshaw, pers. comm., 1988). Mennonite women kept their weight down through weight-loss programs and exercise. Recently, however, the obesity rate of Mennonite women is increasingly noticed by their non-Mennonite neighbors, one of whom said, "It used to be that Mennonite women were always thin, and we were fat. Now, they're as chubby as we are!" (J. Perez, pers. comm., 1991). One Mennonite woman explained, "We spend most of the day cooking, and it's hard not to eat. But our husbands want us thin—that's so hard to do when we're always in the kitchen. It's getting hard to keep them [husbands] happy." The increased obesity rate of Mennonite women could be interpreted as a covert attempt to defy their husbands' control over their bodies.

The preceding examples demonstrate Holdeman Mennonite women's subtle resistance to both private (family) and public (societal) patriarchy. There is no mindless subjugation of self. While the women may appear submissive, their motivations are complex. They reinforce the dress norms while also resisting the image proscribed for them by the ministers. While there is overt submission, on a more covert level there is collective resistance which supports women's dissension. Women work together, within the age-set, to protect themselves from men's control by monitoring their own behavior. Through their own informal control, women protect themselves from male censure and fashion an alternative image to counteract the image proscribed by men.

While individual men spend much of their time alone, women are constantly involved with other women. Friendship between the sexes is exceedingly rare, and interaction between husband and wife is kept to a minimum. As a consequence, men are excluded from women's lives and are intentionally kept in the dark about things of interest to women. Women take advantage of male ignorance and through their age-sets are able subtly to circumvent the rules. Both resistance and reinforcement of the norms are possible because women's age-sets build solidarity. An individual alone is unable to bend the rules, but women as a group are able to make small changes in the dress codes. The result of this corporate resistance is creation of alternatives to male characterizations of both

women's bodies and the social body. These alternatives resist rather than reinforce patriarchal authority.

Conclusions

The constraints on Mennonite women seem overwhelming. However, these women were raised to suppress individual needs and to yield to group control. The formal structure of the Holdeman Mennonite community as a whole is expressed by men, while the informal structure of the women's age-set supports both community norms and some deviances. The age-set is a first line of defense against the structure imposed by men. Clothing is a major source of conflict between men and women. It is the site of struggle—a struggle between the patriarchal social system and the collective agency of the women's age-set groups. It is also a source for building solidarity among women.

In these struggles, it is not only clothing per se that is negotiated. Dress is the site of conflict in which symbolic meanings are negotiated and contested. Dress is a metaphor; it is interpreted as a visual symbol of the suppression of the self to the demands of the community. In this conflict, the physical body becomes a symbol for the social body. In the case of the Holdeman Mennonites, women's bodies become the focus of a symbolic struggle over both personal and group identities— a struggle that draws attention to the ways freedom and constraint go hand in hand.

Freedom and constraint are apparent in conflict over the Mennonite dress code. While men exercise both private and public power over the female body, women help keep each other in line and overlook some deviations from normative behavior. Thus they both reinforce and resist normative constraints. There is a double nature to the agency of Mennonite women. Both actions resist the characterization of a social body ruled entirely by men. Both empower women and build solidarity within the age-sets and for women as a whole.

Religious dogma is used to rationalize admonishing women for infractions of a rigid dress code, since clothing is seen as evidence of either religious conformity or deviance. The greater the deviance from the dress code, the more likely the woman will be reproved by the ministers. The women's age-sets are able to enforce and mitigate that discipline, however.

Resistance of this kind points to the need to go beyond narrowly defined descriptions of agency. A singular focus on either structural constraints or personal agency seems inadequate to analyze the Holdeman Mennonite case. It is through a constant process of negotiation that boundaries are delineated, negotiated, and redefined.

Notes

1. There are about 300,000 Mennonites in the United States today. The Mennonites are prone to schisms, and at least twenty major divisions represent liberal, mainstream, and conservative philosophies. One of the most conservative sects is the Holdeman Mennonites, who number over 10,000 in the United States (Scott, 1986:35). Formally known as the Church of God in Christ, Mennonite, members of this branch are called Holdemans, Holdeman Mennonites, or (by the local outsiders) Mennonites. In this chapter, I generally refer to the group as Holdeman Mennonites. When the term *Mennonite* is used, it refers to the larger body of Mennonites.

2. *Patriarchy* is used here to indicate both a family system in which men control women and children in the private sphere, and a social system, characterized by the formal and public control of society by men. This usage follows Carol Brown's (1981) discussion of private and public patriarchy.

   Brown distinguishes between public patriarchy (i.e., a patriarchal social system) and private patriarchy. She states that private patriarchy includes the individual relations found in the traditional family, in which men have control over women, their labor (productive and reproductive), and their children. However, Brown notes that patriarchy is not just a family system. In the social system, we find public aspects of patriarchy that function to uphold rights and privileges of the collective male sex. A husband's control of his wife's daily life is reinforced by the larger-scale monopolization of the social and economic world by men. In current U.S. family law, private patriarchy intersects with public patriarchy (Brown, 1981:240). In most of the United States today, it is public not private patriarchy that is problematic for women. For the Mennonites, however, public and private patriarchy constantly intersect, which functions to keep power firmly in male hands.

3. For a discussion of clothing as a metaphor of religiosity, see Boynton 1989 and Poll 1962.

4. "Plain dress" is required by most conservative Amish, Mennonite, and Hutterite churches. It illustrates the values of modesty, piety, economy, and simplicity and provides visual testimony to the commitment and fellowship of the group. For further reading on this topic, see Scott 1986.

5. In Holdeman Mennonite society, the major age-sets for women are girls (sixteen and older, unmarried), mothers (married to age thirty-five), and older women (over thirty-five). Mennonite women refer to unmarried young women as girls. Spinsterhood is rare. It is acknowledged that, without a husband, a woman has few options and a nebulous status. The good things in life, family and children, only come to married women.

6. One woman in the community explained this separation in the following way: "well, you want to be with your friends, the ones you grew up with. After all, you can talk to your husband at home." It is only in the homes that the sexes mingle.

7. I've changed the names of persons and places to insure anonymity.

8. Sixty-three of the seventy-eight adult women, both married and unmarried, were interviewed.

9. A person who will not be controlled by the church is expelled and shunned, which means the expelled person is cut off socially and economically from everyone in the group. As a result of this pressure, the person usually begs for forgiveness and returns (85 percent return to the church). During the second phase of my fieldwork I interviewed 95 percent of the ex-Mennonites who lived within a hundred-mile radius of Bend.

10. This situation was highly unusual. The woman was expelled while she and her husband were having marital problems that ultimately ended in divorce. Initially she was unjustly accused of adultery, after which she became bitter and did have an affair. Eventually she left her husband and was denied access to her children, so the women in the community took over their care. In this instance, public and private patriarchy clearly intersected. Only one other divorce occurred in the history of this community.

References

Archer, M. (1988). *Culture and Agency: The Place of Culture in Social Theory.* Cambridge: Cambridge University Press.

Boynton, L. (1986). *The Plain People: An Ethnography of the Holdeman Mennonites.* Salem, WI: Sheffield Press.

Boynton, L. (1989). Religious orthodoxy, social control and clothing: Dress and adornment as symbolic indicators of social control among Holdeman Mennonite women. Paper presented at the American Sociological Association annual meetings, San Francisco.

Brown, C. (1981). Mothers, fathers and children: From private to public patriarchy. In L. Sargent (Ed.), *Women and Revolution: A Discussion of the Unhappy Marriage of Marxism and Feminism.* Boston: South End Press.

Douglas, M. (1970). *Body Symbols.* Oxford: Blackstone.

Douglas, M. (1982a). *Essays in the Sociology of Perception.* London: Routledge and Kegan Paul.

Douglas, M. (1982b). *Natural Symbols.* New York: Pantheon Books.

Emerson, R. M., & Messinger, S. (1977, December). The micro-politics of trouble. *Social Problems,* 25:121–134.

Goffman, E. (1963). *Stigma: Notes on the Management of Spoiled Identity.* Englewood Cliffs, NJ: Prentice Hall.

Goffman, E . (1971). *Relations in Public.* New York: Harper and Row.

Gulliver, P. H. (1968). Age differentiation. In *International Encyclopedia of the Social Sciences.* New York: Macmillan.

Hiebert, C. (1973). *The Holdeman People.* Pasadena, CA: William Carey Library.

Mauss, M. (1936, March/April). Les techniques du corps. *Journal de la Psychologie,* 32: 372–383.

Merten, D., & Schwartz, G. (1982). Metaphor and self: Symbolic processes in everyday life. *American Anthropologist,* 84:796–810.

Poll, S. (1962). *The Hasidic Community in Williamsburg.* New York: Free Press.

Schur, E. (1984). *Labeling Women Deviant: Gender, Stigma and Social Control.* New York: Random House.

Scott, S. (1986). *Why Do They Dress That Way?* Intercourse, PA: Good Books.

Clothing, Control, and Women's Agency

1. What are the subtle changes Mennonite girls and women make to their dress in order to combat the strict dress code set by male ministers?

2. Are changes made by individuals typically successful? Why or why not?

3. List the ways that Mennonite women support each other in their agency against male control of their dress.

78 From Habit to Fashion: Dress of Catholic Women Religious

Susan O. Michelman
University of Kentucky

This article focuses on data with 26 Roman Catholic nuns, or, as those in noncloistered orders prefer to be called, "women religious," who relinquished religious habits for secular dress. It examines dynamics of personal identity announcements and social identity placements that are not congruous. Prior to the 1960s, women's religious orders were quite homogeneous both in exterior manifestations, such as their dress in the habit, and in the purpose and spirit that permeated them (Ebaugh, 1977). Their personal and social persona were one and the same. The life of a woman religious was highly prescribed and routinized. During the 1960s and 1970s, the majority of women in noncloistered orders of the Roman Catholic Church, as part of larger reforms dictated by Vatican II in 1962, relinquished religious habits for secular fashions. Many had worn habits for a large portion of their lives, often between 20 and 35 years, dressing in them from the moment they arose in the morning until they retired in the evening. Their social identities were more outwardly visible than their personal identities, as they had relinquished individuality for social control of their bodies by the Church. From the time that women religious first wore religious attire as

novices, they were instructed to view themselves not as individuals, but as representatives of a group. Their habits symbolized their commitment and vows to the Church, which superseded their individual identities (Griffin, 1975). (See Figures 12.4a and b.)

Prior to Vatican II, which occurred in 1962, many women in noncloistered religious orders came to view the habit in a more negative than positive light. Their perception was that this dress communicated a social identity that inhibited their ability to express personal identities that would allow them to function more fully in secular environments. The habit clearly symbolized their total commitment to their order, but they described it as a social control in their ability to interact and communicate freely as individuals. As described by women in this study, the habit made them feel less than fully human.

Ebaugh (1977), in her research on religious orders, confirmed that the Church did not address personal identity issues prior to Vatican II. She describes the indoctrination of women

Original for this text.

FIGURE 12.4 *Sisters of Providence dressed in (a) modified habit and (b) full habit.*

religious as demanding ideological totalism (Lifton, 1961). In her research, she discussed the mechanisms of social control that made totalism work. The symbolic gesture of exchanging secular dress for black religious garb was "the first symbolic gesture of 'putting off the world' and entering into a new life" (Ebaugh, 1977):

> The uniform was characterized by complete simplicity and modesty, being high-necked, long-sleeved, and ankle length. In addition to the uniform, feminine lingerie was exchanged for simple white cotton underwear, indicating that the postulant was exchanging her womanly enjoyments for austere dress that would now symbolize her as the spouse of Jesus Christ. In addition, henceforth the woman was no longer to be distinguished by dress from the other women in the institute with whom she would live.

Historically, the habit did not start as a symbol of religious life; rather, it was the widow's dress of the day. In the case of the Sisters of St. Joseph, it started with six women in France in the seventeenth century, who went out two by two to minister to the needs of the people (Aherne, 1983). They wore modest black dresses and veils, because women who were widows were allowed more personal freedom than those who were single or married. They could travel without male chaperones. These women were able to circumvent both church and state regulations. This early "habit" was a protection, in a sense, and it allowed them to be free to do the work they wanted. Some of the women in this study felt that, prior to Vatican II, the Church saw the habit as a protection against the "evils of the world." The voluminous layers of black serge and veiling covering their bodies, heads, and necks cloaked both femininity and sexuality. In the eyes of the women in this study, it also suppressed their personal identity. Ironically, whereas the "habit" had historically begun as a way of achieving autonomy, this type of dress had evolved into a way of suppressing personal identity, through the social control of their bodies. It is important to bear in mind that the women in this study did not leave religious orders after Vatican II; rather, they had remained as members and had negotiated their identity within the boundaries of the Church. They negotiated some social control issues with the Church symbolically by discarding the habit for secular dress.

The women in my study dressed in contemporary fashions that made them indiscernible from any other modestly dressed professional woman in American society. Some orders like their members to wear some visible indication of their affiliation as women religious, such as a ring or cross (Ebaugh, 1993), but many of the women in my study did not. As stated above, prior to Vatican II, many women in noncloistered religious orders came to view the habit in a more negative than positive light. Their perception was that dress inhibited their ability to have positive social interactions as people; rather, they were frequently stereotyped by the symbolic nature of the habit. The habit visually symbolized and promoted interactions with others that reinforced this belief.

> Interviewer: If you were sitting there in a habit, I would feel differently. I would feel a little more inhibited, more cautious, more formal.
>
> Respondent: Your experience is the other end of what I'm trying to describe to you about coming out of habit.
>
> Interviewer: You are talking about it being an inhibition for you—an inhibition in social interaction?
>
> Respondent: Yes, it was—because immediately when people saw us, they didn't see us as the individual that you were. They saw you as the woman religious, and they immediately raise you above the human level. We had privilege and prestige, and we were considered to be in a holier state of life. That's not true. I've chosen another way to

live, but it is not a holier way—it's a different way.

At the present time, the work and lifestyles of women religious in active orders are highly liberated in contrast to the period prior to Vatican II. When the habit was relinquished, social control of the body by the Church decreased. For example, today women exhibit a high degree of personal autonomy, many living alone or in small groups instead of orders, fully integrated into the noncelibate lay community (Ebaugh, 1993). Dress, in light of many social changes for women religious, has been critical in not only reflecting, but also helping them to construct social change, specifically by its role in symbolic interaction processes related to the formation and perpetuation of personal identity.

EMERGING FROM THE HABIT: FASHION AND SECULAR CLOTHING

After Vatican II, which was a period of emerging personal identity, the women experienced profound conflicts surrounding dress and its complex relationship with their vow of poverty. The essence of the vow of poverty of spirit is humility, which is facilitated by material poverty (Metz, 1968). The habit had come to be accepted as a visible symbol of humility, while fashion and cultural issues of women's appearance, such as makeup and hairstyle, were historically associated with worldliness and materialism (i.e., fashion). Yet, women religious found themselves visibly reentering the secular world from the perspective of appearance. Because of their vow of poverty, there was little money for clothing. Most of their post-habit attire came as hand-me-downs or from thrift shops or sales.

The following quote is from a woman religious who worked in a career in women's clothing sales for 13 years prior to entering religious training. She expresses ambivalence about her love of clothes:

> I maintained my ability over the years [while in habit] to be a very good shopper. I would go

to Steigers [Department Store]—the girls [clerks] would really get to know me. Many of them I had known throughout the years, and they would know when the bargains were coming in. I became a shopper for several other people, especially in the early days [of transition from habits]. Now I struggle tremendously. I have far too many clothes. I'm good for a while but I have to keep looking. Someone else might not see me as a person that has a lot of clothes.

The habit had obscured visible markers of womanhood, such as the hair and figure. In my interviews, much discussion focused on the personal discomfort and even trauma of reemerging into secular society. Skills related to personal appearance had to be relearned. Hair was discussed frequently as the focus of anxiety. After years of deprivation from air and light under the habit, hair loss was common. In this interview segment, a woman religious discusses her personal viewpoint on hair:

> Respondent: I saw older women buying wigs who had lost their hair because of the habit.
> Interviewer: Was that because of rubbing?
> Respondent: Yes, and also because they didn't get air. Even at night they wore caps.
> Interviewer: Was this a permanent hair loss?
> Respondent: Yes, for some. But for some it was OK [it grew back]. I color my hair. It's something I do for myself. In the 1960s we began to do a lot of more personalized and psychological study of ourselves. The spiritual was always part of it. How can you separate the spiritual and emotional? It's holistic.

The habit had given women religious surprising freedom from the tyranny of appearance experienced by women in North American culture. Women religious were confronted with issues of body weight that had previously been obscured under the folds of black serge. Some women interviewed went on diets. Their awareness of style and fashion became evident. Women made personal choices about makeup,

jewelry, modesty issues (e.g., length of skirt, neckline) and even hair coloring. The move to secular dress had a dramatic impact on both women religious and society in general. "It revealed to the world in general the human being underneath the habit. But more important, it revealed the nun to herself: It was an experience in recognition" (Griffin, 1975).

Women emerged from habit during the turbulent period of the Civil Rights Movement, the Vietnam War, and the Women's Movement. Whether in habit or not, women religious are known for their involvement in social causes. Several women in the study referred to themselves as feminists, noting that historically they were role models for women who chose lives of dedication rather than marriage and family. Women religious also acknowledged their identities as single, professional women, and their continuing conflicts with the patriarchal structure of the Vatican. They have been active participants in social activism and the dual labor market of the parish, where they have frequently, despite achieving higher education than priests, been denied positions of authority and participation in aspects of the liturgy.

Their emergence from habit to secular fashion not only reflected gender controversy within the Church, but also helped women construct new identities as educated and professional women religious, rather than cloistered icons of the Church. Two women in my study referred to identities of women prior to Vatican II as "women of service" or, more derogatorily, "handmaids of the Church." In a symbolic feminist action after Vatican II that coincided with elimination of the habit, many women religious dropped the male component of their chosen names and reassumed the female. The names of male saints who possessed desirable virtues were assigned to the women by their Mother Superior before the women took their final vows:

> There was something else going on…we were changing our clothes and we were also changing our names. It didn't happen like Friday and Saturday, but it happened that we just kind of rebelled against having men's

names—Sister Mary Peter, Sister Mary John, Sister Mary Bartholomew. Many women religious were moving out of their dress identity, and they were changing their names back. All that was happening at the same time.

Discarding the habit was perceived by the women in this study as a positive step toward allowing them to work and interact as human beings while interpersonal distance lessened. In a positive sense, the Church, prior to Vatican II, had viewed the habit as a protection against the evils of the world, yet that caused many women religious to perceive themselves as isolated and inhibited from mingling with the people. The women's bodies were restrained and controlled by the Church within the confines of the habit. Women religious in this study perceived secular dress as essential in allowing them normal, daily, human interactions, which greatly enhanced their ability to provide social service within the community. They symbolically reclaimed their bodies as they discarded the habit:

> From 1983 to 1987, I was in Kentucky in Appalachia. I could never have done down there in the habit what I did in my [secular] clothes. It would have been an absolute impossibility. My freedom would have been restricted. I was living in a county where there were only 30 Catholic families. I didn't go in as a Sister, I went in as a person named Mary.

THEORETICAL ISSUES

Symbolic interaction theory asserts "that the self is established, maintained, and altered in and through communication" (Stone, 1962). Stone widened the perspective of symbolic interaction studies to include appearance as a dimension of communication, usually the precursor to verbal transactions. Furthermore, Stone asserted that appearance is a critical factor in the "formulation of the conception of self" (Stone, 1962). Appearance establishes identity by indicating to others what the individual projects as his or her "program" (i.e., one's social roles of gender, age, occupation). In turn, these are "reviewed" by others, thereby validating or challenging the self (Stone, 1962):

> It [identity] is not a substitute word for "self." Instead, when one has identity, he is situated—that is, cast in the shape of a social object by the acknowledgment of his participation or membership in social relations. One's identity is established when others place him as a social object by assigning him the same words of identity that he appropriates for himself or announces. It is in the coincidence of placements and announcements that identity becomes a meaning of the self and often such placements and announcements are aroused by apparent symbols such as uniforms. The policeman's uniform, for example, is an announcement of his identity as policeman and validated by others' placements of him as policeman.

Stone (1962) describes identity as being established by two processes, apposition and opposition, a bringing together and setting apart. "To situate the person as a social object is to bring him together with other objects so situated, and, at the same time to set him apart from still other objects. Identity, to Stone, is intrinsically associated with all the joinings and departures of social life. To have an identity is to join with some and depart from others, to enter and leave social relations at once."

In contrast to Stone, Goffman (1963) defines personal identity as "the assumption that the individual can be differentiated from all others." From an interactionist perspective, this was a real dilemma for some women religious in habit. Their dress clearly symbolized their total affiliation to their work in the order, but was described by them as "restricting" in their ability to interact and communicate freely. The consequences of these symbolic limitations led to a paradox described by the women as causing them to "feel less than fully human."

Davis (1992) addressed the concept of ambivalence and appearance more directly than other symbolic interactionists who preceded him.

He argued that personal identity announcements and social identity placements might not be congruous. For example, a person might dress as a police officer for a costume party and be incorrectly identified as someone who is actually responsible for law enforcement. Davis (1992), maintaining that dress serves as "a kind of visual metaphor for identity…registering the culturally anchored ambivalence that resonates with and among identities," suggests that personal and social identity incongruity occurs regularly because dress is often an ambivalent form of communication. Davis (1992) is broadly interested in dress and its symbolic relationship to identity, but more specifically, he discusses his theories within the framework of fashion. Davis defines fashion by distinguishing it from style, custom, conventional or acceptable dress, or prevalent modes by stressing the importance of the element of change. While the term "dress" communicates elements of stability, use of the term "fashion" implies the added element of social change (Roach-Higgins & Eicher, 1993).

A symbolic interaction perspective emphasizes social process and meaning(s) and is relevant for explaining how and why these women negotiated their visual and verbal awareness of their appearance (Kaiser, Nagasawa, & Hutton, 1995). When the women emerged as visible females from the self-described "androgyny"[1] of how they felt in the habit, identity conflicts surfaced. Davis (1992) described how dress serves as "a kind of visual metaphor for identity…registering the culturally anchored ambivalences that resonate with and among identities." Ambivalence is acknowledged by Davis (1992) to be natural and integral to human experience and can be exhibited in symbolic issues of appearance.

The dialectic of the women's physical bodies, symbolized by their dress, to the social body of the Roman Catholic Church is a critical one in understanding the power of dress in both reflecting and constructing social change for women religious. For example, both Marx (1967) and Durkheim and Mauss (1963) argued for the dialectic between the "natural" and "social" body. Other social scientists have viewed the body as the *tabula rasa* for socialization. Van Gennep (1960), Mauss (1973), Bordieu (1977), and Douglas (1966, 1970) have argued this dialectic to demonstrate the social construction of the body.

Conclusion

This study of women religious provides a model for examining how changes in enduring modes of dress such as habits can be examined not only in relation to the more predominantly held view of changing social roles, but also from the perspective of personal identity. The relationship between dress and social change must be carefully examined, as with women religious, by examining their relationship to social roles, issues of social and personal identities, and their mediation through the symbol of dress.

Davis (1992) uses the term "fault lines" to describe "culturally induced strains concerning who and what we are" that find expression in dress. Vatican II certainly created an enormous quake for women religious, but the forces of change within orders ultimately came from the women themselves in the form of human agency. Women religious were poised and ready to address issues of roles, identities, and social change.

Note

1. Some women in the study used this word to elaborate on how they felt when wearing a habit. This is not my choice of words. The term "androgyny" is derived from the Greek words "andro" (male) and "gyn" (female). Heilbrun (1964) uses this term to define a condition in which the characteristics of the sexes and the human impulses expressed by men and women are not rigidly assigned. Therefore, the term may be more closely associated with perceptions of identity than solely with characteristics associated with physical appearance.

References

Aherne, M. C. (1983). *Joyous Service: The History of the Sisters of Saint Joseph of Springfield.* Holyoke, MA: Sisters of Saint Joseph.

Bordieu, P. (1977). *Outline of a Theory of Practice* (R. Nice, trans.). Cambridge: Cambridge University Press.

Davis, F. (1992). *Fashion, Culture and Identity.* Chicago: University of Chicago Press.

Douglas, M. (1966). *Purity and Danger: An Analysis of Concepts of Pollution and Taboo.* Washington: Frederick Praeger.

Douglas, M. (1970). *Nature Symbols.* New York: Vintage Books.

Durkheim, E., & Mauss, M. (1963). *Primitive Classification* (R. Needham, trans.). London: Cohen & West.

Ebaugh, H. (1977). *Out of the Cloister: A Study of Organizational Dilemmas.* Austin: University of Texas Press.

Ebaugh, H. (1993). *Women in the Vanishing Cloister.* New Brunswick, NJ: Rutgers University Press.

Goffman, E. (1963). *Stigma: Notes on the Management of a Spoiled Identity.* Englewood Cliffs, NJ: Prentice Hall.

Griffin, M. (1975). *Unbelling the Cat: The Courage to Choose.* Boston: Little, Brown.

Heilbrun, C. (1964). *Toward a Recognition of Androgyny.* New York: Alfred A. Knopf.

Kaiser, S., Nagasawa, R., & Hutton, S. (1995). Construction of an SI theory of fashion: Part 1, ambivalence and change. *Clothing and Textiles Research Journal,* 13(3): 172–183.

Lifton, J. (1961). *Thought Reform and the Psychology of Totalism.* New York: Norton.

Marx, K. (1967). *Capital: A Critique of Political Economy,* 3 vols. New York: International Publishers.

Mauss, M. (1973). Techniques of the body (B. Brewster, trans.). *Economy and Society,* 2(1): 70–88.

Metz, J. (1968). *Poverty of Spirit.* New York: Paulist Press.

Roach-Higgins, M., & Eicher, J. (1993). Dress and identity. *ITAA Special Publication #5.*

Stone, G. (1962). Appearance and the self. In A. Rose (Ed.), *Human Behavior and Social Processes: An Interactionist Approach,* pp. 86–118. New York: Houghton Mifflin.

Van Gennep, A. (1960). *The Rites of Passage* (M. B. Vizedom & G. L. Caffee, trans.). Chicago: University of Chicago Press.

DISCUSSION QUESTIONS

From Habit to Fashion

1. Uniforms (such as a nun's habit) make the wearer easy to identify, but can also create barriers that make accessibility to that person difficult. Can you think of other examples of a uniform dress that create the same effect?

2. Describe the origin of the nun's habit and what freedoms and/or restrictions were placed on the wearer at the time of its origination.

79 Muslim Doll Offers Image of Modesty and Self-Esteem

At first glance, this new girl on the block doesn't give Barbie much of a run for her money. After all, Barbie is everything Razanne is not—curvaceous, flashy and loaded with sex appeal. But that's exactly why many Muslim Americans prefer Razanne, with her long-sleeved dresses, head scarf and, by her creator Ammar Saadeh's own admission, a not-so-buxom bustline.

For Saadeh, the doll not only fills a marketing void but also offers Muslim girls someone they can relate to.

"The main message we try to put forward through the doll is that what matters is what's inside you, not how you look," said Saadeh, who set up NoorArt Inc. with his wife and a few other investors.

The Livonia-based company, founded about seven years ago, sells the Razanne doll [see Figure 12.5] and a number of other toys geared toward Muslim children.

"It doesn't matter if you're tall or short, thin or fat, beautiful or not, the real beauty seen by God and fellow Muslims is what's in your soul," he said.

Razanne has the body of a preteen. The doll comes in three types: fair-skinned blonde, olive-skinned with black hair, or black skin and black hair.

Her aspirations are those of a modern Muslim woman. On the drawing board for future dolls are Dr. Razanne and possibly even Astronaut Razanne. There's also Muslim Girl Scout Razanne, complete with a cassette recording of the Muslim Scout's oath.

What sets Razanne apart from her few competitors is that she "holds a global appeal for Muslim girls," Saadeh said. That image encouraged Mimo Debryn, of West Bloomfield Township, to buy the doll for her daughter, Jenna, four years ago.

"Razanne looks like the majority of women around Jenna," said Debryn. "She loves that doll

FIGURE 12.5 *Razanne doll offers Muslim girls a modest alternative to Barbie.*

and always took care of her, giving Razanne a special place in her room, treating her with respect.

"Jenna never tried to take Razanne's hijab (head scarf) off, though Barbie was usually stripped naked," she said as her daughter, 11, curled up on the couch and smiled.

RAZZANE: NO MOROCCAN BARBIE

In the United States, Mattel, which makes Barbie, markets a Moroccan Barbie and sells a collector's doll named Leyla. Leyla's elaborate costume and tale of being taken as a slave in the court of a Turkish sultan are intended to convey the tribulations of one Muslim girl in the 1720s.

"It's no surprise that they'd try to portray a Middle Eastern Barbie either as a belly dancer or a concubine," said Saadeh, adding that countering such stereotypes was one of his main aims in developing Razanne.

Mattel didn't respond to repeated calls seeking comment.

Laila, the Arab League's answer to Barbie, offered girls of the league's 22-member states a culturally acceptable alternative to Barbie's flashy lifestyle. But she never made it to store shelves. Sara and Dara were launched a couple of years ago—Iran's version of Barbie and her beau, Ken. The two were offshoots of a children's cartoon in Iran.

But Saadeh said those dolls are more "cultural and don't have mass appeal in the Middle East."

Saadeh hopes to capture that market. Razanne will soon be marketed in Kuwait, the United Arab Emirates and make greater inroads in southeast Asia.

30,000 SOLD PER YEAR

The doll is sold throughout the United States, Canada, Singapore and Germany. Saadeh would not reveal the doll's sales figures, but he said retail sales over the company's Web site account for a majority of the almost 30,000 dolls sold per year.

Prices range from $9.99 for a single doll to $24.99 for a set like Teacher Razanne that includes a briefcase and other accessories.

Saudi Arabia's religious police recently declared Barbie dolls a threat to morality, complaining that the revealing clothes are offensive to Islam.

Saudi Arabia and other Middle Eastern countries likely would be attracted to Praying Razanne, who comes complete with a long hijab and modest prayer gown.

Lest people think that she's all about praying, there's In-Out Razanne, whose wardrobe also includes a short, flowery dress she can wear inside the home, in view only of men in her family.

"Razanne represents to Muslim girls that they have options, goals and dreams and the ability to realize them," said Debryn.

Jenna, who recently donned the veil after much soul-searching, said Razanne makes her "feel more comfortable about being a Muslim girl."

DISCUSSION QUESTIONS

Muslim Doll Offers Image of Modesty and Self-Esteem

1. This article is critical of Mattel's Barbie and states that the Muslim doll, Razanne, emphasizes that what matters is what's inside you, not how you look. How does this square with the idea that dress is a powerful communicator? With the message that during a job interview a decision will be made within the first 30 seconds?

2. By implication, what does the article lead you to believe about Barbie? What's inside of her? What messages does Barbie send to young girls?

3. Why might Razanne be commercially successful when the "Just Like Me" doll a few years back was not?

CHAPTER 13

Dress and Technological Change

Kimberly A. Miller-Spillman

AFTER YOU HAVE READ THIS CHAPTER, YOU WILL COMPREHEND:

- The variety of ways technology is used in the image industry.

- How military technology can be used for humanitarian purposes.

- The variety of innovations within the wearable electronics market.

- Ethical issues and technology.

Change is inevitable, especially in fashion. In this chapter we observe the many effects that new technology has on dress and fashion. For example, as the population in the United States grows older, more techniques are developed to keep people looking younger. Botox injections, anyone? How about liposuction or stomach stapling? Technology makes changing the body a futuristic experience compared with a method that was recommended in 1896 (see "Concerning the Ear," Box 1 in Chapter 2). Since young people have grown up with technology, they expect more and more technological gizmos to make life easy and convenient. In addition, most all humans want to change something about their appearance. Short people want to be taller, flat-chested women want to be bustier, and photos of models on the covers of fashion magazines undergo extensive computer retouching. This desire to improve on what nature gives us is called a **cultural universal.** One would be hard pressed to find a culture in any geographic area or in any period of time that did not make changes to the body (see "The Enigma of Beauty" in Chapter 2 for cross-cultural examples).

In this chapter we tie technology to issues of individuality and conformity. For instance, as Western television programs are exported to remote places, women begin to request cosmetic surgery and develop eating disorders in attempts to approximate the Euro-American ideal.

Also in this chapter, we will see how the Internet is changing the way fashion is distributed by bypassing the traditional department store. Technology can affect our lives in strange and unexpected ways. Heightened security at airports after terrorist attacks on September 11 resulted in businessmen who wear high-end footwear being stopped repeatedly for setting off security alarms. And last, several companies are working together to move us into the future of wearable electronics. Consumers, especially younger ones, who want to remain mobile *and* "connected" may be interested in a jacket that contains a personal area network, or PAN, for supporting all those electronic gadgets (see Figure 13.1). Technology is a moving target, and as technology changes, so does fashion.

IMAGE-DRIVEN TECHNOLOGY

Technology that is developed for the purpose of "improving" the body is **image-driven technology.** In other words, it is technology that is driven by the desire to attain a certain image. Breast augmentations and reductions, face-lifts, and nose jobs are a few examples. Those who want to conform to an ideal image use technology. For example, Cindy Jackson has had several surgeries in her personal quest to look like Barbie (see Figure 13.2). Other types of image-driven technology include computer photo retouching to make beautiful models look even more beautiful and Internet technology used to obtain exclusive designer clothes long before they reach department stores.

What is the motivation behind image-driven technology? It can be the desire to be either an individualist or a conformist. "**Individuality in dress**" is an awareness of the norm and a desire to set one's self apart from it (Horn, 1965). Technology can be used to express one's individuality, such as playing music downloaded

FIGURE 13.1 *This $900 ICD+ (Industrial Clothing Division Plus) jacket comes equipped with an MP3 player, cellular phone, headset, and a remote control device.*

Before   After

FIGURE 13.2 *Cindy Jackson in the 1970s before numerous plastic surgical procedures to become* "Barbie" *and again in 2000.*

from the Web from a jacket while snow skiing (Latour, 2000). Conversely, "**conformity in dress**" is the acceptance of or adherence to a clothing norm, or dressing in accordance with the norm of a specified group (Horn, 1965, p. 146). Latin-American women who request plastic surgery to look like a "big-busted, small-nosed variation on the traditional California girl" are using technology to conform to a Euro-American body ideal (see "Bodies à la Carte").

An individualist can buy hot new designer clothing from eBay (see "Chic at a Click"). Early adopters, who want tomorrow's fashions today, can get the latest designer clothes from eBay months before the same designs appear in their local department stores and boutiques. This practice of being the first to obtain the latest designs via the Internet has the potential to radically change the way fashion is distributed and marketed.

Traditionally, designers presented their latest designs on the runways of Paris and New York. Amid all the marketing hype surrounding runway shows, consumers were left salivating until the actual items appeared in stores months later. The Internet has the potential to change that age-old tradition. Now, a small portion of a designer's line can be accessed on the Web in as little as ten days following its runway debut. In addition, eBay representatives serve "eBay-tinis" and provide online shopping tours to socialites and trendsetters as an add-on to the traditional runway show.

There is a downside to this new development, however. Isaac Mizrahi's first attempt at fashion failed for many reasons, but one was how quickly his designs could be posted on the Internet and effectively knocked off (see "The End of Fashion" in Chapter 11). The knockoffs of Mizrahi's designs reached the public long before Mizrahi's *real* designs. Today, Mizrahi is back with a line of clothing at Target stores and an exclusive made-to-order business for movie stars, gala goers, and other women who will pay $10,000 for a dress (Heller, 2003). As Mizrahi notes, more and more people are mixing designer fashions with items from K-Mart and Target ("Cheapskate Chic," 1999). This practice, known as demi-couture, is a new and creative way to wear designer originals. But the bottom line is that distributing designer fashions via the Internet has a formidable impact on the world of fashion.

Chauvin et al. take a hard look at Latin-American women and their requests for plastic surgery. Once the *New England Journal of Medicine* declared silicone implants safe, Latin-American women ran to plastic surgeons in droves, demanding a procedure that just three years prior was rarely requested. The authors of "Bodies à la Carte" provide us with a cross-cultural look at plastic surgery and the spread of the Western ideal of beauty. This homogenization of "beauty," in which one rejects one's own beauty to acquire another's definition of beauty, is the issue at hand.

Jones, in his article titled "The Height of Vanity," tracks young Chinese women as they pursue their dream of being four inches taller. Height in Chinese society equates with beauty and power. However, the process is extremely painful and does not always deliver good results. But the quest must be important to those who are willing to endure the pain and risk of infection for an additional four inches of height. Chinese women are not the only ones using this surgical procedure: a woman from Ohio who suffered social alienation because of her dwarfism underwent this procedure to gain seven additional inches of height (Parker, 2004).

MILITARY TECHNOLOGY USED FOR HUMANITARIAN PURPOSES

When it comes to the creation of new technology, who foots the bill? Technological advances are due in part to university professors who successfully convince large corporations to fund their research. But more likely it is the U.S. military or the space program that deserves credit. Both the space program and the military are often considered expensive programs to run, and taxpayers often complain about paying the bill. One justification for these programs is that the items that are invented as a result enhance people's everyday lives. Can you imagine life without Velcro? We can thank the space program for that one.

"Cutting Edge Humanity" is an article about cosmetic surgery for humanitarian purposes and the use of technology developed for the U.S. military. Besim Kadriu was 21 years old and a student in economics when part of his face was destroyed by a bullet during the Kosovo war. The authors of this article craft an engaging story about a young man, his desire to live, and the technology that replaced what a bullet once removed.

TECHNOLOGY VERSUS TRADITION

Tradition in all fields has a habit of slowing things down. The terms *Western* and *non-Western* are often used interchangeably with *industrial* and *non-industrial* and create boundaries between cultures that embrace technology and those that do not. Cultures are often described by their level of technology. Think of the Egyptian pyramids and the roads and bridges engineered by the ancient Romans. In the apparel industry, one can create a technology continuum with a back-strap loom on one end and computer-operated industrial looms on the opposite end. What one gains in speed and standardization with computer-operated looms, one looses in creativity and variation of handmade items. Colores del Pueblo is an Internet business that helps Latin-American artisans benefit financially from their skills rather than loosing profit to an intermediary (www.coloresdelpueblo.org/index .htm).

Is tradition gender-specific? Women in most Third World countries are considered more traditional than men. Women are often the last to give up their traditional dress and their cultural traditions. As a matter of fact, "women's work" invokes images of slow, repetitive, low-tech labor that takes place in the home while women tend children. "Men's work" invokes images that are fast paced, high production, and high technology. Although not all Third World countries divide labor between the public sphere (male) and the private sphere (female), many do (Barnes & Eicher, 1992).

Tradition is naturally resistant to innovation, and technological change is not always embraced with open arms. For example, a specialty shoe market—toe shoes for ballet dancers—is battling it out between the traditional Capezio and the new Gaynor Miden (Conley, 2002). The Capezio Pointe shoe has all of the characteristics that ballet dancers have counted on for many decades. The new Gaynor Miden Pointe shoe has newer materials, is more comfortable, and costs less to use than the traditional Capezio. However, in the ballet world, where the dancer who suffers the most for her art is considered "best," tradition is not just rolling over and playing dead: it's fighting back.

Golden, author of "Socked by Security," focuses on customer satisfaction in another specialty footwear market—high-end men's footwear. An unexpected consequence of the terrorist attacks on September 11 and the resulting heightened security at airports was the sound of shoes setting off security alarms. Businessmen who travel for a living and wear expensive shoes were repeatedly inconvenienced by security stops. The culprit was a metal shank. Plastic shanks are also used in men's shoes, but are considered inferior by the purists who believe that metal gives the wearer the most support. Metal shanks are the hallmark of conservative footwear companies that have been in business over 100 years, and the controversy to change the shank material from metal to plastic has been a controversial one.

Even the apparel industry is resistant to change. Susan Watkins details two processes, heat sealing and molding, as possible alternatives for the American apparel industry (Watkins, 1995b). Some of these processes have been around since the 1950s and were perfected after initial endeavors. These processes, which are practiced in European apparel industries, are time-efficient and economical. However, adopting these processes would mean changing the way clothing is designed, produced, and marketed in the United States. The American apparel industry evidently is not ready for these changes. Another example of this industry's resistance to change is the fact that most American women are a size 14 or above, yet the apparel industry continues to make clothing that looks good on tall, slim figures.

WEARABLE ELECTRONICS MARKET

Nanotechnology is the science of making electronics as tiny as possible. When nanotechnology companies partner with apparel companies, you get the development of wearable electronics. Everything you can imagine—and probably a few that you can't—

has been tried or is in the process of being tested (see "Ready-to-Wear Watchdogs"). From clothes that "talk" to washers, telling the washer how the garment should be cleaned, to a global positioning system woven into a jacket collar to track a wandering child or an Alzheimer's patient, wearable electronics can do amazing things. There's clothing that adjusts to your changes in size, clothes that change color to match another garment in your closet, children's sleepwear that sounds an alarm if breathing stops, gym suits made in fabrics that absorb odors and can be worn three or four times without offending other exercisers, and fiber-optic wedding dresses or disco trousers that sparkle.

Clothing for specific needs has been the segment of the apparel industry to accommodate consumers outside of the mainstream (Watkins, 1995a). Astronauts, firefighters, handicapped individuals, and elderly individuals are a few examples. Any specialized occupation, such as football players, motocross riders, hockey players, individuals employed in the microchip manufacturing industry, and underwater divers, could fit under the broad umbrella of clothing for specific needs. "Smart" spacesuits can monitor an astronaut's condition. This sophisticated and expensive technology is slowly trickling down to consumers who are willing to pay $200 for a T-shirt (or running bra) that monitors heart rate, body temperature, respiration, and number of calories burned and can warn the wearer of potential heart attack or heat stroke.

ETHICS AND TECHNOLOGY

Ethical issues arise when new technologies are developed. As digital technologies are developed, individuals who work in the image industry must decide how far they will go with it. In the article "The Man Who Makes the Pictures Perfect," Mr. Dangin says that putting an actress's head on a stylist's body would be similar to human cloning and he would not do it. Yet legs are lengthened, thighs are trimmed, and eye color is enhanced routinely in the world of glossy magazine covers. Is it ethical to publish photos that are retouched to the point that they no longer look like the actual model? Is it ethical to promote those images as "real" to young girls who may decide to start severe dieting to be as slim as the models on magazine covers? Mr. Dangin believes that we all want glamour and fantasy, and, besides, the pictures are not reality anyway. They're just paper. But how many young girls know that these aren't real? How many girls can separate an image on a magazine cover from reality? Just because we have the technology to do something, does that mean we *have* to use it? On the other hand, there are resources to help young girls discuss ideas related to the body. Ogle and Thornburg (2003) looked at body-related content of a Web magazine for girls called *Girl Zone* and concluded that the site does offer girls a proactive strategy for coping with beauty ideals and is a model for media that target teens in a socially responsible way. Given the limited options of healthy body images available through popular media, more alternative resources such as *Girl Zone* may help young girls to separate the glamour from reality. Ethical issues are often difficult to resolve. Ultimately, each individual must decide what is in bounds and what is not.

Another ethical issue confronts eBay shoppers. What if you unknowingly buy a counterfeit item off eBay? If that were to happen to you, eBay would reimburse you up to $175 through their insurance program and often you can get more through your credit-card issuer. eBay is doing its best to remove items when they receive complaints from brandholders. But counterfeit items could potentially become a problem when newly minted designs are being offered (see "Chic at a Click").

Ethical issues arise when any licensed medical specialist can legally practice plastic surgery after a few days of training (see "Bodies à la Carte"). Ethically, one would like to know that the person about to perform plastic surgery on her body is competent and well educated about the procedure. There is also an ethical issue related to the type of appearance Latin-American women are choosing. Latin-American women, we are told in the article "Bodies à la Carte," consistently choose a "Nordic fantasy" when requesting plastic surgical procedures. The article refers to this phenomenon as "cultural colonization," or the practice of devaluing your own culture's definition of beauty for another's.

Ellen Goodman (2001) was angered by pharmaceutical companies that produced and marketed drugs to help people lose weight. For people who are more than 30 pounds overweight, a drug that can help you lose weight sounds too good to be true. Unfortunately, it *was* too good to be true, and several people died from taking a drug touted by companies that were aware of the fatal side effects. The pressure to conform to society's standard of slimness evidently enticed obese individuals to try a drug that was not safe.

Summary

Technology and dress is an enormous topic with many avenues for innovation and ethical concerns. Many recently developed innovations are for the purposes of looking—and feeling—young. But technology can also be put to use for humanitarian purposes when victims of war need cosmetic surgery to rebuild a face and a life. Many innovations are in the works that join nanotechnology and clothing or wearable electronics. All new technologies come with ethical issues. The decision of whether to use a new technological procedure or when to use it centers on ethical issues.

Suggested Readings

Conley, K. (2002, December 9). Pointe counterpointe. *The New Yorker*, 69–70, 72–73, 76, 79.

Goodman, E. (2001, June 20). Better dead than fat? Women are targets for foolish choices. *The Des Moines Register*, 13A.

Harris, G. (2003, December 7). If shoe won't fit, fix the foot? Popular surgery raises concern. Accessed August 19, 2004, at www.nytimes.com.

Hatcher, M. (2002, October 8). Fiber-optic dress goes down the aisle. Accessed October 8, 2002, at optics.org/articles/news/8/10/11/1.

Kalb, C., Hayden, T., Figueroa, A., Downey, S., Sieder, J. J., Lauerman, J., Pierce, E., & Roberts, E. (1999, August 16). Our quest to be perfect: Upi don't have to be wrinkled or rich to go under the knife. *Newsweek International*, 32+.

McLaren, L. (2000, July 8). Stretch city. *The Globe and Mail* (London), R17–R18.

Parker, G. (2004, February 14). Woman endures surgeries to lengthen limbs. Netscape News. Accessed March 12, 2004, at search.netscape.com.

Sagario, D. (2001, October 15). Now I lay thee down: Device helps shape skull. *The Des Moines Register*, 1E–2E.

Dress and Technological Change

Objective: Debate ethical concerns related to dress and technology and find the most current information on wearable electronics.

Procedures

1. There are several issues in this chapter that have no clear-cut "right" answer. Having students argue for a position, and then asking them to later argue against the same position, helps students master debating skills.

   To get students thinking about an issue, after they have read and/or discussed an article in the chapter, ask them to make two lists in their notebooks, one a list of reasons in support of a position and the other a list of reasons against the same position. Have students call out the reasons on their lists as you compile a list on the board for all of the reasons in support of and all the reasons against a position. This should facilitate class discussion and make it easier for students to voice their opinion on a given topic.

   Repeat the above procedure several times early in the semester on different issues to encourage students to participate in class discussions. After several of these exercises, move the class exercise to a more formal level of a mock, in-class debate. Ask half the individuals in a class to prepare a debate in favor of a position while the other half of the class prepares a debate against the same position. Announce this exercise and assign positions during the first class meeting of the week and ask students to be prepared by the last class meeting of the week to debate the issue in class. If possible, arrange desks so that students on opposing sides are facing one another.

   Several possibilities for this type of debate are listed below:

   Mr. Dangin regarding photo retouching states that "This is the world we're living in. Everything is glorified. I say live in your time."

   "I need this surgery (i.e., face-lift, nose job, leg lengthening) in order to keep my job or to secure a life partner."

   There is something terribly ironic about women from Latin America wanting to acquire the look of their North European counterparts.

   "I am willing to tolerate a little inconvenience in order to be safe" versus "I want my favorite shoe manufacturer to replace the metal shanks in my shoes with plastic ones."

2. Do a computer search to find out what is currently available in the "smart clothing" market. Use the following terms or a combination of terms to search for current information:

ICD+	Smart garments
Levi-Strauss	Nanotechnology and clothing
Philips NV	Wearable electronics
Technology and clothing	Smart fabrics
Luminex	Textronics
Fiber-optics and dress	DuPont and smart garments

References

Barnes, R., & Eicher, J. B. (Eds.). (1992). *Dress and Gender: Making and Meaning.* Oxford: Berg Press.

Cheapskate chic. (1999, June 11). *The Wall Street Journal,* W1, W14.

Colores del Pueblo. Accessed March 15, 2004, at www.coloresdelpueblo.org/index .htm.

Conley, K. (2002, December 9). Pointe counterpointe. *The New Yorker,* 69–79.

Goodman, E. (2001, June 20). Better dead than fat? Women are targets for foolish choices. *The Des Moines Register,* 13A.

Heller, Z. (2003, March). Movin on up. *Vogue,* 554–561, 593.

Horn, M. (1965). *The Second Skin.* Boston: Houghton-Mifflin.

Latour, A. (2000, September 3). Full wired jacket. *Lexington Herald-Leader,* E1.

Ogle, J. P., & Thornburg, E. (2003). An alternative voice amid teen 'zines: An analysis of body-related content in *Girl Zone. Journal of Family and Consumer Sciences,* 95(1):47–56.

Parker, G. (2004, February 14). Woman endures surgeries to lengthen limbs. Netscape News. Accessed March 12, 2004, at search.netscape.com.

Patel, S. (2003, April). Extreme beauty: Five other incredible treatments. *Marie Claire,* 10(4):98.

Watkins, S. M. (1995a). *Clothing: The Portable Environment* (2nd ed.). Ames: Iowa State University Press.

Watkins, S. M. (1995b). Stitchless sewing for the apparel of the future. In M. E. Roach-Higgins, J. B. Eicher, & K. K. P. Johnson (Eds.), *Dress and Identity,* pp. 270–274. New York: Fairchild.

80   Bodies à la Carte: Passionate for Pulchritude, Latin American Women Are Reshaping Their Form through Plastic Surgery

Lucien Chauvin, Andrew Downie, Uki Goni, Christina Hoag, and Dolly Mascarenas

There are shortages, and then there are shortages. In January, in the middle of Brazil's prime beach season, torrents of women suddenly started showing up in the plastic surgery clinics of Rio de Janeiro and Sao Paulo, demanding an operation that was hardly asked for just three years ago: breast augmentation. [See Figure 13.3.] They wanted bigger busts, and they wanted them now. "It was crazy," says Celia Accursio, a Sao Paulo plastic surgeon who sits on the board of Brazil's Association of Aesthetic Medicine. "People were saying, 'I want the operation done tomorrow.'" Doctors were caught off guard. They frantically called manufacturers seeking extra supplies of implants—to no avail. "Some surgeons had to postpone operations," recalls Accursio. "I'd never seen anything like it." Swept away in a passion for pulchritude, Brazil was hit by its first-ever breast-implant crisis.

Working overtime, manufacturers conquered the short-term demand, but Brazil—indeed, all of Latin America—was given a dramatic warning. Suddenly women are demanding new bodies as never before. [See Figure 13.4.] A craze for aesthetic surgery—on breasts, noses, thighs, eyes, buttocks and everything in between—has been sweeping the region, bringing women (and a smaller percentage of men) to the plastic surgeon's clinic in unprecedented numbers. From the dusty border towns of Mexico to the capitals of the Southern Cone, long lines of patients are forming, people from all walks of life and every level of social status, eager to improve their appearance, their image, their self-esteem—all at the hands of the body sculptors.

The frenzy is democratic: it infects not only the minority of middle-aged, upper-class women who have traditionally turned to plastic surgery but also their young daughters, their middle-class neighbors and even their family servants, who are lining up at clinics in poorer neighborhoods for cut-rate body-sculpting available on a layaway plan. The era of the mass production of appearance is at hand, and Latin America is welcoming it with a smile (chemical peel optional) and open arms.

Like many other phenomena of mass culture, the surgery craze has a strong component of American show biz. As they elect aesthetic surgery, Latin women of all ethnic and racial backgrounds are overwhelmingly choosing

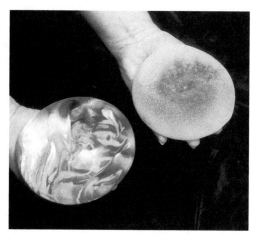

FIGURE 13.3 *Silicone breast implants used in enhancement surgery.*

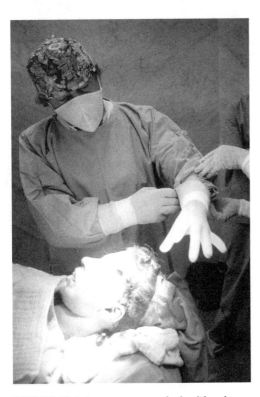

FIGURE 13.4 *A surgeon prepares for face-lift and rhinoplasty (nose job) surgery.*

denly pneumatic Argentine model who formerly had the perfect long, whisper-thin figure that used to be a porteno favorite—before the breast boom. Gomez had enhancement surgery last year. "I am very happy now," she says.

Whether it spreads joy or alarm, the body-shaping trend is a boom that is still growing, and Brazil is at the forefront. Home to one of the world's best and most well-known plastic surgeons, 1960s pioneer Ivo Pitanguy, Brazil has for decades been a mecca for international jet setters seeking a discreet nip and tuck. But then, according to the Brazilian Association of Plastic Surgeons, something more dramatic began to happen. Between 1996 and 1999, the number of plastic-surgery procedures in Brazil jumped 50%, to 300,000. And whereas in the U.S. about two-thirds of all plastic surgery is reconstructive, performed on accident victims and other afflicted people, in Brazil a full 60% is aesthetic, devoted only to changing the body image.

The craze has been accompanied by a full-scale media blitz. New hair! New nose! New breasts! New tummy! New bottom! DON'T MISS CARLA PEREZ'S NEW BODY! screamed the cover of Brazilian Playboy last December. It was the second Playboy cover to feature the singer-TV hostess, and the second in a row to celebrate the debut of a newly enhanced chest. (November's cover featured dancer Scheila Carvalho, who told a reporter that her new breasts were like "two new twin boys—I never get tired of looking at them.") On TV, people from superpopular talk-show host Xuxa Meneghel to Vera Fischer, a soap-opera siren since the 1970s, have talked openly about the body-work they have had done. A small forest of new magazines with names like Plastic and Beauty, devoted to the wonders of plastic surgery, now blare from newsstands. No wonder Juliana Borges, this year's Miss Brazil, seemed startled when her revelation that she had had 24 surgeries—from a tummy tuck and breast implants to mole removals—brought forth an international media storm last May. "All I did was improve a little bit," she explained to ABC News. "Many girls do it."

one look: a big-busted, small-nosed variation on the traditional California girl. "It's Barbie," says Venezuelan beauty-queen trainer Giselle Reyes, who works with the team that prepares the country's international beauty queens. "Baywatch," agrees Argentine celebrity surgeon Jorge Panate. Either way, it's a Nordic fantasy transplanted to the southern parts of the hemisphere.

To Roberto Briceno-Leon, a sociologist who heads the Social Sciences Laboratory Research Center in Caracas, it's cultural colonization. "It's a devaluation of ourselves, putting a higher value on what comes from abroad," he says. But to the women who choose it, it's the reconstructed look rather than its deconstructed meaning that counts. "I was quite flat and missing a womanly attribute I wanted to have," says Florencia Gomez, 21, a sud-

So true. But just as significantly, Brazilian women are usually choosing new bodies with a radically new shape. Traditionally, the ideal feminine figure was deemed to be the guitar-shaped, Sonia Braga outline, with curvy hips and a smaller bust. Call it the Girl from Ipanema look. But today more than a third of all aesthetic surgeries are breast enlargements, turning the guitar into an elongated hourglass—shades of Pamela Anderson. "It's only in the past two years that implants became something to be desired," says Margaret Figueiredo, commercial director of Silimed Silicone e Instrumental Medico Cirurgico e Hospitalar, the Brazilian subsidiary of a U.S. implant manufacturer. Silimed is the only implant maker in Latin America, and supplies two-thirds of the gel-filled orbs that go into Brazilian chests (the other third are imported items). For the company, business is booming. In 1999 Silimed sold 18,000 pairs of implants. It expected to produce about 22,000 in 2000, but demand was so high that the firm manufactured 28,000—a 55% increase—and projects a 40% increase in production this year.

Figueiredo sets the beginning of the big-breast frenzy at November 1998, when the New England Journal of Medicine published a much-heralded article on the health effects of silicone breast implants that declared them safe. One big inhibition to change was lifted. But it's hard to separate that development from another that swept Brazil the next year: the sudden, explosive fame achieved by Brazilian supermodel Gisele Bundchen.

Born and raised in the small town of Horizontina, about 400 km northwest of Porto Alegre, curvy Gisele did not fit the traditional-figure stereotype. Indeed, she had initially been shunned even by U.S. fashion designers as being too top-heavy to wear their clothes to advantage. But within two years of coming to New York City, Gisele had changed the walkway aesthetics of the entire fashion world. After triumphant turns on the Manhattan, London, Milan and Paris catwalks in 1999, Gisele was the model of the moment—and curvy was in.

At home, Brazilians justifiably proud of Gisele's success took note and started dialing for doctors. By March 2000, as Carnaval season

rolled around, change was already in motion. On the glittering floats of Rio's samba schools, the Baywatch babelicious look had won pride of place. Later nicknamed the "Silicone Carnaval," the Rio samba-school parade that year made a star of Angela Bismarchi, 27, a plastic surgeon's wife who showed off her husband's extensive work by painting her enhanced breasts and lipo-suctioned tummy the colors of the Brazilian flag and wearing just a tiny pubic pastie. Mammary mia! The race to the clinic was on.

For all the exhibitionistic benefits, economic anxiety may play a role in the body-shaping trend as well. In the U.S., the number of minor plastic-surgery procedures done on middle-aged professionals went up during the recession of the early 1990s. In Latin America, where economies have been more volatile, photographs are commonly attached to resumes, and newspaper ads for everything from secretaries to accountants demand a "good appearance." Thus in uncertain times, honing one's looks may seem even more necessary. "I had a face-lift in my 50s because my job requires that I look the part," says the 70-year-old editor of a Mexican women's magazine. "I don't think anyone noticed."

Inside the doctor's office, changes were also under way that fed the craze. Dr. Pablo Hidalgo-Monroy, who has been practicing in Mexico City for more than 10 years, credits the growing popularity of 1990s "cosmetic medical" procedures like skin-clearing dermabrasion and doses of Botox (which erases wrinkles by temporarily paralyzing facial muscles responsible for frowning) for stimulating demand for body shaping. "Those procedures make plastic surgery seem less foreign, more everyday," he says. "And once a patient is on the table for a chemical peel, she feels more comfortable asking me, 'Doctor, what can I do about these jowls?'"

Discussion of "lunchtime quickies" at the clinic became staples in women's magazines and brought an ever-younger group of women to the surgeons for a touch-up. "A few years ago, people had plastic surgery to remove either ugliness or old age. Now it is to remain young and vibrant," says Raul Lopez Infante, a well-known surgeon who practices at Mexico City's plastic-surgery pinnacle, the Hospital Angeles del Pedregal.

These less invasive procedures made the business more attractive to medical practitioners looking for new streams of income. Legally, almost any medical specialist can train to perform many cosmetic procedures in just a few days, and patients usually pay for them in cash. One sign of the increased supply of clinics is a drop in prices for nips and tucks. In 1980, for example, an Argentine matron could expect to pay around $30,000 for a face-lift—the cost of a small apartment in Buenos Aires. Today the same operation would cost $4,000 or less, with about half going into the surgeon's pocket after expenses. But even at these prices, plastic surgery brings in big bucks. Taking out an appendix, by contrast, carries a fee of only about $300, and the surgeon might wait months before getting paid by the patient's insurance company.

Of course, $4,000 is still a hefty price for the majority of Latin Americans to pay. So some doctors have found ways to lower the cost even more. In San Juan de Miraflores, a low-income district of Lima, busy Pachacutec Avenue is lined with the offices of low-cost doctors and dentists who do plastic-surgery procedures. And then there is the Miami Center, a clinic offering liposuction for $500 and nose jobs for $120. "The price is negotiable, and we have plans for people to pay in monthly installments," says Elvira Moreno, a medical assistant at the center. She says the no-frills clinic sees about 30 patients a month, mostly for rhinoplasty and breast enlargements.

Dr. Julio Daniel Kirschbaum, president of the Plastic, Reconstructive and Cosmetic Surgery Society of Peru, says this low-cost care is not necessarily of lower quality. "If you work out of San Juan de Miraflores, you have a much lower overhead than in other areas," says Kirschbaum, who runs an exclusive surgery center in the San Borja district of Lima. "Many people confuse price with quality, and one really has little to do with the other." Rich patrons have figured that

out. In Rio, where Pitanguy—still practicing at 74—and his students offer at-cost or free cosmetic surgery at the Hospital Geral da Santa Casa da Misericordia, medical personnel will occasionally discover a middle-class patient hiding out in the crowd, hoping to score good work cheap.

For the wealthier patient, modern plastic surgery offers safer, less invasive procedures that give better results with less obvious scarring. Doctors can now lift a patient's buttocks—even place implants—and leave a mark so small that it will be well covered by any tanga. Ten years ago, getting breast implants left a patient on her back for weeks. Now the surgery requires only seven to 14 days of recovery before stitches are removed. And Latin American doctors have been in the forefront of the surgical advances. "Many techniques you see in the U.S., especially in reducing the amount of scarring resulting from these operations, originally came from Latin America," says Dr. Thomas Biggs, a Houston plastic surgeon and president-elect of the International Society of Aesthetic Plastic Surgery.

To cite just one example, take the technique known as yensie, which uses a patient's muscles to lift breasts without the use of implants. Dr. Manuel Enrique Chacon, President of the Costa Rican Association of Plastic Surgery, invented it. At the annual convention last May of the American Society for Aesthetic Plastic Surgery, an entire Manhattan hotel ballroom packed with doctors was silent as a specialist described a minimally invasive face-lift technique that left only a few small scars deep within the patient's hairline. "Latin American surgeons think of surgery as an art form," says Renato Saltz, a Brazilian-born surgeon who was taught and practices in Utah but regularly visits colleagues in his native country. This year he presided over the first ASAPS convention symposium ever to focus exclusively on work being done outside the U.S. (Latin Americans made up almost half of the presenters.) "I think they are maybe more creative than those in the U.S. or in Europe," says Saltz. "They are less restrained by fear of lawsuits."

But the same freedom that can lead to creativity on the part of a good surgeon can be deadly in the hands of a bad one. In Latin America, a patient often has little redress for faulty or substandard work, and professional supervision is rare. In Argentina's health ministry, health-resources inspection director Dr. Jorge Antoniak is frustrated at having only 26 full-time health inspectors to monitor the entire medical industry, including an estimated 1,300 surgeons—many of them originally trained in other specialties—who perform cosmetic operations. "Doctors do not require any special title or authorization to practice plastic surgery in Argentina," he says. "Any licensed doctor can legally carry it out." Antoniak is also frustrated by a lack of concern for malpractice and fraud on the part of Argentina's legal system. "At one point my office tried to clamp down on a number of plastic-surgery clinics advertising impossible results," he says. "We were unable to obtain a single conviction from the courts." This despite high-profile cases like that of Argentine model Raquel Mancini, who slipped into a coma during liposuction at an unlicensed clinic in 1996 and, after she recovered, never fully regained her career.

The problem is well recognized elsewhere in the region. Mexico, where 1,038 physicians are certified to perform plastic surgery, has an extensive system of regulation. Yet problems still exist, says Dr. Hector Arambula, president of the Mexican Council of Plastic, Aesthetic and Reconstructive Surgery: "Mainly they come from having other specialists trying to do plastic surgery—gynecologists, ear, nose and throat specialists, even dentists and dermatologists." The problems can be even more severe in the continent's backstreet beauty parlors where crude surgery is sometimes practiced. In Lima in 1999 a mother and daughter died from having silicone gel injected directly into their breasts. A hairdresser was convicted of homicide for performing the procedures.

Those well-publicized tragedies haven't deterred consumers a bit. A recent international poll found that the biggest fear about plastic surgery in the U.S. was that something would go mortally wrong in the operating room, while Latin Americans were most afraid they wouldn't get good-looking results. Despite the concerns of sociologist Briceno-Leon, no political party has taken up the antisurgery cause, and there is no widespread debate about the diversion of scarce medical talent from the basic health requirements of a region in urgent need of more and better care.

For the most part, people are content to sit back and enjoy the results. Even surgeons like Brazil's Celia Accursio see all the slicing, pulling, tucking and stitching as "simply fashion. Today, getting implants is banal. It's as if women are going to the hairdresser and getting a different hairstyle." Right now the style is tres, tres bouffant.

DISCUSSION QUESTIONS

Bodies à la Carte

1. Do you think that plastic surgery in the U.S. will ever be regarded as a mundane, everyday occurrence as is already the case in Latin America? Or have Americans already reached that point?

2. Are plastic surgery procedures in your past or in your future? Why or why not?

3. What do you think about the cultural colonization of the Latin-American body type in favor of a "Nordic fantasy" (i.e., big bust,

small nose, Barbie look)? Do you think everyone should have the option to choose a Nordic fantasy? Or do you think people should instead value the beauty they already possess? Give reasons to back up your answers.

4. Does it seem odd to you that Latin-American women would choose to look like Northern European women? What does this do to cultural diversity in the world? Will we all look alike someday?

Won't that be boring? Or will it make interacting with others easier? Give reasons to back up your answers.

5. What are the ethics involved when a medical professional who received a few days of training performs cosmetic surgery for cash or a convenient layaway plan? If it takes months to be reimbursed for taking out an appendix for $300 and cosmetic surgery pays cash at time of procedure, do you see any ethical issues?

81 Chic at a Click: eBay Fashions a Deal with Designers

Shelly Branch and Nick Wingfield

Tomorrow night, when models are set to mount the runway for hot designer Narciso Rodriguez's Fashion Week show, they'll also be doing a bit of tacit marketing for eBay, the online-auction powerhouse.

That's because eBay, a sponsor of Mr. Rodriguez's show, says it has gained dibs to a few dozen items from the designer's fall and spring collections. And unlike the department stores and boutiques that must wait for months to receive their spring orders, eBay says it plans to auction off the chic cache Sept. 25, with Mr. Rodriguez as the seller.

Though the auction is petite—about 40 items—the arrangement between Mr. Rodriguez, a fashion celebrity, and eBay opens up tantalizing possibilities for the future of fashion distribution and marketing. It's also a testament to eBay's rising clout as a purveyor of clothing and accessories. Mr. Rodriguez, 42 years old, didn't return numerous calls for comment.

Launched less than three years ago, eBay's "clothing, shoes & accessories" category now ranks among the top five fastest-growing niches for the company, and is on track to handle more than $1.3 billion in sales this year. By means of comparison, Tiffany & Co. does $1.7 billion at its 120 stores world-wide.

Meanwhile, online high-fashion pioneer Bluefly.com grew its revenue by 33% in 2002, but has yet to end losses. The landscape for Bluefly.com and others won't get any easier: With more than a million fashion items up for sale at any given time, eBay now ranks as the No. 1 fashion Web site in terms of unique visitors and page views by Nielsen//Netratings.

"EBay realized it was becoming an important fashion player in a grass-roots way, so now it is taking more aggressive steps to ensure that it is an important player," says Constance White, a former fashion journalist who holds the new eBay title of style director.

On a typical day, the site logs 53,000 keyword searches for "Louis Vuitton" and 34,000 searches for "Prada." Kate Spade, Coach and

Manolo Blahnik are other favorites. Rarely available items, such as Hermes Birkin bags, have lately been flooding the site, too. Average asking price for the elusive French tote: $10,000.

The existence of counterfeit fashion goods on eBay is a concern, but the auction house hasn't been deemed liable in courts for the sale of fakes. Nevertheless, the company says it's doing its best to prevent fraud by removing listings for questionable items when it receives complaints from brandholders. In many cases, shoppers who unknowingly buy counterfeit goods can get reimbursed for as much as $175 through an eBay insurance program or more through their credit-card issuer.

EBay's fashion thrust comes as online sales in general, and apparel sales in particular, gain traction. Online apparel sales for the month of July rose 44% from last year, to $500 million, according to Internet ratings service comScore Media Metrix. Marketing consultants Forrester Research predict that online sales will jump 19% a year in the coming five years.

EBay's fashion sense represents another potential blow to beleaguered department stores. "It adds to the competitive pressures that they are facing," says Frank Badillo, senior retail economist for the consulting concern Retail Forward Inc., of Columbus, Ohio. "Department stores have to prove they are more than a collection of brands, which is why they are offering more private-label clothes." Mr. Badillo says the growth in eBay apparel sales is part of the larger surge of shoppers using the Internet to find the lowest price.

Based in San Jose, Calif., eBay has been working behind the scenes for its fashion debut, including meeting with the Council of Fashion Designers in New York. The session this past summer, says eBay, was meant to get the group's unofficial blessing to solicit designers for partnerships like the one it arranged with Mr. Rodriguez. Last month, eBay hired Ms. White to help it make contacts in the fashion world, as well as edit a new online style magazine.

This week, eBay representatives are stationed at New York's Bryant Park tents, where Fashion Week is being held. They are serving up special cocktails called "eBay-tinis" and are offering online shopping tours to socialites and trendsetters. EBay also purchased a four-page ad in the current issue of Vogue. "Department stores don't have a department just for you," says the copy.

Unlike the used collectibles that made eBay famous, more than half of the site's fashion goods are brand new: a sign that wholesalers and designers, and not just individual sellers, are taking seriously eBay's fashion might.

Ms. White says eBay has been well-received so far on Seventh Avenue and is optimistic that it can get designers to look beyond regular retailers and to sell a fraction of their collections online.

EBay is redesigning its fashion Web pages to make them more attractive and user-friendly. Visitors, for instance, now can search for goods by size and color, and condition. To lure the likes of Mr. Rodriguez, eBay plans to promote designers on its site. It also refers them the services of an auction manager, who, for varying fees, can coordinate payment collection and shipping. For each item, eBay takes a commission of roughly 5% to 8% of the selling price. Even at the high end of the scale, that's a bargain for most designers. Apparel vendors typically sell their wares to stores for about half of retail value, and often grant sizeable credits or "markdown money" to stores when items don't sell well.

Apparel sellers note that the sheer size of the eBay audience—the company's sites have more than 75 million registered users—is compelling. Immediately after the terrorist attacks of Sept. 11, 2001, Alessandro Mitrotti saw business plummet in his Manhattan designer showroom, Transfer International. So Mr. Mitrotti began emphasizing, with greater luck, sales on his own Web site and on eBay.

"It's almost like a fisherman—you cast your net out and the next morning reel it back and see what you've caught," Mr. Mitrotti says. His online offerings often are unsold merchandise from such department stores as Barneys New York and Saks Fifth Avenue, he says. Other items, worn only a few times, come from runway models.

Chic at a Click

1. What effect do you think selling designer fashions on the Internet will have on the foundation of the fashion business? Does selling their items on the Internet undermine a designer's business? Or does it enhance a designer's business/credibility/visibility?

2. In your opinion, will the department store and their private label clothes always have a place (for instance for technophobes) regardless of the popularity of Web sites such as eBay? Why or why not?

3. Have you ever bought or sold an auction item on eBay? Have you ever bought clothing or accessories online? Why or why not?

82   The Height of Vanity

Richard Jones

In a hospital ward in the southern Chinese city of Guangzhou, patients with large metal frames attached to their lower limbs lumber around slowly leaning on metal crutches for support. Most of them are women; all of them are dreaming of being taller. [See Figure 13.5.]

Fortunately for them, their dream can become reality, thanks to cosmetic surgery that actually increases the body's length. When a 16-year-old British girl named Emma Richards—who wanted to be taller so she could land a job as a flight attendant—had the operation recently, she made headlines in the European press. But in China, the reaction is much more likely to be a shrug.

"There have been at least 600 operations like this. Probably more," says Dr. Liu Bin, a surgeon who performs leg-lengthening surgery on several patients each week. "If we could reach out to more people, then I'm sure it would be much more popular."

For Chinese women, the pressure to be tall invades all aspects of life. Chinese society equates height with beauty and power. Many image-driven companies place height require-

ments on hiring; so do entire branches of the Chinese government (the Foreign Ministry, for example, requires would-be female diplomats to measure at least 5'3"; males, 5'7"). This bias is even more striking socially: Personal ads in the newspapers often include minimum heights.

Leg-lengthening surgery is big business for a select number of doctors who advertise on TV and in magazines, charging an average of $10,000 for the full treatment. This price is by no means cheap: The average Chinese family grosses only $4300 a year.

"If I ever wanted to change my job, it would help if I were taller. A tall girl is always more welcome in a job interview," says a 26-year-old patient named Miao, sitting on her hospital bed. She traveled over 600 miles from her native Chongqing in central China to have the surgery after seeing an ad in a beauty magazine. "Before I read the magazine, I felt as if I had no hope at

Reprinted by permission of Richard Jones/Sinopix.

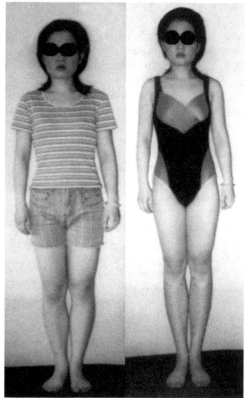

Before   **After**

FIGURE 13.5 *Before (4'9") and after (5'1") photos document the results of leg-lengthening surgery. Leg-lengthening operations are painful and require a recovery period of one year.*

all," she says. "When I saw that advertisement, I saw my future."

"THE PAIN IS UNBEARABLE"

According to Dr. Liu, Guangzhou is "the world center for height-increasing operations," home to hundreds of operations every year. But while surgeons such as Dr. Zhang Yi Qing blandly label the procedure "routine," a better word

might be grueling. A team of five surgeons must spend three hours intensely sawing, drilling, hammering, and grafting. A hole is cut into the patient's leg just below the knee joint, and the bone is sawed in half. "This is the point of bone regeneration," Dr. Zhang explains, pointing to his handiwork on X rays spread out on a light table.

A long metal pin, called a "locked nail," is then inserted into the bone cavity. The nail is banged into position with a metal hammer, and then the frame is secured around the leg. Several holes are then drilled through the patient's leg and into the bone. Finally, the frame is adjusted to force the bones apart and stretch the skin, muscles, and nerves.

This surgery is the longest and is followed by two others: The first, six months later, is a procedure to remove the metal frame, and, once the bone has completely regenerated after a year-and-a-half, a second operation removes the nails.

Leg-lengthening surgery was actually first introduced in 1951 to treat patients whose legs had naturally grown to different lengths, or to fix broken bones that had grown back crooked. Back then, the surgeons didn't use nails, so patients were forced to lie in bed for over a year, waiting for their bones to regrow and strengthen. Today, they are able to walk around after 10 days, the nails acting as temporary bones.

Miao has spent more than six months in the hospital so far. She used to be just over five feet tall and has thus far been stretched to 5'3", growth she confesses was achieved through a lot of agony. "The pain is very hard to take," she says, rubbing her legs. "It was unbearable at the beginning. And now, as my legs have stretched, the pain has come back. I rarely sleep for more than two hours at a time." But mental strain and boredom are the biggest burdens, "much, much, worse than the physical pain. This is a big change to the body, and it affects the mind. One girl down the hall cries all night. She cannot take it."

Miao does two hours of exercises a day, one in the morning and one in the evening, mostly on a stepping machine. She sits in bed massaging her bones and stretching for most of the day.

She also adjusts the frames on her legs three times daily, for maximum lengthening impact. "On a good day," she says, "I can stretch myself by about half a millimeter."

"THIS IS OUR SECRET"

Women who undergo leg-lengthening almost always do so secretly. And many go to extreme measures to hide their secret.

Soong Ling, who lives on the outskirts of Guangzhou, is at the hospital today for a checkup following her operation four months ago. Desperate to increase her 4'9" frame by four inches, the 22-year-old didn't even tell her husband she was having the surgery. "I knew he didn't really want me to have it, so I just did it while he was away on business," she says. "He was really mad when he found out."

Ling says she had the operation because she was jealous that her husband, a tour operator, was always mixing with the "tall and beautiful girls" in the travel industry, who are mostly ex–flight attendants. The extra inches, she says, will increase her self-confidence.

Similarly, Miao, who has now been away from Chongqing for almost six months, lied to her boyfriend, telling him she had taken a new job in Guangzhou. It's common in China to work a long way from home, so he believed her.

"Luckily, he is quite busy and cannot afford the time or the flight to visit," she says.

Her mother, who shares a room in the hospital with her only child, borrowed the $20,000 for the operation. (The cost of Miao's operation is twice the average because her mother is living with her in the hospital during her recovery.) And she is fully complicit in her daughter's subterfuge. "This is our secret," she says. "We're not going to advertise it. It will help with her future. We will be able to pay back the money when she gets a better job. She's very clever, and this will make all the difference."

With few outside visitors and year-long recovery times, rumors and speculation regularly surface in the ward. Miao says there has been gossip that the leading surgeon is so busy that he only operates on one of each patient's legs himself. "Most of the girls say their legs feel very different. Before the operation, my legs used to feel balanced, but now, they feel different and unequal," she says.

Indeed, while doctors crow about a 100-percent success rate, the truth is far different. Surgical complications are a frequent occurrence.

Ling's operation did not go smoothly: The frame infected her leg and created a lot of seeping pus. Antibiotics cleared up the infection in a month, but Ling had to endure several weeks of bedridden pain. Going into the surgery, Ling's only concern was the slight scars it could leave; now, she's realizing that the full implications of her operation were far more complex—and risky. Recently, she found out that one of her legs is now slightly longer than the other.

"Perhaps my husband was right," she says. "At the moment, I regret it."

DISCUSSION QUESTIONS

The Height of Vanity

1. Jones states in this article that "Chinese society equates height with beauty and power." Is it the same in the U.S.? Why or why not?

2. In your opinion, is the amount of pain endured in this surgery and the one year of recovery time worth four more inches in height? Why or why not?

3. If increasing one's height can help you land a job and even a husband—both related to quality of life issues—can leg-lengthening surgery be labeled as vanity? Or should it be labeled as practical?

4. According to Sejal Patel (*Marie Claire*, 2003), the current fashion for crop tops has resulted in women in the U.S. requesting umbilicoplasty, a 90-minute procedure in which an "outie" belly button is put back "in." Other procedures include adding depth or giving a round belly button a more vertical look. Would you be willing to spend $3,000 to $5,000 for one of these procedures? Why or why not?

83 Cutting Edge Humanity: With the Help of Digital Photography and the Internet, Caring Surgeons Rebuild the Face of a Kosovo War Victim

Jonathan Margolis

Thursday April 29 last year, a rainy day in Kosovo, should really have been the last of Besim Kadriu's short life. That morning in the Albanian sector of the town of Mitrovica—a town once again torn apart by communal strife—Serb paramilitaries torched the house the 21-year-old economics student shared with his pregnant wife, Valbona. Watching the inferno from a distance, Kadriu was confident Valbona had escaped Mitrovica, but was unsure where she had fled. He set off on foot for the village of Zaza, a few kilometers away, on a hunch she would be with her two brothers, who lived there. She wasn't, but a large number of armed Serb militiamen were. They were closing in on Zaza just as he arrived. For the second time in a day, Kadriu was facing death.

Thugs in balaclavas surrounded the village in three concentric rings, moving inward to trap the inhabitants in much the same way that small game animals are sometimes hunted in the Balkans. Knowing they were prime targets, Kadriu and a few of the other young men in Zaza tried to escape. They managed to slip through the two innermost cordons undetected.

But as they attempted the third, they were spotted. One of Kadriu's brothers-in-law was shot dead on the spot. Four other men surrendered and were never seen again. Kadriu and the other brother-in-law made a run for the woods. The brother-in-law was shot in the leg but kept running and survived. Kadriu felt a bullet sting his face, fell to the ground and played dead.

The Serbs may have believed they had killed him, or simply have thought it unnecessary to waste any more bullets on the young man. Much of the right side of the face of their previously handsome victim, including his entire nose and right eye, had been removed by the shot. What was left of him resembled a medieval gargoyle after centuries of erosion.

At nightfall, several hours after the Serbs had left, Kadriu ran to the forest and hid. Although he felt nauseated and could sense blood running down his face, there was no pain from the wound. He touched the destroyed area and, in his state of shock, thought the bony sensation was damaged teeth. He realized things were much worse only when he explored the inside of his mouth with his fingers and found it was intact.

A strong-minded, pragmatic man, Kadriu resolved immediately to avoid glimpsing any reflection of himself in puddles left by the rain, even though he needed them to drink from during the 48 hours he remained in the woods. For his psychological survival, this was probably a good tactic. So grotesque were his injuries that when he finally judged it safe to return to Zaza he went unrecognized. People scurried from him in horror until he produced a photo he happened to have in the back pocket of his jeans. It showed him and Valbona smiling for the camera a few months before, at Christmas 1998, days after they had married.

Besim Kadriu still keeps that photo in his wallet as a lucky charm, for while many people would opt for death rather than disfigurement, he considers himself a fortunate man. For one thing, a couple of centimeters further back and that Serb bullet would have hit his brain, destroying his mind as well as his looks. For another, he was reunited with Valbona and survived for three months in the care of relatives—without disinfectants or antibiotics, his only treatment being changes of gauze bandages, when they could be found. He was still avoiding mirrors when troops of the KFOR peacekeeping force arrived to provide some less rudimentary first aid. But luckiest of all—and thanks to the efforts of an American charity doctor and a British military medic with a bag full of electronic gizmos and an Internet connection—Kadriu's face has now been rebuilt by surgeons in Manchester, U.K.

Besim Kadriu thus became one of the first civilian beneficiaries of military telemedicine, the use of digital technology in treating war injuries beyond the scope of army field surgeons. Thanks in no small part to the Internet, he and Valbona are now living in Manchester awaiting the final cosmetic work on his face before resuming life in Kosovo. In the crib in their small apartment is their new daughter, born two days before Christmas.

Telemedicine is a variation on the tradition of referring difficult cases to a specialist—the difference being that the specialist doesn't see the patient, only e-mailed photos of him. With a digital camera, a laptop and a GSM phone wielded by a doctor in the field, the specialist can be across the world, viewing high-definition photos of a wound inflicted perhaps only minutes earlier. It was such technology that made the link between an act of butchery in a meadow in Kosovo and one of medical mercy in a hospital in Manchester.

Before the technology, however, came philanthropy. In June 1999 Dan Clay, a California emergency room physician, set up a clinic in Kqiq, on the outskirts of Mitrovica, for the International Medical Corps, a charity based in Los Angeles. Kadriu soon heard about the new American clinic and, with his wound covered by a gauze pad, went to see "Dr. Dan."

Like every doctor who was later to meet the young man, Clay was shocked by the wound. But he recognized that it was far beyond his expertise to treat. "When I first saw Besim across the room with a large bandage over his 'eye,' I assumed I would be seeing a corneal abrasion or the like," says Clay, now back at the rural St. Helena Hospital in Deer Park, Calif. "But nothing could prepare a doctor for what lay beneath the gauze. I've spent half my career in ERs in some of the most violent cities in America, seen all kinds of mangled human beings, but I've never come across anyone still alive carrying such a horrific injury as Besim."

"I sent him to the Pristina Hospital, knowing full well that what he needed was beyond the capabilities of its surgeons," says Clay. "They, of course, returned him with a suggestion that he be referred for treatment abroad. Unfortunately the channels for such a placement are a bureaucratic obstacle course and were overwhelmed in any event." Clay knew that the recommendation doomed a 21-year-old man to a life with a cruel disfigurement, but "I also knew that I had become his only hope, as I was not prepared to accept that unthinkable notion. So in June, I started face shopping, talking to every KFOR medical officer and every MASH unit I could find, hoping that one would know of a bored plastic surgeon somewhere, or perhaps get as emotionally involved in Besim's case as I was."

Clay soon found a committed colleague in Lieut. Colonel David Vassallo, a British army doctor who had days earlier set up the Royal Army Medical Corps' 22 Field Hospital in a former Serb army base at Lipljan, outside Pristina. Maltese-born Vassallo was equally gripped by Kadriu's plight. "He presented with a gaping hole in his face," says Vassallo, now in Bosnia. "Looking at him made me think of a horror film. To sustain that kind of injury without dying and then to wander around untreated for three months, at risk of infection, was almost impossible to imagine." Like Clay, Vassallo knew there was little he could do for Kadriu, but he's an evangelist for telemedicine, and was eager to prove that a simplified, low-cost system he had been developing with colleagues in the U.K. could work for humanitarian purposes.

The first step in securing medical evacuation for refugees, Vassallo knew, was to get influential doctors abroad so involved in serious cases that they would put pressure on their governments. But he had been unable to arouse much interest from specialists abroad by merely describing cases in letters and e-mails. Vassallo concluded he needed not words but pictures.

Such imaging technology was already in use by the U.S. military, which had been pioneering video telemedicine with hardware costing millions of dollars and requiring a team of specialists to operate. But the equipment and software that Vassallo used—a couple of digital cameras loaned by Japanese camera maker Olympus and his own Toshiba laptop—cost only a few thousand dollars. A satellite phone bought by the British army and Vassallo's account with America Online completed the package. "The principle followed throughout has been, 'Keep it simple' to ensure that the system can easily be used by doctors," Vassallo says. "I damaged the Olympus we used in

Bosnia but was able to buy a replacement [at the military duty-free store] that day. At the same time, the Americans had a whole container load of telemedicine equipment, but the technician was on leave for two weeks so they couldn't use it."

The uncomplicated British system worked. Minutes after Besim Kadriu walked into the hospital in Lipljan with Clay, Vassallo was photographing the Kosovar's ruined face and e-mailing the digital pictures to colleagues at his base at Fareham, near Portsmouth in England. At their suggestion, he e-mailed the pictures to Richard Loukota, a maxillofacial reconstructive surgeon at Leeds General Infirmary in Yorkshire. For a little added emotional pull, Vassallo copied Kadriu's wallet photo of himself and his wife before the shooting and added it to the e-mail.

Loukota was fascinated by the challenge of creating a face from such shattered remains. But he could tell by the photos from the other side of Europe that the lengthy series of operations Kadriu needed would require not only a world-class maxillofacial reconstructive consultant—a kind of superqualified dentist who rebuilds faces—but an ophthalmic surgeon to fashion something that looked like a right eye; an ear, nose and throat doctor to try to salvage what was left of his nose and build a new one around it; and an anesthetist able to keep the patient alive for the 12 hours or more at a stretch that these procedures could take. Moreover, all these professionals would have to be prepared to work on their day off, effectively as volunteers.

The photos from Kosovo were copied and recopied in e-mail from Loukota in Leeds to surgeons across Britain who had responded to a British Medical Journal article appealing for help from National Health Service surgeons for Kosovo victims. The complexities of coordinating surgeons' timetables and the bureaucracy of funding the exercise—even if the doctors worked for nothing, regional health service accountants have to pay for public hospital facilities on a pseudocommercial basis—meant that plans for Kadriu's operation began to coalesce around

Manchester, where the necessary team of specialists could be assembled more swiftly, rather than Leeds.

After Loukota, the first to volunteer to work on Kadriu was Brian Leatherbarrow, an ophthalmologist and oculoplastic surgeon specializing in artificial eyes at the Manchester Royal Eye Hospital. Leatherbarrow downloaded the images from Kosovo to his computer at home in Alderley Edge, a suburb of Manchester. "It was a very good quality image of Besim, and I printed it off and took it to the hospital, where because of stupid technical difficulties within the NHS, my computer is not linked up to the Internet," Leatherbarrow explains. "Apart from being sent the occasional photo in the post, Besim was the only patient whose deformity I have ever seen ahead of time. I can see how it would help enormously as a more common practice."

Soon after, a maxillofacial surgeon at North Manchester General Hospital, Bob Woodwards, joined the team along with ear, nose and throat consultant Prad Murphy and anesthetist Harry Vallance. "My emotional reaction when I first saw Besim was, what a tragedy this is to happen to such a nice young man," says Woodwards. "But his personality shined through all the disfigurement. And for people who practice reconstructive surgery, there's no doubt it was a challenge, a thrill really, thinking to yourself, how can we get this chap into a reasonable state?"

As the doctors were organizing their team, even the bureaucrats searching for a way to make it work were showing the kind of energy people of goodwill can muster for a good cause. The civil servants came up with a formula based on a reciprocal health care arrangement between Yugoslavia and the U.K. that had been concluded long before the war. When a British subject fell ill in Yugoslavia, he would be treated free, and vice versa. The officials declared that Kosovo was still part of Yugoslavia and the R.A.M.C. 22 Field Hospital in Lipljan was temporarily British sovereign territory, so Kadriu could be regarded as a case of a Yugoslav citizen who had fallen ill in Britain. Hospital bills would therefore be picked up by the central government rather than the local NHS, and people in Manchester would have no cause to complain that their health care was suffering because of the treatment given to Kosovo refugees.

It was a useful bureaucratic formula: after Kadriu's subsequent transfer to the U.K. by the R.A.F., the British Home Office used the same logic to bring a further 50 seriously wounded Kosovars for treatment in the U.K. Several of the patients were treated by Richard Loukota—who became so involved in those cases that in the end he was unable to take part in Kadriu's operation.

That operation was finally performed in December—a week before Kadriu's daughter was born—at the sprawling North Manchester General Hospital. It took 15 hours and involved details that sound more like makeshift engineering than surgery. First, Leatherbarrow removed the remains of Kadriu's damaged eye and retrieved its surrounding membrane, which he filled with a piece of fat from Kadriu's hip to create an eye-shaped blob with the remaining ocular muscles attached to it. It will later form a mobile platform for a false eye resembling a giant contact lens. With the machinery for the artificial eye in place, Leatherbarrow then recreated a right upper eyelid using cartilage grafted from the back of an ear and a lower eyelid with skin from the forehead.

Woodwards then took over, exposed the remaining bony parts of the patient's cheek area and screwed in a set of precision titanium plates made to his specifications by a team at University College, London. The missing mid-face soft tissue and skin were replaced with a graft from Kadriu's left forearm, complete with its own artery, which Woodwards stitched into the jugular vein and facial artery, working at times with a microscope to join blood vessels as thin as half a millimeter in diameter. The resulting gap in Kadriu's arm was filled with flesh from his groin.

Murphy, the ear, nose and throat surgeon, then fitted a titanium nasal bone and fabricated a new nose around it from part of the flap from the arm. Fortunately, the nasal passages and linings were still present in residual form, and worked normally after the operation. There was not quite enough spare flesh to give Kadriu his original Roman nose; he now has something shorter and more north-European looking.

The successful operation left a delighted Kadriu looking something like himself again, albeit with a pale flap across his face. Woodwards promises this skin from his underarm will in time become tanned and match the rest of his face—although with Manchester famed for its rain, he will need makeup for a while. Kadriu's face is still swollen and dressed, but the prognosis is that by summer, with his new eye fitted, he will look and feel well enough to go back to Mitrovica.

For the moment, living in an apartment block in Manchester occupied entirely by Kosovar refugees, Kadriu seems a happy man. Valbona tends the baby, swaddling her in Albanian style, and has a support network of other young ethnic Albanian women around her. She is still mourning her brother, who was killed on the escape run with Besim back in Zaza, but nonetheless longs to return to Kosovo.

It is clearly not easy for Kadriu to relate the details of his shooting through an Albanian interpreter, but he is measured and phlegmatic. Emotional reaction overcomes him only at certain moments. When taking a wedding photo from its frame to show visitors, a key falls out from behind the print. "This is key to house in Kosovo," he says tearfully in his newly acquired English. "Now the key is all we have. House gone."

Digital pictures of Besim Kadriu as he recovers continue to flash across the Internet, keeping the band of doctors following his case informed of his progress. A few days after Kadriu's operation David Vassallo, in England on leave, went straight to Manchester, digital camera in hand, to visit Kadriu. The photos were on the Internet by evening.

In California, Dan Clay was especially thrilled to see them. "He looks beautiful," he said. "I think I will always rate downloading those photos from Manchester as one of the greatest moments of my medical career."

Pictures are said to be worth a thousand words, but in this case their value has been far greater. They have proved to be worth a new face—and a new life—for a young man who was left for dead on a lonely field in Kosovo.

DISCUSSION QUESTIONS

Cutting Edge Humanity

1. What is your reaction to the fact that Besim Kadriu remained alive and uninfected from his wounds for three months without disinfectants or antibiotics?

2. How do you feel about technology developed by and for the U.S. military being used for a Kosovo war victim?

3. For all the money that is spent on nonmedically necessary cosmetic surgery, how does that amount compare to plastic surgery used for humanitarian purposes?

84   Socked by Security: Fancy Shoes Trip Up Business Travelers

Daniel Golden

The war against terrorism may have one unexpected repercussion for well-heeled business travelers: fallen arches.

At the Alden Shoe Co. factory here, foreman Steven Tringali broke a 118-year tradition last week when he put a thin, five-inch-long, graphite-and-plastic strip known as a shank onto the cork filler of a brown $450 wingtip. Since 1884, Alden has relied on steel shanks for arch support in its elegant shoes, made of cordovan leather from the rumps of horses. But now it was testing the reinforced plastic in a pair of oxfords made to order for Chicago venture capitalist Allan Cohen.

Mr. Cohen, who has worn Aldens since 1970, had complained that since Sept. 11, the steel shanks set off the metal detectors at the Sears Tower, where he works, and O'Hare Airport. "I'm married to Aldens," says Mr. Cohen, 55 years old, adding that they ease the pain of his arthritic big toe. "But I don't want to be taking my shoes off all the time."

By heightening airport vigilance, the Sept. 11 terrorists and would-be shoe bomber Richard Reid have roiled the $3.1 billion U.S. men's dress-shoe market and prompted a shift in high-end footwear habits. Long the hallmark of quality men's shoes, steel shanks have become their Achilles' heel—to the dismay of purists.

"I'm very skeptical," says Robert Hanney, superintendent at the Alden plant. "I still believe there's more stability in a steel shank."

"We're pretty conservative," adds Alden's president, Arthur S. Tarlow Jr. "There won't be a quick memo that we're changing to nonmetal shanks by Friday." Still, he says, "If this works, it would be fun. I'd like to waltz through security."

Mr. Reid, who was arrested when he was taken off a plane in Boston in December, sailed through airport metal detectors because he was wearing sneakers containing a plastic explosive. Nevertheless, federal guidelines urge travelers to "limit metal objects worn on your person or clothing."

Unlike vacationers in sneakers or sandals, many business travelers set off beeps—and get a subsequent going over from a security guard. Wearying of such pedal profiling, they're selecting footwear not just for fit or fashion but also for its lack of metal content.

Before the terrorist attacks, airport metal detectors were set at such a crude standard that steel shanks rarely set them off. Today, the machines are more sensitive, and more airports have installed the latest generation of detectors, which identify metal content in particular body zones, enabling them to pinpoint footwear as the culprit.

Steel shanks, which cost about 25 cents a pair, bridge the heel and the ball of the foot. Generally, casual and athletic shoes have plastic shanks or none at all.

Women's dress shoes often have steel shanks, but they're smaller than in men's shoes—and less likely to trigger the detectors, though some do. A pair of Nine West shoes worn by Deirdre Allingham, public-relations manager for Symantec Corp. in Santa Monica, Calif., set off a metal detector at Boston's Logan Airport. "It's a little embarrassing, but I don't see it as a major inconvenience. I'd rather be safe," she says.

John Shanley, a shoe-industry analyst for Wells Fargo Securities, used to buy his Johnston & Murphy shoes wholesale direct from Genesco Inc., the manufacturer in Nashville, Tenn. After Sept. 11, he got tired of being stopped at security checkpoints and running through airports to catch flights with his briefcase in one hand and his shoes in the other.

So Mr. Shanley recently bought four pairs made by Allen-Edmonds Shoe Corp., of Port Washington, Wis.—even though he had to pay retail (between $200 and $300)—because its shoes have an unusual shankless design. "I'll probably go back to Johnston & Murphy when they offer a plastic-shank shoe in my width," he says.

Allen-Edmonds's chief executive, John Stollenwerk, attributes a small portion of the company's 15% increase in revenue this year to refugees from steel. "'We don't set off metal detectors'—that could be the theme of an ad campaign," he says.

On a recent U.S. business trip, Francisco Rivero, an analyst for a Mexico City financial group, was frisked from coast to coast because of his steel-shank Cole Haan shoes, made by Nike Inc. of Beaverton, Ore. "I'll never use these shoes again to travel," says Mr. Rivero. "It's a nightmare. You have to remove your shoes, which takes extra time. Then you stand on the worn carpet, and who knows what you're standing on?"

Deluged with complaints, several high-end manufacturers are pondering plastic—formerly regarded as sacrilege. Mason Shoe Co. in Chippewa Falls, Wis., is considering a changeover to plastic in its E. T. Wright brand calfskin shoes, despite what it calls formidable retooling costs. "We're in the customer satisfaction game," says men's merchandiser Clark Woznicki. "If your customers are frustrated they have to take their shoes off when they're traveling, they may think twice about buying your product next time."

Johnston & Murphy introduced fiberglass last fall in its top-of-the-line Crown Aristocrat model, although it says the decision was made before Sept. 11, and had to do with the lighter weight and improved flexibility of the new shank. Michael Goudie, manager of its Boston retail outlet, says metal detectors are a "big issue" for customers and the new $275 shoe is selling well. Timberland Co., which specializes in more casual wear, is also replacing metal shanks with plastic, citing security hassles as a reason.

Airlines—as well as manufacturers—are eager to soothe customers. At the Delta Shuttle at LaGuardia Airport, travelers who trigger the detectors, including one woman on a flight to Boston Tuesday morning, are supplied with footstools and shoehorns. Once removed, shoes are placed on what looks like a silver platter to await screening. At America West's request, Allen-Edmonds donated 250 shoehorns for the airline's Phoenix hub.

Pilots and flight attendants, who have to clear security daily, are fed up. Whenever David Sorensen shops for boots, the US Airways pilot brings a heavy magnet—his own portable metal detector—so he can screen out those with steel.

Delta pilot Mike James says he has been "stopped and frisked enough times" to know his Rockports set off metal detectors. (A spokeswoman for Reebok International Ltd. In Stoughton, Mass., which makes Rockports, says the company is "looking" at nonmetal shanks for Rockports but prefers steel because it's "crucial in stiffening the shoe.") When Mr. James approaches a checkpoint, he takes the shoes off and puts them on the conveyor belt through the X-ray machine. Then he breezes through the detector in his stocking feet. He says he'll buy new shoes soon and is polling other pilots to find out which shoes have plastic shanks.

"I've done some research," he says. He is leaning toward Florsheims. But Thomas Florsheim Jr., chief executive of Weyco Group Inc., the parent company in Milwaukee, says it uses steel in some shoes and has had about half a dozen complaints from pilots.

Alden, which has annual revenue of $10 million to $20 million, boasts an eclectic client mix. It makes field boots for the Massachusetts

State Police and black loafers for Brooklyn retail stores catering to Hasidic Jews. It briefly tested — and rejected — nonmetal shanks a decade ago when security was stepped up during the Gulf War.

There the matter rested until Allan Cohen made a desperate bid two months ago to pass through the O'Hare detector without taking off his shoes. Thinking it might help to lower his metal level, he removed his glasses and put them in a bin rolling through the X-ray machine. But the bin toppled over, smashing the glasses. "I stewed a little bit and decided to do something," Mr. Cohen says.

Mr. Cohen is a managing director of First Analysis Corp., a private equity firm. It manages a fund that has a majority stake in Performance Materials Corp., a California maker of plastic footwear components. Mr. Cohen hooked up Alden with PMC, which provided a variety of reinforced plastic strips. At a sales meeting, Mr. Tarlow snapped one prototype in half.

But another sample survived the snap test — and went on to the factory floor. After Mr. Tringali glued it to the cork, he covered it with the outer sole. In 10 days, the shoes will be ready for Mr. Cohen's next trip through the airport metal detector.

DISCUSSION QUESTIONS

Socked by Security

1. Mr. Cohen was a demanding consumer while Ms. Allingham was willing to tolerate a little inconvenience in order to be safe. Whose position do you agree with and why?

2. Should consumers of the high-end footwear market be accommodated with plastic shanks (which is believed by the manufacturer to be an inferior product) or should these consumers be more tolerant of inconvenience for the sake of air safety for all travelers?

3. When a conservative company that has been successful in business for 120 years gets targeted by an unlikely event like 9/11, how easy is it for that company to change? Why?

85 Ready-to-Wear Watchdogs: 'Smart' Garments Keep Track of Vital Signs, Hide Odor

Susan Warren

Novelist John Jurek published a mystery, "KaeLF Skin," last fall featuring "smart fabric" underwear that can pleasure, addict, injure and even kill the wearer.

As it happens, the fiction isn't all that far from the truth.

The first generation of garments that couple nanotechnology—the science of making electronics on the tiniest of atomic scales—with high-tech fabrics to create "smart clothing" is beginning to roll out.

Motorola Inc. is working on developing clothing that can "talk" to washing machines, giving instructions on how the garments should be washed. Chemicals giant DuPont Co. and textiles concern Burlington Industries Inc. also see potential for a huge new market in clothing that looks like the same old thing but functions more like an appliance.

On the horizon: Expanding the waistline of your pants with a push of a button. Adjusting the color of a sweater from blue to green to match a favorite skirt. Tracking a wandering child through a global-positioning system woven into his jacket collar. Clothing a baby in sleepwear that sounds an alarm if breathing stops.

Last year, Burlington, of Greensboro, N.C., paid just under $10 million for a 51% stake in Nano-Tex Inc., a company using nanotechnology to engineer fabric that resists wrinkles and stays drier.

At Nano-Tex's laboratories outside San Francisco, researchers play basketball every day in the same socks, engineered with molecular-scaled sponges that absorb the rancid hydrocarbons responsible for body odor. The sponges are designed to release the smelly stuff only when they meet up with detergent in the washing machine. With this new fabric, "you could wear the same gym suit three or four times" without offending other players, says David Soane, chief scientific officer.

At DuPont, Wayne Marsh, a manager in the company's central research department, has been guiding efforts to engineer new fibers that can function as conductive "wires," as well as react to signals from electricity, heat or pressure. DuPont scientists have tinkered with the traditional circular shape of fibers to make them oval, square, or triangular. These shapes enable microscopic "wings" of different materials to be added to the core fiber, like blades of a propeller; the doctored material can then be made to contract or expand, loosening and tightening clothing, or making it warmer or cooler depending on what the wearer desires.

These fibers, already appearing in some new high-performance fabrics, will ultimately combine with electronic devices to enhance fashion as well as function. For instance, conductive, winged fibers could change the reflective quality of specially dyed fiber/cloth so that it changes color on command from an electric signal.

"The clothes that we wear might not look like the uniforms on the bridge of the Starship Enterprise, but they will be able to do the same things," DuPont product manager Stacey Burr says.

The Wilmington, Del., company hopes such research will to renew its fibers businesses.

DuPont's specialty-fibers business constituted $3.5 billion of the company's $28 billion of sales in 2000, while its slow-growing polyester and nylon businesses brought in another $7 billion. The now-tiny area of smart fabrics, or "textronics" as DuPont calls it, is considered an ideal opportunity for leveraging the company's knowledge in chemistry, textiles and electronics.

Scientists at the Massachusetts Institute of Technology are approaching smart clothing from the electronics side, trying to find ways to meld devices like phones and computers into garments. They have attracted several corporate sponsors to help fund their research, including Philips NV of the Netherlands, which last year collaborated with Levi Strauss & Co. to introduce a jacket with a built-in cellphone and MP3 player. Though briefly marketed, the system proved too cumbersome, observers say.

Last month, MIT researcher Steven Schwartz traveled to Russia to test a "smart" space suit outfitted with wearable computers. The suit, built in collaboration with Boeing Co., is designed to monitor the astronaut's condition while providing information and feedback during space walks outside the space station. Mr. Schwartz's pet project is the "smart vest"—an undergarment made with flexible conductive fibers that could be used as a kind of motherboard for plugging in wearable devices.

In New York, technology start-up Sensatex Inc. hopes to roll out an athletic T-shirt that will monitor heart rate, track body temperature and respiration and count how many calories the wearer is burning. It could even warn of a potential heart attack or heat prostration. Such a shirt might have prevented the recent death from heatstroke of football player Korey Stringer, the company says.

Sensatex moved into the "smart shirt" business after buying an exclusive license to technology developed at Georgia Institute of Technology for the military to monitor battlefield soldiers.

The company's first smart-shirt prototype is a T-shirt-like garment that looks and feels like a soft, ribbed-cotton knit. But the cotton and spandex cloth is interwoven with conductive fibers that can receive and transmit data from embedded sensors to a special receiver the size of a credit card. The "transceiver," worn at the waist, stores the information and can transmit it for playback to a cellphone, home personal computer or a wrist-mounted monitor.

Worn by an elderly person, the shirt could monitor vital signs or signal a dangerous fall. A GPS unit could locate a wandering Alzheimer's patient. Baby pajamas could be fashioned with a cellphone, so anxious parents could call home from the theater to listen to their infant's breathing, check his heart rate or even sing a lullaby.

For now, though, Sensatex says it is focusing on the fitness arena. The company's chief executive, Jeffrey Wolf, says he is working with sports organizations to test the athletic T-shirt on professional players by the end of the year. Also in the works: a version that could be used for weight-loss or fitness training. The company expects the T-shirt to sell initially for around $200.

DISCUSSION QUESTIONS

Ready-to-Wear Watchdogs

1. Since most of the new technology related to dress is expensive when it first becomes available ($900 for an ICD+ jacket and $200 for a T-shirt), how likely are consumers to purchase it?

2. Usually, technology comes down in price as more people buy it. Will it be the same for wearable electronics such as those mentioned in this article?

3. What are some of the differences between manufacturing straight technology (i.e., technology not attached to clothing) and manufacturing technology that is part of clothing?

4. Do you think male consumers will be willing to pay more for their workout suits to avoid having to wash clothes after each use?

86   The Man Who Makes the Pictures Perfect
Kate Betts

Madonna and J.Lo depend on him. Annie Leibovitz and Steven Meisel won't print a picture without him. Anna Wintour and Graydon Carter shell out many thousands of dollars a year for his services. He's arguably one of the most powerful men in fashion, but he doesn't sit in the front row or wear designer clothes, and you certainly won't find him on the Style network coughing up deep thoughts about Gwen Stefani's Super Bowl outfit.

Come to think of it, though, there is probably no one who has such a close knowledge of Gwen Stefani, down to the pores of her powdered cheek.

This behind-the-scenes magician, more intimate with celebrity flesh than a personal trainer or a masseur, is Pascal Dangin, the digital retoucher for fashion's and Hollywood's most famous photographers. Some refuse to work with anyone else. On the glossy side of the newsstand just this month, he tweaked the covers of W, Harper's Bazaar and Allure.

In a field where designers, photographers and stylists want to be celebrated for their every flourish of innovation no matter how dubious—topless models with vacuum cleaners, anyone?—the French-born Mr. Dangin, the founder and chief executive of the foremost photo retouching business in the country, Box Studios in New York, cultivates his anonymity.

"I never want to talk about my work, because it's kind of taboo," he said. "The people who benefit from my work do not benefit from me talking about it."

While photo manipulation is more prevalent than ever in this digital age, when many laptops come with software to help get the red out of your mother-in-law's eyes, the extent of retouching practiced by glossy magazines is still little understood by readers. At the same time, insiders offer a shrug of indifference: of course the camera can be made to lie. Do you really think that's Kate Winslet's figure on the cover of British GQ this month?

"Hey, everybody wants to look good," said Mr. Dangin (pronounced dawnh-GANH). "Basically we're selling a product—we're selling an image. To those who say too much retouching, I say you are bogus. This is the world that we're living in. Everything is glorified. I say live in your time."

Although most newspapers, including The New York Times, forbid the distortion of news photographs in a lab or on a computer, at fashion magazines it has long been standard to throw in a little digital pixie dust to make a model's eyes bluer, her teeth whiter, her legs slimmer. Periodically, such highly tweaked images stir controversy, proving that the retoucher's skill is still viewed as something of a dark art. Ms. Winslet, who is well known for waxing content about her healthy womanly figure, was at the center of the latest flare-up when she complained of being overly slenderized for the GQ cover. "The retouching is excessive," she was quoted as saying in The Daily Mail. "I do not look like that, and more importantly, I don't desire to look like that."

Dylan Jones, the editor in chief of British GQ, defended the retouching. "I really don't see anything sinister in this," he said by e-mail. "It's been going on for years. Essentially we all want glamour. We all want show business." A second controversy arose around the body-positive Ms. Winslet when Women's Wear Daily reported two weeks ago that her head had been digitally placed on the torso of a slimmer stylist on the cover of the January issue of Harper's Bazaar. The report was denied by the magazine and by a spokesman for Ms. Winslet.

That episode suggests that there are some lines that the image manipulators at glossy magazines will not cross. Mr. Dangin has on occasion pieced together a cover photo by putting the model's head on a different picture of her own body, but he rejects the Dr. Frankenstein brand of photo splicing.

"I would not put an actress's head on a stylist's body—no!" he said. He said it would be too hard to make such a composite convincing, and acknowledged that it would also raise an ethical question. "People can get very upset," he said. "They put it in the same pool as human cloning."

Retouching was once an obscure and narrow practice by photographers who would cover skin and body imperfections in their prints using tiny brushes. Now it entails whole new realms, drawing on the power of computer technologies to improve light, color and contrast in photos, not to mention thighs and heads. Mr. Dangin retouches and prints the work of a dozen leading fashion photographers, including Michael Thompson, Mr. Meisel, Craig McDean, Steven Klein, Inez van Lamsweerde, Mario Sorrenti and David Sims. He also works with a handful of art photographers like Philip-Lorca diCorcia. Some photographers refuse to work with anyone else.

"He is much more than just a technician who removes pimples," said Mr. McDean, who had Mr. Dangin flatten the background and simplify the colors in a Madonna portrait to create a 50's look for the cover of Vanity Fair last year. "He's a thinker, too. He's not someone who just pushes a button. There's some kind of soul in it, which is very rare. He can physically express himself through the computer."

The color, flesh tones and bodies aren't the only things tweaked in photos. Sometimes the composition isn't real, either. One example is in last fall's ad campaign for "The Sopranos." Although it seems that the photographer, Ms. Leibovitz, shot the entire cast around a table, she actually took them separately, and Mr. Dangin assembled the images in his computers.

Photographers and art directors swear by Mr. Dangin's ability to marry a deep knowledge of photography with technology. "Before I met Pascal, I couldn't do so many different kinds of lighting," said Patrick Demarchelier, a prolific shooter of Harper's Bazaar covers and fashion advertising. Because of Mr. Dangin's ability to correct the harsher aspects of dramatic lighting, he said, he has been able to go beyond conventional studio lights. "He has introduced a new brand of photography that didn't exist before," he said. "Without Pascal, a lot of photographers would not exist today."

For all his technological expertise, it is Mr. Dangin's rapport with photographers and his slow, meticulous pace that seem at the center of his success. "Some photographers won't work unless he does the retouching and printing," said Raul Martinez, a partner in the advertising firm of A/R Media in New York, who often works with Mr. Meisel. "He has real personal relationships with them, and they trust him."

For somebody who devotes his time to glossing up the images of others—at fees of $500 for an inside magazine page up to $20,000 for a cover image requiring lots of digital cutting and pasting—Mr. Dangin is decidedly unpolished. His tobacco-stained teeth have not been whitened, and despite his stature and success, he wears grungy brown corduroys, a Champion sweatshirt and New Balance sneakers every day. An unruly mass of finger-in-the-socket curls belie his background as a hairdresser.

Watching Mr. Dangin at work at his Box Studios on Broadway near Spring Street, which employs 40 people, is like ducking behind the curtain to see the last stage in the manufacture of film and fashion celebrities. In a pitch-dark loftlike room packed with high-definition computer monitors and light boxes, more than a dozen retouchers hunch over keyboards clicking and pointing and drawing. A huge Oz-like computer server buzzes in the background. The wizard himself sits at a giant triptych of screens. If the one in the middle is the canvas, then the two side screens are like palettes holding the software icons and files of images.

At any given moment, Mr. Dangin juggles about 10,000 files. Not long ago he was tending to an ad campaign for Cover Girl cosmetics that uses Angela Lindvall, a model; a Leibovitz image to promote the next "Sopranos" season; and a Steven Klein portrait of Madonna for a magazine cover.

"This part is too light, so I am going to basically start to burn it in and bring in more density," Mr. Dangin said, scribbling with a stylus on a computerized drawing pad as he adjusted the color and contrast in a photo by Adam Bartos, an art photographer. "It's about changing light. Think of this as a virtual darkroom, where you would expose parts of the photo to make it denser. Only in a darkroom, that would take five hours, and here we do it in an instant."

In a culture in which image is a major commodity, the paradox of appearing natural on film is nothing new. As far back as the mid-19th century, the photographer Mathew Brady employed retouchers to improve formal portraits. In the early 20th century, Man Ray used innovative techniques like solarization, and in the 1930's and 40's the Hollywood photographer George Hurrell elevated actresses like Jane Russell and Joan Crawford into icons of glamour by lengthening their eyelashes, smoothing every wrinkle and blemish and highlighting their hair.

Taking a cue from Hurrell, Richard Avedon retouched many society portraits by hand, famously extending the neck of Marella Agnelli in one to make her look literally like a society swan. More recently, artists like Cindy Sherman have used retouching and manipulation to transform identity completely—a process that is now common, but has not always been embraced. In 1997, the fashion photographer David LaChapelle squabbled publicly with one of his subjects, the actress Mira Sorvino, when he transformed her image digitally into a facsimile of Joan Crawford for Allure.

These days, anybody can retouch a photo. Web sites like Photo-Brush and the Pixel Foundry sell software that teaches photo-manipulation techniques, which are also described in books like Scott Kelby's "PhotoShop 7: Down and Dirty Tricks." As a result, almost any photo and image, both personal and public, can be retouched: high school yearbook pictures, family Christmas cards and online dating head shots.

Which raises the perennial question about Mr. Dangin's work: how much is too much? Is straightening your child's teeth on a Christmas card in the same category as straightening the teeth of a celebrity mother of septuplets, for which Newsweek was criticized in the late 1990's.

The only certain answer is that the line between what is in bounds and what is out is a moving one in the digital age. Grabbing a printout from a recent Yves Saint Laurent ad campaign, Mr. Dangin shrugged. "This world is not reality," he said, fingering the print. "It's just paper."

The Man Who Makes the Pictures Perfect

1. The dividing line between what is acceptable in photo manipulation and what is not has not been firmly established by the image industry. For instance, photo retouching could be defined as techniques that enhance but do not drastically change an image, while photo manipulation could be defined as techniques that drastically change an image. Dangin has established a line he personally will not cross in his own work. Do you think his self-imposed standards are enough? Or is it just splitting hairs? Should photo manipulation be regulated? If so, who should regulate it? Where do you draw the line between acceptable and unacceptable photo manipulation practices? Why?

2. Dangin, founder and chief executive of Box Studios, states that "This is the world we're living in. Everything is glorified. I say live in your time." Do you agree with him? Why or why not?

3. Similar to the controversy over human cloning, just because we have the technology to manipulate photos does that mean we *have* to use it? Why or why not?

CHAPTER 14

Future Trends

Mary Lynn Damhorst

AFTER YOU HAVE READ THIS CHAPTER, YOU WILL COMPREHEND:

- How forecasting the future of dress in society is a useful endeavor.

- Why it is necessary to make several alternative rather than single forecasts for dress in the future.

- How multiple factors influence future trends.

What will you be wearing in the year 2020? Will your attire resemble a space suit, with high-tech, shiny fabrics inspired by clothing adapted and invented for colonists on the moon or Mars? Will we need to wear actual space suits to protect ourselves from elevated levels of pollution here on Earth? Will our garments and accessories have communication systems and voice command computers engineered into the materials? Or will the hottest fashions be similar to what we wear today as a result of a nostalgic revival of 1990s styles? Chances are, clothing in 2020 will not be radically different from what we wear today, except for new silhouettes and fashion details reflecting the times and fiber innovations reflecting technological trends. But who knows?

We cannot know exactly what people will be wearing next season or three years from today. But we can look at today's trends and other data that give probable indications of what societal conditions will be 20 to 50 years from now. Those projections are a type of thinking that can help us imagine what life and dress will be like in the future. To do a respectable job of such "futuring," we must always keep in mind, however, that we are dealing with probabilities. Forecasts about the future must be tentative, and multiple probabilities or possibilities must be examined. For example, in the 1982 book *Fashion 2001* by Lucille Khornak, forward-thinking designers proposed what they thought would be in fashion about 20 to 25 years into the future. Knowing what we know today, over 20 years later, we can see that none of the designers was completely correct. But across their imaginative forecasts, a number of designers' ideas were quite right. Their forecasts in sum, rather than one individual prediction, helped us look into the future.

Futuring is not about making specific and detailed predictions. Instead, we will look at a few present-day trends and consider several directions in which those trends might go in the future. We are making **forecasts** rather than **predictions**; forecasts are estimations of probable occurrences based on present and past information. We will have to be diligent about not thinking too linearly, however. Only a very few trends are linear, with continuing increases or decreases over time. Most trends happen in cycles, spurts, and curvilinear waves. Sometimes exponential increases occur, blowing the trend way out of existing proportions. And unpredictable or catastrophic events can disrupt and change life, such as the destruction of the World Trade Center on September 11, 2001. Who would have thought that shoes would become potential weapons and that airline travelers' shoes would be examined in great detail before passengers are allowed to embark on commercial airplanes?

Thinking about the future helps individuals and organizations, such as retailers and apparel producers, plan for what might happen. Such planning can help any of us in choosing career directions, selecting educational experiences, and making investments, as well as helping organizations plan business strategies and shape policy. Thinking about the future is also a lot of fun and a great mental workout, requiring the juggling of multiple ideas and data at one time while allowing for creative leaps of imagination. And thinking about future possibilities can make things happen. If we examine possibilities and consider any of them desirable, we might be more apt to make them happen.

Future forecasting could go in endless directions. Therefore, for this chapter, we will establish some parameters for choosing what to consider. We base our forecasts on the assumption, which is possibly flawed, that during the next 50 years the world as a whole will not experience any catastrophic changes that destroy much of life on Earth or radically alter human existence as we know it today. For example, we will not consider what might happen if worldwide nuclear devastation occurs; if global warming becomes so severe that only the Arctic regions are inhabitable; if a worldwide economic collapse occurs, rendering all monetary systems useless; if a giant comet strikes Earth; or if beings from outer space take over Earth and make us all slaves. Some of these situations might be interesting to ponder, but we will not entertain these possibilities here, just for the sake of limiting our projections.

Instead, we will look at technological, population, and social trends that are already starting to happen and that most probably will affect our lives during the next 20 years. Four trends we examine include:

1. the increasing proportion of ethnic minorities in the U.S. population;

2. the increasing proportions of older people in many nations throughout the world;

3. the technological innovation of the Internet, which, as it vastly expands our access to diverse ideas about appearance and customized designs, might influence how we dress and how we manage the presentation of ourselves; and

4. technological innovations, such as genetic engineering, which may allow selection or manipulation of appearance characteristics in unborn children.

We will discover that all of these trends are, to some extent, interconnected. No cultural trend occurs in isolation. In addition, we will try to consider a few alternative projections for the future. Although data may indicate a strong possibility for a future trend, we can never know what might occur to radically alter what seems most plausible now. Probable trends may pan out in ways we never could have suspected. So, thinking about the future requires consideration of alternative possibilities to help us remember that we can only make projections; we cannot look into a crystal ball and predict exactly what will happen. Thinking about multiple futures helps individuals, businesses, government, and organizations to plan flexibly for changes to come.

TRENDS IN ETHNICITY AND CULTURAL IMAGES OF ATTRACTIVENESS

Over the next 50 years, substantial increases in the proportions of ethnic minority groups in the United States appear to be a certainty. There may be some geographical regions of the United States in which only limited ethnic diversity occurs, perhaps because of historical patterns of migration to an area, racism, or exclusionary social and political practices in the local area. However, to remain a viable and livable part of society, any community in the United States must at least do business with the rest of the country and the world. Individuals or communities that cannot operate within the conditions of pluralism will not be effective or successful in the increasingly multicultural society that is and very likely will continue to be the United States of America (Wellner, 2003). Career options will be limited for individuals who cannot interact successfully with diversity. That is one forecast we can make with a great amount of certainty.

The 2000 U.S. census updated the population projections listed in Table 14.1. For the first time in a U.S. census, individuals were able to claim multiple categories to reflect mixed race and ethnicity. Minority representation in the United States was probably undercounted before 2000, in part as a result of prior census data-collection methods that did not allow indication of mixed heritage. But even the 1990 figures painted a

TABLE 14.1

Census results and projections: Ethnic representation in the U.S. population

	1990	2000	2010	2050
European-American	75.6	69.1	68.0	50.5–56.0
African-American	11.8	12.3	12.6	13.8–14.2
Latino-American	9.0	12.5	13.8	22.0–25.7
Asian-American	2.8	3.6	4.8	7.0–9.2
Native American	0.7	1.0	0.8	0.8–1.0

Note: 2010 and 2050 figures are projections based on 1990 census data. 1990 and 2000 figures are census findings.
Source: Day, 1996; U.S. Census Bureau, 2000.

picture of increasing ethnic and racial diversity in the United States. According to estimations based on 1990 census data (Day, 1996), the proportion of European-Americans in the United States could be approximately 50 percent by the year 2050 (see Table 14.1). As a result, the United States is rapidly moving to a situation in which there is no ethnic majority group. What consequences will increases in diversity have on how people dress and how they think about their bodies?

In a society with a pervasive diversity of skin colors, body shapes, and facial features, ideals of attractiveness are apt to change. Let's imagine three scenarios or possibilities of what could happen: (1) true equality, (2) white supremacist takeover, and (3) white backlash.

True Equality

This first scenario is probably too optimistic. Although 2050 seems far away, this scenario might take well over 100 years to become a reality. If ethnic minority groups increase proportionately in the U.S. population and increase their educational and occupational achievement, by 2050 the United States might see greater levels of pluralism and decreasing white or European-American hegemony. With diversity characterizing men and women in powerful and successful positions in society, standards of attractiveness should also tend to diversify. Ethnicity may cease to be an issue in assessing attractiveness. A wider variety of facial features and skin colors would be seen in models and glamorous celebrities. People from diverse ethnicities will have a greater impact on fashion trends. We are already seeing evidence of this scenario (see "Generación Latino" in Chapter 10). Will greater variety in heights and weights also be seen as attractive in men and women? Forty-five years is a short time to escape the shackles of thinness standards. But appreciation of greater variety in body shapes may begin to become evident as diversity in racial characteristics is appreciated. The apparel industry would pay more attention to a diverse array of body sizes and shapes, as well as to differing style preferences across groups (see Figure 14.1).

White Supremacist Takeover

An opposite scenario foresees a rising tide of ethnic protectionism among the shrinking white, European-American majority over the next 45 years. Threatened by affirmative action policies, increasing numbers of minorities in positions of power and achievement, and government policies favoring diversity in schools and other public institutions, wealthy groups of white European-Americans seeking to hold on to privilege and opportunities afforded in the prior hegemonic situation may band together to influence business leaders, politicians, religious leaders, and media moguls to support new policies and practices that tend to exclude minority groups from the upper echelons of society. Claiming that acceptance of diversity has weakened the nation and reduced its productivity and leadership on the world scene, these white supremacists might increase their support base among whites who feel lost and fearful in a nation of increasing diversity. Supremacist media "plots" would unfold to emphasize and idolize whiteness, diminish inclusion of nonwhite appearances in the media, and seek passage of laws and public policy that do not favor or accommodate ethnic minority groups in any way. A portion of the mainstream fashion industry, owned by white supremacist leaders or threatened by boycotts from supremacist consumers, might move to ignore needs of ethnic minority consumers and the inclusion of diversity in advertising. This scenario

FIGURE 14.1 *Benetton has been committed to ethnic diversity of models in its ads.*

seems counter to today's trends emphasizing ethnic marketing and minority group influences on fashion (see "Generación Latino" in Chapter 10). Under future conditions of a weak economy, high crime rates, and terrorism, fringe elements in society can grow in influence if their message helps to allay fears of a segment of the population that feels its quality of life is diminishing. Protest and violence may erupt throughout the nation as a response to escalating exclusion of minorities, further convincing the supremacists that ethnic minority groups must be controlled and segregated from whites and positions of power.

White Backlash

A third possibility could be that increasing diversity in the population could move toward emphasis on ethnic minorities as attractive and anything European-American as unattractive, unfashionable, and unappealing. Diversity could become popular and acceptable only if it is not white. Such a backlash against European heritage could send youthful whites into a frenzy to acquire darker skin tones via excessive sun tanning or staining lotions. Those who could afford it might seek physicians who dispense drugs that darken skin color all over the body. Entertainers and sports stars with ethnic minority heritage would lead fashion trends. Fashion magazines would include few white models. Those who looked European in heritage might be considered "uncool," poor, or elderly.

We can see that each of these scenarios leads to a different projection of trends and consequences for dress and attractiveness standards. What will emerge remains to be seen.

INFLUENCE OF AGING POPULATION ON CONCEPTS OF BEAUTY

In Chapter 9, we projected that about 16 percent of the population would be 65 years and older in 2020. A historically unprecedented number of individuals will move into that age group after 2020 in the United States, Canada, Japan, and many countries in Europe. Within 10 years after that, all baby boomers will be above 65 and the proportion of older consumers will be even higher, depending on birth and death rates over the next 30 years. How will these countries deal with so many older individuals? Three following possibilities are proposed: (1) aging will become fashionable, (2) the older population will be seen as a pariah that drains resources from society, and (3) older persons will be viewed as highly diverse.

The Fashionable, Aged Baby Boomer

With relatively many individuals in their elder years, the fashion and cosmetics industries may pay substantial attention to aging consumers. Perhaps attractive images of older men and women will appear in apparel and cosmetics ads. Designer and brand name clothing, specially designed for the changing aging body, may become common. "Gray power" could become increasingly important to politicians, businesses, and cultural institutions. It might even become chic to be 60-something or 70-something. Aging might be seen as "graceful" and beautiful in its own way, a time to retire and explore activities one has always wanted to pursue. Perhaps some fashion trends would start with innovative baby boomer consumers and be picked up by young adult fashion opinion leaders inspired by plucky, independent oldsters.

Old Is Out

In contrast, deep and long-lasting economic recession could wipe out retirement savings and push a substantial proportion of older people below the poverty level. Social Security and Medicare could disappear. Welfare systems, stretched beyond their capacities, would take limited care of the impoverished multitudes. The great numbers of impoverished elderly might be seen as a burden on society rather than attractive as a market segment. The fashion industry would probably ignore this lifespan group to a great extent, leaving it out of advertising, product development focus, and marketing efforts in general.

Instead, the fashion industry might continue to focus on youthful markets. By 2020, technological developments might make cosmetic surgery less expensive and less painful, giving more individuals an incentive to sculpt their bodies to desired youthful shapes and condition. Exercise equipment, in combination with drug therapies, may make muscle toning and development easier. The body could, in essence, become more readily malleable. Fashionable sleek bodies may be clothed in spray-on materials or synthetic skins to show off every muscle and curve (Richards, 1997).

Older people who could afford to might procure all techniques available to look as youthful as possible. But the elevated levels of poverty and low incomes among the old may leave many out of the quest for a youthful-looking body. Body dissatisfaction among older people in general might soar if many think that they could do something to make their appearance more youthful but could not afford to do so. Problems such as anorexia, bulimia, and drug misuse related to appearance management might increase among older consumers.

Diversity among Older Segments

What is quite probable by 2020 is a blend of the prior two scenarios. Some middle-aged and older consumers might embrace the new technologies of beauty and chase relentlessly after a medically chiseled, youthful, trim body. Other baby boomers, a generation questioning the status quo to the end, might reject artificial means of looking young and insist on aging naturally. They would wear their wrinkles and gray hair as badges of honor. These radical elders might begin to forge new meanings of aging for generations to follow.

TECHNOLOGY AND THE CONSUMER

The technology of cosmetic surgery and innovations in age-retarding and youth-enhancing drugs will continue to develop over the next several decades. Bioengineering of human babies may help to prolong life and shape appearance. People around the world will continue to negotiate the meanings and acceptability of these procedures and products for modifying the body. Each cultural group may derive different or particular meanings for these technological advancements. Technology is also changing the way we shop and get fashion information; this may have a profound impact on how we dress and how we feel about our bodies. First, we will consider the potential impact of the Internet on dress.

Customization and Multiple Modes of Access

Computerized systems are currently under development to make virtual images that capture actual measurements, proportions, movements, and the appearance of the real human body. These three-dimensional images can already be combined with images of apparel to help designers adjust style design for size variations, help consumers electronically "try on" clothing to see how it looks on them before ordering an actual garment, and eventually will allow consumers to order a custom-made garment that perfectly fits their actual bodies and their personal tastes (Gray, 1998). Computers could someday translate computerized body measurements into pattern adjustment commands that guide robotized production systems to cut and sew a garment to fit an individual person precisely. In addition, the computerized system could allow the customer to select fabric, color, and style details such as sleeve length, pant leg fullness, and pocket style from an array of options offered through the system. Not only would fit be customized, but the consumer would take part in designing the style of garments she or he wants. This process is called **co-design** (see Fiore, Lee, & Kunz, in press; Lee et al., 2002). Apparel industry experts often refer to custom-fit garments ordered through a mass retailer or producer as "made-to-measure" (Gellers, 1998). Garments ordered through a mass retailer or producer for which the consumer has made personal style design choices are referred to as **mass customized** (Pine, 1993).

Much of this ordering of mass customized and made-to-measure apparel could be done at home through the Internet via online catalogs, at mall kiosks, or in retail stores.

The customer might have a file containing a computerized image of his or her body; the image could easily be updated for a small fee at a local mall shop with imaging equipment. Or we might eventually be able to stand in front of our personal computers with built-in camera connections that would record our current body dimensions. The bandwidth of phone or cable line connections between home and Internet would have to be ample to provide enough speed and capacity to effectively use three-dimensional images on home computers, and equipment advances and access to pipelines with increased image speed and clarity are already on their way. Made-to-measure and mass customized apparel is available today (Coia, 2003; Lee & Chen, 1999), but advances in computerized imaging and production systems probably will make customized apparel more readily accessible and less expensive sometime during the next 20 years.

Certainly, there are many consumers who will never attempt to buy anything through the Internet, much less order a garment customized to their body size and their style preferences via computer (Fiore et al., in press). Only a tiny minority (about 9 percent) had purchased apparel through the Internet by early 1999 (Yoh et al., 2003). But over a third of online shoppers had purchased apparel via the Internet by 2001 (Pastore, 2001), and apparel is now one of the top five most purchased product categories ("Online Spending," 2003). Today, few consumers have garments custom-made on a regular basis, and computerized robotic systems for customizing fit and style are not yet fully operable. So why should we believe that these modes of shopping will play any substantial role in how consumers shop within the next 20 years?

First of all, population segments that are more inclined to purchase by mail are increasing in numbers. Aging individuals are more apt to experience health conditions that make shopping in stores very time-consuming and physically inconvenient. The majority of individuals in their 60s and 70s in the year 2020 will have had experience using computers, because of present and upcoming job demands. For most of these consumers and consumers of all younger ages, using the Internet will be a common experience. Furthermore, more women will probably be working in jobs other than homemaking, leaving little time for women and their families to get out and shop. With the aging population and increasing diversity in ethnicities in the United States, garment size needs are also becoming more diverse, but it will be extremely difficult for most store retailers to stock the wide array of clothing sizes necessary to fit their customers.

At present, most Internet catalogs tend to be simple electronic versions of printed mail-order catalogs. Interesting and creative innovations will be needed to lure more consumers onto the Internet. Some Internet stores allow the customer to dress an illustrated model shaped somewhat like the customer with different items from the catalog to see how a combination of pieces will look together. Front and back views, close-ups, and the ability to see a product in each color further differentiate some Internet apparel sites from mail catalogs. Yoh (1999) has found that many consumers would be attracted to the Internet if there were indexing services that would find similar items (e.g., navy blazers) across all shopping sites. They are also interested in being able to upload images of themselves as models to see how garments would look on their body size and shape. Easy search, comparison, and try-on features for some consumers might compensate for the wait to receive a garment by mail rather than through immediate, in-store experiences. And mail systems may speed up. Mass customization of fit is beginning to attract more customers; Land's End has found that four of its top-selling products are in the customized fit category (Coia, 2003).

Would availability of made-to-measure infinite sizes help some consumers feel less discriminated against or left out because of non-normative body size or shape? And will an "underclass" of people who cannot afford made-to-measure apparel develop, marked as lower status by their imperfectly fitting clothing and off-the-rack wardrobes? Both positive ramifications for some individuals' body satisfaction and negative effects on others' self-esteem could be the result of made-to-measure advances.

Chances are that a variety of modes of shopping will continue to be used through the next 20 years. Made-to-measure apparel will require extensive development of computer systems and new retail systems. For example, what happens if you purchase a custom-fit garment that was made specifically for you but you want to return it? What will the retailer do with your rejected, perhaps oddly sized garment? And how will the average consumer deal with the expanded array of choices if mass customized style choices become common? Will retailers need to provide style consultants who can help the choice-overloaded consumer make decisions about what style details to order in a customized garment? Recently, Lee (2004) found that consumers were more likely to go back to a simpler customization site for children's clothing, even though they were very satisfied with the performance of a more complex site. Until the average consumer is socialized into making many co-design choices, simpler and more limited customization options may be the best approach for introducing innovative customizing systems.

Internet catalogs can take the consumer directly to the manufacturer or designer. Will some designers develop such close connections with consumers that they ask regular online customers to "vote" on new seasonal offerings? With such bypassing of traditional retail buyers as gatekeepers to style selection, will consumers gain more direct impact on style options available to them? Individual choice and innovation may be facilitated by direct and personal connections with designers. Style design could become highly individualized if customized ordering for made-to-measure apparel becomes more affordable. How will that influence fashion diffusion? Will fashion changes become even more rapid when designers are linked directly to consumers and can propose new style ideas any time of the year?

The eventual changes in the fashion system that could result from widespread use of electronic catalogs and made-to-measure and mass customized ordering are almost too immense to comprehend, but certainly intriguing. Increased variety and diversity in appearances and more uniqueness in what can be purchased could certainly emerge. Would more people develop independence and confidence in ordering styles they want rather than conforming to fashion trends? Or would major segments of the population be confused and crave dictation of styles by mainstream fashion designers? Perhaps all of these trends could occur simultaneously. The fashion system will probably become increasingly complex during the twenty-first century.

GENETIC ENGINEERING: CONSEQUENCES FOR APPEARANCE?

Medical advancements in genetic engineering that will change the way we think about birth and control over disease and human characteristics are likely to be available at increasing rates during the twenty-first century (Stock, 2002b). Some of these interventions may be applied to people after they are born, but altering the genetic makeup of a live person will be difficult and limited in scope. The easiest and most effective approaches may be conducted on embryos before implantation in the womb.

Sex selection is already a possibility. It is outlawed in some countries, such as Britain, but the practice is legal in the United States and has not yet led to a notable imbalance in selection for either girls or boys (Stock, 2002a). Modifications to prevent disease, improve health, and increase longevity also will be possible (Stock, 2002b). Will parents go so far as to modify their child's intelligence and physical strength? And what about aesthetic characteristics such as eye, hair, and skin color? Or height and weight? Elimination of the obesity gene may become a common choice because of its connection to other potential health problems.

"**Germinal choice technology** refers to a whole realm of technologies by which parents influence the genetic constitutions of their children at the time of their conception" (Stock, 2002a, p. 17). Embryo screening for certain diseases and sex selection is already possible. Farther into this century, **germline interventions,** in which genetic alterations are made to the egg, sperm, or first cell of an embryo, will become safer (Stock, 2002a). In essence, an artificial chromosome will be attached to the genetic structure to enhance the capabilities of the individual in some way.

A great variety of human characteristics can be genetically modified, so parents will have to make very complex choices. Their choices may be limited by monetary resources, but will limiting on the basis of who can afford these interventions become an ethical concern when disease control is involved? And what are the political and personal consequences for the enhanced versus the unenhanced? Will some parents make some choices for their children that challenge our sense of parental rights—choices that incapacitate the child in some way? Germline modifications raise a huge array of questions and concerns. Societal dialogue about this technology is sure to expand exponentially in the near future.

Now it's your turn to imagine some scenarios for the future of these technologies. The following learning activity asks you to focus on the consequences of germinal choice technology for appearance. Many of you could be the parents making some of these choices.

ON TO THE FUTURE

We cannot be sure if any of the above trends will actually materialize. As with any forecasting exercise, only time will tell. Nevertheless, pondering the future is a good exercise in using some of the theories and ideas we have encountered throughout this book. Two things are pretty much a certainty in the future, however: (1) changes in society and people's lives are bound to occur, and (2) dress will reflect those changes in some way.

Summary

In this chapter we have examined brief scenarios built around four future trends: minority ethnicity in the United States, the aging population, customized and computer-purchased apparel, and biomedical engineering. Three alternative scenarios relate to projected increases in diversity in U.S. minority ethnic populations. We considered how attractiveness standards and appearances might be affected if alternative situations of true equality among ethnic groups, white supremacist dominance, and reverse discrimination against European-Americans occur. Three scenarios examine what might happen to attractiveness standards and fashion trends as a result of increasing proportions of older individuals in many industrialized countries around the world. Possibilities include older consumers having some influence on fashion trends or becoming undesirable and considered a drain on society. A mix of those two situations could occur.

Internet shopping systems, combined with made-to-measure and mass customization, were considered for possible impacts on the fashion process and individuality and conformity in self-expression through dress. The last trend we considered is genetic engineering or germline choice technology. The potential for this technology during the first half of the twenty-first century is introduced. A learning activity invites thinking about the consequences of the technology for appearances and society.

LEARNING ACTIVITY
Designer Selves in the Future

Objective: To imagine the consequences of genetic engineering for appearance and to critically think about the consequences of these possibilities for society.

Procedure

Work in small groups to imagine what the future will be like 50 years from now. Assume that:

- Genetic engineering of children is common and has been so since about 2030. Before conception, fertilized eggs can be implanted in mothers after the eggs are selected to be free of genetic proclivity for physical disorder and obesity. Height, weight, hair color, eye color, skin color, and other appearance attributes can also be selected—for a price.

- Many people born later than 2000 have received medical treatments early in life that will extend the aging period. Some people in their 50s look and feel like they are in their 20s and 30s. Some will probably live to be 120 years old, and many will be reasonably healthy and independent well past 100.

- An amazing array of cosmetic surgery options is available. Cosmetic surgery is cheaper, safer, and more painless than it is today.

Write a plausible future based on the three assumptions above. In your story of the future (a scenario), attend to the following issues:

1. What will beauty standards be like 50 years from now?
2. What will happen to young people whose parents cannot afford genetic selection before birth?
3. Who will be likely to be the people who choose not to get treatments to extend or mask the aging process for themselves or their children? How will they be treated?
4. Think about how these conditions will affect health insurance, dating and marriage, fashions, social status systems, etc.
5. Now that you have thought out your scenario, do you think that scientists should be allowed to develop these technologies in the United States? Can they be stopped from doing so? If they can be impeded, will a black market or foreign source arise for these treatments? Or should society take some other approach to dealing with these technologies?

Use your imagination!

References

Coia, A. (2003). Channeling e-tail resources. *Apparel*, 44(12):18–20.

Day, J. C. (1996). Population projections of the United States by age, sex, race, and Hispanic origin: 1995–2050. U.S. Bureau of the Census, Current Population Reports, P25-1130. Accessed July 27, 2004, at www.census.gov/prod/1/pop/p25-1130/.

Fiore, A. M., Lee, S., & Kunz, G. (in press). Individual differences, motivations, and willingness to use a mass customization option for fashion products. *European Journal of Marketing*.

Gellers, S. (1998, July 8). Made-to-measure: Raising the stakes for better clothing. *Daily News Record*, 9, 16.

Gray, S. (1998, February). In virtual fashion. *IEEE Spectrum*, 35:18–25.

Khornak, L. (1982). *Fashion 2001*. New York: The Viking Press.

Lee, H. H. (2004). Antecedents and consequences of satisfaction with a mass customized Internet apparel shopping site. Unpublished doctoral dissertation, Iowa State University, Ames.

Lee, S., & Chen, J. C. (1999, December). Mass customization methodology for apparel manufacturing with a future. *Journal of Industrial Technology*, 16(1). Accessed August 5, 2002, at www.nait.org.

Lee, S., Kunz, G., Fiore, A. M., & Campbell, J. R. (2002). Acceptance of mass customization of apparel: Merchandising issues associated with preference for product, process, and place. *Clothing and Textiles Research Journal*, 20(3):138–146.

Online spending keeps growing in Q3. (2003, October 1). Accessed November 1, 2003, at www.bizrate.com/content/press/release_rel—147.html.

Pastore, M. (2001, January 16). Consumer continues online purchases. Accessed September 13, 2004, at www.clickz.com/stats/markets/retailing/article.php/560781.

Pine, B. J., II. (1993). *Mass Customization: The New Frontier in Business Competition*. Boston, MA: Harvard Business School Press.

Richards, R. W. (1997, October 14). Fashion 2027. *The Advocate*, 744:103.

Stock, G. (2002a, July/August). Choosing our genes. *The Futurist*, 36(4):17–23.

Stock, G. (2002b). *Redesigning Humans: Choosing Our Genes, Changing Our Future*. Boston: Mariner Books.

U.S. Census Bureau. (2000). Accessed January 13, 2002, at factfinder.census.gov.

Wellner, A. S. (2003, April). The next 25 years. *American Demographics*, 25:24–27.

Yoh, E. (1999). Consumer adoption of the Internet for apparel shopping. Unpublished doctoral dissertation, Iowa State University, Ames.

LIST OF READINGS

Abu-Nasr, D. (2002, October 20). Men hear Saudi women's unmentionable details. *Lexington Herald-Leader*, A13. *Chapter 6*

Agins, T. (1999). What happened to fashion? Introduction to *The End of Fashion: The Mass Marketing of the Clothing Business*, pp. 1–16. New York: HarperCollins. *Chapter 11*

al-Shaykh, H. (1994). Inside a Moroccan bath. In P. Foster (Ed.), *Minding the Body*. New York: Anchor Books. *Chapter 9*

Bader, J. L. (2000, July 2). All that's bare is fit to wear, so why the stares? *The New York Times*, 4(Sec. 4). *Chapter 6*

Beauty and hygeine: XV.—Concerning the ear. (1896, August 29). *Harper's Bazaar*, 29(35):724. *Chapter 2*

Bellafante, G. (2003, January 26). Young and chubby: What's heavy about that? *The New York Times*, 1(Sec. 9). *Chapter 2*

Betts, K. (2003, February 2). The man who makes the pictures perfect. *The New York Times*, 1(Sec. 9). *Chapter 13*

Boynton-Arthur, L. (1993). Clothing, control, and women's agency: The mitigation of patriarchal power. In S. Fisher & K. Davis (Eds.), *Negotiating at the Margins*, pp. 66–84. New Brunswick, NJ: Rutgers University Press. *Chapter 12*

Branch, S., & Wingfield, N. (2003, September 15). Chic at a click: eBay fashions a deal with designers. *The Wall Street Journal*, B1. *Chapter 13*

Brodman, B. (1994). Paris or perish: The plight of the Latin American Indian in a Westernized world. In S. Benstock & S. Ferriss (Eds.), *On Fashion*, pp. 267–283. Piscataway, NJ: Rutgers University Press. *Chapter 4*

Bulla, T. (2000, March). T'ween spirit. *Earnshaw's*, 54–56. *Chapter 8*

Chauvin, L., Downie, A., Goni, U., Hoag, C., & Mascarenas, D. (2001, July 9). Bodies à la carte: Passionate for pulchritude, Latin American women are reshaping their form through plastic surgery. *Time International*, 158(1):26. *Chapter 13*

Coleman, C. (2000, February 2). Just playing doctor? Shorter coats make residents feel naked. *The Wall Street Journal*, Sec. A. *Chapter 7*

Cottle, M. (1998, May). Turning boys into girls. *The Washington Monthly*, 32–36. *Chapter 5*

Creager, E. (2002, May 27). Move over, Tupperware: Botox parties sweep the country. *The Des Moines Register*, Sec. E. *Chapter 9*

Dalby, L. (1983). Kimono schools. In *Geisha*, pp. 290–292. Berkeley: University of California Press. *Chapter 3*

Damhorst, M. L., & McLeod, H. (2004, original for this text). A clothing gift program for low income women: Corporate giving with an impact. *Chapter 7*

Damhorst, M. L., Jondle, K., & Youngberg, K. (2004, original for this text). How personnel interviewers see women's job interview dress: A 2002 update. *Chapter 7*

Dickinson, A. (2000, November 20). Measuring up. *Time*, 154. *Chapter 5*

Duke, L. (2002, February). "Just because it's a White magazine...doesn't make it a bad magazine:" African American readers and "mainstream" teen magazines. Adapted from Get real!: Cultural relevance and resistance to the mediated feminine ideal. *Psychology & Marketing*, 19(2):211–233. *Chapter 8*

Edwards, A. (2000, March). How black can you be? *Essence*, 96, 100, 153–154, 156–157. *Chapter 7*

Edwards, L. (1993, May 30). Worldly lessons. *The New York Times*, C1, C9. *Chapter 12*

Farr, B. A. (1999, original for this text). Plus-size modeling: The industry, the market, and reflections as a professional in the image industry. *Chapter 11*

Fassihi, F. (2003, July 28). In Tehran, boutiques stock hot outerwear under the counter. *The Wall Street Journal*, A1, A8. *Chapter 11*

Golden, D. (2002, August 1). Socked by security: Fancy shoes trip up business travelers. *The Wall Street Journal*, A1, A5. *Chapter 13*

Gray, R. (2002, January 11). Goodbye briefs, hello jammers. *The Des Moines Register*, C1, C6. *Chapter 6*

Grealy, L. (1994). Pony party. In *Autobiography of a Face*, pp. 1–13. Boston: Houghton Mifflin. *Chapter 8*

Hall, S. S. (1999, August 22). The bully in the mirror. *The New York Times Magazine*, 31–35, 58, 62–64. *Chapter 8*

Harris, P. (2001). Learning the language of my daughter's hair. In J. Harris & P. Johnson (Eds.), *Tenderheaded: A Comb-Bending Collection of Hair Stories*, pp. 43–49. New York: Simon and Schuster. *Chapter 4*

Hart, J. (1998, June 8). Northampton confronts a crime, cruelty. *Boston Globe*, A1, A12. *Chapter 5*

Hayt, E. (1997, April 27). For stylish Orthodox women, wigs that aren't wiggy. *The New York Times*, 43, 48. *Chapter 12*

Healy, P. (2003, September 2). Reading, writing and body waxing. *The New York Times*, 1(Sec. B). *Chapter 8*

Hegland, J. E. (1999, original for this text). Drag queens, transvestites, transsexuals: Stepping across the accepted boundaries of gender. *Chapter 5*

Hymowitz, C. (2003, September 16). Female executives use fashion to send a business message. *The Wall Street Journal*, B1. *Chapter 7*

Jervis, L. (1998). My Jewish nose. In O. Edut (Ed.), *Body Outlaws: Young Women Write about Body Image and Identity*, pp. 62–67. New York: Seal Press. *Chapter 10*

Jones, R. (2003, April). The height of vanity. *Marie Claire*, 92–94, 96, 98. *Chapter 13*

Kaiser, S. B. (1999, original for this text). Identity, postmodernity, and the global apparel marketplace. *Chapter 3*

Kershaw, S. (2000, April 19). The skullcap as fashion statement. *The New York Times*, 1(Sec. B). *Chapter 12*

Kletter, M., & Braunstein, P. (2001, January 4). Racy school fashions under fire. *Women's Wear Daily. Chapter 6*

Kolata, G. (2000, October 18). No days off are allowed, experts on weight argue. *The New York Times*, 1(Sec. A). *Chapter 2*

Kozar, J. (2004, original for this text). Older women's attitudes toward aging, appearance changes, and clothing. *Chapter 9*

Kugel, S. (2003, October 5). Urban tactics: And Bloomingdale's returns his calls. *The New York Times*, 4(Sec. 14). *Chapter 11*

Lacayo, R. (2001, December 3). About face: An inside look at how women fared under Taliban oppression and what the future holds for them now. *Time*, 34–49. *Chapter 12*

Life in plastic. (2002, December 21). *The Economist*, 365:20–22. *Chapter 5*

Lubow, A. (1999, November 14). The shadow designer. *New York Times Magazine*, 124–127, 140. *Chapter 11*

Lynch, A. (1995). Hmong American New Year's dress: The display of ethnicity. In J. B. Eicher (Ed.), *Dress and Ethnicity: Change across Space and Time*, pp. 255–267. Oxford: Berg Publishers. *Chapter 10*

Mandava, B. C. (1998). To Apu, with love. In O. Edut (Ed.), *Body Outlaws: Young Women Write about Body Image and Identity*, pp. 68–77. New York: Seal Press. *Chapter 2*

Margolis, J. (2000, March 6). Cutting edge humanity: With the help of digital photography and the Internet, caring surgeons rebuild the face of Kosovo war victim. *Time International*, 155(9):40+. *Chapter 13*

McEnally, M. (2002). Princess for a day. In *Cases in Consumer Behavior*, Vol. 1, pp. 57–65. Upper Saddle River, NJ: Prentice Hall. *Chapter 4*

Mead, R. (2002, March 18). Shopping rebellion: What the kids want. *The New Yorker*, 104–111. *Chapter 8*

Merrick, A. (2001, May 11). The pared-down prom dress. *The Wall Street Journal*, B1, B4. *Chapter 6*

Michelman, S. O. (1999, original for this text). From habit to fashion: Dress of Catholic women religious. *Chapter 12*

Michelman, S. O. (1999, original for this text). Is thin in? Kalabari culture and the meaning of fatness. *Chapter 2*

Michelman, S. O. (2004, original for this text). Reveal or conceal? Examining the meaning of modesty in post-modern America. *Chapter 6*

Miller, K., & Hunt, S. (1999, original for this text). It's all Greek to me: Sorority members and identity talk. *Chapter 3*

Miller-Spillman, K. A. (2004, original for this text). Playing dress-up: Childhood memories of dress. *Chapter 8*

Mithers, C. L. (1994, December). A new look at beauty, aging and power. *Glamour*, 92(12):184–185, 246–249. *Chapter 9*

Morgado, M. A. (2004). Refashioning the Hawaiian shirt. Adapted from "From kitsch to chic: The transformation of Hawaiian shirt aesthetics." *Clothing and Textiles Research Journal*, 21(2):75–88. *Chapter 11*

Munson, K. (2003, February 14). Erasing love never easy with tattoos. *The Des Moines Register*, 1E–2E. *Chapter 4*

Muslim doll offers image of modesty and self-esteem. (2003, October 8). Associated Press. Accessed January 13, 2004, at www.msnbc.com/news/977700.asp. *Chapter 12*

National Institute on Media and the Family. Fact sheet: Media's effect on girls: Body image and gender identity. Accessed May 18, 2004, at www.mediafamily.org/facts/facts_mediaeffect.shtml. *Chapter 2*

Newman, C. (2000, January). The enigma of beauty. *National Geographic*, 100–121. *Chapter 2*

The new puritans. (2002, December 21). *The Economist*, 99–101. *Chapter 2*

Ogle, J. P., Eckman, M. J., & Leslie, C. A. (2004, original for this text). Dress and the Columbine shootings: Media interpretations. *Chapter 4*

Palmer, B. (1999, August 15). True colors. *New York Times Magazine*, 24. *Chapter 3*

Peck, D. (2003, June). The weight of the world. *The Atlantic Monthly*, 38–39. *Chapter 2*

Prystay, C. (2002, May 30). As China's women change, marketers notice. *The Wall Street Journal*, A11. *Chapter 11*

Ralston, J. (2001, November). The high cost of beauty. *Parenting*, 132, 134, 137, 139–140. *Chapter 8*

Respers, L. (1996, February 22). Day-care dress up not amusing to boy's dad. *Baltimore Sun*, 1A. *Chapter 5*

Rich, C. (1983/1990). Ageism and the politics of beauty. In B. MacDonald & C. Rich (Eds.), *Look Me in the Eye* (2nd ed.), pp. 139–146. Duluth, MN: Spinsters Ink. *Chapter 9*

Sagario, D. (2001, August 30). A web of deceit: Internet sites encouraging anorexia draw alarm from the medical community. *The Des Moines Register*, 1E–2E. *Chapter 2*

Sciolino, E. (2001, November 18). Hair as a battlefield for the soul. *The New York Times*, 5(Sec. 4). *Chapter 6*

Sciolino, E. (2003, February 7). In Iran's hair salons, the rebels wield scissors. *The New York Times*, 4(Sec. A). *Chapter 5*

Stacey, M. (2000, November). Your mother, your body. *Shape*, 20(3):76, 80, 82. *Chapter 4*

Stapinski, H. (1999, July). Generación Latino. *American Demographics*, 63–68. *Chapter 10*

Sterngold, J. (2000, June 28). Taking a new look at uniforms and their impact on schools. *The New York Times*, Sec. B. *Chapter 8*

Stevens, D. G. (2000, May 7). Casino gives workers look they can, must live with. *Chicago Tribune*, 1, 16(Sec. 1). *Chapter 7*

Sullivan, T. (2003, July 6). India examines color of beauty. *Des Moines Sunday Register*, 3A. *Chapter 3*

Symbols in school. (2003, Spring). *Intelligence Report*, 109:70, 72. *Chapter 3*

Trebay, G. (2000, August 20). Scrawn to brawn: Men get muscles, or pray for them. *The New York Times*, 1(Sec. 9). *Chapter 5*

Trice, D. T. (2003, August 12). Complex issues of complexion still haunt blacks. *Chicago Tribune*, 1A. *Chapter 10*

Wall, M. (2002, July 7). Health to pay: Pressures push jockeys to extremes for weight loss. *Lexington Herald-Leader*, C1, C13. *Chapter 7*

Wallace, A. (2002, September). True thighs. *More*, 90–94. *Chapter 9*

Warren, S. (2001, October 10). Ready-to-wear watchdogs: "Smart" garments keep track of vital signs, hide odor. *The Wall Street Journal*, B1, B3. *Chapter 13*

Wickens, B. (1999, January 11). Proud to be big: The fat fight back against insults and discrimination. *Maclean's*, 62. *Chapter 2*

Wickliffe, V. (2004, original for this text). Black hair—black times. *Chapter 10*

Winge, T. M. (2004, original for this text). A survey of "Modern Primitive" body modification ritual: Meanings of pain. *Chapter 4*

Yamanaka, L. (2001). When Asian eyes are smiling. In V. Nam (Ed.), *YELL-Oh Girls! Emerging Voices Explore Culture, Identity, and Growing Up Asian American*, pp. 171–174. New York: Quill. *Chapter 10*

LIST OF PHOTO CREDITS

Chapter 1

Figure 1.2a *Universal (Courtesy Kobal).*

Figure 1.3 *Photo from Goudge, B. S. (1985). Attributions for job acquisition: Job skills, dress, and luck of female job applicants. Master's thesis, Iowa State University, Ames.*

Figure 1.4 *Kim MacDonald / Habitat for Humanity International.*

Figure 1.5 *Ed George / National Geographic Image Collection.*

Chapter 2

Figure 2.1 *Beauty Mask © 1992 Stephen R. Marquardt. All rights reserved.*

Figure 2.2 *© National Gallery, London.*

Figure 2.3 *Photo by Larry White.*

Figure 2.4 *© Tim Graham / CORBIS.*

Figures 2.8, 2.9 *Courtesy of Susan O. Michelman.*

Figure 2.10 *Albert Moldvay / National Geographic Image Collection.*

Figures 2.11, 2.12 *Photos by Jodi Cobb. Reprinted by permission of The National Geographic Society.*

Chapter 3

Figure 3.1 *Courtesy of Fairchild Publications, Inc. Photographer: Donato Sardella.*

Figure 3.2 *Courtesy of Mary Lynn Damhorst.*

Figure 3.3 *© Zits Partnership. Reprinted with special permission of King Features Syndicate.*

Figure 3.5 *AP / Wide World Photos.*

Figure 3.8 *© Michael S. Yamashita / CORBIS.*

Chapter 4

Figure 4.1 *AP / Wide World Photos.*

Figure 4.2 *STONE SOUP © 2004 Jan Eliot. Reprinted with permission of UNIVERSAL PRESS SYNDICATE. All rights reserved.*

Figure 4.3 *Photo by Clarence E. Damhorst.*

Figure 4.4 *© Jim Cornfield / CORBIS.*

Figure 4.5 *Courtesy of Fairchild Publications, Inc.*

Figure 4.6 *Viking braid scalp tattoo (2003, left), Celtic knot scalp (back) tattoo (2003, right), photographed by Theresa M. Winge.*

Figure 4.7 *Jasin Boland / MPTV.net.*

Chapter 5

Figure 5.1 *Courtesy of Susan O. Michelman.*

Figure 5.2b *The Metropolitan Museum of Art, Bequest of Sam A. Lewisohn, 1951 (51.112.2). All rights reserved, The Metropolitan Museum of Art.*

Figure 5.3 *© Royalty-Free / CORBIS.*

Figure 5.4 *Courtesy of Jane E. Hegland, South Dakota State University.*

Chapter 6

Figure 6.1 *Courtesy of Fairchild Publications, Inc.*

Figure 6.2 *Courtesy of Susan O. Michelman.*

Figure 6.3 *Photo by Tina Yee, Copyright 2001, The Des Moines Register and Tribune Company. Reprinted with permission.*

Figure 6.4 *www.modestprom.com.*

Chapter 7

Figure 7.1 *Carhartt, Inc.*

Figures 7.2, 7.3, 7.4 *Photo collages courtesy of Mary Lynn Damhorst.*

Figure 7.6 *Courtesy of* Lexington Herald-Leader.

Chapter 8

Figure 8.2 *Courtesy of Mary Lynn Damhorst.*

Figure 8.3 *Courtesy of Jihye Park.*

Figure 8.4 *Lynn Johnston Productions, Inc. / Distributed by United Feature Syndicate, Inc.*

Figure 8.5 *Girl Zone Corp., www.girlzone.com.*

Figures 8.6, 8.7 *Courtesy of Kimberly A. Miller-Spillman.*

Figure 8.8 *© Michael Roberts / Macohochi Photography.*

Chapter 9

Figure 9.2 *Illustration by Rob Hernandez. Copyright 1992, Los Angeles Times. Reprinted with permission.*

Figure 9.3 *Andrew Eccles / jbgphoto.com.*

Chapter 10

Figure 10.1 *Courtesy of Huntington Historical Society, Huntington, NY.*

Figure 10.2 *Photo by Annette Lynch, University of Northern Iowa.*

Figure 10.3 *Courtesy of Vanessa Wickliffe.*

Figure 10.4 *Courtesy of Sandra Jones.*

Chapter 11

Figure 11.1a *Courtesy of Fairchild Publications, Inc.*

Figure 11.1b *Courtesy of Fairchild Publications, Inc. Photographer: Kyle Ericksen.*

Figure 11.2 *Courtesy of Fairchild Publications, Inc.*

Figure 11.3 *© Bradley Smith / CORBIS.*

Figure 11.4 *© 1998 Don Doll.*

Figure 11.5 *AP / Wide World Photos.*

Figure 11.6 *Illustration by Crystal Morris, based on a sculpture by Duane Hanson in the collection of the Scottish National Gallery of Modern Art.*

Figure 11.7 *Based on an illustration in* Rubbish Theory *by Michael Thompson, 1979, p. 45. Reprinted by permission of the International Textile & Apparel Association.*

Figure 11.8 *www.vintagehawaiianshirt.net, © anachronistic productions.*

Figure 11.9 *Photo by E. J. Carr.*

Chapter 12

Figure 12.1a *Courtesy of Fairchild Publications, Inc.*

Figure 12.1b *AP / Wide World Photos.*

Figure 12.3 *Illustration by Mary Lou Carter.*

Figure 12.4 *Courtesy of Susan O. Michelman.*

Figure 12.5 *AP / Wide World Photos.*

Chapter 13

Figure 13.1 *Courtesy of* Lexington Herald-Leader.

Figure 13.2 *© Cindy Jackson Ltd., www.cindyjackson.com.*

Figure 13.3 *© Najlah Feanny / CORBIS SABA.*

Figure 13.4 *Photo by Jodi Cobb. Reprinted by permission of The National Geographic Society.*

Figure 13.5 *Reprinted by permission of Richard Jones / Sinopix.*

Chapter 14

Figure 14.1 *© 2003 Benetton Group SpA. Ph. James Mollison.*

AUTHOR INDEX

SUBJECT INDEX

Co-design, 531
Collagen, 62
Collective selection theory, 409–410
Collectivistic cultures, 8
College sororities, 71, 83–87
Color, 71
  red, 73
  See also Skin color
Colores del Pueblo, 496
Columbine school shootings
    media coverage, 108–109, 144–152, 206, 207
  backlash to, 148–149
  Columbine Report, The, 150–51
  further hypotheses, 146
  locating cause, 147–148
    dress as facilitator claim, 148
    social tensions/revenge claim, 148
    subcultural group claim, 147
  reconstructing the crime, 145
  solutions proposed, 149–151
    RESPECT patches, 150
    school dress codes or uniforms, 149–150
Communication, 67–69
  See also Nonverbal communication in dress
Communication systems, 525
Communists, 407
Community activity dress, 277
Computers, 339
  voice command, 525
Concerned Women of America, 213
Concrete operations, 262
Confederate flag symbol banned in schools, 207
Confirmation/first Holy Communion dress, 277
Conformity
  in appearance, 263, 268, 337
  in dress, 494
  versus individuality, 8–9
Confucianism, 449
Confusion in dress, 93–94
Consumer, and technology in dress, 531
Consumer choice, 408, 421–428

Consumer lifestyles, 330
Consumer markets, ethnic minority, 406, 428–430
Consumer power, 332
Contemporary cultural "moment," 75–77
Contemporary dress, 8
Context
  dressing out of, 78–79
  of nonverbal communication use, 72–75
Corporate culture, 241
Corporate dress code, 237
Corporate expansionism, 167
Corporate giving, Sears Roebuck & Co., 250–259
Corsets, 155
Cosmetic surgery, 14, 333, 493, 494, 495, 498, 501–506, 511–515, 531
  for men, 164, 331
  nose jobs (blepharoplasty), 63, 373, 377–379, 384–386, 493
  See also Blepharoplasty surgery; Botox; Nose jobs; Plastic surgery
Cosmo Girl (magazine), 208
Cosmopolitan dress, 188
Costuming, 279–280
Council for Christian Colleges and Universities, 212
Counterfeit items, 497–498
Creativity in dress, 94–96
Credit card debt, 339
Critical thinking about the body, 14
Cross-dressing, 157–158, 180–192
  background and definitions, 180–182
  boundaries of, 187–188
  the drag queen, 185–186
  experimentation by boys with feminine dress, 72–73, 156, 264
  in religious and mythological traditions, 189
  in theatre, 189
  the transsexual, 182–183
  the transvestite, 183–185
  understanding, 186–187

Cultural assimilation, Hmong Americans, 374, 388–395
Cultural biases, 23
Cultural ideals, 15
  in the U.S., 15–22
Cultural perspective, 3–5
  artifacts, 5
  beauty, aging, and power, 343–347
  in cross-cultural context of body ideals, 46–47
  mentifacts, 3
  modesty and immodesty, 198
  significance of dress, 135–137, 139–142
  sociofacts, 4–5
  See also Body in cultural context
Cultural system in fashion, 406–407
Cultural universals, 493
Culture obsessed with youthfulness, 333, 352–354
Curtis, Jamie Lee, 348–351
Customization and multiple modes of access, 531–533

D

Dances Sacred and Profane (documentary), 131, 133
Dani women in Irian Jaya, 2
Day care, experimentation by boys with feminine dress, 72–73, 156, 172–173, 264
Delia's Inc., 268
Deodorants, 70
Department-store buyers, 439–444
Dermatologists, 14
Designer clothing, 494, 497, 506–508
Designer selves in the future, 535
Designers, 6, 494
  and retail buyers, 408, 439–444
Developmental stages, 260
Diabetes, 21
Dieting, 2
Diffusion of fashion, 6, 409
Discount brands, 339
Discourse process, 104

Faith-based social initiatives, 212
Fake furs, 77
Family celebrations, 279
Family vacations, 279
Fantasy play dress, 280–281
Fashion, 2, 5, 403–447, 454
    and capitalism, 143
    and change, 492
    for Chinese women, 438–439
    cultural system, 406–407
    defined, 90, 404–405
    eBay and designer clothing,
        494, 497, 506–508
    and female executives, 237–238
    haute couture, 135
    and the Internet, 493, 494, 495
    Japan's contribution to, 309
    knockoffs, 495
    mainstream fashion industry,
        410, 421–428
    marketing morality, 412–413
    men's advertising, 301
    micro-macro continuum, 405
    and middle age, 333
    minimalism in exposure,
        209–210
    and modesty in dress, 210,
        213–215
    negotiation with others, 408–410
    negotiation with self, 410–411
    provocative, 209–210
    and rubbish theory, 404, 409,
        415–420
    system, 407–408
    traditional runway shows, 494
    trends, 266, 403–404
    trickle-across diffusion, 409
    trickle-down theory, 409
    trickle-up theory, 374, 410
    trickling up, 374
    and work dress for women, 232
    See also Megatrends in fashion
Fashion 2001 (Khornak), 526
Fashion magazines, 5, 20
Fashion models, classes of in teen
        magazines, 323–324
Fashion system, 407–408
Fashion Takes Action (FTA), Sears
        Roebuck & Co., 250–259
    background and overview,
        250–252

confidence in work clothing,
        254–256
    procedures, 252, 254
    self-esteem and self-confidence,
        254
    women beneficiaries, 252, 253
Fathers
    bonding with children, 105,
        112–115
    experimentation by boys with
        feminine dress, 72–73,
        156, 264
Feminine passing transvestism,
        184
Feminist movement, 156
Fetishistic transvestism, 184
Films, 5
Fire-fighters, 497
First Holy Communion dress,
        277
Fitness, 29
    See also Working out
Food obsessions, 34–39
Forecasting, 526
Formal dress in the workplace,
        218
Formal operations, 268
Frail recluses, 334, 335
Frameworks for viewing the body,
        14
Frederick's of Hollywood, 202
Freedom of Speech clothing
        label, 208
Friends (television show), 20
FTA. See Fashion Takes Action
        (FTA), Sears Roebuck &
        Co.
Fubu brand, 207
Fundamental religious beliefs,
        195–197, 448, 451–452
    Bible colleges, 466–470
    and evangelicalism, 213, 467
Funerals, 73
Future trends, 525–536
    aging population, 530–531
        diversity among older
            segments, 531
        "gray power," 530
        old is out, 530–531
    customization and multiple
            modes of access, 531–533

designer selves in the future,
        535
    genetic engineering, 533–534
    race and ethnicity, 527–530
        increases in minority groups,
            527
        true equality, 528
        white backlash, 529
        white supremacist takeover,
            528–529
    technology and the consumer,
        531

G
Game dress, 263
Gang-related imagery, 194, 206,
        207
Gangs, youth, 71, 87–88, 284
Gap-bridgers, 410
Gatekeepers, 408
Gauguin, Paul, 155
Gay bashing, 157, 178–180
    See also Homosexuals
Gay/Straight Alliance, 179
Gaynor Miden Pointe shoe, 496
"Gazing-at-the-Sun," 130
Geisha, 98–100
Gender, 153–192
    appearance, 153
    boundaries of, 180–192
    and cultural ideals, 16–17
    differences in, 16
    equality in, 177
    in fundamental religions, 451
    historical perspective of dress,
        158–159
    media effect on girls, 18–19
    roles and dress, 4, 104
    and sex definitions, 154
    sexism, 156–157
    as social construction, 154–155
    and socialization, 263
    stereotypical book and media
        images, 156, 157
    traditional roles, 337
    in the workplace, 220–221
    See also Men; Sexuality;
        Women
Generation effects in adulthood,
        337–339
Generation X, 123, 338–339

Generation Y, 123, 339
Genetic engineering, 533–534
Genocide, 141
Gentlemen's Quarterly
(magazine), 194
George clothing label, 210
Germinal choice technology, 534
Germline interventions, 534
G.I. generation, 337
G.I. Joe, 154, 162–163, 168
Girdles, 59
Girl Zone (online teen magazine),
269, 497
Girls
back-to-school preparation,
215–217
back-to-school shopping, 268,
315–317
and Barbie, 168–169
beauty pageants for, 265,
286–289
body image, 17, 18–19, 21,
53–55, 266
diet and exercise, 267
facial disfigurement, 268,
303–306
and fathers, 112
makeup, 266
media effect on body image and
gender identity, 18, 269
and mothers, 116–118
prom dresses, 195, 202–203
See also Women
"Glass ceiling," 219
Global apparel marketplace,
89–98
ethics of, 77
Global capitalism, 97
Global marketplace, 22
Global positioning system, 497
Global warming, 526
Globalization of female beauty, 23
Good Housekeeping (magazine),
17
Goodie Mob, 403
Grammar of nonverbal
communication in dress,
70–71
"Gray power," 530
Great Britain, race in, 372
Great Depression, 337

Great Power era, 337
Groove Camp brand, 292
Group association in dress, 74,
104
Group dress, 104, 107, 109–110
Guatemala, Maya people in, 108,
135–143
Guatemalan Indians, 135
Gym attendance as religion, 14,
22, 29–33

H
Hadith, 449
See also Islam
Hair, 196
and African Americans, 373,
396–402
and black culture, 240
color products for, 14, 332
issues in Islam, 170–172,
199–200
loss of, 14, 16
transplants of, 14, 164
workplace requirements, 235
Halakha, 196, 463
See also Orthodox Jews
Hand gestures, 68
Haptics, 68
Harper's Bazaar (magazine), 17
Harrah's Casinos, 234
Hasbro, 168
Hate crimes, Northampton,
178–180
Haute couture, 135
copies in Wal-Mart, 209
Hawaiian shirts, 404, 409,
415–420
as durable, 418–419
refashioning, 419–420
as rubbish, 418
rubbish theory, 416–417
as transient, 417–418
Hazing, 299
Health
and fitness, 30–31
in late adulthood, 334
and obesity, 21
See also Working out
Health clubs, 29
See also Working out
Healthy hermits, 334, 335

Healthy indulgers, 334, 335
Hearing channel, 70
Heart disease, 21
Hebrew Bible, 450
See also Judaism
Hebrew Institute of Riverdale in
the Bronx, 197
Hedonic power, 16
Hegemony, 4, 107
Height
Chinese women, 495, 508–511
men, 219
Hermaphrodites, true, 154
Heterosexuals, 21, 157
High heels, 20, 23
Hinduism, 449
Hip-hop, 206, 207, 403
Hippie look, 2
Hispanics
Barbie, 167
consumers market, 374, 379–383
hegemonic power, 21
See also Latino culture
Histories of clothing and the
body, 336–337
Hmong Americans, 374, 388–395
American New Year, 390–393
ethnicity, 389
Lao Hmong dress, 389–390
Holdeman Mennonites clothing,
control, and women's
agency, 452, 470–483
background, 470–471
formal control, 475–476
history, 473
informal control, 476–478
power and resistance, 471–473
shaping an alternative image,
478–479
study community, 474–475
See also Mennonites
Homosexuals, 21, 264
gay bashing, 157, 178–180
and school dress, 206–207
See also Bisexuals; Lesbians;
Sexuality
Hook hanging, 130
"Hot box" and jockeys, 249
Hot Topic clothing label, 208
Hutterites, 481
Hypodescent rule, 372

dress and cultural survival,
139–142
Latino culture, 379–383
See also Hispanics
Leg-lengthening surgery, 508–511
Legitimation of subcultures, 108
Les Tout Petits brand, 292
Lesbians, and ageism, 357
Liberty College, 467
Lifespan process, 336–337
Lifespan stages, 260, 336
Lifestyles, 6
of consumers, 330
Limited Too specialty chain, 292
Lip reductions, 63
Liposuction, 14, 62, 63, 164
Lipsticks, flavored, 70
Little Mermaid, The (movie), 156
"Looking glass self" process, 104
Lopez, Jennifer, 21, 68
Low-income women, clothing gift
program, 222, 250–259

M

"Made-to-measure," 531–533
Madonna, 194
Magazines, 5, 20
and diversity, 267, 317–329
Mail-order shopping, 331, 335
Mainstream, 4, 107
Mainstream fashion industry, 410,
421–428
Mainstream teen magazines,
317–329
African American readers,
318–319
background and definitions,
317–318
classes of models, 323–324
cultural relevance, 321
how girls read, 320
race matters, 320–321
racial identity theory, 319
reading against the mainstream,
324–325
Major life events, 330
Male action dolls, 297–298
Management jobs, 219
women in, 225
Manheim, Camryn, 21
Market segment analysis, 340–341

Marketing morality in fashion,
412–413
Marriage, 105–106, 330
first, 330
meaning and stability of, 338
socialization to, 106
See also Weddings
Masculinity ideology, 295
Mass customization, 531–533
Mastectomy, 16
Mattel, 168
Mature people, 334
See also Adulthood
Maya people in Guatemala, 108,
135–143
Meanings of dress, 2, 5
messages in, 75
Media
adolescents in, 268–270
Columbine school shootings
coverage, 108–109,
144–152
critical analysis of, 17–22
effect on girls' body image and
gender identity, 18, 269
images in, 17–22, 266, 269, 270
and modesty in dress, 210
subculture, 133
and subcultures, 108–109
See also Advertising
Medical personnel dress, 221,
224–246
short-coat rule, 244
Medicare, 530
Megatrends in fashion, 424–427
people stopped dressing up, 425
top designers stopped gambling
on fashion, 426–427
values changed regarding
fashion, 425–426
women let go of fashion,
424–425
Megatrends in U.S. culture, 406
Memories of childhood and
adolescent dress, 271,
274–283
Men
and aging, 332, 336
body building, 30, 163–165
body ideals, 16–17, 29–39
body images of, 154, 266, 332

bonding with children, 105,
112–115
cosmetic surgery for, 164, 331
dress codes, 16
for casino workers, 221,
234–236
dress in, 71–72
with eating disorders, 154,
162–163
height in, 219
Islamic, 171, 199–200
power of, 16
restricted code of appearance,
158
swim team attire, 195, 204–205
and vanity, 158–159, 163–165,
173–178
See also Gender; Sexuality
Mennonites, 194, 195, 448, 449,
450, 452
background and history of, 481
Men's footwear, 496, 516–518
Men's Health (magazine),
173–177
Men's magazines, 173–177, 300,
302
Men's work, 496
Mentifacts, 3
Mentors, 332
Micro-macro continuum in
fashion, 405
Middle adulthood, 332–334
body changes in, 332–334
empty nest syndrome, 332
peak income earning years, 332
Middle childhood, 261
Military technology, 495, 511–515
Minimalism in exposure of skin,
209–210
Minis, 2
Minoan artifacts, 17
Minorities, 373
consumer markets, 406,
428–430
fashions from, 339
increases in, 527
Puerto Rican Day parade, 209
stereotypes of, 374, 374–376
See also Ethnic groups; Race
and ethnicity; Skin color
"Mirror Boy," 293–303

Miss Heilala Beauty Pageant, 23
Mizrahi, Isaac, 495
Model agencies, 58
Modeling industry, 431–432
Models, plus-size, 73, 430–437
Modern Primitive
  body modification, 107–108,
    127–134
  Fakir Musafar, 129
  pain and spiritual
    transcendence, 131–132
  ritual hook hanging, 130
  ritual piercing, 129–130
  subculture, 128–129
  Sun Dance, 130–131
  3-D implants, 131
Modes of access, 531–533
Modesty and immodesty, 5, 70,
    193–216, 449, 452
  cultural differences in, 198
  in postmodern America, 210–216
  and religion, 195–197
  theories of modesty, 193–195
Moles, 14
Monah Li girls line, 291
Mongoloid, 372
Monkey Wear brand, 292
Monotheism, 449
Moore, Demi, 25, 26, 27
Moral taboos, 70
Morality, 452
Mormons, 195, 197
Moroccan baths, 336–337, 363–370
Mortality, fears of, 345, 355
Motherhood and aging, 346
Mothers, bonding with children,
    105, 116–118
Moushka Bambino, 290, 291
Movies, and modesty in dress, 210
Mrs. Doubtfire (movie), 157–58
MTV, 206
Multicultural societies, 9, 527
Multiculturalism, 239
Multiple modes of access, 531–533
Multiple roles, 7
Mummies, 132
Musafar, Fakir, 129
Muslim societies, 154, 155–156,
    170–172, 193–194, 195–196
  crescent symbol banned in
    schools, 207

Razanne, 449–450, 452,
    490–491
women-only shopping centers,
    201
See also Afghanistan; Islam;
    Saudi Arabia

N
NAAFA. See National Association
    to Advance Fat Acceptance
Nano-Tex Inc., 519
Nanotechnology, 496
  See also Technology and dress
National Association to Advance
    Fat Acceptance (NAAFA),
    56
National Network for Women's
    Employment, 251
National Survey of Adolescent
    Males, 295
National Waiters Association,
    235
Native Americans, 108, 135–143
  berdaches and cross-dressing,
    189
  Sun Dance, 130–131
Negotiation of meanings, 409
Negotiation with others in
    fashion, 408–410
Negotiation with self in fashion,
    410–411
Negroid, 372
New wave styles, 339
Niche markets, 406
Nondiscursive behavior, 68
Nonverbal communication in
    dress, 67–102
  channels of transmission
    (senses), 70
  context of use, 72–75
  dressing out of context, 78–79
  elements of dress signs, 71–72
  grammar, 70–71
  meanings of dress messages, 75
  nonverbal communication,
    68–69
  present-day cultural "moment,"
    75–77
North American Plains Indians,
    130
Northampton, 178–180

Nose jobs, 63, 373, 384–386, 493
  See also Blepharoplasty surgery;
    Cosmetic surgery; Plastic
    surgery
Nostalgia, 75, 76
Nuclear devastation, 526
Nuns, 197, 450, 452, 453, 483–489

O
Obesity, 16
  in boys, 162–163
  in children, 265
  and health, 21
  in men, 162
  as public-health problem,
    42–44
  See also Body weight
Occupations
  specific, 221–222, 244–246,
    246–250
  See also Workplace
Older people, 334
  See also Adulthood
Older women's attitudes toward
    aging, 359–363
  appearance concerns, 361–362
  background and method of
    study, 359–360
  clothing importance with age,
    360, 362
  independence increases with
    age, 360–361
One-drop rule, 372
Online teen magazine, Girl Zone,
    269
Orthodox Jews, 195, 196–197,
    450, 452, 454
  See also Judaism
Osbournes, The (cable television
    show), 105
"Other" defined, 133
Ötzi, 132

P
Pacific Sunwear, 208
Pain
  Modern Primitive body
    modification, 107–108,
    127–134
  and spiritual transcendence,
    131–132

PAN. *See* Personal area network
Pantsuits, for women at work, 225
Parental rights, 534
Parents
    bonding with children, 105,
        112–115, 116–118
    experimentation by boys with
        feminine dress, 72–73,
        156
    single-parent households, 331
Paris and fashion, 135
Patriarchical societies, 21,
    451–452, 470–483
Paul Frank brand, 292
Peak income earning years, 332
Peer groups, 266, 267, 268
Penis augmentation, 164
Performance art, 108
Perfumes, 70
Person perception, 220
Personal area network (PAN),
    493
Personal values, 2
Petit Bateau brand, 292
Pharmaceutical industry, 498
Photo retouching, 493, 497–498,
    521–524
Physical attractiveness in job
    interviews, 220
Physical disabilities, 16, 220, 497
Physicians' dress, 244–246
    short-coat rule, 244
Physiological senses, 70
Piaget, Jean, 262
Piercing, ritual, 129–130
Pigmentation problems, 336
Pitt, Brad, 15
Plains Indians, 130
Plastic surgery, 62–63
    Latin American women, 494,
        495, 498, 501–506
    See also Blepharoplasty surgery;
        Botox; Cosmetic surgery;
        Nose jobs
Play with dress, 263, 264–265
    childhood memories of dress,
        274–283
    experimentation by boys with
        feminine dress, 72–73,
        156, 264
Pluralism, 9, 10

Plus-size modeling, 73, 430–437
    the image industry, 435–436
    the modeling industry, 431–432
    the plus-size market, 432–435
Plus-size range, 406, 430–437
Political correctness, 5
Political idealism, 338
Political resistance against
    dominant group, 107
Politics, of ageism and beauty,
    355–358
Pollution, 525
Polynesia, 23
Polysemic, 69
Polytheism, 449
Pop culture
    buff males, 301
    and modesty in dress, 211
Pop stars, 194
Porn Star clothing label, 207–208
Postmodernism, 75, 76, 77, 268,
    339, 406
    and the global apparel
        marketplace, 89–98
    meaning of modesty, 210–216
Postoperative transsexuals, 182
Poverty, 530
    children living in, 262
Power
    and aging, 343–347
    and cultural ideals, 15–16
    and sexual harassment, 157
Predictions, 526
Pregnancy
    cultural standards over time,
        25–27
    in the workplace, 220–221
Prejudices, 3
Preoperative transsexuals, 182
Present-day cultural "moment,"
    75–77
Prestige, 218
Primary and secondary sex
    characteristics, 154, 266
Primitive body modification,
    107–108, 127–134
Princess Diana, 25, 26, 27
Priscilla, Queen of the Desert
    (movie), 158
"Pro-Anorexia!" Web site, 40
Programs of dress, 7

Prom dresses, 195, 202–203
    and modesty, 215
Promostyl, 290, 292
Protestantism, 450
Proxemics, 68
Puerto Rican Day parade, 209
Punk styles, 339
Purging, 2

Q
Quant, Mary, 2
Questioning of rules, 75, 76–77,
    268, 339, 406

R
Race and ethnicity, 371–402
    ethnicity and appearance,
        373–374
    ethnicity defined, 373
    future trends, 527–530
    and identity, 239–240
    race and appearance, 48–53,
        372–373
    race defined, 372
    symbols in schools, 81–82
    See also Ethnic groups;
        Minorities; Skin color
Racial identity theory, 319
Racism, 373
Rampage Girls, 291
Rap styles, 6, 76–77, 87–88, 339,
    410
Razannne, 449–450, 452,
    490–491
"Rednecks," 81–82
Reference groups, 106–109
Relationships and dress, 2,
    103–152
    discourse process, 104
    group dress, 104, 107, 109–110
    "looking glass self" process,
        104
    marriage, 105–106
    media and subcultures,
        108–109
    parents and children, 105
    reference groups, 106–109
    self-indication process, 104
    significant others, 104,
        105–106
    subcultures, 107–108

Traditional dress, 8, 69, 407
  modern indigenous people,
    137–138
Transsexuals, 157–158, 182–183,
  189, 190
Transvestites, 157–158, 183–185,
  189, 190, 264
Trend forecasting services, 290
Trends in fashion, 403–404
  See also Future trends
Trickle-across diffusion, 409
Trickle-down theory, 409
Trickle-up theory, 374, 410
Trousers Up label, 291
True equality, 528
Tweens, 266, 290–292
  description of, 290–291
  profit potential, 291
  tailored retailing, 291–292

U
Uniforms, 4, 109
  and Columbine school
    shootings, 149–150
  game dress, 263
  in schools, 149–150, 263,
    284–285
  in the workplace, 219, 221
  See also Dress codes in schools;
    Workplace
Unisex, 158
United States, modesty in
    postmodern America,
    210–216
Universal Royalty National
    Pageant, 289
Urinary elimination, 336

V
Values
  personal, 2, 3
  of society, 2, 3
Van Doren, Mamie, 5, 6
Vanity Fair (magazine), 25, 26, 27
Variety in lives of early adults,
    331
Vegan, 207
Veiling of women, 195–196, 449,
    454
  Afghanistan, 449, 456–461
  See also Muslim societies

Victor/Victoria (movie), 158
Vietnam War, 338
Visiting grandparents, 279
Visual channel, 70
Visual cues in dress, 2
Vital signs, 496–497, 519–521
Vogue (magazine), 17, 194
Voice command computers, 525
Vuitton, Louis, 5, 6

W
WADL. *See* Witches Anti-
    Discrimination League
Wal-Mart, 209
Warts, 14
Wearable electronics market,
    496–497, 519–521
Web
  and Generation Y, 339
  Girl Zone (online teen
    magazine), 269, 497
  See also Internet
Weddings, 106, 120–127, 278
  See also Marriage
Weight. *See* Body weight
Weiss, Rabbi Avi, 197
Welfare systems, 530
Western dress, 188
What We Wore (Melinkoff), 2
"Whirling dervishes," 133
White backlash, 529
White supremacist takeover,
    528–529
White-collar dress, 219
Wigs, 14
  for Orthodox Jewish women,
    196–197, 450, 454,
    463–466
Will & Grace (television show), 4
Williams, Serena, 21
Williams, Venus, 21
Witches Anti-Discrimination
    League (WADL), 297
Women
  agency, 452, 470–483
  and aging, 331–332, 335, 336,
    348–351
  bonding with children, 105,
    116–118
  business dressing, 158
  of color, 4

as cross-dressers, 188
dress codes for casino workers,
    221, 234–236
dress, 71–72
  for job interviews, 220, 221,
    222, 225–233,
    250–259
  in the workplace, 218
elaborated code of appearance
    for, 158
female executives, 221,
    237–238
"glass ceiling," 219
hair issues in Islam, 170–172,
    199–200
height in Chinese, 495,
    508–511
Kalabari people, 44–47
larger body size, 4
Latin-American, 494, 495, 498,
    501–506
in management roles, 225
Mennonite, 194, 195
in Muslim societies, 154,
    155–156, 170–172,
    193–194, 195–196,
    449–450
older women's attitudes toward
    aging, 334, 359–363
positive role models for, 19
power of, 16
single in late adulthood, 336
sizes of, 496
in Third World countries, 496
women-only shopping centers,
    201
working outside the home, 331
  See also Gender; Girls;
    Sexuality
Women Employed, 235
Women's work, 496
Work roles and dress, 104,
    218–219
Work-appropriate clothing for
    women reentering the
    workplace, 251
Workforce 2000, 239
Working out, 17, 163–165, 266,
    267, 293–303, 339
  in gyms, 29–33
  See also Exercise

Workplace, 217–259
    ascribed roles, 220–221
    blacks in the corporate arena,
        239–243
    dress codes for casino workers,
        221, 234–236
    female executives, 221, 237–238
    interviewing a professional,
        222–223
    specific needs clothing, 220
    specific occupations, 221–222,
        244–246, 246–250
    women's job interview dress,
        220, 221, 222, 225–233,
        250–251
    work roles and dress, 104,
        218–219

    See also Business appearance
        norms; Dress codes;
        Uniforms
World dress, 8
World religions. *See* Religion and
    dress
World War II, 337
Wrangler, 77
Wrappers, 154

X
XOXO girls line, 290

Y
Yanomano people, 9
Yarmulkes, 461–463
YM (teen magazine), 317–329

Yoga, 31
    See also Working out
Young people, and body weight,
        17, 18–19, 21, 53–55
Youth gangs, 71, 87–88
Youthfulness, culture obsessed
        with, 333, 352–354

Z
Zeitgeist, 406, 408